THE U.S.A. A history of
its people and society
to 1877

VOLUME I

The Dorsey Series in American History

America is hard to see
Robert Frost

THE U.S.A. *A history of its people and society to* 1877

VOLUME I

Peter d'A. Jones
University of Illinois—Chicago Circle

1976

THE DORSEY PRESS Homewood, Illinois 60430

Irwin-Dorsey Limited
Georgetown, Ontario
L7G 4B3

© THE DORSEY PRESS, 1976

All rights reserved. No part of this publication may be reproduced, stored in a retrieval system, or transmitted, in any form or by any means, electronic, mechanical, photocopying, recording, or otherwise, without the prior written permission of the publisher.

4 5 6 7 8 9 0 K 5 4 3 2 1 0 9

ISBN 0-256-01801-4
Library of Congress Catalog Card No. 75–26102
Printed in the United States of America

LEARNING SYSTEMS COMPANY—
a division of Richard D. Irwin, Inc.—has developed a PROGRAMMED LEARNING AID
to accompany texts in this subject area.
Copies can be purchased through your bookstore or by writing PLAIDS,
1818 Ridge Road, Homewood, Illinois   60430.

BEAU FLY
The most American

Personal message to student readers

I wrote this textbook to help readers come to grips with American history. Before you plunge into reading it, perhaps you should think about what a textbook is. What has been my approach in writing this one? You certainly have a right to know something about what I have tried to do, and about the difficulties of writing a survey textbook covering the whole of American history. If student readers write to me about the book, care of the publisher, I shall be very pleased.

Teachers adopt textbooks out of need rather than out of choice. Some guide or survey is needed, because there is so much history to learn. But every teacher realizes that textbooks have to condense and summarize, omit some topics and explain others. It is a difficult task to decide what to select from a mass of data, themes, and ideas, and even more important, what sort of questions to ask of this selected material. Writing this textbook during the last few years has taught me over and over again the old lesson that, in studying history, framing the questions is at least as important as the answers you get.

For instance I made a deliberate decision to give less attention to traditional political details and descriptions of battles in order to leave room for social, ethnic, and economic questions. You will find all the wars highly summarized in this book, but I give more space to how people made their living, how cities grew, and how dissenting groups organized themselves and felt about America. If you are understandably fascinated by Civil War battles, you will need to use a specialist book in addition to this text. This is not because I do not like military history (my weakness, like that of most historians I know, is that I like *all* history, but life is not long enough to master everything, and no manageable textbook is able to include it all).

So be careful and cautious when you use a textbook in any field, mine not excepted. After all, what is a textbook? It is merely a tool. It cannot begin to tell you "all you need to know" about American history. A bad textbook will bore you, and may "close off" the debate on controversial or unresolved issues by pretending to offer a balanced or middle-of-the-road view, sliding between two conflicting opinions. There are few either/or questions in history. Professional historians disagree widely on countless issues. This is sometimes disturbing to students, but others find it exciting.

The U.S.A.

I have tried to give you as many of the opposing or differing arguments as space allows, without claiming to "solve" each issue in turn. At the same time, a good text should stimulate the reader to investigate a given topic further on his or her own, in deeper books and sources. I have allowed myself to express my opinions and views in this textbook—in every case it is clear which are my conclusions or attitudes and which are the "facts" or conclusions of others. A book without opinions is tedious and lifeless. Am I too hard on Jefferson? Too soft on Truman? Too brief on your favorite topic? A large number of historians have read this book in its many stages of evolution. I have taken their advice throughout the book—frankly, I did tone down my views of Jefferson, and point out some of the various criticisms made of President Truman. But I kept my own style and changed very few fundamental ideas.

What I hope I am offering you, therefore, is a fresh, sometimes mildly revisionist, textbook-with-views. I believe very deeply, after 20 years of teaching American history in various parts of the United States and Europe, that it is easier to learn history from such a book than from the traditional, sitting-on-the-fence, cautious sort of survey text. You may even learn more from reacting *against* a book; you will surely remember more. How much history do we remember from our course work? Is it as high as 50 percent? Or as low as 10 percent? We can all remember disagreeing or strongly agreeing with, or simply being surprised by, fresher views of traditional topics.

I have been a student for a long time; I know how hard it is to remember details, and how hard it is to come to your own conclusions about an issue before you have fully absorbed the material, especially when you have other subjects to learn besides American history. That is why I have tried to shape the whole book itself as a learning guide.

Each chapter has a theme, which is built-into the chapter title and the many side-heads. The side-heads are gathered together at the opening of each chapter. You can use them as a guide or outline when you take notes. Use them in conjunction with the index, which I made as detailed as possible: The index should be ideal for locating facts and for taking notes. Read a chapter quickly first—skim it. Then using the side-heads and index take your notes as you need them, flicking back and forth readily between the grouped side-heads at the opening of the chapter and the index. I have found that students rarely use indexes enough. Reading a book is not a simple process of starting at page one and ploughing through it to the bitter end. Move back and forth within the book. Get to know it. Remember, it is a tool.

Sometimes you will need other sources for term papers and for personal research on topics that interest you. I avoided the long, unread book-lists found in some texts. Instead I decided to make my own careful selection of books for further reading and to place a short list at the end of each chapter. Usually the first book cited is longer and more detailed—a source book or major study. This is followed by four or five paperbacks which elaborate on some of the themes and subthemes in the chapter. Of course, these books themselves contain bibliographies. You can begin with one of my chapters, go on to study one or two of my selections for additional reading, and then follow up on further reading they recommend. The journey is without end. It is always fascinating, and it brings constant rewards and enlightenment. A society that does not know its own history is like an autistic child, tragically cut off from reality and a sense of identity.

Note to teachers

My goal has been to produce a textbook "with opinions," a mildly, but not wildly, revisionistic, more personal sort of survey. Having taught the subject since 1956 I am convinced that such a textbook is necessary, not only to attract the imagination of the modern student generation, but to use as a learning device, to enable students to remember ideas and events, dates and facts, through a more active involvement with the author and the ideas and opinions of the teacher.

I will not overstate the degree of freshness in my book, for I have striven to retain the basic known and familiar structure of the story. The text is enlivened however by use of modern idiom and by many cross-references and allusions to contemporary matters and values. I often adopt international, comparative angles of vision when handling American themes, such as the Revolution, industrialization, radicalism and other topics. I have tried to avoid making this methodology too overt or obvious. I firmly believe that the study of history is in itself a liberal education, if approached with a broad view. History is the core for any modern student curriculum.

There is no question that as a field of study American history is much more challenging for teacher and student today than ever before. Some branches of historical writing have become technical, even mathematical, like that sort of economic history which calls itself "Cliometrics" or the New Economic History. The New social history and the New political history also demand more sophisticated methodology and understanding. They apply concepts from other social sciences—sociology, economics, psychology, and related disciplines. We know that historians have always been expected to display a kind of omniscience, or at least omnicompetence, since everything on earth (and beyond) has a history. Yet there are good reasons for students and teachers, researchers and authors, not to be too disheartened or overwhelmed.

First, *any* reading of history, however brief or intermittent, brings instant rewards and widens our human understanding, our sense of self and of group and national identity, and our feeling about humankind in general. We share this pleasure from reading history, whether or not we have a grasp of technical economic theory, statistical method, or whatever. Second, history remains the possession of every American, however technical the practitioners become. Many Americans can dabble, enjoy, and gain insight. Like politics, American history belongs ultimately to the people. Our job as teachers and writers is to clarify, elucidate, illustrate, and spread knowledge of history to as broad a spectrum of citizens as possible.

To help in this formidable task I have prepared a special sort of *Teacher's Guide* to go with this textbook, containing such aids as model tests, hints on how to judge essay examinations, and—unique to such guides—model answers. Some of these ideas I learned while lecturing on History Curriculum and Teaching Methods to an informed and experienced audience of high school and junior college teachers in a special summer school arranged by Smith College and the High School of Northampton, Massachusetts, back in the Johnson years of the 1960s when the federal government funded such valuable schemes. I certainly learned as much, probably more, than I imparted in those sessions. I also learned a great deal as an Educational Testing Service exam grader for Advanced Placement, and as a designer of the Graduate Record Examination in History for some years. The teaching of American history is an enterprise at many levels, and all of us who are involved could afford to get to know each other better. High school, junior and community college teachers and the faculty of 4-year universities and graduate schools, as well as professional testers and educators, need each other's help and experience in the enterprise. I happily acknowledge my indebtedness to all those colleagues I have known.

Acknowledgments

It gives me pleasure to acknowledge the fact that this survey textbook of American history is based solidly on years of reading the many works of scholars in the field. My students, my friends, and my colleagues know how much I owe them. My experience and knowledge of American history has been enriched by those I have taught, counselled, and communicated with over the years at several American institutions including Tulane University, Smith College, the University of Illinois at Chicago Circle, Columbia University, the University of Massachusetts at Amherst, the University of Hawaii, Hartford College for Women, and elsewhere. Abroad, I wish to thank my colleagues and students at Manchester University (England), the University of Warsaw (Poland), and the University of Düsseldorf (Germany).

I wish to thank the many readers who gave their time to reviewing the manuscript of this book over the years of its evolution: John G. Clark, The University of Kansas; Robert A. Divine, The University of Texas at Austin; Stanley M. Elkins, Smith College; Justin Kestenbaum, Michigan State University; Lawrence Leder, Lehigh University; Harold C. Livesay, The University of Michigan; Arthur Mann, The University of Chicago; Howard H. Quint, University of Massachusetts; Norman K. Risjord, University of Wisconsin; and Ronald E. Shaw, Miami University.

In particular, I especially want to thank Professor Kestenbaum, who not only gave the manuscript a valuable reading but helped with some of the illustrations for Volume II; I am deeply grateful for his advice and knowledge of the field.

Above all, the author is in debt to Dorsey Press staff, who had to put up with the vagaries of international mails, my travels and delays, and what became several years of writing and rewriting in Chicago, Honolulu, Warsaw, Düsseldorf and London.

The dedication page speaks for itself.

Winnetka, Illinois
December 1975

PETER D'A. JONES

Note on bibliographies

I have tried, as explained in my "Personal Message to Student Readers," to avoid the cumbersome list of books attached to most textbooks by carefully selecting five or so books as additional reading for each chapter. One book is made the major choice for more detailed reading; four or five books follow, invariably available in cheap paperback editions.

The readings are selected not as a guide to sources for this survey but purely for their merit in stimulating further interest in the subjects of each chapter. Selection is a painful process, given the wealth of writing by recent scholars in the rich field of American history. Dates cited are usually of latest paperback editions.

Contents

List of maps   xxiii

PART I
Americans created

1. The Old World rediscovers the New   3

   Who discovered the Americas? Europeans rediscover the New World. Viking expansion: "Vinland the Good." The Indians of North America. Great variety of Indian cultures. The shock of culture contact. Christopher Columbus, Admiral of the Ocean Sea. A Paradise of islands. Gold fever and the Spanish Empire. Christopher Columbus and ecology. What lay behind Columbus? Beginnings of modernization. Modernization and the European colonizer. The idea of America's "lack of a feudal past."

2. The cultural baggage of Europe   21

   Cultural differentiation in the New World. The struggle for North America. Britain's rivals: New Netherlands and New Sweden. Britain's rivals: New France. The peopling of New France: Champlain and Colbert. Englishmen cross the Atlantic. The cultural baggage of the colonizers. English merchant capitalism: The "revolution of expectations." Economic expansion and alienation. Tudor politics: The "rights of Englishmen." The Tudor legacy: Religious compromise. Virginia: The discipline of a new environment. The "starving time." The tobacco colonies: Virginia and Maryland. Afro-American beginnings: Slavery in Virginia. The first colonial assembly: The Virginia Burgesses. Maryland: Feudalism fails to transplant. Puritan utopias: The settlement of New England. A polity of Saints: The Mayflower Compact. A society of Saints: Congregation and township. Puritan Commonwealth: Massachusetts Bay. Puritanism and the pursuit of moderation. Puritan social and family values. Economic growth and change in New England. Colonies react to events in England. Puritanism comes down to earth. The witches of Salem. New proprietary colonies. The North American colonies in 1688.

3. American provinces of Britain   51

   The English Revolution of 1688 and the colonies. Emergence of a colonial system: Mercantilism. Growth of colonial political controls.

Economic life-styles: American merchants. Bills of exchange. Economic life-styles: Southern planters. Economic life-styles: Subsistence farming and handicrafts. Territorial expansion: The Westward Movement in the 18th century. The struggle for Canada. France and the American West. The tides of war on the frontier. North America becomes British. White over red: The Indian trauma. Puritans and Indians. The clash of Indian and white values: Landownership. The London government and the Indians. Economic expansion and American society in the 18th century. Power of the colonial elite. Social tensions and class struggle. The Great Awakening and the American mind. Rise of Deist beliefs. Jonathan Edwards: Science and God. Social and political implications of the Great Awakening. Religion and the Revolution.

4. A Revolution for Home Rule 77

A political revolution. The American fear of an English conspiracy. The view from London. Problems faced by England after 1763. Making the colonies pay: Interest-group politics. Growth of American separatism. Alienation, Phase I: Taxation and confrontation. Violence and united action: The Stamp Act Congress. Alienation, Phase II: Violence pays. The Boston Massacre: First blood. Crispus Attucks: Black martyr. Alienation, Phase III: Stalemate, 1770–73. Alienation, Phase IV: Open struggle renewed. The Quebec Act and Canada. Political organization: First Continental Congress. Lexington and Concord: The first "federal government." A republican world-view: The Declaration of Independence. Alienation, Phase V: Warfare. Long Island and Valley Forge. Saratoga. Organizing the war effort. Capturing the Midwest. Yorktown. The Peace of Paris, 1783. The Loyalists: Patriots or traitors? The Revolution as a colonial "war of liberation." A Lockean revolution which actually happened. What if the Americans had lost? Mercantilism and American growth. England fought for an unattainable end.

5. The Revolution contained 102

How did one create a new nation in 1783? Natural Law and separation of powers. Origins of Federalism: Revolutionary government. New state constitutions: Government by assembly. A nation of states? Fear of executive government: The Confederation. The public domain: Individualism and capitalism unleashed. The Territorial system. The movement for stronger centralism. Economic interest-groups behind the new constitution. Revolution and containment. Sectional issues: Slavery. Fears of social breakdown. The "Critical Period." Thinking continentally: The Founding Fathers. National pride and foreign affairs. Federalist techniques: Pressing for a new constitution. A closed room in Philadelphia. Struggles within the convention. The federal constitution: The Preamble. Federalists versus Antifederalists: The battle for ratification. How did the Federalists win? The Bill of Rights. Private property and public welfare.

PART II
Majoritarian democracy

6. The Federal world-view   133

   The Federal style. National feeling and the arts. The plan for a capital city. The Federalists take over: Washington and Madison. Hamilton's plan for national economic development. The rebirth of mercantilism: Hamilton's radical economics. Hamilton creates the American variant of "capitalism." Public credit: The mysteries of "funding" and of "assumption." The first Bank of the United States. The U.S. Mint: Decimal coinage. The futuristic *Report on Manufactures*. Hamilton's prejudices lose him Southern support. The birth of party: Federalists versus Democratic-Republicans. Party strife in the election of 1792. Impact of the French Revolution. The dilemma of neutrality. From one war scare to the next, 1793–95. The Jay Treaty, 1794. Washington's "Farewell Address," 1796. The succession struggle: The election of 1796. Crisis in U.S.–French relations, 1797–98. The threat to civil liberties: Alien and Sedition Acts, 1798. The election of 1800: The miracle of peaceful transfer of power. The fate of the Federalists.

7. The Agrarian Dream   157

   Dream and reality. The dream transforms itself. Jefferson, the national expansionist. Rustic America: Life on the Southern frontier. A diet of corn. Louisiana: Traces of French culture. Frontier life in the Ohio country: The first prairie. The Mississippi. Jefferson in power: The realist. Gallatin and federal aid. Party discipline and frugality. Jefferson and the courts: Judicial nationalism. Threat of secession: The "Northern Confederacy." Burr kills Hamilton, 1804. From success to failure: Jeffersonian foreign policy. Failure of the embargo policy. Internal contradictions of "Jeffersonian Democracy." Red, white, and black: Racism in Jefferson's utopia. Confining slavery to the South. Passing the Republican torch: Madison. Complex motives for war with England. War of 1812: National honor and independence. New England threatens: The Hartford Convention. The Creek War, the Battle of New Orleans, and peace. American nationalism in the saddle.

8. The pursuit of happiness   186

   Material growth of the nation. Expansion of the market economy. Sources of economic expansion. The man–land ratio. Scarcity of capital. The Transportation Revolution. The first toll roads. The canal mania. Benefits and disadvantages of canals. The steamboat age. Rails and steam: The iron horse. Public enterprise and private profit: Aid to railroads. Americans in foreign trade. American merchant seamen. The Yankee clippers. A loss of momentum. Revolution in manufactures. Samuel Slater's first mill. Lowell's "Boston Associates." Why did not the South industrialize? Spread of new industrial techniques. Heavy industry: Coal and iron. A variety of small industries. The "American system of manufacture": Mechanization. The revolution in agriculture. Commercial farming in the Old Northwest. Scientific agriculture. Farm processing plants. The Cotton Kingdom. Plantation slavery. Life of the slave. Slave breeding. Did slavery pay? Long-term retardation of the southern economy caused by slavery. The noncotton South. The growth of economic sections. The "happiness of pursuit."

9. Trying to define the Federal system 227

The spoils of government. Monroe: The Republicans go Federalist. The "Era of Good Feelings" versus an era of factionalism. The new nationalism: Economic and judicial. The capitalist Supreme Court. The new nationalism: Territorial and racial. Andrew Jackson and the Indians. The Supreme Court fails the Indians. Black slavery and the Missouri Compromise. The Monroe Doctrine: Peak of Republican nationalism. New politics: The revolt against the caucus. John Quincy Adams and the American System. The Jacksonian Revolution: 1828. Andrew Jackson and the symbols of democracy. Who was Andrew Jackson? What does a "democratic" president do in 1828? The men around Jackson. The West and Daniel Webster. The South and Calhoun. A Jefferson birthday dinner, 1830. The theory of disunion: Calhoun's "concurrent majority." Nullification and the threat of force. Jackson's war on the U.S. Bank. The jealousy of state banks. Death of the Bank. What was the outcome of the Bank War? How "democratic" was Jacksonian Democracy? Rotation in office and the spoils. Jackson and the underprivileged. The Indian "Trail of Tears." "Making it": The world of Jackson.

10. Revivalism and radicalism: America as Utopia 257

The radical style: Facing up to slavery. Radical groundswell: Origins. Romanticism: The cult of Nature. Radical ideas in education. Revolution for the American child: Horace Mann. Heredity versus environment. The American worship of self-improvement. The High Culture: Transcendentalism. Brook Farm: Elite commune. Emerson: Mysticism, self-reliance, and cultural nationalism. The religious impetus: Evangelicalism. The cult of "Love." Beecher and Finney. Religious undercurrents: Anti-Catholic prejudice. Communes: The search for Utopia. Shakers and Mormons. Secular utopias: New Harmony and Nashoba. French phalanxes and communities. Sexual radicalism: Oneida. Women's leadership in a galaxy of reforms. Seneca Falls Convention, 1848. Labor and capitalism. Humanitarian reforms: The Jacksonian underworld. The Cold-Water Army. Reform as a way of life.

11. Frontier nationalism 285

The party politics of expansionism. Birth of Manifest Destiny. The growth experience reinforced. Frontier nationalism: Canada. Election of 1840: Professional campaigning. Frontier nationalism: The Pacific Northwest. The Polk Doctrine. Oregon and Asia. The Americanization of California. Frontier nationalism: Middle Border and Southwest. Slavery and Texas annexation. Frontier nationalism: The war against Mexico. Mexico is halved. Triumphant nationalism. The Mexican War and the Civil War. The Wilmot Proviso and the election of 1848. Zachary Taylor favors statehood for California and New Mexico. Whigs, Democrats, and the Compromise of 1850. The Fugitive Slave Law. The territorial issues: "Popular sovereignty." The Compromise in practice. The role of Texas. Aftermath of the Compromise: Election of 1852. Further fruits of expansionism: The Ostend Manifesto. The slavery question reopened: Kansas–Nebraska. Civil War in miniature. The Republicans and the ideology of sectional conflict.

12. The survival of the Union   309

Love of Union versus secession. A conflict of sections? Former sectional issues: Banking and tariffs. Internal improvements: The allegiance of the West. From anti-slavery-extension to abolitionism. Evolution of abolitionist thought. Gradualism and immediatism. Black and white abolitionists. Abolitionism becomes political: The gag rule and the Liberty party. The drift to Civil War: Dred Scott. Radical stereotypes: Cavalier and Yankee. The slave and the Negro. The emergence of Abraham Lincoln. The Lincoln-Douglas debates. Escalation: John Brown's raid. The last straw: Lincoln's election. Lincoln and the secession crisis: Upper versus Lower South. The Upper South and last-ditch compromise. Jefferson Davis and the Confederacy. The final issue: Federal bases in the South. The South shoots first: Fort Sumter, April 1861. War strategy: The odds. First Bull Run and naval blockade. The campaigns of 1862: Second Bull Run and Antietam. Diplomacy and slavery. Origins of the Emancipation Proclamation. Campaigns of 1863: Chancellorsville and Gettysburg. Vicksburg: Cutting the Confederacy in two. Troubles on the home front: The Radicals, draft riots, and the election of 1864. The final campaigns: Chattanooga; Sherman's March. The ending: Appomattox and Lincoln's death. Was it worth it?

PART III
A nation of strangers

13. From slavery to serfdom: The unreconstructed South   347

Who won the Civil War? Reconstruction: An unusual idea. If Lincoln had lived. Fears of the Republican Radicals. Andrew Johnson and Confederate Reconstruction. Negro and Radical dissatisfaction rises. The battle for Negro civil rights: White violence. Civil rights amendments. Election of 1866: The coming of Radical Reconstruction. Impeachment of President Johnson. The political arms of the Radicals. Negro education. The hooded Klan. Black reaction to Reconstruction: What did Freedmen want? Why were ex-slaves not given land? Collapse of Negro land schemes. Election of 1868: The 15th Amendment and women's rights. Strange death of Reconstruction. Why did the North acquiesce? Myths of Reconstruction. Was Radical Reconstruction "corrupt"? Why did Reconstruction fail? Southern cultural nationalism. The Redeemers and the New South. Control of blacks in the New South: The Supreme Court. Black accommodation: Booker T. Washington.

Appendixes

Appendix A	The Declaration of Independence	iii
Appendix B	The Constitution of the United States	vi
Appendix C	Growth of U.S. population	xviii
Appendix D	Admission of states	xix
Appendix E	Presidents and vice presidents	xx
Index		xxv

List of maps

Map		Page
1	Diffusion of Indian cultures in the New World	4
2	Military campaigns of the Revolution	94–95
3	The War of 1812	179–81
4	The Missouri Compromise	233
5	The "Trail of Tears"—Removal of the Five Civilized Nations to Indian Territory under the Acts of 1830 and 1834	254
6	Trans-Mississippi trails	290
7	Alignment of states in the Civil War	311

PART I
Americans created

1

The Old World rediscovers the New

Who "discovered" the Americas? . . . Europeans rediscover the New World . . . Viking expansion: "Vinland the Good" . . . the Indians of North America . . . variety of Indian cultures . . . the shock of culture contact . . . Christopher Columbus: Admiral of the Ocean Sea . . . a Paradise of islands . . . gold fever and the Spanish Empire . . . Christopher Columbus and ecology . . . what lay behind Columbus? . . . beginnings of modernization . . . modernization and the European colonizer . . . the idea of America's "lack of a feudal past."

Who discovered the Americas?

The Americas were discovered by the ancient ancestors or precursors of the people Columbus called "Indians." They were not East Indians, but this did not stop Columbus from naming them. He needed to find some part of Asia. The expense of his expedition westward had been justified by the search for a new course to the rich trade of China and Japan. The natives Columbus actually found have nevertheless been called Indians ever since. At least their distant ancestors, like the real East Indians, were Asian.

Most scholars now accept the idea that the predecessors of the many Amerindian tribes crossed over the region that is now the Bering Straits and Alaska from Asia into North America toward the end of the era of the last ice cap. Exact dating is still not possible. The polar ice cap receded for the last time 10,000 to 15,000 years ago, though even earlier evidence of human settlement in North America has been uncovered. Bones of extinct sloths, camels, and horses, along with human remains such as spear-throwing shafts and camp fire debris, have been found in cave sites in Nevada and New Mexico, which indicate the existence of *Homo sapiens* in North America at least 20 to 25,000 years ago. Men could have crossed the Bering Straits region 30,000 years ago or even earlier.

This migration took place in successive waves over the space of much time, perhaps a few thousand years. Ancient men migrated southward from Alaska, passing the Isthmus of Panama into South

3

Map 1. Diffusion of Indian cultures in the New World

© 1961, American Heritage Publishing Co., Inc.
Reprinted by permission from The American Heritage Book of Indians by William Brandon.

America around 10,000 B.C. These nomadic game-hunters had spread to the southern tip of that continent by 7,000 B.C. In the high Tehuacán valley near Mexico City archaeological findings reveal a shift from purely hunting toward settled farming and the domestication of plants, some time between about 7,000 and 5,000 years before Christ. Hunting remained important, but domesticated corn has been found in Mexico that is about 7,000 years old. By 2,500 B.C. the Mexican aborigines lived in settlements, had begun making pottery, and were domesticating not only crops but animals. Around 900 or 800 B.C. they were building temple mounds and using irrigation. The great Aztec and Inca cultures destroyed by the white invaders of the 16th century were irrigation civilizations.

The waves of migration out of Asia, the dispersion of tribes over North America and their differentiation into distinct linguistic groups and subgroups, and their onward move into Central and South America over thousands of years, is a most remarkable story. Added to it is the theory of Thor Heyerdahl and the Kon-Tiki expedition of 1947 that "Indians" from Peru sailed out across the Pacific in primitive balsa rafts and settled the islands of Polynesia. This whole *diffusion theory* of the first settling of the New World by the ancestors of the Amerindians would have to be drastically revised, or even scrapped, if someone were to discover evidence of primitive man in the Americas. But so far no evidence whatsoever of pre-*Homo sapiens*, or of his close cousins in evolution, the great apes, have been uncovered in the Western Hemisphere. From the very beginning, it seems, the Americas were a land of "immigrants."

Europeans rediscover the New World

The European explorers of the late 15th and 16th centuries merely rediscovered the New World. In Central and South America the Spaniards encountered very ancient and advanced cultures in the Aztecs and Incas. On the other hand, long before the 15th century different Europeans had seen the New World. The *idea* of the New World had been well known for several centuries in Europe. Welsh claims to

Prehistoric sagebrush sandals, about 9,000 years old, found in Fort Rock Cave, Oregon

University of Oregon

have discovered North America are usually discounted since they are based on the alleged exploits of a Prince Madoc, the son of the Lord of North Wales, Owen Gwynned, who appears to have had no son at that time. Irish claims seem the most credible. The first Europeans to sight North America may well have been missionary monks sent out by the Celtic Church in Ireland. There is no hard evidence, but these intrepid monks did cross the northern seas from the 6th century on, reaching Iceland, which they named *Thule*, in the year 795. Irish stories and legends helped to prepare the way for the more permanent settlers, the Viking voyagers from Scandinavia who colonized Iceland around the year 870 A.D.

Viking expansion: "Vinland the Good"

The Vikings fanned out from northern Europe in the 8th and 9th centuries, moving into Britain and Ireland, France, through the Straits of Gibraltar into the Mediterranean and on to Italy, North Africa and the Arab lands, and further north, crossed the Baltic and moved down the great rivers of Russia to the Black Sea. Viking settlements around Kiev were the predecessors of medieval Russian civilization. The "Norsemen" founded Norman culture in France. Logically, part of these astonishing achievements was the pressure to move westward across the northern Atlantic to Iceland, Greenland, and ultimately to North America. There is now sufficient historical evidence that this migration took place.

Apart from merely military plunder, the Vikings were deeply motivated by the forces of population pressure and land hunger at home. When they settled, the warriors developed into hardy traders and farmers. Iceland was a thriving republic by the year 930. It traded wool, cloth, hides, falcons, and various other goods in demand to Scandinavia and to Britain. On the west coast of England the port of Bristol, centuries later a major port for the English colonies of North America, was already a vital market in the 10th century for Viking trade. In those years Iceland also had a remarkable representative assembly, the *Althing*. The population was about 30,000, made up of Vikings and Celts.

According to the evidence of the ancient poetic *sagas* the first Viking to sight the shores of North America was a merchant, driven off course from Greenland. Eric the Red colonized Iceland in 985; his son, Leif the Lucky, having heard of the earlier merchant's first sighting, bought a boat to explore the coast more thoroughly. Leif found what he described as lush grasslands, timber stands, salmon, and grapes somewhere along the North American coast and he named the region "Vinland the Good." This was about the year 1,001 A.D. Ten years later Leif's brother-in-law, a rich Icelandic merchant called Thorfinn Karlsefni, sailed south from Greenland and established the first permanent European settlement in North America, so far as we know.

What is the evidence for this story? Some details are given in the Icelandic sagas. Though they conflict with each other, careful scholarly interpretations have helped to piece the story together. The two chief sagas of American interest (recently retranslated by the scholars

M. Magnusson and H. Pálsson) were written down from the oral, story-telling tradition in the late 12th century (the *Greenland Saga*) and the mid-13th century (*Eric's Saga*). The two sagas are supported by other evidence, including documents of earlier vintage, many cross-references in ancient European literature and historical, geographical, and climatic inferences. There seem to have been *several* expeditions of Vikings to North America.

At least one authentic Viking settlement has been dug up in northern Newfoundland at a site called L'Anse aux Meadows. Its contents have been dated by radiocarbon and other techniques at about 1,000 A.D. They include seven or eight dwellings, a smithy, an anvil, nails, bronze fragments, and other evidence of Viking origin. Was this Vinland the Good? It is still too early to say. One thousand years ago the climate in this region was much warmer, which is why some investigators favor Labrador as the original Vinland. Others think that the New England coast further south is more likely. Over the decades the climate deteriorated badly and by the late 15th century the Norse parent-colony was almost eliminated from Greenland itself. The Viking settlement on Greenland was tiny by then, starved and poverty-stricken. At this same period of history Columbus was "discovering" the warm, tropic isles of the West Indies and telling the world he had found the route to Asia.

Centuries of settlement and humanization of the New England coast has made it unlikely that any evidence can remain there of possible Viking colonies, although little systematic searching has been undertaken. Deep inland, as far west as Minnesota, what was allegedly a Viking stone with lettering was claimed to have been discovered in 1898. This *Kensington Runestone* can be seen by tourists for a price at Alexandria, Minnesota, but it is not generally accepted as authentic by scholars. Its lettering describes a not impossible Viking expedition into the heartland of the American Midwest. There are also many other tales and scraps of unauthenticated evidence.

One of the most convincing sections of the sagas describes the Amerindians. The Vikings called the natives of North America *Skraelings* (savages) and their attitude to them was little different from that of later English invaders in New England or Virginia to the Indians. The Vikings cheated the Skraelings, say the sagas, using sharp trading practices and rewarding the natives' friendliness with violence and war. The Indians were described as tough, black-haired, broad-cheekboned, and fierce peoples who used canoes and catapults and ate a sort of dried meat (perhaps the same known to the Anglo-Americans later as pemmican). Who were these Skraelings?

The Indians of North America

Indians in North America were far fewer in number and less technologically advanced than Indians in other parts of the Americas. The greatest Indian population concentrations and highest cultural achievements were in Mexico, Central America, and the Andes Mountains, where they supported themselves with a remarkable agricultural and irrigation technology. Estimates of pre-Columbian Indian popula-

Prehistoric ritual twig deer, about 3,000 years old, found in the Grand Canyon

Arizona State Museum

tions differ very widely. A most recent demographic estimate claims a population in Mexico alone as large as 25,000,000 for 1519, far higher than earlier guesses. Other accounts suggest a range of from 8 to 15,000,000 Indians for all the Americas, 9 or 10,000,000 for Mexico alone. The U.S. Census of 1960 estimated a population of 523,591 Indians in the United States; guesses for the total number of Indians in the New World as a whole today range between 15 and 25,000,000.

Historians agree more closely on the figures for *North* American Indians at the time of Columbus. Apparently under 1,000,000 Indians lived in what later became the United States, perhaps 900,000 or less. In the North the chief population centers were along the Pacific coast (mainly a fishing and hunting culture), in the Southwest (farming), and on the Atlantic coast, where the Indian population was least dense. Along the Atlantic, more lived in the Southeast than in the Northeast. Thus the Puritans of the 17th century would encounter the fewest Indians in this so-called empty continent.

Great variety of Indian cultures

Indians were of course not "all alike," though fearful European invaders refused to make adequate distinctions. Perhaps as many as 600 Indian subcultures existed and 6 major language groups with hundreds of dialects. The 20th-century Hollywood Indian hopelessly confuses many life-styles, mixing Plains Indians (always dominant in movies) with others. Yet some of the Plains tribes with their feather headdresses, war dances, and tepees, did not even see a white man until the mid-19th century.

Indian cultures differed widely. In the Pacific Northwest, tribes like the typical Kwakiutls developed the longhouse, totem pole, carving and painting, hunting and fishing cultures, with social stratification and the elaborate gamesmanship of the *potlatch* ceremony—a complex ceremonial exchanging of gifts in a spirit of intense rivalry and display. In the Southwest the Pueblo mortar and stone apartment houses sheltered almost classless and rigidly theocratic communes. The fiercer Apache and Navajo warrior nomads, descendants of 12th-century migrant Athabascans from Canada, who surrounded and harassed the Pueblos, themselves evolved into more settled sheep farmers in the 17th century. In the Northeast the hunting and farming tribes with their wigwams and cult of manliness developed systematic self-torture in some instances as part of their religious beliefs. The warlike semi-monarchies of the Southeast knew no wigwams or tepees, but instead built thatched-roof houses, as did the Natchez tribe, for instance, in Mississippi. These and other Indian tribes knew little or nothing of each others' existence except when raided or shifted off their customary lands by enemy tribes in time of war.

The adventures of St. Brendan—German woodcuts of 1499 depict the Irish monk on his voyages of discovery

The Viking map,
now a suspected
forgery

Thule ultima

Tartarata fluuius

Imperiu[m] Tartaroru[m]

Kytauo

Mogog

Magog Anain

Mare Orientale

Insula Sub aquilone

Taurus

Magnu[m] mare Tartaroru[m]

magnus lacus

Iacal

Iuuam

Tartaria magn[ific]a

Postrema Insula

Samara

Terra Indica

mare Indicum

Ierusalem

Alexandria

Chaura Acca

[O]ceanus

Sinaicus mons

Imperiu[m] Basra

mare Indicum

Ethiopia

Garbar superior

Ethiopia

The U.S.A.

The higher cultures of Central America and Mexico exerted considerable influence on those North American Indians nearest to them, in the Southeast of what was the later United States. For example, in the lower Mississippi valley an ancient Indian culture called by archaeologists the Mound Builders has been shown to have shared similar carving and modeling motifs and designs with those of ancient Mexico. The Mississippi mounds are more simple earthwork versions of the developed pyramids of Mexico. These mysterious Mound Builders seem to have been overrun by tougher tribes of Iroquoian stock from further north, who were ancestors of the Indians of the Southeast called by English colonizers the "Five Civilised Tribes": Chickasaws, Choctaws, Cherokees, Creeks, and Seminoles.

The shock of culture contact

The invasion by European white men, mainly Spanish in the 16th century, Dutch, French, and English in the 17th, brought demographic catastrophe to the native Americans. Diseases spread by Europeans, such as tuberculosis, venereal disease, typhoid, measles, and the murderous smallpox, wiped out thousands, in some areas millions, of Indians. Besides such epidemics the Indians were reduced by war; by harsh forced labor in the Spanish colonies (the brutal *mita* slave-labor system in the silver mines of Peru was disastrous); and by what anthropologists call "culture shock": the low birthrates and generalized apathy of subject peoples.

The full extent of the trauma is not known. The relatively small sailing ships of the Spaniards and of the English settlers who came

Pueblo Indian dwelling—Cliff Palace, Mesa Verde, Colorado, built about 1073–1262 A.D.

much later must have seemed like miraculous, huge canoes to the Indians. The over-dressed, strangely bearded Europeans with their horses, sheep, and "hot-mouthed sticks," their wheels and tools, were a shock to the Indians. The story is often told that the Aztecs of Mexico thought the Spanish conqueror Cortés was their white-skinned avenging god, Quetzacoatl, coming from the sea. Not only among the Aztecs and Incas, but also among the Indians of North America, communalism ran deep and proved a weak defense against the arrogant and self-confident, profit-seeking individualism of the Europeans, Spanish, and English alike. The clash of cultures was profound—and profoundly unequal.

To handle the subject of conquest, historians have invented the phrase "depopulation ratio." The demographic impact of the invasions is not fully known. Some scholars claim a depopulation ratio of 20:1. If, indeed, one can accept 25,000,000 as the Mexican population of 1519 (the date of Cortés's landing at Veracruz), reduced to a mere 1,000,000 by 1605, the depopulation was even more tragic, and the ancient centers of Amerindian civilization suffered a holocaust worse than that of the European Jews in the 20th century. By 1650 it appears, the worst was over, at least in the Spanish colonies. The impact of British colonization was beginning to be felt at that date.

It has occasionally been suggested that British invasion was more destructive to the Indians than Spanish settlement, partly because the Spanish policies were tempered by certain institutional restraints, such as the Catholic Faith, with its insistence on the individual souls of Indians and on conversion. There is little evidence to justify this claim despite the noble work of men like Father Bartolomé de Las Casas in support of the *New Laws* of 1542 to protect Indians in Spanish possessions. The difference, if one existed, was chiefly in numbers. The British met relatively few Indians and most were wiped out or driven westward. In Spanish America millions of Indians perished but there were too many for complete annihilation to take place. For the Spanish, moreover, the Indians were an essential labor force in developing gold and silver mines. Where the Spanish met fewer Indians, as in the West Indies and the Caribbean, the natives were wiped out even more thoroughly than in British North America and were replaced by imported African slaves. It remains true, however, that there was more race mixing in Spanish and Portuguese America. By the 19th century a large middle group of *mestizo* (Indian-European) peoples were rising to economic and even some political power in South America at a time when the U.S. was still pursuing its racist Indian "reservation" policies.

Christopher Columbus, Admiral of the Ocean Sea

Columbus is justifiably praised as a great hero, the man who broke through the water barrier to the New World. Modern attitudes, however, force us to see him in another, less flattering light as an ecological disaster for the New World. His crass lust for gold, his brutal treatment of the Indians and their environment, set the pattern for later invasions and occupations by Europeans.

Born apparently in Genoa around 1451, Columbus came from a

modest weaver's family, but somehow gained an education, most likely in Portugal where he settled about 1485, and learned Latin, Spanish, and the arts of navigation in which the Portuguese excelled. He voyaged as a sailor over the Mediterranean for some years and appears to have gone as far as "the island of Tile" (*Thule:* the Iceland of the Vikings) in 1477, if we can believe his *Journals* as transcribed by his eulogist and critic, the Spanish priest, Las Casas.

Equipped intellectually and through experience as a sailor, Columbus determined to sail westward across the Atlantic to find a new route to the rich trade of the East. This idea was less original and audacious than it seems in his *Journals,* since educated Europeans had known for some decades that the globe was round or pear-shaped and that the wealth of the Orient, China, Cipango (Japan), and the fabled golden cities of the Great Khan, described by Marco Polo, could be reached by traveling westward. Of course, no one was sure how far the journey was, or what dangers lay in between. Columbus was a magnificent sailor and a truly courageous and single-minded leader.

For some years Columbus begged various monarchs (Portugal, Spain, England, France) to finance his voyage. Finally, after saying no several times, Queen Isabella of Spain agreed to help him. She was probably encouraged to do so by the spirit of national feeling engendered in Spain in that same year with the fall of Granada (January 1492) and final expulsion of the Moors, along with the Jews, from the peninsula. Columbus sailed on the 3d of August and made first landfall in the New World on the 12th of October in the sunny Bahamas, at an island he called San Salvador (present-day Watling's Island, a British colony).

A Paradise of islands

The Bahamas were beautiful and warm, and inhabited only by a few peaceful Arawak Indians; but they contained no obvious gold deposits, so the *Santa Maria,* the *Pinta,* and the *Niña* sailed on. Columbus skirted the northern coast of Cuba, keeping a lookout for the splendid cities of the Khan and convincing himself that this was Japan. On the island he called Española (present-day Haiti and the Dominican Republic) he settled a colony of men from the wrecked *Santa Maria,* and instructed them to look for gold. He returned to Spain, taking seven Indians with him and other evidence to support his exaggerated, wondrous tales. The following year his second of four voyages to the Caribbean passed by way of the Antilles, the Virgins, Puerto Rico, Jamaica and southern Cuba (1493–94). On a third trip (1498–1500), Columbus discovered Trinidad, the mainland coast of Venezuela and the great Orinoco River, which he claimed as one of the four famous rivers that were said to irrigate the Garden of Eden. Increasingly frustrated at not having located Japan and China, Columbus pitched his claims very high: he had discovered the "earthly Paradise" itself.

To judge from his early descriptions of the island of Española, this was indeed a Paradise—one that Columbus and his followers soon despoiled. "This island and all others are very fertile to a limitless degree," he wrote in a famous letter. ". . . there are many harbors on the coast of the sea, beyond comparison with others which I know in Christendom, and many rivers, good and large, which is marvellous. Its lands are high . . . and all are accessible and filled with trees of a thousand kinds. . . . And the nightingale was singing, and other birds of a thousand kinds in the month of November there where I went. There are six or eight kinds of palm . . . large tracts of cultivable lands, and there is honey . . . birds of many kinds, and fruits in great diversity." But, above all, more important to Columbus than such natural beauty: "In the interior are mines of metals, and the population is without number."

Scholars have estimated the population of Española may have been a million; by 1509 the Spanish incursion had reduced the Indians to perhaps 14,000. It is ironical to read Columbus in the light of this knowledge, particularly his view of the Indians as "handsome," "very marvellously timorous" and peaceful, "so guileless and so generous with all they possess." What happened to this "land to be desired, and once seen, never to be left"?

Gold fever and the Spanish Empire

The Spanish *conquistadores* went to the Americas in military expeditions, supported by the Church and the State, to loot the New World of its gold. The Church's aim of "spiritual conquest" was overshadowed by the gold fever of the conquerors, though in Bartolomé de Las Casas at least one priestly leader emerged with different life goals. Las Casas drew a flattering portrait of Columbus, but reserved the right to criticize his treatment of the Indian populations of the Caribbean. Other priests also struggled to preserve the Indians from the cruelty, forced labor, and diseases of the Spanish. Eventually the Church itself grew fat on the colonies, and succumbed to moral lethargy.

Over a century later the English went to America also; they sought gold, at least in Virginia. What saved England was that they failed to find any. The Spanish found tons of treasure, and being unable to absorb it into their still-feudal economic structure at home, eventually collapsed under its weight. True, the material basis of Spain's Golden Age and of the baroque splendors of the Spanish American colonies, was the treasure of the New World. But the flood of new treasure brought inflation in Spain without any real growth of the economic "infrastructure" necessary for sustained growth (better roads and transportation, better education and technology, new industries, a more efficient bureaucracy). The Spanish economy declined; the nation had to import products she had previously sold abroad (such as armaments); even the family monopolists who maintained exclusive control of colonial trade ended up as fronts serving foreign masters. In the 18th century Spain fell from her great-power status and was replaced by England and France, though her empire was still enormous.

Christopher Columbus and ecology

Never has the single-minded pursuit of gold and silver—obvious, tangible wealth—produced more perverse results. Spanish gold-lust had much to do with Columbus himself, who negotiated with Isabella

The U.S.A.

an unusual personal contract, an almost absolute dictatorship in perpetuity for himself and his heirs over all the lands he discovered. His two brothers were also given grand titles and positions, and with this contract behind him, Columbus became a tyrant, treating all around him as his creatures. On Española, dissent was put down by brute force. The Indians were mercilessly exploited, despite the opposition of Las Casas. Columbus imposed a monstrous and unworkable labor system, a compulsory gold levy per head, the tribute to be collected by local Indian leaders, *caciques*, who were to pay with their lives for any failure to produce. Widespread torture and mutilation failed to bring forth the mythical gold from the island's interior: there simply was not enough placer gold to meet Columbus's demands. This terrible system helped to wipe out the Indian population very rapidly.

Las Casas, who exaggerated his case for effect (the priest has been blamed for beginning the "Black Legend" of Spanish cruelty in the New World), claimed that 3,000,000 Indians were annihilated between 1494 and 1508—an impossibly high figure. But many thousands did vanish. Even Columbus himself was shocked, on his return to Española, at finding the island almost depopulated. By 1570 the Caribbean and the parts of the Spanish Main touched by Columbus and those who came after him, had been reduced from a tropical paradise to a condition of shabby poverty. Columbus and his brothers were shipped home in chains in 1500, when a new governor, sent out to Española after many complaints, found Spaniards hanging in gibbets at the harbor mouth. Yet the Admiral managed to regain court favor within a few months and was dispatched on his fourth and final mission to the New World. On this voyage (1502–4), he explored the coast of Central America from Panama to Honduras and extended the impact of Spanish colonialism to ancient Meso-America and the "Spanish Main." He died in relative obscurity in 1506, aged about 55, never having found the fabulous wealth of the East. Santo Domingo claims to have his remains.

Little was left of the Indian civilization he helped destroy. The Spanish conquistadores moved their attention to the vastly greater wealth of Mexico and Peru and found the treasure that Columbus had so desired. In the silver mines they exploited far greater numbers of Indians. Meanwhile along the Caribbean the former Spanish settlements were already being recovered by lush tropical vegetation, 30 or 40 years before Englishmen settled in Virginia. Natural beauty returned, to cover the sores of what was left of a vanished Indian culture.

What lay behind Columbus?

The historical timing of Columbus's voyages was not accidental. The colonial settlement of the New World was the product of early modern European history. Within the space of an incredible 40 *years*, from 1488 when the Portuguese navigator Bartholomew Diaz rounded the Cape of Good Hope and pointed the way to the trade route to India, to 1522 when another great Portuguese, Ferdinand Magellan (or rather, the survivors of his party) completed the first recorded circumnavigation of the globe, all the preliminary explorations were made of Asia, Africa, and the Americas. Magellan was killed in the Philippines; yet his voyage had already proved before his death that the Americas were not merely a physical extension of Asia, but truly a separate "New World" lying between Europe and the Far East.

The Western Europe that produced these magnificent global explorations was a subcontinent in a special phase of its history. The nations of Western Europe were undergoing the process of modernization. A whole cultural revolution lay behind Columbus—indeed a series of overlapping, interlocking, and mutually reinforcing revolutions: religious and philosophical, scientific and technological, geographic, political, and economic. Many of these changes began before

The Timucuan Indians of St. John's River, Florida, through British eyes (John White, 1585)

British Museum

the Renaissance got under way and long before Martin Luther pinned his *Theses* on the church door at Wittenberg in 1517 and began the Reformation. A deep-rooted set of transformations brought Europeans out of feudalism and manorialism into the modern world of statist-nationalism and commerce. The "Great Discoveries" of 1488-1522 were both a symptom and a part of this complex cultural upheaval.

Beginnings of modernization

The deepest revolutions take place in the minds of men and women. At the very core of the modernization revolution was a changing concept of the Universe and of Man, a new human self-image, a restructuring of basic religious and philosophical beliefs. We think of the 18th century as the Age of Reason and Enlightment, but those years saw the coming to fruition of older ideas and struggles. The modern rationalist, individualist, and scientific view of man arose naturally out of the Catholic Faith itself, out of the thoughts and experiments of devout monks. As early as the 13th century the English monk Roger Bacon (1214-94) proclaimed: "Truth is the daughter, not of Authority but of Time." His experiments in alchemy and the natural sciences taught Bacon, as no doubt he taught his Oxford students, that the application of human reason would reveal many, if not all, secrets in time. He felt no antipathy between his science and his faith, no sharp distinction between secular and religious authority such as plagued later centuries.

Bacon's students no longer regarded college as the place one attended to be told the origin, function, and inevitable destiny of mankind, as laid down in authorized texts. The medieval age of faith and fixed human knowledge was giving way to reason and a new sense of progress, of the gradual accretion of new knowledge and the unfolding of ideas never dreamed of in the accepted sources. In the following century a devout German cardinal and monastic reformer, Nicholas of Cusa, (1401-64) hinted that the Universe was not fixed but very indeterminate, perhaps infinite. And the great Polish priest-astronomer Nicholas Copernicus (1473-1543) overturned generations of belief by establishing the sun as the center of the Universe, with earth merely revolving around it. His *De revolutionibus orbium caelestium* (1543) appeared some years after the New World colonies of Spain had been founded and about 20 years after Magellan's circumnavigation of the globe. First, there was a whole "New World"; second, the earth was round; and now, third, it revolved around the sun. Neither earth nor perhaps even man himself was the center of the Universe.

Such radical ideas took decades to sink in and be fully accepted. Nearly a century later the Italian scientist Galileo Galilei (1564-1642) was tortured by the Church and forced to deny his confirmation of Copernicus. The Church decreed that the earth did not revolve around the sun, whatever Galileo's original mathematical computations, based on sightings with his astronomical telescope, had pretended to prove. The two worlds of faith and science were now opposed. By the late 15th century the Italian Renaissance was creating a new secular culture in great painting and sculpture, medicine, science, literature, and thought, which would spread from northern Italy throughout Europe: a body of knowledge and of fresh attitudes far removed from established theology. Ironically, the Church herself had been the first great patron of the artists. Michelangelo, Botticelli, Dante, Petrarch, Machiavelli, and, above all, that perfect example of the all-around genius called the "Renaissance man," Leonardo da Vinci exemplify the cultural explosion called the Renaissance.

At the more humble level of technology, the geographical discoveries were made possible by such breakthroughs in navigational aids as the sextant and the mariners' compass, though many explorers sailed into the unknown without them. Improvements in map-making were a great help and advances in ship design from the 15th century on produced vessels like the Portuguese caravel, with its newer hull and its greater number of sails and masts. It was now easier to sail to windward, and the open galley and oars became obsolete. The caravel was a 50-ton, 3 or 4-masted vessel, lateen-rigged, with a castle at the stern. The Spanish galleon was broader, larger and heavier. Both now had rudders by which to steer more accurately.

No single invention had more impact than printing. From the 14th century, larger scale manufacture of cheap rag paper, and from the mid-15th century, the use of movable metal type, brought a flood of publications. Millions of printed books took the place of the few thousand hand-made works of art that formerly were the world's reading matter. Knowledge of the world was made available suddenly, to a wide market, as books were translated into Latin and then into vernacular languages. The Bible itself did not escape this treatment; retranslation led to new critiques by scholars like Erasmus. It was now possible to question at least the text of the Bible.

The European invasion of the Americas came at this precise historical moment. The colonizers were confident, aggressive, energetic, nationalistic people who thought of themselves as the product of a new civilization and science, superior to the old. The native peoples of the Americas could offer little resistance to this aggression. Colonists of the 17th century, for example, despised the Amerindians because they lacked a written language. Could the people of Shakespeare's England intermix with illiterate "savages"?

Modernization and the European colonizer

The political engine of the new culture was the nation-state. Centralizing monarchs concentrated power in their own hands and created state bureaucracies and rational administrations subject to their personal control. National identity gradually became a major shaping force in history, buttressed by national literatures in vernacular tongues, by clever political and economic theories to justify dynastic rule (Divine Right of monarchy and mercantilism), and in the case of Britain, by a newly separated national Church, free of Rome. Local and communal identities began to be pushed into the background, though they did not yet fade away. Men came to see themselves on two levels: first, as *individuals*, second as members of a nation. Nationalism was a powerful device for conquering the New World. In England it was supported by an economic revolution at home. So the cultural pride and feelings of immense superiority already felt by the European conquerors of the New World was enhanced by nationalist fervor. Nothing would be permitted to step in the way of Progress and the advance of the Europeans.

The idea of America's "lack of a feudal past"

It would be wrong nevertheless to exaggerate the difference and the cultural gap between "medieval" and "early modern" society. After all, the roots of the cultural revolution of modernity which helped to create America went back deep into the medieval European past, as with the example of Roger Bacon. It is often said that the United States and British America which preceded it were somehow "born free," and entered the world scene without feudal attributes. Technically, "feudalism" should refer to certain specific institutions of medieval Europe, especially a form of landholding in which local lords or "vassals" hold land in exchange for giving military service to overlords or kings. Serfs, legally tied to the soil, worked for the vassals and went with the land title to new owners. This sort of feudalism, and, indeed, aristocratic landlords, an Established, state-supported Church, and a fixed, caste-like peasantry, were certainly absent, or died out rapidly, in British America. The Americans were effectively free of direct monarchical rule for most of the time, and no single church could lay a dead hand on thought and conduct for very long. In practice, however, historians who talk of America's lack of a feudal past imply more than this—her relative freedom from a great variety of social attitudes, institutions, and ideas in the European past. The word feudal can be oversimplified or made too all-embracing. Colonial America owed much to medieval Europe. Essential links between the medieval and modern world are inescapable.

It is true that the men and women who settled North America were "modern" in distinctive ways and regarded themselves as such. They also retained many medieval habits, ideas, and ways of doing things. Canada and the United States, as well as Mexico, Brazil, and other South American nations, owed debts to the legacy of Europe's medieval past and to the "cultural baggage" the Europeans brought with them to the New World.

Bibliography

S. E. Morrison. *The European Discovery of America: the Northern Voyages,* A.D. *500–1600.* New York: Oxford University Press, 1971.

M. Magnusson and H. Palsson. *The Vinland Sagas.* Baltimore: Penguin Books, 1965.

A. M. Josephy, Jr. *The Indian Heritage of America.* New York: Bantam, 1969.

Howard M. Jones. *O Strange New World: American Culture, The Formative Years.* New York: Viking, 1964.

Charles Gibson. *Spain in America.* New York: Harper, 1968.

2

The cultural baggage of Europe

Cultural differentiation in the New World . . . the struggle for North America . . . Britain's rivals: New Amsterdam and New Sweden . . . Britain's rivals: New France . . . the peopling of New France: Champlain and Colbert . . . Englishmen cross the Atlantic . . . the cultural baggage of the colonizers . . . English merchant capitalism: the "revolution of expectations" . . . economic expansion and alienation . . . Tudor politics: the "rights of Englishmen" . . . the Tudor legacy: religious compromise . . . Virginia: the discipline of a new environment . . . the "starving time" . . . the tobacco colonies: Virginia and Maryland . . . Afro-American beginnings: slavery in Virginia . . . the first colonial assembly: the Virginia Burgesses . . . Maryland: feudalism fails to transplant . . . Puritan utopias: the settlement of New England . . . a polity of Saints: the Mayflower Compact . . . a society of Saints: congregation and township . . . Puritan Commonwealth: Massachusetts Bay . . . Puritanism and the pursuit of moderation . . . Puritan social and family values . . . economic growth and change in New England . . . colonies react to events in England . . . Puritanism comes down to earth . . . the witches of Salem . . . new proprietary colonies . . . the North American colonies in 1688.

The rediscovery of the Americas and the subsequent colonization by the European powers brought a world shift of population and economic investment. Not until many decades later, in the 19th century, would the full extent of this mass global relocation of human resources and culture be felt, with the great migration of Europeans to North America and the rise to world power of the United States.

Cultural differentiation in the New World

The colonizers did not approach the New World in the same way or at the same time, nor did they meet the same problems of geography, climate, and preexisting Indian cultures. The earliest Spanish military conquerors created separate kingdoms in the Americas, each in-

The U.S.A.

dependent of the other though all directly under the throne of Castile. The Spanish enslaved and enserfed the Indians but eventually intermixed with them. French trappers and traders who came later and further north were closely controlled by the state regulations of the mercantilist minister, Colbert, who aimed to build a "New France" in Canada as a state-directed extension of old France. The French traded and intermarried with the Indians of Canada, but not enough Frenchmen ever emigrated to make New France a reality. In contrast, the British settlers and religious utopians were left alone by their government for many years. Colonization was organized by private businessmen and religious groups. The British attempted some conversion of the Indians to Protestant Christianity, but for the natives of America the major result of the coming of the British to North America was war, disease, and near-extinction.

Historical timing deeply affected later colonial histories. The Spanish settled their colonies in the 15th and 16th centuries during the era of Divine Right absolutism and hereditary family rule. Brazil was not developed by Portuguese sugar planters until the later 17th and 18th centuries. The British were late comers also, and some of them, the Puritan pioneers, for example, were products of the intense revolutionary and religious turmoil of the late 16th and 17th centuries. They were worlds apart in style and action from the conquistadors of Spain of a century or more earlier.

A consequence of Europe's rediscovery of the New World was to be, in the long run, the overshadowing of Europe itself; but such an outcome was entirely unlikely in the 17th and 18th centuries. Moreover, at that time, it was not North America, but Central and South America, which dominated in the New World and in the minds of Europeans. While French Canada was not much more than a string of impoverished trading posts in a vast wilderness, and the British settlements in New England and Virginia were still struggling for their physical survival, a magnificent culture flourished in Spanish America. Great urban centers supported arts, crafts, and letters; famous universities shared in the major intellectual movements of the day; the Catholic Church patronized the arts and built gorgeous churches and baroque cathedrals which stand today as perfect examples of transatlantic civilization in this period. The Spanish colonies, with their resources of gold and silver and their captive native labor-force, were rich and powerful. As for North America, the British held the West Indies far more highly than the whole of British North America; the London government regarded the true wealth of America to be in the tropics.

The struggle for North America

The nation-states of Europe nevertheless were prepared to fight for control of the northern half of the continent. Much of North American history in its first two European centuries was determined by the ups and downs of dynastic rivalries in Europe. The contest east of the Mississippi became part of a worldwide war between the two major powers, England and France. Other colonizers—the Dutch, the Swedes, and later on, the Russians in the 18th century—held only brief authority. In 1763 eastern North America became indisputably British, yet a mere 20 years later Britain lost the newly united states.

Britain's rivals: New Netherlands and New Sweden

The Dutch were a nation of seamen, merchants, and skilled craftsmen, who attained a peak of world economic power and influence in the mid-17th century. They derived peculiar energy from nationalism, partly the result of their bloody struggle for independence from Spanish rule. Militarily free by 1595, the Dutch nation became formally independent in 1648. They had pioneered as merchants in far corners of the globe when they were cut off from continental European markets in the course of the long war with Spain. The Dutch designed and built the world's best merchant fleet. They explored the Russian Arctic, the Far East (particularly Southeast Asia), the Indian Ocean, South Africa, and the Americas. In Brazil, for instance, they developed sugar plantations more successful than those of the Portuguese; they came to control the northeast of the territory (Pernambuco) until thrown out in 1654. Their adventure in North America, New Netherlands, was but a small part of these global activities.

The Dutch colony where New York City now stands began with a government grant of 1621 to a trading group, the Dutch West India Company. Actual settlement in the New York area began in 1624. The first leader, Peter Minuit, bought Manhattan Island from the Indians for a famous sum of $24 in 1626 and began the town of New Amsterdam on that site. The colony failed to prosper on the fur trade, and a succession of unpopular governors culminated in the last, Peter Stuyvesant. The colony's basic problem was insufficient population: ordinary, hardworking Dutch folk did not care to emigrate to a settlement dominated by the large landholdings of favored grantees, the great *patroons*. The Company had offered large land grants along the Hudson to the patroons in order to attract speedy settlement, but these soon established themselves as semifeudal lords, armed with perpetual family tenure. The patroons kept strict control of their dues-paying tenants and regulated the law courts and all local offices. Moreover, New Netherlands could not offer to poorer men the lure of gold and silver as could Mexico or Peru. The slightly more favored British colonies of the Connecticut area raided and harassed the Dutch. Eventually in 1664 a British fleet conquered New Netherlands, renaming its town New York.

The Dutch had earlier taken over in 1655 a very small, deeply conservative, and pious, fortresslike, Lutheran settlement on the Delaware River—New Sweden. The British thus swallowed both their minor rivals, Dutch and Swedish, with one gulp. Among other contributions, the Swedes and Finns gave British America the log cabin. In the Hudson Valley of New York Dutch cultural influence remained strong and left traces in architecture and family names. For decades after 1664 great families like the Van Rensselaers, the Schuylers, and the

The U.S.A.

Van Cortlandts wielded authority, and in the 20th century two Roosevelts became presidents of the United States.

Britain's rivals: New France

The two chief rivals for North America, Britain and France, shared the advantage of being latecomers. Roughly a hundred years behind Spain and Portugal in the colonization game, they enjoyed an extra century of experience, knowledge, and economic development that gave them a strong home base to build viable settlements in the New World. When the Spanish invaded the Americas the Spain of Ferdinand and Isabella was still medieval, divided, and a mere group of petty kingdoms under the throne of Castile. The Britain of the Stuarts and the France of the Sun King, Louis XIV, presented more effective centralized monarchies.

French interest in North America dated from 1524 when the Italian explorer, Giovanni da Verrazano, was financed to sweep the coast from north to south, looking for the fabled "Northwest Passage" through America to the Far East. Jacques Cartier established French claims on Newfoundland and the Gaspé Peninsula a decade later. Montreal was noticed as an Indian site in 1535. A French settlement in Quebec failed in 1542 and the region was abandoned by them for half a century. Further south, French Protestants at Fort Caroline in Florida (near present-day Jacksonville) were eliminated after only one year by a Spanish raiding party in 1565. The Spaniards were more firmly entrenched in Florida at their colony, St. Augustine—the oldest, continuously inhabited European settlement in the United States today.

So, at the opening of the 17th century France still had no real colonial foothold in America. She had been slow to colonize, since policymakers were intensely involved in European politics, wars of religion, and dynastic struggles with Spain. French fishing fleets mined the cod off the Grand Banks, sailors traded furs from Indians along the

Dutch America— New Amsterdam in the 17th century

Museum of the City of New York (from the cyclorama in the Dutch Gallery)

North American coast, and the French role was limited to piracy and occasional explorations.

The peopling of New France: Champlain and Colbert

Quebec, the future French capital, was finally established by the pioneer, Samuel de Champlain, in 1608. Motivated by a grand vision of a New France in North America, Champlain extended French territorial claims much further to the West—as far as present Wisconsin—and took part in Indian disputes. He supported the Algonquins in wars against the Iroquois, choosing sides badly, since the Iroquois never forgot, much to the joy of the Dutch and English later. The hopes of Champlain were defeated, however, by that perennial problem of North American colonization, lack of people. He died in 1635, his ambitions unfulfilled, at a time when English Puritans were streaming into New England in numbers. The Canadian "man-land ratio" remained unsatisfactory: the relative shortage of settlers was a retarding factor in Canada's growth throughout the 18th and 19th centuries.

French planners did understand the problem. Cardinal Richelieu chartered the *Company of 100 Associates* in 1627 to encourage emigration but it failed miserably on a first venture. British pirates captured its little fleet (1628) and took Quebec (1630). The Company's land grant was unrealistic: it stretched in theory from Florida to the Arctic, from the Atlantic to the Great Lakes. Yet the charter required a mere 4,000 emigrants over a period of 15 years. Like the English, Richelieu thought more of the West Indies (with their sugar and rum) than of North America. France also ran a profitable slave trade in the tropical waters of Guadeloupe, Martinique, and Guiana.

A sharp policy change came with the new leadership of Louis XIV's finance minister, Jean-Baptiste Colbert (1661–83), who was the leading exponent of the economic theory of dynastic rule, *mercantilism*. The goal in this theory was to build up national economic power by maintaining a constant favorable trade balance and acquiring colonies to exploit them for their raw materials. Mercantilism involved a host of central government regulations of the economy. A central Council of Commerce controlled the chartered trading companies. Planned emigration to Canada was hoped for and soldiers serving in the colonies were required to marry. The merchant fleet, the navy, and colonial defenses were all to be strengthened. Colbert's development plan for the colonies ran up against the residual feudalism of French land policy. Like the Dutch patroon system, the French *seigneurial* system in Canada was a modified version of French feudal tenure in which the king gave large grants to local lords (*seigneurs*), who subdivided their estates into farms controlled by *roturiers* and worked by peasant laborers called *habitants*. In practice it was difficult to force the *habitants* to pay their dues and taxes to the seigneurs and their compulsory tithes to the Church. The wilderness always beckoned and local administration was far from effective. The landholding system nonetheless cramped emigration of ordinary folk from France. The seigneurs' control over local courts and over military service lapsed. Feudalism of this sort was never successfully transplanted from France. The population of New France remained sparse even though the native birthrate was high and the French intermixed more freely with the Indians than did the British.

Englishmen cross the Atlantic

Several years before the Dutch and French pioneers, as early as 1497, John Cabot set sail to the West out of Bristol port toward the New England coast. It took another 80 years before Sir Francis Drake circumnavigated the globe (1577–80), and before three Englishmen, Martin Frobisher (1576), Humphrey Gilbert (1583), and John Davis (1585), sailed to North America again, seeking the way through to Asia. Confusion reigned: Sir Humphrey Gilbert, for example, annexed a fishing village on Newfoundland and claimed the region for Queen Elizabeth I, despite Jacques Cartier's earlier claim on behalf of France.

In the more hospitable lands to the south, the failure of Sir Walter Raleigh's "Lost Colony" of Roanoke (on the present North Carolina coast) revealed one clear lesson: exploration and colonization were two distinct and different sorts of enterprise. Successful settlement would take money and careful planning. Raleigh was behind three experiments at Roanoke—1584, 1585, and 1587. The last was a genuine attempt on his part to establish a true colony made up of men, women, and children, with a plan of government. This version, the "Lost Colony," produced the first English child born in America, Virginia Dare—a *creole*, the French or Spanish would have called her, meaning a child born of European-born parents in the New World. Virginia would have been three in 1590, by which date no trace of anyone was left, only the name "Croatoan" carved on a tree. Presumably some members had been carried off by a local Indian tribe, the Croatans. The historian S. E. Morison points out that Elizabethan words occurred in the Indian language, including surnames from the Lost Colony and that the tribe produced several blue-eyed, fair-haired offspring. Regardless of what became of this group, permanent colonization waited upon an economic revolution at home in the late 16th and early 17th centuries and it would be the fruit of business enterprise and organization, not simple adventuring.

The cultural baggage of the colonizers

All colonial cultures are a mixture in varying degrees of the culture of the invaders and the invaded. The lessons taught by Indians were invaluable, but in the case of the colonies settled by the English in the 17th century the importance of the "cultural baggage" they brought with them seems overwhelming.

This English baggage was economic, social, political, and religious. All of it was part of the rich Tudor legacy, left by the 16th century to the 17th. The New England and Virginia ventures were unmistakably the offspring of English political traditions, of the English Reformation—with its own special national character, and of English merchant capitalism. Political and religious forms to be adopted in the American colonies would reflect the experiences and ideas already

From Father Louis Hennepin,
A New Discovery of a Large Country
in America, *London, 1698*

The first picture of Niagara Falls, 1697

hammered out in Tudor England (both the future Virginia House of Burgesses and the Mayflower Compact would share such roots). And unlike the state-controlled, city-state colonies of Spanish America or the planned Colbertist ventures of New France, British America was first settled by private joint-stock companies. They were organized to make a profit out of taking settlers to the New World, supplying them with goods, and selling their colonial products in Europe.

Stuart England, and therefore the colonies founded in the 17th century, inherited from the Tudors an economic revolution. This "Industrial Revolution of the 16th Century," as it has been named, brought great expansion of old established industries, like woolen cloth production, shipbuilding, and house construction, and the growth of new industries on a relatively large scale, like coalmining, iron manufacture, copper and brass-founding, and production of armaments. Behind this industrial growth lay a necessary expansion of demand: Britain threw off its long dependence for markets on Northern Europe and sought new outlets wherever she could find them, in the Mediterranean, in Spain, and in her colonies in the Caribbean and South America. Britain's natural rivals were the Dutch and the French.

At home, demand was stimulated by native population growth. Meanwhile war and disturbance on the Continent gave English manufacturers, investors, and traders a distinct advantage. The immigration

English merchant capitalism: The "revolution of expectations"

of persecuted minorities from the Continent, especially Protestants and Jews, brought to England some of the most skilled artisans and businessmen who founded several of her basic industries. Native labor mobility was also high and was the result partly of the enclosure movement in the countryside that drove peasants into the towns looking for work. Former common and peasant lands were being taken over by large farmers.

During the first half of the 16th century exports of traditional English broadcloths doubled or tripled. In the second half, English manufacturers developed the finer and lighter "New Draperies" to capture new markets outside Northern Europe. It was through selling this cloth that the English merchants gradually displaced the Dutch in the Mediterranean area. On another trade front the English cannily and deliberately infiltrated the Spanish colonial trading system, both legally and by piracy, and they exploited it for England's use. The great Spanish Empire became an economic colony of English industry. Spanish wools and dyes were imported and then sold back to Spain in the more profitable form of finished cloth. English products were re-exported from Spain to Spanish America and thus the treasures of the Spanish New World flowed ultimately into English pockets—even when English pirates did not steal them on the way. England and Spain warred, but the small kingdom defeated the Spanish Empire's great Armada in 1588, staving off invasion. By 1655, when England took Jamaica from Spain, she was more concerned with the French. (Britain had an old understanding with Portugal; and English merchants had also infiltrated the Portuguese economy.)

Economically, England needed the New England area of North America for its essential naval stores. Timber was increasingly scarce in England, where the iron industry consumed more charcoal, and land was cleared for population growth. The Royal Navy itself had consumed large sections of forests in shipbuilding programs. English merchants also entered the rich slave trade of the Caribbean area and, like the Dutch before them, built sugar plantations.

The boom years created what economists call a "revolution of expectations." Prosperity and growth raised the horizons of many Englishmen and fired a growing nationalism, too. For most individuals these raised life-expectations would be inevitably frustrated. Like other periods of growth, this one abounds in social tension and alienation as well as in the more obvious "Elizabethan exuberance," optimism, and vitality. Progress did bring poverty—as with the large number of landless peasants, pushed out by the enclosure movement in which large landlords converted former cultivated land to sheep pasture to supply wool for the booming cloth trades. Also, an unusual inflation came with the economic growth. General price levels rose roughly four- or five-fold from the mid-16th to the mid-17th century.

Economic expansion and alienation

Economic growth can be as unsettling to the social order as economic depression. Expansion is almost always accompanied by inflation, which disturbs a whole range of established values and norms. For example, the Puritan leader John Winthrop deeply believed in the task of serving God at home in England. Yet he finally convinced himself of the necessity of emigrating to Massachusetts Bay in 1630 and salved his troubled conscience with various arguments, economic as well as religious. His three sons all came of age and needed to be given land in order to survive in English society; this halved Winthrop's personal landholdings. His prosperity as an attorney in London was no longer certain. In England, said Winthrop, a decent man had a tough struggle merely to "keep sayle with his equalls." The times were out of joint. Men could no longer maintain their inherited station.

The causes of the massive price rise are not yet fully agreed upon by scholars. Influx of Spanish-American treasure alone cannot explain it, since the increased money supply was balanced to some degree by the increased output of goods and services. Prices began to rise before the influx of treasure. In England a local cause was Henry VIII's lavish spending of his father's wealth. Henry debased the coin of the realm so often that it came to contain a mere one sixth of its former silver content; he sacked the monasteries and melted down their gold and silver objects to coin the metal. The seizure of Church properties and land during the Reformation has been said to have caused fully one third of total English national wealth to change hands. This social revolution created the newly rich and helped to widen still further the gap between rich and poor. Inflation hit the poor and the modest the worst. Outside the Church, the rich became richer and there were more of them; the poor were relatively poorer and they were more in evidence. Wages did rise, but lagged behind the price rise—which gave a further windfall profit to employers of labor, speculators, merchants, and manufacturers, and stimulated even more economic expansion. Whatever its causes, inflation and growth created social dislocation in England.

In an age of inflated values (and monetary values, when inflated, affect many other values in a culture), men will suffer the treadmill effect: the sinking feeling of being forced to run hard, just to stand still. Winthrop's "keeping sayle" in the 17th century was as painful as "keeping up with the Jones's" in the 20th century. Winthrop, and others like him of varying religious persuasions, grew pessimistic about things English. Perhaps his dismay at the state of English religion reflected some of his own status anxiety and his fears of the changes in mass values. For the truly poor however, for the dispossessed peasantry, there was little need to devise elaborate justifications for leaving England. Those who did so, usually as indentured servants, agreed to a sort of short-term slavery in order to emigrate. The vast majority were forced to stay behind.

Despite the displacements and growing pains of economic expansion, at some date the English people learned to live with economic change. The nation broke through to modernity. People learned not only to suffer or to enjoy economic growth but to *expect* it. This radical conversion, even taken by itself, helps to differentiate the colonial experience and ethos of the English from that of the Spanish or the French.

Tudor politics: The "rights of Englishmen"

The Tudor *political* legacy was equally differentiating. The political basis of the sudden burst of British power in the 17th century was the achievement of national unity, a consolidation that had taken place under the Tudors between 1485 and 1603. The Tudor monarchy had become less absolutist than the Spanish or French. The Crown allied itself with the economic revolution, deliberately encouraging it through charters to private companies. British pirates were supported in their attacks on Spanish trade lines. The State was directly involved in some industries at home. The Tudors built up an alliance of Crown, local gentry and middling groups in the shires, and City of London merchants. The power and influence of the feudal landed nobility were reduced. The Protestant Reformation was welcomed for its more individualistic theology and for the Divine sanction it appeared to give to secular "callings," though the Tudors themselves remained ambivalent about their private theology. Henry VIII's struggle was with the Pope rather than with the Faith.

The key to the success of the Tudor alliance was local government. The system of local administration by direct Crown nominees almost destroyed the feudal nobility. Counties were governed by *Lords Lieutenant,* each a Crown appointee, wielding the power to supervise the local militia in support of the king. Two posts inherited from feudal times were transformed to support the monarchy: *sheriffs* were empowered to collect taxes, administer County Courts and run elections to Parliament, while *justices of the peace* wielded a wide range of powers and performed the major functions of local government. Thus the chief organs in the localities were tied to the Crown. The titles of local government offices in the United States today—the sheriff, the justice of the peace, and also the county coroner—derive from Tudor practice.

At the national level the Tudors were prepared to use the feudal institution of Parliament whenever they needed extra support, as in Henry VIII's daring decision to break with the Pope, or in Elizabeth's war with Spain. This was good short-run tactics but poor long-run strategy: it weakened the authority of the monarchy. Parliament grew stronger than Tudor rulers had intended. In the 17th century as the idea of government *by consent* emerged the political balance of power began to alter. Elizabeth I had adopted warm-hearted rhetoric when she needed help in facing a threatened invasion by the Spanish Armada in 1588, but her words came to be taken literally:

. . . I do not desire to live to distrust my faithful and loving people. Let tyrants fear. I have always so behaved myself that under God I have placed my chiefest strength and safeguard in the loyal hearts and goodwill of my subjects . . . .

Government without consent became un-English. The "English birthright" was firmly established by 1603 in village and town governments with their host of petty offices open to men of varied background and with the jury system, the sheriffs, and the J.P.'s.

What the Tudor system left out, the onrush of history after 1603 would soon provide. The English revolutions of the 17th century—the Puritan Civil War and Cromwell's theocracy, the Stuart Restoration of the monarchy, and the Whig Revolution of 1688—lifted Britain out of the general European 17th century mode. This was not yet full constitutional monarchy with a democratic legislature and a government responsible to an elected assembly, but England was far in advance of Spain or of France, where Louis XIV, who did not die until 1715, remained convinced that his personal authority came from Heaven and his ancestry direct from Adam. Moreover, British nationalism was less a matter of dynastic bombast or military thrills and more one of common Englishmen boasting to the world about their superior freedoms. The "rights of Englishmen" were a firm foundation for a popular nationalism and a strong in-group identification which has survived over the centuries, and they were a central feature of the cultural baggage of the colonists in North America.

Queen Elizabeth's patent that authorized Raleigh's expedition of 1585 revealed in its language the existence of a consensus in England, a general belief that Englishmen enjoyed superior rights to men elsewhere. These rights were guaranteed in the new colony: settlers were promised

all the privileges of free denizens, and persons native of England . . . in such ample manner and fourme as if they were borne and personally resident within our saide Realme of England.

The Tudor legacy: Religious compromise

The English Reformation was as much nationalist as religious in meaning, particularly to the Tudors. Elizabeth, last of the line, was excommunicated by the Pope when she put down a rising of Northern earls and executed about 800 Catholics, yet she remained some sort of Catholic. She was equally tough with the extreme Protestants, like the Browneists who wished to do away with bishops within the Church of England, not merely throw off the Pope and his cardinals. Elizabeth could not accept this radical notion of church government through local congregations. She steered a middle way between Papists and Puritans. Her compromise national faith was founded on Thomas Cranmer's revised Prayer Book, the Acts of Supremacy and Uniformity of 1559, and the 39 Articles of Faith of 1563.

The more radical Puritans, who would purify the Anglican Church, still loved their queen; but she stood for a religious revolution that had stopped halfway. Some moderates were willing to keep the Anglican bishops so long as the Church was purged of Papist ideas. The radicals were either self-governing Congregationalists or Presbyterians, supporting church government by elders and councils. Most radical of all were the Quakers, who rejected even the authority of the local congregation in favor of the conscience, or "Inner Light," of each individual person.

The English who settled the American colonies brought with them these factions and divisions. Virginia was largely moderate and Anglican; New England was colonized by separatists like the Pilgrims, who had already abandoned the Anglican Church before leaving England, or by nonseparatist Puritans, like the main body of emigrants who sailed to Boston in 1630 with Winthrop and still considered themselves members of the national Church of England. Not all of Winthrop's fellow-colonists stayed; religious factions soon appeared. As explained by Captain John Smith of Virginia in his *Advertisements for the unexperienced Planters of New-England*, published almost as these events took place (1631):

Some could not endure the name of a bishop, others not the sight of a cross nor a surplice, others by no means the Book of Common Prayer.

But the "noble Governor" John Winthrop, wrote Smith, acted wisely in allowing the separatist Congregationalists to join their coreligionists in the earlier Pilgrim colony of New Plymouth. "Some two hundred" others, disgruntled and clamorous, he sent back to England. Six or seven hundred remained. In later years the Puritans would prove less wise and tolerant: they would persecute the dissident Quakers. The colonies saw the coming not only of various Protestant factions, but also of Jews and Catholics. Jews arrived in 1654 with the Dutch; the first synagogue was built four years later in tolerant Rhode Island. Catholics first settled Maryland.

The religious legacy of the Tudors meant for the British American colonies a rare degree of religious diversity. This pluralism did not always make for harmony or early success. Once more the legacy of the English past clearly differentiated British America from the colonies of Spain or France. Diversity, independent-mindedness, and factionalism characterized the English settlements from the beginning.

Virginia: The discipline of a new environment

The colorful adventurer Captain John Smith (1579/80–1631), first coined the name "New England" and helped to chart that region's coast, but his main contribution was as a pioneer settler further south in Virginia. His stay was brief—he left after serving as leader (President of the Council) for one year, 1608–9. Yet Smith was outstanding for his practicality, his detailed empirical observations of the terrain and Indian life, and his knowledge of what it took to survive on the edge of the New World. Captain Smith had an overall vision of the possibilities of America as a setting for a new civilization, a vision not to be found in most pioneers of his day, whose chief desire was for quick riches.

Two groups of emigrants acting under a joint-stock company charter issued in 1606 tried to settle the North American coast. One group sailed from Plymouth, England, to the Maine coast. Like Raleigh's earlier attempt, this one failed through lack of follow-up in supplies and financial backing. The second, more solidly underwritten by rich London merchant speculators, landed at Jamestown, Virginia, in 1607. Smith sailed with them, though from the start he was troubled by the type of person who was emigrating. The company was overloaded with "gentlemen," who would not work and had no idea of how to cope with life on the frontier. Smith was mutinous on board ship and was not released from custody until after the group had landed.

The Virginia Company, apart from its ineptly chosen Council, faced enormous constraints of geography. Capital, tools, and labor skills were very scarce. The rewards for the London investors were small; the venture cost them about 100,000 pounds sterling, on very long odds. No gold was discovered, only "fool's gold" (iron pyrites). The colony could find little of cash value to export and it was some years before the tobacco crop would begin to pay off. Further north and later, the Boston and New Plymouth colonies at least had religious zeal to hold them together, but the Virginia settlers were not persecuted minorities. They were a mixture of types: middle-of-the-road Anglicans, get-rich-quick gentlemen, and hardworking artisans seeking a life of dignity and material comfort. Captain Smith saved the colony from vanishing. He imposed a tight labor discipline on all members, whatever their station: all who ate must work.

Smith resisted the short-term, profit-seeking outlook of the Company investors. From comfortable London headquarters they made impossible demands on the colonists—to locate gold mines, find the Northwest Passage, search for Raleigh's Lost Colony. "In over-toiling our

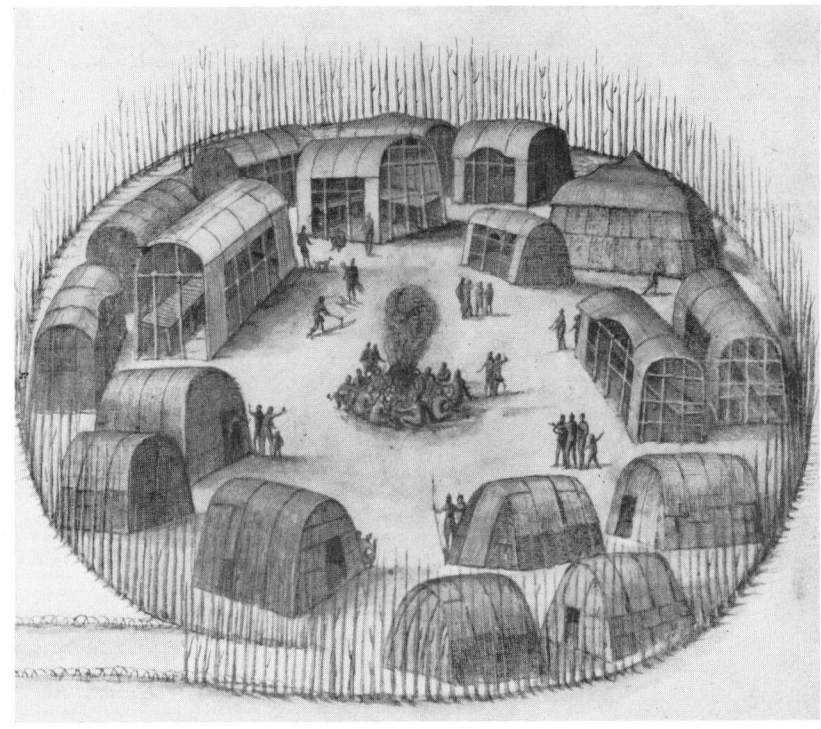

Virginia—an Algonquian village near Roanoke, 1585

British Museum

The U.S.A.

Pocahontas saves John Smith, 1607

From T. de Bry, America, 1634

weak and unskillful bodies, to satisfy this desire of present profit, we can scarce ever recover ourselves from one supply to another," Smith complained in a letter home. The colony was dependent on each supply ship; but the sailors who brought provisions often ate up most of them before leaving. Instead of gentlemen and sailors, sent over at great expense, Captain Smith suggested bluntly:

When you send again, I entreat you rather send but thirty carpenters, husbandmen, gardners, fishermen, blacksmiths, masons, and diggers up of trees . . . than a thousand of such as we have.

The energies of a new colony should be channeled into building up food supplies for the winter, especially Indian corn. The principal aim was not to search for some mythical El Dorado or silver mine, but to survive. Smith's outlook was in sharp contrast to that of many explorers, who followed the poor example of Columbus.

The "starving time"

The year after John Smith returned home the Jamestown settlement suffered its worst catastrophe of bad government, bad luck, and bad relations with the Indians who could have helped them. This terrible "Starving Time" (1609–10) more than halved the colony and brought the little town to ruin. Malnutrition (the corn supply rotted), disease, and violence almost wiped out the whole colony. They abandoned Jamestown, but halfway down the river were met by an incoming supply ship with a new governor, Lord De la Warr. Virginia was saved.

Other colonies suffered "starving times" (Plymouth, Bermuda, and Barbados, for example). Yet Virginia was to be one of the wealthiest in North America. The Virginia Dynasty was to dominate colonial and United States politics and society for decades to come, and produce four of the first six U.S. presidents. The original natural wealth of this beautiful land would win through in the end. Chesapeake Bay, as seen through the eyes of Captain Christopher Newport on that lovely April morning of 1607, vies with Leif Ericson's vision of Vinland the Good. Newport saw "fair meadows, goodly tall trees, . . . fresh waters." Turkeys, oysters, cultivated Indian corn, tobacco, strawberries four times the English size, abounded. Yet Englishmen starved in the midst of plenty and "died like dogs" from "cruel diseases, such as swellings, fluxes, burning fevers." What they needed above all, to please London and to keep up the supplies from England, was something to export for cash.

That something was tobacco, first exported from Jamestown by John Rolfe in 1614. Rolfe was close to the Indians: he married chief Powhatan's daughter, Pocahontas, in 1614—the same girl lauded by Captain John Smith for having saved his life in 1607. But more lay behind the decision of the Virginians to grow tobacco for export than this personal story. The colonists experimented with various exports, including tobacco, grain, grapes, naval stores (for which they set up sawmills), glass, and iron. Their economic organization was altered in 1616 and 1618 and private ownership in land was introduced, through the "headright" system, to create more incentive. Previously, land had been jointly held and cultivated; the profits were to be split. The headright system allowed 50 acres of land to each colonist who subscribed 12½ pounds sterling to the colony. Another 50 acres was available for each person who would settle in Virginia; and 50 more acres for those who would agree to pay the passage of another emigrant to the colony. Thus each colonist was himself a sort of living share in the company—an "adventure" they termed it, rather than the modern corporate word, "share." After 1616 the colonists worked harder for their individual profits than they had ever worked for the community store.

The tobacco colonies: Virginia and Maryland

In 1624 the Virginia Company failed financially. It made no profits and the Indian massacre of 1622, led by Powhatan's brother, Opechancanough, was a tragic setback. In 1621 the Privy Council prohibited the public lotteries through which the Company had raised extra funds in southern England. Bankrupt, the Company lost its charter, and the State took over Virginia directly. Virginia thus became England's first Crown Colony.

Company or Crown-controlled, the fundamental problems in America did not change. Of these the central issue was labor scarcity and land abundance. As tobacco became popular in Europe, the growing export demand brought the institution of African slavery to the tobacco colonies. Other means of meeting the labor shortage were tried: the headright system was continued after 1624; the technique

The U.S.A.

of allowing private groups to develop sections of Virginia under "patents" from the colonial government was extended. Convict labor was used, though Virginians came to object to this, and much *indentured* labor: people without means selling their labor for a number of years, to have their passage paid. Indeed, evidence indicates that at first black African labor was on an indentured basis. Out of these attempts to meet the labor problem, two basic institutions of Southern life emerged: the plantation system and black slavery.

Afro-American beginnings: Slavery in Virginia

"About the last of August came in a Dutch man of warre, that sold us twenty Negars," reported John Rolfe in 1619. Thirty years later there were about 300 Africans in a total white population for Virginia of about 15,000. Their numbers were still small, but the evidence is that already Negroes were being treated differently from other indentured labor and servants. Some blacks, at least, were held as *perpetual* slaves and their children were born into slavery in America. After 1660 it became clear: slavery, written into the law codes of Virginia and Maryland, was soon supported by strict regulations against racial mixing.

North America was not the site of the first large-scale enslavement of Africans by the English. This happened in the Caribbean sugar

A tobacco plantation

Arents Collection, New York Public Library

islands, where native Indian labor had been wiped out already, as we have observed. Thousands of Africans were bought from black traders in Africa and shipped to Barbados, the Leeward Islands, and after 1655, to Jamaica, where they were literally worked to death on English sugar plantations and simply replaced by other Africans. The first black revolt against English overseers broke out in Puritan territory, ironically, on Providence Island (off the Central American coast), as early as 1638. In the Caribbean the English had few qualms about using human slaves.

Inhibitions against slavery also evaporated in North America, as indentured labor proved inadequate in the tobacco areas and it became clear what profits were to be made in the trade. Tobacco dynasts flourished, the number of slaves grew, and the system became deeply entrenched as a whole way of life. It was not planned that way in 17th century Virginia or Maryland; slavery simply grew up. But in the Carolinas, its institution was more deliberate and calculated: in the 1690s Barbados planters planned the introduction of slavery there to cultivate rice plantations. Consequently the South Carolina slave codes became the most harsh, modeled on the grim Barbados precedents.

Successful use of slavery as a labor system by the Portuguese and Spanish may have helped convince Englishmen that the system could pay. This is not to "spread the blame" for an evil system: after all, English and Dutch traders, among others, sold many of the slaves to the Spanish colonies in earlier decades. Certainly the words "Negro" and "mulatto" were taken from the Spanish. The English may well have called the blacks "Indians": they tended to use that word widely —calling the Hawaiians that they came across in the late 18th century "Indians." In any case, slavery survived and grew because it worked; it filled the labor gap. The English did not stop to calculate detailed costs, still less the social costs. No other labor was forthcoming in sufficient quantity. Ironically, the more slaves were used, the less likely it was that floods of free European labor would appear to compete for the slaves' jobs.

Colonial economic survival and growth depended on the export trade. By the 18th century most export crops were produced by black labor. The contribution of Africans to American history is thus incalculable from the earliest days.

The first colonial assembly: The Virginia Burgesses

While Virginia struggled for economic life, the "rights of Englishmen" did not entirely die. The colony submitted to a firm political hand after 1611, to save it from factionalism. But in 1619 under Governor Yeardley the House of Burgesses was created—a one-chambered body made up of elected representatives, two from each town and patented plantation, which sat with the governor and his nominated council. Geographical distance and local needs made the Company government system ludicrous and at the outset the Burgesses began to exercise two basic functions of government: the right to initiate legislation, and the right to control the purse. These rights other nations have taken many decades of bloodshed to attain. In Virginia they came fairly easily. The Burgesses were a long way from democratic government of course, but this elected committee of the elite of the colony was also no more rubber stamp for the governor or the Company.

Remarkably, the Burgesses were allowed to continue after the assumption of Royal control in 1624, along with the headright land grant system. In later years the assembly became bicameral and the elected section withdrew to meet separately. Many leaders of the future American Revolution were trained in this college of representative government, including Washington, Jefferson, Madison, and Monroe. The lower house of the assembly began a struggle for power, paralleling that of the House of Commons within the English system in London. The House of Burgesses was an unusual creation in a 17th century European colony. The Spanish-American *cabildos* were created earlier, in the 16th century, and were elective; but their scope, as town councils with limited powers, was very restricted, and by the 17th century the councillors were purchasing office. The Burgesses expressed the "rights of Englishmen" and were a sign of the comparative political maturity of British America.

Maryland: Feudalism fails to transplant

Meanwhile Virginia's neighbor, Maryland, was created in 1632, personal gift of Charles I to a Catholic aristocrat, George Calvert, Lord Baltimore. Maryland was the first noncorporate settlement, a feudal-type domain. But just as the Virginia Burgesses began to grasp the initiative, so the settlers of would-be feudal Maryland insisted on their Englishmen's rights. In theory the Calverts were absolute rulers of Maryland; in practice the conditions of the frontier environment and the attitudes of the emigrants from England made this unworkable.

A mainly Catholic settlement was established at St. Mary's in 1634, and Baltimore's brother, Leonard Calvert, set up a semi-feudal government. The early years of Maryland's history were very troubled, chiefly with military conflicts against claimants to Calvert territory from Virginia. The raiding grew worse during the Puritan revolution in England, when Calvert almost lost his colony to invaders and his charter to political opponents in England. In fact, Protestants did emigrate to Maryland, and in 1649 under a Protestant deputy governor the assembly passed a religious Toleration Act. The Calverts had been forced to permit an elective assembly, which, like the Burgesses, took a hand in introducing new laws. The toleration granted was limited to all Trinitarians. By then, however, the colony was heavily Protestant in population, and in 1654 the Puritan parliament in England intervened, threw off the authority of the proprietors, and denied civil rights to all Catholics in Maryland. A short civil war in the colony was won by the Puritans, though after a period of political confusion another Calvert, Philip, became governor in 1660.

Maryland, like Virginia, became dependent on tobacco exports. Catholic gentry, who emigrated from Britain with their families and servants, developed large land grants. They were a local elite though most immigrants were yeomen farmers paying only nominal rents to landholders. Tobacco plantations, using African slaves, soon developed. Tensions between Catholics and Protestants and between the Calverts and the assembly and smaller farmers were always worse when tobacco prices were falling, as in the 1660s. Despite the restoration of the Stuart monarchy in England in 1660, anti-Catholic feeling did not die in Maryland and two rebellions were crushed in 1676 and 1681. The Whig Revolution of 1688 and the absence of Lord Baltimore, who was in England trying to solve complex boundary disputes with Pennsylvania and Virginia, led to a final successful coup by the Protestant Association in 1689. The assembly governed until 1691 when Maryland temporarily became a Royal Province and the Anglican Church was established. In Maryland, age-old English religious battles had been refought.

Puritan utopias: The settlement of New England

The religious colonies that were settled in New England reacted as violently as did Maryland to political changes in England in the volatile 17th century. Their colonization was organized, like that of Virginia, by joint-stock private enterprise companies, but their driving force was religious idealism. Whether this idealism can be considered truly "radical" or truly "conservative" is a matter of one's theological point of view. The dissidents emigrated to build a new church and a new society, with a fresh start: a "City Upon a Hill." They thought England was backsliding, going to the Devil, and that those who did nothing would suffer torment for their inactivity. As we have observed, many Puritans had no wish to abandon the Church of England entirely, though its residual Romanism, its language, style, and rituals displeased them. They would merely purify the church from within and by the example that they would set of a better society in the American wilderness. They would live according to God's law in the New World.

The Pilgrim Fathers went much further. They were tough "independents" who had already forsaken the Anglican Church before leaving England. They had set up new churches and had been persecuted for it. Their uncompromising and exclusive spirit was characterized by Captain John Smith, himself an orthodox Anglican:

This absolute crew, only of the Elect, holding all (but such as themselves) reprobates and castaways.

One group of these self-chosen people, William Brewster's separatist congregation at Scrooby, Lincolnshire, escaped to Leyden in Holland in 1609. Ten years later Brewster's people set sail for America via England, where they picked up more supporters. From the outset their voyage was beset by calamities and was badly underfinanced. One ship alone—the *Mayflower*—managed to complete the journey.

Off course, these Pilgrim Fathers took the historic decision to settle at Plymouth where they had accidentally made first landfall. The Pilgrims held no official royal charter to this land, merely a patent from the Virginia Company, whose territory did not extend this far north. Since the patent was meaningless, Plymouth Plantation was an extralegal affair from the beginning—not that the Pilgrims had any desire to settle in Anglican Virginia anyway. Here was private initiative with a vengeance, a sharp contrast with the state-regulated and state-planned colonial ventures of New Spain or New France.

A polity of Saints: The Mayflower Compact

With no charter to guide them and serve as a nucleus for political institutions, the Pilgrims were obliged to experiment. They created a political society of their own choosing. On board ship 41 adult males drew up the unprecedented Mayflower Compact while they rested offshore near what is now Provincetown, Cape Cod. Non-Pilgrim members—"strangers"—had threatened to go their own way when ashore, so the company resolved the crisis by written agreement on November 11, 1620.

The Pilgrim Fathers literally enacted what later generations would term the "Social Contract." In this ideal concept, the legitimacy of all government rested ultimately on the consent of the governed, on majority will. They pledged, "in the presence of God and of one another," to:

covenant and combine our selves togeather into a civill body politick; . . . and by vertue hearof to enacte, constitute, and frame shuch just and equall lawes, . . . from time to time, as shall be thought most meete and convenient for the generall good of the Colonie: unto which we promise all due submission and obedience.

They tempered their individual freedoms with the obligation of *obedience* to the government they themselves would choose. In England such notions were still very novel; not until 1690 would John Locke's *Second Treatise* formalize the concept, and not until 1762 in the case of Rosseau's famous *Social Contract*.

The agreement on the *Mayflower* in 1620 was the first recorded example of Americans writing themselves a paper constitution. Many others followed, e.g., Roger Williams' "covenant" at Providence in 1636, and ultimately the Federal Constitution adopted in 1787. The idea was not new to the Pilgrims. Church "covenants" had been common for some years. Dissident members anxious to form a new church of their own would usually draft a covenant or pledge, to stick together, obey the elders, and support the church at all times. In Scotland, for example, the "Covenanters" were those Presbyterians who bound themselves solemnly together to oppose Catholicism by the Covenant of 1581. Each separatist Puritan church had its covenant. The Pilgrims had already signed several since the Scrooby church was first formed.

What form of government did the Mayflower Compact produce? A limited representative system, in which the "freemen" (original signers, of whom only 20 survived the first six months) had the vote, and from time to time enlarged their number by admitting their children as they grew up, servants whose indentures had been worked out, and others. The freemen met annually in General Court and elected a governor each year. William Bradford won election for 31 years in a row. The Court was a legislative assembly and a supreme court of law combined. As the colony grew geographically, local government also became necessary. The seeds of American self-government were sown early and deep in New England as in Virginia.

A society of Saints: Congregation and township

The idea of the fellowship of the *congregation,* bound together by the covenant, was at the heart of all Puritan political and social thought. The way they ran their church was the model for secular affairs, the "City Upon a Hill." Government in New England did not become openly theocratic, in fact the Puritans were careful to separate Church and State, but the influence of religion and of its ministers was always deep. Every political decision, like every Puritan personal life decision, was saturated with the consciousness of God and His law. The sanctity of the will of the congregation probably saved Puritan society from becoming priest-ridden.

The very physical organization of the New England colonies expressed Puritan religious beliefs. In New England people settled in compact communities, in contrast with Virginia or Maryland, where the plantation, large land grants, the tobacco crop, and African slavery created a decentralized pattern of independent homesteads. Each New England town was built around a village green—the Common—and a church. The Puritan authorities frowned upon indiscriminate settlement of individuals in the wilderness. Even the "strangers" who signed the Compact agreed not to wander out on their own. The town was patterned closely on the medieval English manor, another illustration of the direct transplantation of Old World, feudal institutions. The township expressed the congregational-covenantal spirit and made possible the closer control by the Puritan community of the lives and behavior of its members, a matter crucial to all sectarian utopias.

Unlike the Virginians, the Puritans lived in close communities. Their families were large, and their houses small, with little individual privacy. Family life was a sort of small-scale public life. Community values dominated. The church and the government felt entirely free to regulate personal conduct and guide morals, or to intervene in family disputes and instruct individuals how to behave. This broad definition of government received support from public opinion, for one moral law governed all.

The New England town was a consensual community, a village of Old England, but without a squire or local lord. The church, to which all belonged, was created on the spot, and had no inherited hierarchy. In the *town meeting* most adult males could vote, dispute, and debate, as the number of freeholders was widened. Society in all its parts was interrelated in one religious organism under God: the individual, the micro-society of the family, and the wider society of the township.

Puritan Commonwealth: Massachusetts Bay

Thus the New England town was an instrument of social control, but one supported by the public. Its later decay was associated with the decay of Puritan faith: cause and effect were intertwined.

Half of the Pilgrim expedition had lost their lives before the first six months passed. Only friendly Indians kept the little colony going. Plymouth survived and grew strong enough to attract migrants from its bigger Puritan cousin, Massachusetts Bay, and to ward off marauding Indians. Yet by 1691 most members were glad to be absorbed into Massachusetts Bay colony: the economic, political, and strategic advantages of union were too obvious and the early sectarian tension between the two settlements had by then abated.

The larger colony began with a company charter of 1629 granted by Charles I to a group of rich Puritan capitalists and property owners. Historians have claimed that the "Protestant ethic" of the Reformation sanctified the rational pursuit of individual profit-making and therefore stimulated economic growth and capitalism. If ever a group of leaders illustrated this hypothesis, the men who came with John Winthrop to Boston in 1630 fit the bill. Many of them were well-to-do. They left England for conscience' sake, but they were determined to make the new colony succeed in a businesslike fashion, and they invested their wealth in the venture.

Their timing was fortunate. In its first ten years, Massachusetts Bay received about 20,000 immigrants. English persecution of Puritans (the regime of Archbishop Laud), combined with depression in the cloth trade and continuing inflation, helped to solve the critical labor scarcity problem faced by all new colonies. This "Great Migration," building on the firm basis of the original expedition (17 ships, and 1,000 emigrants), put Massachusetts on the map almost instantly. Immigration slowed after 1640 when a Parliament called in London seemed to promise more civil rights for Puritans; but the outflow picked up again later. These immigrants (not all were Puritans) did not seek gold or furs; they came planning to settle and to farm. They gave themselves to the New World, to build a new "Commonwealth."

The political form of this Commonwealth came from the company's charter. By some oversight the original royal document did not state where the Company should meet, so its officers boldly took the charter with them to New England. Massachusetts became the first company colony *not* to be officially administered by absentee directors thousands of miles away in London. The Puritans were a self-regulating colony. Twelve original "freemen" of the Company formed the first civil government and elected their own governor and his assistants. They all met in General Court. By May 1631 this small oligarchy was broken and all church members were admitted to voting and to some participating rights in civil affairs; they all became "freemen." Within three more years the pattern of liberalization we have already noticed in Virginia and Maryland was followed in Massachusetts. The General Court won lawmaking powers and reaffirmed its right to elect the governor. In 1644 the Court was now a bicameral body with a lower house composed of elected members from each town. Political rights were still restricted to church members, however.

John Winthrop, four times governor of Massachusetts between 1629 and 1649, was a dedicated moderate who resisted the utopian separatism and self-righteousness of New Plymouth. Winthrop believed that one could not make the world a better place by running away from it. The decision for him to leave England had been very difficult. He was no perfectionist, as were the radicals he felt forced to banish from the colony. This world could never be made perfect; the most one could do, Winthrop felt, was to *strive to do the right thing*.

Puritanism and the pursuit of moderation

The preacher Roger Williams, for example, was clearly a subversive radical from Winthrop's point of view. Williams attacked the charter. He claimed that the government had no rights in religious affairs. This threatened the entire venture of Massachusetts Bay, so the General Court, supported by Winthrop, ordered Williams to leave. During the winter of 1635 Williams went off to join the Narragansett Indians and to create his own settlement at Providence, which eventually became the colony of Rhode Island. Williams' later record was magnanimous: he remained true to his word and kept Providence open to men and women of various shades of belief. He developed a fairer relationship with the Indians than did most Puritans. But in his split with Governor John Winthrop in 1635 he had insisted rigidly on the narrow pursuit of his own personal holiness. For Winthrop this sort of atomistic individualism was a sin. Williams threw off the English churches; then he escalated his revolution by rejecting the Puritan churches of Massachusetts; finally he ended up, absurdly, "communicating" (sharing worship) with no one but his own wife. As leader of his own colony, Williams relaxed and came closer to Winthrop's position of allowing to others the sort of individual freedom and dignity he always demanded for himself.

In 1638 another dissident, Anne Hutchinson, was also exiled after she defied the Puritan consensus and community bond by deliberately holding religious meetings and preaching the gospel at her own house. Mistress Hutchinson threatened the colony with *Antinomianism*: the doctrine that the conversion experience of the elect placed them outside the conventional moral rules; they could be guided by a personal conscience and had little need of orthodox ministers or the necessity of doing "good works" to reveal their inward holiness and acceptance by God. She built up a sizable following and won over the young governor, Sir Henry Vane. This alarmed Winthrop, who fought a strong election and replaced Vane in 1637. Anne Hutchinson was tried, excommunicated, and banished. She went off with her husband and family to Roger Williams and established the town of Pocasset. This remarkable woman was murdered by Indians in 1643. The Puritans saw God's hand in this.

John Winthrop,
Puritan leader

American Antiquarian Society

Puritan social and family values

Many Americans today still think of Puritans as drab, narrow-minded, sexually repressed, witch-hunting bigots. This distorted view reflects the arrogance of later ages, a false sense of moral progress, and the influence of satirists who have defined Puritanism as "the haunting fear that someone, somewhere, might be happy." The Puritans were very likely as "happy" as any generation. Their lives were not markedly drab. Their everyday clothes were often gaily colored, though formal dress would be dark. Men like John Winthrop, scion of the English country squirearchy, were accustomed to their huntin', shootin' and fishin.' Winthrop drank and ate well and enjoyed God's gifts without excess. Puritans were rarely bigots in the sense of having closed minds. They loved to talk, to argue, debate, and think things through again—as did Winthrop—within the limits of their theological framework.

The family structure of the Puritans, according to recent historical scholarship, was not very different from that of present-day America. The Puritan family was "nuclear" and consisted of man, wife, and their own children, rather than being an "extended" family which included many less-close relatives. The chief contrast with today was that Puritans had many more children and childhood came to an official end much sooner, at about the age of seven. Young people were not forced into family-arranged marriages, though family approval was more necessary for love-matches than is now the case. Puritans married later on in life, and older people were more respected than nowadays. The family performed many functions such as schooling and job-training and served as a micro-model of the larger Puritan society, subject to interference if deemed necessary from church and state and by community values. A large number of Puritan parents farmed out their children to other families to ensure that their affection for them would not impede the children from being properly disciplined and trained.

Economic growth and change in New England

The Puritans and "strangers" survived, as did colonists elsewhere, by developing cash export crops. The soils of New England were poor and stony and would support only subsistence farming of corn, together with some sheep and cattle grazing around Narrangansett and the island shores. Luxury furs could be traded from the Iroquois but the real basis of the Puritan economy became pine and cod. Massachusetts Bay lived off its own immigrants for a while, keeping them supplied with the basic necessities of food and housing. When the Great Migration tailed off however, cattle and lumber prices declined. In the 1640s the Puritans turned to external markets. All along the North American coast from Nova Scotia to the West Indies they supplied cattle, lumber, and fish to other colonists. Their trade extended to the Azores, Portugal, and Spain. They avoided or ignored the British legal restrictions imposed by the Navigation Acts, which sought to limit colonial trade in England's favor.

The shipping of other peoples' goods led New Englanders to begin a shipbuilding industry, on which England herself soon became heavily dependent. The soft white pine of northern regions, Maine and New Hampshire, converted into usable timbers by backwoods sawmills, was in great demand for building, for fuel, and for potash and pearlash for the glass and soap industries at home and in England. American ships' timbers and masts were considered superior by the Royal Navy. Meanwhile the fishing ports like Boston, Salem, and Gloucester flourished in the supplying of cod to Catholic Europe and fish scraps as cheap slave food to West Indies planters. Fish were so abundant that Puritan farmers used them for fertilizer. Captain John Smith reported in 1631:

In Virginia they never manure their overworn fields . . . but in New England they do, sticking at every plant of corn a herring or two.

In the 18th century, sailors from Nantucket and New Bedford developed the large whaling industry. The soil being poor, New Englanders farmed the ocean.

The expansion of New England and the creation of additional colonies was brought about by increasing prosperity and by religious disagreements. Roger Williams gained a charter for Rhode Island in 1644. Rev. Thomas Hooker's factious congregation left Cambridge, Massachusetts, in 1636 after a personality struggle among leaders and moved into the beautiful Connecticut Valley at Hartford. The *Fundamental Orders* of 1639 united Hartford with nearby settlements. Later the ultra-orthodox colony at New Haven was joined to these, and Connecticut colony was thus created. In 1679 the settlements north of the Merrimac River also broke away from Massachusetts and were chartered as the separate royal colony of New Hampshire.

Colonies react to events in England

By the mid-17th century the British colonies were firmly established, with growing population and exports; but they remained tied culturally and economically to the Mother Country and reacted to each political change at home. Virginia was affected the least by the climactic events—the Civil War, the Puritan Commonwealth of Cromwell, the Stuart restoration of the monarchy and the Glorious Revolution of 1688. Virginians cared not who governed England, so long as the English continued to smoke more tobacco. Maryland, in contrast, reacted violently to English events and suffered her own miniature civil war, as we have seen.

New Englanders formed a loose, defensive alliance to fight the Indians and Dutch in 1643. Massachusetts dominated the group and began to test its own independence. Nathaniel Ward's famous new code of law, the *Body of Liberties* of 1641, was a sort of declaration of *legal* independence and in 1646 even John Winthrop, under strong criticism for persecutions of non-Puritans and for ignoring English legal precedents, brought himself to declare:

Our allegiance binds us not to the laws of England, any longer than while we live in England.

In 1652 Massachusetts went so far as to ignore the London Parliament and become an independent "Commonwealth."

When King Charles I was beheaded (1649), and the English Puritans came to full political power after years of persecution and frustration, Massachusetts suddenly felt itself to be at the center of world events. The little colony was engulfed in a new zealotry, and began cruel persecutions of dissidents, especially Quakers, with their individualistic, "Inner Light" doctrine of personal roads to salvation. Quakers were banished, some had their ears cut off, and four were hanged, including Mary Dyer, a disciple of the late Anne Hutchinson. This happened in the space of four or five years (1656–61). The Stuart restoration of 1660 brought Charles II to the English throne and an abrupt change of course.

Puritanism comes down to earth

By the late 17th century New England's leaders could no longer afford to be so exclusive. External and internal forces, erosion and corrosion, brought the "declension" of Puritan faith. The first generation of pioneers, the "Visible Saints," like John Winthrop, John Cotton, and Thomas Hooker, were mortal and passed away. The Puritan *sect* could not maintain its early zeal and impetus; it was forced to become a more orthodox Congregational *Church*.

The Stuarts brought external pressures to bear, as they tried to tighten the royal grip on the colonies. Charles II nullified the Massachusetts Bay charter in 1684. The next year his brother, James II, imposed one form of government over the region, the short-lived *Dominion of New England*. Governor Edmund Andros ruled without benefit of any local assemblies until the colonists overthrew the Dominion, with the coming of the Whig Revolution of 1688 and the removal of James. In 1691 the Puritan leadership was forced to accept a new Massachusetts charter which based the franchise on property ownership instead of membership in the Congregational Church. Secular-minded liberals took over Harvard College and the clergy felt deeply threatened. A general secularization process was under way, partly the result of economic change and the rise to social power of a large class of merchants and traders.

The very economic success of the Puritans proved to be their undoing. Prosperity and population growth made it impossible to restrict settlement to the planned, contiguous township pattern. The rules were relaxed for Thomas Hooker's out-migration as early as 1636. Expansion entailed social tension and class differentiation in certain New England towns: there was population pressure, and actual scarcity of good land—an ironic circumstance for any American colony.

The old pioneer faith could have withstood such forces perhaps, but rival beliefs waxed strong, despite attempts to suppress them. The Baptists flourished in Rhode Island and Presbyterians and Quakers would not be stilled. Fewer faces were seen in congregations; steps had to be taken to attract the young to the true faith. So in 1662 the *Half-Way Covenant* was agreed upon in Massachusetts, making it easier for second-generation Puritan offspring, who had never suffered the molding influence of persecution, to become members of the church. The original exclusiveness of Puritan membership was based on proof of religious *conversion*, offered by the would-be member and examined by the church committee. Now, second-generation Puritans could stay in church and even baptize their own children without such stringent proof of personal religious experience. They were still not permitted to vote or to take the Lord's Supper—but the floodgate was opened. Soon, in the Connecticut Valley, Rev. Solomon Stoddard began preaching full membership for all Godly folk, and in Boston itself the Brattle Street Church admitted all and sundry from 1699. The utopian phase of Massachusetts history came to an end.

The witches of Salem

The outburst of witch-hunting at Salem in 1692 was a body blow to Puritan orthodoxy. Some adolescent girls, apparently as a prank, feigned hysteria and accused their half-Negro, half-Indian family slave of having bewitched them. The woman was flogged until she "confessed" and named accomplice witches. Before the frenzy ended, 14 women and 5 men were hanged (not burnt, as in Europe), and one male victim of this judicial murder was pressed to death because he would not plead guilty or not guilty. Many prominent Puritan leaders and divines went along with these proceedings, which involved inadmissible ("spectral") evidence, rigged confessions, secret torture, and totally unfair defense procedures.

How can one explain this mass delusion? Puritanism was caught off balance in 1692. The new charter rights of the previous year that were granted to nonmembers and the secularizing forces that were at work threatened the orthodox and the clergy. There were temporary economic problems, including property conflicts. A raid against the Catholics in Quebec had failed. Increased social tensions produced violent outbursts in several colonies, such as Bacon's Revolt of 1676 in Virginia and Leisler's uprising of 1689 in New York. However, one needs more than this to explain the Salem affair.

Mass delusions have been fairly common throughout history. Mass suggestion episodes are not limited to religion, though witchcraft delusions occurred throughout Europe in this same period. There was perhaps little that was uniquely Puritan about the Salem tragedy. The trials began in the spring, but by October the madness was recognized and the court dissolved; 150 accused witches were released from jail. Full restitution was done to the victims' families, and judges and juries confessed their folly. The entire colony held a day of shame and fasting in January 1697. This, at least, was very "Puritannical."

New proprietary colonies

When the humane William Penn was asked to take action against dangerous witches in his colony, he replied cleverly that he could not, because "there was no law in Pennsylvania against riding on broomsticks." Pennsylvania was one of the new colonies created after the Restoration, and it came to rival Massachusetts and Virginia on the British American scene. These new settlements were owned by proprietors: the joint-stock company colonies simply had failed to make a profit in the New World (though in India the British East India Company clung on until 1858).

Charles II gave generous grants of land to Stuart supporters, and in rapid succession the Carolinas (1663), New York and New Jersey (1664), and then Pennsylvania (1681) were formed. Years later, Georgia was colonized by the philanthropist James Oglethorpe (1732) as a haven for debtors and the unemployed. The Carolinas followed the American pattern: feudal land grants could not survive unchanged, because the English aristocrats who were given the land understood the need to attract and then to placate settlers. The Carolinas were intended as a buffer against possible Spanish military expansion from the South. To be of any profit to their proprietors the lands had to be settled and farmed; so religious toleration, generous headrights, and local representation came swiftly if not without political conflict between Tidewater and backcountry. The New York grant was not immediately settled. The owner, James Stuart, became king in 1685. Dutch settlers were still strong in the Hudson valley and Manhattan area; in fact, Dutch power had returned to New York very briefly during the Anglo-Dutch Wars (1673–74). The patroon landed elite was outflanked by migrations of New Englanders into upper New York in the 18th century, facilitated by English friendship with the powerful Iroquois Confederacy. James had already begun the history of New Jersey with a large section grant to a couple of his cronies in 1664.

The Quaker convert, William Penn, received the Pennsylvania grant in 1681 in payment for an old Stuart debt to his father. His colony was in many ways the best planned and most rationally settled of them all.

He advertised openly for religious refugees and minority dissidents, like the German Mennonites who settled Germantown in 1683, or the Dunkards, triple-immersion Baptists, who joined them there in 1719. Penn gave his people liberal land grants, freedom of worship, and local political representation. Immigrants swarmed in. The Quakers did not countenance the idea of a permanent servant class; they ultimately refused to allow African slavery, and most of the labor that entered was free or temporarily indentured. Penn's single-bodied assembly was based on a wide franchise. He aimed to attract free, white labor and build a society dominated by a majority of independent small freeholders. Pennsylvania soon became a microcosm of the future United States: a *plural society*. Its population was made up of so-called Pennsylvania "Dutch" (Southwest Germans and Swiss, who settled in southeast Pennsylvania); Quakers (mainly English and Welsh, concentrated around Philadelphia, and controlling trade and politics); other sectarians, and in the 18th century, Scotch-Irish in the Cumberland Valley and West. In accordance with his acquired religious faith, Penn made a famous treaty of peace and friendship with the Indians, though this Indian policy did not survive. Philadelphia, his City of Brotherly Love, grew to become the largest North American city of the 18th century and second in size only to London within the British Empire. For ten years after the Revolution (1790–1800) it was the capital of the new American nation and for much longer its cultural and financial center. Among New World cities, however, Philadelphia was still far behind Mexico City, or Lima, Peru.

The North American colonies in 1688

By the time of the Whig Revolution of 1688 in England, the British had a string of settlements down the Atlantic coast of North America. Their origins were varied, but they were all independent-minded, diverse, factious, and resistant to royal controls. Immigration of common folk in large numbers characterized these settlements, helped by schemes like the indenture system, under which those without funds agreed to labor for periods of from four to seven years in repayment for their passage and minimum keep. One estimate is that over half the emigrants to the American colonies went in this fashion, as bound labor. Their conditions of work were not good, though markedly better than those experienced by the African slaves who went in chains to the New World. In addition there were forced white emigrants—convicts, vagrants, political prisoners of Cromwell (Irish and Scots defeated in battle), and even people deliberately kidnapped by unscrupulous labor "brokers" to meet the growing demand for labor in the colonies. In the following century large numbers of Scotch-Irish, Highland Scots, and Germans would go to the colonies, along with about 200,000 African slaves. These numbers distinguished the British settlements from those of the French further north in Canada.

Even by 1688 the Americans had built up a store of political experience in the management of tricky relationships among assemblies, governors, short-lived "Dominions," and royal prerogatives. Soon they would be up against more powerful odds, the prerogatives of the House of Commons. Early political maturity thus differentiated the British colonies, as well as the unusual economic origins of the population, religious diversity, and a spirit of factionalism.

Bibliography

C. L. Ver Steeg. *The Formative Years, 1607–1763*. New York: Hill & Wang, 1964.

J. Lankford (ed.). *Captain John Smith's America*. New York: Harper, 1967.

W. F. Craven. *The Southern Colonies in the 17th Century*. Baton Rouge: Louisiana State University Press, 1949.

E. S. Morgan. *The Puritan Dilemma: The Story of John Winthrop*. Boston: Little, Brown, 1958; *The Puritan Family*. New York: Harper, 1956.

Paul Goodman (ed.). *Essays in American Colonial History*. New York: Holt, 1972.

3

American provinces of Britain

The English Revolution of 1688 and the colonies . . . emergence of a colonial system: mercantilism . . . growth of colonial political controls . . . economic life-styles: American merchants . . . bills of exchange . . . economic life-styles: Southern planters . . . economic life-styles: subsistence farming and handicrafts . . . territorial expansion: the Westward Movement in the 18th century . . . the struggle for Canada . . . France and the American West . . . tides of war on the frontier . . . North America becomes British . . . white over red: the Indian trauma . . . Puritans and Indians . . . the clash of Indian and white values: landownership . . . the London government and the Indians . . . economic expansion and American society in the 18th century . . . power of the colonial elite . . . social tensions and class struggle . . . the Great Awakening and the American mind . . . rise of Deist beliefs . . . Jonathan Edwards: science and God . . . social and political implications of the Great Awakening . . . religion and the Revolution.

The 18th century was one of general prosperity and demographic growth for the British colonies in North America. From being scattered settlements they evolved into mature, though distant, provinces of Britain. Yet while they consolidated and matured within the British framework they also began to move away. Gradually and imperceptibly the transplanted British colonists became self-consciously American. Historians cannot agree on the exact timing of this transformation. Its alchemy remains mysterious, if logically unsurprising.

The English Revolution of 1688 and the colonies

With the Whig Revolution of 1688 in Britain a crucial step took place in the slow evolution of constitutional monarchy and government by consent. James II was replaced by William and Mary. On being invited to take the throne they were obliged to accept limitations on royal power. These limitations, written down in the Bill of Rights of 1689 and the Act of Settlement of 1701, greatly strengthened the hands of Parliament. The philosopher John Locke returned from political exile in Holland and promptly published two *Treatises on Civil Government* to justify this Whig Revolution. He adopted Social Contract and Natural Rights arguments. These philosophical ideas entered directly into the colonial political mind and became an indestructible part of American political thought from that day to this.

The Whig Revolution was vindicated by John Locke's statement that all governments are limited by the Natural Rights of the people: if a government violates these rights, it can be overthrown. In 1689 Parliament was of course pleased with this rationalization. Some decades later, when the American colonists would use the notion against Parliament itself in 1776, the Natural Right of revolution would be denied. Meanwhile a great lawyer, Chief Justice Sir Edward Coke, had prepared the way through case decisions he had made earlier in the century. While the English Parliament struggled for "Supremacy" within the political system, Coke confronted both King and Parliament with the deeper doctrine of the *supremacy of law*. The King was beneath no man but he reigned only "under God *and the law*," said Coke in 1608. Thus "the King in his own person cannot adjudge any case." This remarkable constraint was put forward by Coke half a century before Louis XIV established his despotism in France, 80 years before the Whig Revolution, and 12 years before the Mayflower Compact. In *Dr. Bonham's Case*, 1610, Coke informed Parliament that it, too, must obey the common law:

When an Act of Parliament is against common right and reason, or repugnant, or impossible to be performed, the Common Law will control it, and adjudge such Act to be void.

Coke's last phrase implies *judicial supremacy* and foreshadows the later American notion of a Supreme Court with power to invalidate acts of the legislature.

In 1688 the English Parliament won certain rights from the monarchy that were *not* automatically extended to the English living in the colonies. These included complete freedom of debate inside Parliament (Parliamentary privilege), control over its own procedures and qualifications for membership, regulation of contested elections, and the power of the purse. The last, financial control, the colonists won by default. Colonial governors were dependent on local assemblies for their income. The London government never began a permanent "Civil List" for any colony—a guaranteed annual revenue to pay the costs of colonial government. But power of the purse was not *formally* conceded to the colonial assemblies by Parliament. It would become a fundamental issue between London and the colonies in the American Revolution: "no taxation without representation."

Beyond the question of appropriations, Parliament had asserted its supremacy in England. Was it also to be supreme in the colonies? Many colonists did not think so. As John Adams declared: "The authority of Parliament was never generally acknowledged in America" (1775). Thus the Whig Revolution of 1688 exacerbated the political struggles going on within the American colonies and merely changed the focus of transatlantic politics. The future contest was to be with the House of Commons, not with the king. Locke's ideas, Natural

Rights and individualism, the rule of Science and of Reason, found a ready audience in the colonies. Americans became more Whiggish in practice and more suspicious of the executive branch of government than the British were at home.

Emergence of a colonial system: Mercantilism

British national self-interest cut across lines of belief and ideology. Like the Spanish, the British wanted to exclude foreign nations from trade with their American colonies and also to make the colonies serve the Mother Country as sources of raw materials and as markets for finished products and goods made in England. So a series of special Acts of Trade were passed, defended equally by Oliver Cromwell's Puritan government and the Stuart monarchy which followed it.

The so-called Navigation Acts that were begun by Cromwell in 1651 and continued in more stringent form by the Restoration monarchy in 1660, 1663, and 1696 contained nothing that was essentially new. Trade controls with the aim of diverting the flow of commerce in the national interest dated back as far as 1381 in English history. However, the enormous growth of international trade in the later 16th and 17th centuries and the propaganda of the mercantile theorists brought a set of comprehensive regulations. There were many Navigation Laws and literally hundreds of amendments and additions over the course of the 17th and 18th centuries. For example in 1621 Virginia was forbidden to export her tobacco to any country but England, and in 1624 the tobacco could be shipped only in English vessels. It had been common practice for years to exclude foreigners from colonial trade, but the 17th century produced a coordinated policy.

The act of 1660 had two major aims: first, to protect and encourage native British and colonial shipbuilding, domination of the carrying trade, and training of merchant seamen. Therefore goods shipped either way among Britain and her colonial possessions in Asia, Africa, and America could be moved only in British-owned (including colonial) vessels. After 1662 this regulation was tightened, to demand British-built vessels for most cases. The crew of such vessels must be mainly British. The second part of the 1660 measure aimed at controlling for the Mother Country the supply of raw materials from the colonies. It listed specific "enumerated commodities" which could be exported from the colonies only to other British possessions or to Britain herself. These enumerated articles included tobacco, sugar, cotton, ginger, and dye woods. Since products like sugar and tobacco were demanded in continental Europe, the act gave a great advantage to merchants at home in England who controlled the reexport of these goods to the continent. The list of enumerated goods was lengthened over the years.

The Staple Act of 1663 meanwhile controlled colonial imports from Europe. All such imports were to go first through ports in England and Wales, then be reshipped to the colonies in British vessels. This was necessary partly because England could not force other European nations to ship their exports to England only in British ships. Goods crossed the English Channel or North Sea in the ships of those nations who were selling the products (these nations also had shipping regulations); but from England and Wales across the Atlantic, the London government theoretically had full control. Evasion and piracy were widespread and an important adjunct to colonial trade. Legal exceptions to the Staple Act included the permissible direct colonial importation of salt (for the fisheries), and of wines from Madeira and the Azores; and servants, horses, and foodstuffs from Ireland and Scotland. Colonial customhouses and admiralty courts were expanded to administer and police this complex system.

Mercantilist theory viewed world trade as fixed in quantity: one nation could only increase its trade at the expense of another. Trade was thus a sort of "cold war," sometimes leading to hot war. The theory assumed permanent scarcity, rather than the reality, which was enormous expansion of world trade. The Cromwellian Act of 1651 produced war with the Dutch, for one example. Gradually the private enterprise freedom under which the colonies had been founded began to recede. Increasing trade and population growth in the colonies brought the desire by the Crown to impose some order on the empire. In 1696 the *Board of Trade and Plantations* replaced a former subcommittee of the Privy Council and began to exercise overall supervision of colonial affairs. This step came two centuries after Spain had created its board, the *Casa de Contratación* of 1503. English regulations were less rigidly enforced than those of Spain: for example, fish, grain, and rum were left free of restriction and these were essential to colonial trade.

Boston in 1764

Bostonian Society

Growth of colonial political controls

The growth of administrative machinery after the Navigation Acts and the creation of the Board of Trade presaged the development of a sort of "constitution" or political framework for the colonies as a whole. At the center of the system was the Board of Trade, acting as a "think tank" for policymakers and made up mainly of eight salaried Crown appointees. "Ministerial" is perhaps more precise than "Crown" here—meaning that they were controlled by the policies of whichever ministry was at present in power. Very slowly, England was developing a cabinet system of government, though changes of ministries still reflected changes in personal political factions rather than in policy goals. In the colonies the governors were usually ministerial appointees. Except for Connecticut and Rhode Island, which kept their company charter status and elected their own governors, and Pennsylvania, which remained a proprietary colony, the colonies were Crown-controlled by the mid-18th century.

The process was as follows. Maryland, after constant political and religious unrest, was made a Crown colony in 1691, though it reverted to the Calverts (now Protestant) in 1715. New Hampshire became royal in 1679, New York in 1685, Massachusetts (combining Plymouth and Maine) in 1691, Pennsylvania (briefly) in 1692. East and West Jersey were united and governed by New York, 1702–38; New Jersey emerged as a separate royal colony in 1738. South Carolina became a Crown colony in 1721; North Carolina in 1729. London controls were mainly formal; Sir Robert Walpole's policy of *salutary neglect* towards the Americans, "letting sleeping dogs lie," as he is reported to have said, encouraged the independent spirit already deeply entrenched in the colonies.

In North America the actual powers of colonial governors were restricted in practice, whether or not they were elected or appointed. Ambiguously, the governor had to represent and to symbolize the King's authority and majesty while at the same time he was responsible for his actions to the colonial assembly which paid him. He even had to go occasionally to London to plea for colonial demands. It was an impossible task. Colonial control of the purse strings severely limited the governor's power, even though in theory his office combined all the royal prerogatives and more, as commander-in-chief, head of the law courts, head of the legislature, and chief executive. Hypothetically there was no Separation of Powers in the colonies. The governor had more authority than the king enjoyed at home. The harsh reality was that any governor's influence depended upon his political acumen, his skill and willingness to play off colonial interest groups against each other, and his ability to pack the Council with powerful local men and to manipulate the assembly by clever use of patronage.

In Britain Sir Robert Walpole had founded in the early 18th century a successful administrative system based on extensive use of patronage —government jobs and preferment, sinecures, contracts, and lavish donation of titles. Too often, in fact, the London government used the American colonies as mere patronage pastures. Shrewd colonial governors could occasionally still the rhetoric of dissident colonists ("No taxation without representation!" or "The rights of Englishmen!") by careful use of the appointments list. Colonial politics were intricate and sophisticated. The complex disputes among colonies and among assemblies, governors, and Crown officials within colonies, prepared the Americans for the Revolution and for the nation-building process which had to follow it, by training them in the necessary political and organizational skills.

Economic lifestyles: American merchants

The Americans also received essential training in economic skills and after the Navigation Acts and attempts by the Board of Trade to formalize controls over the colonial economy, they devised ingenious channels of trade to obviate mercantilist regulations. By the 18th century a roughly three-fold differentiation could be observed among the 13 colonies: Northeast, Middle Atlantic and the South. Each section had different economic problems and served different functions within the system. The persistence of these differences through the centuries has been a feature of U.S. history.

New York and New England owed their livelihoods partly to the ocean. New England, we have observed, supplied cod, lumber, naval stores, and ships to England. The Northern merchants carried the products of other nations all over the globe and opened up the Far East to world commerce. They shared in the famous "triangular trade" between themselves, the West Indies, and West Africa, which interchanged molasses and black slaves. Specie and molasses were imported from the West Indies to the colonies. The molasses was processed into rum; the rum, together with metal trinkets, was sold on the coast of West Africa for slaves. Then followed the dreadful "Middle Passage," the run from Africa to the Caribbean in which slaves were packed into 18 inches of space apiece, with little headroom, all chained together. Hundreds, if not thousands, died of disease, fear, and shock. Some committed suicide.

In this manner New England merchants helped to bring slaves to the Caribbean. The circularity of the historical process is to be seen in the fact that the West Indies turned to plantation sugar production in the 1640s, precisely when the first cycle of immigration (the Great Migration) of Puritans to New England was tailing off. The northern colonies had excess products of their own to trade in the Caribbeans and a poor balance-of-payments with England. Meanwhile the Middle Atlantic settlements from the Hudson to the Potomac rivers played an important role as grain producers—the "bread colonies" of North America. Their grain met the growing demand of colonial cities like Philadelphia, New York, and Baltimore, and they shipped it via the coastal trade to neighboring colonies. Dutch and German immigrant farmers had introduced to the relatively unsophisticated Middle colonies an advanced European form of commercial agriculture, based on individual homestead farms carved out of the wilderness and worked with free (or temporarily indentured) labor. These homesteads were quite unlike the slave plantations of the South, which owed their existence

*Chase Manhattan Bank
Money Museum*

A Bill of Exchange signed by Robert Morris

partly to an all-year-round working climate and partly to the tobacco crop.

By the mid-17th century the Middle and Northern colonies were thus trading grains, flour, fish, meat, cloth, and lumber to the West Indies, bringing back the molasses for rum manufacture, and specie and gold. Specie (or hard money: gold and silver) was desperately short at all times in the colonies. The London government discouraged creation of currency in America though colonies occasionally ignored this prohibition. Yet the colonial economy grew rapidly, needed more cash to transact business, and was always losing specie to England because coin was drawn off by the adverse balance of trade. The colonists constantly needed to import more than they had to export. A clever way was worked out to avoid some of these problems. First, the colonists imported and used the currency of other nations when they could get it—Spanish pieces especially. Second, for their supplies in the West Indies they accepted paper bills. The latter were sugar *bills of exchange*—I.O.U.'s earned in England by the sugar planters for their sugar sales. With these bills the Northern merchants bought the goods they needed in England. The bills merely returned to England from the Caribbean via the North American colonies.

New England and the Middle colonies also traded directly with Britain and with southern Europe, selling fish, lumber and naval stores to England. The colonists added indirectly to their trade with the Mother Country by sailing their two-masted brigantines to the Mediterranean, trading fish and other products for fruits, wines, spices, and salt. These luxury items they sold on the English market, keeping to the letter of the Navigation Laws, and returned home with much-needed British tools, supplies, books, and manufactured goods of all

Bills of exchange

types. In this way they greatly expanded colonial trade and helped to avoid the crippling problem of specie shortage.

In its attempts to restrict colonial trade the London government merely helped to create a class of skillful and enterprising American traders. These traders performed a whole series of economic functions which in such preindustrial days had not yet become specialized or separated. Triangular trading patterns provided exchange for trade with Europe, but also for trade among the colonies in America. In modest offices and with minimal clerical or accounting aids, colonial merchants handled real estate deals, engaged in international financing, investment brokering, banking, and insurance underwriting; managed rum distilleries; made loans; bought, used, and sold ocean-going vessels; bartered, stored, bought, and sold and exchanged all types of products, both wholesale and retail. The Americans were always in debt to merchants in Bristol or London and were always extending simple "book credit" for routine transactions at home. They made the wheels of colonial economic life turn, and in so doing also prepared the way for independent nationhood.

Economic lifestyles: Southern planters

The Southern colonists had less need of Yankee ingenuity in order to survive. They had a more favorable trade balance. Their exports to England and to continental Europe through English ports, exceeded their imports. Unlike the Middle colonies, which produced goods in competition with England and therefore ended up trading with the Caribbean and southern Europe, the Southern planting colonies did not compete directly with the Mother Country. They were classic colonies: they complemented the English home economy and provided materials not otherwise readily available to the British, like rice, indigo, and tobacco. In North Carolina naval stores such as pitch, tar, and resin were made by black slave labor in rivalry with New England. The Southerners had a better trading position, protected within the British Empire, a guaranteed market, and an excellent growing season. Their climate was suitable for slave labor, which had to be housed and fed all year round and would have been unprofitable in the northern winter. The South with its rich, fertile soil was the wealthiest section of British North America and of the United States for about 250 years.

The most valuable cash crop was tobacco, grown in Virginia, parts of Maryland, and later in North Carolina. Tobacco was cheap to transport on the numerous waterways of the Chesapeake Bay country because of its high cash value in relation to its bulk. Virginia leaf had an absolute advantage over other tobaccos in quality and price. As a cash crop, shipped raw to England to be handled and resold there at a good profit, tobacco fitted very well into the mercantilist view of the world. Soon after John Rolfe's first export of the crop in 1614 a tobacco craze developed that led people to grow it in the streets of Jamestown. Highly profitable, tobacco created a one-crop "kingdom" and supported an entire way of life based on plantation slavery.

The monoculture of tobacco depleted the soil and mined it of its natural wealth after about seven years. This encouraged constant crop migration and abandonment of used-up land. Given the abundance of land in the 17th and 18th centuries, however, it is unrealistic to expect better conservation attitudes from the Virginia planters. The five years preceding the outbreak of the American Revolution saw the height of 18th-century tobacco output. The fortunes of many elite families were made by then.

In South Carolina other staples were featured. An upland crop, indigo (a much-valued blue dye), and a lowland crop, rice, complemented each other as cash exports. Indigo was first introduced to Charleston from the British West Indies (Antigua) in 1742 and soon became designated a staple crop. The English government encouraged its production with a bounty to planters of six pence a pound. South Carolina was exporting over 1 million pounds a year by 1770. Indigo planters suffered from American independence when they lost their bounty. Rice first came to Charleston, it is said, from Madagascar in 1694. Its cultivation spread into adjoining North Carolina and Georgia, along tidal coasts. Rice plantations became a major source of income here before the Revolution and supported an even larger aristocracy after 1820 with the invention of steam threshing. Like the tobacco crop, rice and indigo were grown with African slave labor. By 1763 about half the population of Virginia and perhaps two thirds of South Carolina was black. Cotton did not become a major crop until after the Revolution.

It would be a mistake to imagine that most American colonists were engaged in commercial output. Foreign trade did provide the early mechanism of economic growth and the accumulation of capital for investment; but large numbers of settlers, North and South, lived outside the market for most of the year. On the frontier everywhere, families struggled merely to survive, growing their own food crops and keeping a few animals. The self-sufficient homestead was common, buttressed by *usufacture* (home manufacture).

Economic lifestyles: Subsistence farming and handicrafts

Apart from the shipbuilding industry and iron manufacture, most 18th-century colonial needs were met by production in the home and on the plantation, on a part-time, unspecialized basis. Those who could afford European goods bought them. But hard-wearing, everyday cloths, such as *fustians* and *jeans* (mixtures of cotton and linen, or cotton and wool), were woven at home. The relative lack of industry meant that town and countryside presented less of a sharp antithesis than in later years. Townsfolk owned farms and tilled the land. No one was very removed from the soil.

Even the very advanced colonial iron industry was still rural in character. In the 17th century it was scattered over the colonies, from Massachusetts to New Jersey. After about 1720 the industry expanded more rapidly and migrated from the sites of old bog-ore furnaces to the Appalachian mountains, from New York to Virginia. The iron industry did not use coal but used timber (charcoal), since the abundance of forests made this fuel very cheap. Colonial ironmasters increased output four-fold between 1771 and 1775; they produced

The U.S.A.

The busy hands of an agrarian society—18th-century crewel work

Colonial Williamsburg Photograph

30,000 tons of iron in the year of Lexington Green. England herself had fewer forges and furnaces than the colonies and tried to limit the manufacture of iron products beyond the pig-iron stage by the Iron Act of 1750. An early forge, first built in 1646, may be seen today at Saugus, Massachusetts.

Territorial expansion: The Westward Movement in the 18th century

Economic expansion was general throughout the American colonies and was based in part on a large native birthrate and continued immigration of new settlers. Germans, Welsh, Scotch-Irish from Ulster (driven out of Northern Ireland by rising rents and English persecution of their Presbyterian faith), Huguenots from France (who settled in South Carolina and became an Anglican planter elite), and more African slaves, all added to colonial population in the 18th century. Americans began to spread out West of the fall line; they crossed the Appalachians and stretched the horizons of the colonists.

The London government looked askance at this westward movement, which was likely to bring confrontations with the Indians and with the French in the Mississippi and Ohio valleys. Who was to control this vast new frontier? The matter became a major issue in the disputes between the colonists and England before the Revolution. The colonies themselves were determined to keep control over land grants in the West. To undercut any attempts by the London government to claim the West, Virginia had given out almost 3 million acres to great Tidewater families by 1754. Rival "land companies" were created by speculators to colonize the new West, like the Ohio Company (1747), authorized by the English Privy Council, and its rival, created by Virginia in 1749, the Loyal Company. Virginia, Pennsylvania, Connecticut, and other colonies also sent out companies as the century progressed. The legendary Daniel Boone began exploring the Kentucky area in 1767; his Wilderness Road trip of 1775, for the Transylvania Company, took him from North Carolina through the Cumberland Gap into Kentucky, where he founded the first American settlement there, Boonesborough, and made a treaty with the Cherokee.

The fears of the British were correct. These American expeditions did bring conflict with the Indians and with the French. In the Pennsylvania backcountry, for example, the French built a line of forts to ward off the Americans. Virginia sent out young George Washington with a force to investigate in 1753. He came back warning that the French intended to take the whole Ohio Valley.

The struggle for Canada

The colonists managed to agree among themselves and with the London policymakers on one matter at least: Britain must oust the French from Canada. The struggle with France in North America was for Britain only a part of a global rivalry which began in the late 17th century and did not cease until 1815 with the second and final defeat of Napoleon. The Great Power rivalry produced a series of complex European wars: King William's War, 1689–97 (called in Europe the War of the League of Augsburg), Queen Anne's War, 1702–13 (the War of the Spanish Succession), King George's War, 1740–48, the American phase not breaking out until 1744 (the War of the Austrian Succession), and the French and Indian War, 1756–63 (the Seven Years' War).

Each of these conflicts produced side wars in North America. Sometimes battles were fought along the American frontier when no official war was in progress in Europe. These local American wars concerned two main issues: control of the rich fur trade and the mastery of the Ohio Valley. Mainly Protestant Anglo-American forces were pitted against Catholic Frenchmen, each side fearing encirclement by the other and using Indian allies where possible. Warfare was brutal and "irregular," with use of ambush, guerilla activities, and massacre of outposts, including civilians.

France and the American West

From their Canadian base the French explored the Mississippi Valley southward, moving down to the Gulf coast and establishing New Orleans in 1718. The explorer Robert Cavalier de La Salle had claimed the entire valley from the Appalachians to the Rockies for France and called it Louisiana, after his king, Louis XIV (1682). Thus the French laid claim to a vast territorial empire in North America, that swept round from the Gulf coast northward and eastward as far as the Gaspé peninsula of eastern Canada. The French theoretically hemmed in the Thirteen Colonies behind the Appalachian barrier.

This French Empire was hollow: nothing much more than a chain of scattered forts and claims, held together shakily by Indian treaties. Over its enormous area a population of only about 12,000 French traders and trappers wandered, manned blockhouses, and mixed with Indians. In contrast, the population of the Thirteen Colonies multiplied —from under 5,000 (1630) to a quarter of a million (1700) and then to two and three-quarter millions (1780). At the time of the last great confrontation and defeat of the French in North America (1763) an English population of under two million faced a French population of at the most 65,000.

The French Empire looked proud on the map, and later in the 18th century great explorers pushed its outer limits even further, to reach Spanish territory in the Southwest (New Mexico) and to the Black Hills of South Dakota (Pierre Vérendrye, 1743) in the Northwest. Only the Rocky Mountains halted this remarkable advance. Yet, as an amused Governor Thomas Dongan of New York said, on hearing that the French king claimed his colony because it was watered by rivers that rose among the Canadian lakes:

He might as well pretend to all the countries that drink claret and brandy.

This was an empire of canoe trails and of *coureurs de bois*. It was decades away from economic development or genuine colonization and settlement.

The tides of war on the frontier

Wars ebbed and flowed on the American frontiers down to 1763, with no clear advantage for either side. Indian tribes, caught between the two rivals, were obliged to take sides. Disease, the white man's alcohol, and warfare wiped out entire tribes. New Englanders attacked *Acadie* (Nova Scotia), and further west threatened the town of Quebec. With Indian allies, the French harassed the borders of New England and New York.

In 1713 the Treaty of Utrecht ended Queen Anne's War and did seem to make a territorial difference. Hudson's Bay Territory was handed over to England along with all Newfoundland and most of Nova Scotia. The French were the losers and had a right to feel encircled in Quebec. Also, the English extended their sovereignty over the powerful Iroquois Confederacy—a remarkable alliance of five, later six, Indian nations, mainly in the upper New York region, whose authority spread to the Great Lakes and even as far south as Tennessee. The Confederacy numbered only about 15,000; but it kept the French out of the crucial Mohawk Valley. Though technically neutral, the Iroquois were friends of the English; in later years they supported England against the colonies in the Revolutionary War.

After the bad losses of 1713, the French decided to fortify New France more heavily. Their attempt to control Indian tribes backfired: it involved them in bloody campaigns against the Fox (Wisconsin) and the Chickasaws (Louisiana and Tennessee). In 1745 a further blow was the first loss of their allegedly impregnable fortress, Louisburg, on Cape Breton Island. Despite early military victories in the French and Indian War, France came out badly. Fort Duquesne (later Pittsburgh) fell, then control of the St. Lawrence was lost to the English, and finally, in one of the famous battles of military history, the British General James Wolfe captured Quebec in 1759. The Royal Navy played its part and three English and colonial armies converged on Montreal in 1760. The French Empire in North America was toppled.

French defeat did not make the whole of North America become British. Large parts of the continent were still Spanish in 1763, and would remain Spanish or Mexican down to the 1840s. The Russians, too, were exploring the Pacific coast in the 18th century. From Russia, Captain Vitus Bering discovered Alaska and the Bering Strait in the years 1728–41. In his wake, Russian fur traders settled in the Aleutian Islands and Alaska. Their exploits stimulated the Hudson's Bay Company to pioneer in the great Northwest and to claim all Canada west of the Rockies by 1789. Anxious Spain sent feelers up the Pacific coast from Mexico and missions were settled at San Francisco in 1775 and

North America becomes British

The Anglo-French struggles for North America— the Battle of Louisburg, 1745

The John Carter Brown Library,
Brown University

Nootka Sound in 1789. The Russians held Alaska however; the town of Sitka, founded by Alexander Baranov, was their capital until 1867 when the territory was purchased by the United States.

Meanwhile, the enormous region called Louisiana was ceded by France to Spain in 1762 by the secret treaty of Fontainebleau as compensation for war losses. From the source to the mouth of the Mississippi, and west to the Rockies, Louisiana covered over 800,000 square miles. Spain gave up the region again in 1800 and Jefferson hastily bought it from Napoleon two years later.

New France was eliminated after 150 years of struggle. Overwhelming economic and population odds and British sea power did the trick. The French could not attract enough emigrants to man their ambitious territorial empire. After 1763 the problems of this territory were handed over to the British administrators. Many French *Canadiens* stayed put and took their chances with British rule, thus laying the foundation for modern Canada as a bicultural society.

White over red: The Indian trauma

France survived its loss of empire. Those who suffered most were the Amerindians. Early in the history of white-Indian culture contact the fear of Indians as wild savages had given way, in face of the evidence that many were farmers and had lessons to teach the English. Individual Indians, like Pocahontas in Virginia or Squanto, who taught the Pilgrims how to trap beaver and plant corn in New Plymouth, later became legendary folk heroes in the mythology of colonization. But early scruples on the part of the whites soon faded. The Dutch of New Amsterdam had gone out to America intending to purchase any land they used and to treat the natives decently. They traded with the Iroquois but they did not intermix, and after some conflicts Governor Kieft offered the first bounty for Indian scalps. The Indians of southern New York were eliminated.

In Jamestown the English followed the urging of James I and for a while tried to convert the Indians to the Anglican faith. An Indian war in 1622 put an end to these experiments; there was to be no more peaceful coexistence. Indian tribes were now regarded as fair game and beyond the protective reach of Natural Law. The "rights of Englishmen" clearly did not apply to Indians, and they seemed to prove the point in 1644, when their leader, Opechancanough, picked up where he left off in 1622, and organized a desperate attempt to drive the white invaders out of his country. Five hundred white colonists perished before the braves were utterly crushed. Though sporadic Indian warfare dragged on for over a century, Virginia was never so seriously threatened again. In Catholic Maryland, the Jesuits hoped to establish missions to the Indians (like their *reducciones* in 17th-century Paraguay), but the Calverts, though sympathetic to the Indians, suspected Jesuit power. In the Carolinas and Georgia also, white-Indian relations seemed less abrasive. Charleston depended on Indians for its rich fur trade and Oglethorpe, the Georgia philanthropist, dealt fairly with the Creeks. In the 18th century there was much evidence of Indian enslavement of blacks and Indian bounty-hunting of runaway African slaves for the whites. Some racial intermixing of whites and Indians took place in the Southeast.

Puritans and Indians

Puritans came to regard the Indians as Hittites, sent by the Devil to test the faith of God's chosen people in the howling wilderness. They did not intermarry. They thanked God for the plague of 1616 which killed off many Indians before the Pilgrims landed and did not regret the later plague of 1633 in Massachusetts. A loving God had cleared the way for His Saints: this was a "providence." Faithful Squanto was forgotten until a later generation. Not all Puritans felt this way. The dissident Roger Williams went to the lands of the Narragansett; he defended the Indians' rights to their hunting lands, as well as to their cultivated fields and camps. Another Puritan, John Eliot, did try to convert the Indians and translated the Bible into his own Anglicized written version of Algonquian in 1661—this was the first Bible published in North America. But even Williams refused to view the Indian medicine man (the *powwow*) at work; he thought it was dangerous to watch the Devil.

As 1622 was the turning point in Virginia, the Pequot War of 1637 was the last blow to good white-Indian relations in New England. The colonies combined forces to wipe out this fierce tribe, also hated by other Indians. They had the aid of Roger Williams' allies, the Narragansetts, in the mopping-up operations in the woods. Puritan thankfulness to God seems excessive to modern ears:

It was a fearful sight to see them frying in the fire and the streams of blood quenching the same, and horrible was the stink and stench thereof. But the victory seemed a sweet sacrifice, and (we) gave praise thereof to God. (*Governor Bradford of Plymouth describing the last battle.*)

The Pequot village had been surrounded at night and set ablaze. The Puritan divine, Increase Mather, told his congregation to pray to God, "that on this day we have sent 600 heathen souls to Hell." This harsh attitude should not be too readily stigmatized as "racism" however. In England of the 17th century public burnings of heretics and public executions were quite familiar.

Another war broke out in 1675, led by the Wampanoag chief, King Philip. This time the Narragansetts supported Philip against the people of Massachusetts. The Indians could no longer endure the impositions of the whites—their abuse of Indian property rights, their enforcement of capital punishment for blasphemy, and their insistence on the Sabbath. About 1,000 colonists lost their lives as settlements were ravaged. The Puritans responded with grim vengeance. Chiefs were beheaded, hundreds sold into slavery in the West Indies, and King Philip was actually drawn and quartered and his skull impaled for all to behold. The failure of King Philip's War broke the back of Indian resistance. They were forced into confined villages, disarmed, and strictly supervised. Their decline was swift thereafter.

One chief, Cannonchet, was captured after his village, with the women and children, was burned. He was ordered to be beheaded and his last speech is recorded to have been:

> I was born a prince. If princes speak to me I will answer. Since none are present, I am honor bound to keep silent. Oneko, the noble son of Uncas, shall be my executioner.
>
> I like it well, for I shall die before my heart is soft, or I have spoken anything unworthy of myself.

Many American Indians did not die "before their hearts were soft." They were corrupted by the subservient life that Cannonchet wished to avoid.

The clash of Indian and white values: Landownership

Whites had superior technology and weapons; they were charged by a sense of mission, individualism, and superiority; they were determined to farm and to settle. Thus the Indians were swept before them, confused, divided, and outgunned. Nothing frustrated the Indians more than the white man's strange concept of individual land *ownership*. This was an idea unknown to Indian values. One could borrow the land for a season; one could have the *use* of the land, but no individual could own it. The English notion of *transferable fee title* in land—the ownership and salability of land and the recording of all this on paper—baffled the Indians. Throughout the history of American-Indian relations this misunderstanding prevailed, down into the 19th century. The Indians recognized usufruct (use rights), and use-right boundaries, but land never became a chattel. For the English however, land ownership and private property were deeply identified with liberty and the Lockean rights of man. These two views were antithetical.

The coastal tribes of the Northeast were wiped out altogether without trace. Further inland, more numerous and more advanced tribes managed to survive. The Iroquois still exist in New York and Canada. In the Southeast the Cherokee maintained a high level of white-assimilated culture until the 1830s, but this did not save them from eventually being pushed out.

In addition to decimation by disease and war, a major result of white intrusion was massive geographical shifting of the surviving tribes. Intertribal conflict became worse with the use of white-supplied guns, and alliances with French or English. As white colonists pushed westward, before them moved the tribes, one pressing against another: it was an Indian westward movement. Eventually they reached the Great Plains. For example, the Dakota saw their first wild horses running free in 1722, and on the Plains a new culture was born, based on horse and buffalo. The Indians now became the unsettled nomads that the whites had accused them of being in earlier years, in order to steal their lands for "better" use.

The London government and the Indians

Indians were often confused by the diversity of white men. They learned to distinguish in time, like the Chippewa chief in Niagara who favored the French (1678):

When the Frenchmen arrived at these falls they came and kissed us. . . . We lived like brothers in the same lodge . . . They never mocked at our ceremonies, and they never molested the places of our dead. Seven generations of men have passed away and we have not forgotten it.

The Iroquois liked the English, but in time many tribes came to hate both nations and to agree with the judgment of a Delaware chief, Teedyuscung, who said of one Anglo-French treaty in 1756:

The kings of France and England have settled this land so as to coop us up in a pen. This very ground under me was my land and inheritance, and is taken from me by fraud.

The Delawares had not been consulted.

Among the Americans, each colony had its own Indian policy and resisted interference from London. The English wanted to impose order on this chaos and to centralize Indian affairs and place regulations on white traders. There should be one uniform land-grant policy. So London devised the first real plan of government by a colonial power over a native people. General Braddock was made commander-in-chief of all forces in America (British and colonial), and the Board of Trade appointed two full-time "Indian agents": one for the northern tribes and one for the southern. These men were sympathetic to Indian values. In the South, agent Edmund Atkin criticized white traders as "the loosest kind of people, . . . despised and held in great contempt by the Indians as liars." The Indians, in contrast, despite their "misguided passion of heroism" were "humane, hospitable and equitable."

The Indians might have been better off had England won the War of Independence. The English showed humanity in 1763 when an Ottawa Indian and ally of the French, Pontiac, could not accept the French defeat in North America and organized an Indian confederacy to ravage the Anglo-American settlers. Fighting on a wilderness front 1,000 miles broad, "Pontiac's Conspiracy" kept the whole West in fear, from Virginia to Niagara. Many forts were destroyed and Pontiac besieged Detroit. He was defeated by Redcoats, but he was pardoned. The English *Proclamation of 1763* was issued in part to protect Indian rights to their lands west of the Appalachians. Further white settlement there was prohibited and whites illegally occupying Indian lands were to move back. Procedures for purchase of land were to be regularized.

This Proclamation is often portrayed merely as an irritant to the Americans or as a measure to favor Quebec at the expense of the Thirteen Colonies. From the viewpoint of Indian history, however, 1763 was a high-water mark of British policy.

The fiat of the British government could not have kept back the American colonists for very long though it may have protected the Indians more. Economic expansion and population growth went on. New towns sprang up in the East and older centers thrived. Boston, Salem, and Newport became good-sized towns. In the South, where

Economic expansion and American society in the 18th century

society was less concentrated, Charleston dominated South Carolina. Philadelphia (40,000 population) and later New York City rose above all other centers. Where no towns existed in the North and West the influence of town culture made itself felt through the growing newspaper and pamphlet press, trade and professional organizations, colleges and fraternal clubs. The legal profession played a large role. The colonies could boast of eight or nine colleges, 25 newspapers, and a prosperous book trade before the Revolution.

Growth and change produced dislocation, the rise of new social groups to power and prestige, and much social tension. Colonial America was rich and varied: Dutch-German homestead farms, rice fields, villagelike tobacco plantations, sawmills, fishing ports, iron forges and slitting mills, tanneries, shipyards, distilleries, workshops, market towns, southern "courthouse towns," indentured laborers and rich merchants, black slaves and grandees, Indian villages and frontier forts. Amid this variety it seems that the early fluidity of social class lines began to vanish. In Maryland, for example, class lines hardened within 30 years after 1637: to "get on," the settler now had to move west or migrate to South Carolina or Georgia. In Virginia the House of Burgesses was controlled by an Anglican planter elite which domi-

A great colonial schoolteacher, David Dove of Philadelphia

The Historical Society of Pennsylvania

The Henry Francis du Pont Winterthur Museum

Plural America—a young Dutch-American girl

nated the major committees. This elite down to the American Revolution combined family lines, wealth, and education and managed to set the tone for the social and cultural life of the colony.

In the Middle and North, as the second and third generations began to inherit wealth, local gentries also appeared, though less unified. A large merchant class emerged, forceful and independent-minded, and jealous of its acquired status. Foolishly, English policymakers alienated this proud and powerful group—with men like John Hancock, the Harvard graduate who inherited his father's firm and whose sloop, *Liberty,* was burned by customs men in 1768, becoming a symbol of British oppression. Merchants played a large part in the American Revolution. Only three men of artisan background signed the Declaration of Independence. One was Benjamin Franklin, son of a candle- and soap-maker, who quit school at the age of ten to work as a printer. His *Poor Richard's Almanack* (1732–57) was the Bible of self-help and social mobility. Its success reflected the fact that real opportunity did exist in colonial America and was supported by public opinion. Whatever was happening to the social structure, Americans did profess deep beliefs in social equality and selection by merit rather than blood lines. Estimates of colonial real wages have placed them at 30 percent to 100 percent higher than in England. Poverty was the exception rather than the rule. As late as the 1830s the French observer Tocqueville could claim:

> Wealth circulates with inconceivable rapidity, and experience shows that it is rare to find two succeeding generations in the full enjoyment of it.

Workingmen were more lucky in the Northern and Middle colonies, where there were no African slaves to compete with free labor and depress its status. No skilled worker faced any insurmountable barrier to social advancement; merit and hard work would bring social rewards to carpenters, blacksmiths, shipwrights—as, for example, silversmiths like Paul Revere Sr., a Huguenot refugee apprentice from the Channel island of Guernsey.

Desperate shortage of labor forced indentures to be shortened and cut down apprenticeships from the traditional English seven years, to three. Not only young men, but women also stood a better chance at improvement in the colonies. Widows readily took over their husbands' businesses, inns, smithies, workshops. Massachusetts and Connecticut went so far as to offer a measure of basic public education, to extend these opportunities to the children of immigrants also.

Power of the colonial elite

Colonial America was far from democratic however, and the worker had little protection. His economic well-being was dependent on the continued growth and expansion of foreign trade. When the economy failed, he suffered. The large merchant had a cushion of wealth to fall back upon; the plantation owner had his resources. Depression filled the debtors' jails of colonial towns with small men. Consequently, after about 1763, the "mechanics" became a radical political force in town life. They demanded such reforms as free public education, abolition of debtors' jails, rotation in public office, and the vote for all taxpayers.

Pennsylvania was the most politically democratic; New England was only imperfectly democratic; and the Southern colonies were imperfectly aristocratic. Far more forceful in keeping political controls over the lower orders were the coastal gentry of the tobacco and rice colonies. Status-conscious merchants of Boston, Newport, or Philadelphia, rich merchants and speculating landowners of upcountry New York, and well-to-do lawyers everywhere, were unable to implant the quasi-aristocratic code that was embodied in the "southern way of life." This code was based on caste and rural values (as in Latin American colonies) and on the plantation house and black slavery. In Virginia, the undisputed ruling class were the great tobacco planters (as they were in Tidewater Maryland). Baltimore, a growing city with middle- and lower-class groups, might offer some political and social opposition to the planter aristocracy of Maryland in future years.

South Carolina was a virtual city-state. Charleston society ruled the roost. Whatever their humble social origins in England, the Southern upper class, aided by slavery, tried to reproduce English "county" life, with the big house of the squire and the subservient peasantry. But it was not easy for American planters to spurn the life of trade, as their models were supposed to in England. That great Virginian, William Byrd I, for example, did not find it beneath his dignity to trade hardware to the Indians. His more famous son, the diarist, William Byrd II (1674–1744), member of the Royal Society, intimate of English literary figures such as Congreve and Wycherley, friend of the Duke of Argyll, graduate of London's Middle Temple law courts, and owner of a pretty mansion, Westover, with a library of almost 4,000 volumes, made his daily bread in the humble world of speculation, dealing in minerals and crops. The would-be "Cavalier" South was always a fragile creation. At least half the white emigrants to the Southern and Middle colonies were humble indentured laborers. Most of Virginia's "First Families" were of English and Scots merchant stock. Late 18th-century Virginia was a society of small farmers, two thirds of whom did not use slaves or indentured labor.

Americans were a factious and ill-tempered lot. Equality of opportunity did not produce a stable or harmonious society. Sectional and class tensions produced outbreaks of violence. All sorts of rivalries split the colonists: religious, political, economic, and geographic. Boundary quarrels; recurrent outbreaks of hostility between the eastern seaboard areas, which were more developed, richer, more commercial, and the western frontier farms, less developed and often in debt to eastern creditors; frontier discontent over inadequate protection against Indians; hatred of taxes—these and other grievances tore apart the social fabric on many occasions. In Nathaniel Bacon's Rebellion (Virginia, 1676) backwoods farmers, frustrated by falling crop prices and Indian raids, went on the warpath. The local Indians were the scapegoat but some of Bacon's men also had radical ideas about tax and voting reforms. Almost a hundred years later these frustrations still boiled over. In Pennsylvania the Paxton Boys—backwoodsmen allegedly scared of Indian marauders—took up arms in 1763, massacred a peaceful village of Christian Indians and marched on Philadelphia, threatening to kill every Indian they met on the way.

Social tensions and class struggle

Politically, the Tidewater often kept the West underrepresented in the assemblies. An East versus West civil war broke out in North Carolina in 1771, when the backwoodsmen (called Regulators) arose to complain of this manipulation. They were put down by militia and their leaders were hanged. The Establishment had been severely threatened, because the Regulators won control of the lower assembly. As late as 1794, when the United States was 11 years old, the western counties of Pennsylvania refused to pay excise taxes on domestic spirits. They tarred and feathered tax collectors, just as if they were representatives of the old colonial power. A militia force marched into western Pennsylvania but found only a few of the insurgents of this Whisky Rebellion.

Little wonder that in London the policymakers thought of American colonists as dangerous and ungovernable people, or that the Founding Fathers who wrote the American Constitution spent so much time

The Great Awakening and the American mind

considering the perils of faction and anarchy and how to contain them.

In an era of economic growth and social change perhaps the deepest stirrings and most profound dislocation took place in colonial religious beliefs. A series of great religious revivals swept through the colonies in the 1730s and 40s, challenged the existing religious establishments everywhere, and split the denominations. By one estimate a quarter of a million Americans were converted and 350 new churches were opened.

American revivalism was part of an international movement evident in Germany and England during this period, but it had native colonial roots. The religious zeal that had carried the pioneers over to the New World had waned by the early 18th century. Puritan orthodoxy had slipped with the Half-Way Covenant (1662) and suffered setbacks with the charter of 1691 and the Salem witch trials the following year. The religion of wealthy Boston merchants lacked the fire of earlier days. Even in Pennsylvania, respectable, rich Quakers grew complacent and conservative. Secular influences crept in. In Europe the ideas of the *Enlightenment,* derived from a new faith in Science and in Human Reason, emphasized the power of the human mind to gain

American popular faith in science—amateurs inspired by Benjamin Franklin experiment with electricity

Library Company of Philadelphia

knowledge of and even to begin to control the physical world through experimentation, empirical study, and liberation from belief in "miracles." Faith in science was bolstered by the discoveries and descriptions of men like the English mathematician Sir Isaac Newton (1642–1727), whose Universe was run on mechanical laws susceptible of human understanding. Few thinkers yet found the idea of God unnecessary to the working of human institutions, but the reliance on organized, churchly religion and on priests began to erode. Man's Reason was to be the guide to all problems—scientific, technical, even moral and social. God himself could be approached through rational ways. The vengeful God of Calvin began to give way slightly before the more benign God of Progress, called by the greatest American exemplar of the Enlightenment spirit, Thomas Jefferson, the "benevolent Governor of the world."

Superstition, miracles, witches and demons, revelations and specters, and divine intervention were no longer acceptable to the Enlightened as sources of evidence or authority. Only a tiny minority of well-educated and well-traveled Americans were affected during colonial days by the Enlightenment, though in the late 18th century they numbered among them Benjamin Franklin and Thomas Jefferson. In the face of religious erosion and relaxation of dogma Americans could go one of at least two ways: towards embracing the new rationalism, or back to the old-time religion in a revival of pristine virtues and beliefs. Masses of Americans took the latter road in the *Great Awakening*.

The Great Awakening peaked in the years 1739–40 when the English revivalist preacher George Whitefield toured the colonies in an electrifying campaign, exhorting sinners to confess, stirring up huge crowds to paroxysms of shrieking, moaning, and writhing. Whitefield was short on theology and long on homely stories and tricks to play on the secret guilt feelings and deep piety of his audiences. But the wave of revivalism began before Whitefield—as early as the 1720s among Dutch Reform congregations in East Jersey, led by Theodore Frelinghuysen. After the first major wave in the 1730s and 40s came the Methodist period of the 60s and 70s. Reverberations were still being felt at the time of the American Revolution and new revivals appeared at the turn of the century.

Rise of Deist beliefs

The broader theology and dogma of the later revivals was easier to understand and to follow. Methodism began to spread to America from Britain after 1766, bringing the solace of religion as well as its ethics and manners to a far greater number of people. But this easier dogma undoubtedly encouraged the secularizing trend that Frelinghuysen and others had fought against. It was a logical step from the hazy Arminianism of the revivalist frontier to *Deism:* the belief that there was a God, but he was a sort of super-engineer of the universe, and the empirical physical sciences were his means of "revelation." Deists, of whom the most radical was Tom Paine, had no need of the supernatural, nor of the Creation, nor of the Trinity. Jesus Christ was to be admired for his ethics; his divinity was irrelevant or denied.

Deism was not a popular or organized movement. Its attitudes arose naturally out of those of the Enlightenment. In the 19th century a large Unitarian movement was influenced by Deist notions. Deists disliked the excessive religious "enthusiasm" and the emotionalism of the revivalists, the concept of ecstatic conversion. For them this was all superstition, ignorance, and in a pet pejorative word of all rationalists, "metaphysics." However, revivalist religion survived and performed important functions. Down to the present day great revival meetings have served as a cathartic group-therapy experience, quite apart from their religious meaning. They have given an immediacy to personal religious experience, and on the isolated frontier a sense of community and belonging.

Jonathan Edwards: Science and God

In New England the revival began in a town of western Massachusetts, Northampton, and was led by Jonathan Edwards. This great preacher was quite unlike any other revivalist: he combined the most sophisticated knowledge and attitude about science with the burning zeal of the religious convert. Edwards took over the Northampton Congregational Church from his grandfather, Solomon Stoddard, who had already made it famous. Stoddard had encouraged extensions of the Half-Way Covenant and Edwards came to oppose this. In the years 1733–35, when Edwards was aged 30–32, Northampton experienced an intense revival of faith, a reversion to earlier Puritan Calvinist beliefs. Edwards rejected the loving, easier-going God of Benjamin Franklin and Jefferson, the notion that Man had the power to save himself by good works, *Arminianism* as this more liberal and less exclusive faith was called, and the idea that any believers besides the Elect could be truly saved. Edward's sermons were vivid and startling. He deliberately jolted the congregation into the realization of God's enormous power and the terrifying fate that awaited most men. By contrast, God's mercy would thus be highlighted. Taking good advantage of his early scientific studies at Yale (Edwards was an accomplished scientific observer from the age of 11 and knew the works of Locke and Newton well), he compared miserable, impotent Man to the insects.

Jonathan Edwards recharged Calvinism. His beliefs in ineradicable Original Sin, in severe restriction of salvation to the Elect and in Man's incapacity to change anything, seem strangely un-American. In 1750 the congregation asked him to leave Northampton and he spent seven years on the Massachusetts frontier, preaching his unlikely doctrines to pioneers and Indians at Stockbridge before he was made president of the new Presbyterian college at Princeton, New Jersey (1758). He died of a faulty smallpox inoculation at the age of 55.

Social and political implications of the Great Awakening

Edwards was a brilliant intellectual. The revivalists who followed him were often less educated and usually more liberal and more careless in theology. With the coming of the dogma of "good works" and of Methodism, most marked after the Revolution, the followers of Edwards embraced the Arminianism he had opposed. Mass conversions and hazy dogma shook up the religious establishment in each colony. Sects grew while older churches lost authority. Presbyterians and Baptists were early winners, appealing everywhere to the lower orders —the thousands of colonists the other churches had failed to reach. On the frontier there were few if any churches or ministers before the great revivals. The audience was unchurched.

The congregational system in New England and the Anglican elite in Virginia were challenged. Once persecuted and weak, the sects now rode the crest. To train the larger numbers of missionaries and ministers they needed, each group built its colleges: Presbyterian Princeton, Dutch Reform Rutgers, Baptist Rhode Island (later Brown University), and others. Losses suffered by the Anglicans probably helped to weaken the link to England and prepare the way to Revolution. So did the democratic overtones of the new theology, the leveling implications seen in the bitter rejection by Rev. John Wise of Ipswich, Massachusetts, of an attempt to centralize authority in the Congregational ministry. "Democracy is Christ's government in Church and State," said Wise. He won his fight to keep alive in church governance the traditional New England congregational principle. From congregational control American theology would evolve toward belief in the priesthood of all believers, the ultimate "democracy" in religion. Wise, the son of an indentured servant, maintained that the people were the true source of power and that all men were naturally equal.

Religion and the Revolution

A new sociology of religious belief and observance came into being, determined by social class. The middle and upper classes tended to stay Congregationalist, Anglican, or at most Presbyterian by the late 18th century. Sectarians tended to be lower class or poorer farm and frontier types: thus was created the Baptist South. When the Revolution came, the northern Anglican clergy feared they would be swamped by the Congregational establishment once the English link was broken. In the South the Anglican Church would be disestablished, though most Southern clergy and laity were staunch Whigs and did not support the English. Quakers were officially pacifist and neutral. Methodists were few in number and were still missionary reformers *within* the Church of England: John Wesley, the English founder of Methodism, considered himself to be an Anglican and did not establish separate Methodist "societies" until 1784. It seems doubtful that lower-class Methodists would support the Loyalist side, however. Presbyterians, Congregationalists, and—in the South—the Anglicans supported the American Revolution.

Generally, nonconformist Americans had built up over the years a deep suspicion and fear that the Church of England would one day succeed in reestablishing itself as the official faith all over the colonies, as happened briefly in Massachusetts, for instance, in 1684. By law, Anglicanism was established in Virginia, Maryland, the Carolinas, Georgia, New York City, and nearby counties. Throughout the 18th century agitation to create a colonial episcopate was successfully opposed not only by the majority of colonists, who were nonconformists, but also by Anglicans in the South, who wished to choose their own clergy—not have them imposed by the Church in England. This struggle came to a climax in the years 1763–65 in a bitter pamphlet war that certainly helped to increase Anglo-American tension in the pre-Revolutionary period. The new state governments created by the rebels in the late 1770s disestablished the Anglican church everywhere except in Virginia, where it was not disestablished until 1785.

The maverick religious thinker whom most Americans would not follow was Tom Paine, however much they liked his anti-British writings. Paine's *Age of Reason* (1794–95) seemed to be an open attack on the Bible. He took his rationalism and Deism much further than did other thinkers like Franklin or even Jefferson. Free-thinking Jefferson did defend Paine, but the radicalism of his friend on religious issues alienated most Americans. Despite his great personal contributions to the Revolution Paine died in obscurity. Though he was out of touch with the religiosity of Americans, in his unquenchable optimism Tom Paine was very "American." Who but a man of that day and age could open his book *The Age of Reason* with the spirited statement:

I believe in one God and no more; and I hope for happiness beyond this life.

That confidence and matter-of-factness lay behind the American Revolution.

Bibliography

C. L. Ver Steeg. *The Formative Years, 1607–1763*. New York: Hill & Wang, 1964.

W. Jordan. *White Over Black*. Baltimore: Penguin, 1969.

W. E. Washburn (ed.). *The Indian and the White Man*. New York: Doubleday: 1964.

Carl Bridenbaugh. *Myths and Realities: Societies of the Colonial South*. New York: Atheneum, 1963.

Perry Miller. *Jonathan Edwards*. Greenwood reprint, 1973.

4

A Revolution for Home Rule

A political revolution . . . the American fear of an English conspiracy . . . the view from London . . . problems faced by England after 1763 . . . making the colonies pay: interest-group politics . . . growth of American separatism . . . alienation, Phase I: taxation and confrontation . . . violence and united action: the Stamp Act Congress . . . alienation, Phase II: violence pays . . . the Boston Massacre: first blood . . . Crispus Attucks: black martyr . . . alienation, Phase III: stalemate, 1770–73 . . . alienation, Phase IV: open struggle renewed . . . the Quebec Act and Canada . . . Political organization: First Continental Congress . . . Lexington and Concord: the first "federal government" . . . a republican world-view: the Declaration of Independence . . . alienation, Phase V: warfare . . . Long Island and Valley Forge . . . Saratoga . . . organizing the war effort . . . capturing the Midwest . . . Yorktown . . . the Peace of Paris, 1783 . . . the Loyalists: patriots or traitors? . . . the Revolution as a colonial "war of liberation" . . . a Lockean revolution that actually happened . . . what if the Americans had lost? . . . mercantilism and American growth . . . England fought for an unattainable end.

The debate over what the American Revolution was all about may never end. Each generation brings its own experience and outlook to bear, offering new insights. Continuous research brings new information to consider. Not so long ago historians insisted that the Revolution was a social upheaval at home in the colonies, as well as a war to throw off the shackles of Empire. This interpretation called into question the very meaning of the word "revolution," given the obvious contrasts with more radical and bloody revolutions, such as those in France (1789), Russia (1917), and China (1948). The American Revolution witnessed no "Reign of Terror" and Thermidorian reaction as in France, no bloody and extended civil war as in Russia, no mass executions of property owners as in China. Despite social tensions among the colonists, the American Revolution did not develop into open class warfare, and did not produce complete destruction of the existing social order as in Russia or China. Admittedly, Loyalists were drummed out; some lost their property and were tarred and feathered. But in France a few years later, 2,600 people were guillotined in Paris alone. What was "revolutionary" about the American war?

A political revolution

Some social, economic, and religious changes were accelerated by the Revolution. Essentially, however, the colonists fought for Home Rule—for a logical extension and formalization of the *political* rights they had gradually accumulated since 1607. The Revolution of course had its economic, social, and intellectual origins, as well as its political drives. All sorts of irritations endangered the colonial relationship; in fact, one could argue that all colonial relationships are inherently unstable, although some have survived for centuries.

As the situation between London and the colonies deteriorated with each new confrontation after 1763, old grievances were dragged out and turned to use in argument, and some new ones were thrown in for good measure. The fundamental disagreement, however, was over the colonists' right to a degree of *self-government*, or home rule. They had enjoyed a large measure of independence for many years. The real protagonists were not the allegedly despotic king versus the liberty-loving colonists, despite the abuse George III received in the Declaration of Independence; but the English House of Commons, which prided itself on its own rights and liberties, versus the fearful and suspicious American rebels.

The American fear of an English conspiracy

Attitudes polarized after 1763, and analysis of the rich pamphlet literature of the period suggests that many Americans had built up a remarkable "conspiracy theory" about the intentions of Britain. This is not to say that American fears of England were groundless and foolish. Later acts of the London government seemed to vindicate the colonists' suspicions. But the pamphleteers surely exaggerated the "conspiracy" and did much to increase the alienation between the Americans and London. They asserted that there was a sinister plot in England, worked out by the king, Commons, Lords, ministers, and bishops to destroy American liberties and to "enslave" the colonists. The core of this evil plot was the group of men surrounding the king: his ministers and court favorites, a corrupted cabinet of self-seeking cabalists.

Some of the evidence for this conspiracy was to be seen, it was claimed, in the agitation to establish an American episcopate. The activities of the Anglican *Society for the Propagation of the Gospel in Foreign Parts*, begun in Maryland in 1701 by Thomas Bray, a commissary sent out by the Bishop of London, were regarded with great suspicion. There was also allegedly a plot against the sacred principle of an *independent judiciary*. Colonial judges, it was pointed out, had never been permitted that life-time tenure granted to judges in England since 1701. Thus in 1759 the English government vetoed an act of the Pennsylvania legislature granting tenure to judges and in 1760 a battle broke out in New York over the same issue. Another pamphlet war ensued; colonists demanded the traditional "liberties

A Bishop sent from England is rejected in America

The John Carter Brown Library, Brown University

and privileges" of Englishmen. However, an English executive order of December 1761 denied tenure to all colonial judges.

Evidence piled up against the evil "ministerials." The defeat of the French in 1763 and attempted colonial reforms, necessitated a larger colonial bureaucracy—more administrators, customs officers, and so on. The colonists saw this build-up of bureaucrats as another part of the conspiracy, rather than as the necessary civil service for a larger and more efficient Empire. Or they despised the new "place-men" as corrupt political appointees, out to make money in the colonies. American dislike for people on the public payroll, still an effective prejudice today, has very deep historical roots.

The conspiracy theory explained that the "junto" in London was aided by juntos in the colonies themselves: subversives at home. Some colonial governments (e.g., that of Thomas Hutchinson, the last royal governor of Massachusetts) were buttressed by local patronage machines that allegedly endangered liberty by controlling all three branches of government, executive, legislative, and judiciary. A mob sacked Hutchinson's house during the Boston riots over the Stamp Act of 1765. His views were certainly conservative financially and pro-English politically. Private letters he had sent to England demanding a limitation of "what are called English liberties" in the colonies, were read out publicly by the fiery radical, Sam Adams. Of course, patronage politics held the political system together in England herself; but colonial leaders, even moderates like Benjamin Franklin, came to despise the corruption and venality of England.

The last piece of the conspiracy jigsaw puzzle seemed to be put in place when the English established a standing army in Boston. Nothing was hated more in England, after the experiences of the 17th century and the great debates of the 1690s, than the idea of a permanent, standing army in peacetime. Yet the colonists became so restive in Massachusetts in 1768 that two regular infantry regiments were sent out and garrisoned in Boston. Troops defending the frontier were one thing; troops stationed in peaceful towns were another. The colonists asked: what was the secret purpose of these forces? When the troops were withdrawn, the anger subsided temporarily. But the fear remained.

The view from London

The fabric of the colonists' conspiracy theory was thus made up of the threat of Anglican bishops, of a controlled judiciary, of a larger and corrupt colonial bureaucracy, of local patronage political machines subservient to London, and of a standing army. In 1765 the Stamp Act added another live issue: unconstitutional taxation. These matters were sufficient to bring confrontation. That the charges were exaggerated and the fears not realized did not matter.

How did the view look from London? The same problems were seen from an entirely different angle of vision. The Americans had long been regarded as turbulent and factious: they disagreed amongst themselves, sometimes violently, about religion, territorial boundaries, political and economic rights; they resented rational suggestions about a unified Indian policy, or a rational land settlement policy, and hated to pay taxes even for their own defense against Frenchmen and Indians. The English national debt soared; the colonists would not pay their fair share.

Was there a conspiratorial junto of King's ministers out to enslave Americans? This alleged junto was but the executive committee of the legally authorized, parliamentary government of England. It changed as ministries changed. It was the embryo of the later English *cabinet system*, which was to be the hallmark of democracy and party government. Colonists could not be expected to grasp this evolution, of course, any more than contemporary Englishmen at home. On the other hand, if by junto Americans meant the *Board of Trade*, what was this body to Englishmen but the policy-making department for the colonies, vital to the rational, orderly, and efficient administration of British possessions in various parts of the world, not merely in British North America?

As the crisis developed between the Mother Country and the Thirteen Colonies, English administrators became convinced that the colonies must be held at all costs. They became locked-in to this belief partly through national pride, partly through fear that loss of the American colonies would be a disastrous blow to Britain. In fact, the British Empire recovered very swiftly from losing the American war: a second empire was conquered, bigger than the first, and an industrialized England grew to world economic dominance. The colonists thus had their conspiracy fear, the English had their determination not to let go.

The year 1763 can be viewed as a special turning point in Anglo-American relations—a point of no return. English acquisition of the French Empire in North America brought to an abrupt end the English policy of "salutary neglect" towards the colonies, and required a reappraisal of the place of what was now a united "British North America" within the entire imperial system. Consequently London began to enforce old laws and pass new regulations to bind the Americans closer to the Empire. England tried to reclaim its lost authority precisely when the colonists themselves began to feel their own separate identity. She lost her grip by tightening it.

This is a plausible scenario. But it overlooks deeper historical continuities: English policy was changing *before* 1763, and American separatism had roots before that date. The great 19th-century American historian Francis Parkman said: "With the fall of Quebec began the history of the United States." This view tries to explain too much. There is ample evidence to suggest that the colonies would probably have broken away fairly soon even if there had been no French and Indian War.

Problems faced by England after 1763

Various interest groups in Britain actually shaped colonial policy. The Treasury emerged as a dominating force quite early. Britain was revenue-minded in its attitude to the colonies in the 1660s, a century before the defeat of France. In the face of strong American resistance to the Navigation Laws and of the evasion of customs duties, there was not much hope of making the colonies a paying proposition. In the early 18th century England left the Americans more alone, though as early as 1754 a junior minister, Charles Townshend, first put forward his plans for colonial reforms embodying the increased taxes which in 1767 would provide confrontation between London and the colonists.

Making the colonies pay: Interest-group politics

We have seen how Britain tried to create a colonial "system" after about 1688. Mercantilist regulations and attempted political controls did not get very far. Part of the problem was that private interests and the ins-and-outs of domestic English politics were allowed to determine policies toward America. Other colonies besides the Thirteen vied for attention in London. Americans often felt passed by in favor of the West or East Indies, or later, of Canada. There was intense intercolonial jealousy.

Though few colonists envisaged independent nationhood as the answer to the quarrel over the Stamp Act, the cultural and psychological roots of American national consciousness go back at least to the

Growth of American separatism

1730s, if not earlier. The ideology of the American Revolutionaries was by that date fully formulated. Ironically it grew out of English political ideals and practices. Americans were litigious and factious but they shared a unifying cultural tradition: preponderantly British, Calvinist in faith, agricultural in pursuit. The colonists were also united by their great degree of material success. This gave firm foundation to their deep belief in Progress, the perfectibility of mankind through improved institutions and environment, and the rational and pragmatic aspects of Enlightenment thought. In effect, Americans were "enlightened" before the Enlightenment. Meanwhile, trade, communications, religious and professional organizations and common political problems brought Americans together many years before 1776. Even an American dialect distinguished many of the colonists.

Viewed in a wider, international historical context, what is usually called the "American" Revolution was, after all, but the first of a series of liberal revolutions which, by stages, created the modern world and embodied the ideologies of modern times. The War of Independence opened up about 50 years of intense turmoil and change in world history: the French Revolution, the various South American revolutions, and that profounder economic and social revolution spreading outward from Britain—industrialization.

Alienation, Phase I: Taxation and confrontation

Faced with the doubling in size of its empire in North America and of its national debt (now about 140 million pounds sterling), the English government took the first of a succession of moves destined to alienate the colonists. The *Proclamation of 1763*, already noted as the high-water mark of a relatively humane English policy toward the Indians, created provincial governments for the former French and Spanish possessions, Quebec, and East and West Florida. While Indian affairs were put under direct ministerial control, white settlement west of the Alleghenies was theoretically prohibited. No one could prevent colonists from moving west of the Proclamation Line in fact, neither civil servants sitting in London, nor chief Pontiac's warriors. All the Proclamation did was to help convince Americans that the London government was out to assimilate Canada and was prepared to sacrifice the interests of the Thirteen Colonies if need be. The new frontier line and the later Quebec Act of 1774, if effective, would surely have fenced in the Americans more comprehensively than former French military encirclement. The conspiracy fears seemed justified.

What a later age would call "confrontation politics" came with the blundering ministry of George Grenville. His reactions to colonial events were ill-judged rather than malicious. He cracked down on smuggling, that very English activity openly encouraged, as we have seen, in the 17th century; it now cost the English government large sums each year in Treasury losses. Grenville tightened customs collections, particularly the duties on molasses, which clearly favored the British West Indies sugar planters over the New Englanders within the colonial trade system, and hurt the triangular trade so essential to American economic growth. Under a Molasses Act of 1733 the colonists were supposed to pay duties on sugar syrup imported from the West Indies to be made into rum. Grenville's *Sugar Act* of 1764 halved the 1733 duty levels but demanded that they be collected for a change. This would stimulate rum production in the West Indies and damage American distillers. Since New Englanders were prohibited from issuing paper money, the very life-line of trade was endangered.

In the Northeast, if not in the Southern colonies, merchants took up the cry of "No taxation without representation!" The Sugar Act was a *revenue* measure, a tax device to create income for the government, rather than a normal trade regulation act. Colonists were angry when the revenue itself was spent on establishing a standing army in America—which Grenville foolishly undertook. Despite bitter colonial opposition, he now extended the revenue functions of these indirect taxes still further. Precisely when he should have retracted, Grenville advanced. The Stamp Act of 1765 hit almost everyone, but those most affected by it were the articulate and educated elite. The act taxed newspapers, pamphlets, legal documents, and licenses. Obviously, Parliament did not think its own cherished rights of free speech and consensual government applied to Englishmen living in the colonies. As an income-creating tax the stamp duty was useless. However innocent in political motive, the act seemed to deny time-honored rights to the colonists. The political arguments which Americans were so skilled in using against governors of the colonies were now raised against England. Americans *rejected the power of Parliament*, however supreme it may be in England, to raise taxes in America without providing for adequate participation in the decision-making by Americans. At the same time the colonists confused the London government by refusing the idea of being represented in the London Parliament. The House of Commons had coolly deliberated and voted 245 to 49 to tax the colonists without asking their opinion. This was no isolated act by a royal tyrant. The Americans feared that more was to follow.

Violence and united action: The Stamp Act Congress

John Adams, the Massachusetts lawyer and a Whig, attacked the Stamp Act as a clear link in the English conspiracy, which exposed British political and ecclesiastical intentions in America. Adams declared that feudalism was not yet dead in England. The Stamp Act, he said in 1765, was merely part of a larger "design":

to strip us in a great measure of the means of knowledge . . . and to introduce the inequalities and dependencies of the feudal system by taking from the poorer sort of people all their little subsistence and conferring it on a set of stamp officers, distributors and their deputies.

The evil stamp officers were soon mobbed, tarred, and feathered by irate colonists. Leaders of hotter temper than John Adams organized a secret radical group in Boston, the Sons of Liberty. Their aim was mob-manipulation. Spurred by the wilder rhetoric of James Otis and the superb propaganda skills of Samuel Adams (John's more radical cousin), mobs burnt the homes of suspected officials and sacked

Governor Hutchinson's mansion. Parades, effigies, bonfires, slogans, and riots followed. Innocent people often suffered. Who were the guilty? The language of James Otis was larded with anti-Semitic and anti-Catholic overtones, for example. The radical Otis denounced the local elite of Rhode Island as a:

> little dirty, drinking, drabbing, contaminated knot of thieves, beggars and transports . . . made up of Turks, Jews and other infidels, with a few renegade Christians and Catholics.

When political confrontation takes place in history, all sorts of suppressed rages and feelings are released.

The movement spread and upper-class colonists became involved. Merchants boycotted English imports. In the Virginia House of Burgesses the moderates struggled to contain the element led by Patrick Henry and others; they passed five of Henry's inflammatory "Virginia Resolves," but dropped the two most radical statements before petitioning the king.

The first united action of the colonists against the new economic policy came at the behest of Massachusetts, which called the Stamp Act Congress of 1765. Meeting in New York, 27 delegates from 9 colonies drew up a Declaration of Rights and Grievances. Though divided as to means, the delegates agreed on ends: opposition to the Stamp Act. Their "Declaration" was a logical, direct descendant of English precedents, particularly of Chief Justice Sir Edward Coke's famous *Petition of Right* of 1628, which sought to wrest from Charles I four basic freedoms: no martial law in time of peace; no quartering of troops in private homes; no imprisonment without due cause; no taxation without consent of Parliament. These chickens of 1628 now came home to roost in America.

Alienation, Phase II: Violence pays

Resistance and mob violence paid off. In London the merchants complained about postwar depression and the decline of colonial export trade; they petitioned Parliament. A brief new ministry of Lord Rockingham tried to win over the colonists and reverse Grenville's trend. The Stamp Act was abolished. Parliament, however, still bristled at the impudence of Americans and undermined Rockingham's policy by passing a Declaratory Act (1766), to remind the colonists that the English legislature remained supreme in all colonial matters. Political in-fighting in the House of Commons continued to affect policy toward the colonies. Charles Townshend became Chancellor of the Exchequer and tried once more to implement his policy of "making the colonies pay."

Townshend proposed to throw over decades of colonial precedent. He would free colonial governors and their staff from dependence on colonial purse strings by paying them directly from London out of funds derived from taxes in the colonies. Governors would thus become direct creatures of Parliament and of the ministry rather than spokesmen for the colonies. Such a radical idea enraged colonial leaders like Otis, Sam Adams, and Patrick Henry. The battle was

John Hancock, merchant for independence

The Bettmann Archive

suddenly renewed. Violence reappeared and a bitter pamphlet war was fanned. Townshend's new duties included a whole line of previously untaxed imports: tea, glass, lead, paper, paint, and other necessities. Northeastern merchants boycotted English imports once more and were supported this time by Southern merchants.

Massachusetts again took the lead. The *Circular Letter* which it sponsored in 1768 and which passed from colonial assembly to assembly, was banned by the English, and subsequently was openly supported by the assemblies in angry defiance. The *Letter* was a fairly mild rehash of ideas to be found in John Dickinson's *Letters from a Pennsylvania Farmer,* which distinguished taxes for revenue from normal taxes for regulation of trade. Dickinson was a moderate Philadelphia lawyer, concerned with "precedent" and due process. But he isolated the real culprit as Parliament:

If the Parliament succeeds in this attempt, other statutes will impose other duties . . . *without any other limitation than their pleasure.*

The British did not handle this new outbreak of resistance very wisely. They tried to respond with firmness. New Vice-Admiralty Courts were added to regulate trade. A separate American department of State was created under the unsympathetic Lord Hillsborough. A Board of Customs Commissioners was sent out to Boston, which was reinforced with troops. The Commissioners were despised. Attitudes polarized, and the opposition to English policies united Americans across class lines. For example, John Hancock was accused, probably justly, of smuggling in Madeira wine; his sloop *Liberty* was confiscated. This became a useful excuse for more town riots, drunkenness, and orgies of window smashing. The customs officers took refuge.

Behind the scenes, Samuel Adams kept up the pressure against the authorities. He urged merchants to maintain the British boycott; those who would not, got their houses stoned or were roughed up. Each incident became a weapon for maximum publicity—as in February 1770, when a mob attacked a Tory house and an 11-year-old boy (Seider, or Snyder) was shot. Adams quickly arranged a large public funeral for the young victim and turned him into a martyr for liberty. By March of 1770 all the ingredients of violent confrontation were gathered in Boston: clever radical organizers, anxious merchants, divided and confused townsfolk, hated customs men, crowds of young apprentices and merchant sailors eager for the fray, and a body of nervous troops led by young officers.

The Boston Massacre: First blood

Sam Adams's Sons of Liberty needed an incident. It came in early March. Three or four days of individual confrontations began with a fight between soldiers and ropemakers on March 2d. On the night of March 5th three separate crowds gathered and people eventually converged on King Street. Crowds armed with cudgels and looking for trouble taunted the troops, snowballed them, and threatened them. One isolated young sentry was surrounded near the Custom House by a group of rowdy apprentice wigmakers, yelling "Lobster!" at him (the way that 200 years later young people would yell "Pig!"); this soon became a big crowd. The sentry had to be rescued somehow; in this way came the Boston Massacre, the first "battle" of the War of Independence.

The redcoats were hated and almost powerless. They could not be used unless civil authorities asked for them; throughout the affair the latter were conspicuously absent. A mere 600 troops had to keep order among 16,000 well-armed townspeople. Boston had no street lights, but the cold night of March 5th was lit by a bright moon in 1770 when eight nervous British soldiers defied the mobs, the constant noise of tolling church bells, and the general uproar, to try to reach the young sentry.

The troops lined themselves up at the Custom House. Their problem now was how to get the sentry back to the safety of the Main Guard, their headquarters. They were held at bay by a crowd of about 400, who jeered, told them they were too scared to shoot (the soldiers were quivering with cold and fear), and threw various objects at them. A thrown cudgel knocked down one soldier to the ice. He fired off his musket either angrily or accidentally. Indiscriminate firing followed. It is not clear to this day if the officer, Preston, ever gave the command to fire. He strenuously denied the charge at the later enquiry in which John Adams took part. Five civilians died and three or four were injured. That was the sum total of the "massacre." For days thereafter Sam Adams and the Sons of Liberty virtually controlled the town.

4 / A Revolution for Home Rule

Crispus Attucks: Black martyr

A hero of the Revolution and one of the first two Americans to die for independence was a man of mixed blood, Crispus Attucks. He has long been considered a hero of Black history. In fact, Attucks remains a mystery man. We do know he was about 47, six-foot-two, and probably came off a Nantucket whaler. He may well have been partly Indian, a Natick, as well as partly Negro. On the fatal night of March 5th Attucks was living in Boston under the assumed name of Michael Johnson and claiming that he came from Nassau in the British Bahamas.

It is clear that Attucks knew what he was doing and did not die accidentally. He was no spectator but a leader of the crowd. Perhaps he had high hopes of possible freedom for his people, we simply do not know. Boston Negroes were politically active and had petitioned the Massachusetts assembly for freedom from slavery. One white leader, James Otis, supported black demands. Otis stood for abolition as early as 1764. As it turned out, however, Attucks and the Boston blacks may have been better off under continued English rule. The United States kept slavery; the British eliminated it wherever their power could reach.

Alienation, Phase III: Stalemate, 1770–73

After the shock of 1770 both sides pulled back: it was clear where that route was leading. Townshend was replaced by the pragmatic politician and master of patronage, Lord North. He promptly abolished all the Townshend duties except the one on tea. Among the colonists the return of trade and prosperity created apathy; and inter-colonial quarrels over western land claims, the Indians, and religious establishment kept them busy. In North Carolina, for instance, the backcountry Regulators marched in 1771, provoking a sectional civil war—western backwoodsmen versus Tidewater elite.

Wealthier, more conservative, Whig colonists were shocked by mob excesses, though they had themselves strongly opposed the standing army and the Townshend duties. How could the radicals keep the pot boiling? Sam Adams kept the Boston Town Meeting stirred up against the customs men; he established in each town the famous system of "Committees of Correspondence," a revolutionary technique later borrowed by the French in 1789. A local network of radical cells was thus built up and spread to the planter radicals of the South. In Virginia, Patrick Henry had defied both the English and the conservative planter oligarchy; an uncompromising frontier lawyer, Henry's flaming oratory ("Give me liberty or give me death!") had already matched that of Sam Adams. Further South, a young aristocratic radical, Christopher Gadsden, also kept anti-English sentiments alive.

The Committees of Correspondence—basic machinery for organizing a revolution—waited to seize the initiative, if another British blunder should occur. In 1772 the *Gaspee* incident helped a little. A group of Rhode Islanders burnt a customs schooner which had run aground near Providence. The colonists closed ranks and for lack of evidence nobody could be convicted. The British government could surely be relied upon to make a major error sooner or later, since

The U.S.A.

policy was often the outcome of inner parliamentary maneuvers on issues irrelevant to American affairs.

Alienation, Phase IV: Open struggle renewed

At this stage the English government did not choose to "let sleeping dogs lie" once more and the alienation between the colonists and London advanced a step further to the point of open conflict. In unthinking disregard for the colonial situation, Lord North began a new round of confrontation politics, with the Tea Act of May 1773. Passed chiefly to aid the powerful but financially ailing East India Company, the measure removed the duty on tea in England, though still keeping the colonial duty, and allowed the company's own agents to sell tea in the colonies, instead of selling it through auctions in London to independent merchants. The East India Company was overstocked with tea at the time and wanted to get rid of it. But the act hurt the American merchants and middlemen in the colonies and was yet another example of London placing the interests of some other powerful lobby above that of the Americans. Ironically, the result could well have been cheaper tea for the colonial consumer, though the company, having been given this monopoly of the trade, was clearly free to manipulate tea prices at any later date.

Colonial merchants were up in arms over the Tea Act. Mobs blocked tea unloadings in American ports like Charleston and Boston. Men dressed as Mohawk Indians dumped tons of tea into the harbor in the carefully staged Boston Tea Party of December 1773. The English, pushed to the limit by the behavior of the Bostonians, closed the port altogether, reduced civil liberties, and restricted the role of the assembly by the Boston Port Act and the so-called Intolerable Acts of

The Boston Tea Party

The Bettmann Archive

1774. Said George III: "The die is cast. The colonists must either triumph or submit." Troops were to be quartered in private homes, rioters were to be tried in England rather than in the colonies, and the port of Boston could not reopen until the East India Company had been paid for its lost tea. Some merchants were ready to pay up, but the radicals held firm and forged colonial unity.

The deeper meaning of these events was that the "American interest" was ill-represented in London. West Indies sugar planters, East Indies merchants, even French Canadians seemed to do better as a parliamentary pressure group. In fact, English trade was much less dependent than it formerly was on the Americans. English producers had developed Eastern and continental European outlets. In the words of Edmund Burke, the American colonies had become merely "the tennis ball of faction."

The Quebec Act and Canada

The government hoped to win over the French Canadians by a policy of calculated generosity, however angry the Americans became. The Quebec Act of 1774 enlarged the borders of Quebec to include the entire territory between the Ohio and the upper Mississippi. American fears about the Proclamation Line of 1763 were now realized: they were to be cut off from western outlets. It was as if the French were back.

What seemed worse, Catholics were allowed to hold office in Quebec, the Catholic Church was legalized, and its tithes acknowledged. The land grants of the great seigneurs were guaranteed. Trial by jury and other English ways were not to be imposed on French culture. The act was a charter of French Canadian civil rights. Frenchmen sat on the governor's council—while in England, itself, Catholics did not win such rights until 1829. The small but growing band of English merchants who controlled Quebec's trade were irritated and alarmed as the early goals of "Anglicizing" the French were dropped. Once more, it seemed that American interests were flouted in favor of someone else. Hostile to the Canadian situation, one of General George Washington's very first steps on taking over the Continental Army was to order an invasion of Canada. Thus the Quebec Act produced the first stage of the Anglo-American war, before the major part of the War of Independence proper got under way. Colonial forces besieged Quebec City and were repulsed in the spring of 1776.

Political organization: First Continental Congress

In September 1774, delegates from all the colonies but Georgia met in the Congress at Philadelphia. A radical maneuver pushed through tough economic sanctions against London, to be enforced throughout the colonies by local "Committees of Safety" (a title reminiscent of Leisler's Revolt of 1689, and used later by the French Revolution). The radical "Suffolk Resolves" were rushed to Philadelphia by the courier for the Massachusetts Committee of Correspondence, Paul Revere, in one of his lesser known rides, and was hastily approved. The Resolves nullified the Intolerable acts, urged the creation of a revolutionary government in Massachusetts and demanded the establishment of an armed colonial militia.

A more conservative approach was Joseph Galloway's Plan of Union which sought to unite the colonies with Britain in a kind of federal system, the Americans having their own president and congress. The radicals narrowly defeated this plan and then went on to expunge it from the very records of the convention. From all this something new was emerging, evident in Patrick Henry's symbolic declaration:

> I am not a Virginian, but an American!

The response to radical activities was good. The moderates were intimidated. The issue for many Americans was no longer freedom from arbitrary taxation or from standing armies or customs commissioners but freedom from Britain: self-government. The rejection of Galloway's plan clearly indicates a change of heart by many colonists. The ideal of independent, *republican* self-government had appeared. After the Philadelphia meetings, John Adams wrote his *Novanglus Letters* (1774–75) which put forward the theory that the American colonies were *not* subject to the London Parliament because they were not part of the British "realm"; each colony was itself an independent realm, owing allegiance only to the king. We have observed earlier

The Battle of Lexington, April 19, 1775

New York Public Library
(engraving by Amos Doolittle after Ralph Earle)

that the Spanish empire had been so constructed. Historians can see Adams's theory as a preview of later English "dominion" theory, by which in the late 19th and 20th centuries the empire evolved into the British Commonwealth of Nations.

Lexington and Concord: The first "federal government"

In Massachusetts a revolutionary committee was already training troops when fighting broke out against the redcoats on April 19, 1775, at Lexington. A party had been sent out by General Gage, the new Massachusetts governor, to seek and arrest the merchant John Hancock and Sam Adams and locate an arms cache at nearby Concord. On Lexington Green eight American "minutemen" were shot. At the North Bridge in Concord the English were halted by armed farmers. They were routed and picked off by marksmen all the way home, losing 273 men, to a colonial loss of 93. Gage was soon surrounded in Boston, and all over the colonies royal governors and councils fell from power.

The first federal government was the Second Continental Congress (May–June 1775) which created an army of the "United Colonies" under General Washington, issued paper currency, and named a committee for foreign relations. Gage broke out of Boston with heavy losses to his "Ministerial" forces (as the colonists called them), in the battle of Bunker Hill (June 1775), and the United Colonies began their unsuccessful siege of Quebec. When the Congress petitioned George III he merely declared a state of rebellion. The last links of colonial loyalty to the Crown disappeared. From then on the king would be deliberately pictured in colonial propaganda as a ruthless tyrant.

A republican world-view: The Declaration of Independence

The rebels, pushed by the Sons of Liberty and by radical thinkers like Tom Paine, developed a republican image of the world. Their original hopes for some sort of limitations placed on the English monarchy, and greater freedom from the Parliament, now gave way. Many Americans had come to equate liberty with republicanism and national independence. Their political and philosophical problem would be how to relate the public-good aspects of republicanism with their traditional, highly individualistic pursuits of "life, liberty and happiness." The tension between the public and the private has remained a major theme of American thought.

The Revolution had become irreversible, because American thought had moved into a different stage altogether. Tom Paine's brilliant polemic, *Common Sense*, appeared in January 1776, and its timing was as perfect as his rhetoric. Paine denounced George III as "the hardened, sullen-tempered Pharoah of England," and "the royal brute of Britain." He totally identified liberty with national independence and a republican form of government. Reconciliation was out of the question: "The last cord now is broken." In *Common Sense* Paine offered his own design for a "continental form of government." He would stop short at "nothing but independence."

Rhode Island and South Carolina cut royal ties; the Congress urged the colonies to adopt new state constitutions (May 1776); the Middle colonies gave way under pressure from the South and New England.

Finally, on July 4, 1776, the Declaration of Independence brought Americans to the point of no return. As Benjamin Franklin told John Hancock on that day in a wry *bon mot:*

We must indeed all hang together, or most assuredly, we shall all hang separately.

This was no time for very subtle interpretation of events, and the Declaration simply laid all the blame for everything on George III, "a Prince . . . unfit to be the ruler of a free people." The large role played by Parliament in this alleged conspiracy to impose "an absolute Tyranny over these States" was not alluded to at all. The main author, of course, was Thomas Jefferson, though a committee and, later, Congress itself made changes—principally, they cut out Jefferson's dramatic attack on human slavery. It took him about two weeks to compose the first draft, while lodged at the home of a German immigrant bricklayer in Philadelphia.

Jefferson was deeply concerned, as the Declaration states, to give "a decent respect to the opinions of mankind"; he listed most of the grievances, some imaginary, that had plagued the colonists for years, in order to justify to the world at large why they had decided to rebel and throw off their legal government. Yet it was not the listing of the sins of George III that impressed later generations, but Jefferson's brilliant *preamble*. In that brief introduction, amazingly succinct, are all the notions he and his generation *took for granted*. It embodied in a few noble sentences the whole tradition of Coke, Locke, Natural Law, and the Enlightenment. For Jefferson, even God is "Nature's God." Five "thats" synthesize the political philosophy derived from social contract and Natural Law theory:

1. "that all men are created equal"
2. "that they are endowed by their Creator with certain unalienable Rights"
3. "that among these, are Life, Liberty, and the pursuit of Happiness"
4. "that, to secure these rights, Governments are instituted among Men, deriving their just Powers from the consent of the governed"
5. "that, whenever any form of Government becomes destructive of these ends it is the Right of the People to alter or to abolish it, and to institute new Government"

These five assertions, taken to be "self-evident," form the bedrock of American *political liberalism*. Later they profoundly influenced the French Revolution and the colonial revolutions in Latin America. The two most radical and disturbing propositions were that all men were created equal, and that unjust governments should be overthrown. The "right to revolution" has frightened many 20th-century Americans, who have rejected this part of their democratic political birthright.

Alienation, Phase V: Warfare

"These are the times that try men's souls," wrote Paine in December 1776. "The summer soldier and the sunshine patriot will, in this crisis, shrink from the service of their country." However there were to be rougher times for the United Colonies (for instance, the coming winter of 1777 when Washington's men suffered at Valley Forge) before ultimate freedom and victory. It was to be seven years before the final peace treaty was signed with Britain—13 years after the Boston Massacre.

The war ebbed and flowed and was ultimately decided by sea power and the aid of the French. At the outset the United States had neither of these and the outlook was poor. She had no navy, though several patriots had argued for one, especially Paine; she had to make do with odd ships of various sorts (34 by 1777) and the help of many privateers and pirates who attacked the British shipping lanes for profit. French intervention alone brought in bigger ships on the colonial side. Despite the exploits of American captains like John Paul Jones, sea power and French aid were virtually the same thing.

The American army was also hastily contrived, though the farmers, tradesmen, and citizen-soldiers did have the advantages of long experience in frontier wars, knowledge of Indian scouting and guerilla warfare, intimacy with the vast terrain, and fine marksmanship with better guns. The American rifle was better than the English ungrooved musket. Washington's worst problem was not even indiscipline, though his men rarely recognized rank, but simple shortage of troops. His armies never exceeded about 21,000 men at one time. This many American Loyalists fought for the British, though not all at the same time.

Long Island and Valley Forge

Before the Declaration of Independence, the chief military actions were the unsuccessful raid on Quebec (which did, however, bother the British and divert their strength) and Washington's long siege of Boston (July 1775–March 1776). Sir William Howe then evacuated Boston and moved British headquarters to New York by sea. Washington followed him but lost the battle of Long Island in August 1776 and was forced to retreat through New Jersey to Pennsylvania, avoiding any major confrontations. Two small American victories there (Trenton and Princeton, 1776–77) lifted the rebels' spirits; but the following September, Lord Howe occupied Philadelphia itself, former site of the Congress. Washington suffered more setbacks at Brandywine and Germantown and went into winter quarters at Valley Forge, 1777–78, where his luckless men alternately froze and thawed out, having inadequate clothing and shelter. It was difficult to prevent desertions and to hold them together. Only Washington's iron will and personal example stood in the way of dispersion.

Saratoga

Meanwhile the tide of war had turned in the North, where a British plan to divide the states by driving a wedge both up and down the Hudson Valley came to failure. The English general, "Gentleman Johnny" Burgoyne, invaded from Canada, recaptured Ticonderoga, but was then forced to surrender his army at Saratoga in October 1777. It was partly the fault of Lord Howe, who had moved on to take Philadelphia instead of ascending the Hudson from New York to trap the

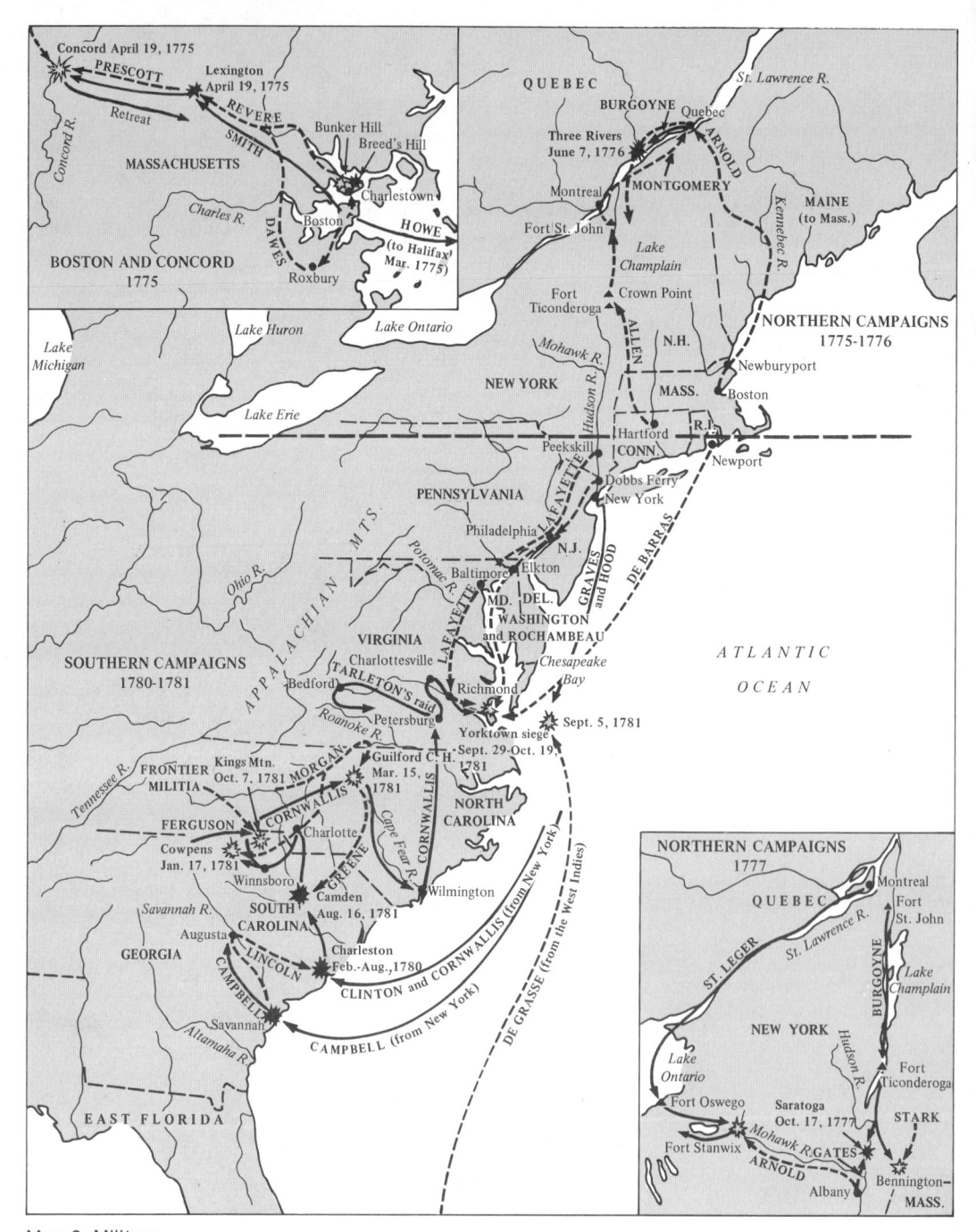

Map 2. Military campaigns of the Revolution

4 / A Revolution for Home Rule

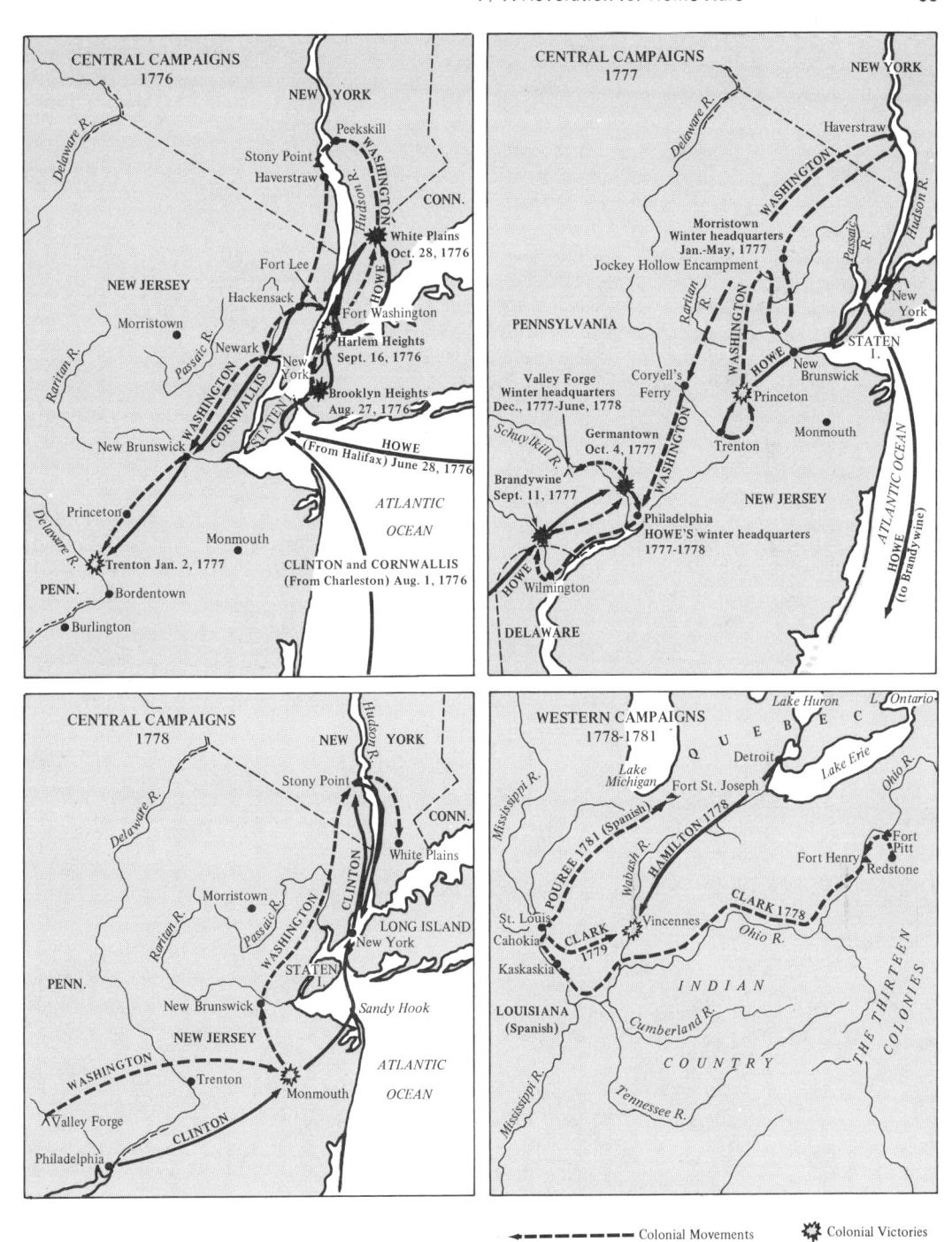

Gruver, *An American History, Volume 1 to 1877, 1972,*
Addison-Wesley, Reading, Mass.

The U.S.A.

Americans with a pincer movement. Thus the colonists, led by Horatio Gates with the help of Benedict Arnold, achieved a stunning victory and Burgoyne went home in disgrace. The English general achieved more success as a playwright than as a commander.

Organizing the war effort

Saratoga was a turning point in the war, for the success persuaded the French to enter on the American side. Doubtless they were also encouraged by the organization of an American government in the Articles of Confederation (November 1777), though, articles or not, the colonists did not cooperate very well throughout the war. No state, for example, imposed additional local taxes to help pay for the war. Financing the war was thus very difficult, and the new confederacy was little better off financially than the former United Colonies. Revenues were scraped together by asking individual colonies for supplies, or by use of lotteries and prize money from captured vessels. Continental currency was issued, but its value fell because there was no gold or silver behind it—hence the classic phrase, "not worth a Continental." Eventually John Adams and Benjamin Franklin managed to acquire foreign funds: loans from the French, Dutch, and Spanish. The efficient way to pay for any war is through direct taxation, but throughout its history the United States has failed to do this adequately. In all its major wars, down to World War II, revenues came partly from taxes, but mainly from loans, usually at high interest rates.

After Saratoga, the British withdrew from Philadelphia (June 1778) and moved back to New York to plan a "southern strategy." On the way, Washington's troops harried them. The Americans were by then better trained—by Von Steuben, a self-styled "baron," who had been a captain in the Prussian army of Frederick the Great, and by other foreign officers. These included two famous Poles—Count Casimir Pulaski, the cavalry general who was killed at Savannah in 1779, and Thaddeus Kosciuszko, the military engineer who survived and later became a Polish national hero—and the French aristocrat, the Marquis

The "Continental" dollar, whose falling value gave rise to the popular phrase "not worth a Continental"

Smithsonian Institution

de Lafayette, a general at the age of 19 and the only foreigner to be given honorary U.S. citizenship directly by Congress (without naturalization) until it was also granted to Winston Churchill.

Capturing the Midwest

The French fleet arrived in July 1778 but an initial scheme of Washington's to invade Newport, Rhode Island, from sea and land was foiled by bad weather. The war began to get very nasty as it lengthened. Atrocities and reprisals became common. For example, Loyalists and their Indian allies murdered frontier settlers in 1778. In February 1779 George Rogers Clark, who in earlier times had explored the Illinois and Ohio country, captured the fort of Vincennes from the British and thus secured the whole of what became known as the "Old Northwest" (much of the modern Midwest). The Proclamation Line of 1763 and the Quebec Act of 1774 were now abruptly consigned to ancient history. Never again would the Old Northwest be a serious threat to the Americans, though some feared a possible invasion from that region during the War of 1812.

June of 1779 brought Spain into the war on the American side; the Spanish hoped to seize Gibraltar and to win back Florida. In the fall, John Paul Jones carried the American war right to England's own back doorstep in a famous sea battle off the coast of Yorkshire in the North Sea—the famous encounter between the *Bonhomme Richard* and the *Serapis*. The battle was an unusual sight for British provincial eyes.

Yorktown

Meanwhile the British southern campaign was a great initial success. They quickly grabbed Georgia. Charleston also fell in May 1780 with the rest of South Carolina following. Subsequent British operations in the Carolina backcountry brought them up against the tough American mountaineers who routed the Tories at the battle of King's Mountain, North Carolina, in October and at Cowpens in January 1781. Frustrated by the apparent stalemate, General Lord Cornwallis invaded Virginia, ravaging the countryside and burning towns. In late summer he retired to Yorktown to await reinforcements. Lafayette, who had refused to risk his poorly trained troops in open battle, wrote Washington that Cornwallis might be trapped.

The denouement came. Sea-power and French cooperation were essential, but the plan was well conceived by Washington, who raced southward from New York in a brilliant forced march. It was the outstanding move of his command (in pitched battles he had not been brilliant, since he lost more than he won). The French navy under Admiral De Grasse bottled up Chesapeake Bay and ferried allied troops to Yorktown. Washington and the French general Rochambeau began a siege of the city in late August. There were 16,000 troops outside the town and 36 French warships in the bay. Cornwallis wisely surrendered on October 19, 1781, and the war was virtually over.

In London the British government had given up on the costly American war. North resigned and was replaced by Lord Rockingham in March 1782. The new government began peace negotiations.

The Peace of Paris, 1783

The Peace of Paris was a complex set of international agreements, delayed by the play of European politics. Contrary to the American self-image that its diplomats were innocents abroad treating with wily Europeans, the clever and skilled American negotiators (Franklin, John Adams, and John Jay) kept an eye on their own national interests, cut out the French, and signed a separate peace with England. The British granted independence and diplomatic recognition to the United States, with the Mississippi as its western border. They thus severed Canada from the rich Ohio valley lands and shaped the future of that nation by forcing Canadians to develop the country north of the Great Lakes. Florida, however, went to Spain.

A number of clauses would cause future disputes. Boundaries were left vague in parts of the West and in the New Brunswick region. The property rights of Loyalists were to be restored by the United States, but this was not carried out. Neither did Britain fully withdraw its troops from military forts in the Northwest. American fishing privileges off the Canadian coast of Newfoundland and the St. Lawrence would recur as an international issue. On the whole the treaty was, however, a massive victory for the young republic and a vindication of their stand.

The Loyalists: Patriots or traitors?

Some scholars claim that at least one third of the American colonists did not support the war against England. Many were simply too busy coping with the wilderness and the soil. After the war about 100,000 "United Empire Loyalists" emigrated; they moved to Canada (about 40,000 of them), the West Indies, and Britain. The Loyalists strengthened Canada's suspicions of the United States and helped build a growing Canadian nationalism.

The result of this migration was the Canada Act of 1791, which divided the colony into upper (English) and lower (French) Canada, each with a separate assembly and style of law and government. This institutionalized what would be very grave bicultural problems for the future of Canada.

What of these Loyalists, some of whom were roughed up and drummed out of town by the American rebels, and many of whom lost their property and never regained it? Clearly, they were "traitors" only in the sense of having lost the war—not in the sense of having turned coat in the middle, like a Benedict Arnold, who negotiated with General Clinton to turn over West Point for a price (20,000 pounds sterling). Such a large exodus must reveal a genuine confusion on the part of many Americans as to where their loyalty belonged. A man like Joseph Galloway, a colleague of Franklin, whose Plan of Union was defeated in the First Continental Congress by only one vote, but who remained loyal and emigrated to England in 1778, could not justly be called a common traitor. The "Patriots," of course, bitterly denounced all Loyalists and Tories—Tom Paine even claimed that all the prostitutes in New York were Tories!

Few of the victorious rebels considered that according to their own theories of Natural Law, social contract, and government by consent, the Loyalists were well within their natural rights in refusing to serve against England. What is more, since American nationhood was not yet formed, to what were these people disloyal? The entire question of loyalty and treason would continue to dog the Republic in the early national period of its history and even long afterward.

The Revolution as a colonial "war of liberation"

Recently it has been claimed that the American Revolution was essentially an early historical example of a colonial "war of liberation." However, if this is true, the conditions were very special. The American colonists were in arms against their own culture, not against a truly foreign power. The Revolution was fought at the outset over differing interpretations of the one shared British Constitution. The colonists no doubt felt themselves to be truer to the 17th century Lockean ideals of Britain and they thought that the Mother Country had become corrupted by the 18th-century patronage system. British colonial administration with all its faults was nevertheless probably the most advanced and most enlightened of any colonial system, and was one within which the Americans had developed unprecedented liberties and rights and a high level of prosperity and material culture.

The colonies struggled not against George III, the "royal brute of Britain," but against Parliament and the ministry. It seemed as if the Divine Right of Kings had been supplanted by the Divine Right of the House of Commons. Yet the Americans rightly regarded themselves as direct descendants of those parliamentarians whose struggles had established the prerogatives and rights of the English lower house. Americans had secured for themselves the basic "rights of Englishmen" and representative assemblies and had written documents, charters, and compacts to validate them. Colonial political history was but a chapter in the evolution of the British Constitution.

This was a strange "war of liberation" indeed. It was fought against a relatively liberal and advanced society, in order that the colonists could fulfill themselves and become whole, along much the same lines as those they had already been following. American self-determination was the historical fulfilment of the English revolutions of the 17th century.

A Lockean revolution which actually happened

Since American political ideas were derivative and part of the English stream of thought and were not particularly radical, what was revolutionary about the American Revolution? At least three elements were revolutionary in their effects. The American war was the first successful colonial uprising to throw off a Mother Country. Second, Americans became republicans and rejected the monarchical tradition, though at this stage they were not conscious democrats in any modern sense. In an era when kings and aristocrats still held sway in the traditional societies of the world, American republicanism was indeed regarded as revolutionary, even though American society had its own elite and political power was not widely dispersed. Third, Americans were prepared to go much further than were the English theorists in carrying out Locke's ideas in the real world by actually constructing a government along his lines. They were aided by having a favorable setting of economic opportunity, growth, mobility and pluralism. The Americans made a Lockean revolution and saw it through.

So far as the techniques of how to stage a revolution are concerned the Americans taught the world the methods of mass agitation, underground organization, and propaganda. They showed how a revolutionary governmental structure could be built. Their conventions, constitutions, and the federal system which emerged out of the Second Continental Congress and the Articles of Confederation were all precedents for future revolutions, like those of France in 1789 and the Central and South American nations in the early 19th century.

What if the Americans had lost?

If England had won the war could she have won the peace? Could she have maintained control over such an area and such a factious people? Tom Paine said in 1776:

> There is something very absurd in supposing a Continent to be perpetually governed by an island.

The center of such a large empire may well have moved west anyway, out of London. High rates of colonial population growth meant that America was outstripping England precisely at the moment of the Revolution. Americans were reproducing themselves every 25 years. Britain was also growing but less fast. What contradicts this thesis most is that the Industrial Revolution was also taking place in Britain. New economic power enabled Britain to build a second empire and to hold onto almost one quarter of the globe for many years longer.

Mercantilism and American growth

Clearly the mercantilist "restrictions" of the British Empire did not hold back the American colonies very seriously. If the colonists lost financially through the Navigation Laws and other policies, their loss was not substantial. Tobacco planters seemed to earn still more after 1783 than before, the need for reexport through English ports now being removed. But American shippers lost badly after the Revolution because they faced the Navigation Laws of other nations and no longer enjoyed the protected market of the Empire. It was a very heavy loss for American merchants to be excluded after 1783 from the rich British West Indies trade. Shipbuilders were also poor after the coming of independence: England had been their major market. Rice and indigo exports both fell and the growers lost their subsidy from the London government. The American iron industry declined seriously, likewise losing its chief outlet.

The American economy was saved only by the outbreak of general war in Europe after the French Revolution. The sudden leap in European demand and the necessary elimination of foreign trade restrictions during the war gave the United States its golden opportunity to trade with all sides. As a neutral trader the new nation began to prosper again. Meanwhile the American domestic market was growing, and the Revolutionary war had helped to stimulate native industries, despite the destruction felt in some regions. The munitions, glass, pottery, leather, and paper industries were all boosted during the War of Independence. The war also affected the social climate, built new fortunes, and prepared the way for the burst of American entrepreneurship in the 1780s and 90s.

What can be said about English bureaucratic trade regulations of the colonies is that they operated unevenly against different groups, classes, and colonies. They seemed capricious. The Americans grew to hate them more as a symbol of their own lack of self-determination and national manhood than for their actual economic effects or costs.

In sum then, the American colonies resorted to violence chiefly for political and intellectual reasons as well as for cultural motives which were harder to measure. They claimed a plot by the London governing cabal to deprive the colonies of all the rights they had built up over 150 years. The English administrators feared the effects of the loss of empire in America. Maybe, as the French commentator Tocqueville said in the 1830s, the Americans were "born mature." Certainly the English in attempting to maintain permanent authority by the London Parliament in America fought for an unattainable end.

England fought for an unattainable end

E. S. Morgan.   *Birth of the Republic, 1763–89.* University of Chicago Press, 1956.

Bibliography

J. T. Main.   *Social Structure of Revolutionary America.* Princeton University Press, 1956.

B. Bailyn.   *Ideological Origins of the American Revolution.* Harvard University Press, Cambridge, 1967.

B. Quarles.   *The Negro in the American Revolution.* New York: Norton, 1973.

A. Heimert.   *Religion and the American Mind from the Great Awakening to the Revolution.* Cambridge: Harvard University Press, 1966.

~5~

The Revolution contained

How did one create a new nation in 1783? . . . Natural Law and separation of powers . . . origins of Federalism: Revolutionary government . . . new state constitutions: government by assembly . . . a nation of states? . . . fear of executive government: the Confederation . . . the public domain: individualism and capitalism unleashed . . . the Territorial system . . . the movement for stronger centralism . . . economic interest groups behind the new constitution . . . revolution and containment . . . sectional issues: slavery . . . fears of social breakdown . . . the "Critical Period" . . . thinking continentally: the Founding Fathers . . . national pride and foreign affairs . . . Federalist techniques: pressing for a new constitution . . . a closed room in Philadelphia . . . struggles within the convention . . . the federal constitution: the Preamble . . . Article I: Congress . . . the Constitution, Article II: inventing an Executive Branch . . . Article III: the Supreme Court . . . the Constitution, Articles IV to VII . . . Federalists v. Antifederalists: the battle for ratification . . . how did the Federalists win? . . . the Bill of Rights . . . private property and public welfare.

How did one create a new nation in 1783?   To fight for independence is one matter, to know what to do with it is another. The United States has been called "the first new nation." How did men go about creating a new nation in 1783?

The Founding Fathers did not operate in a vacuum. They had many historical precedents, dating back to the Mayflower Compact and earlier. They shared certain conventional political values and their Revolution itself had set the stage by deciding several questions about the future shape of the new nation. The Revolution threw off Britain and rejected the monarchy, forever as it turned out; Alexander Hamilton toyed briefly with the notion of monarchy but gave it up in favor of the Federal presidency created in 1787. The American Revolution made republicanism into the new orthodoxy, from which the nation has never swerved. John Locke's ideas had been assimilated by the ex-colonials but had been Americanized in the process. For Locke's three aims, "life, liberty and property," the Declaration of Independence had substituted, "life, liberty and the pursuit of happiness." Locke was made more egalitarian and even more individualistic by the Americans, who could dare to expect human happiness as a by-product of a scheme of government.

Revolutionary principles, however, were no blueprint for a new nation. In truth, the Revolution decided very little about the form the new nation would take after 1783. The Founding Fathers looked back to pre-Revolutionary political experience. Their fundamental ideas were already part of the liberal conventional wisdom of the late 18th century: separation of powers among the executive, legislative, and judicial branches of government; checks and balances wherever possible; independence of the law courts as an essential condition for real justice; separation of Church and State; the Rule of Law. Such beliefs they took for granted. In addition there was the great body of practical experience deriving from the years of congregational-covenantal government, colonial company charters, the ideas and precepts of the English 17th-century revolutions, the evolution of the colonial constitutions, and a long line of theoretical sources and commentaries.

Natural Law and separation of powers

Apart from John Locke, Sir Edward Coke, and the great British legal scholar Blackstone, the men of the 1780s were familiar with the works of various European philosophers and lawyers. Two outstanding theorists of Natural Law were popular and widely read among 18th-century Americans: the Dutchman Grotius, who founded the basic principles of international law in the early 17th century, and the German scholar Pufendorf. One of the best-read books of the period was an unoriginal but useful textbook synthesis of various Natural Law treatises, the French writer Burlamaqui's *Principes du Droit Naturel* (Principles of Natural Law, 1748). Naturally, John Locke and, even more immediately, Tom Paine were the chief popular conduits for such ideas.

The French liberal critic Montesquieu, an Anglophile like so many French liberals of his day, spread the notion that the British government was a successful example of separation of powers and checks and balances. Basically, Montesquieu was inaccurate in his analysis

After liberty, what? The first exultation—Revere's Liberty Bowl

Museum of Fine Arts, Boston

of the way the British political system worked at that time, but his writings were influential. Though the three branches of government were not truly separated in the British model they were made so in the new American state and federal constitutions.

Origins of Federalism: Revolutionary government

Out of the American Revolution and post-revolutionary years came the creation of the United States as a federal system of republican government. For the origins of this Federalism we can go back to the Continental Congress, the Declaration of Independence, and the Articles of Confederation, to the ways in which the revolutionaries managed their government during the war. The Continental Congress had acted *as if* it were a true national government, not a mere temporary war alliance among colonies in revolt. This preceded the Declaration of Independence, which the Congress itself wrote and adopted.

The Declaration was ambiguous in wording. Did it speak for 13 independent states or for the "United Colonies," one nation? It spoke of "We . . . the Representatives of the United States of America, in General Congress, Assembled," but it also said that "These United Colonies are, and of Right ought to be, Free and Independent States." Still, the intention of the Declaration seems clear, as was the action taken under it: Americans did not behave as if they planned to create 13 separate nations once the war was over.

Already it had been the Congress which demanded that the colonists form themselves into new states and write new constitutions. Four of them had obeyed this suggestion from the central governing body before the Declaration of Independence was even signed—a strong argument for those who claimed that the Union preceded the states.

New state constitutions: Government by assembly

Formal separation of powers was built into the new state constitutions but usually the legislative branch was dominant. This system of government by elected assembly arose from the fear of executive power, born in the colonial period. It was based also on faith in "the People" and in their ability to choose wise representatives. After experiencing the turmoil of revolution and war not all Americans sustained this faith. The Founding Fathers had good reason to fear "mobocracy"; Hamilton favored a hereditary upper house for the new nation. However, republicanism and elected assemblies survived.

The state constitutions were more liberal and democratic than the federal constitution which followed. Most had a separate Bill of Rights, which set forth explicitly the individual freedoms not to be violated by the government. All the states except Georgia and Pennsylvania chose to become bicameral. Governors lacked appointive powers, could not veto acts of the assembly, and were usually subjected to annual elections. Having rejected the English king and the power of the parliament, and having thrown out royal governors, the states did not intend to recreate such power. However, excessive fear of the executive branch, as in the French Revolution, can prove to be as dangerous to liberty as excessive fear of "the People" and the legislature.

5 / The Revolution contained

Independence Hall, Philadelphia

United Press International

A nation of states?

The argument over whether the Union preceded the creation of the states or not was more than academic. In view of later threats of state secession from the Union, the coming of the Civil War between the states in the 1860s, and the use of states' rights arguments against federal power throughout the 19th and 20th centuries, the historical question of which came first, Union or states, has been rehashed many times. Though it was the Continental Congress which urged the colonies to transform themselves into states, and though it was colonial military unity alone which made it possible for all the states to become free, many Americans insisted that the United States remain a "nation of states." Certainly the Articles of Confederation of 1777 did not establish a *strong* central government. The long struggle between

"Federalists" and "Antifederalists" (i.e., centralists and states' rights advocates) in the 1780s centered on this issue.

There was of course no absolute answer to this question. Over the decades the debate became a question of degree: *how much* authority should go to the federal government and how much be left to the states, and indeed, to the individual? Time and again, warring statesmen looked back to history to support their views, particularly to the character of the Confederation government which preceded the adoption of the federal constitution.

Fear of executive government: The Confederation

Created by vote of Congress in the fall of 1777, the Confederation was based on earlier suggestions by Benjamin Franklin, whose Albany Plan for inter-colonial cooperation dated back to 1754. Other leaders, like Tom Paine in *Common Sense,* had demanded a much stronger union. The motion to create the Articles of Confederation was that of Henry Lee of Virginia, a disgruntled aristocrat, a Son of Liberty, and a man whose earlier motion had led to the adoption of the Declaration of Independence. Lee, however, soon became a major Antifederalist and an opponent of the yet stronger federal union of 1787. The Articles of Confederation blended well with Lee's spirit of states' rights individualism.

Like the state constitutions, the Articles were suspicious of executive power, though they did ignore separation of powers in one sense by creating only one central body, Congress, with no distinct or separate executive branch or federal judiciary. Little authority was delegated to that Congress. There was no president, no supreme court, no police power, and no real sanction for federal authority. The Congress did have authority over questions of peace and war, but could not raise taxes to pay for such a war. It could appoint diplomats and raise troops but had no means of supporting either. Congress could issue money but could not buy bullion. It was allowed to borrow money on the credit of the confederated states. Unlike the later federal system, the Confederation did not claim direct legitimation by the people of the united ex-colonies; it worked only indirectly, through the state governments. Congress had no way of enforcing its wishes or desired policies upon the individual states. Its own delegates were not directly elected but chosen by state assemblies and paid by them, if at all. In other words, members of the Confederation Congress were merely representatives of the state governments.

Each state had one vote in the Congress and nine states must agree before any important measure could be taken, such as declaration of war or conclusion of treaties, appointments, and borrowing of funds. For any alteration of the basic Articles, complete unanimity was required. On the other hand, Congress did have control of all Indian affairs and assumed the power to create executive departments (foreign affairs, finance, war, admiralty, and the post office). Though public lands were not mentioned specifically in the Articles, Congress took them over.

In view of the many achievements of the Confederation, historians tend nowadays to emphasize less the weakness of the Articles as a orm of federation. But its successes, such as waging a successful war against Britain, were achieved because the Congress ignored its formal impotence and acted *as if* it had more legitimacy and power. Formally the Confederation was, in George Washington's words, "a shadow without substance." As Tom Paine said, the "continental belt" was still "too loosely buckled." Some of the new state constitutions had been legitimized in special *constitutional conventions*, a fresh departure in the technique of participatory government. The Congress lacked such a mandate. Nevertheless, with imagination and daring, it took command of western land settlement.

The public domain: Individualism and capitalism unleashed

The colonies and states were badly divided by disagreement over western lands. All Americans were interested in the West, even those who took no notice of politics and paid only modest attention to the Revolution. Some states claimed contiguous territory stretching westward for hundreds of miles. A rational solution to the decades of violent rivalry over the West was finally reached when Virginia decided to cede its land claims to Congress. Other states followed suit after 1784. This vast new "public domain" gave future federal governments a valuable and rich source of income, and buttressed the policy of unifying Indian affairs under Congressional control.

How was Congress to administer these enormous lands? There were no precedents except the management of the British Empire, and Americans never considered "colonizing" these so-called empty lands. On the contrary, it was taken for granted that the western territories would eventually evolve into separate and independent states, equal partners in the Union. The public-land policy laid down by the Confederation formed the basis of U.S. territorial growth until much of the continent had been absorbed by the Republic.

The Land Ordinance of 1785 established systematic surveying and title procedures for the public domain. The norm was to be the six-mile-square township, subdivided into one-mile-square sections (640 acres). The land was to be sold at not less than $1 an acre, increased in 1796 to $2 an acre. Congress was keen to sell the land quickly: it needed the revenue and favored rapid economic growth. Consequently, the individual small family farmer, beloved of Jefferson's agrarian dream, was for the most part let down by the ordinance. The *minimum* sale allowed was 640 acres. Few small farmers had $640 to spare in 1785 (or $1,280 in 1796). When initial land sales proved slow, Congress became anxious and was easily persuaded by lobbyists of large real-estate speculators and some equally impatient state governments to *disallow* retail sales. The small man was cut out in favor of the large middleman, the land wholesaler.

Control of public-land sales passed rapidly into the hands of large capitalist "Land Companies." Public land was released in huge "parcels," up to five million acres at a time, for only a few pennies an acre. The land corporations speculated by buying it and then reselling it, broken down into manageable parcels, on credit, at much more than $1 an acre. The profits were enormous, though some companies went bankrupt. The companies pressured Congress to provide rules for orderly government in the West in order to accelerate land resales to genuine settlers. In response to agitation by the private Ohio Company for law and order, Congress enacted the Northwest Ordinance in 1787.

The Territorial system

The Northwest Ordinance of 1787 provided for the government of the lands between the Ohio and the Mississippi rivers, the Old Northwest, so long disputed with France, with the Indians, and then with Quebec. Under the "Territorial" system an area with a population of at least 5,000 free adult males could be organized as a Territory of the United States, under a federal governor, a legislative council, and a locally elected house of representatives. The courts would be staffed by federal judges. There was an obvious modeling on British colonial administration here; but once the territory attained a population of 60,000 free residents it could request admission to the Union as a full-fledged state. In the Northwest, slavery was to be prohibited. In 1790 the Southwest was similarly organized, but slavery was guaranteed there. The Old Northwest and the Old Southwest were thus tied into the future sectional struggle over slavery from the beginning.

The western lands stretching to the Mississippi were hastily carved up and settled by ambitious, impatient Americans and by eager land corporations. An interaction of political need, capitalist profit-seeking, and national vision produced this remarkable plan for continental development. Government was the handmaid to capitalism and to an unleashed individualism which would allow nothing to stand in its way—neither qualms about human slavery nor sympathy for the Indian tribes. This was a new nation in a hurry.

The movement for stronger centralism

Whatever the relative strength of Congress and the states within the system, the permanency of the Union itself was not questioned The "Articles of Confederation and Perpetual Union" (the phrase was Benjamin Franklin's) reflected the national pride of Americans and a high degree of confidence for 13 ex-colonies, which had only just dissolved an imperial union 170 years old. Men like Franklin, Washington, James Madison, and Alexander Hamilton came to feel that much stronger central authority would be needed to make the United States respected by the British and other foreign powers, to give it good standing with international creditors and bankers, and to preserve the very liberties for which the Revolution had been fought Others however, feared that a too-powerful Congress would endanger not only states' rights but individual freedoms as well; they carried over from pre-Revolutionary days a deep suspicion of officeholders and even of elected officials.

Behind the centralist versus states' rights schools of thought also lay economic interests. Men of wealth and property had much to gain from a stronger form of government.

Economic interest-groups behind the new constitution

Some writers today, following the lead of the Progressive Era historian, Charles Beard (*Economic Interpretation of the Constitution* 1913), claim to see a clear alliance among wealthy Americans of the 1780s, Northern merchants and Southern planters, conspiring to ensure their own continued dominance of American politics and society by framing a conservative federal constitution. A strong central government could protect the rights of creditors and property-holders, fund the national debt, and pay off handsomely those who owned government bonds. Charles Beard created a storm in 1913 by accusing the venerated Founding Fathers of being politically influenced by their private ownership of Revolutionary War bonds, often bought from their original owners at a much-reduced price. The new federal government they established after 1787 paid off the bonds at par value. In Beard's view and in later derivative variations by New Left historians in the 1960s, the Constitution was a conservative ploy: a document foisted onto the silent, proletarian, farming majority by a decided minority of wealthy and self-interested men working in close cooperation.

The Founding Fathers would have been startled that Charles Beard thought it so important to expose economic motivations. The shocked reactions of his critics, their defenders, would have amused them. For the Fathers had a more sophisticated grasp of political economy than the moral platitudes of the Progressive Era or of the 1960s would allow. They took economic interest for granted. James Madison's brilliant *Federalist No. 10,* written to defend stronger centralism, expounded the economic interpretation of politics long before Karl Marx, the Old Left, or the New. Of course, they were not corrupt, and gross cases of self-interest would have been unacceptable to them, but in 1787 their class interests and the nation's goals were closely identified.

What were their interests? Those Americans who were involved in the growing market economy, who had products to sell at home or abroad, desired a stronger federal government, able to impose duties on foreign imports, levy taxes, and regulate interstate and foreign trade. This group included most merchants, those of the large planters who exported their crops, commercial farmers, bankers and speculators, real-estate dealers, and most of the eastern seaboard townsfolk of all classes, even mechanics and artisans. In New York City, for example, the urban workers supported the new federal constitution. Meanwhile those Americans not directly involved in the market economy, such as subsistence, frontier farmers, and families in the West and backcountry, had less interest in or apparent need of a more powerful congress and executive. These were closest to the Jeffersonian ideal. The demand for strong government cut across simple class lines. The division was between the commercial and noncommercial, those who took part in the market economy and those who did not. More important, the demand for firm government was not merely economic, but is best understood within the wider context of the drive for "containment."

Revolution and containment

In history revolutions are commonly followed by periods of containment. This is no "iron law" of revolutions, but it has happened frequently. After the violence and upheaval comes the search for order. Old social and economic forces and traditions reassert themselves. For instance, in the early 19th century after the colonial revolutions in Latin America came a period of creole containment. Members of the creole elite had allowed themselves to be radicalized enough to lead the independence movements against Spain and Portugal, but once the wars were over they reasserted their controls in each nation and clamped down on the Indian peasants, the poorer whites, and the mixed races. Thus the revolutions at home were kept within limits acceptable to the elite.

Containment was less blatant and class conflict less obvious in North America, but it took place all the same. With the exodus of the Loyalists, all Americans were Whigs of some sort or another after 1783. The Whig elite was never monolithic, which complicated the American version of containment.

The American Revolution could not have been won by the radicals Sam Adams, Patrick Henry, and the Sons of Liberty, acting alone. The colonial elite, the merchants, planters, lawyers, clergy, and intellectuals, had to become radicalized. After the war these groups had less to hold them together. There was enough agreement to produce the federal constitution of 1787, though not all the elite supported that document. Patrick Henry was a notable opponent, and he was no economic radical. On the other hand, Tom Paine, who was undoubtedly radical, strongly favored the new constitution and federal power. Paine's view of the future of the United States coincided with that of Alexander Hamilton on this point, if on no other.

Sectional issues: Slavery

Containment in the United States was complicated also by sectional and interstate conflicts. It was a miracle that the new republic survived at all. Individual states constantly bickered over boundary lines and western lands and engaged in open economic warfare with each other. New York, for example, imposed harbor duties on all ships from Connecticut and New Jersey; New Jersey retaliated by taxing a lighthouse essential to New York's port. This sort of spirit of "independence" could soon destroy the common cause. Some states found issues to unite them against others along sectional lines.

Within and across state lines, social class interests and group interests threatened disruption. Urban mob violence, deliberately encouraged in the fight for independence, threw up an underworld of the "inarticulate": merchant seamen and fishing crews, exemplified by Crispus Attucks, servants, "mechanics" and artisans, unruly apprentice boys, like the wigmakers of the Boston Massacre. Some of the upper classes feared this Revolution could go too far and overturn the social order. The Founding Fathers were very conscious of the dangers of the mob. While this was, of course, a *class* motivation to support stronger central government it was much more general than Beard's specifics about war bonds.

No issue kept the Whig elites more divided among themselves than human slavery. Whites in the South, where the slavery-plantation social system was already entrenched even in these pre-cotton days, were scared by wild talk of abolishing slavery. Yet many "moderates" of the revolutionary generation had slavery on their Enlightened and Republican consciences. Men like Thomas Jefferson, who himself owned slaves, could not miss the glaring contradiction between the rhetoric of liberty and the real facts of black slavery. Tom Paine, reliably radical, attacked slavery in one of the first pieces he ever wrote in America. Even at this early stage in U.S. history, slavery created a North–South sectional division; the institution being permitted in the Old Southwest and not in the Old Northwest.

Fears of social breakdown

Fears of possible social breakdown accelerated the movement toward a stronger federalism. The Fathers certainly saw their Constitution as a technique of *social* containment. They argued that the economy was in decline and that social upheavals were imminent. The most frightening evidence was Daniel Shays' Rebellion of 1786 in Massachusetts—perfectly timed to convince the waverers that stronger helmsmanship was called for. Captain Shays was a Revolutionary War veteran who emerged as leader of the dissident, frustrated farmers of central and western Massachusetts, people who were prepared to face up to a civil war rather than continue to suffer economic misfortunes, unaided and unheeded by the weak government of the Articles of Confederation. The authorities seemed more eager to tax Shays than to pay him for his years of military service. The war-time prosperity on

Shays' Rebellion —brawl between Massachusetts government supporter and rebel

The Bettmann Archive

the farms had vanished. Caught by falling farm prices, rising taxes, pressure from wartime creditors, and demands from all sides that payments be made in specie (people would not accept depreciated paper), the small farmers took action.

Captain Shays' men had one idea: close the courthouses, and stop further foreclosure actions against mortgaged farmers who could not pay their debts. When brother rioters were convicted, it also became necessary to attack and close down the criminal courts. Open warfare broke out between the rebels and state troops in January 1787 and lasted for six weeks or so. Shays failed to capture the famous arsenal at Springfield and his forces were scattered into the hills during heavy snows. Bloody and bitter, Shays' Rebellion passed like a shock wave through American society. What had happened to the ideals of the Revolution?

The "Critical Period"

Was the economy really in decline? Historians still cannot agree what was happening in the 1780s. There is much evidence of economic growth and prosperity. During the war British forces had destroyed parts of Georgia, Virginia, the Carolinas, and New Jersey; they had also carried off slaves and commandeered crops in the South in spasmodic raids between 1778–81. But manufacturers far from the battle areas did well as a result of war demand and the nonimportation agreement; overall tobacco output rose, and so did the output of cotton, wool, and foodstuffs. A free flow of French, and, ironically, of British, gold raised farm prices and brought an era of inflation and prosperity.

With the war's end came the usual postwar depression. How long and how severe it was and who was most affected is not yet clear. Some individuals made huge war profits and founded family fortunes which outlasted any postwar slump. Others rose more meteorically, like Robert Morris, signer of the Declaration of Independence and Superintendent of Finances, 1781–84, who sometimes used his own money to help pay for the war expenses of the frail Confederation government, but who ended up in debtors' jail for three years (1798–1801) and died in obscurity for all his pains. Morris was simply not liked because he had become so rich and was so successful a speculator.

The currency shortage was a general condition which hurt many people. Some states printed paper money in a desperate attempt to keep up outstanding public payments. The impact was inflationary and therefore most useful to debtors, small businessman, and farmers and bad for creditors, who would be repaid in currency of less value. It was the failure of Massachusetts to issue paper money that partly occasioned Daniel Shays' uprising.

The pro-Constitution people, or Federalists, probably exaggerated economic problems. The 1780s saw much growth. Canals, turnpike highways, and bridges were built. The first experiments with textile mills began. American banks were opened, like the Bank of Pennsylvania (1780), which soon evolved into the powerful Bank of North

America (1781), and banks in New York and Boston. The land-boom created by the land ordinances of 1785 and 1787 brought new resources into the growing American market.

Thinking continentally: The Founding Fathers

Another sort of interest, less crass than simple economics, which motivated certain of the leaders of the constitutional movement was very personal and built into the career-structures of some men, army officers for example. Leading Federalists had often served the nation, rather than their own state alone. They were cosmopolitans, well-educated, and better-traveled than most. The Antifederalists were usually men of local interests, absorbed in state-level affairs. From their point of view the United States had survived for ten years already and did not need such a drastic alteration of its form of government as that proposed in 1787, even if some changes were called for.

Personal drives and careers thus made nationalists out of some men, localists out of others. Not that the *leaders* of the Antifederalists were so unlike the Federalists: they were by no means poor farmers or backwoodsmen themselves. Ultimately, in the ratifying conventions, some Antifederalist leaders abandoned the people they were supposed to represent; they had never stood firm in favor of paper money, as they should have as spokesmen for debtor farmers.

The classic example of a nationalist by career and temperament was the nation's top soldier and official hero in his own lifetime, General George Washington. He could never have been expected to oppose the new federal constitution—quite apart from the fact that he was the obvious choice for the first president under it and the army he led would not be properly paid until the weakly financed Confederation was replaced. Washington's army was on half-pay. His tremendous prestige carried many Americans with him into the nationalist camp. Fears of what this new executive office of "president" would mean soon vanished—upon the reflection that it most likely meant, in the first years, President Washington.

National pride and foreign affairs

The Confederation was weakest where it hurt national pride the most: in foreign policy. Anyone who had served in foreign affairs or, like Benjamin Franklin had gone to Europe cap-in-hand to ask for loans, felt most keenly the need for stronger government. Even Thomas Jefferson, despite his reservations about the new constitution, admitted to feelings of impotence as the Confederation's ambassador to France.

England was contemptuous of her ex-colonies and jeered that they could never govern themselves. Other powers were hard to handle in trade negotiations, since the Confederation could not bind its own states at home to obey treaties. Spain after 1783 controlled the Louisiana territory and Florida and financed Indian raids in the South while placing trade restrictions on Americans in New Orleans, the essential outlet for the West. The Confederation had no means to stop Spain or to protect settlers in the Tennessee and Southwest country. Some Americans looked to Spain for frontier protection.

Nationalists were humiliated at such loss of face. This, combined with dissidence at home like Shays' Rebellion, caused Washington to declare himself "mortified beyond expression" that the United States should appear "ridiculous and contemptible in the eyes of all Europe." He feared that the British were laughing up their sleeves.

Federalist techniques: Pressing for a new constitution

By the late 1780s the nationalists were bent on a change in government, a major overhaul by regular or irregular means. They were determined to avoid altogether the Articles of Confederation. Men of high caliber inspired their hopes: *Washington;* his ex-aide, *Alexander Hamilton,* a well-married, prosperous New York lawyer of humble origins and brilliant mind, for whom good government meant elite control; *James Madison,* philosophical Virginia planter and intimate of Jefferson, widely read in the science of politics—the "father of the Constitution"; *Robert Morris,* the Superintendent of Finances who tried in vain to win a limited taxing power for the weak Confederation (the import duty plan of 1781) and then resigned in despair in 1784; the rich and cynical *Gouverneur Morris* whose political ideas paralleled Hamilton's, and whose stylistic pen shaped the final version of most of the Constitution in Philadelphia; *James Wilson,* Scots-born Philadelphia lawyer and rebel pamphleteer, who argued forcefully at the Convention for a new government armed with authority derived directly from the people, not merely indirectly from the states. Less emphatic about federal power was *John Rutledge,* lawyer from Charleston, South Carolina, who tried to fight for stronger centralism but also wished to preserve a large measure of states' rights.

From 1780 onward the nationalist plan was to avoid the existing Confederation Congress by the simple expedient of calling an entirely separate *constitutional convention.* Some hinted at firmer tactics, including a possible military coup. Such coups plagued other newly independent ex-colonies in later years. The coup idea had support from the Morrises, Hamilton and a few generals. Anxious creditors and angry, unpaid army officers were a likely brew. But George Washington flatly rejected the idea in 1783 and without him nothing was possible at that time. Washington did circularize the states with a personal plea for stronger government, but they took no action. Two years later, at Madison's behest, a meeting of commissioners was held at Washington's Mount Vernon estate allegedly to debate mutual problems of navigation on the Potomac. That set the ball rolling.

The meeting led to a five-state conference at Annapolis, Maryland (September 1786), on "commercial" matters. Hamilton, as the unlikely New York delegate, introduced a resolution to ask Congress and the states for a bigger convention to "render the constitution of the federal government adequate to the exigencies of the union." Congress ignored the plea at first, but along came Shays' Rebellion and by the next session all the southern states, Pennsylvania, and New Jersey had led the way in electing delegates. The Confederation Congress found its hand forced and legalized the matter, calling the convention to meet in Philadelphia in May 1787. The nationalists had won their

Washington, Lafayette, and Tench Tilghman at Yorktown (painting by C. W. Peale)

Maryland State House, Annapolis (M. E. Warren photographer)

objectives and even trapped a reluctant Congress into blessing the idea.

What Congress ordered, however, the nationalists had little intention of discussing. They were told to meet for

A closed room in Philadelphia

the sole and express purpose of revising the Articles of Confederation and reporting to Congress and the several legislatures such alterations . . . as shall, when agreed to in Congress and confirmed by the states, render the federal constitution adequate. . . .

They did not debate the Articles at all but wrote a new and different constitution, which they did not submit to Congress and the states but to the American *people* in especially elected state ratifying conventions.

For four months through the heat of summer (May–September 1787) the 55 delegates met behind closed doors in Independence Hall. Jefferson called them "an assembly of demi-gods." This they were not. But few eras of crisis have turned up such a brilliant group of leaders. They were men of vision. Most of them were committed to some form of stronger government before they went to the Philadelphia meetings. The delegates were the sort of men that Hamilton described in a famous letter to Washington in April 1783: "men who think continentally."

Two thirds of the delegates were trained in the law and ten were practicing judges. Such men were aware of precedent and past experience, as well as of Grotius, Locke, and other political philosophers. Eight members had signed the Declaration of Independence. Seven had been state governors and 39, congressmen. Over half would serve under the new system they were about to create. Two would become president of the United States. Thomas Jefferson and John Adams were absent in Europe serving as diplomats.

Among the delegates 31 were college-educated, 3 were professors, and 2 were college presidents. Classical allusions flew thick in this debate. Yet the delegates were not essentially theorists but practical men, rich in legal, administrative, and political experience. The source of most of their opinions and prejudices was America's past experience. From this historical experience they did not choose to wander very far.

The federal constitution which they wrote was a triumph of containment. It contained in two senses: it *embodied* and it *restrained* the political ideals and experiences of the revolutionary generation. The Founding Fathers tried to summarize for future Americans, in a sensibly brief document, the accepted wisdom of their day and to build its principles into a set of viable institutions. They found that the essence of viability was *compromise*. The outcome, however, was a victory for the nationalists.

One patriot worthy portrayed by another—Thomas Jefferson by Kosciusko

The Henry Francis du Pont Winterthur Museum

Struggles within the convention

The nationalists faced two major hurdles: first, a genuine and widespread American distrust of all executive authority; second, deep rivalries and fears among the states—big versus small states, North versus South, western fears, disagreements over trade. Well-prepared, they came early, armed with the *Virginia Plan* (mainly Madison's work), and they swung into action without any delay. Not until June were the nationalists checked, by William Paterson's small-state *New Jersey Plan*.

Like James Wilson of Pennsylvania, Madison desired a truly national government, not a feeble creature of the jealous state legislatures. The mandate for such a government had to come directly from the people, the individual citizens of the United States, not through the state governments. The Virginia Plan, therefore, totally ignored the existing Articles, gave broad powers to a new central government, and based representation in this new Congress on population. Madison expected to disarm much criticism and talk of possible "tyranny" through the use of a two-chamber system, separation of powers, and checks and balances. These familiar ideas and practices were now to be extended from the state to the federal level. The one-chamber, unseparated congress created by the Articles was not considered. (Benjamin Franklin favored unicameralism, but in this he was not heeded.)

The idea of relating representation in Congress to population size created tremendous opposition in the convention from the small states, which feared they would be swamped by the large states like New York, Virginia, and Pennsylvania. The *New Jersey Plan* of Paterson, who later developed into a more Federalist-minded Supreme Court justice, took a different tack. Paterson proposed no great changes but a mere amendment of the Articles and a system based on a one-chamber Congress, one state-one vote. During the long, hot June days the convention was "scarce held together by the strength of a hair." Dissolution seemed imminent. The 81-year-old Benjamin Franklin, a skilled conciliator and a man twice the age of over half the delegates, saved the day by engineering the "Great Compromise." Franklin had to give up his own pet notions such as a plural executive, but exemplifying the spirit of compromise, he steered through the plan whereby the states would have equal representation in the Senate, irrespective of size, wealth, and population, while in the House of Representatives the guide would be population. This ingenious system has not been questioned ever since. The opposition of the small states evaporated overnight, their fundamental patriotism taking over. The rest of the New Jersey Plan was not heard of again.

The federal constitution: The Preamble

The strong rejection of the Paterson plan accelerated the rest of the debate. As the proceedings wore on the delegates became more "federalized" in spirit. They created a new national legislature, executive, and judiciary. Federal law, composed of three parts, the Constitution, acts of Congress, and international treaties, was made the supreme law of the land, enforceable in federal courts. Federal law was to override state laws. The federal government was given fundamental powers, called later by Chief Justice John Marshall the powers of "the sword and the purse"—power to make war and treaties and to tax, and power to regulate trade. Congress was finally to be financially independent of the states, through its own taxing power, and was to be able to forestall any economic warfare among the states, through its commerce power.

The Preamble *to the Constitution, in very direct and dramatic fashion, makes clear what a revolution in government was now proposed.*

> We the People . . . do ordain and establish this Constitution for the United States of America.

This opening phrase cuts out the states from the process and gives instant legitimacy to the new government. Patrick Henry of Virginia was angry: "Who authorized them to speak the language of We the People, *instead of* We the States?" *he asked at the Virginia ratifying convention in 1788. Defenders made it clear that* We the People *was not mere arrogance on the part of the Philadelphia delegates. It applied not to them, but to the popular voters at the future ratification conventions to be called by each state; they would accept or reject the Constitution. The people alone, not the state governments, had the legitimate authority to institute a new form of government.*

The Preamble was also radical and emphatic in its succinct outline of the goals of government: more perfect union; justice; domestic tranquillity (echoes of Shays' rebellion); common defense; the general welfare (an expansive and broad category for the future); and securing liberty for generations to come. This was vague and general, yet comprehensive. Out of its studied ambiguity much future constitutional development was possible.

Article I: Congress

The importance of the legislature is seen in the length of Article I— over half the Constitution. Yet the Fathers had no intention of creating "government by assembly." Congress was to debate, not do; its job was to make the laws, not carry them out. Article I has had a successful history, with few basic changes in its 10 sections.

1.	*Two chambers*	Congress separated into a House of Representatives and a Senate.
2.	*House*	Elected every two years (minimum age of members— 25 years, 7 years a citizen, state residents). States get representatives according to their population; states with slaves to count three fifths of them as "population" for the purposes of estimating the number of representatives; untaxed Indians do not count. Population census to be taken every ten years for this apportionment of seats. The House chooses its own officers; it alone can bring charges of impeachment.

Delegates were agreed that the lower chamber should be based on population numbers in the states. The nationalists, led by Madison, began by wanting both houses so-based. The need to know how many voters each state could legally claim thus created the need for a national head count; it was the first national census and in many ways one of the best of any nation. From its first report of 1790, the U.S. Census has been an essential in American life. Manufactures were added in 1810. Today it gives a wealth of factual information for economic and social uses. The treatment of slaves as three fifths, and the casual exclusion of Indians altogether from the accountable population of a state, left two massive problems for the future to resolve.

> 3. Senate   Two members per state, chosen by state legislatures for six-year terms (minimum age of members—30 years, 9 years a citizen, state residents). Vice president presides over the Senate, casting a vote only in case of a tie. Senate alone can try impeachments, on charges brought by the House.

Conceived of as an upper house, the Senate from the outset became superior to the House. Its greater freedom from periodic elections, and its greater powers (approval of treaties and of judicial and executive appointees), attracted men of ability and education. The Senate was closer to the Executive and the Supreme Court and more removed from grass-roots politics. The 17th Amendment (1913) finally broke the 19th-century link between state assemblies and the Senate, by providing for direct popular election of senators by the voters in each state. Alexander Hamilton, among others, had envisaged a hereditary upper house, like the British House of Lords, whose power included voting on money bills. The U.S. Constitution gave the lower house control over money bills (Article I, Section 7).

> 4. Sessions   At least once a year, from the first Monday in December, unless summoned earlier by the president.

This section was not innocuous: it affirmed the right *of the legislature to meet regularly—a question fought over between kings and parliaments for many years.*

> 5. Qualifications of members   Each house to be the judge of the qualifications of and the elections of its own members; and to print an official journal of debates.

A reflection of the ancient struggles between executive and assembly can be seen in this section also. The right of the voters to know what was said and have a record of debates was affirmed. The more tricky principle of self-policing by elected bodies, though well-established in Whig political theory by 1787, can have strange side effects. The principle is intended to keep the elected assemblies free from executive interference; but in fact some of the most famous cases have involved the legislature *itself overturning the decisions of the voters. The case of John Wilkes in England was notorious to Americans of the Revolu-*

tionary era, since Wilkes posed as a radical and supported the rights of the colonists. The House of Commons refused to seat him in 1768, although the Middlesex voters elected him three times in a row. More recently, in the U.S. House, the Milwaukee Socialist Party leader, Victor Berger, was refused his seat, though the voters reelected him three times in 1918–19. (*The states often copy the federal government in exaggerated fashion, and at this same period of the post-World War I "Red Scare," the New York legislature unseated five legally elected Socialist members.*)

6. *Separation of powers* — Congressmen to be paid from federal funds; to be free from arrest for anything said in Congress; to hold no other government office while a member of the Congress.

This was meant to free Congressmen from dependence on state funds, as under the Articles of Confederation, and to prevent corruption. The corruption problem is increasingly important as the federal government becomes more involved in every aspect of the economy.

7. *Revenue bills* — All finance bills to originate in the House of Representatives (because it was more popularly elected). This was a concession to the large states in the compromise.

Section 7 also laid down procedures for passages of laws through the House and Senate, signing by the president, and the means for a veto. A president's veto of a bill can be overridden by a two thirds vote of both houses: this is not easy to obtain and few vetoes are in fact overridden. Here the sacred principle of separation of powers *is clearly violated, and the president plays a vital role in the legislative process. Since no bill becomes law until he signs it he can effectively stop it. This power was not used extensively until Andrew Jackson began rejecting bills he did not like; previously, only bills thought to be unconstitutional were rejected.*

8. *Enumerated powers* — Specific listing of the powers of Congress include: power to tax and impose duties; borrow money; regulate commerce (the vital "commerce clause"); control naturalization and bankruptcy; coin money and fix weights and measures; establish post offices and post roads; issue patents; create courts below the Supreme Court (Article III); adjudicate maritime and international law; declare war; raise an army and navy (appropriations for only two years at a time); control the militia; locate the federal capital; and, a final clincher, pass all laws necessary to carry out these enumerated powers.

The commerce clause *has been the most heavily used and supported. Apprehension over interstate economic warfare was a major source of discontent with the articles among nationalists in the 1780s. Section 8 (and Section 10) set up a "free trade area," or common market of the*

United States, that proved basic to American economic growth—the key to which in the 19th century was home demand.

The final clause of Section 8 has been very controversial. It was delightfully ambiguous: who would decide what laws were "necessary and proper" to enable the government to function? This was a ground for bitter disagreement between strict constructionists and broad constructionists. Hamilton subsequently thought it "necessary and proper" for the United States to establish a national bank, federally chartered. Jefferson did not; and neither did Andrew Jackson, who vetoed the Second Bank in the 1830s. Over the decades, the broad constructionists have won out: the functions of central government have grown enormously. Usually the Congress has been pushed by the Executive in this growth (as in the New Deal of the 1930s).

Section 8 also attracted attention from the nationalist Supreme Court led by John Marshall. He affirmed Hamilton's broad construction views in 1819 (McCulloch v. Maryland), and he began to define Congressional controls over interstate commerce in 1824 (Gibbon v. Ogden).

9. *Slavery* — The slave trade was to be left alone by Congress until 1808 (apart from an import duty of $10 per head). This section also included a guarantee of habeas corpus; prohibition of bills of attainder (political deprivation of civil rights without fair trial); direct federal taxes apportioned according to population (used to fend off an income tax until as late as 1913); and a disclaimer of titles of nobility.

The agreement on the slave trade, together with the allowance of three fifths voting-power equivalency for slaves in Section 2 of this article, and the fugitive slave clause of Article IV, Section 2, was an unappetizing if not a disgraceful compromise of the ideals of republicanism and the Revolution. The South would not have stayed in the Union, however, without these safeguards: the Carolinas and Georgia would have walked out. So the African cause was not taken up either by Federalists or by Antifederalists and the blacks were sold out at the start of the new nation's history. It is possible, though not probable, that a much smaller republic could have been launched without the slave states.

10. *State prohibitions* — Individual states were prohibited from various activities: making treaties; issuing money; impairing the obligation of contracts; imposing import and export duties; making war independently.

Among these prohibitions, the Founding Fathers felt most strongly about trade duties and possible impairment of contracts (i.e., debtor relief laws). Colonies and states had sometimes protected debtors from their creditors. They passed stay laws (*delaying court action*), or tender laws, as in Rhode Island, where politically powerful indebted people made creditors accept inflated paper as legal repayment of loans made in good faith. The Fathers certainly preserved their own upper-class interests in banning such laws; in this they were "conservative." Yet it must be admitted in all fairness that no economy can long survive in which debts are not repaid and contracts fulfilled.

Article I has been changed by five amendments, numerous Supreme Court cases, and several federal laws. In respect to voting rights, Section 2 had allowed all those who were qualified to vote for members of the lower chamber in their state to vote for the federal House of Representatives. The 14th and 15th amendments gave added protections to the Negro voter after the Civil War (though ineffectively); the 19th Amendment gave the vote to women (1920); and the 24th outlawed the poll tax (1965). The 17th Amendment abolished the indirect election of Senators (1913). On the whole, this long article of the Constitution, containing so many basic principles of American government, has stood the test of time very well.

The Constitution. Article II: Inventing an Executive Branch

The Founding Fathers invented a wholly new Executive, in four modest sections. Even in the Virginia Plan, the ideas were vague on what the form of the executive should be. Some, like Franklin, favored a plural executive, a sort of government by committee; others, an officer chosen by Congress alone. A few would not have been displeased with a sort of constitutional monarch. What evolved, the American presidency, was an ingenious device—a monarch-prime minister elected for four years. Article II was finally voted through the convention toward the end of its long sessions.

1. Presidency	President and Vice President; four-year terms. Qualifications for president: minimum age—35 years, native-born, 14 years resident. Electoral College system of election; salary; oath of office.

The Electoral College system was altered by the 12th Amendment (1804), and the Founders' hopes to have a nonpolitical selection of the chief executive vanished with the early rise of the party system. Party *is the one element not dealt with in the Constitution at all;* yet the party system has made the entire construction work. *The* oath of office *was placed directly in the Constitution by its thoughtful writers.* (Curiously, when President John F. Kennedy was assassinated in 1963 no one in the entourage knew where to find the oath to administer to the vice president, Lyndon Johnson. He finally took the oath on board the president's jet, and the succession was then assured.)

2. Powers of the president	Commander in chief and head of the cabinet officers. Power to pardon; to make treaties (with "advice and consent" of Senate); and to make appointments (also with advice and consent of Senate) of diplomats, judges, and executive officers.

This section again links two branches of government, executive and legislative, through the Senate's approval of appointees and treaties.

> 3. Duties — The president reports to Congress on the "State of the Union"; recommends legislation; may call special sessions of Congress; receives foreign representatives; oversees "that the Laws be faithfully executed."

The most powerful clause here is the president's power to initiate legislation. It once more links the allegedly "separated" powers, executive and legislative, and gives the president the authority he needs to launch a real program. So, "the Congress makes the laws" has come to mean that the Congress (usually) votes on the laws, which originate as ideas in the Executive office.

> 4. Impeachment — Only once has a president been impeached (Andrew Johnson in 1868), and even he was not convicted. Section 4 seemed to be a dead letter for decades until the idea of impeachment arose again in 1973.

The power and responsibility of the presidential office have grown so much in recent years that Hamilton and Madison would not recognize it today. It is often claimed that Andrew Jackson was the first modern president, but even the reluctant Thomas Jefferson expanded the office by his actions, such as the purchase of Louisiana by which he doubled the size of the Republic. However, the presidency has also known periods of decay, as after Reconstruction or during the 1920s.

Article III: The Supreme Court

An unintimidated court system is essential to any democracy. The courts of law must be independent and judges must be free of political pressures in their decisions. At the same time, a truly national government needs its own national courts, enjoying complete legal supremacy and uniform responsiveness throughout the land. This the Confederation did not have. Article III created a national legal system, headed by a Supreme Court, whose law, along with treaties and statutes, was supreme over all state laws. Thus the three principles of independence, supremacy, and uniformity were built into the court system.

> 1. Supreme Court — One Supreme Court, but Congress *may* ordain lesser courts; judges hold office "during good behaviour"; their salaries are guaranteed.

Opposition to the creation of lesser courts (the New Jersey Plan), produced a compromise at Philadelphia, whereby Congress was permitted, but not told, to create such courts. The compromise was very short-lived, since the very first Congress immediately established U.S. District Courts (Judiciary Act, 1789). Judges hold office "during good behaviour"—which means permanent tenure, not subject to the whim of the Executive. Readers will remember from an earlier section that colonial judges did not enjoy this independence.

2. Coverage of national courts	National courts cover all cases under national law (Constitution, statutes, and treaties), cases of maritime law and cases involving foreigners. They also mediate and determine cases among and between the individual states of the Union. Trial by jury is guaranteed
3. Treason	Precisely defined, so as to avoid vague, political charges being brought against citizens.

Readers will notice that one of the Supreme Court's greatest powers —judicial review *of laws passed by Congress or by the states*—is not mentioned in Article III. Nationalists assumed this authority, especially Justice John Marshall. Having a written Constitution, the new republic obviously did need some agency with the power to determine disputes that were bound to arise over the interpretation of specific clauses. Nationalists argued that this agency was certainly the highest national court in the nation, charged, in Section 2 above, to handle cases of constitutional law. Through this channel the Court came to nullify legislation it regarded as "unconstitutional"; the general public, however, found that what Justices rejected in one period they would accept in another. A crucial early case of John Marshall's was Marbury v. Madison (1803), *in which he invalidated part of the Judiciary Act of 1789. No other court of law in the world had this power to invalidate legislation.* This was "checks and balances" with a vengeance, but was it "separation of powers"?

The Constitution: Articles IV to VII

Article IV of the Constitution dealt with what lawyers call "conflict of laws": the "full faith and credit" clause demands that the states recognize each other's laws. The Supreme Court acts as the sole court of last resort. Section 2 provides for extradition, but also includes the infamous fugitive slave clause, *put in at Southern insistence to make it legally necessary for free states to return escaped slaves to slave states.* The writers could not bring themselves to use the word "slave" openly in this new Constitution for a democratic republic. The coy phrase "Person held to Service or Labour" was adopted instead. James Madison did object, *when in Section 4, the U.S. guaranteed the republican form of government to each state.* Did a slave state have a genuine republican form? *he wondered.*

Article IV also admitted new states to the Union, rejecting suggestions that larger states be split up; any state could ask the federal government for aid against domestic violence (though the modern government has a tendency to move in, unasked, in certain cases). Ways of amending the Constitution were given in Article V. Other forms of constitutional evolution, especially judicial review, have greatly supplemented the need for the cumbersome amendment process.

Article 7 allowed the Constitution to become operative immediately nine states had ratified it.

The supremacy clause: Article VI

Article VI, however, was of fundamental importance. Its "supremacy clause" *was the keystone of the nationalist-centralist arch. The Constitution and the statutes and treaties of the United States were made* "the supreme Law of the Land"—"any Thing in the Constitution or Laws of any State to the Contrary notwithstanding."

Federalists versus Antifederalists: The battle for ratification

At the end of August 1787, the Philadelphia delegates had no desire to submit their creation to the severe test of unanimous approval by 13 jealous state legislatures and by the existing Congress (which would have to agree to destroy itself). So they abandoned an earlier plan of "recommending" to Congress a convention system of ratification and built the idea into the Constitution itself in Article VII. In the state conventions which followed came the greatest battle over the merits of the new Constitution and the emergence of two distinct parties.

The word *federal* signifies in political science "plural," as opposed to "unitary," forms of government. The U.S. federal system, however, is more unified than some other federated systems, such as that of Switzerland. The Swiss system can be typed as a *con*federation, a looser, more plural form. In 1787 a confusion of terms arose because the nationalists deliberately took as their title "Federalist." Some voters

Triumphant float celebrating Alexander Hamilton and ratification of the federal constitution

Brown Brothers

were misled, since the real federalists were the opposition, who did not want such a strong central executive and congress. Hamilton added to the confusion by attacking what he called the "bigotted idolizers of State authority," meaning those who supported strong states' rights. He defended the Federal Constitution in the name of the plural sharing of power. The *Federalist* papers which Hamilton wrote with Madison and Jay could have been titled more accurately the Nationalist or Centralist Papers. With this terminological ploy the nationalists put their opponents at a disadvantage, for the only title they were left with was the rather lame "Antifederalist."

North Carolina and Rhode Island did not come around to ratifying the Constitution until 1789 and 1790. The other small states, satisfied with the Great Compromise and in need of federal protection, ratified more readily—these were Delaware, New Jersey, Connecticut, Maryland, and Georgia. The big political fights took place in the big states: Massachusetts, Virginia, and New York, and also in smaller New Hampshire. Sometimes only the narrowest margin secured the Constitution's acceptance, e.g., 30 to 27 in New York in July 1788. Yet from the moment it became the law of the land the Federal Constitution of 1787 has been worshiped as holy script. Some of those who had opposed its passage became its most ardent venerators and fought thereafter to ensure that the document was to be interpreted very strictly, according to the letter of the law.

How did the Federalists win?

The Federalists represented a continental vision. They also stood for those economic and social groups which would gain most from the new system. The Antifederalists, it now appears, were the subsistence pioneers and small farmers of the backcountry hills and upland plains, who rarely had anything to market. Since these people were the majority of Americans in 1787, how did the Federalists win?

First, many Antifederalists did not bother to vote. Only about 160,000 people altogether voted in the crucial election for delegates to the ratifying conventions: perhaps *one fifth* of adult males. Since the small, backcountry family farmer was less politicized, despite his violence on specific, *local* issues, the Antifederalists wasted much inarticulated strength.

Second, while their opponents were not fully mobilized, the Federalists were, and had superior organization and political management. "Management" sometimes meant that in certain states the conventions gave disproportionate delegate strength to the coastal regions that favored the new constitution. Federalist speakers and writers played on fears of mob violence and economic disorder—though the nation was generally well-fed and there was a great boom going in western lands. Whatever economic distress existed was as much caused by the after-effects of the Revolutionary War as by weak central government. The Federalists were strategically located and their propaganda, of which the brilliant *Federalist* papers are the finest example, was excellent. They made a weapon out of local issues where they could, e.g., threatening a secession of New York City from the rest of the state, unless the Constitution was accepted. Their arguments were already fully worked out at Philadelphia, and the opposition, though it may have represented the *majority* opinion of all Americans, was much slower to organize. On occasion, the Antifederalists began their main propaganda thrust in a state only *after* the decision had been made to adopt the Constitution.

Third, the Antifederalists suffered from not having a clear and simple position. A negative platform is hard to defend; and many of them agreed with the Federalists that some strengthening of the government was desirable. So their case against the Constitution was only one of degree, of the amount, of centralization. They were forced to campaign on the grounds that they did not like *certain parts* of the Constitution (say, the Preamble's general welfare clause or the supremacy clause). Subtleties make difficult propaganda.

Fourth, the rapid acceptance by six states, including two crucial ones where there was tough debate, created what political observers today call a *bandwagon effect,* pressuring others to follow suit. In order, the first six were Delaware, Pennsylvania, New Jersey, Georgia, Connecticut, and Massachusetts (December to February 1787–88). The press was generally pro-Federalist too. But the major single element was the Federalists' promise that they would add a *Bill of Rights* once the Constitution became a reality. At first some Federalists had opposed a Bill of Rights, but this wise promise brought over many waverers who feared loss of individual liberties under the new presidential-congressional system. The first ten amendments stilled their fears.

The Bill of Rights

The Bill of Rights finally cut the ground from under Antifederalist opponents of the Constitution. No doubt, Federalist resistance to the idea had created suspicions, too, for almost every state had such a bill attached to its constitution. These bills claimed for Americans the "rights of Englishmen," going back to Magna Charta of 1215, and through all the later victories, like the English Bill of Rights of 1689.

Originally the federal bill (it was not a "bill" formally, taking this name from the state bills) contained 12 amendments, but the first two did not get ratified. The successful ten were as follows:

1. No religious establishment; freedom of speech, press, assembly, and petition.
2. Free militia; right of citizens to bear arms.
3. No quartering of troops in peacetime.
4. No unauthorized searches, seizures, or arrest warrants without cause.
5. The famous *Fifth Amendment:* grand jury for all capital crimes; no double jeopardy; no self-incrimination; no loss of property without just compensation.
   (*This amendment, meant to protect people's rights, was turned against them during the McCarthy anticommunist witch-hunt of the 1950s. Those who claimed the protection of the amendment*

against self-incrimination were even more incriminated by being vilified as "Fifth Amendment Communists." Even a written Constitution cannot definitely assure the citizen of his rights. Another example, from this same amendment, is the loss of property clause: at the state level many Americans in recent years have had their houses and land taken by roadbuilding authorities for compensation they did not regard as fair—under the legal doctrine of the state's "eminent domain.")

6. Speedy jury trial in criminal cases with right to defense counsel.
7. Common law suits of over $20 value have right of jury trial.
8. Prohibition of excessive bail or fines, and of cruel and unusual punishments.
   (The last was applied to capital *punishment by legal reformers in the 1960s.)*
9. Any rights not mentioned are retained by the people.
10. Powers not delegated to the federal government nor forbidden to the states are reserved to the states or to the people.

Private property and public welfare

The Constitution was an act of social and political containment. It favored those who favored it—the Federalists whom Thomas Jefferson later attacked as "monocrats." They believed in profit-taking, private property, rule by the wealthy and educated, government encouragement to commerce and speculation, and a strong national government able to cope at home and represent the nation well abroad. If, despite the explanations given, it is still hard to believe that they could foist these ideas on an unwilling farm population, perhaps one must consider another aspect. Was nationalism a dead issue with the farmers and backwoodsmen? Did not many of these reforms affect *all* classes? In other words, whatever their motivation, were the framers of the Constitution tempered by the Bill of Rights—that great Antifederalist victory—wise or unwise?

The answer lies of course in the longevity and flexibility of that Constitution over the years and in what greater centralism achieved for *all* Americans, not merely for select groups. For example, abolition of state powers to impose tariffs created a vast national, free trade market that would guarantee the prosperity of future Americans, even while it favored at the moment the Eastern merchants. Clearly the Constitution was a complex mixture of public concern and private profit, a product of open debate on political theories and of crude political leverage. Economically it contains a characteristically American confusion of private-profit capitalism, individualism, and public programming for rational economic development.

From John Marshall's point of view, the adoption of the Constitution was simple common sense. As he said, the Articles of Confederation were useful, but only because they "preserved the idea of Union, until the good sense of the Nation adopted a more efficient system." The Constitution *was* more efficient. It protected property more efficiently than did the Articles, for instance. In the American legal system property rights became more strongly guarded, lawyers say, than in any code since the Romans. Yes, the Declaration of Independence had replaced John Locke's "property" with Jefferson's "pursuit of happiness" as the third goal of government; but the ownership of property, especially land, was for Americans the underpinning of all, including the hedonistic individualism of the "pursuit of happiness." Property, liberty, and happiness became indistinguishable in the American creed of the 19th century.

Bibliography

G. S. Wood. *The Creation of the American Republic, 1776–1787.* New York: Norton, 1972.

Clinton Rossiter. *1787: The Grand Convention.* New York: New American Library, 1968.

J. T. Main. *The Antifederalists.* Chapel Hill: University of North Carolina Press, 1961.

R. B. Morris. *The Emerging Nations and the American Revolution.* New York: Harper, 1972.

P. H. Smith. *Loyalists and Redcoats.* New York: Norton, 1972.

PART II
Majoritarian democracy

6

The Federal world-view

The Federal style . . . national feeling and the arts . . . the plan for a capital city . . . the Federalists take over: Washington and Madison . . . Hamilton's plan for American economic development . . . the rebirth of mercantilism: Hamilton's radical economics . . . Hamilton creates the American variant of "capitalism" . . . public credit: the mysteries of "funding" and of "assumption" . . . the First Bank of the United States . . . The U.S. Mint: decimal coinage . . . the futuristic *Report on Manufactures* . . . Hamilton's prejudices lose him Southern support . . . the birth of party: Federalists versus Democratic-Republicans . . . party strife in the election of 1792 . . . impact of the French Revolution . . . the dilemma of neutrality . . . from one war scare to the next, 1793–95 . . . the Jay Treaty, 1794 . . . Washington's Farewell Address, 1796 . . . the succession struggle: the election of 1796 . . . crisis in U.S.–French relations, 1797–98 . . . the threat to civil liberties: Alien and Sedition Acts, 1798 . . . the miracle of peaceful transfer of political power: the election of 1800 . . . the fate of the Federalists.

The Federal style

The federal constitution of 1787 established the United States as a new nation to be reckoned with on the world stage and inspired a generation of Federalists to nurture and to manage its growth. This brilliant first generation of nationhood had a distinctive *world-view*, a far-reaching and comprehensive vision of the shape of things to come for the United States.

With the election of George Washington as first president in 1788, the Federalist leadership presented the nation with well-formulated, detailed plans for its future and for its place in world affairs. James Madison and Alexander Hamilton clothed the bare bones of the Constitution with flesh. Together, and a little later in opposition, the two men created the administrative institutions and machinery essential to the proper working of the Constitution. They moved from the political anatomy of the Constitutional framework to the political physiology of creating a real working government. Foreign affairs were largely directed by George Washington and through his style and his

Copley's "Brook Watson and the Shark", 1778

Museum of Fine Arts, Boston

presence he lent a certain stuffy dignity to the new office of the presidency.

National feeling and the arts

The new Federal style was captured on canvas by the American artist Gilbert Stuart in his elegant, life-size bust paintings of Washington, Madison, and other dignitaries of the day. Stuart did not limit himself to painting the Federalists, of course (he portrayed Jefferson, for example); but his work shared some of their characteristics: realism, cool technical competence, command over the materials, and a fateful taste for high living. He was trained in London by Benjamin West (court painter to George III, and president of the Royal Academy from 1792), another early American artist.

A surprising number of artists managed to make a living in late-18th-century America. Like Stuart, the better-known among them were trained abroad, lived by painting local worthies at home, and owed much to Thomas Gainsborough and Sir Joshua Reynolds. At least one, however, the intellectual entrepreneur Charles Willson Peale, took a deep interest in nature, landscape, and the American physical environment. This motivation would produce in the mid-19th century a distinguished native group, the Hudson River school. Meanwhile, Peale painted at least seven portraits of Washington, along with pictures of lesser Whig gentlemen. At that time, the nationalist spirit in painting was limited to portraying the Revolutionary heroes. Thus, John Trumbull, son of the Connecticut governor, is said to have painted about 250 portraits. His patriotic *Battle of Bunker's Hill* (1785) and his later mural in the new national Capitol, *The Declaration of Independence* (finished in 1794), perfectly express the spirit and style of the day.

In the late 18th century an "American" architecture began to emerge. Like painting, it was supported by solid bourgeois prosperity and the patronage of the wealthy and by the rise of American national self-consciousness. Thomas Jefferson was a major influence—ironically, since the classical style he favored is sometimes called "Federal." Jefferson and the classical revivalists of his day adopted a more chaste style and rejected the American architecture that had grown up in the century—American baroque, exemplified by the wooden, white-steepled New England churches fashioned after Christopher Wren, or by the brick of Independence Hall, or the baroque plan of Williamsburg, capital of Virginia from 1699.

Jefferson's *Notes on Virginia* (1784) demanded a new American public architecture, one more grand and suitable for a new republic. The following year, work began on his monumental Virginia State Capitol in Richmond (which had replaced Williamsburg in 1799). The Capitol, "American Roman," fronted by six massive columns with Ionic capitals and a large entablature, contrasted sharply with the more modest charm of Independence Hall. The classical revival dominated public building for some years, its major technical exponent being the English-born Benjamin H. Latrobe (1764–1820), the chief

American artist
—Charles Willson Peale

Pennsylvania Academy of the Fine Arts, Joseph and Sarah Harrison Collection

The U.S.A.

Greek Revivalist, whom Jefferson, as president, named surveyor of public buildings. Latrobe's Greek forms were to be seen in the Bank of Pennsylvania and the Second Bank of the United States, both in Philadelphia, and in America's first Roman Catholic cathedral in Baltimore. Latrobe took over the architectural plans to build a national capitol.

The plan for a capital city

"Federal City" was the nationalist vision of a new capital for the young Republic. It was meant to fulfill and to symbolize the Federal style, but the city grew only slowly. Its name was changed to Washington. To locate the city it was necessary to avoid political rivalries between states and existing cities, such as Philadelphia, the acting capital from 1790 to 1800, and New York, the capital from 1785 to 1790. A wholly *new* city would therefore be created. It was a daring and imaginative idea.

The choice of site was finally part of a political deal made by

L'Enfant's plan for Federal City

Stokes Collection, New York Public Library

Hamilton, Madison, and Jefferson at a dinner party in 1790. Madison had split with Hamilton over the latter's financial policies. Hamilton promised to swing a bloc of Northern votes in favor of a southern site for the new city if Madison would withdraw his opposition in the House to the payment of state debts by the federal government. The precise location was the choice of George Washington, and Maryland and Virginia gave the land to create a Federal District of Columbia.

Washington selected a French engineer who had fought for the American side, Major Pierre Charles L'Enfant, as overall designer of the city. L'Enfant was aided by a brilliant Negro mathematician and astronomer, Benjamin Banneker, sometimes called the "Black Poor Richard" because he issued an Almanac like Franklin's from 1791 to 1802. Latrobe worked on the buildings with intermissions until he retired in 1817, and also on the rebuilding after the destruction during the War of 1812. Washington remained an unpaved village for many decades. Congress would not pay for L'Enfant's grandiose radial design. His plans were unearthed in 1901 and partly carried out, and he was reburied with honor in Arlington National Cemetery in 1909.

The Federalists take over: Washington and Madison

The Federalists smoothly assumed that it was their natural right to govern the new nation. George Washington was chosen as president by a sizable majority of the electoral college. He gained 69 votes; his closest runner-up and therefore the vice president, John Adams, received 34. Washington took the job with triumphant support from the populace but with personal misgivings and anxieties. He made the muddy, eight-day trip to New York City, he said, like "a culprit who is going to the place of his execution." His first inaugural speech was stammered and awkward. He did not know what to wear, not having yet decided to be formal: European court stockings, silver-buckled shoes, a dress sword—decorating an American homespun suit. This uncertainty soon vanished. Washington developed a natural style of his own, graceful, slightly stuffy, proud, and courtly. He came to be driven around in a canary yellow coach drawn by six cream horses. Washington was determined to make the executive office respected. Though he did not interfere much in legislative matters and preserved a strict separation of powers, this fair-minded if somewhat intellectually limited man firmly established the office of the presidency. Rapidly, Washington fell under the influence of James Madison and Alexander Hamilton and was "Federalized."

Power went with drive and personality: three great men dominated the shaping of the American political system, Hamilton, Madison, and Jefferson. The chief figure for the first five months or so was Madison. Jefferson was away in France as a diplomat and did not accept the office of Secretary of State until January 1790, arriving in New York not until March. George Washington controlled foreign affairs: Jefferson could at most only share responsibility in this area. The president sometimes overruled his judgment. In contrast, Hamilton, as Treasury Secretary from September 1789, had close links with Congress, to whom he was supposed to report according to an arrangement insisted upon by Madison. In his reports Hamilton helped to mold the nation's institutions. Madison wielded authority through his influence on Washington and from his seat in the House of Representatives. He became the link between the executive and legislative and took a large part in Congress's creation of the departments of the executive branch: Treasury, State, War, Attorney General, and Postmaster General. Madison ushered through the Bill of Rights and introduced the first federal tariff of 1789. In the House he was behind the crucial Judiciary Act of 1789 which carried out Article III of the Constitution by creating 3 circuit and 13 district courts and gave the Supreme Court power of judicial review over the state courts.

President Washington, however, made the key appointments to these newly instituted offices. Both Washington and Madison agreed on the need to keep the executive branch separate. The cabinet officers thus did not develop into an executive committee of the government responsible to the legislature, as was happening in England with the evolution of the parliamentary "cabinet system." Washington did not convene the cabinet collectively in regular sessions. Each Department Secretary had his own separate responsibilities to the president. Madison, again, was the one who had insisted that the Chief Executive have the right to fire cabinet officers at his own discretion, though they were to be appointed with the approval of the Senate. No cabinet, as such, really existed in the first years.

Madison's influence was chiefly in his sway over Washington. His old rival in Virginia, Patrick Henry, had prevented his being elected to the Senate, so Madison had to work out of the lower chamber: but his strength was evidenced in the fact that he wrote much of the president's inaugural speech and the congressional response to it also. As for the Bill of Rights, these ten amendments grew largely out of the proposals Madison submitted to Congress in June 1789. In the House he prevented the Judiciary Act from being chopped up by saving the provision for district courts. This young Virginian was in truth a sort of activist political scientist. As a man he lacked presence, being small and unprepossessing, but his impact on the shaping of the nation was extraordinary.

Hamilton's plan for national economic development

Alexander Hamilton can best be understood in terms of modern economic *planning*. He was an economic activist, a builder, a man committed to development; and though he helped shape the American nation, Hamilton died frustrated. His visions far exceeded the political possibilities of the times. Today he would surely be a United Nations project director for underdeveloped nations, or an energetic president of some vast Common Market for Europe or Latin America, or a global population planner. No doubt he would be equally frustrated.

Jefferson, the liberal who came from a privileged, landowning family, accused Hamilton, the "bastard brat of a Scotch peddler" (as John Adams cruelly observed), of being a secret monarchist and an autocrat. By personality, Hamilton was autocratic; great planners

6 / The Federal world-view

Federal Hall
New York, 1789

Stokes Collection,
New York Public Library

usually are. He was brusque and impatient; his own tremendous work capacity did not allow him to suffer fools gladly. He must have swallowed hard many times as he dealt with the slower-witted Washington, without whom nothing could be accomplished. Hamilton was decidedly conservative in his social and political outlook. He had no time for the "mob" and the pretensions of democracy, but hoped to make the new federal government work by binding the upper classes of wealth, blood, and talent to it through economic ties. The economic theory behind his planning was not new.

Hamilton's early life was hard. Born in the West Indies in 1757, the bastard son of a bankrupt Scots merchant and his mistress, a French Hugenot married lady, he was abandoned by his father at the age of eight. He worked from age eleven as a bookkeeper in a counting-house on the Danish island of St. Croix and was saved from a life of obscurity by his employer and a local Presbyterian minister who sent him to New York, hoping he would train as a doctor and return. In 1773 he entered King's College (Columbia) and became involved immediately in the struggle against Britain. In 1776, at the age of 19, Hamilton was in command of an artillery company and fought alongside Washington, becoming his aide-de-camp with the rank of lieutenant colonel. In 1780 he married into one of the best New York families, the Schuylers. He became a member of the Continental Congress in 1782 and was admitted to the bar in 1783. His earliest legal work was a defense of federal as against state authority.

This was *Rutgers* v. *Waddington,* 1784. Hamilton, in a remarkable defense, three years *before* the federal constitution was written, took the attitude adopted by Article VI, the supremacy clause. He asserted blankly that the peace treaty with Britain was supreme over the laws of New York state; that the Union preceded the states; and that if individual states failed to recognize national treaties, everyone would suffer. Hamilton won a partial victory, but he pressed too far in asking the court to overturn a state law. America was not quite ready for judicial review. Yet it is clear that Hamilton's *Federalist* position was worked out in his own mind long before the delegates went to Philadelphia to prepare a stronger constitution and before his colleagues misappropriated the title "Federalist."

The rebirth of mercantilism: Hamilton's radical economics

Hamilton's economic ideas were not new, though he was well aware of the revolution in economic thought that was taking place, largely stimulated by Adam Smith's *Wealth of Nations* (1776). He took his policy recommendations from past British practices and mercantilism. Hamilton's use of these old ideas was, of course, different. He was a *neo-mercantilist,* adopting doctrines to suit his need, as any sensible policymaker must. He had no confidence at all in "general systems" of thought or in monolithic, theoretical views.

Hamilton did *not* believe in laissez-faire, as did Adam Smith, and

Philadelphia's Chestnut Street Theater, 1794

The Metropolitan Museum of Art, bequest of Charles Allen Munn, 1924

could not accept Smith's hope that if everyone pursued his own personal profit, an "invisible hand" would somehow reconcile these many pursuits to fit the national good. In his plan, the *government* must provide the "hand." Nor did he accept Smith's dogma of free trade. Smith argued that if each nation specialized in what it was good at, and bought from abroad products that other nations could make better or cheaper, all nations would be the richer. Hamilton thought this was a pleasant enough theory: but, in practice, other nations were all discriminating against U.S. products. This was the reality. Moreover, he argued that America would forever remain a colony of Europe—a mere exporter of foodstuffs and raw materials to the more advanced nations—if it concentrated solely on farming. Like 20th-century exposers of "imperialism," Hamilton realized that Smith's free-trade dogma was fine for England, an advanced nation, but did not pay off for the United States, an ex-colony of farmers. He would certainly accept the modern view, that free trade was a subtle form of imperialism if insisted upon among unequal nations. So he demanded tariffs, not only for revenue but also for *protection* of home producers against cheaper foreign products. Hamilton wanted to protect America's "infant" industries. (By the later 19th century his arguments were distorted to protect mature, rich industries.)

It is perhaps strange to think of Alexander Hamilton, that conservative Anglophile, as a profoundly *radical,* anticolonial thinker; but he was. Few observers notice this radical aspect of his economics. A constant theme of his economic arguments is the idea of a *domestic market*—which must be developed to free the nation from dependence on other powers. His tariff protection aimed to stimulate home industries; once they got started, a large domestic market would keep the economic expansion going. In this analysis he was entirely correct. A key to American economic growth proved to be the large home market. Thus he favored immigration. The government must encourage trade, industry, banking, transportation, and technology, or the United States would remain 200 years behind the advanced nations of Europe. His nationalist economics, we may call it *radical mercantilism,* was close to the later views of the German 19th-century theorist Friedrich List, who lived in the United States from 1825 to 1832. In his own day the closest theorist was probably the Scot, Sir James Steuart (1712–80). While the English had used mercantilist theory to exploit the colonies, Hamilton twisted these ideas to the new nation's advantage.

Hamilton creates the American variant of "capitalism"

Hamilton is forever associated with the rise of "capitalism" in the United States. Capitalism has many meanings. American capitalism was never fully the capitalism of Adam Smith, the laissez-faire, no-government-intervention, free-trade model. Hamilton gratefully accepted some of Smith's arguments: the need to develop markets; the benefits of "division of labor" (specialization) and of the use of machinery to increase output; the need for "internal improvements." Many mercantilists, however, could accept such notions—Colbert

The U.S.A.

(whom we met in an earlier chapter) could have in 17th-century France.

Against the state regulation of the details of economic life, high tariff barriers, favorable trade balances, dependent colonies, Adam Smith opposed his radical views. Smith rejected state authority and the centralism of mercantilist theory, in favor of unfettered economic individualism and private initiative. But the mercantilism that Smith detested was the machinery of royalist, dynastic, and aristocratic rule —the royal (or Parliamentary) interference in economic life, which the American colonists had thrown off in the Revolution. The "state" that Hamilton now proposed should do the regulating and encouraging was the new republic. Though Hamilton's opponents feared his "aristocratic" leanings, after him American capitalism became an amalgam of mercantilist and Smithian notions. In the American variant of the capitalist model, free-enterprise capitalism, as such, never really existed (whatever 19th- and 20th-century boosters might claim). The federal government and the state governments, too, were to play crucial parts in American economic development. American capitalism was Hamiltonian.

Public credit: The mysteries of "funding" and of "assumption"

Hamilton launched his comprehensive, integrated plan in a series of brilliant *Reports* to Congress. The first (January 1790), on the *Public Credit*, asked Congress to pay off the foreign debt in full; to "fund" the domestic debt at par (that is, to pay American holders of governments bonds in *new*, long-term government bonds, with guaranteed interest payments and assured future maturation); and to assume responsibility for paying off the Revolutionary War debts of the states in the same way. Most people realized that the national debt to foreigners had to be paid up properly or the United States would not be able to borrow again. But the second two proposals created a furor. Madison objected to the new government paying the American bondholders at par, i.e., the face value of the bonds or certificates when they had first been issued during the war. Who would get this money? Not the men who had originally lent the needy Confederation their funds for the war effort. The value of the bonds had been driven down by inflation and by doubts about the viability of the Confederation; speculators had bought them at much lower prices. Now Hamilton proposed rewarding these speculators at par. He was accused of corruption. He did allow his Assistant Secretary, William Duer, to give information ahead of time to speculators, but there is no evidence at all that Hamilton enriched himself. He died leaving a modest estate.

Madison thought Hamilton's plan of repayment at par was very unfair. He suggested that the payments be somehow shared among the first holders and the present owners and that the government should not pay the face-value price but the highest price the bonds had attained. This idea was unworkable. The paper had changed hands many times and the administration of Madison's scheme would have been impossible.

Why did Hamilton insist on full repayment? He was guided by more than crassness. Hamilton believed it vital to build strong public support for the new Constitution; pleased investors would surely support the new system and instill in others confidence in the economy. The federal government must prove its good faith and credit with home as well as with foreign capitalists. Hamilton wished to tie local capital to the national government, so he also demanded the federal assumption of the states' old debts as well. This idea angered the states that had few outstanding debts and those that had paid them off, like Virginia. It pleased states like New York, New Jersey, Massachusetts, and South Carolina, which still owed heavy debts. Hamilton's *Report* passed the Senate by two votes and the House by three, after a six-month debate.

The first Bank of the United States

In December 1790 Hamilton confronted Congress again. His new *Report* demanding a national bank outraged Madison and Jefferson. As a director of the Bank of New York, Hamilton found it easy to believe that banks were "nurseries of national wealth." A nation of farmers who regarded all financial transactions with suspicion could not readily accept this view. Hamilton, of course, was correct; no nation can develop without adequate banking facilities. American fears of banks, and particularly of a central bank, probably set back economic growth. Hamilton's opponents failed to see that a strong central bank—a semipublic corporation—could discipline the wilder activities of private banks and help to impose decent banking standards on the nation.

England had created a central bank, the Bank of England, as early as 1694. Hamilton wanted such a bank to perform certain *economic* functions: act as fiscal agent of the government; aid in tax collection; help foreign-exchange operations and flotation of government loans; provide stability for a uniform paper currency; and expand commercial credit by offering investment loans to business, in a nation still short of capital. Above all, he thought it would perform the *political* and *social* function of strengthening the federal government by linking the wealthy and educated segments of society to the administration.

The origins of our two-party system are to be seen in the deep opposition to this idea of the national bank. The Jeffersonian "Republicans," as they were to call themselves, insisted that banks increased speculation and usury, led to a drain of hard specie because of the competition of paper money, and diverted needed capital to industry and commerce and away from farming. Deep down, they feared *monopoly* and the old colonial, royal grants of privileges for trade to certain favored people. Hamilton argued that the Bank of the United States would not create monopoly, since each state was still free to charter state banks as it wished. Madison and Jefferson took a purist, strict-construction stand on the Constitution, though Madison had favored a broad-construction in the earlier *Federalist* essays. The Bank proposal passed the Senate quickly; it was Madison's leadership in the House that delayed the bill. He claimed that the Philadelphia convention of 1787 had specifically excluded the right of incorporation of a bank from the "enumerated powers" given to Congress in Article

I, Section 8. Hamilton denied this. While Jefferson's written opinion to President Washington said:

> The incorporation of a bank and the powers assumed by this bill (July 1791) have not, in my opinion, been delegated to the United States by the Constitution.

Hamilton's unequivocally declared:

> It is unquestionably incident to sovereign powers to erect corporations.

Hamilton insisted that the Congress was given not merely "express," enumerated powers, but "implied" powers (the last paragraph of Section 8). His reply to Washington was very long, detailed, and thorough. The president signed the bill into law and virtually became a Hamiltonian Federalist from that moment.

The Act of 1791 chartered the Bank of the United States for 20 years with a capital of $10 million, one fifth of it subscribed by the federal government. The Bank could issue notes up to the amount of its total capitalization, and the government would accept such notes in commercial transactions (payment of taxes) so long as the Bank was ready to redeem them in hard specie. No interest charges were to exceed 6 percent. The Bank was an immediate success, but hostility to its work came from numerous banks now chartered by the states, and because 75 percent of the national bank's stock fell into foreign hands (though foreign stockholders could not vote). In 1811 Congress allowed its charter to lapse. Hamilton had failed to win over its sectional opponents. The original act was passed by rigid sectional votes—the *yeas* nearly all Northern, the *nays* Southern.

The U.S. Mint: Decimal coinage

The central bank was the keystone of Hamilton's arch. He felt, rightly or wrongly, that his whole economic plan for the nation would stand or fall by the Bank of the United States. He went on, in June 1791, to propose, successfully, the creation of a U.S. Mint that would provide specie by coining gold and silver at a ratio of 15 to 1,[1] and would establish the *U.S. dollar* (roughly equivalent to the Spanish milled dollar in value) and the decimal system. He hoped to solve the problem of a desperate shortage of specie which had plagued the colonies because the English would not allow a colonial mint. Curiously, much of this new American specie drained away to the West Indies, because the ratio of 15:1 overvalued silver. Gold disappeared from circulation. American silver dollars, though lighter than Spanish milled dollars, were accepted at face value in Spanish-America and many of them ended up there. The conduct of American economic life came to rest heavily on the paper notes issued by private commercial banks. The United States did not issue paper money until the first "Greenbacks" of 1862.

---

[1] 15:1 ratio means 15 times as much silver in the silver dollar as there was to be gold in the gold dollar. The value of the dollar was established at 24.75 grams of gold. The ratio created a definite comparison between the value of gold and the value of silver. The *Mint Act* was passed in April 1792.

The futuristic *Report on Manufactures*

Funding and assumption, the national bank, the mint, these were all accepted with a struggle, but Hamilton's greatest *Report*, the visionary projection of a future industrial and urban America, was firmly rejected. The *Report on Manufactures* (December 1791) establishes Hamilton as a clear-minded prophet of America's future wealth and condition. He spent two years of work and research on the paper, with the advice and help of the economist Tenche Coxe, who had already published his own survey of existing manufacturing. To this Hamilton added knowledge gained from correspondents in various parts of the nation.

The *Report* envisaged a sort of "state capitalism": a paternalistic, neomercantilist, federal government, urging and regulating economic growth through an integrated program of protective tariffs (he suggested 21 increases in rates and 5 reductions on raw materials); premiums and bounties (direct government subsidies to approved industries—like the colonial bounties given by the English to indigo growers); encouragement to inventors; inspection by the government to maintain production standards, as in 17th-century France; improved roads and canals ("internal improvements") with federal aid; and use of the central Bank of the United States, whose funded debt was a major source of capital for investment.

Hamilton realized that his major hurdle was the *agrarian myth* and the farming reality by which most Americans lived. He took pains to respond to that worship of the soil and of the farmers and that distrust of commerce and cities of which Jefferson made much political use. Seeing the shape of things to come in Holland and France, and in England, which was undergoing the world's first industrial revolution from the 1790s, Hamilton pointed out that total reliance on agriculture would in the end reduce the United States "to a state of impoverishment." His study of America's resources convinced him that the United States could become economically powerful among world nations because their "political and natural advantages authorize them to aspire" to "opulence."

Hamilton's prejudices lose him Southern support

"Opulence" of the kind Hamilton desired did not interest the Southern slaveholding planters. While the massive restructuring of society that his plans called for struck most Americans with horror, the Southerners were especially opposed. The immediate effects of his changes seemed to be to profit a small minority of Eastern, Northern, urban, monied, commercial Americans. To a nation of rustics or isolated plantation owners, he spoke of coal mines, copper, lead and iron workings, and textile machinery.

Hamilton was prejudiced against Southern planters and their lifestyle. Opposing slavery, he helped to organize the New York Manumission Society in 1786. He despaired at the plantation system, which tied up needed capital in land and slaves and maintained a backward-looking society at a low level of technology. This was the antipathy between "capitalism" and the slavery-plantation culture. So Hamilton failed to make any move to placate the South, or in his planning to meet any of its sectional needs and fears halfway. It was no accident that his two major opponents, Madison and Jefferson, were Virginians. More politically astute than he, they built up a North-South political alliance.

The birth of party: Federalists versus Democratic-Republicans

The Founding Fathers decried the "evil" of "faction" and "party" and thought they had provided for a nonparty presidency in the Constitution. But they were factious and party-minded themselves. George Washington feared and opposed the spirit of party division, yet parties were born in his administrations, first in the struggle over Hamilton's program and then over foreign policy.

Parties proved to be necessary to make the system work. James Madison, in the *Federalist No. 10*, had argued that the size and variety of the American republic would prevent the emergence of national party spirit, because there would be too many different parties. No one group of "factious leaders," no one issue—"a rage for paper money, for an abolition of debts, for an equal division of property, or for any other improper or wicked project" as he put it—would dominate the nation as a whole. Madison was wrong. It was because no single faction could control Congress and implement a given policy that parties emerged. An *alliance* of interests, compromising some aims in order to unite for others, could elect a president. Thus was party born. In 1800 the Federalists were brought down by a new party alliance.

James Madison was the first to realize the full sectional and economic implications of Hamilton's plans and broke with him after a working relationship of eight years. Madison lined up votes in Congress against Hamilton's funding scheme, suffered a political setback, recouped, and continued the job of building an anti-Hamilton group in the House. The Antifederalists gained very little out of the political deal over the location of the federal capital and in the fight over the Bank they lost again. But the "Great Collaboration" between Madison and Jefferson was forged at that time, and it was the nucleus of the Democratic-Republican (Antifederalist) "party." The Antifederalists were sometimes called "Madisonians." Until Washington's retirement in 1796 they had no chance of defeating Hamilton. Though he left the cabinet in January 1795 and resumed his Manhattan law practice, Hamilton's political influence remained powerful.

The feud between Jefferson and Hamilton, so painfully evident by 1792, was personal and sometimes vicious. Jefferson was an expert name-caller. A great and liberal mind, he nonetheless saw people in terms of Good and Evil. Hamilton, in turn, regarded any attack on his economic plans for America as blasphemous. The two men hit out at each other via anonymous newspaper articles written by journalists, throughout the second half of 1792—Jeffersonians in the *National Gazette* and Hamiltonians in the *Gazette of the United States*. The feud soon had politicized the conduct of American foreign policy and torn apart the first cabinet in U.S. history. Not even George Washington could bring the two men together, though he tried several times.

Two worthies—Hamilton and Adams, c. 1791, portrayed by C. W. Peale

Independence National Historical Park Collection

Party strife in the election of 1792

Washington was eager to retire to Mount Vernon in 1792. He was dismayed by the bitterness of political faction, especially the fight in the press. Neither side could trust the other enough to allow the president to retire, so Madison and Hamilton, with Jefferson's approval, prevailed upon Washington to stand for reelection. The president was returned to office by a unanimous electoral college vote (three abstentions).

At the vice presidential level, however, a tough party contest took place. In the fall Jefferson made an alleged "botanizing" trip to New York state where he talked to Governor George Clinton, a staunch states' rights man and an anti-Hamiltonian. The Democratic-Republicans favored Clinton for the vice presidency and as a runner-up to Washington he won 50 electoral college votes, as against 77 for the Federalist, John Adams, who was reelected. The Jeffersonians thus revealed they had political pull in the North: a Virginia-New York political axis had appeared.

Impact of the French Revolution

The Revolution which broke out in France in 1789 had repercussions in many nations. In Britain the political leader Edmund Burke first supported the Revolution, then turned against it. Tom Paine, who became an honorary French citizen and sat in the French revolutionary assembly for a while, strongly opposed the execution of King Louis XVI in January 1793 and the mass executions of the Reign of Terror. He was jailed and missed the guillotine only by the accident of falling sick in his cell. Burke wrote his famous *Reflections on the French Revolution* in 1790, foreseeing the excesses that were to come. Paine continued to defend the French Revolution. His *Rights of Man* attacked Burke directly (1790–92).

Similar divisions of opinion were to be seen in the United States. Federalists took a position like that of Burke. Jefferson defended Paine and the French Revolution and came to believe that his own party was the embodiment of liberty, republicanism, and morality. Jefferson denounced the evil "monocrats," genuinely fearing for the Republic. He warned Americans against this sinister "sect" that was conspiring to overthrow American principles and to "Anglicize" the Constitution. In return, the Hamiltonians attacked him as a wild, pro-French, atheist radical. Jefferson would have liked to enlarge Congress and give more representation in that body to farmers, as opposed to what he called "stock-jobbers" and "King-jobbers." The second phrase was certainly less justified than the first. The Federalists denounced the events in France and the *Rights of Man*, while the more extreme Jeffersonians abused George Washington mercilessly. They demanded a *new* American Revolution, saying that the first had been betrayed by those admirers of privilege and aristocracy, the Federalists. Of course this situation was not like that in France and despite the bitter rhetoric any strong action was unlikely. Partisanship was most virulent during elections.

For foreign affairs, however, the division was significant. Jefferson's group generally favored France and Hamilton's favored England. Both men went far in their views—Jefferson gave some information to the French diplomat Genêt, and Hamilton, more seriously, negotiated secretly with a British agent, Major Beckwith. Though the aim of his secret dealings with Beckwith, who listed Hamilton as agent "No. 7", were always, in his own view of what was best for the American national interest, Hamilton undoubtedly sought to undercut Secretary of State Jefferson and exert influence over U.S. foreign policy in favor of friendship with Britain. No modern Treasury Secretary could behave in this way. Hamilton realized that for U.S. economic survival, as well as for the survival of his own domestic programs and hopes, *continued trade with Britain was vital*. The British were in fact less hostile to the United States than most historians have thought. American trade was important to England (the United States was her best customer), and her foreign problems at the time were enormous. Hamilton's dealings probably had little impact on the course of events, and here George Washington was the moderator. However "Federalized" he may have become in domestic matters, foreign policy was a province Washington fully controlled. In economic terms it is true that the federal government depended for its income on revenues from trade duties, and the bulk of the trade was with Britain.

The dilemma of neutrality

War broke out between France and a varying combination of allies in 1793. Most Americans wanted to stay out of Europe's wars. In 1776 the United States drew up a model treaty to be used as the basis for any treaty to be made by the new nation with a foreign power. This plan first defined "freedom of the seas" in international law with some clarity; it demanded for neutral nations the right of free passage of all nonmilitary goods in time of war and the right to trade with combatants. The doctrine "free ships make free goods" was strongly defended by American merchants and the United States emphasized this in its early treaties with Holland, France, and Prussia. When war broke out among the Powers in 1793 the United States therefore hoped these principles of free neutral trading in noncontraband, nonmilitary goods would be upheld.

Washington declared American neutrality in 1793. Personally, he was inclined to isolationism despite his feeling for France, his gratitude for French help in the American Revolution, and his friendship with men like Lafayette. Technically, the French-American alliance of 1778 was still in force, but France was glad to have the United States act as a neutral, since the Americans had no navy and could not help France in a military way. Consequently they were more useful bringing neutral supplies. The French were desperate for flour and grain. The neutrality of the United States should have pleased England for much the same reasons, but, in practice, the two nations never agreed on the true definition of neutral rights, or on what goods could be called "contraband." Thomas Jefferson's view of neutrality would have allowed more aid to France; so as to help out the French he deliberately slipped a vague definition of "contraband" into the neutrality declaration announced by Washington in 1793. However, he resigned from Washington's cabinet in December 1793 on the issue of France.

Caught between the Powers, the United States moved from one war crisis to the next, alternately fearing and hating England and France. A French crisis came first in 1793, when an overzealous minister, Citizen Edmond Charles Genêt, began commissioning privateers on U.S. soil and sending them out to prey on British ships. Genêt's Republican friends, Madison and Jefferson, were embarrassed by such open activities of a nonneutral sort. Washington had to ask the French to recall Genêt. When the new French minister arrived, along with papers for Genêt's arrest, Washington relented and refused extradition. Genêt settled down in the United States and married the daughter of Jefferson's New York political ally, Governor Clinton.

From one war scare to the next, 1793–95

The Genêt episode illustrates the growing party polarization over foreign policy in several ways. During the furor, local grass-roots Jeffersonian Republican organizations sprang up, called *Democratic Societies*. The Federalists detested them, and President Washington smeared them by linking them with the Whisky Rebellion of 1794, the taxpayers' revolt in Pennsylvania, with no justification. Even John Adams objected to this tactic.

A crisis arose almost immediately with England. On November 6, 1793, the English issued a severe Order in Council, ordering the seizure of all vessels, neutral or French, carrying products of the French colonies or trying to supply those colonies. This was a direct blow to American merchants, for at the outbreak of war with England the French had lifted all normal restrictions on trade by foreigners with their West Indies colonies. The English view was based on the "Rule of 1756": that trade not normally open to neutrals in time of peace was not open to them in time of war. War loomed between the United States and England. The Caribbean was alive with Yankee vessels, and the Royal Navy and the local admiralty court judges in the British West Indies lost no time in seizing American ships and looting them in the name of "contraband" trading with the French colonies—whether or not the ships were in fact going to the French islands. American seamen were jailed and sometimes forced ("impressed") into the British navy. Meanwhile in the Northwest, Indian warfare on the American frontier brought renewed charges of Canadian plotting, and British troops had still not evacuated the frontier outposts, as promised under the terms of the Treaty of Paris of 1783. (Peace came to that region for a while with the Treaty of Greenville of 1795, agreed between General "Mad Anothony" Wayne and local chiefs.) Even Federalists were angry with England. Washington sent Chief Justice John Jay to London to negotiate.

The Jay Treaty, 1794

John Jay's treaty of 1794 with the British was denounced by the Jeffersonians as a sellout. In the House, Madison fought a last-ditch stand against the treaty and seemed to go so far as to demand control

Folk art—an American home of 1786 seen through the cross-stitch art of a ten-year-old girl, Anne Anthony

Museum of Fine Arts, Boston

over foreign policy by the lower chamber. President Washington had held back the treaty for four months before daring to offer it to the Senate. Jay had managed to get the British to agree to evacuate the Northwest frontier posts by 1796 and to accept joint commissions to resolve issues like the Maine boundary dispute, claims for the seizure of U.S. vessels, and the payment of unsettled pre-Revolutionary War debts owed to English merchants. But nothing was said about payment to the United States for the slaves who escaped with the British in 1783 or about the painful subject of impressment. Since both countries were to enjoy "most favored nation" treatment in each other's trade, Americans could now enter the trade of the British *East* Indies, the market of India. On the other hand their right to trade in the rich West Indies market was so beset with special clauses as to be ineffective.

The Jay Treaty did not clarify the question of neutral rights, though it was probably the best treaty either side could have expected at that juncture. Madison's threat to refuse appropriations only caused George Washington to stand firm on his rights as chief executive to make treaties. Jeffersonians in general, and Virginians in particular, hated the treaty provision for the payment of outstanding prewar debts to English merchants, since their own slave losses were ignored. The Senate passed the treaty after a debate along party lines.

The following year the *Pinckney Treaty* was drawn up with Spain (1795–96). This gained more concessions for Americans. Spain guaranteed the free navigation of the Mississippi to its mouth and the right of deposit, without fee, at New Orleans. Previously the Spanish had tried to cut off the American West from the sea outlet at New Orleans and had not allowed American traders to "deposit" (store) their goods at that port for trans-shipment elsewhere. The Spanish also agreed to recognize the 31st parallel as the northern boundary of Florida and promised to restrain the local Indians from making frontier raids. The Pinckney Treaty was a triumph for those in the more western states. In earlier years some of them had flirted with the Spanish authorities for adequate frontier protection. Kentucky and Tennessee were now certain to stay American, if that was ever in doubt. The frontier drive to the Mississippi was inevitable. Trade down that river grew so rapidly that it alarmed the Spanish. They delayed opening the port of New Orleans to American traffic until 1798 and then closed it again in 1802. Angry American traders spoke of seizing New Orleans, but the entire Louisiana Territory passed from Spain to France in that same year and its purchase by Jefferson in 1803 effectively terminated any further need for a "right of deposit."

Between them, Jay and Pinckney had managed to neutralize the war crises with England and Spain. The Federalist foreign policy stratagem of staying out of Europe's wars and making profit by trading with both sides had produced excellent results in terms of U.S. prosperity. But foreign policy crises were by no means over. They took up much of the time of the incoming president, John Adams. The major war scare arose ironically with America's old ally, republican France.

The U.S.A.

Washington's "Farewell Address," 1796

George Washington gave up the nation's helm at a sad time in his own life. He had been deeply hurt by personal attacks from the press. Also, an open letter published by Tom Paine from Paris in 1796 accused Washington of letting his old friend languish in a French jail for months. Washington's "Farewell Address," a noble document, was not a true address, since he did not give it orally, but was a press release of 1796. In it Washington looked ahead to the basic principles that should govern the nation's conduct. He warned Americans of the dangers of sectional factions and of party and foreign alliances. Though he did *not* use the famous phrase "entangling alliances" (it came from Jefferson's first inaugural), he did beg the nation to "steer clear of permanent alliances with any portion of the foreign world." Temporary agreements were understandable; but Washington devoted a long section to the evils of playing favorites with foreign powers.

Earlier, he emphasized the basic *interdependence* of the four great geographical sections of the nation: North, South, West, and Atlantic states. But when Washington spoke of the "baneful effects of the spirit of party," the dangers of sectional conflict, and the "insidious wiles of foreign influence," the Jeffersonian Republicans could read between the lines. For them this meant: no permanent alliances (i.e., with *France*); no political parties (i.e., *Republican*). The hand of Alexander Hamilton was heavy in the authorship of the farewell. It was based partly on one draft by Madison and two by Hamilton.

The Farewell Address told the world that the American Revolution was over. In Washington's mind, the great revolution whose army he had proudly led, despite its universal significance in the history of human liberty, was to be a local affair. It was to be kept a struggle with England, now terminated, and not turned into a worldwide liberal upheaval led by Americans. The Revolution had achieved national unity; it had introduced the republican form of government; it must be preserved against faction, sectionalism, and foreign intrigue. The Revolution was to be contained and entrenched at home. George Washington thus embodied the spirit of containment.

The succession struggle: The election of 1796

Many political revolutions in the world have reverted to dictatorship when the revolutionary governments failed to achieve the essential miracle—the *peaceful transfer of power between succeeding administrations*. The political situation in the United States was dangerously unsettled at times after 1783, but the miracle of peaceful transfer was achieved in 1796 and again in 1800. In the United States, unlike elsewhere in the Americas later, the army never gained sufficient power or inclination to subvert the constitutional process laid down in 1787. George Washington squashed hints of a coup d'état in 1783. For that alone he is worthy of a place of honor, besides his many other gifts and achievements.

The election of 1796 was the first to be contested on both levels by parties. The Federalist candidate was John Adams, supported by Thomas Pinckney of South Carolina, who was included for geographical balance, and was known to the public for his treaty with Spain.

The Jeffersonian Republicans put up Jefferson, supported by Aaron Burr of New York. Under the nonparty rules of the electoral college (voters did not vote for president or vice president separately until passage of the 12th amendment of 1804), Adams became president, with 71 votes, and his political opponent, Jefferson, became vice president, with 68 votes. Pinckney and Burr received 59 and 30 votes, respectively. The candidates had been hand-picked by congressional leaders in an informal fashion.

In this tough and sometimes vicious campaign, the unpopular Alexander Hamilton had too many enemies to feature as a candidate. Nonetheless, he did scheme to manipulate the voters and to fix the electoral votes so as to keep out Adams. Hamilton suffered press exposure of his moderately active extramarital sex life. Jefferson was again excoriated as a libertine French anarchist. John Adams stood for a moderate Federalism, nationalism, and a degree of suspicion for monied men. He tried to reconcile Jefferson as his vice president, and sought to forge a bipartisan administration, but failed. Adams's main achievements as president were undermined by the Hamiltonians and were negative, though not less important for all that: he struggled to avoid war and to resist the pressures of faction at home.

Crisis in U.S.–French relations, 1797–98

War hysteria built up against the French, when their anger at the Anglo-American treaty made by Jay encouraged them to step up *French* seizures of U.S. vessels on the high seas and in ports. The new French revolutionary government (called the Directory) would not accredit the U.S. minister. Agents of the French foreign minister,

First brick house west of the Alleghenies— William Whitley house, Kentucky, 1787–94

Kentucky Department of Public Works

Talleyrand (called X, Y, and Z in dispatches) tried to persuade President Adams's negotiators to "loan" France a large sum and donate a "gift" to Talleyrand, in return for a French willingness to negotiate. John Adams covered himself politically by revealing the documents to Congress and U.S. public opinion was inflamed against France. Adams himself was angry and jingoistic at this stage, and Congress authorized him to raise an army of 10,000. The U.S. Navy Department was created. For two years France and the United States fought an undeclared naval war (1798–1800) and the extreme "High" Federalists pressed Adams for open war. Alexander Hamilton dreamed of leading a U.S. army into Florida and Louisiana. This scared President Adams enough to convince him of the need to try once more to negotiate with France. In 1799 he sent off another team to Paris which did complete a peaceful agreement. France recognized American neutral trading rights.

The threat to civil liberties: Alien and Sedition Acts, 1798

The Federalists took advantage of the war crisis to attempt to suppress opposition editors and close off debate before the coming election of 1800. Fear of aliens was genuine among the Federalists; they were not the representatives of newcomers or of the underdog in American society. The Jeffersonian Republicans were more attractive to Irish, English, and French immigrants. A number of French immigrant journalists became vitriolic against Adams. The Naturalization Act of 1798 extended the residence requirement for U.S. citizenship from 5 to 14 years and banned from citizenship any alien whose nation was at war with the United States at the time of his application. A further Alien Act and an Alien Enemies Act gave the administration the power to deport suspected aliens without trial if the president thought them a danger to "peace and safety," and to deport *enemy* aliens in time of declared war. The last seems a reasonable measure (it was never invoked, since war was not declared); the first act was effective for only two years. Given the reality of French spying in America, the legislation can be understood. Republicans felt, quite rightly, that it was a direct assault on them as a party. The Sedition Act was more dangerous to civil liberties: it authorized fines and imprisonment for those who joined "unlawful combinations" to oppose the government or plot against it, or those who published "any false, scandalous and malicious writing" that would bring the government, Congress, or the president into disrepute. Under this act 25 Republican editors and publicists were arrested and ten were convicted. Jefferson later pardoned them all and Congress paid them back their fines with interest after the Republican electoral victory of 1800.

The four acts taken together encouraged and expressed fear of aliens and of "conspiracy." They set back American civil liberties, restricting freedom of speech and of the press and giving somewhat arbitrary power to the president. Republican editors were harassed by prejudiced judges, such as Judge Samuel Chase, a man Hamilton himself had attacked for corruption in 1778 and whom Congress would see fit to impeach in 1804. The danger however was in a possible Republican overreaction. John Taylor of Caroline considered the possibility of dissolution of the American Union, but both Jefferson and Madison managed to restrain their followers. The two allies drew up state resolutions, Madison's adopted by Virginia and Jefferson's by Kentucky. Because he was vice president Jefferson kept his authorship secret to avoid charges of impropriety (and to escape the Sedition Act). Jefferson's resolution used the angry word "nullification," later taken out by the Kentucky legislature. Madison used the idea of "interposition"—the individual state could "interpose" its sovereign power to prevent a threatened "usurpation" of power by Congress or the administration. "Nullification" was used in later decades by the South to justify secession, and was an unfortunate word. Both Jefferson and Madison had helped to construct the American Union and were not about to dissolve it. Kentucky and Virginia expressed their loyalty to the Union along with the resolutions. Perhaps Jefferson would have been on stronger grounds standing on the Bill of Rights amendments, which protected individual liberties, and trusting to the courts for justice, however Federalist they were in personnel.

Hamilton talked fiercely of "putting Virginia to the test" if she tried to oppose federal laws, and of subdividing the larger states. Virginia planned to call up 5,000 militiamen. President Adams's resistance to both sides, the small size of the federal forces, popular hatred of a standing army and of the taxes to sustain it, and the coolness of other states, all prevailed to prevent a serious breakdown. The Congressional elections of 1799, however, brought Federalist victories in both houses. Whether this reflected popular favor for the Alien and Sedition Acts or popular backlash against the Kentucky and Virginia resolves is hard to determine.

The election of 1800: The miracle of peaceful transfer of power

The crisis passed and in 1800 political power was transferred peacefully and through the electoral process, to the opposition. Jefferson called it the "Revolution of 1800" (because he won the election). The American voters were told to choose:

GOD—AND A RELIGIOUS PRESIDENT

or impiously declare for:

JEFFERSON—AND NO GOD!

Despite such extravagances, Jefferson managed to squeeze 73 votes from the electoral college as against Adams's 65. But the trouble was that the man Jefferson hoped would be his vice president, Aaron Burr, also won 73 votes. The election was therefore thrown to the House of Representatives, where it took 35 ballots for them to select Jefferson as president and Burr as vice president. In a statesmanlike action which helped to cost him his life later, Alexander Hamilton threw his support, for what it was worth, to Jefferson, his arch rival. Hamilton was already alienated from John Adams, had suffered a political setback in New York, and detested Burr, whom he attacked as "an embryo Caesar." Later events proved his judgment correct, but it was an unusual election in which Hamilton pressed members to support Thomas Jefferson. His final estimate of Jefferson was shrewd indeed: he saw him as a moderate given to radical rhetoric, which is the way the French revolutionaries also viewed Jefferson. Said Hamilton:

He is as likely as any man I know to temporize . . . and the probable result of such a temper is *the preservation of systems.*

Perhaps the real revolution of 1800 was not Jefferson's coming to power—in practice his administration was not so different from its predecessors—but the way the contest was organized. Party managers at the local and state level brought in the vote with the aid of party newspapers, pamphlets, rallies, and meetings. The candidates were chosen by congressional leaders meeting in formal *caucus*, a system which would prevail down to 1824. The coming of the two-party system had rendered the electoral college unworkable and the 12th Amendment was introduced to reform it. After 1800 the Republican party caucus was very powerful: its choices were unquestioned.

The fate of the Federalists

The Federalists were already weakened before the election of 1800. They were internally divided by John Adams's policy of moderation over the civil liberties struggle. In Congress after 1800 they were reduced to a rump of New England reactionaries. However the Federalist Party was still active outside New England too, in New York, Delaware, and elsewhere. They ran candidates for the presidency in every election down to 1816. De Witt Clinton of New York made a good showing against Madison in 1812. They finally died out after the War of 1812.

In its various aspects *nationalism* did not die with the defeat of the Federalists in 1800. In one of his last moves Adams appointed the staunch Federalist John Marshall of Virginia to be Chief Justice of the Supreme Court (January 1801). For 34 years Marshall imposed *judicial nationalism* on the country and defended the federal government's prerogatives against states' rights and strict construction. In foreign policy the Federal world-view was firmly entrenched for years to come.

Bibliography

J. C. Miller. *The Federalist Era, 1789–1801.* New York: Harper, 1960.

Marcus Cunliffe. *George Washington, Man and Monument.* New York: New American Library, 1958.

R. Hofstadter. *The Idea of a Party System, 1780–1840.* Berkeley: University of California Press, 1969.

J. R. Howe, Jr. *The Changing Political Thought of John Adams.* Princeton University Press, 1966.

S. M. Lipset. *The First New Nation.* New York: Doubleday, 1963.

7

The Agrarian Dream

Dream and reality . . . the dream transforms itself . . . Jefferson, the national expansionist . . . rustic America: life on the Southern frontier . . . a diet of corn . . . Louisiana: traces of French culture . . . frontier life in the Ohio country: the first prairie . . . the Mississippi . . . Jefferson in power: the realist . . . Gallatin and federal aid . . . party discipline and frugality . . . Jefferson and the courts: judicial nationalism . . . threat of secession: the "Northern Confederacy" . . . Burr kills Hamilton, 1804 . . . from success to failure: Jeffersonian foreign policy . . . failure of the embargo policy . . . internal contradictions of "Jeffersonian Democracy" . . . red, white, and black: racism in Jefferson's utopia . . . confining slavery to the South . . . passing the Republican torch: Madison . . . Madison's alternatives to war . . . complex motives for war with England . . . War of 1812: national honor and independence . . . New England threatens: the Hartford Convention . . . the Creek War, the Battle of New Orleans, and peace . . . American nationalism in the saddle.

Dream and reality

Jefferson's vision in contrast with Hamilton's was of a United States which would remain a land of farmers, a republic of free, independent family homesteaders. This agrarian dream was close to the American reality of 1800. Most Americans did live on farms, with few amenities or comforts. They had little contact with the outside world of intellect and art, trade, and politics, either of the Federalist or Republican variety. Jefferson doubled the size of the country with the purchase of Louisiana in 1803, hoping that the addition of such vast territory would increase still further the preponderance of farmers and pioneers in American society and thus swamp the commercial and financial interests of the North and East. The new West he had acquired would become, he hoped, an "empire for liberty." The nation changed more rapidly than he expected and Jefferson adapted himself toward the end, accepting if not embracing industry, commerce, and their concomitants, mainly in the interest of national prestige and growth. His nationalism overcame his agrarianism.

The new president *walked* to his own inaugural from a Washington boardinghouse. He brought simplicity and democratic manners to the White House, in contrast with the Federalists. But at home Jefferson lived very well. His mansion at Monticello was an oasis of elegance, gadgetry (much of it of his own devising), and good living—gourmet food and imported French wines. It was suported by a bevy of slaves. Jefferson was an intellectual, a man of wide learning and world travel. The rural America he wished to represent and to preserve did not live so comfortably and was far less sophisticated. Life on the frontier of Georgia, or out west in Tennessee and Kentucky, was simple and crude. In Jefferson's day everything just over the Appalachians was "west." It took about 22 days to journey from the "western" settlement of Nashville to Philadelphia. The Boston–New York stagecoach (before turnpike highways) took three adventurous days over rough and muddy tracks. Until the coming of the steamboat Jefferson's beloved pioneers had to give up a full four *months* of their lives to travel upstream from New Orleans to Louisville or Cincinnati, one month to go downstream.

This was the double jeopardy of the Agrarian Dream. A nation that followed Jefferson's ideal and stayed agrarian could not advance fast enough either to provide comforts for its people or to feature in the world of nations. Both these elements meant much to Jefferson. Moreover, an agrarian economy would always be a dependent economy— an *economic* colony if not a political one. America would remain dependent on the more advanced industrializing nations of Europe, sending them her raw farm staples and buying back more expensive and more profitable finished goods. More than this, even to make the Agrarian Dream itself a success, the farmer would need better roads and better transportation. But the Transportation Revolution brought with it industry and cities.

The dream transforms itself

The Jeffersonian creed did not stand still. Jeffersonians controlled the White House from 1800 until 1825 under the successive presidencies of Jefferson, Madison, and Monroe, all three of them Virginians. This "Virginia Dynasty" enjoyed a virtual one-party, or at most one-and-a-half party, system for a quarter of a century. In his last two campaigns Monroe was almost unopposed. The divisions *within* the party now served to express the divisions within the nation, a common feature of one-party systems. The Jeffersonians split apart in 1824. The followers of John Quincy Adams of Massachusetts called themselves "National" Republicans, those of the new Western candidate from Tennessee, Andrew Jackson, called themselves "Democratic" Republicans. Before this, Jefferson had modified his economic thinking and in his second administration adopted a neomercantilist position not far from that of his old rival Hamilton. The Virginia Dynasty "Federalized" itself in the face of changing economic realities.

Jefferson, the national expansionist

After 1800 the frontiersmen pushed out to the Northwest, South, and Southwest. New states entered the American Union and altered the political as well as the geographic and economic balance of the nation. Eleven states were admitted, 1791–1821:

On the *Northern* frontier: Vermont entered in 1791; Maine not until 1820.

On the *Western* frontier: Kentucky (1792), Tennessee (1796), and Ohio (1803) came in succession. Then after a brief pause, Indiana (1816), Illinois (1818), and Missouri (1821).

On the *Southern* and *Southwestern* frontier: Louisiana (bringing with it a touch of French culture in 1812), Mississippi (1817), and Alabama (1819).

Thus America was geographically transformed in the years of Jeffersonian Republicanism. Beyond the Mississippi River lay all the vast Louisiana Purchase regions still to be tamed.

As president, Jefferson soon set aside his doubts about the use of federal power and realistically encouraged territorial expansion and rapid settlement, not only buying Louisiana but sending out Lewis and Clark on their western explorations of 1803–6 with congressional funds. Jefferson's nationalism far outweighed his localism. He inspired the tradition of frontier nationalism and armed it with his justifying phrase—*empire for liberty*—the root idea of later "Manifest Destiny."

So Americans exploited their huge internal continental empire, sweeping before them the Indians, and subjugating the terrain in the name of democracy, liberty, and progress. The flaw in their rationalization was the continued existence of human slavery at the heart of this expansionist democracy. Was black slavery to be spread, along with democracy and progress, throughout the continent?

A series of measures governed the sale and distribution of public lands, which became a major cause of economic growth in these years. The Ordinances of 1785, 1787, and 1790, the Public Land Act of 1796 and Article IV of the Constitution provided for township surveys, for the "territorial" system of temporary government, and for admission of new states. As Western politicians entered Congress and as virgin lands were settled, powerful lobbies managed to bring down the price of public lands and to reduce the unmanageable size of the basic lot offered for sale. Federal lands fell below the high $2 an acre price set in 1796, mainly because only 50,000 acres of federal land had been sold by 1800 and pioneers could often buy much cheaper public lands from the individual states at 50 cents an acre. Reforms of federal sales in 1800 brought down the price, began progressive reduction in the unit size of lot (down to 160 acres by 1804), allowed purchase of land on only 50 cents an acre down payment, and extended credit up to four years. While these changes made the lands more available to poor farmers, they also encouraged speculation, many more taking up land for which they could not pay. Land *companies* became the major purchasers and real estate dealers became as dominant and as wealthy in American society as Eastern merchants or Southern planters. These land "speculators" performed essential middleman services and helped to accelerate the settlement of the lands. Usually the companies carried out minimum improvements and rationalized the process of pioneering.

In the Lower South, the frontier was almost a separate society, quite

Rustic America: Life on the Southern frontier

outside and beyond the plantation experience of the Virginia dynasts of the Upper South. On the rough frontier of the deeper South and Southwest a burgeoning democracy, soon to be set back by the spread of cotton culture and of sugar and rice plantations, flourished for a while and left a later legacy to Populism. The poorer farmers lacked churches, schools, and most of the facilities of civilization to be found in the North. Their major contact with the outside world was the ubiquitous Yankee peddler. After 1800 a new wave of religious revivals spread out of Logan County, Kentucky, and featured vast camp meetings which provided poor Southern backwoodsmen with some vital *social* as well as spiritual needs. The "old-time religion" of the South was more than a moral revival, though it did also bring the faith to the many who were unchurched on the frontier.

This *Cumberland Revival,* as it is often called, since it fanned out from the Cumberland Valley of Kentucky and Tennessee, brought a narrow but vital moral fervor to a savage frontier. Our 20th-century critical attitude to its rigid, straitlaced, guilt-ridden Sabbatarianism should be modified as we remember the rough nature of the society it sought to penetrate and reform—a frontier of eye-gouging, drunken, desperately isolated, and poverty-stricken people. In the land of the

Johnny Appleseed's grave

S. E. Pallone for the Fort Wayne-Allen County Public Library

Camp revival meeting

Kennedy & Lucas lithograph, New York Historical Society

Bowie knife, the clan feud, and the lynching mob, crowds of up to 25,000 folk would bring their bedding and food and stay the week, as at the Cain Ridge meeting of 1801 in Kentucky, to listen to a series of day-and-night hot-gospelers. The orators were usually Methodist or Baptist, sometimes renegade Presbyterians like the Scotch-Irish ranter, Rev. James McGready. The crowd would chant hymns, work itself up into paroxysms of guilt, mysticism, and ecstasy and end up sobbing, screaming, dancing, oblivious to the world, barking like dogs on all fours, succumbing to the "jerks." The campfires, torches, music, and overnight vigils were a form of emotional release, an escape from the bleakness of frontier life and the soul-destroying hard labor it took just to stay alive.

Since formal education was not a highly held Southern value and only the gentry could afford it, the religious life of the frontier was also its chief *intellectual* outlet. Most of the revivalist preachers were fastidiously ignored or spurned by the college-educated ministers of the major Episcopal, Congregational, and Presbyterian churches further north. While not men of letters, these often crude gospelers did share in the general religious trend away from emphasis on the Enlightenment and man's reason. Moreover they stood for a natural democracy in religion, the salvation of all men and women of good will. They rejected notions of predestination and the salvation of the elect. They gave more scope to Free Will and a liberal Arminianism. For a frontier roughneck to be "saved," only repentance and faith were required. The niceties of theology were perhaps lost on many of the new preachers, be they nominally Methodists, Free Will Baptists, or "Universalists." But they were expert crowd-rousers who knew their people and they appeared to live intimately with Jesus Christ. Gradually, as their leaven spread, the established churches became affected and influenced by them. The newer sects began to make themselves more respectable, to develop their own denominational colleges and to build up a more informed and educated clergy.

A diet of corn

The social and economic gap between the Southern planters and the poorer farmers widened with the spread of cotton plantation culture to the Deep South and Southwest. The predominant small farmer grew a variety of subsistence crops to keep himself alive and perhaps a few acres of low-grade tobacco or upland cotton for cash sales on the market. His life was simple and his major staple was corn, a monotonous diet, however his wife varied the form: fried, roasted, boiled; as cornpone, spoonbread, or muffins. A little bacon, with sweet potatoes and peas, gave some variety. The average diet of white farmers in the South was not all that different from that of the plantation slaves.

As slaves rose in price because of growing demand for cotton in England, the chances of a poor farmer "making it"—building-up a nest-egg and buying a few slaves to ape his planter superiors—became less likely. From frontier log cabin to plantation mansion became more difficult, especially after about 1820. Meanwhile, below the sturdy farmer class was a smaller group of several thousand "hillbillies" and "crackers." These "poor whites," who formed a permanent part

Charleston, South Carolina, 1831 (painted by S. Barnard)

The Mabel Brady Garvan Collection, Yale University Art Gallery

of the Southern scene, eked out an existence on cracked corn and wildlife, and suffered from malnutrition, diseases like pellagra, hookworm, and rickets, and from cultural deprivation. The myth later built up of the "cavalier" South and the large, white-pillared plantation Big House, with its superior culture, concealed such realities. The "crackers" and "clay eaters," like the African slaves, did not figure in the Agrarian Dream.

The purchase of Louisiana in 1803 added French culture and several thousand Roman Catholics to the American population and gave the nonurbanized South another city, New Orleans. Within 20 years the French language was dying out in places like St. Louis, which was swamped by German immigrants in the 1840s and 50s, and the up-river towns of the Mississippi. The French architecture of New Orleans was largely destroyed by those fires which plagued all American cities, but the Spanish buildings survived, and as a port the city attracted immigrants of various nationalities. A degree of racial mixing unusual for North America kept New Orleans distinct from other American cities. There were additions of French blood with the influx of emigrants and refugees from Canada (the "Acadians," who became known as "Cajuns"), from Haiti (the French colony that was taken over by black slave rebels led by Toussaint L'Ouverture in 1791), and from France (torn apart by the Revolution and Napoleon).

Louisiana: Traces of French culture

The sugar plantations of Louisiana thrived under American rule and the mansions of the country around New Orleans were among the finest in the South. It is probably a myth, however, that French slavery of Africans was less harsh than American slavery, a myth encouraged by the greater ease of race-mixing among the French, the "octoroon balls," and acceptance of mulatto offspring and mistresses in society life. When New Orleans experienced one of the worst slave revolts in 1811, the blacks were put down by troops and many impaled black heads lined the Mississippi as a warning to others. It is too easy to confuse lack of sexual distance with less onerous exploitation. The French-speaking slaves on sugar plantations were little better off than slaves elsewhere.

Louisiana managed to keep its French law (it adopted the Napoleonic Code), its parish system of local government, and its Catholicism. Protestants moved in, of course, but the Catholics were not entirely overrun as they were further north. There, the scattered American Catholics of the Old Northwest were formed into a large diocese in 1808. The first Catholic diocese was the entire nation, under Bishop John Carroll (Baltimore, 1789), who became an archbishop in 1808. Later on, new dioceses were added, mainly in the 1840s and 50s with the influx of Catholic Germans and Irish. In 1789 Bishop Carroll founded Georgetown University, the nation's first Catholic college.

Planters, farmers, and squatters from North Carolina and Virginia moved over the mountains in Tennessee and Kentucky. From there, they or their offspring could move either south, into the frontier country of Mississippi and Alabama with its rich limestone soil, or north,

Frontier life in the Ohio country: The first prairie

across the Ohio River to the Indiana and Illinois country. Here, as one advanced northward, the American prairie appeared, not exactly "treeless," but much less wooded than Tennessee–Kentucky and much flatter. Its immense potential was not to be realized until later, with the coming of the Erie and Ohio canals and the railroads, which opened up the Midwest to wider markets in the United States and abroad. This terrain, the Old Northwest (Ohio, Indiana, Illinois, Michigan, and Wisconsin), was geographically the northeastern part of the great Central Basin, one of the world's richest farm areas, created about 25,000 years ago when a late glacial ice cap scooped out the Great Lakes and pushed soil ahead of it from Canada, depositing it in the future American Midwest, sometimes up to 300 feet deep.

American pioneers emerging from the wooded east and south onto this rolling plain, covered with tall, shoulder-high grass, were perplexed. They were unused to this sort of country. For 200 years they had learned to carve farms out of forest lands, to girdle and burn trees, and plough round the stumps, and to depend on timber for many uses. Their ploughs could not cut into the tough prairie sod. For some years, therefore, the Old Northwest was valuable mainly for *livestock grazing* rather than arable agriculture. Today, northern Indiana and Illinois are the center of heavy industry and steel manufacture. Most Midwesterners have never seen tall prairie grass—it has long since vanished—and they are unaware that this was indeed the first American prairie.

New Englanders tended to dominate the settlement of the northern sections of the Old Northwest, and Southerners, the settlement of the southern, more wooded sections. The New England small town with its white-steepled church and schoolhouse, and an occasional college, was reproduced all over the Midwest, while closer to the Ohio River in southern Indiana and Illinois, Southern style homes and "courthouse towns" prevailed, and there was a characteristic neglect for education. Much of the northern Ohio lands were part of Connecticut's "Western Reserve," about 3 million acres of Revolutionary War claims, absorbed into the Northwest Territory in 1800. Larger cities would soon rise on this Midwestern frontier, like Cleveland on Lake Erie, founded as early as 1796, and Cincinnati on the Ohio, which had a meteoric rise as a meat-packing town. The future metropolis of Chicago remained a mere village and was wiped out in the Fort Dearborn massacre during the War of 1812.

The Mississippi   The umbilical cord of the Midwest was the Ohio-Mississippi river system which drained south to New Orleans. This great navigation system, together with the heavy migration of Southerners to the Ohio country, tied the new West of the post-1800 years to the southern states. First came the *keelboat era*, through the 1820s, then the years of the more effective steamboat. The keelboats were shallow vessels up to 80 feet long and 10 feet wide, maneuvered by pole and oar and an occasional sail, and they were an essential part of frontier and river life for 3 decades. At least one brawny keelboat man, Mike Fink (c. 1770–1822), lives on as an American legend. Like countless river characters, Fink was killed in a brawl.

The policy of territorial expansion pushed by President Jefferson soon caused the original 13 colonies to become somewhat overshadowed. This can be seen symbolically in the migration patterns of two key families, the Lincolns and the Davises. Jefferson Davis, future president of the Southern Confederacy in the Civil War, was born on the Kentucky frontier within a hundred miles and within a few months of Abraham Lincoln. The Davis family migrated westward but then turned south to the rich new lands of Mississippi, where they built a plantation fortune. The Lincoln family moved to Kentucky from Virginia (having moved in earlier generations from Massachusetts), but Abraham's ne'er-do-well father turned north and eventually settled in Illinois where his son took up law.

Jefferson in power: The realist

What did Americans want in 1800? The election was a poor guide to opinion, being so close that it was thrown to the House for decision. What most Americans probably wanted in 1800 was not very different from what John Adams had tried to give them—stable government, economic growth, and a generation of peace with Europe. Thomas Jefferson inherited the international and domestic problems of Adams and was at first astonishingly successful. His personal style and overt convictions fitted the national temperament precisely. He was shrewd and realistic and pursued a policy of deliberate conciliation. His character, correctly estimated by Hamilton, was far from "radical." Jefferson *in office* was less partisan, less caustic. His largeness of mind and broad national vision were seen at their very best.

The first Jefferson inaugural promised a "wise and frugal" government and freedom from "entangling alliances." Jefferson declared: "We are all republicans, we are all federalists." A contemporary called the speech a "lullaby." The president set out to woo New England and its rich merchants. He kept the Hamiltonian system intact, of course (there was no real way of abandoning it now that it was firmly entrenched). The Bank of the United States prospered under Jefferson, and various states also chartered private banks. The tariff was kept; otherwise the federal government would have had little or no revenue. He did manage to persuade Congress to wipe out the Judiciary Act of 1801 and thus reduce the number of judges. The hated whisky tax was eliminated, as was the Naturalization Act. Jefferson appointed the brilliant Swiss, *Albert Gallatin* (1761–1849) to be his Secretary of the Treasury in 1801.

Gallatin and federal aid

Gallatin pressed for federal aid for economic development in a very un-Republican fashion. He stayed in the Treasury for 13 years, serving Madison too, and in 1808 wrote his farsighted, visionary *Report on Roads and Canals*—a report Hamilton himself might have enthusiastically endorsed. Gallatin realized that private business could not provide quickly enough the immense social overhead capital that European nations had managed to build up over centuries of history. He therefore proposed extensive federal aid to road and canal construction through land grants to private corporations given from the public domain. The federal government did adopt his system of direct governmental intervention in 1850; the individual states, much earlier. An unfavorable man–land ratio and capital shortage could retard the growth of the young nation, said Gallatin, the Democratic-Republican. He demanded a large appropriation of $16 million for internal improvements, for: "The General Government alone can remove such obstacles."

Such a long-term plan for national economic development through federally funded enterprise was not matched in U.S. history until the 20th century. Congress did not approve the $16 million, but Gallatin had also pushed for the purchase of Louisiana and for western exploration, both of which bore fruit.

Party discipline and frugality

Jefferson genuinely tried to keep his promise of frugality. Besides the whisky tax he cut military appropriations very low, both for troops and for ships. He did not like the nation to have a large navy, and left it defended by a handful of gunboats. When the pirates of the North African ("Barbary") coast attacked American merchant shipping, however, and the Pasha of Tripoli declared war on America, Jefferson did not take it lightly. The U.S. navy defeated the pirates soundly in the war of 1801–5. The daring exploits of commanders like young Stephen Decatur were stimulating for national prestige, as well as for votes. Once more Jefferson's nationalism overrode his deep regard for minimal government and a small military establishment. He was caught in the classic bind of the small-government protagonists. Many years later, in a totally transformed setting, President Eisenhower would face fundamentally the same philosophical dilemma.

The largest step away from frugality was the *purchase of the Louisiana Territory* for a mere $15 million in 1803. Regarded as Jefferson's greatest single achievement, in fact he had little to do with it except to give it his approval. The purchase came almost by accident, as a result of changes in European politics, though several Americans, such as Gallatin, had wanted to acquire the region earlier. Louisiana was not strictly Napoleon's to sell (the Spanish disputed the sale for years afterward to no avail) but the deal was so advantageous to America that niceties were swept aside. Jefferson himself had qualms of conscience about his authority to buy the area, but thought in the end that "metaphysical" questions of constitutionality should not prevent a move so obviously in the national interest. Congress, by approving the funds for the purchase, gave its implicit consent, and Marshall's Supreme Court was not about to raise any serious legal objection. In the case of *American Insurance Company* v. *Carter* (1828) the power of the administration to take over territory was justified by the treaty and war provisions of the federal constitution.

Louisiana was acquired because Jefferson felt that the projected transfer of the region from Spain to France in 1802 represented a threat to U.S. security. As it worked out, France "held" the vast territory for only a few brief weeks. Worried that France might take control over New Orleans and that American frontiersmen might react with violence, Jefferson told his minister in Paris, Robert R. Livingston, to negotiate for free navigation of the river and use of the port. A surprised Livingston was asked by the foreign minister of Napoleon, Talleyrand, "What will you give for the whole of Louisiana?" (April 1803.) Concurrently, Jefferson had already sent Monroe to France to try to buy New Orleans and some territory to the east, but Monroe was a day's drive away from Paris when the deal was negotiated. He had been authorized by Congress to spend up to $2 million for New Orleans and West Florida (secretly he could go as high as $10 million). Finally the United States spent $15 million for the entire region, stretching from the Mississippi to the Rockies. No doubt the American representatives exceeded their authority in buying Louisiana for a song, but one cannot imagine any American turning the offer down.

Despite the $15 million for Louisiana, Jefferson was able to reduce the national debt from $83 million to $57 million by the end of his second term. Disciplined party majorities in Congress saw him through, and party organization at the state level was firmed up. Jeffersonians were best organized in states like New York where the two parties were evenly matched and grass-roots participation was called for. They made clever use of the party press, especially the *National Intelligencer*, edited by Samuel H. Smith. At the national level the congressional party caucus maintained unity. The president was not slow to use the patronage power in order to rid himself of the many Federalist appointees and to reward his party supporters. Jefferson boosted the patronage system as much as Andrew Jackson did later, according to recent research. Jefferson hit his opponents hard. He dismissed almost half of all federal officeholders and put only Republicans in their place. Even his economy cuts in the army and navy had political implications, since Federalists lost their jobs.

Jefferson and the courts: Judicial nationalism

Jefferson's anger was aroused by the last-minute appointments of the outgoing president, John Adams. Allegedly Adams appointed a group of "midnight judges" on his last day of office, staying up late to do so. The truth was that the Judiciary Act was not approved until three weeks before Adams gave up office: He could not have created judges under it any earlier. He worked until 9 P.M. on his final day, March 3, 1801, signing the commissions of army officers, justices of the peace, and other judicial appointees but authorized only three judgeships. Still, Adams gave jobs to Federalists alone and thus saddled the incoming government with potentially hostile officeholders.

In 1803 a case came up before Chief Justice John Marshall, appointed a month before Adams left the White House. Jefferson ordered his Secretary of State, Madison, to withhold the commission of one Adams appointee, William Marbury. In the famous case *Marbury* v. *Madison,* Marbury asked the Supreme Court for a writ of *mandamus* (like an injunction) to order Madison to give him his commission as justice of the peace for the District of Columbia. The Court held unanimously that:

1. Madison had no right to withhold the commission, which was legal and signed.
2. The Supreme Court, however, had no jurisdiction in the case and could not issue a writ of *mandamus* because:
3. Section 13 of the Judiciary Act of 1789 which authorized the Court to issue such writs was unconstitutional and null and void.

Marshall's decision was clever. He avoided a confrontation with the Republican executive on what was essentially a minor case (for Marbury, himself, the post of justice of the peace was financially "insignificant"), but he widened the whole affair to assert the right of the Supreme Court to *nullify* acts of the legislature—the principle of judicial review. His legal basis for declaring that section of the Judiciary Act unconstitutional was not very strong: he argued that the Founding Fathers gave the Supreme Court original jurisdiction only in specific instances. In fact, the Constitution describes the areas of Supreme Court appellate jurisdiction but goes on to add "with such exceptions and under such regulations as Congress shall make." Congress, it appears, could enlarge the Court's powers if it chose to do so. Marshall denied this interpretation. No other act of Congress was nullified by the Supreme Court until the Dred Scott slave case of 1857, but in his remaining years Marshall continued to build the Court's prestige and to push the principles of judicial nationalism.

Threat of secession: The "Northern Confederacy"

In the early 1800s the future of the American Union was still uncertain. When the Louisiana Purchase seemed a possible threat to the political status of New England as a section, the most extreme Federalists of Massachusetts began plotting possible secession. They were led by Senator Timothy Pickering, former Secretary of State for John Adams. Pickering counselled separation of the North from the South and West early in 1804, and the creation of a "Northern Confederacy." He realized that, for success, New York and then Vermont, New Jersey, and Rhode Island would need to be added to the hard core made up of Massachusetts (the "Essex Junto") and Connecticut (the "River Gods," or High Federalist elite). Many Federalists would not go along with the idea, including Alexander Hamilton, Fisher Ames, and John Quincy Adams. In desperation the conspirators turned to Hamilton's mortal rival, Aaron Burr. A New England delegation approached Burr, who was running for the governorship of New York in April 1804, and asked him if he would take New York into their proposed Confederacy if he were victorious. It all came to nothing very rapidly, for Burr could not win in New York state without Federalist aid, and Hamilton scotched that. Burr lost and the idea of a Northern Confederacy evaporated.

The affair had a bitter aftermath. It added to the tensions between Hamilton and Burr, who could believe that he had lost two major political offices, the presidency and the New York governorship, due to Hamilton's interference.

Hamilton provoked Burr to a duel. In February, before the New York election, he had called his enemy "a dangerous man, and one who ought not to be trusted with the reins of government." He would not respond favorably to Burr's demands for an explanation and on a bright summer morning (July 11, 1804) the two men fought a duel at Weehawken, New Jersey, on the Palisades overlooking the Hudson River. As Hamilton's last letter to his wife reveals, he felt it was murder to kill in a duel and deliberately withheld the first shot. He played the code of courage to the end. Burr had no intention of missing and shot Hamilton in the abdomen. Hamilton suffered agony and did not die for 30 hours. He was barely 50.

So America lost one of its great statesmen, entirely unnecessarily. Hamilton's judgment of Burr proved to be correct. Jefferson had abandoned Burr after the 1800 election and gave him no patronage or encouragement (which was partly why Burr ran for the New York governorship). He dropped Burr as a running mate in favor of George Clinton of New York. When he was returned to the White House in the 1804 election, Jefferson did give patronage posts to Burr's friends in the Louisiana territory. The failure of the Northern Confederacy enabled Jefferson to win every New England state except Connecticut, and every other state in the Union but Delaware. He got 162 electoral college votes to only 14 for the Federalist nominee, C. C. Pinckney. Clinton became vice president, having run for that office against a Federalist under the terms of the new 12th Amendment (September 1804), which provided for separate ballots for president and vice president.

Burr's career was not yet over. He became involved in a series of shady negotiations in the years 1805–7 which included a deal with

Burr kills Hamilton, 1804

New Orleans in 1803 (painted by Boqueto de Woieseri)

Chicago Historical Society

The duelling ground at Weehawken, New Jersey

*Stokes Collection
New York Public Library*

the British minister, Anthony Merry, to dislodge the western states from the Union, and in another plot with General James Wilkinson, the U.S. commander in Louisiana, and others for vague military actions in the West. Wilkinson double-crossed Burr, and the latter was captured in Alabama in February 1807 on his way to freedom in Spanish territory. His treason trial opened in August and was notable because it became in part a struggle between John Marshall and Jefferson. Marshall tried to order President Jefferson to attend as a witness but Jefferson set a presidential precedent by refusing to appear.[1] Burr was eventually acquitted.

From success to failure: Jeffersonian foreign policy

The second administration was dominated by foreign affairs. The lull in warfare abroad ceased. The Napoleonic Wars broke out in 1803 in Europe, a land power (France) being opposed by a sea power (England). It was a total war that involved blockade and therefore deeply affected neutrals. Jefferson, despite his dislike of entangling alliances, became entangled. He insisted on preserving and exercising America's neutral trading rights. In the course of this policy that, ironically, was intended to defend U.S. merchants, American farmers suffered. Behind the policy lay Jefferson's national pride and his overestimation

---

[1] Many decades later, in the Watergate scandal that involved President Richard Nixon and his staff, Nixon refused to hand over presidential papers and tapes of conversations that could be germane to the trial of his aides (1973–74). Jefferson's precedent in refusing to appear before Marshall's court became of more than historical significance. (Nixon agreed to obey if ordered to by a "definitive" command of the Supreme Court.)

of Europe's dependence on American exports, which was itself a partial reflection of that pride. Jefferson decided to apply economic sanctions to enforce America's will. A series of confrontations with Britain came after 1805 on the issues of neutral trading rights, naval blockades, and impressment. In 1805 the *Essex* case decision of the British courts made it more difficult for Americans to prove legally the principle of a "broken voyage," by which they had successfully traded between France and her West Indies colonies by breaking the journey in American ports. Henceforth all U.S. vessels so trading would be liable to British seizure.

The United States responded with the Non-Importation Act of 1806 which prohibited the import of many British manufactures. Jefferson refused to submit to the Senate or sign a humiliating treaty the British had proposed in 1807. Napoleon had responded to the British blockade with his own Berlin and Milan Decrees of 1806–7, establishing the "Continental System," which was supposed to seal off Europe to British trade. Napoleon's was a mere paper blockade. Jefferson's chief problem lay with the British policy of seizure and impressment. The British Orders in Council of 1807 forbade *all* trade with France except through British ports: Theoretically it wiped out neutral trade.

Like Adams before him, Jefferson was under pressure to declare war. When the British frigate *Leopard* had opened fire on the U.S. vessel *Chesapeake* off the Virginia coast after its captain refused to submit to search (June 1807), 3 U.S. sailors were killed, 18 wounded, and 4 carried off as alleged British deserters. (The matter was not settled until 1811.) Caught between the two Powers, Jefferson pushed the crisis one stage further with his own drastic retaliation, the Embargo of 1807. This forbade American vessels from leaving port for foreign shores and was Jefferson's response, short of war. Economic sanctions have rarely worked throughout history and this one backfired: it hurt New England far more than Britain. Two lean winters were suffered in the Northeast, bringing renewed threats of secession and nullification. Jefferson's own Virginia and Kentucky Resolutions and his threat of "interposition" used in 1798 came back to haunt him.

The Republicans enforced nonimportation against British imports very harshly, as repressively as ever British colonial authorities had carried out regulations of trade. New England arose in opposition and was momentarily "re-Federalized" in spirit. These measures did not succeed in pressuring the English, but they did split the Republicans as a party at home. Never again were the Jeffersonians as united as they had been under his first administration.

Failure of the embargo policy

The embargo and nonimportation may have been Jefferson's bloodless alternative to war, but their impact at home and on U.S. trade was harsh. Within a year U.S. imports were cut to under one half; exports were reduced to one fifth. The $5 million-worth of tobacco and the $14 million-worth of cotton exported in 1807 were down to $1 million and $2 million, respectively. Lossses in the reexport and carrying trades were not recouped, though exports of native American products

The U.S.A.

By the Virtue, Firmness and Patriotism of
JEFFERSON & MADISON,
Our Difficulties with England are settled—our Ships have been preserved, and our Seamen will, hereafter, be respected while sailing under our National Flag.

New York Historical Society

The revocation by Madison of Jefferson's disastrous embargo, 1809

did begin to recover by 1809. The economic retaliation policy resulted in idle vessels, deserted quays, and unemployment. Merchants were sometimes ruined. Empty coffeehouses, the normal centers for trade and talk, contrasted with crowded debtors' jails. In New York city alone, 1,300 men found themselves in debtors' cells, after business failures.

In the course of time opposition to the embargo and nonimportation policy brought some reform, but Jefferson took no part in this. The problem of neutral trading and of economic sanctions was left to Madison to tackle after 1808. Perhaps Jefferson could have avoided some suffering if he had been prepared to *compromise* over neutral rights, instead of imposing such sweeping prohibitions. But Madison did little better with this problem and ended up at war with England, which was worse.

Internal contradictions of "Jeffersonian Democracy"

The inner contradiction of Jefferson's agrarian, democratic dream was the anomaly of his minimal-government, decentralized goals in an increasingly commercialized society that depended on world trade. His nation of farmers was expansive and nationalistic; its needs could only be fully met at this stage through multilateral trade and territorial growth. The farmers themselves, as well as the planters, needed credit and better transportation. They pressed hard for expansion into Florida and the Southwest and Northwest. Various pressure groups demanded central banking, the right of deposit at New Orleans (before 1803) and safety on the high seas from search and seizure. All these demands implied stronger national authority and ultimately more taxes and appropriations.

Jefferson came around to accepting some of these ideas. He abandoned pure agrarianism for a sort of neomercantilism that favored tariff protection and federal encouragement to economic development. Increasingly, he came to depend on Northern votes in Congress. "Purer" Jeffersonian Republicans than Jefferson began to pull away. The brilliant, malicious John Randolph of Roanoke, for example, was one who fought all measures that smacked of nationalism—the U.S. Bank, tariffs, the embargo, and annexation of Florida. John Taylor of Caroline, the arch-agrarian and scientific farmer, was a staunch defender of states' rights come what may. Larger sectional interests were also becoming clearly distinguishable: the West, New England, the Middle Atlantic states and Virginia. Jefferson's vision of a *balanced economy* was now closer to that of his old rival, the late Alexander Hamilton.

However, Jefferson never came around to dropping his party loyalty. As late as 1811 he could still claim:

. . . the Republicans are the *nation*. . . . The last hope of human liberty in this world rests on us.

In one major act of 1807 Jefferson reasserted his libertarian beliefs: the abolition of the international slave trade. The impact of this reform on Negroes was unfortunate in some ways. The act cut off legal slave imports and thereby it inadvertently encouraged slave breeding and the domestic slave trade within the United States. It did not attempt to prohibit slave trading among the states under the interstate commerce clause of the Constitution. This would have been difficult to enforce, in any case.

Red, white, and black: Racism in Jefferson's utopia

The place of the Amerindian was assured in Jefferson's Agrarian Dream. That of Africans and their American descendants was doubtful. Like many of his generation Jefferson detested slavery but thought that Africans were probably genetically inferior. He looked on Indians as white men with copper skins who only needed education and training to be fully assimilated one day into the white world as equals. "Let our settlements and theirs meet and blend to intermix and become one people," he suggested in 1803.

In contrast, Jefferson was not ready to adopt such an environmentalist and racially liberal view about blacks. He would abolish slavery, but feared the race mixing and conflict that he felt would occur if the freed Negroes remained in close proximity to whites. Jefferson's fear of black-white race mixture has been closely studied in recent years and one writer has linked the fear to an alleged phobia that Jefferson had about women in general. Whether this is true or not, there is heavy circumstantial evidence, reexamined in 1972, that Jefferson fathered several mulatto children by his light-skinned slave, Sally Hemings. Her entire family was given special treatment on his estate and were eventually liberated, an unusual step for Jefferson, who unlike Washington, Randolph, and others, did not generally free his slaves. He may have been a kinder master than many, but he bought and sold slaves, had them lashed, and advertised for runaways like any other slave owner.

Sally Heming's light-skinned family was born between 1795 and 1808. It was over a decade earlier that Jefferson had published his influential *Notes on Virginia* (1784), which summarized the known biological, intellectual, and allegedly scientific arguments used against Negroes. This work became a general source book for "evidence" of black racial inferiority. Jefferson opposed "mixture of color" in America in private correspondence during the last year of his life, 1826. The *Notes* places the African low on the roster of the accepted Linnaean biological charts of Jefferson's day. Late-18th-century science searched for order and hierarchy in the Universe (the "Great Chain of Being" theory) and in that order Negroes did not feature well. Jefferson characterized Negroes as being sexually uncontrolled and intellectually incapable and brushed aside evidence to the contrary. These two principal charges have pursued black Americans down to the 20th century.

Confining slavery to the South

Jefferson's feelings about Negroes weakened his position on slavery as an institution. He could foresee its abolition only gradually, with adequate compensation for the property rights of slave owners, and he hoped this would be followed by the removal of freed blacks back to Africa ("colonization," as it was called). Without this colonization, he thought race war would break out in the United States and undesirable miscegenation (race mixing) would take place. These stipulations made it almost impossible *financially* to abolish slavery, though throughout his life Jefferson continued to press for resolutions in favor of emancipation. As late as 1824 he put forward a scheme for liberating all children of slaves, to be paid for by the federal government. Negroes would no longer be *born into* slavery in the United States. Since slave imports had been made illegal, this meant that slavery as an institution would die out in time. This policy, of course, was never adopted; it took a bloody civil war to remove slavery from the American scene.

Slavery spread during Jefferson's day, along with the frontier and cultivation, to Kentucky, Tennessee, Louisiana (where it already existed at the time of its purchase), and the Southwest. It was, however, excluded from the Old Northwest (Ordinance of 1787). Jefferson had introduced his own act in the Confederation Congress in 1784, the year of publication of his *Notes on Virginia*. That act would have banned slavery throughout the American West by 1800, Southwest and Northwest alike, but it failed by one vote when a sick member from New Jersey stayed home. If it had passed, American history could have been different thenceforward: there might have been no contest over the extension of slavery into the territories and perhaps no Civil War. "The fate of millions unborn," cried Jefferson, was left "hanging on the tongue of one man, and heaven was silent in that awful moment."

Though slavery was not "dying" in this period, the Founding Fathers did manage to hem it in and to limit the institution to the Deep South and Southwest. Had the Fathers not excluded slavery from the Midwest and had they not abolished the slave trade in 1807, slavery might have spread throughout the Republic. By about 1830, antislavery pressure and economic factors had eliminated slavery in the northern states, and voluntary manumissions, economic circumstances, and propaganda also brought a sharp decline in the use of slave labor in the Upper South, if not in slave-trading to the Deep South. Thus slavery became a beleaguered institution concentrated in the Deep South and in the boom lands of the Southwest. It was a form of labor "peculiar" to those regions. Racial *discrimination* short of actual slavery existed over a much wider area, of course.

Passing the Republican torch: Madison

James Madison, who defeated the Federalist candidate Charles Pinckney in 1808, was a fitting successor to his friend of many years, Jefferson. Madison gained 122 electoral college votes to Pinckney's 47. He was a consistent nationalist and was troubled by such issues as the matter of strict versus broad construction of the Constitution in areas like internal improvements. As president, he urged Congress to devise plans for a national scheme of roads and canals, but then felt constrained to veto the appropriations bill to carry out his suggestion, thinking it would require a constitutional amendment to legalize such a step. This appropriations bill of 1817, ironically, was offered by John C. Calhoun of South Carolina, who later became the classic states' righter.

Madison defended the Union against all hints of secession or separatism, even by Jefferson in 1798. Between the clarities of Alexander Hamilton and the clarities of Thomas Jefferson, Madison the political scientist was always trapped. In his favor one must add that things were never as clear as his two companions saw them. Madison's two terms were almost totally taken up by foreign affairs and war. Here his policy in the face of foreign crises and the problems of U.S. neutrality was to extend the goals of Jefferson: Madison stood for *peace before war, but war before submission.*

Complex motives for war with England

The War of 1812 was to a great extent the end result of the years of tension over the question of neutral rights. The Napoleonic Wars dragged on in Europe between England and France and their allies. The issue of the rights of neutrals had never been resolved. Madison inherited a delicate situation between the United States and England over Jefferson's policy of economic sanctions, imposed to force the English to respect American rights and to cease impressment and illegal searches on the high seas. National honor was not the sole cause for war, however; a younger generation of nationalist politicians, several from the West, demanded forceful action against England. These "War Hawks," as they were called (the word "hawk" is old in

American usage), were territorial expansionists. Some eyed Canada, others wanted to push U.S. boundaries outward in a southern and western direction toward Mexico and the Floridas, a move which presumably would also extend slavery as an American institution.

Led by Henry Clay of Kentucky and John C. Calhoun of South Carolina, the War Hawks worked on the theory that two elements prevented the emergence of a *wholly American* republic of North America: the Indians and "foreign"-held areas, such as Canada. Neither the Indians nor the Canadians agreed with this theory. The War Hawks demanded a tough policy against Indians and territorial pressure against the Canadians, Texas, and Florida. The issue of Canada was made clear in Congress, when an anti-war Republican, John Randolph, complained in 1812:

Agrarian cupidity, not maritime rights, urges the war. . . . We have heard but one word—like the whip-poor-will, but one eternal, monotonous tone—Canada! Canada! Canada!

Western expansionism was certainly one motivation for the U.S. declaration of war in 1812. Yet, threats on Canada were often as much a military weapon to use against England as any real intent to assimilate that vast territory. Americans did not have much to bargain with against England, and Canada seemed the most available soft spot. There was some justification for American frontier fears about English interference in the Northwest. For example, when Governor William H. Harrison of Indiana Territory led 1,100 men

Dolly Madison

New York Historical Society

against Chief Tecumseh's federation of Indians at the Battle of Tippecanoe (November 1811), he found unpacked British rifles. Tecumseh, aided by his brother, the Prophet, planned to unite the tribes in one great, moralistic, disciplined religious revival and to drive out the whites. Though he failed, it was evident to Americans that the English had still not relinquished their hold in that region despite the treaty of 1783.

Westerners were not the only ones who shared in a general Anglophobia. President Madison's major weapon with which he hoped to defend U.S. honor and foreign trade—without going to war against either the French "Continental System" or the English restrictive Orders in Council—was the same as Jefferson's: economic sanctions. Madison's first crisis was with France, which had been seizing hundreds of American ships. The Non-Intercourse Act of 1809 affirmed that the United States would trade with all nations except France and England and offered to reopen trade with whichever of these two warring powers would lift its own restrictions against American merchants. More subtle was Macon's Bill No. 2 of 1810, which lifted all restrictions, but offered to reimpose them on the enemy which would not begin free trading with Americans once more. This polite blackmail did not work very well. Madison was defrauded by both sides. An Anglo-American agreement of 1809, under which Britain would not impress men from American ships and the United States would begin trading with England again but not with France, was all but signed (the Erskine Agreement), when the English Prime Minister, George Canning, rescinded it. The French also made an offer that turned out to be false. By 1811 it was obvious that economic sanctions alone were not effective in bringing recognition and justice for American merchants.

To Congress and the president alike, Britain began to appear the more arrogant of the two enemies. Its use of mediocre diplomats and its vacillation seemed to show contempt for American opinions or possible reactions. Continuing impressment and the indignities suffered by Americans on the high seas at the hands of the Royal Navy strengthened the attacks of the pro-war group in Congress. True, British sailors often *did* desert and join up in the American merchant navy, but the Royal Navy "press gangs," which boarded United States ships seeking deserters, often grabbed any sailor they could find who could not prove American citizenship.

By 1812 American anger over impressment was high and Madison's war message to Congress cited impressment and British trade restrictions (the Orders in Council) as the major causes of war. The war vote in Congress was close. Studies of voting patterns by sections reveal no clear geographical alignments. States involved in the carrying trade opposed the war with England, while states producing farm goods for export favored war. The War of 1812 was largely a question of national honor, to show the world that the American experiment in republicanism would prevail, in the face of English doubts. Republicans feared that growing dissent at home would unnerve Americans and give power to the Federalist minority whom they accused of conspiracy to overthrow the republican form of government. It was necessary for Congress to stand firm, to declare war on England, and to put an end to foreign comments about the viability of American institutions. For its part, England would not concede on the Orders in Council until the very last minute and then too late. News of a British offer came after war had been declared.

In later years (1827) Madison said the war could have been avoided if the English had acted sooner. Congress was divided. But the Republican party rallied round and supported Madison in his stand of 1812. Certain party advantages were seen in having a war with England at this juncture, as a very frank letter from a Vermont Republican judge, Royall Tyler, explained in May 1812:

A declaration of war will confound the Federalists; . . . derange their present plans which are calculated only for political campaigns; introduce new topics of conversation; invite many Federalists into the army—and soldiers are always patriotic in time of war; it will relieve commerce from the embargo, and . . . break the mercantile phalanx; and above all it will place the opposition on slippery ground, and drive them to silence or rebellion. I do not fear the latter.

Tyler's letter was most shrewd, though some Federalists were driven into thoughts of rebellion. The Federalist group still identified their own rule with the national interest, while the Republicans identified their own party with republicanism in general.

War of 1812: National honor and independence

Whatever ideological, party, or economic motives pushed Americans into war, the English government left the U.S. the narrow choice of alternatives: submission to a form of quasi-colonial trade regulation or resistance. As John Quincy Adams observed:

In this question something besides dollars and cents is concerned. [We have] no alternative left but war, or the abandonment of our right as an independent nation.

As Andrew Jackson put it:

We are going to fight for the re-establishment of our national character.

For these reasons the War of 1812 has been termed the "Second War of Independence."

The United States of 1812, however, was unready to fight for anything very efficiently. The regular army of under 7,000 was eventually strengthened by the addition of state militia, but some state governments still refused to allow their troops to serve outside state borders. On the Niagara frontier in October 1812 the New York militia would not leave its state by crossing to the Canadian side of the river, and the regulars therefore lost the battle of Queenston Heights to the Canadians. This was a narrow view of states' rights and duties. Mean-

7 / The Agrarian Dream

Map 3. The War of 1812

The U.S.A.

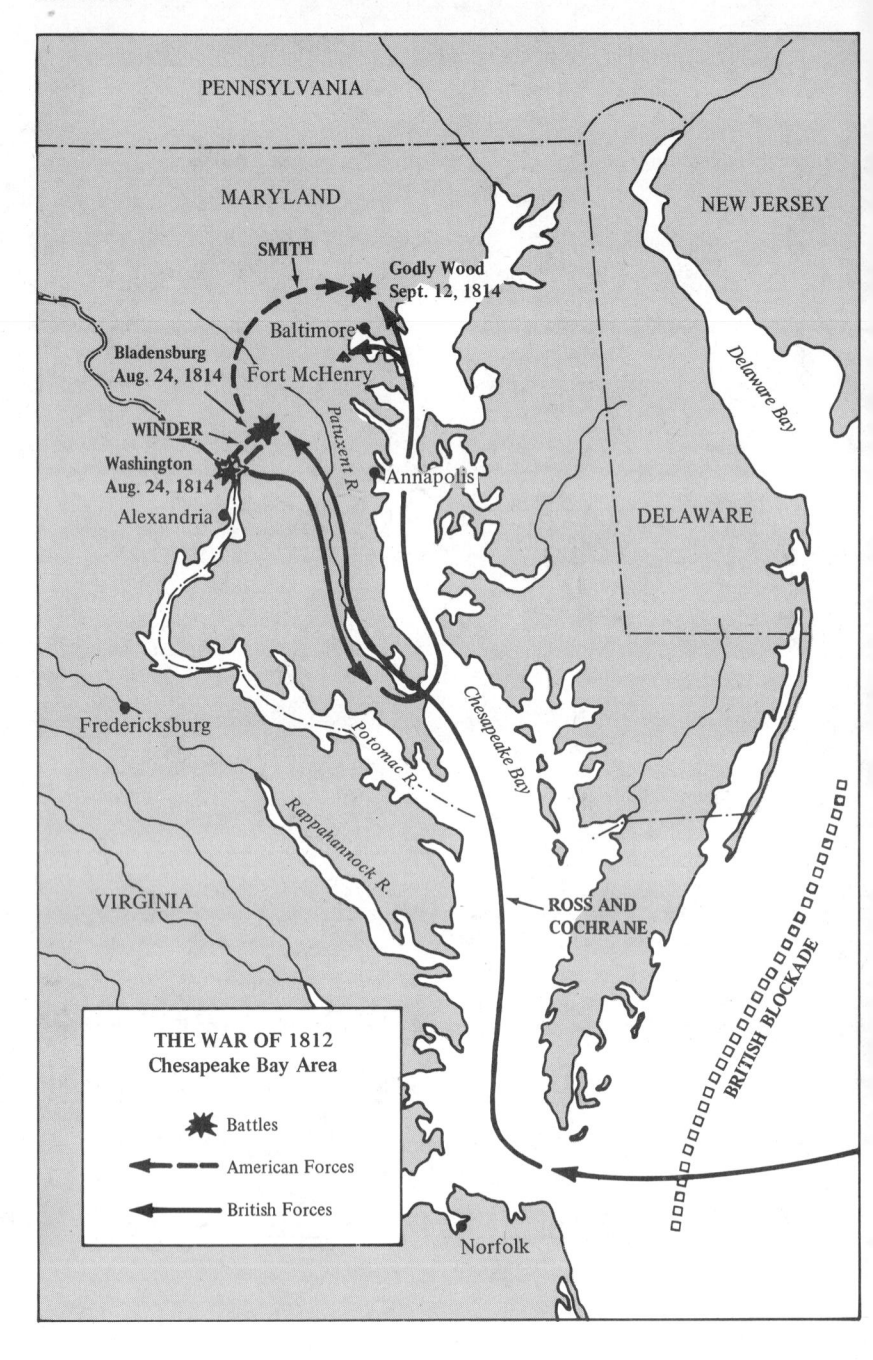

THE WAR OF 1812
Chesapeake Bay Area

- ✸ Battles
- ⟵ --- American Forces
- ⟵ British Forces

Locations shown: PENNSYLVANIA, MARYLAND, NEW JERSEY, DELAWARE, VIRGINIA; Baltimore, Fort McHenry, Annapolis, Washington, Alexandria, Fredericksburg, Norfolk; Delaware Bay, Chesapeake Bay, Patuxent R., Potomac R., Rappahannock R.

Battles:
- SMITH — Godly Wood, Sept. 12, 1814
- Bladensburg, Aug. 24, 1814
- WINDER — Washington, Aug. 24, 1814
- ROSS AND COCHRANE
- BRITISH BLOCKADE

7 / *The Agrarian Dream* 181

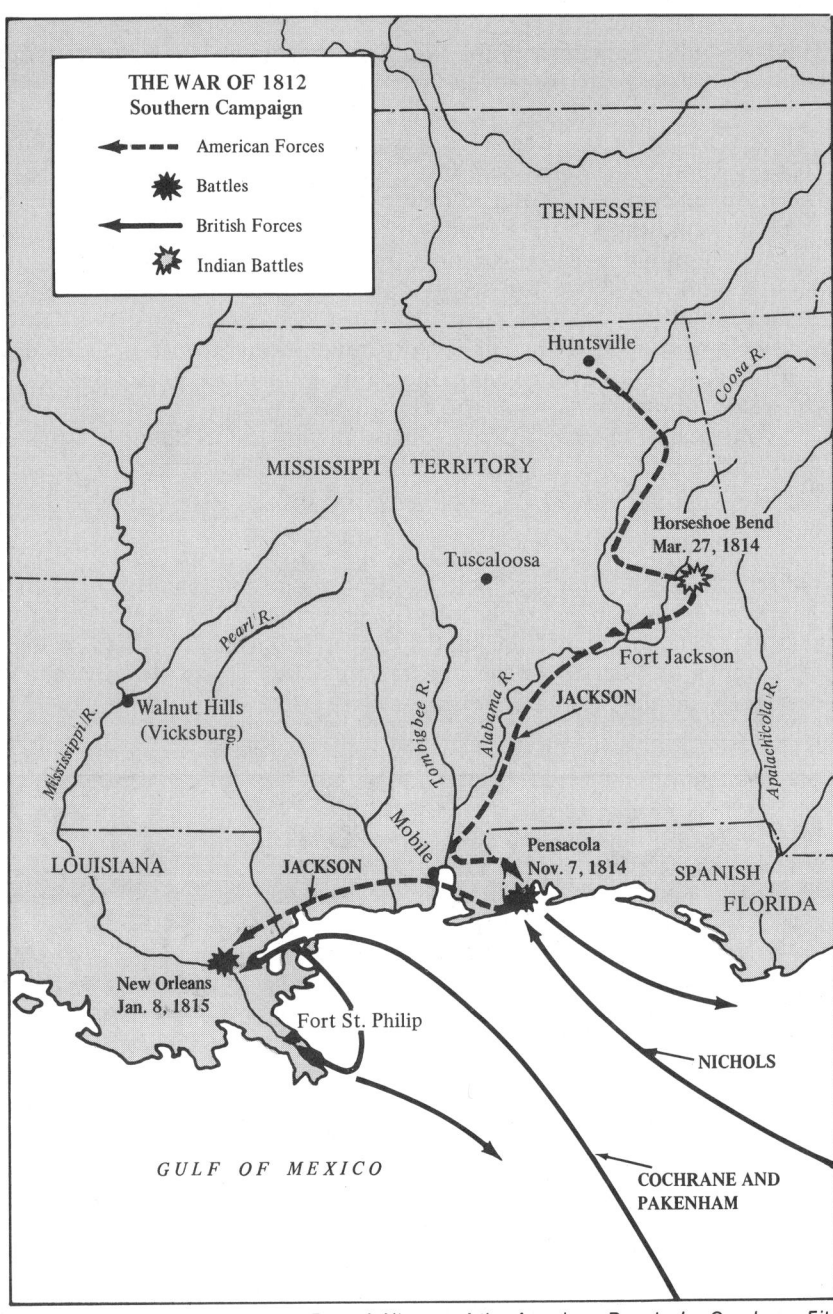

**THE WAR OF 1812
Southern Campaign**

- - - ← American Forces
✸ Battles
← British Forces
✸ Indian Battles

TENNESSEE

Huntsville

Coosa R.

MISSISSIPPI TERRITORY

Horseshoe Bend
Mar. 27, 1814

Tuscaloosa

Fort Jackson

Pearl R.

JACKSON

Walnut Hills
(Vicksburg)

Mississippi R.

Tombigbee R.

Alabama R.

Apalachicola R.

LOUISIANA

JACKSON

Mobile

Pensacola
Nov. 7, 1814

SPANISH
FLORIDA

New Orleans
Jan. 8, 1815

Fort St. Philip

NICHOLS

GULF OF MEXICO

COCHRANE AND
PAKENHAM

From *A History of the American People* by Graebner, Fite
& White. Copyright © 1970 by McGraw-Hill, Inc. Used
with permission of McGraw-Hill Book Company.

The U.S.A.

while, at the federal level, Congress made no efforts to appropriate funds to build up the navy, the War Department was inadequate, and most American generals proved incompetent until near the war's end. General William Hull, for example, surrendered Detroit with all its supplies intact to the Canadian hero, Isaac Brock, in August 1812. General Henry Dearborn led a large American army against Montreal but his own men forced him to turn back in the winter.

Such weaknesses were Canada's good luck, for the U.S. population of about 8 million outnumbered the Canadians of half a million, about 16 to 1, and only 5,000 British regulars were kept in Canada in 1812. Some Canadians did feel sympathy with the American cause. Two members of the legislature of Upper Canada fought on the U.S. side. But the vast bulk of Canadians, including even those "late Loyalists," the recent immigrants from the United States into Ontario, resented the Americans and struggled to maintain an independent existence for Canada. It has been a miracle of Canadian history that the nation has survived absorption by the expansive and powerful nation to its south.

Toward the end of the war the United States, with its control of Lakes Erie and Champlain, held the whip hand and could ravage the Niagara region and go freely into Upper Canada. The explosion of a powder magazine caused the deaths of over 100 Americans and incited U.S. troops to burn down the Parliament building and the governor's residence in the Canadian capital, York (Toronto), in 1813. The

The British burn Washington, D.C., 1814

Library of Congress

British later retaliated by burning parts of Washington, D.C. The war in the North was bloody. The conflict strengthened the resolve of those Canadians who wished to remain separate from the United States and damaged Canadian-American relations for some years to come.

The British-Canadian forces had fallen back in the Old Northwest region after W. H. Harrison's victory at the Battle of the Thames in Canada in 1813 and their loss of Indian support after Tecumseh's death. In the East, however, they controlled Maine and had been reinforced by 16,000 regulars in the summer of 1814. Their planned offensive to push down the Hudson Valley and divide the Americans was prevented. The Royal Navy maintained a successful blockade of the Atlantic coast. Individual exploits by courageous American ships, the U.S.S. *Constitution* defeating H.M.S. *Guerrière*, for example, did much to raise morale and add to the growing pantheon of American national heroes, but did not substantially affect the outcome of the war.

New England threatens: The Hartford Convention

Hatred for "Mr. Madison's War" was strong in parts of New England among Federalists and among merchant interests badly affected by the disruption of trade. In the presidential campaign of 1812 Madison was returned to office, but the Federalists threw their support to an insurgent Republican, De Witt Clinton, mayor of New York City and Lieutenant-Governor of the state, who captured all New England and the Middle states except for Vermont and Pennsylvania. In December 1814 a special convention met at Hartford, Connecticut, called by the state assemblies of Connecticut, Rhode Island, and Massachusetts, and by special state conventions in New Hampshire and Vermont. Their aim was to discuss revamping the Constitution.

This Hartford Convention demanded various constitutional amendments: to limit the presidency to one term, to nullify federal conscription laws, to create defense machinery independent of the federal government, to prohibit all embargoes of over 60 days' duration, to require a two thirds vote of both houses to declare war, to restrict the admission of new states, and some other sectional demands. The moderate Federalists kept control at Hartford so the threat of secession or disunion was never very serious; they headed it off. The ending of the war—the Peace of Ghent and Andrew Jackson's belated victory at New Orleans—made the recommendations of the Convention instantly redundant.

The Creek War, the Battle of New Orleans, and peace

Through his victory over the Shawnee at Tippecanoe in 1811, General W. H. Harrison assured his later election to the U.S. presidency (in 1840), but Harrison was outclassed as an Indian fighter by Andrew Jackson of Tennessee. When Tecumseh visited the Creeks in Alabama in 1811 and the Creeks subsequently rose on the southern frontier in 1813, Jackson had more than enough excuse to begin the process of eliminating the Indian tribes of Florida and the Southwest. Jackson's Tennessee militiamen fought several pitched battles and finally destroyed the Creek-Cherokee stronghold at Horseshoe Bend on the Tallapoosa River, in what became Alabama, in March 1814.

The Indians were forced to accept the Treaty of Fort Jackson. They agreed to vacate the Alabama region and to give up two thirds of all their ancestral lands in the Mississippi Territory. This region was opened up immediately to white settlement, much of it becoming cotton boom land. Jackson's conquests opened up the rich black soils of the Mississippi floodplains, greatly extending the life of slavery and the plantation system in the United States. Very rapidly the states of Mississippi and Alabama were admitted into the Union, following Louisiana. By the 1820s these three states were the very heart of the Cotton Kingdom.

Meanwhile, Andrew Jackson was victorious over the seasoned, but sickness-weakened British forces at the Battle of New Orleans, fought in January 1815, two weeks after the war had been officially ended by the peace signed at Ghent, Belgium, on Christmas Eve 1814. News of the treaty did not even reach New York until February 11th. The famous victory had no impact on the peace terms, but it did add to Jackson's personal legend. He went on to defeat the Seminoles in Florida (1816–18) and then brashly occupied Florida, ignoring Spain's feelings in the matter. When the U.S. bought Florida, Jackson became its first governor (1821). The way was now open for his election to the U.S. presidency in 1828.

The treaty of Ghent made no mention of maritime rights, the alleged major cause of the war. With the termination of the war among the European powers in the spring of 1815 the question of neutral trading rights became irrelevant. They did not reappear as a cause of international unrest until the American Civil War. Instead of maritime rights the treaty dealt with boundary issues and fishing rights. All conquered territories were to be restored. Commissions were to be created to handle Canadian-U.S. boundary matters though the questions of the Oregon boundary and military power on the Great Lakes were left alone. The document did not mention impressment, search and seizure, or indemnities, but the Senate accepted it immediately and unanimously. This had been an unpopular war.

American nationalism in the saddle

Despite American mismanagement the War of 1812 was a psychological victory for frontier nationalists and for the new generation of Jeffersonian Republicans like Andrew Jackson. It produced a sort of isolationism in America: an attitude of leaving Europe's affairs behind (let the British tangle with them), and committing Americans to the development of the Western Hemisphere. The outbreak of the wars of independence in Latin America brought forth the Monroe Doctrine of 1823. This said, in effect, "Hands off America!" while the steady, steamroller drive for internal empire crushed the Indians in its path, smothered the moral issue of black slavery, and accelerated the economic revolution which Americans universally hailed as Progress.

Expansive nationalism was in the saddle.

Bibliography

Marshall Smelser. *The Democratic Republic, 1801–15.* New York: Harper, 1960.

Merrill D. Peterson. *Thomas Jefferson and the New Nation.* New York: Oxford University Press, 1970.

Bernard De Voto. *The Course of Empire.* Boston: Houghton Mifflin, 1964.

R. Horsman. *Causes of the War of 1812.* New York: Barnes, 1970.

I. Brant. *James Madison and American Nationalism.* Princeton: Van Nostrand, 1968. (A very brief introduction; for more details see Brant's *The Fourth President,* Indianapolis: Bobbs Merrill, 1970.)

8

The pursuit of happiness

Material growth of the nation . . . expansion of the market economy . . . sources of economic expansion . . . the man–land ratio . . . scarcity of capital . . . the Transportation Revolution . . . the first toll roads . . . canal mania . . . benefits and disadvantages of canals . . . the steamboat age . . . rails and steam: the iron horse . . . public enterprise and private profit: Aid to railroads . . . benefits of the railroads . . . Americans in foreign trade . . . American merchant seamen . . . Yankee clippers . . . a loss of momentum . . . revolution in manufactures . . . Samuel Slater's first mill . . . Lowell's "Boston Associates" . . . why did not the South industrialize? . . . spread of new industrial techniques . . . heavy industry: coal and iron . . . variety of small industries . . . the "American system of manufacture": mechanization . . . revolution in agriculture . . . commercial farming in the Old Northwest . . . scientific agriculture . . . farm processing plants . . . the Cotton Kingdom . . . plantation slavery . . . life of the slave . . . slave breeding . . . did slavery pay? . . . long-term retardation of the Southern economy caused by slavery . . . the noncotton South . . . the growth of economic sections . . . the "happiness of pursuit."

Material growth of the nation For most Americans the phrase "pursuit of happiness" meant the rapid material growth of the nation. The earlier Jeffersonians had questioned the commercial values of Hamilton. They shared his passion for American economic growth but viewed it more narrowly in terms of frontiers and farms. After the 1812 war, the *economic revolution* came to the United States and did not limit itself to the expansion of farming or to the values of the Agrarian Dream.

In personal terms, the pursuit of happiness meant the pursuit of individual independence and the winning of a degree of material comfort and security for American families, based on the ownership of land and of private property. Thus a down-to-earth, healthy materialism suffused the culture and was taken entirely for granted by Americans of different classes and opinions. Government was seen as a device to secure this material well-being and happiness, and its job was to promote economic growth.

Expansion of the market economy

No economic revolution is possible when the market sector is small, and the typical person is a farmer or frontiersman, a jack-of-all-trades who makes his own clothes, mends his own tools, and grows his own foods. For many years, even down to the Civil War, a large, though decreasing, number of Americans remained outside the market economy: they did not produce a marketable surplus, at least not regularly. They worked merely to subsist and stay alive, not to sell their products to others. These subsistence families, scattered geographically, provided no basis for a breakthrough in economic growth.

People will not abandon subsistence production, and begin to *specialize* in making one or two products for sale unless there is some assurance of a market for their work. As Adam Smith said in 1776: "Division of labor is limited by the extent of the market." That is, economic growth depends upon specialization in production for the market (division of labor), which depends in turn on how large the market is itself. In the 18th century Paul Revere could make a decent living in the town of Boston; he would have starved on the frontier if he had remained an engraver and silversmith. The size and nature of the market in turn depends upon two factors: (1) the *population*—is it scattered or concentrated in towns? and (2) *transportation*—how soon and how reliably can goods be shipped? If there is no concentrated market or town, transportation can virtually create a market. For example, the mail-order business was developed by ingenious Americans in the late 19th century to sell products to scattered farm families by use of the improved U.S. mail system and a large catalog of products (Montgomery Ward, 1872). In the antebellum years, the Transportation Revolution—turnpike highways, canals, and railroads—helped to create markets and to link the farmer with the town. Improved transportation and the growth of towns are essential to the extension of the market.

Already in the early 19th century, *regional differences* related to these factors began to appear. The plantation and farming South and Southwest developed fewer towns and poorer transportation than the Middle Atlantic states, the Northeast, and Midwest. The South became a "colonial" region: it produced one or two crops for export (via Northern factors), but saw little economic development itself. The market economy did not grow appreciably in the South, while in the Ohio country, as we have observed, frontier cities sprang up, and in the Northeast the beginnings of industrialization were seen in New England. The Old Northwest developed a *commercial agriculture*, selling meat and grains to the South and East; but not all the profits were drained off—money was plowed back into the Midwest region and put into canals, railroads, and city growth. This happened far less in the South.

Sources of economic expansion

Different sectors of an economy grow at different periods. The chief source of early U.S. growth was the income derived from foreign trade. By the mid-19th century the source of growth was the home market. Foreign trade rarely rose to more than 7 percent of national output; the U.S. economy became remarkably autonomous and self-sufficient, though trade was useful in providing the means of foreign exchange. Colonial and early national America, however, was heavily dependent on foreign trade. The economic recession partly caused by Jefferson's Embargo of 1807 forced some American investors to shift capital out of trade and into home manufactures—cotton mills, for example—and began a premature industrialization movement at home. This trend relapsed with the influx of British goods after the peace of 1814.

The twin bases for U.S. development were human resources and physical resources, a growing population and vast virgin lands.

The man–land ratio

Alexis de Tocqueville, the French political analyst, was stunned by the natural wealth of the American West. In 1835 he wrote of the "inexhaustible fertility" of the Mississippi Valley, that "most magnificent dwelling-place prepared by God for man's abode." The rich continent "seemed prepared to be the abode of a great nation yet unborn" even in pre-colonial days. Americans have certainly been fortunate compared with some nations in the richness of their resources. But natural wealth may remain untapped for centuries, as it did in the New World. Resources must be developed and drawn into an economic system. This takes labor and social organization. The rate of development depends upon the man–land ratio. Too large a population and too few resources, e.g., 19th-century Ireland, spell disaster. Too small a population to develop natural resources, e.g., for a long time, Canada, spells retardation. One cannot give a mathematical figure for an optimum man–land ratio, because of the variety of historical and geographical circumstances. For example, the *level of technology* affects the ratio; some resources, like uranium, or oil, or aluminum, remain outside the market for centuries until technical advances create a demand for their exploitation. So the man–land ratio is never fixed; it is dynamic. If oil had been struck in mid-19th-century Ireland, that country's man–land ratio and its entire economic and social history would have been totally transformed.

The man–land ratio is a relationship between two of the three classical "factors of production," resources, labor, and capital. In antebellum America, two of these three factors were always relatively scarce—labor and capital; one was always abundant—land. The relative scarcity of labor in the United States is said to have kept the nation as a *high-wage economy*, for those who worked for wages. Labor scarcity also encouraged the invention of a host of labor-saving devices and stimulated the very early application of technology in the United States. Technical advances come slowly in nations that have masses of cheap peasant labor (e.g., India). American "know how" and mechanical ingenuity, which was already renowned by 1850, was to a great degree the child of necessity.

In colonial America economic growth, and certainly the growth of towns, was probably *retarded* by the abundance of resources and land and the relative shortage of labor. In contrast with French Canada the

American population was far from scarce and its early reproduction rate was high. It is no accident, however, that large-scale economic growth came to the United States in the 1830s and 1840s with large-scale emigration from Europe. The technical roots of modernization go back at least to the 1790s; the political roots, to the free-trade market created by Article I, Section 9, of the federal constitution; the psychological and social roots, to the impact of national independence and the natural growth-rate of the native population. But the economic revolution after about 1830 was associated with immigration and the transportation revolution. The peopling of the United States began in earnest at that time.

The young nation also lacked capital in the sense of man-made physical resources—tools, machinery, plant, and buildings—and in the plain sense of money. Financial resources of all sorts—currency, bills and notes, stocks and bonds, and all forms of credit—were very scarce in early America. An economy needs more credit forms and money as it expands, but the traditional attitude of rural Americans toward banks and finance did not encourage the development of efficient financial institutions to provide the necessary credit for growth.

Scarcity of capital

Throughout colonial history there was a chronic shortage of currency and the British restricted export of specie to America. Local assemblies printed paper money from time to time, with inflationary effect. Frontier farmers and other debtors in the colonies liked paper money, because it depreciated in value, and over time they would be paying back less in real value than they had borrowed. Creditor merchants opposed paper issues and were against any other inflationary measures that would erode the value of the loans they had made. This was the root cause of the monetary struggle which reverberated through the 19th century and climaxed in the 1890s.

For physical capital (consumer goods and capital goods) the young nation was dependent on England, as it was in colonial days. Only gradually were the necessary skills and industries built up for the home manufacture of the many tools and aids needed in clearing the wilderness, commercializing farming, and constructing the towns. For one example, as late as the 1850s the United States was still importing the rails it used for railroad track. Heavy foreign investment, mainly English, helped to develop the early canals and railroads, and as late as the 1880s the range cattle industry was dependent on British investors. It was this scarcity of capital of both sorts, physical and financial, that brought *government intervention* in the American economy at local, state, and federal levels, with land grants and stock purchases to encourage private venture capital and to promote economic development.

In the early years however, labor scarcity was more crucial than capital scarcity. The initial stages of development of any frontier nation are labor-intensive. The acts of clearing and settling and the labor of pre-mechanized farming take brawn and sweat more than capital. An undeveloped economy, and early America was more of an *unde-*

veloped economy than an *under*developed one, requires a heavy input of gross labor, before it is even prepared to assimilate inputs of capital investment and technology. The need for labor was greater than the need for capital. This situation underscores once more the early readiness of Americans to adopt labor-saving devices and mechanization, and their dependence on the immigration of fresh citizens of working age from abroad. It also underlines the true extent of the contribution made by the labor of enslaved Africans to American material growth, and the toll of masses of Irish, German, and other European immigrants of the pre–Civil War years. Black and white, theirs is the human story of economic growth.

The Transportation Revolution

Foreign exports played a strategic role down to 1860; America's wealth was first generated in the holds of Yankee merchant vessels. But the home market expanded even more dramatically than did foreign trade, due to population growth (in absolute size and in urban concentration) through natural increase and immigration, and due to the building of an efficient transportation network linking the regions. While the United States of 1790 was a small, divided group of ex-colonies with a population of under 4 million and a doubtful economic future, that of 1860 was already a major economic power. Its industrial techniques won the admiration of the British, its exports were vital to world trade and its people had multiplied eight-fold to well over 31 millions.

Pioneer Americans were restricted in travel to waterways and to crude "traces," or trails. They penetrated slowly to the interior along the lines of navigable streams and used the most-frequented and safest overland routes. Trails were essential to frontier life. Rough dirt tracks linked eastern settlements while longer exploratory western traces had been pioneered since the late 18th century.

Daniel Boone's "Wilderness Road" passed over the mountains into the lush bluegrass lands of Kentucky in 1775 by way of the Cumberland Gap, a pass through the Appalachian barrier at the southwest point of the present state of Virginia, where it meets Tennessee and Kentucky. The spot is now a National Park. Another long trail went to the Mississippi at Memphis, the "Bluff City," by way of Nashville, Tennessee. Two trails ventured into the Far West to the picturesque border town of Santa Fe, New Mexico, just beyond the Sangre de Cristo range of the Rockies. One, an old Spanish route, linked St. Augustine, Florida, on the Atlantic coast all the way to Santa Fe. A second joined the town of Independence, Missouri, to Santa Fe, going by way of Kansas and the Great Plains. This trace, developed by the U.S. Army in 1825, was commonly known as the Sante Fe Trail and was used by stagecoaches until replaced by rail connections in the 1870s. Meanwhile the Northeast was connected by trails from the Hudson Valley in New York up to Lake Erie and to Lakes George and Champlain and then by way of the Hudson-Mohawk valleys to Lake Ontario, using stream and portage.

The first toll roads

The American invasion of Canada during the War of Independence used the Lake Champlain route, but military campaigns during the War of 1812 revealed the poor conditions of American roads, stimulating the entrepreneurs to create joint-stock companies to build "turnpike" highways. Turnpikes, modeled on English examples, recouped their high costs by charging tolls. The first was built in Pennsylvania, 1792–94, from Philadelphia to Lancaster. Its 62 miles cost about $465,000. This *Lancaster Pike* made good profits because it was vastly superior to existing roads and people were willing to pay. The Pike had a good gravel surface on a firm stone foundation and was well located in a populated, growing region. Not all turnpikes did well during the 30-year flurry of building which ensued, though state governments hastily intervened and issued hundreds of charters promising the construction of thousands of miles of roads.

New York State alone, keen not to be outrivaled in the rush to the West, claimed 135 trust companies by 1811. These managed to complete building 1,500 miles of toll highways. Pennsylvania's 86 chartered trusts constructed 2,200 miles. The movement stimulated bridge design, new construction and engineering techniques, business organization, and large-scale financing. It brought together state legislatures and private businessmen in an association which was to remain typically American.

What about the role of the federal government? The first significant "internal improvement" at the federal level was the work financed on the *Cumberland Road,* authorized by Jefferson's second administration in 1806 but not actually begun until 1811. The plan was to connect Cumberland, Maryland, with the Ohio River, and thus to open up the Ohio region and the upper Mississippi with a good highway. This federal road did not fulfill its goal of reaching St. Louis. By 1838, after 30 or so acts of Congress, a failed attempt to impose tolls, and the spending of about $7 million, the "National Road" stretched as far as Vandalia, Illinois—a bare 50 or 60 miles from the Mississippi at St. Louis.

In spite of heavy political opposition from strict-constructionists, the National Road brought economic prosperity and local growth along the length of its 834 miles of all—weather surface. It cut the time of travel from Baltimore to the Ohio River at Wheeling from eight days to three. It became a chief artery to the West and the Ohio country. With the coming of canals and passenger railroads the importance of the National Road declined, though a later federal highway followed its trail in the 20th century.

The decline of the turnpikes set in before the advent of real competition from railroads, because the trusts only averaged profits of 2 or 3 percent on investment. The pikes, moreover, could not provide a cheap enough method of *long-distance* transport for very bulky or perishable goods. Cargoes with low value to bulk ratios found the canals more feasible, while perishables could depend on the faster railroads. People tried various means to evade payment of tolls; they even built "shun-pikes" around tollgate areas. Meanwhile, a short-lived boom of *plank roads* took place. The idea of using timber surfacing, copied from Russia and Canada, apparently was first adopted in New York State in 1844. Plank roads proved useful for short-distance uses in heavily settled regions where timber was plentiful and cheaper than stone and gravel. They did not last well, on average about seven years. As late as a road census of 1904 some plank roads were still in use, but in general they died out after the 1850s.

The canal mania

The turnpike era was followed and overlapped by the years of canal mania which peaked before 1850. The outstanding technical achievement was the construction of the Erie Canal by the state of New York. From 1777 onward, proposals were heard to join the Hudson River to the Great Lakes by water and to create a vast water highway to the Midwest of the continent—a new "Northwest Passage." But nothing was done until 1817, despite the example of the British canal mania of the 1790s. In 1817, when the New York legislature sanctioned the building of a Hudson-Erie canal, the scheme was subscribed by British investors. The canal was completed by 1825—360 miles at a cost of over $7 million. Tolls collected as the canal was being finished had already exceeded interest charges on the original loans. The Erie Canal

The Erie Canal

New York Public Library

was a magnificent economic success. Tolls were not removed until 1882 by which time the state had collected about $120 million in revenues. The canal stretched from Albany to Buffalo. It turned New York City into one of the world's greatest ports, serving the massive hinterland of the Midwest. Branch lines brought local prosperity, boosted towns, and encouraged migration and settlement.

"The success of the Erie Canal," said H. V. Poor's *Railroad Manual* (1868), "had an electric effect upon the whole country, and similar works were everywhere projected." A canal mania broke out, which became highly speculative and evaporated in the crash of 1837. The Erie Canal cut travel time from New York to Buffalo from 20 days to 6 and reduced costs from $100 to $5 per freight ton. New York state farmland doubled in value as the western half of the state came into effective contact with the port of New York. Manhattan itself doubled its population in the decade 1820–30 and came to dominate the Eastern seaboard, outrivaling Philadelphia. Despite railroad competition, especially in long-haul traffic, freight tonnage on the Erie Canal continued to increase to its peak year of 1880. "Clinton's Big Ditch," as the canal was nicknamed after Governor De Witt Clinton, brought a huge return on a daring investment by the state government, in the teeth of political opposition and engineering hazards.

Cities and states in the East competed frenetically. Pennsylvania, Maryland, and Massachusetts, anxious about the status of their great ports, Philadelphia, Baltimore, and Boston, hastened to charter trunkline canals. Massachusetts failed to build a waterway to the Hudson and never did manage to divert trade and traffic from New York to Boston. Pennsylvania built a canal from Philadelphia to Pittsburgh at a cost of about $10 million (1806–34). Maryland, in spite of aid from her sister state, Virginia, did not complete a canal along the Potomac that was supposed to connect Baltimore with the Ohio River. The state spent $11 million between 1828 and 1850 but the canal never crossed the mountains beyond the town of Cumberland. In its rush, Maryland competed with itself: the Baltimore and Ohio Railroad (first rail contact with the West) was begun in 1828 with state aid.

The nation's longest canal, over 450 miles, was built in the Midwest: the Wabash and Erie (1832–43), which spanned the state of Indiana diagonally, joining the southwest tip (Evansville, on the Ohio River) with Lake Erie at Toledo, Ohio. Meanwhile, the Illinois River was connected by water to Lake Michigan and to the upper Mississippi River system at the Iowa border. The canal mania of the 1830s and 40s thus linked up the Great Lakes–Mississippi–Ohio waterways and joined the lakes to the Hudson. Built chiefly as *public* schemes (they were very expensive to dig and build), the canals were not private enterprise in any real meaning of that phrase, but a form of "social overhead capital" (or "infrastructure," as economists now say), which private capital funds could not have covered. The incessant pressure of an expanding society kept pushing the canals outward, though the railroads were close on their heels.

Benefits and disadvantages of canals

Canal mileage thus grew from nothing to 1,270 miles (1830), doubled to 3,320 miles (1840), and then slackened in growth rate to a total of 3,700 miles (1850). Superior to the mule train and wagon for the transportation of heavy, bulky, massive cargoes like grain, ore, and flour, the canals were less useful for passenger traffic, though immigrants often had no other alternative. A frightful description of such a canal trip taken by Andrew Carnegie and his family in 1848 can be found in his *Autobiography*. The journey from New York to Pittsburgh in pre-railroad days took three weeks, via the Hudson River, the Erie Canal to Cleveland, then by canal to Beaver, and by steamboat up the Ohio to Pittsburgh! The family was almost eaten alive by mosquitoes. Canals, like later railroads, not only transported goods more efficiently and cheaper than by road; they often created traffic where none existed before. The state canal that linked Cincinnati to Toledo, for one example, shipped 3 million bushels of grain and 125,000 barrels of pork in its first year of operation (1845)—though neither pork nor grain traffic had previously existed in this section of the state. Canal ventures thus opened up former wilderness, forests, mines, farmlands, stimulated production, diverted existing trade into new channels, increased its flow, and created new markets.

It has been suggested that the railroads were premature and not entirely necessary to American economic growth and that they pushed out the canals too soon. Could canals have done the job of the railroads? Canal traffic is slow and cumbersome, very subject to changes in the weather, especially to snow and ice, which is heavy throughout that New York–Midwest region for several months of each year. Moreover, while it is impossible to measure the social and economic gain brought by fast passenger traffic on railroads, such gains must include more effective business organization and management and labor mobility. Canal companies often overbuilt; they stimulated the financial crash of 1837 in which many states reneged on foreign debts and some disavowed further public investments.

With canals, as with turnpike highways, regional differences were marked. Few of either were built in the South in comparison with the Northeast, Midwest, and Middle Atlantic states. The Northeast dominated in toll roads as in canal-building (few turnpikes were ever built in the Midwest). The Upper South (Maryland) finished about 300 miles of toll highway by 1830; Virginia and South Carolina accomplished some building. The Deep South, reflecting its dispersed plantation system, its skewed income distribution with a few persons holding most of the disposable wealth, and its low degree of urbanization, paid little attention either to toll roads or to canals.

The steamboat age

Travel by animal-drawn canal boat was slow. But as early as 1807 the steam revolution hit the river trade, when Robert Fulton first took out his *Clermont* on the Hudson river. Fulton was an all-around inventor and publicist of the canal age. After 20 years abroad, where he designed an early submarine, the *Nautilus* in 1801, he returned to the United States and built the *Clermont,* with financial help from

Jefferson's ambassador to France, Robert R. Livingston. The boat was described by an observer as a "backwoods sawmill mounted on a scow and set on fire"; its sidepaddle wheels were driven by a steam engine made by Fulton's British friend, James Watt. The steamboat combined various ideas of previous pioneers, including John Fitch, whose *Thornton* provided regular service on the Delaware River for some time after 1790. Nevertheless, successful commercial steam navigation really began with Fulton's triumph of 1807.

By the end of the 1812–14 war steamboats were common on eastern rivers and had attempted the trip from Pittsburgh to New Orleans. By the 1850s the *upstream* journey from New Orleans to Louisville was reduced to five days. The famous race of 1870 saw the *Robert E. Lee* beat the *Natchez* by steaming from New Orleans to St. Louis in 3 days, 18½ hours. Meanwhile, the cost of fares fell as much as 75 percent, and by 1850 about 600 steamboats were in use on the western river system, serving frontier cities. Many were over 300 feet long, and carried 400 passengers. After the gold discoveries of the 1840s and 50s steamboats appeared on California and Oregon rivers. Some of these incredible, top-heavy, narrow-hulled boats actually rounded Cape Horn to reach the Far West, belching smoke and sparks all the way.

Government aid to steamboats was small—unlike the promotional activity devoted to canal and railroad construction and to turnpike highways. Steamboat companies did not receive land grants, and (except in Georgia) governments did not buy their stock. Government engineers though, did improve river navigation and in 1850 the federal Steamboat Act was passed to regulate traffic. Steamboats were doomed once the railroads established good *through* routings, though at first the need for river connections between rail points had stimulated more steamboat navigation. Steamboats survived on lakes and across harbors (e.g., Lakes Erie and Michigan and Long Island Sound). The railroad gave better speed, more direct routes and all-year-round travel, little affected by seasons and weather.

Rails and steam: The iron horse

Americans took up the British example of railroad-building much faster than they had adopted canals. From the early 1830s onward the rail network began to spread in the East. In the words of the Southern economic writer, T. P. Kettell:

The excitement in relation to canals and steamboats was yet at its zenith, when the air began to be filled with rumor of the new application of steam to land carriages and to railroads. . . . In 1825 descriptions came across the water of the great success of the Darlington Railroad, which was opened to supply London with coal, and which had passenger cars moved by steam at the rate of seven miles per hour.

Seven miles per hour! This was a revolutionary speed. Even before the famous Stockton-Darlington line had been completed in England, several native American experiments had taken place. As early as 1804 Oliver Evans proposed steam wagons for use on the Lancaster turnpike. He promised that they could carry 100 barrels of flour at 3 miles an hour, but he was rejected. The success of the Darlington line in England and of the Rainhill Trials of 1829 in Lancaster were a great encouragement to American entrepreneurs. "The most animated controversy sprang up," wrote Kettell, ". . . [and] with the national energy of character, the idea had no sooner become disseminated than it was acted upon."

The first engine to operate on a commercial track in the United States was British-made, the *Stourbridge Lion*. It was too heavy for American needs, as were most British engines imported at that time. The first commercial railroad, the Baltimore and Ohio, used a lighter U.S. engine designed by Peter Cooper, the *Tom Thumb*, in 1830. Meanwhile, Americans continued to experiment with horse traction and even with sails. The South remained relatively backward in transportation matters compared with the North and the Midwest, but state governments there did promote railroads; in fact the second commercial line in the U.S. was built to connect the port of Charleston, South Carolina, with the Savannah River. The idea was to cut off the port of Savannah, Georgia, with this line and divert the rich cotton traffic to Charleston. The Charleston and Hamburg Railroad claimed to be the longest in the world in 1833 (136 miles), though it was soon outstripped.

Intercity and interstate rivalry helped to pattern the railroad growth of the North, as it had patterned canal construction. Massachusetts rapidly chartered three railroads to fan out from Boston in 1831; ten years later that city had a through rail connection with the Hudson River and the rich Great Lakes trade—something it had not achieved by canal. In the 1830s Pennsylvania also gained advantage by starting four railroads, which went in all directions from Philadelphia. The city was connected to Trenton, Reading, and then to Baltimore. By 1840 all the eastern states had considerable mileage except Maine, and most major cities were connected; railroad mileage equaled canal mileage. Ten years later, the Appalachian barrier had been crossed by iron tracks. Total rail mileage was 3 times as large: about 9,000 miles.

The first through rail connection to the Great Lakes was made in 1850 by the New York Central. Chicago was linked to New York three years later and St. Louis in 1855. The great Mississippi was bridged in 1855. In the 1850s, New Orleans was joined to Chicago, and Memphis was linked to the Atlantic coast of Virginia. The question now was: How soon would the iron horse reach the far Pacific coast and link together the two great oceans?

Congress would have to agree before such a vast railroad construction scheme could be undertaken. Its capital cost was far beyond the means of any private enterprise company. Initial investment would be very heavy before any profits would result. Since the 1820s Americans had dreamed of a great transcontinental railroad spanning the nation, though at this date, much of the West was still officially Mexican. Politicians divided on sectional lines and argued constitutional issues, while cities and states fought each other in desperate rivalry for a share in the projected lines and in the rich future traffic. Three towns on the edge of the settled frontier—Chicago, St. Louis, and Memphis—all claimed the right to a transcontinental rail terminal. Whichever won would experience great real estate growth and population expansion.

In 1855 a railway had been built across the Isthmus of Panama, to expedite traffic to the Pacific coast without making the long and perilous sea journey around Cape Horn. The secession of the South and the coming of the Civil War strengthened the new Republican party, which immediately pushed ahead many pro-capitalist, economic growth measures, including the federally aided transcontinental railroad.

Public enterprise and private profit: Aid to railroads

Secretary of the Treasury Albert Gallatin suggested a comprehensive development plan as early as 1808. He said that growth would be retarded by lack of adequate capital and by an unfavorable man–land ratio ("the extent of territory compared with the population," as he put it). Only the "General Government" could avoid these obstacles to growth. In the case of railroads, the U.S. federal government stepped in massively in 1850. In the 1830s private funds initiated many railroad schemes; in particular, British investors funded loans at fairly high rates of interest to build American railroads. Individual state governments gave charters which allowed wide privileges to railroad companies and imposed few restrictions on fares or service. Some states overcame traditional American fears of private monopoly and privilege and granted outright monopoly rights to certain lines. Among them were Georgia, South Carolina, Louisiana, Kentucky, New Jersey, and Massachusetts. One example, the Camden and Amboy Railroad, was allowed the exclusive right to provide rail transportation between Philadelphia and New York. City and state rivalries and the scramble for profit and progress led to tax exemptions, free grants of rights-of-way, and other privileges being donated to railroad promoters.

Individual states gave outright financial aid to private rail corporations. Public tax money was spent by towns, county governments, and states to buy railroad securities. States were indebted to railroads by $43 million in 1838, the year after the crash of 1837 in which several states had failed to repay their debts to foreign bondholders. Local aid probably exceeded the states' total. In the antebellum South railroad investments reached $144 million, an estimated 95 percent of which (1861) was derived from state and local governments. In addition, the states gave away millions of acres of public land; Texas alone donated 5 million acres to encourage railroad builders.

Before the act of 1850 the federal government promoted railroads mainly through tariff aids and having the U.S. Army engineers survey and map land. They even directed the construction of some lines, free. Congress wiped out tariffs on imported British rails and other necessities (1830–43). Then in 1850 Gallatin's original idea of large federal land grants from the public domain became a reality. An alliance in Congress of Western and Southern members produced this act to create a north-south rail link down the Mississippi Valley, linking

Chicago to Mobile, Alabama. The 1850 act gave federal land to the states of Illinois, Alabama, and Mississippi, which were then to give it to the railroad corporations in strips six miles wide on each side of the proposed track in alternate sections. The firms could sell the land or sell bonds secured by mortgage on the land. By using the states as intermediaries the federal government sidestepped tricky questions of constitutionality over its role in the economy.

This first massive federal grant, almost 4 million acres, eventually became part of the Illinois Central and the Mobile and Ohio Railroads. The companies agreed to transport federal troops and property without charge and Congress was to fix mail rates. Following this precedent Congress had doled out about 18 million acres to 45 firms, using 10 states as intermediaries by 1857. After the Civil War federal grants dwarfed these figures. Railroading became a form of "public enterprise for private profit."

Americans in foreign trade

International trade brought in foreign exchange and made it possible to import goods while the Transportation Revolution metamorphosed the economy. Cotton was the chief component of trade from the War of 1812 to the Civil War. Down to the Panic of 1819 southern cotton was a third of total U.S. exports; in the 1830s it rose to two thirds; it remained over half until 1861. Traditional U.S. exports to Europe—tobacco, rice, naval stores, lumber, and fish—declined as a proportion of foreign trade. Grain and flour from the Middle Atlantic states, about one tenth of exports down to 1820, declined altogether for a while.

The economic growth of the post-1814 years through the 1830s was supported by rising prices for American cotton based on growing British industrial demand. Even during the boom years of the 1850s, where many other elements were involved such as the industrial revolution in New England, gold discoveries in the Far West, waves of immigration, and the westward movement, the rising statistics of cotton output and cotton exports were the best guide to the general well-being of the U.S. economy.

Where did American exports go? About half of them went to Britain as that nation underwent its industrial revolution in the first half of the 19th century. Other nations were slower to industrialize; France took about one sixth of U.S. exports. The West Indies, no longer an important U.S. outlet as they had been in the past, bought a steadily falling proportion. Eli Whitney's cotton gin, patented in 1794, was perfectly timed: It increased the output of cleaned cotton on Southern plantations precisely when the demand for cotton in England was about to increase enormously due to technical changes in spinning and weaving. The cotton textiles of Lancashire became the key growth industry of the English industrial revolution and the key export staple of the United States became raw cotton. The two were heavily interdependent until the Civil War and beyond. The cotton trade formed a pillar of an emerging Atlantic Economy. In this *international economy* large-scale migration of factors of production—labor, capital, and knowledge—took place from the 1840s on.

The depression after the Crash of 1819 reduced foreign trade in the 1820s. The major wealth-producing changes of those years took place internally, such as the completion of the Erie Canal and the success of the steamboat, which boosted the growth of two major ports, New York and New Orleans. The recovery of foreign trade was slow to about 1830. Then followed a seven-year trade boom.

American merchant seamen

Foreign trade expansion of the 1830s, the result of a general growth of U.S. population and of productivity, was boosted by tariff cuts, international trading agreements, and a growing domestic surplus of foodstuffs turned out by American farmers. The trade boom ended in the crash of 1837—an international breakdown of the Atlantic economy.

At the peak, U.S. imports had mounted to $129 million and exports to $190 million. Within three years trade recovered again, though total figures fluctuated until about 1846. In that year famine broke out in Ireland, where the potato crop, the main source of food, failed. The British government increased its demand for imported American grain to save the Irish from starvation. Sir Robert Peel, the Prime Minister and a free-trader by conviction, abolished the infamous "Corn Law" of 1815 which had taxed imported grain. Nonetheless many Irish starved; thousands emigrated to the U.S. Those who stayed and survived did so with the aid of American grain.

Meanwhile, world events also spurred U.S. commerce. Gold discoveries in Australia, Colorado, and California coincided with falling U.S. tariff barriers. Innovations appeared in ocean transportation. So the 1840s saw an abnormally high construction of American ships to meet growing trade demands. The steamship arrived, and regular steam services brought New York nearer to Liverpool and to northern Europe. Steamships were not fully competitive with sail on the Atlantic routes however until the 1850s and 60s.

The regular transatlantic "packet" lines took 30 or 40 days to reach Britain in the era before steam. For very special trade, specifically the movement of tea, Americans designed the famous clipper ships. These beautiful, three-masted, narrow-hulled ships were much faster than packets or steamships. Six times as long as they were broad, with concave, racing sides and a tremendous height and spread of sail, the Yankee clippers could not carry a very large payload. Too expensive for any ordinary cargoes, they could be made to pay only with cargoes of high value in relation to bulk. Donald McKay's *Flying Cloud* raced from Boston to San Francisco in 89 days, 8 hours, in 1854. By contrast the novelist R. H. Dana's voyage on the square-rigger *Pilgrim* (Boston–Santa Barbara) had taken 150 days in 1835–36. This was the voyage he dramatized in *Two Years Before the Mast*. When Dana re-

The Yankee clippers

turned to California by steamship in 1859, the San Francisco harbor was crowded with clipper ships.

Yankee clippers speeded up transfers between the east and west coasts. But beyond this great economic and social contribution, their chief significance was in Oriental trade. Americans had taken the lead in opening up the Far East to the Western nations, as with the sailing of the U.S. *Empress of China* in 1784. In 1836 American traders won special rights in Siam; wars between England and China in the 1840s and 50s gave Americans the chance to capture a larger share of the China trade and Chinese ports were more open to all comers after 1844. The British finally relaxed their age-old navigation laws in 1849, allowing the fast Yankee clippers to compete with English ships in carrying tea to London, where the first delivery of a season's crop always brought a high price. Five years later, Commodore Matthew Perry broke Japanese cultural isolation and dragged that nation out

A Japanese view of the Perry mission

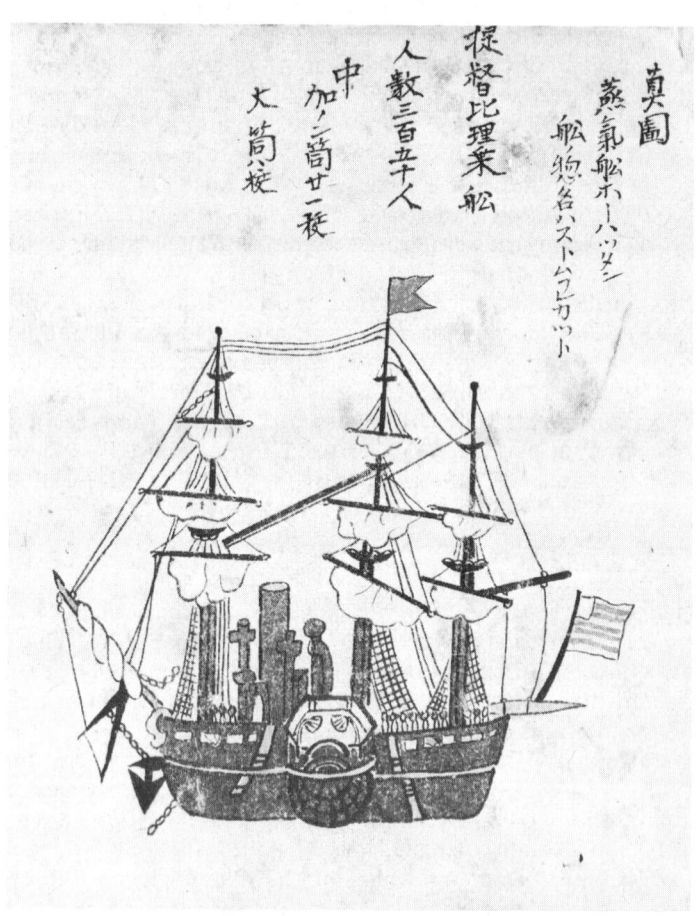

The Honolulu Academy of Arts, anonymous artist, gift of Mrs. Walter F. Dillingham in memory of Alice Perry Grew

Commodore M. C. Perry—Japanese woodcut

of its self-spun cocoon into the world arena (1854). By the 1850s American merchants were buying, selling, and shipping in all parts of the globe from Hawaii to Zanzibar, from the Far East to Europe, and in all oceans.

The mid-century boom in ship*building* was based partly on America's cost advantage in cheap timber. As time wore on, forests near the Atlantic coastal ports were depleted of pine and oak. Timber prices rose and marginal types of timber had to be adopted. Yankee craftsmen fell back on the less suitable chestnut and birch. As the price differential declined, British buyers began to seek sources in Europe and bought from Scandinavian and Russian suppliers. The clipper ship could not survive changing economic conditions. Peculiar historical circumstances had given clippers their ephemeral advantage as carriers of high value, perishable goods. The gold discoveries in California (1849) and Australia (1851), international war, in the Crimea as well as in China, and the European revolutions of 1848—all had favored the Yankee clipper, which dominated the trade of a brief era. Another combination of historical circumstances eliminated the clipper. The shipping of bulky goods across the Atlantic—grain, flour, meats, manufactures, steel, and iron rails—could not be done by clippers. The cheap, mass transportation of immigrants also was left to the newer steamships. Meanwhile, trade routes changed. For example, Brazilian coffee plantations opened up and captured the U.S. market at the expense of Oriental tea. The United States became mainly a coffee-drinking nation.

A loss of momentum

The Crash of 1857 and the coming of the Civil War accelerated the relative decline of the American merchant marine in general as compared with that of Britain. The shipbuilding industry was unready for the changeover to steel ship production. Even before 1860, British clipper designers were catching up on the Yankees. The coming of metal ships gave Britain the edge since she had the world's largest and most advanced iron and steel industry and therefore had a huge cost advantage in shipbuilding for years to come. What happened then to U.S. capital? The American investors abandoned shipbuilding and put their money in fresh outlets: manufacturing, railroads, and the like. Americans now paid all their attention to the home market, to the internal economic empire of the continent.

Revolution in manufactures

The shipping boom of the 1840s and 50s, immigration and population growth, the influx of foreign capital, gold discoveries, land sales, rising export prices, and the government-promoted transportation revolution, and great buildup of social overhead capital—all helped to stimulate an industrial revolution in New England, centered there, as it had been 40 or 50 years earlier in England, on the textile industries. The beginnings of industrial society in the Northeast were tentative; but the railroad expansion into the Midwest in the 1850s brought a diffusion of manufacturing technology and a real "take-off," to use the phrase of the economist W. W. Rostow, into industrialism that was sustained thereafter. Once begun, industrialization is irreversible. The transformation from a farming and shipping society to a manufacturing society, from merchant capitalism to industrial capitalism, did not take place overnight in New England; its roots were deep. But the rate of change accelerated in the 1840s and 50s. American population increased four-fold between the end of the War of 1812 and the end of the Civil War, while the volume of manufacturing output went up twelve-fold and its value eight-fold. These absolute increases came with changes in the scale and technique of industrial organization, increased specialization, and deeper local concentration of industry. Gradually, industrialism altered the structure of society.

Massachusetts cotton textiles led the revolution. As in Britain in earlier decades, woolen textiles followed the example of cotton. Would-be woolen manufacturers faced greater technical difficulties, more craft conservatism (woolens were an old industry, cotton quite new), inelastic raw material supplies, and less elasticity of demand. The first attempts to manufacture woolens under the factory system suffered from the competition of higher quality imported British woolens and cheaper English cotton goods. The experiment at Hartford in 1788 which Hamilton made use of in his *Report on Manufactures* soon failed. Americans continued to make their own coarse homespuns for use at home and to buy finer imports for other use. The War of 1812 did stimulate a growth of woolen mills and the introduction of merino sheep improved wool quality and increased raw material supplies. There were about 2,000 woolen factories in the United States by 1860 compared with 100 in 1820. American farmers kept their handlooms at home, however, until late in the century. (In Britain too, handloom weaving persisted very late). In the 1850s wool textile output increased by over 50 percent and was worth about $40 million in

1860. But cotton textiles were already valued at three times that amount ($115 million) and had a faster rate of growth.

Americans were no longer content to ship out their raw cotton for the British to manufacture into cloth and products and sell back to them at a high profit. The highest rates of profit are always taken in the latest stages of the productive process. Gradually, home cotton mills took an increasing share of the South's cotton output. In New England several famous ports, like Salem, known in the past for its cod fisheries and for exotic imports of Arab coffee and Sumatra pepper, became mill towns in order to survive.

The diffusion of the industrial revolution to the United States began almost as soon as it originated in Britain. From the 1780s Americans attempted to copy and adapt English cotton spinning and carding machinery. English laws forbade the export of machinery, and industrial espionage was therefore practiced. In the most famous case, the craftsman Samuel Slater slipped out of England in disguise in 1789, taking with him in his head his knowledge of the new machine processes learned as an apprentice in the Derbyshire textile mills of Jedediah Strutt. Immediately, Slater teamed up with the firm of Almy and Brown, Providence, Rhode Island, merchants who were trying their luck with textile manufacture. Behind them was the capital of the

Samuel Slater's first mill

Workers on their way to the factory

Winslow Homer, Library of Congress

wealthy Moses Brown, a Quaker merchant. The state of American technology can be inferred from the letter Moses Brown wrote to Slater in December 1789, asking for his help:

> We have from Ireland a man and his wife, who are spinners on the jennies, but we are destitute of a person acquainted with the frames. We shall be glad to be informed what quantity of yarn your mills spin in a day on one spindle. What number of spindles a lad can, or does attend, and at what age? How your roping is made . . . ? Whether the cotton is soaped before carding . . . ? What are the wooden rollers . . . covered with? Ours have been done with calf-skin. On what the spools play and run . . . ?

In an agreement of April 1790, Slater joined the firm to establish a water-powered cotton textile mill at Pawtucket, Rhode Island. Slater was only 21, a blunt, outspoken, inner-directed, hardworking person of great drive. The association was a success and he became involved in other projects, weathered the bad trade years of 1807–9 and prospered during the 1812 War. He again survived the postwar depression and introduced power machinery at Pawtucket in 1827. Slater died in 1835. His American career and associations perfectly illustrate the theme of the emergence of manufacturing capitalism out of merchant capitalism. One of his mills still stands in Pawtucket as a textile museum. Its architecture and appearance is remarkably like the still-standing historic mills of his native Derbyshire.

In Slater's day there was much opposition to the very idea of manufacturing, and capital was scarce. Many ventures failed through ignorance of technology and poor management. The merchants and bankers who experimented with manufacturing had to learn new tricks and take great risks. To set up a textile mill they had to learn about factory discipline and labor organization, the finding of adequate labor, building and maintaining complex machinery, training foremen and superintendents, scheduling production in some regular way, analyzing costs in more sophisticated forms than they had previously known. Strict accounts had to be kept in double-entry bookkeeping. Consumers had to be attracted. Only the larger, more heavily capitalized urban mills did well. Small rural spinning mills failed by the dozen.

Lowell's "Boston Associates"

The secret of success, then, was in having enough capital and being well organized. The most famous of the successful firms was the Boston Manufacturing Company, supported by several big local names like Appleton and Jackson and under the business leadership of Francis Cabot Lowell. These "Boston Associates" invested $600,000 in a factory at Waltham, Massachusetts, over a 6-year period. The "Waltham Plan" of operation, which began in 1813, was a unified management of all the major productive processes from spinning of raw cotton to dyeing of finished cloth, within a single, integrated plant and with a single marketing agency. The labor force down to the mid-1840s consisted of New England farm girls. As the region's agriculture declined because of the competition of the growing Midwest, the girls went out to work in the factory towns. They helped to keep the farm mortgage payments going, or they put a brother through school. Then they returned home. The girls were not usually part of a permanent factory class. So, under Lowell's plan, they were housed by the company in special dormitories. An early form of the "company town" was born.

The Boston Associates made money even during the bad years after 1814 when British imports once more flooded into U.S. ports. They could compete with Lancashire cottons because they specialized in a coarser-weave, cheap, standardized, hard-wearing fabric (cotton shirtings and sheetings), easy to mass produce in New England with the help of relatively unskilled farm girls. Such cloths were in great demand throughout rural America. At the town of Lowell, the Merrimac Manufacturing Company with a similar plan of organization turned out tough calicoes. By the 1820s it pioneered the large-scale use of water-powered machinery with improved dams, metal gears, and leather transmission belts. The old, clumsy, timber cogs and shafts vanished. The waterpower of several New England streams produced a crop of mill towns—Lowell, Lawrence, Manchester, Nashua, and others. Very soon, emigrants from New England took the new system of textile manufacturing with them as they spread out into the Mohawk and Hudson valleys. By 1830 the United States had 800 cotton mills; by 1860 there were 1,100. Mainly in Massachusetts, these mills devoured 423 million pounds of raw cotton from the South in 1860.

Why did not the South industrialize?

Why did manufacturers not locate their mills in the South, closer to the supplies of raw material? There were attempts to root the textile industry in Georgia and the Carolinas, but without much result until the 1880s. By then the New England industry was old and its plants were becoming obsolete; the South could rival it by beginning a brand new industry in the Carolinas, usually with electric power and more modern machinery.

In the 1840s and 50s the North had distinct advantages as a potential manufacturing region, the South had distinct, cumulative disadvantages. New England had a free labor force and when the farm girls gave out, European immigrants poured in. The South had slaves. Industrialization is theoretically possible using a slave force, but historically improbable. Moreover, the main cost of his labor force to a Northern employer was simply the wage bill; slaves and their families were maintained all year-round. (The dormitories soon vanished from New England as immigrant labor replaced the New England farm girls.) The South, also, was economically dependent on the North; its own capital was not mobile and free for investment in factories, but tied up in the ownership of slaves and land. Only Northern capital or foreign investment was available to develop industry in the Southern region. The South lacked a middle class and was low on social overhead capital, such as public education and transportation facilities. Banks and exporting concerns were in the North; New England merchants like the Lowells and Browns knew the ropes financially and had European connections already well established for trade credits. There was a commercial elite in Boston and New York; port installations were developed; the scene was set for economic change.

Finally it was not uneconomic to transport raw cotton to New England for manufacture into cloth—cotton is not like a metallic ore or a fuel. As a raw material it does not lose weight or get used up in the manufacturing process. It is foolish to move ore or coal to somewhere else, and then burn it all up at that spot; for this reason industry moves *to* the coal and ore fields. But the New England merchant capitalists bought raw cotton, and made cloth in their own region. In other words, so far as the Southern planter was concerned, New England was another foreign power, like England, which imported the South's raw materials and sold her back finished products. Those Southern agitators who complained before 1861 that the South was becoming an economic colony of the North were correct in principle, though no sinister conspiracy had brought this condition about.

In any case, the South's chief customer in 1860 was still Britain, not the North. Though the number of cotton mill spindles in New England leaped from 20,000 (1800) to over 5 million (1860), Britain's total was around 21 million.

Spread of new industrial techniques

The Northeast had a favorable "factor endowment" (mix of available resources, capital, and labor) for industrialization, and from the textile industries new techniques spread to other sectors. The region had river waterpower in New England with its many streams; coal and iron ore in Pennsylvania; a large reservoir of labor skills and ability to attract immigrants; banks and financial institutions; good ports; concentrations of population in several well-established cities and towns. In the 1850s the textile industries became localized in certain places and the size of individual textile companies grew. These large firms developed national markets rather than merely local outlets. In this prototype industry, many skills were learned which could be applied elsewhere.

Economic growth is a chain reaction. Economists talk of "backward and forward linkages." Such linkages grew out of the textile industries, *forward* in the productive process, toward transforming the clothing trades, for example, and *backward,* creating greater demand for factory machinery, machine tools, timber, coal, and iron. So the manufacture of cloth became a great American industry with many other industries dependent upon it. In turn, the manufacture of textile *machinery* for those factories became a major heavy industry.

Bottlenecks which have to be solved in one industry may produce innovations that can be applied to other industries. Thus, many engineering lessons were learned in building the first canals and railroads, and in textiles, the sewing machine was a product of two streams of influence. Elias Howe invented the sewing machine (patented 1846) from the experience he gained as an apprentice in a cotton textile mill in Lowell and his later training as an instrument maker

The Singer Company

Singer sewing machine—the home model of 1859

in Cambridge. His machine, improved upon by Isaac Singer, revolutionized the mass clothing industry and thus stimulated further demand for textiles. Immigrants provided both the labor force and the consumer force for this mass clothing. But Howe's machine was then applied to the boot and shoe industry, with equally revolutionary impact, with Lyman Blake's sole-stitching patent of 1858. Like textiles, boot and shoe manufacture was concentrated in Massachusetts.

As the Industrial Revolution spread over the world, those nations which had coal and iron and could develop steam-power survived and grew; those which lacked these resources fell behind in the race for economic power. Thus the Netherlands, a once-great world economic power, declined in the later 18th and 19th century, while Britain and the United States became strong. From the 1830s to the 1860s U.S. coal and iron output went up 20-fold. By 1860 the iron industry was second to textiles.

The first stage of U.S. industrialization, however, did not see extensive dependence on either coal or iron, and steam power was applied, in the main, only to transportation. The early steam railway engines burned timber, not coal. This would have been impossible in Britain, where timber was scarce. Though the U.S. iron industry was second in manufacturing, its dollar value of 1860 (about $42 million) was about a third of textiles ($115 million). Meanwhile flour and gristmills turned out foodstuffs valued at $223 million. The United States was still a farming nation in 1860. The age of steam power and of iron and steel did not come until after the Civil War.

Heavy industry: Coal and iron

The U.S.A.

The changeover from charcoal to coke smelting in the U.S. iron industry came much later than in timber-scarce Britain, not only because the United States had plentiful forests but because American furnaces after about 1840 began to use anthracite coal. Though timber was cheap, the labor of converting it into charcoal for use in iron furnaces was not. To the east of the Alleghenies were seams of anthracite coal. This would not make good coke, but it could be used directly in iron making, since it contained little sulfur. The sort of coal that was good for making coke—bituminous coal—lay to the west of the mountains and contained impurities like sulfur, which produced a poorer quality of pig iron. Charcoal pig iron was better, though more expensive; anthracite pig iron became dominant before the Civil War. After the war, the vastly increased demand for iron and steel and a westward shift of the industry brought in the use of bituminous coke, and supplies were mined with lower phosphorous content. The demand for native rails now made it economically feasible for native ironmasters to adopt great rolling mills and coke-burning blast furnaces. The first American heavy iron rails were rolled successfully in 1845. Pressure on Congress brought a high tariff on imported British rails. With the British virtual monopoly broken, the essential "big boost" came for the U.S. iron industry.

Availability helped to delay the mining of coal. Deposits further west remained untouched for some time. Eastern anthracite mines were exploited earlier for use in iron making, after David Thomas perfected a technique for using anthracite at the LeHigh Crane Ironworks in Pennsylvania (1840). About 150 anthracite blast furnaces were at work by 1856 and anthracite coal mining had quadrupled.

In 1856 Henry Bessemer in Sheffield, England, made his breakthrough in the manufacture of cheap steel in quantity—the Bessemer converter. In a few years this revolutionized the industry. Steel, containing intermediate carbon content between pig iron and wrought iron, was more useful than iron for a large range of products, being

Tin bathtub with seat and soap holder, c. 1870

Allen County Historical Society, Ohio

more malleable and stronger. In time steel would replace iron in mass uses: railroad tracks, steel girders, bridges and tunnels, though initially Bessemer's "mild steel" had too little carbon. The process was simple though dramatic: In the huge converter (a massive crucible) the molten iron was decarbonized into molten steel by having a stream of air forced through it, burning out the "impurities." The process is spectacular to watch, particularly when the converter is tilted and the molten steel pours forth. The basic idea had been invented independently five years earlier by a Kentucky ironmaster, William Kelly.

The greater use of coal from the 1840s on brought *concentration* of industry on the coalfields, and the U.S. iron making process lost forever its rural character and setting. Over half of U.S. pig and manufactured iron was being made in Pennsylvania in 1860—the state with the large anthracite coalfields. Ohio and New Jersey were second and third. Pig iron output was almost 20 times as large as in 1810. The metal was used in a great variety of industries and jobs: farm implements, machinery, steam engines, rails, small arms (subsidized by the federal government ever since 1792), and a mass of domestic hardware, such as stoves. A million iron stoves were being sold every year by 1860. From the 1830s on, improvements in the American stove enabled it to serve both as a cooking stove and a house heater, and some sort of central heating system was already known, with pipes from the stove taking hot air up into bedrooms. English visitors, accustomed even in those days to more spartan conditions of self-imposed misery, were already complaining of American hotels being "overheated."

Despite these changes, in the antebellum years the characteristic of American industry was not the domination of large heavy-industry firms, but a great variety of small enterprises of all sorts. The French observer Tocqueville noticed:

A variety of small industries

What most astonishes me in the United States is not so much the marvellous grandeur of some undertakings, as the innumerable multitudes of small ones.

This was a shrewd observation. It should remind us not to emphasize one or two major innovations, such as the Erie Canal, in trying to explain America's economic growth before 1860. A great and general popular enthusiasm for all kinds of projects and "undertakings" was in the air of America in the 30s, 40s, and 50s. The changes were widespread and often small. The average business was not a large partnership but a family affair. The age of the corporation had not yet arrived, though the prototype was here in the railroads.

In the 1850s the "American system of manufacture" became known abroad. In 1851 the British held a major industrial fair, the Great Exhibition in London at the Crystal Palace, a great iron and glass building, itself an architectural innovation. Exhibits there from the U.S. were very successful, particularly the Colt revolver (patented much earlier in 1835) and the new McCormick reaper. Even the London

Times was forced to admit that the ex-colonials had achieved something at last:

> Their reaping machine has carried conviction to the heart of the British agriculturist. Their revolvers threaten to revolutionize military tactics.

In 1853 and 1854 the British sent official teams to the United States to investigate economic progress here and report back to Parliament. The teams were impressed by the size of the American home market and by the high average wealth and well-being of Americans. They admired the beginnings of standardized mass production of some factories and acknowledged the mechanical ingenuity of the people. How did the English experts explain this higher level of technical competence of Americans? They said *public education* was the key.

> Bringing a mind prepared by thorough school discipline and educated up to a far higher standard than those of a much superior social grade in society in the Old World, the American working boy develops rapidly into the skilled artisan, and having once mastered one part of his business, he is never content until he has mastered all.

Public education hardly existed in England in 1854 and the first national public education act to provide elementary schools for the British masses was not passed until 1870. It was natural therefore that English observers would seize upon this factor.

The "American system of manufacture": Mechanization

But the essence of the "American system" was mechanization and division of labor—a principle explained by Adam Smith in 1776. Americans carried these principles through, to include standardization and interchangeability of parts and the rough beginnings of rational workshop layout to allow for a useful flow of materials through the factory. The English took note of this in their report:

> In the adaptation of special apparatus to a single operation in almost all branches of industry, the Americans display an amount of ingenuity combined with undaunted energy which as a nation we would do well to imitate, if we mean to hold our present position in the great market of the world.

England should "imitate" the United States! America's labor scarcity and lack of a large under-class of peasants or workers available as cheap labor were bearing fruit. Labor-saving devices and technical ingenuity characterized the American scene already.

> The Committee also observed that everything that could be done to reduce labor in the movement of materials from one point to another was adopted. This includes mechanical arrangements for lifting material, etc., from one floor to another, carriages for conveying material on the same floor, and such like.

Three years after this report, E. G. Otis, the American inventor, went one step further and created the passenger elevator (1857). In the future this would make it possible for men to build multistory buildings—the skyscrapers. The combine harvester and the tractor were also still to come, all fruits essentially of the same tree.

An early form of interchangeability of parts was used by Eli Whitney in 1800 to meet the contract deadline for a federal order for 10,000 muskets. A Connecticut gunsmith, Simeon North, had worked out a similar scheme (having the guns made up of easily assembled interchangeable parts) for manufacturing pistols in 1799. The notion spread to various light industries, such as clockmaking, which had long been a source of technical ideas.

Experiments with automatic machinery with some degree of self-regulation had taken place in the flour-milling industry in the late 1780s, with Oliver Evans's brilliant adoption of a conveyor belt system, a mill elevator, and a gravity-fed grinding process. Evans was a pioneer in the manufacture of machinery. He began making steam engines at the Mars Iron Works in Philadelphia as early as 1803. By the 1830s machine shops were fairly common in New England; by 1860 they were common throughout the North. They produced reapers, mowers, plows, clocks, guns, locomotives, steam engines, textile machinery, printing presses, sewing machines, and many other devices without which economic advance would not have continued. Many of these workshops were not large. Like the railroads, these shops were the prime educational institutions of the growing industrial society so far as its technical know-how was concerned. By 1860 the goal of mechanization was generally accepted; it seemed almost synonymous with "Americanization," at least in the Northeast. This was the "American way."

The revolution in agriculture

Much of the gross national product of 1860 was made up not of manufactures but of the output of flour mills, meat-packing plants, tanneries, and breweries, all of them involving the *processing of farm products*. Despite the industrial takeoff in the Northeast, most Americans were avidly absorbed in pursuing happiness by exploiting as fully as they could their most abundant factor of production, the soil. Two fundamental changes transformed American farming in the early 19th century. First, the area of cultivable land increased enormously. Second, scientific farming began. There were ups and downs in farm prices, but the secular trend was up, and markets at home and abroad for foodstuffs seemed bottomless. Land values shot sky-high in the Old Northwest, and after about 1830 slave prices mounted in the Deep South and the Old Southwest. Additions to U.S. territory more or less kept up with the doubling of the population each decade; 6 Americans per square mile in 1800 had become 11 per square mile in 1860. The man–land ratio remained relatively unchanged in the nation as a whole, though land became of higher value in towns and in all areas of agricultural development.

The American farmer and planter manipulated his resources to maximize his chances of survival and success. He tended to "use up" the soil—land being relatively abundant and labor scarce. American agriculture became *extensive,* not intensive as in Europe. Yields per acre were not very high, compared with more intensive systems; but overall farm output was considerable. The antebellum farmer has been criticized for "wasting" the soil, "mining" it of its nutrients and then moving on, as the cotton planters abandoned the Upper South for the Deep South and the rich lands of the Mississippi Yazoo floodplains. But the criticism is misplaced.

Commercial farming in the Old Northwest

We have noticed how the Old Northwest was settled by pioneers from the Northeastern states, by later European immigrants from Britain, Germany, and Switzerland and by Southern backwoodsmen moving North across the Ohio. The regional population (Ohio, Indiana, Illinois, Michigan, and Wisconsin) stood at 7 million by 1860. The great wealth of this area was tapped more fully after the Erie and Ohio canals and the railroads opened it up to wider markets, initially for livestock products, later for grain.

The fertile prairie soil of this part of the Central Basin of North America was topped by a thick, heavily matted sod. Existing plows could not break it. The comparative shortage of trees convinced the first pioneers that the land was barren. At first they used it for grazing livestock. The eastern part of the region (Ohio, southern Michigan, and Indiana) were not unlike the countryside they already knew further east. Here the basic unit remained the family farm.

Gradually, suspicions of this new prairie land were overcome, for improvements in technology made it easier to conquer. The prairie needed a heavy metal plow with a long, sloping moldboard to turn the sod over. Many Americans experimented with new plows, e.g., Jefferson and Daniel Webster. In 1819 Jethrow Wood designed a cast-iron three-piece plow made of interchangeable parts. But the first commercially successful, all-steel plow that broke the prairie was John Deere's patent of 1847. In the days of pre-Bessemer steel, the Deere plow was expensive, but its value was high to the farmer and plows like it came into use in the 1850s.

Meanwhile, labor scarcity and the heavy nature of farm tasks stimulated a wide range of other labor-saving devices. Many hand processes were mechanized before the Civil War and a host of patents were taken out for mowers, reapers, threshers, drills, horse-drawn rakes, feed grinders, and so on. The expansion of the iron and steel industry helped. Two men, Obed Hussey (1833) and Cyrus McCormick (1834), independently patented similar machines for reaping. After about 1855 McCormick's machines dominated. Around 100,000 reapers were at work by 1860, though their greatest application came after the Civil War. Meanwhile the new threshing machine made the ancient hand-flail threshing floor system, inherited from Europe, totally obsolete. Mechanical threshing spread after Hiram and John Pitts introduced their thresher in 1837. The work was often done by migrant crews, traveling around the countryside at harvest time. Mechanization transformed American farming and made commercial production possible on the prairie.

Scientific agriculture

The application of science ("book learning") to farming did not make as much headway as that of mechanization. The farmer was not interested in conservation, fertilization, and planning. As Thomas Jefferson had said years before:

In Europe the object is to make the most of their land, labor being abundant; here it is to make the most of our labor, land being abundant.

Some idealistic, progressive farmers who were aware of the scientific changes made in agriculture by advanced experimenters in Europe—men such as Washington, Jefferson, and Livingston—did apply scientific principles. New methods of fertilization, animal breeding, and crop rotation were introduced on their farms. The statesman Henry Clay, protagonist of the "American System" for national economic development, first brought Hereford cattle to the United States in 1817. British shorthorns and Devons improved American beef cattle; dairy stock was improved after the introduction of Ayrshires, Jerseys, and Guernseys. Spanish merino sheep (for their fine wool), and British breeds of hogs and sheep (for their pork, lamb, and mutton) were also imported and bred. The fiery Confederate, Edmund Ruffin (1794–1865), who fired the first shot that opened the Civil War at Fort Sumter, South Carolina, and committed suicide because the South lost, was a pioneer soil chemist. His famous *Essay on Calcareous Manures* appeared in 1832.

Gradually the ox was replaced by the horse. A popular breed of heavy draft horse in the United States was the Percheron, brought in from France in 1839. Another was the English Clydesdale. The first American-bred horse was the Morgan, a light, general-purpose animal, developed in Vermont by Justin Morgan. The Morgan horse descends uniquely from one bay stallion (1795–1821) of unknown ancestry. Out in the West, wild horses roamed, descendants of the horses first used by the Spanish conquistadores. Their coming revolutionized the life of the Plains Indians.

Agricultural societies, schools, and journals sprang up in the early 19th century. County fairs played an important social and educational role, and government aid began in a very small way. The pioneer scientific farms of the Founding Fathers, however, were allowed to fall into decay. Jefferson's son-in-law was the first to adopt the technique of contour plowing in the Piedmont region at Monticello, but the estate was in poor condition when he died. Washington's Mount Vernon was also allowed to decline. In 1860 American farm education still had far to go and the extensive nature of agriculture did not stimulate the adoption of more scientific methods.

Still, the basis of a mechanized, commercial farming was laid by 1860. Farm tools and machines of 1860 enabled a man with a two-horse team to complete about ten times the work he could have done by hand in earlier years. The heavy cereal croplands developed in Indiana, Illinois, and Wisconsin were replacing Kentucky and Tennes-

The U.S.A.

see as America's granary. Almost half of the total grain crop of 1860 came from the five states of the Old Northwest.

Farm processing plants

The closer association of farmer and city and increasing commercialization were seen in the rise of the processing industries. Western farm products flowed east by canal and rail after about 1825. Cattle and hogs were no longer driven to Eastern markets on the hoof. Meat-packing plants sprang up at points of trans-shipment, like Cincinnati, a nodal center, which became known as "Porkopolis." After the 50s, other centers supplanted Cincinnati as new farm areas opened up beyond the Ohio country. Chicago, Kansas City, Omaha, in turn became meat-packing centers and distribution capitals. In time the meat-packing industries spun off many by-products—leather goods, fertilizer, glue, soaps, fats, and so on. Flour-milling centers grew in towns situated on great river systems: Cincinnati, Louisville, St. Louis. The grain elevator made its appearance in grain storage and shipment cities. The first was developed by Joseph Dart in 1842 and soon improved upon by Chicago shippers. Once the railroad reached Chicago, the city outrivaled Buffalo as a grain shipping center.

The dairy industry also witnessed technical changes before the Civil War, with the factory production of cheese and butter, the rise of the canned milk industry and the large-scale production of ice

St. Louis in 1854

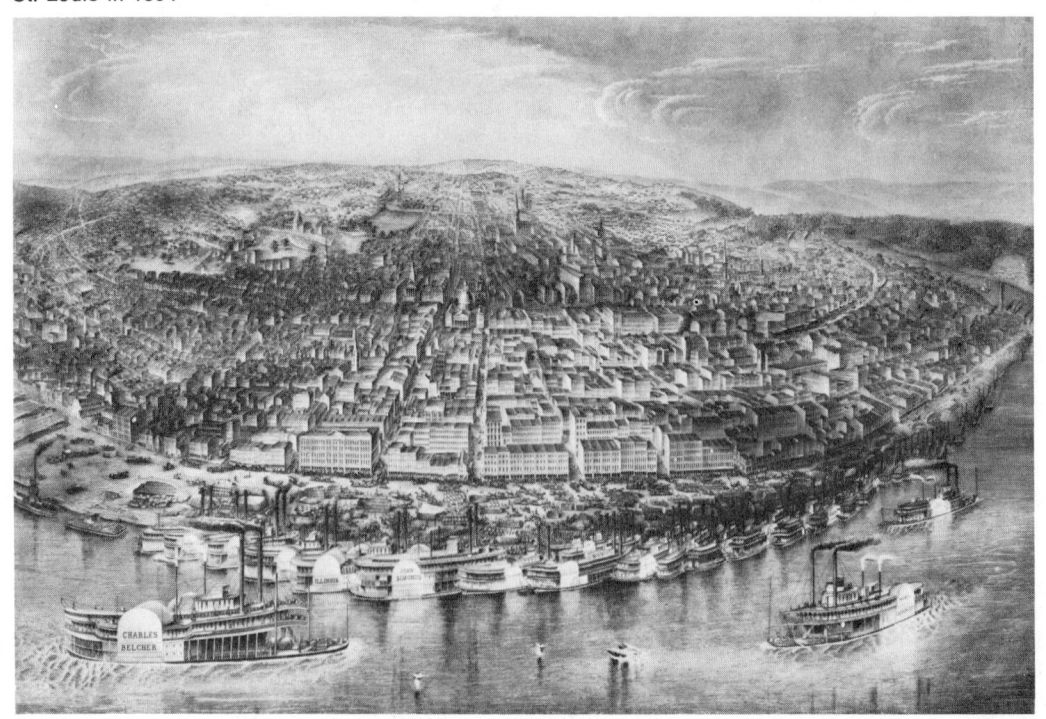

Missouri Historical Society

cream. Canning would be given a boost by the needs of the Union Army during the Civil War, though public suspicion of canned foods remained high—justifiably, since much had still to be learned about the technology and botulism was common.

While farming in the Old Northwest became specialized for the market and became a business, in the Old Southwest, which was settled slightly later, cotton became king.

The Cotton Kingdom

As men had left the tidewater lands and moved to the Piedmont in earlier years, so the Upper South as a whole suffered relative decline and real economic depression. The chief impulses in the drive to the Southwest were the invention of Whitney's cotton gin (1793) and the general American nationalist and expansionist fervor that had helped to create the 1812 War. Spain was ejected from Florida and Texas and the Creek and Cherokee Indians were forcibly removed to western reservations with little impunity. Thus "land hunger" drove planters from the relatively eroded Upper South to the Mississippi floodplains and the tributary lands of rivers like the Yazoo, rich in thick, black, waxy loams. Mississippi, Alabama, and Louisiana formed the core of the cotton kingdom in the 1820s. Here richer planters often drove poorer families off the best lands, and some of the smaller farmers migrated north across the Ohio. As the new planters tried to ape the life of the Big House and plantation further east, and developed large operations with many slaves, the "poor whites" were shoved aside and those who stayed to eke out a bare existence on inferior and hilly soils became known as "hillbillies" and "crackers." Their numbers were not large, though later economic changes in the South would help to create more of them.

Cotton was the very life of most of the 7 million free whites and 4 million black slaves of the South in 1860, or at least, of those living in the Deep South and Southwest. While in colonial days the larger plantations had depended on tobacco crops, indigo, and rice, the coming of the cotton gin, the Industrial Revolution in England, and the

TABLE 1
Population growth and Western settlement, 1790–1860

Year	Total population	Nonwhites	Old Northwest*	Old Southwest†
1790	3,929,000	757,000	—	110,000
1800	5,297,000	1,002,000	55,700	405,900
1810	7,224,000	1,378,000	272,500	913,000
1830	12,901,000	2,329,000	1,501,500	2,033,000
1850	23,261,000	3,639,000	4,521,700	3,881,000
1860	31,513,000	4,521,000	7,382,000	4,729,000

*Including Ohio, Indiana, Illinois, Michigan, and Wisconsin.
†Including Kentucky, Tennessee, Mississippi, Alabama, and Louisiana.
Source: *Historical Statistics of the United States* (Washington, D.C.: U.S. Bureau of the Census, 1960), Series A-2 and A-46; Peter d'A. Jones, *Economic History of the United States Since 1783* (London, 1956), p. 25. Figures adapted for this table.

The U.S.A.

TABLE 2
Admission of Western states, and state population, 1790–1860

			Population			
State and year	1790	1800	1810	1830	1850	1860
Old Southwest						
Kentucky (1792)	74,000	221,000	406,000	688,000	982,000	1,156,000
Tennessee (1796)	36,000	105,000	262,000	682,000	1,003,000	1,110,000
Louisiana (1812)	—	—	77,000	216,000	518,000	708,000
Mississippi (1817)	—	8,900	40,000	137,000	606,000	791,000
Alabama (1819)	—	70,000	128,000*	310,000	772,000	964,000
Old Northwest						
Ohio (1803)	—	45,000	231,000	938,000	1,980,000	2,340,000
Indiana (1816)	—	5,600	24,500	343,000	988,000	1,350,000
Illinois (1818)	—	2,400	12,300	157,500	851,000	1,712,000
Michigan (1837)	—	2,700	4,700	32,000	397,700	1,184,000
Wisconsin (1848)	—	—	—	31,000†	305,000	776,000

* 1820.
† 1840.
Note: A study of both tables shows, among other things, how at first the Old Southwest grew faster than the Old Northwest, but was outstripped after 1850.
Source: Jones, *Economic History of the United States Since 1783*, p. 25.

later emergence of the textile industry nearer home in Massachusetts, made cotton king. Cotton was the most valuable Southern crop by 1820 (less than 350,000 bales); its output doubled each decade to a total of 4 million bales by 1860. By then, two thirds of all black slaves were engaged in growing it; the crop was also two thirds of all national exports in value.

Two kinds of cotton were cultivated in the South, long staple and short staple. The fine-fabric, long-staple cotton was grown chiefly on the sea islands off the coast of Georgia and South Carolina. It had come to the United States from the Bahamas in about 1786. This was not, however, the fiber which made the South famous as a cotton exporter, for its yield per acre was low, about 150 pounds, and it demanded highly skilled pickers. At the height of production in the 1820s, long-staple output only reached about 11 million pounds a year. This high quality "sea island" variety could not be produced in sufficient quantity to meet the growing demand of the British textile market. The hardy, short-staple variety, grown in the upland and interior, was restricted in output until Whitney's gin made it possible for the short-staple fiber to be mechanically separated from the seed with comparative ease. Thereafter, the upland cotton became the major export variety and kept England's mills going.

Whitney was a Connecticut Yankee and a Yale graduate who lived on a plantation near Savannah, Georgia, for a short time. There he devised his fairly simple gin, much like a hand clothes-wringer in looks. The device was not very difficult to build, and was simple to operate. It was easily pirated. Whitney made little personal profit out of the machine. Few young graduates have been able to write home, as did Whitney in September 1793 to tell their family they had just made a major invention. "Dear Parent," he wrote to his father, ". . . I presume, Sir, you are desirous to hear how I have spent my time since I left College." The time was well spent. The impact of the cotton gin on the economy of the South, on the maintenance and extension of African slavery, and on the growth of U.S. trade were enormous.

. . . all agreed that if a machine could be invented which would clean the cotton with expedition, it would be a great thing both to the Country and to the inventor. I involuntarily happened to be thinking on the subject and struck out a plan of a Machine in my mind . . . I made one before I came away which required the labor of one man to turn it and with which one man will clean ten times as much cotton . . . This machine may be turned by water or with a horse, with the greatest ease, and one man and a horse will do more than fifty men with the old machines. It makes the labor fifty times less. . . .

One slave instead of 50: Given the rising prices of slaves in the South the saving was very great. By August of the next year, 1794, Whitney was reporting home with excitement that he could not make machines fast enough to meet the swelling demand and the increased supply of raw cotton waiting to be cleaned. In later years the gin was improved upon, and with it a slave could work 350 pounds of cotton a day.

The more tricky problem of a machine for *picking* cotton in the fields was not solved until the Rust brothers' machine of 1925, a century and a quarter later. Cotton bolls ripen unevenly at different times. Slaves could plant and cultivate more cotton than the same number of them could pick, and for years acute labor shortage was felt at cotton-picking time.

Plantation slavery

American slavery was originally a solution to a labor problem. It became the basis for a whole way of life. The pursuit of happiness of the white majority implied perpetual slavery for the black minority. In the South as a whole, however fewer than 3 percent of the whites lived in families which owned 20 or more slaves. This top 3 percent of the large slave-owning class owned more than half of all the slaves in South. The average Southern white, about 2 million of them, lived in families owning 4 or 5 slaves. It has been estimated that at least 50 percent of the cotton crop was farmed by men who could not afford over 5 or 6 slaves and who worked alongside them in the fields. This small a number of slaves does not call for a middleman white overseer.

A minimum of about 20 slaves was necessary to make the employment of an overseer economically feasible. Since the average black field hand of the 1850s could look after about 10 acres of corn and 10 of cotton, the minimum economic size of a large plantation would have to be about 400 or 500 acres, if one includes space for living, uncultivated waste space, and so on. In fact, under 3 percent of all farm units in the South were bigger than 500 acres. So the myth of the cavalier South, dominated by large plantations and huge gangs of slaves worked by cruel overseers, is not statistically correct. Those planters who moved to the Southwest frontier in particular were yeomen farmers, "men on the make." In Louisiana, the elite sugar planters did manage to maintain large estates and mansions and some examples remain as tourist sites today. But even in the Southwest, the usual planter was not an "aristocrat," but a hard-working farmer with a handful of slaves.

Within this general picture of economic modesty, the larger plantations stand out—like the 2,000 acre cane-sugar holdings of the delta land of Louisiana, which employed large numbers of African slaves and involved extensive capital investment. In the 1830s steam-powered sugar machinery could cost up to $14,000. This was "industrial slavery." Socially, the thousands of yeomen planters who made up the bulk of the Southern population gave way before the large planters. The big slaveholder was socially dominant: He exerted strategic economic and political pressure over the white majority who copied his way of life and thought as closely as they could afford. The middle-class whites competed socially with the big planter on the one side and the poor whites and black slaves on the other. They succumbed to strong leadership and came to identify closely with the white elite.

Life of the slave

In the North, slavery had never emerged on a large scale. Accident of geography helped to produce this condition; even in colonial days there was already a strong contrast between the Northern family farms, carved out of the wilderness of deciduous forests and the Southern plantation way of life. Most slaves in the North were in domestic service; they were gradually freed. The trading of slaves persisted in New York and in New Jersey as late as the Missouri Compromise of 1820. Yankee ships supplied the slaves to Southern markets, of course.

Even after 1808 the foreign slave trade continued illegally. It has been estimated that around 1,000 slaves a year were illegally imported. Northern cash and ships made this possible. After the Civil War, Yankee captains were still trading slaves to Brazil, Cuba, and elsewhere. The "guilt" of slavery rested on many shoulders, North and South.

It is often said that slavery as a labor system was declining in the South after the War of Independence and would have died out but for the surge of English demand for raw cotton and Whitney's gin enabling the U.S. to supply it. Certainly the boom of the Southwest in the early decades of the century sealed the fate of slavery. The institution was not about to die by the 1820s and as the South hardened in its attitude, overtly pro-slavery arguments and rationalizations were invented. The myth of inherent African inferiority was fastened in the white public mind. Economic necessity and common sense dictated generally that slaves should be housed, fed and clothed adequately—according to the living standards of the day, which were low in the South, even for whites. Usually, slaves worked either by fixed hours, like the overworked factory workers of industrial England at that time or by *stints*, the completion of set tasks. Their food was coarse and lacked variety. On the other hand, the daily diet of many country people, for instance peasants in 20th-century Spain and Italy, or North Africa, is often of this sort. In the South at that time, slaves, poor white farmers, overseers and even better-off yeomen farmers, all wore coarse homespun cotton and cowhide and ate corn bread, hominy grits (boiled maize), salt pork, chitterlings (intestines), and vegetables (black-eyed peas and others) only in season. Much of the "soul food" made known by black Americans today was eaten by blacks and whites in the Southern states for decades before the Civil War and after it.

The slaves were housed in windowless log cabins in the countryside, in "quarters" in the cities. They probably labored no longer hours than did the "wage slaves" of the North in the textile mills or the pioneers who worked from dawn to dust on the prairie lands of Iowa. The Irish peasants, who began to emigrate to the United States in the 1830s and 40s lived more precarious and uncertain lives and died more often of malnutrition. But none of these other groups were *permanent* slaves. Moreover, though common sense would demand that the owner treat his slave property well, common sense did not always prevail. It is true, as Southern apologists for slavery argued, that the slave was housed, clothed, fed, together with his family all year-round, whatever happened to the price of cotton or sugar. In the North, the factory "hand" was subject to instant dismissal and his fate was determined by market forces. But the chattel slave was a mere piece of saleable property. Legal discriminations against him were built up rapidly and became clearly racist, rather than economic in character. Slavery was no longer merely a labor system. Studies reveal that free Negroes, whether in the North or the South, had little protection under the law; they were pariahs. Few laws protected slaves against assault, mutilation, even murder. Slaves could not own private property nor could they legally marry and have legally recognizable families. Often they were denied the right to education or to attend church. Religious ceremonies were held out in the woods.

The personal degradation and lack of spiritual freedom of American slaves has been compared to the dehumanization of the inmates in the Nazi concentration camps. Others say American slavery was in fact no worse than slavery elsewhere—for instance in Brazil—for the evidence does not show that Latin Americans or the French were gentler to their black slaves, however different may have been their sexual attitudes. But the system of chattel slavery in the South made the slave utterly dependent on the white master in the Big House, made it difficult for slaves to build a firm family structure and family values, and denied to the black male his human role as head of family, father, husband and breadwinner. Above all, the crushing paternalism of the master class, however "benevolent" in goal, was pernicious and corrosive. What is remarkable is how many slaves survived this system, emerging as whole personalities and even as leaders of their people in the abolitionist movement and in religion.

Slave breeding

One ghastly feature of slavery was the *domestic* slave trade. We have seen how difficult it would have been to check this trade entirely, despite the abolition of the international slave trade in 1807. Jefferson himself bought and sold Africans. But the relative decline of the Upper South as slave plantation country and the simultaneous growth of the Deep South and Southwest as cotton spread created ideal conditions for a lively slave trade from Virginia, Maryland, and North Carolina to states that were desperate for cotton workers—like Alabama, Mississippi, Louisiana, and parts of Texas. There seems to have been outright *breeding* of slaves, though the evidence is difficult to evaluate. In Maryland, Kentucky, and Virginia there are examples of incentives being offered to Negro mothers—gifts of land, separate cabins, cash bonuses, clothes, rest periods, even a promise of ultimate freedom—in return for childbearing. Under American slavery, of course, any children were automatically slaves and the property of the white owner. This was the system which Jefferson sought to eliminate with his reform of 1824. On the other hand, women of both races, black and white, tended to begin childbearing at an early age in the South, North, and West alike, with or without incentives.

The Upper South exported an estimated 180,000 slaves in the 1840s, and another 230,000 in the 1850s to points further South. Given a rough average price of about $800, this made an enormous traffic with high profits for speculators, traders, auctioneers, and any would-be breeders. The slave-trading profession was looked down upon by upper-class whites in the South. Yet out of that trade came great fortunes and famous Southern family names, like the De Saussures, Gadsdens, and Ryans of South Carolina. Centers of slave-auction traffic were Charleston, Savannah, Memphis, and New Orleans, though smaller markets existed in towns like St. Augustine, Florida. Slave trading was a very noticeable and disturbing occupation in the very heart of the District of Columbia and brought constant critical comment from visiting Europeans and diplomats.

Did slavery pay?

In recent years economists have studied slavery as an economic institution and tried to determine whether the system was profitable or not. Did plantation slave-owners make money out of the unfree labor system? Would they have been more successful with free labor? Southern defenders of slavery in pre-War days claimed that only Negroes were adapted to subtropical labor in the fields and that slavery was the best system for the administrative control of Africans in large numbers. The slavery system made possible division of labor and internal economies on the plantation. But these arguments were weak, for whites did work in the Southern fields, in fact most of them did, and large gangs of supervised slaves were the exception, not the rule. The question is not that free white labor could *not* have done the job of developing the Southern cotton economy; humans of all races are very adaptable to climatic changes. Was the slave system profitable for the white planters? Earlier claims, based on plantation account books and other evidence, indicated that slavery was dying (for the second time) before the Civil War broke out and that it was no longer a viable institution. But a reexamination of slavery operations in the light of modern capital theory reveals that the slave was a profitable proposition considered as a capital investment, and taking into account his initial cost, his life expectancy, annual maintenance costs, and variations in productivity per head. An investment in slaves compared favorably with an investment in the New York Stock Exchange of the antebellum years, taking an average of returns on available securities.

The complex cost structure of the Upper South in this period of rising prices and falling soil fertility of the area made investment in slaves a more doubtful proposition. Here the slavery system was kept going by breeding and the domestic trade. Prime field hands rose in market value from about $250 (1790) to $1,800 or more (1860). Those who made the best profits out of slavery were the owners of plantations of optimum size, well situated on good soils, as in Mississippi during the 1850s. Here slavery *was* profitable. In all cases, profits depended on the skill of the manager and on the market judgment shown by the buyer. Smart speculators could make heavy profits in capital gains by shrewd purchases and resale; of course, they could also suffer heavy losses if erratic cotton prices brought a temporary drop in slave values. It seems clear that Southern planters themselves were never driven to consider an alternative to the slave-labor system, which seems to indicate that slavery was not on the point of collapse in the 1850s.

Is the profit motive the only reason for the survival of human slavery in the American Republic so late in history? Obviously not. Slavery was above all a *social* system. The possibility of abolishing it and putting the two races on a more equal footing was never further from the mind of Southern whites than in the 1850s. The more that Northern white and black reformers attacked slavery the more the Southerners defended it. In 1831–32 when the British-led world antislavery movement was at its height and following Nat Turner's violent and bloody slave revolt, the Virginia assembly did debate the idea of abolition. The move was blocked by considerations of the cost of compensation to owners and the difficulties in shipping freed Negroes out of the state. Whites could not conceive of allowing freedmen to stay in Virginia. Individual Virginians freed their slaves, like John Randolph of Roanoke, who liberated 400 in his will when he died. By the 1850s though, the idea of general abolition was no longer debated in the South.

Slavery "paid" in the 1840s and 50s in selected areas of the South. Its general long-term impact was bad however. Apart from the technical problem of inadequate labor supplies at cotton-picking time, the high capital investment cost of slaves impeded the accumulation of normal regional capital. There was little capital left free for investment in mechanical improvements or local industries, town growth, or transportation. Thus the impact of the agricultural revolution was less felt in the Southwest than in the Northwest and throughout the South

Long-term retardation of the southern economy caused by slavery

the level of technology was low. Frederick Law Olmsted, a one-time experimental farmer and the pioneer landscape architect who gave the United States several of its great urban parks, visited the South on three occasions and observed the terrible lack of even the simplest hand tools. After buying land and slaves some planters had no cash left for a plow; the fields had to be dug by hand. The contrast was stark with the rapid development of mechanized farming in the Midwest in the 1850s. McCormick was perfecting the reaper while some southern farms were limited to medieval technology.

Plantation slaves, despite the adaptability of many and their general know-how, were deliberately uneducated and they were ill-suited to economic production under market conditions of unstable demand and changing technology. The use of an oppressed slave-labor force almost dictated the *monoculture* of cotton, rice or sugar, the unyielding dependence on one-crop specialization. So slavery underpinned the condition of the South as an *economic colony*, a dependent agrarian society, whose economic well-being would fluctuate with world market prices for agricultural staples. Low urbanization, relatively poor intra-regional transportation, low immigration from outside, decentralized settlement patterns—all these elements, the opposite of which helped the North and Midwest to grow, kept the South relatively retarded.

Comparative lack of opportunity in the South, caused by the skewed income distribution, rigid social stratification and the slavery system, discouraged Europeans. In 1860 only 3.4 percent of white Southerners were foreign born, and this proportion had fallen to just over 2 percent by 1900. In contrasting New England the figures of foreign born were 15 percent (1860) and 26 percent (1900). Similarly, the South was fighting against the census returns. Her population did not keep up with the rest of the nation—as the tables given earlier indicate. In 1790, North and South had roughly two million each. By 1860 the North had under 20 million and the South 11. Slavery alone does not account for this difference, but the institution had much to answer for in terms of secular retardation of the regional economy.

The noncotton South

Plantation slavery supported the cultivation of other cash crops for export besides cotton. Rice and sugarcane were both best managed on a large scale with "industrial slavery." On these large plantations the field hands tended to be reduced to the status of a mere tool, like Northern factory hands. Slave trading was common here, families were often divided, and brutal punishments more known and less restrained by social custom or closeness between black and white. The intermediary of the overseer, who was often recruited from the embittered poor white class, made the situation much worse than it might have been. Sugar workers at harvesting and processing times labored an 18-hour day. On the large plantations, however, the house slaves were better treated, closer to the whites, and better educated. Often they considered themselves socially superior to the field hands. Their numbers were small in relation to the total slave population.

Other Southern crops—tobacco, corn, wheat, hemp, and livestock—

did not justify the expense of a large slave force. Three slaves could manage about 50 acres of hemp. Therefore in the border states (Kentucky, Maryland, and Missouri, for example) the very word "plantation" was almost obsolete by the 1850s; men spoke of "farms." In Georgia and the Carolinas, *rice cultivation* was very capital-intensive and demanded large, concentrated slaveholdings, sometimes up to 700 slaves per unit. In the mid-19th century the peak of rice output was reached on the Atlantic coast; the region never fully recovered from the ravages of the Civil War and the destructive Union armies. The rivalry of the rice lands of Louisiana, Texas, and Arkansas, and in 1906, a series of terrible storms, destroyed many of the seaboard rice plantations that were left. They became tropical game preserves for wealthy Northern industrialists.

Sugar estates were capital-intensive. Cane sugar was introduced to Louisiana by Jesuits from Santo Domingo, and slave revolts on that island in 1791–95 brought an influx of French planter refugees into Louisiana. Among them was the soldier, Jean Etienne Boré, who discovered how to granulate sugar from cane juice in 1795. Boré made a profit of $12,000 on his first crop. One famous sugar plantation, Magnolia, about 50 miles South of New Orleans, was well located on rich delta soil. Its records indicate an acreage of 2,200, a slave force of about 100, and a gross income of $148,000 in 1861. Louisiana sugar planters suffered the competition of the West Indies, as well as the impact of climatic hazards (tropical storms and diseases like yellow fever) and unstable world prices. The federal government stepped in to protect them with a tariff against foreign sugar in 1821.

In the Kentucky bluegrass region, in central Tennessee, and in Missouri, *hemp* was an important local cash crop. It was liked on the frontier because it supplied a coarse homespun cloth in wide use. In the 1820s the hemp growers, like the sugar planters, were protected by a federal tariff. The statesman Henry Clay made federal tariff protection a central plank in his platform for the "American System"; it so happens he had also married a hemp heiress. Meanwhile, the South's traditional crop, tobacco, faced an uncertain history after the War of 1812. Jefferson's embargo, the war itself, and foreign competition hit tobacco planters badly. Not until after 1840 were new species of leaf and better curing methods developed on newer tobacco lands. Planters abandoned the eroded Tidewater, moved to the Piedmont and even over the mountains into Tennessee, Kentucky, and as far as Ohio. Virginia and North Carolina were worried by this migration, but the new improvements helped to double the tobacco crop in any case and trebled it in the 1850s. By 1860 the United States was what it long remained, the world's greatest tobacco-growing nation. These cash crops for export—cotton, sugar, rice, tobacco, hemp—were the South's best-known crops.

The chief crop grown in the South, however, was none of these, but *corn*. In acreage, total weight, and total value, corn exceeded other crops. Grown by slaves as a side crop on cotton plantations and by white yeomen farmers and poor whites all over the region, corn was the essential food crop that kept the South alive, though it did not enter into foreign markets. The Upper South did "export" corn to the Southwest. As usual in this pre-1860 period of U.S. history, the subsistence, home-use sector, remained the largest. Much of American society still remained outside the market or devoted a good deal of its energies to nonmarket activities.

The growth of economic sections

Long before 1860, the economic revolution and the opportunistic pursuit of happiness had produced more or less distinct sections within the American nation. These sections were at the same time both hostile rivals and heavily interdependent. Nationalism underlay economic growth and growth in turn helped to bind the nation together. Yet three great sections were now clear: the North, the South, and the West. Each had different comparative advantages; each began to specialize in commercial output.

The South was devoted to plantation and farm staples for export to foreign nations and to the Northeast. Its food supply was bought largely from the West by way of the Mississippi; its manufactures from the Northeast by sea. The West came to specialize in grain and cattle to feed the other two sections and eventually Europe as that continent industrialized. New England and the Middle Atlantic states performed the same function that England had performed in colonial days. They supplied the West and South with finished goods, with capital and equipment, with commercial and building know-how, and with foreign imports and immigrants. They became a little England and the West and South their colonies.

After 1814 a pattern of sectional interdependency became clearer. The river steamboat helped. Domestic trade flow before the 1830s depended on the Mississippi-Ohio system. The West was bound to the South, and western products floated down the great river through Arkansas, Tennessee, Mississippi, and Louisiana, very often being sold long before they reached New Orleans. Goods were landed informally (European observers marveled at the casual nature of American docks) and sold on the way. New Orleans meanwhile shipped cotton, rice, sugar, and other commercial staples to the North by sea. Bulky products from the East could afford to go west only by sea and the Mississippi system before the 1830s.

In the 1830s and 40s this cord between West and South was cut. Turnpikes, canals, and railroads went east-west, rather than north-south. The Western farm frontier was linked to the commercial East by the Erie Canal, the New York Central, and other companies. Major economic flows changed direction. New Orleans never became a truly great port as did New York. Trade between West and South still rose in *absolute* figures, pushed up by normal growth of population. The 1850s was a prosperous decade on the river systems. New York's port activities were less than those of New Orleans at this time, but the latter would soon fall behind. Three southern ports, Mobile, Charleston, and Savannah, were also busy, shipping staples to the North by the coastal lanes. By 1843, however, Buffalo, New York, was trans-

Bustling New York port—the South Street Pier in 1850

Brown Brothers

shipping more western farm produce eastward via the Erie Canal than the port of New Orleans could receive each year from its water-fed hinterland. For the expanding western trade, the Mississippi river water-link had become inadequate. Population and farms were concentrating in the Ohio country and beyond. The statistics of the trade of Buffalo tell the whole story, with a moral for the beleaguered South: 1836—139,000 barrels of flour and 500,000 bushels of grain shipped from the West; 1860—over 1 million barrels of flour and over 31 million bushels of grain from the West. The volume of trade at the river port of St. Louis destined for shipment downstream to New Orleans declined in the 1850s. The Transportation Revolution had cut off New Orleans from its taproots.

The "happiness of pursuit"

Changing economic dependency patterns of the sections had much to do with the outbreak of the Civil War and more to do with its outcome. To some degree the war was a sectional conflict, with the West as the balancing element. The unlimited pursuit of happiness had wrought fundamental structural changes in the American nation before 1860. Americans worshiped the very activity of the pursuit as much as its fruits; perhaps it should be called "the happiness of pursuit."

Bibliography

G. R. Taylor. *The Transportation Revolution.* New York: Harper, 1968 ed.

P. W. Gates. *The Farmers' Age.* New York: Harper, 1968.

S. Bruchey. *Roots of American Economic Growth.* New York: Harper, 1968.

S. Elkins. *Slavery.* University of Chicago Press, 1968 ed.

Hugh G. Aitken. *Did Slavery Pay?* Boston: Houghton Mifflin, 1971.

9

Trying to define the Federal system

The spoils of government . . . Monroe: the Republicans go Federalist . . . the "Era of Good Feelings" versus an era of factionalism . . . the new nationalism: economic and judicial . . . the capitalist Supreme Court . . . the new nationalism: territorial and racial . . . Andrew Jackson and the Indians . . . the Supreme Court fails the Indians . . . black slavery and the Missouri Compromise . . . the Monroe Doctrine: peak of Republican nationalism . . . new politics: the revolt against the caucus . . . John Quincy Adams and the American System . . . the Jacksonian Revolution: 1828 . . . Jackson and the symbols of democracy . . . who was Andrew Jackson? . . . what does a "democratic" president do in 1828? . . . the men around Jackson . . . the West and Daniel Webster . . . the South and Calhoun . . . a Jefferson birthday dinner, 1830 . . . the theory of disunion: Calhoun's "concurrent majority" . . . nullification and the threat of force . . . Jackson's war on the U.S. Bank . . . the jealousy of state banks . . . death of the Bank . . . what was the outcome of the Bank War? . . . how "democratic" was Jacksonian Democracy? . . . rotation in office and the spoils . . . Jackson and the underprivileged . . . the Indian "Trail of Tears" . . . "making it": the world of Jackson.

The spoils of government

Americans viewed Government as a device for securing individual Happiness as promised in the Declaration of Independence. Or at least they thought Government should guarantee the conditions under which Happiness could be Pursued.

They disagreed about what those conditions were: protective tariffs or free trade; central banking or local banking; liberal land policies or less generous land policies; aid to "internal improvements" or none —these policy matters divided men and women in this age of rapid economic growth and expansion. But few Americans were ideologues and few held rigidly unchangeable views on these issues; there was a give-and-take which made the art of politics (the art of getting things done) possible. Americans were pragmatic and practical rather than theoretical in their politics, thus Jefferson could wield the power of the nation, despite his anxiety for local rights; and both Henry Clay and John C. Calhoun could have abrupt and public changes of position on major issues. Government was to be manipulated. Abstractions like states' rights and strict or broad construction went by the board when powerful sectional interests were at stake or when the unfettered pursuit of material Progress seemed threatened. Generally, Americans did not reject the use of government power, despite their tough individualism; they only opposed its use by others.

The hidden theme of the period from the War of 1812 through the age of Andrew Jackson was therefore: *What is government for? Who is to benefit from its actions?* In these years Americans were simultaneously nationalist and provincial; they pursued national purposes and fought bitterly for sectional and private interests. Usually sectionalism is said to have been stronger than national unity before the Civil War. Yet the political system did operate to restrain the most extreme and most separatist sectional forces, as in 1820, 1833, and 1850. The "miracle" of peaceful transfer of political power at each election finally broke down in 1860–61 with the election of Lincoln on an anti-slavery-extension platform. No further compromise was then possible, in spite of valiant efforts by border states representatives. Southerners were finally convinced that with Lincoln's election, the role of the federal government was to be radically redefined to their gross disadvantage.

Monroe: The Republicans go Federalist

As during the Revolution and the struggle over the adoption of the federal constitution, *national* consciousness was strongest in the upper reaches of government, weakest at the lower levels of state and locality. James Monroe, elected easily to the presidency in 1816 as the logical successor to Jefferson and Madison, shared Jefferson's nationalism. Monroe, the last of the "Virginia dynasty" to occupy the White House, was an orthodox Jeffersonian partisan. He had been a successful states' rights, anti-Federalist senator, Governor of Virginia, and ambassador in Europe for Washington and Jefferson. During the War of 1812 he served as Madison's Secretary of State. His career line paralleled that of his master and ex-law teacher, Jefferson, and encouraged Monroe to *think nationally,* as it had encouraged Jefferson.

Nationalism brought with it a Hamiltonian revival under new, more popular, and less elitist auspices. This Republican neo-Federalism was seen especially in the younger men who surrounded Monroe—like John Quincy Adams, exponent of a strong national foreign policy, and W. H. Crawford, John C. Calhoun, and Henry Clay, "War Hawks" of the 1812–14 years. A "new nationalism" was thus born: a middle-class, commercial-minded, economic growth-conscious nationalism, that produced Henry Clay's "American System" and buttressed the economic revolution described in the previous chapter.

The "Era of Good Feelings" versus an era of factionalism

Monroe's years have been called an "Era of Good Feelings" partly because American national security was assured abroad by renewal of friendship with England, the amicable settlement of Canadian boundary issues, and growth of Anglo-American trade. The Royal Navy, in truth, gave free security to the U.S., since it dominated the oceans at that time and the national interests of the English and of the U.S. were similar. The English, eager to enter South American as well as North American markets, favored a strong and independent United States. Thus the demilitarization of the Great Lakes was begun in 1817 and the 49th parallel was recognized as the U.S.-Canadian border as far as the Rockies, with joint Anglo-American occupation of the Oregon region. Meanwhile, Jackson's military exploits in Florida and the Adams-Onis Treaty with Spain (1819), gave Florida to the U.S. for a mere 5 million dollars. In view of the presence of the British navy and the growing turmoil in Spain's own Central and South American colonies, all of which became independent nations in the 1820s, that nation was in no position to resist the territorial ambitions of the Americans.

Security was one aspect of the Era of Good Feelings. Another was alleged to be a sort of consensus at home, under the one-party system. The Missouri Compromise of 1820 was supposed to have settled the question of slavery in the Louisiana Purchase. Yet bitter political infighting took place, as the economic revolution and western expansion brought sectional conflict and as the tide of popular opinion rose against the old elite politics of the caucus and the dynasty. Out of radical ferment, especially in the West, emerged Jacksonian Democracy. Monroe's second administration was more characterized by factional struggle than by good feelings, though he was readily reelected in 1820, winning all electoral college votes except one. Thereafter no one could hold the Republican party together. The Jacksonians came to reject many of the economic notions of Henry Clay. They saw themselves as the true heirs of Jefferson. In this purist self-image, they would turn the party around again, back to the true faith and away from neo-Federalism. John C. Calhoun of South Carolina also split with his former War Hawk colleague Clay; he eventually abandoned nationalism in favor of strict states' rights. Though Calhoun was to clash with Jackson in 1833 in a head-on collision between federal and state power, the Jacksonians received much Southern, pro-slavery support. But their day did not come until the election of Andrew Jackson in 1828.

The new nationalism: Economic and judicial

The new popular nationalism assumed various forms—economic, judicial, territorial, and racial. *Economic nationalism* was stimulated by the material growth of the nation. State aid to enterprise was mainly motivated by local rivalries; federal aid was driven also by a national vision. Apart from federal aid to canals and railroads, which the Republican nationalists still felt queasy about, the Washington government helped banks by giving charters, and purchasing stock in the two banks of the United States. One was Hamilton's Bank of 1791, whose charter was allowed to lapse in 1811; the Second Bank was chartered in 1816, a gift of Madison's change of heart on the subject of central banking. The Second Bank was three times bigger than the First. Madison also signed the first truly protective tariff, that of 1816, another step which appeared to bring him nearer to Hamiltonianism.

Meanwhile the Panic of 1819 and the depression which followed brought demands for federal intervention to aid specific groups. The Land Act of 1820 made land more easily available—still sold at auction with the minimum price cut to $1.25 an acre, and with minimum lots of 80 acres. The Tariff of 1824, pushed by Henry Clay, could be supported by arguments of a nationalist variety. *Judicial nationalism,* adopted by the Supreme Court, was a policy which tended to strengthen the hands of the federal government in economic affairs. The John Marshall Court made a series of careful decisions of crucial economic significance which placed it clearly on the side of active promotion of business enterprise. Marshall asserted the Court's authority as a third branch of national government, in *Marbury* v. *Madison* (1803) when he affirmed the Court's right to invalidate acts of Congress as unconstitutional. This interpretation was extended to the invalidation of state laws in 1810 by *Fletcher* v. *Peck.* Marshall's centralizing tendency was extended by decisions which favored the growth of capitalism.

The capitalist Supreme Court

The Court protected risk capital and placed private property on a pedestal as a supreme value above all others. *Sturges* v. *Crowninshield* and *Dartmouth College* v. *Woodward,* both in 1819, made the contract clause (Article I, Section 10, of the Constitution) the protective bulwark of vested property rights in the U.S.—a condition demanded by the vigorous, enterprising "men on the make" who were leading the forces of economic revolution. In *Fletcher* v. *Peck* Marshall voided a Georgia law rescinding an original state land grant, as a violation of the federal contract clause. In the *Dartmouth College* case, when the state of New Hampshire tried to amend the college charter in order to increase the number of trustees and, in effect, turn the college into a state university, Marshall defended the college charter as a *contract.* The college, he argued, using Associate Justice Joseph Story's distinction between public and private corporations, was a private corporation and immune from state control. Daniel Webster defended the college before the Court, and ended with the famous line: "It is, sirs, a small college, yet there are those who love it." The case was not considered important at the time, but the corporation argument used by Story and Marshall created a precedent used many times over to protect business from interference.

In that same year, 1819, the Court used the "implied powers" clause to uphold the constitutionality of the Second Bank of the U.S. in *McCulloch* v. *Maryland.* In one of his most openly nationalistic decisions, Marshall declared that the state of Maryland had no power to tax the notes of a federal branch bank. Five years later, in *Gibbons* v. *Ogden* (1824), Marshall overturned a steamboat navigation monopoly given to Aaron Ogden (as agent for Robert Fulton's patent) by the legislature of New York. Construing the "commerce clause" (Article I, Section 8) very broadly, Marshall asserted sweeping powers for Congress over all aspects of interstate commerce and virtually excluded states from the field. He fortified the commerce clause argument with the clause which empowers Congress to promote science and the useful arts. Obviously, Marshall was opposed to local monopolies that could restrict the spread of new technology and enterprise, and he thought that trade rivalries between the states were against the national interest.

The expansion of the new American nation took place at the expense of others. The losers were to some extent the English and the French, to a great extent the Spanish, and most of all the Amerindians.

The scourge of the Indians was Andrew Jackson, who led a punitive raid against them and against escaped Negro slaves in Florida. The "Florida solution" to the Indian problem was simple. Jackson helped to bring the white man's vengeance against the Creeks, and the humane policies of Oglethorpe in 18th-century Georgia were now forgotten. Naturally, hatred of Indians did not spring from nowhere; life on the southwestern frontier for white settlers could be terrifying and tragic. Indian uprisings in the Mississippi Territory and the Florida borderlands climaxed in the Fort Mims massacre of 1813, near Mobile. Jackson hastily took the lead of some Tennessee militia and fought several battles with the Creeks in the winter of 1813–14. After a terrible defeat at Horseshoe Bend in 1814, the Indians capitulated and were forced into a treaty which ceded two thirds of all Creek lands. This Treaty of Fort Jackson was of doubtful legality, being signed on behalf of only a small segment of the tribe. The problem was that the white and Indian notions of land "ownership" were so opposed in principle that any treaty was a mere imposition by force of arms. Jackson was magnanimous with one chief, Red Eagle, who came alone to his headquarters and faced him down.

The new nationalism: Territorial and racial

General Jackson, I am not afraid of you. I fear no man, for I am a Creek warrior. . . . you can kill me, if you desire. But I come to beg you to send for the women and children of the war party, who are now starving in the woods. Their fields and cribs have been destroyed by your people. . . .

Jackson let Red Eagle go free. The moral of this story is that, though about 900 warriors were killed at Horseshoe Bend, the real enemy of the Indian was hunger and the destruction of his farm economy by the whites. As Red Eagle is alleged to have said: "If I had an army, I would yet fight, and contend to the last: but I have none; my people are all gone. . . . Once I could animate my warriors to battle; but I cannot animate the dead." The Creeks (or Red Eagle's section of them, called Red Sticks) were outgunned and outmaneuvered.

Jackson's Indian policies represented the white Tennessee frontier. He spoke for trans-Appalachia. In a well-known letter to President Monroe in March 1817, Jackson urged toughness toward the Indian.

Andrew Jackson and the Indians

He wanted to overturn the principles of American Indian policy laid down since 1789: "The utmost good faith shall always be observed towards the Indians, their lands and property shall never be taken from them without their consent." The principle was rarely kept and "just" wars were a frequent excuse for land-grabbing. Yet George Washington had hoped to establish a clear demarcation line in the West between Indian and white territories (like the English line of 1763); he was against indiscriminate white settlement on the frontier. In time, he expected, the game would vanish and the Indians would disappear. Jackson refused to wait, not necessarily because he hated Indians, but because he was an impatient nationalist.

In truth the Indians had destroyed most of the game but they had not disappeared; land patents given to Tennesseans proved useless when the whites discovered Indians on the lands. Jackson wrote angrily to Monroe:

The game being destroyed, as acknowledged by all, the right of possession, granted to the Indians for the purpose of hunting ceases, and justice, sound policy, and the constitutional rights of the citizen, would require its being resigned to him.

The argument Jackson used here was based on the myth that all Indians were hunters, not farmers. The whites would put the land to "superior use." But Jackson was even franker in a later passage:

I have long viewed treaties with the Indians as an absurdity. . . . Is it not absurd for the sovereign to negotiate by treaty with the subject?

Here spoke the authentic voice of the white frontier. Monroe accepted the hunting argument. "The hunter or savage state," he wrote back to Jackson, "requires a greater extent of territory to sustain it, than is compatible with the progress and just claims of civilized life." "Progress" and "civilization" demanded the ouster of the Indians.

The Supreme Court fails the Indians

Marshall's Court went along with the image of the Indians as savage hunters, though his conscience was uneasy. Marshall, unlike later theorists, wished to treat the Indians as separate nations, with their own laws, rather than as an automatically inferior, subject race. In *Worcester* v. *Georgia* (1832) he declared:

America was inhabited by a distinct people, divided into separate nations, independent of each other, and of the rest of the world, and governing themselves by their own laws.

But the Court was willing to go along with the superior use rationalization, derived from the Swiss jurist E. de Vattel (*Law of Nations*, 1758), which stereotyped all Indians as nomadic hunters. In 1823, in *Johnson's and Graham's Lessee* v. *McIntosh,* Marshall also justified the "ultimate dominion" of the white man over Indian lands, on the argument that, "However extravagant the pretension of converting the discovery of an inhabited country into conquest may appear; if the principle has been asserted in the first instance . . . and if the property of the great mass of the community originates in it, it becomes a law of the land." In other words, America was not "empty" when the white man came but it was too late now to alter things. Fait accompli! The Court thus failed the Indian as it would later fail the Negro.

James Madison's fears about the instability of the patched-up compromise on slavery contained in the Constitution came to a head in 1819–20 when the slavery question was a matter of dispute between the sections. Slavery became mixed up with the fierce sectional politics over land policy and the struggle for benefits. Congress could not legally make laws regarding slavery within the existing states, but in the new western Territories it had jurisdiction. Each time a new Territory was created a crisis broke out. If the Territory permitted slavery it was likely to keep that institution intact upon entering the Union as a state. This would add to the Southern votes in Congress. The population and power of Dixie was relatively declining and it would be further affected by any new free Territory and state added to the Union because that was likely to result in two new antislavery Senators and a number of Representatives. This struggle produced both the crises and political compromises of 1820 and 1850.

Black slavery and the Missouri Compromise

Map 4. The Missouri Compromise

Redrawn from Life History of the U.S., Vol. 3, p. 123.

While the South developed more rigid arguments about the alleged benefits of slavery to civilization, the question of the admission of Missouri arose. Would the new state be free or slaveholding? In 1819 the Union had 11 free and 11 slave states. Since 1791 the entry of new free and slave states had balanced each other. In the Missouri-upper Louisiana Territory, slavery was an old institution going back to Spanish days though the region had only about 3,000 slaves. Representative James Tallmadge of New York tried to prohibit slavery in the Territory: no new slaves would be admitted to Missouri and the children of existing slaves would go free on reaching the age of 25. The House passed the Tallmadge amendment (having a Northern majority); the Senate rejected it.

Heated debate lasted into 1820 and was resolved by Henry Clay's Compromise. This admitted Missouri as a slave state; balanced it off by admitting Maine which was lopped off from Massachusetts in the North; and forbade slavery in what was left of Jefferson's Louisiana Purchase area, north of 36° 30′. Southerners were quieted with the hope that both Florida and Arkansas would soon enter the Union as slave states. The nation breathed a sigh of relief. Shortly thereafter a new Negro republic was founded in Africa by free Negroes from the United States, sent there by the American Colonization Society (established in 1817). The republic of Liberia named its capital Monrovia, after the U.S. President.

The Compromise held the peace for a generation, but for Jefferson, who died six years later, aged 83, Clay's clever deal was like a warning "firebell" in the night; some day, he feared, the bell of slavery would toll the knell of the American Union.

The Monroe Doctrine: Peak of Republican nationalism

While Monroe's second administration witnessed growing political factionalism, his foreign policy was increasingly nationalistic. He crowned it with the Monroe Doctrine of 1823. American territorial nationalists were disturbed by Russian adventures in Alaska and by the possibilities of European intervention in Central and South America, where colonies were fighting for their independence. Russians explored the Pacific coast of North America in the 18th century and employed a Dane, Vitus Bering, to map the Arctic shores. He discovered Alaska and the Bering Straits, 1728–41. Russian fur traders settled the region and led by Alexander Baranov, virtual governor of Russian Alaska until 1817, they established the capital of Sitka in 1799. A Russian Orthodox cathedral was later built there (this 118-year-old church was destroyed by fire in 1966). By the early 1820s Russian settlements were expanding southward down the coast. In 1789 the Hudson's Bay Company had laid claim to all of the West beyond the Canadian Rockies. Only the Spanish "threat" had been removed: In the Adams-Onis Treaty of 1819, Spain gave up its Pacific Northwest ambitions. A Spanish mission had been founded at San Francisco as early as 1775, and a settlement much further north at Nootka Sound in 1789.

The true originator of the Monroe Doctrine was the tough-minded, nationalistic John Quincy Adams. As Secretary of State, he wrote Monroe's message to Congress. The suspicious and proud Adams also rejected a British proposal, made by his counterpart, George Canning, of a joint Anglo-American warning to the Continental powers not to intervene in the Americas. Britain had split with its former European allies (France, Austria, Prussia, Russia) after they had plotted a counterrevolutionary intervention to restore absolute monarchy to Spain. The French pushed for the right to intervene and restore Spanish power in the New World colonies. Canning was ready to ally with the U.S. to redress the balance of power in Europe, but Adams refused to approach France and Russia behind England's skirts. In any case he was suspicious that England wanted some deal with Spain over Cuba (Americans had their eyes on that island). Adams acted alone. Congress had already recognized the independence of Colombia and Mexico in 1822, and Chile and Argentina in January 1823. As early as July 1821 Adams had firmly resisted the Tsar's claim to Pacific Northwest territory as far south as the 51st parallel in Oregon country. He bluntly told the Russian ambassador (July 1821): "The American continents are no longer subjects for *any* new European colonial establishments."

This rhetoric was repeated almost exactly in the Monroe Doctrine, the message to Congress of December 2, 1823. The American continents were no longer to be subjects for colonization by European powers; any threat to do so would be considered a threat against the security of the United States; *existing* colonies would not be interfered with by the United States. In addition the United States would not intervene in the internal affairs of European states or take part in European wars in which U.S. interests were not involved.

The declaration was brusque, even gauche. To some extent it was not necessary, since Canning had managed to get the French to renounce the idea of intervention in Latin America two months earlier. The Doctrine was a "paper tiger": the United States had no means of militarily enforcing its claims. The British navy was the main line of New World defense. But the true importance of the Doctrine would come in later years and its inner significance was not lost on the young republics of Latin America. From the moment of their birth, the Monroe Doctrine began that troubled relationship, shot through with U.S. paternalism and misunderstanding, which would govern the intercourse between the Latin American nations and their northern neighbor.

New politics: The revolt against the caucus

John Quincy Adams won the election of 1824 only via a decision of the House of Representatives. With the termination of the Virginia dynasty in Monroe came an open challenge to the one-party, Republican elite, caucus politics which had dominated the nation for so long. The post-1819 depression also helped to arouse new democratic, grassroots forces at state and local levels. Relief for debtors, prison reform, labor union organization, strikes, all reflected the growing social tensions of the day. Quasi-two-party systems emerged at state levels and extensions of the franchise, largely through abolition of property-owning qualifications for voters, came in the new constitutions of western states, and as reforms in older states—for example, Connecticut (1818), Massachusetts (1820), and New York (1821). In the 1820s several states held constitutional conventions to reform their basic laws and to meet new demands. The rhetoric of "democracy" was heavy in those conventions, where ideological battles were bitterly fought out. The right to vote, representation, the right to hold public office, the establishment of religion, the duties of government—these and other fundamental issues were re-debated in a more egalitarian and majoritarian age. The rights of property were not seriously questioned (though some conservatives feared so) because the political reformers of the 1820s proclaimed the United States to be a middle-class society in which property was widely distributed.

The new dissent was reflected at the national level in the presidential election of 1824. After a long regime, the Republican party was breaking up. Party discipline was weak and the party caucus crumbling. The elite did choose its candidate, the neo-Jeffersonian, William H. Crawford of Georgia. There was no outstanding Virginian available. Crawford was opposed, however, by three other Republican contenders, Adams of Massachusetts, Clay of Kentucky, and Calhoun of South Carolina. Calhoun attacked the caucus system as undemocratic and he was not far off the mark, for despite the pleas of the aging Madison and Jefferson only a bare one third of the Republican party Congressmen attended the caucus meeting called in February 1824. They nominated Crawford. Calhoun dropped from the race to settle for the vice presidency.

In local Tennessee politics a dark-horse candidate was thrown up as the state nominee for president—Major General Andrew Jackson, the hero of the Battle of New Orleans and of the Indian wars and senator from Tennessee, 1823–24. All the candidates were thus Republicans and no states' rights or Federalist leader emerged. Jackson's name kindled instant enthusiasm across the nation. In Pennsylvania the party had originally leaned toward Calhoun but now switched to Jackson and named Calhoun its vice presidential candidate instead. Other states jumped on the Jackson bandwagon. In the election Jackson carried Pennsylvania, the Carolinas, and much of the West. He won 99 electoral college votes, while Adams received 84, Crawford 41, and Clay 37. Calhoun was elected vice president with little real opposition. The popular vote was: Crawford 46,618; Clay 47,126; Adams 108,740; Jackson 153,544. Though Jackson won the highest number of the popular vote and of the electoral college (a plurality), he needed a *majority* of the electoral votes in order to gain the White House. The 12th Amendment directed that the election be decided by the House of Representatives, each state having one vote and choosing the winner from the top three candidates.

Crawford was partially paralyzed though his campaign did not entirely die. Clay being fourth was excluded, but exerted influence on the outcome as the Speaker of the House. Clay leaned toward Adams, the

New England economic nationalist, seeing him as being closer to his own views than was Jackson. When Adams was chosen and then nominated Clay as his Secretary of State, the irate Jacksonians cried, "Corrupt bargain!" General Jackson immediately began to plan his campaign for 1828 and soon took into his camp Vice President Calhoun and the New York leader of the Crawford group, the canny professional, Martin Van Buren, the "Little Magician."

John Quincy Adams and the American System

Henry Clay's personal ambitions now reached their nearest approach to fulfillment. He never won the presidency though he was a candidate in 1824, 1832, and 1844. His American System was as much a personal political platform as it was a plan for national growth. He swung into action to push the American System, aiming to unite sectional blocs around his policies: tariff increases, the Bank of the United States, and federally aided internal improvements. He wished to unite the Ohio Valley with New England. High tariffs would protect American industries from foreign imports and help to stimulate the growth of cities and of immigration as well as to build up a skilled native work force. In turn, this body of consumers would provide the necessary market at home for American farm output. Clay had a place in his scheme for everyone: worker, business leader, farmer and planter, banker, and trader.

Southern planters, however, opted out of the American System. Very sensibly, they felt that Clay's hopes were unreal: It would be decades before New England's infant textile industry could absorb all of the South's great raw cotton output and meanwhile the planters depended on the English market. Clay's proposed high tariffs on imports would make it difficult for the English to continue to buy cotton, since their exports to the United States would be reduced.

The defection of the South from Clay's system meant the loss of Jackson and Calhoun. The Jackson-Calhoun-Van Buren forces now called themselves "Democrats" and the two-party system was reborn: National Republicans versus Democrats. The Democrats were well organized. They tried to subvert President Adams's legislative program in Congress. All Adams could achieve was a lengthening of the National Road, minor improvements to harbors and rivers, and the Tariff of 1828, called the "Tariff of Abominations" in Calhoun's state of South Carolina. Foreign policy successes of Adams were also meager. While the English leader Canning agreed to extend the joint Anglo-American accord on Oregon, he still smarted from the treatment Adams had meted out to him over the Monroe Doctrine and so he killed all hopes of enlarging U.S. trade in the British West Indies. Adams's hopes of asserting U.S. hemispheric leadership at a Pan-American meeting in Panama were scotched by Congress.

The well-meaning, honorable Adams even failed in his Indian policy. Wishing to treat the Creek and Cherokee with honor, he annulled a fraudulent treaty (Indian Springs, 1825) which was designed to take away 5,000,000 acres of tribal lands. Governor Troup of Georgia called out his state militia in defiance of federal authority.

Jackson, Webster, and Clay (engraving by John Sartain)

New York Historical Society

Fortunately for Adams, he was able to save face because the Indian tribes agreed to certain land cessions. Tragically, in the meantime Georgia had asserted its sovereignty over the Cherokee and greedy white farmers began pushing them off their lands. Andrew Jackson entertained few doubts about what was best for the Indians. The moment he took office in 1829 he overturned the sympathetic policy of Adams and totally rejected Indian land claims in Georgia. Jackson felt that he understood what the "needs" of the Indians were: removal and separation from the white race.

The Jacksonian Revolution: 1828

The election of 1828 was indeed a turning point in the history of American politics, not because it heralded the "Age of the Common Man" but because it marked the advent of organized mass politics. The growth of the electorate, the widening of the franchise, and the state constitutional reforms which preceded this election prepared the way for the *politics of party* and of professional organizers. If this was not necessarily an Age of the Common Man it was surely an age in which his vote was demanded and sought. Since the electors were more popularly chosen, printed ballots now appeared and party organization was built at the local and state level. Politics became the role of the professional. Martin Van Buren of New York typified the new breed, while Jackson himself was no amateur at the game.

The transportation and communications revolution, the rise of the party manager to manipulate the mass electorate which was still semiliterate, the adoption of campaign tours, party rallies, newspapers and party symbols, deliberate appeals to ethnic, economic, and sectional prejudices—many aspects of modern U.S. political life openly emerged. Gentry control was forced to yield.

Jackson and the Democrats easily defeated John Quincy Adams and the National Republicans in 1828. In the electoral college Jackson won 178 votes to Adams's 83. Calhoun, with 171 votes, was equally readily elected as Jackson's vice president. The heavy support for the Democrats came from the South and West, though Jackson did carry Pennsylvania and, by a narrow margin, New York. The latter was delivered by Martin Van Buren helped by William L. Marcy, the two bosses of the "Albany Regency," a political machine built on patronage.

Here was a classic example of the new politics with its open appeal to sectional interests and its political sleight of hand. Party managers had grasped that New England was a lost cause and would go for Adams, as the South and West would go for the winning combination of Jackson and Calhoun. A play must be made for the crucial Middle states. Pennsylvania iron manufacturers wanted high tariffs to keep out British products. Since the House Committee on Manufactures was controlled by Jackson men, that group deliberately recommended very high tariffs on imported iron and raw materials and played down the demands of the New England textile mills for higher duties in imported woolens. When New Englanders reversed their previous free-trade stance and voted for the bill, the Tariff of Abominations passed in May 1828. Though Calhoun and Southerners in general (especially South Carolinians) were angry with the tariff, Jackson landed on his feet for he could appear to the Middle states as a supporter of tariffs and of the American System, which he was not. The tariff question and the cry of a corrupt bargain between Clay and Adams defeated the National Republicans in 1828. The campaign was scurrilous and personal.

Andrew Jackson and the symbols of of democracy

Jackson's inaugural on March 4, 1829, symbolized these political changes. He went out of his way to *walk* from his hotel to the Capitol for the ceremony (as Jefferson had walked in 1801). Then he took a horseback ride, *caudillo* style, to the White House. The reception there was wide open. The muddy boot on the satin chair was a far cry from John Quincy Adams. But was this in truth the reign of "King Mob" as some feared? Or merely the manipulation of popular sentiment? It was clear who was in charge as seen in the shrewd stratagem used to get the unruly mob out of the White House: A punch barrel was placed strategically on the lawn. If this was a political "revolution," it was one from the top.

Jackson was the first outsider, and the first man from the "West," to become president. This was a new political generation. The sources of its support did reflect the profound economic changes that were taking place in the nation: population migration and economic development. Political power shifted from the countinghouse, the Eastern merchant, and banking house, to the farmhouse, the factory—but what of the planter? There were deep ambiguities in "Jacksonian Democracy." People called: "Jackson, Calhoun and Liberty!" and "Let the Freeman speak!"; and they added, "don't forget to bet all you can!"

Jackson's appeal cut across many old lines of allegiance such as the

Federalist-Republican divisions. He was Unionist but not "nationalist" in Clay's sense. He came to stand for state economic activity but not federal economic intervention. A flat anti-internal improvements program would never have appealed to the West. He lacked sympathy with radical reformers such as feminists or abolitionists and held intellectuals in contempt. Yet he stood strong against monopoly and "privilege." Jacksonianism implied greater equality *of opportunity*, rather than equality. Indians and Negroes did not figure in his philosophy, though he appealed to small farmers, small businessmen, urban workers, and the "men on the make" everywhere, and could count on Southern planter support. His appeal to the small capitalists and men on the make is curious, for Jackson's economic policies acted to retard growth if anything.

Who was Andrew Jackson?

Andrew Jackson, "Old Hickory," "King Andrew," the "Gineral," was no poor, illiterate, uncouth Tennessee backwoodsman, despite the many myths that have surrounded him. He was a well-to-do planter, lawyer, land speculator, and professional soldier. He farmed a fair-sized estate near Nashville, which began with a nucleus of 650 acres and 8 or 9 slaves (eventually he owned about 150) and used the only cotton gin in the vicinity. His mansion, "The Hermitage," was impressive, if not palatial. He was a passionate breeder of racehorses and a solid member of the upper class. Things were not always this way with Jackson. He was born of Scotch-Irish immigrant parents on the South Carolina frontier in 1767. The American Revolution, in which he fought at the age of 13, left him orphaned and scarred by a brutal British officer. After the war he lived with relatives, leading a rough and riotous life, gambling, drinking, and learning a little law on the side. Eventually he became an attorney at the age of 20, wooed and wed his beloved (but not completely divorced) Rachel at 24, and settled near Nashville.

Jackson was driven by ambition and the quest for fame. He served in the Tennessee House, then as Congressman, and later as a Tennessee supreme court justice. By conviction and temperament, Jackson was a Jeffersonian agrarian, but he split with Jefferson for a while over the Aaron Burr affair, and quit the national arena. He reappeared as a successful war hero against the Creeks and as the triumphant victor over the British at New Orleans in January 1815. The Battle of New Orleans gave Jackson extraordinary publicity and popularity which he kept alive by periodic tours of eastern cities. In spite of his vaulting ambition and his upper-class way of life, Jackson became the hero of large sections of the new electorate, the exemplar of frontier virtues and of American opportunity. Not noticeably "democratic" in sentiment before he became president, Jackson took on a more aggressively democratic stance thereafter, particularly following his reelection in 1832. He became a popular champion, if not consistently a champion of the populace. His political strength was his image of simplicity and directness, an image which masked deep shrewdness and calculation. Even his famous temper (he fought many duels, killed one man, and carried a bullet in his chest all his life) could be used to good purpose to cajole an opponent.

Yet beneath these complexities Jackson was indeed driven by great simplicities: worship of personal honor, love of country, determination to protect the Union. Never above using the parochial states' rights argument to win a local political argument, Jackson nonetheless placed the Union above the states. In his inaugural, twice in the same sentence, he emphasized this: *"The Federal Constitution must be obeyed,* state rights preserved, our national debt must be paid, direct taxes and loans avoided, *and the Federal Union preserved.* These are the objects I have in view, and regardless of all consequences, will carry into effect." (Emphasis added.)

Jackson's program was vague. He said little about what he would do, more about what he would *not* do. What does an avowedly "democratic" president do in 1828? The range of alternatives was not great, perhaps, but Jackson was in any case no radical. The "isms" of the day did not appeal to him. He had little or no contact with social thinkers such as Emerson or Hawthorne, or the feminists and abolitionists. *George Bancroft,* (1800–91) the great nationalist historian, did not become active in Jacksonian politics in Massachusetts until the 1830s. An intellectual, trained at Harvard, Berlin, and Göttingen, Bancroft was a rare man, who became the Democratic patronage boss of Massachusetts and, in 1845, Secretary of the Navy for President Polk. But Bancroft did not influence Jackson at all. In contrast to the younger man's travels and education, the only time Jackson left the United States was to invade Spanish Florida.

What does a "democratic" president do in 1828?

Many of Jackson's achievements were negative and his office was marked by frequent presidential vetoes. Yet he expanded the powers and the prestige of the presidency and was the first president to veto laws not only because he thought them unconstitutional but because he did not like them. Thus he killed the bill to build the Maysville Turnpike in 1830 and the bill to recharter the Bank of the United States. Jackson tried to strengthen the states and transferred federal funds from the federal bank to state banks in 1833. It was Henry Clay's idea, in an act of 1836, to distribute surplus federal funds to the state governments. Jackson signed a mild tariff reform bill in 1832, but he strongly resisted the defiance of the state of South Carolina in 1833. Do these measures make up a "People's Program"?

No doubt Jackson's concept of freedom was limited and negative: it meant freedom *from.* He lacked the visionary quality of some later statesmen and could not contemplate a positive federal government acting to create freedom *to.* But at all times Jackson felt himself to be the true representative of the "People" and his attitudes were not far removed from theirs. His concept of freedom has persisted in American history, supported by a growing economy and a society which has offered opportunity for individual advances. American freedom

Martin Van Buren

Chicago Historical Society, daguerreotype

has largely meant the freedom to be left alone, the right to pursue individual goals, unhampered by officialdom: in other words laissez-faire for those fortunate enough to be able to enjoy it.

The men around Jackson

Jackson chose an undistinguished official cabinet, except for Van Buren. Other men around him could be used for advice; these included old Tennessee friends, journalists like Amos Kendall of Kentucky, and Francis P. Blair, who was to edit the party organ, the Washington *Globe*, and Roger B. Taney, a Maryland political organizer, whom Jackson rushed through a series of public offices (Attorney General, Treasury Secretary, and finally, Chief Justice, to replace Marshall). These men came to be called the "Kitchen Cabinet." Their importance should not be exaggerated, for Andrew Jackson was always the real boss.

In Jackson's first administration two men stood out: Van Buren and Calhoun. They were bitter rivals but Van Buren was certain to win from the start because Jackson was already suspicious of Calhoun. Jackson, however, had needed the Southern support that Calhoun's vice presidency brought. Van Buren methodically froze out Calhoun from the inner circle, insofar as this was necessary. Van Buren's sectional political strength lay in the New York–Southwest axis he had helped to forge. Calhoun's hopes of constructing a firm political base on an alliance of South and West was doomed to ultimate failure because of the impact of the ongoing transportation revolution.

The West and Daniel Webster

One reform that the West did expect its "People's candidate" to produce was cheap land. With rapid settlement, much of the good land had been taken up in the near-West and East. Jackson himself had bought land in Tennessee before it became a state in 1796 and then sold it at a much higher price after settlers moved in. At $1.25 an acre, fertile land was a good buy, but poorer soils were not. Westerners demanded a cut in the official land price to enable marginal lands to come under development. Their champion was the Missouri senator, Thomas Hart Benton, an ardent Jackson man, though he had fought a wild brawl with Jackson back in 1813. Benton's plan was to "graduate" the price of land, lowering it the longer the land had been on the market unsold. Another scheme was "preemption": the right of squatters to claim public land, on which they had worked improvements, at the minimum federal price. This did not *lower* the price of the land below the $1.25 an acre minimum but it did enable them to avoid competitive bidding.

In December 1829 Senator S. A. Foot of Connecticut touched off a raging debate on land policy by suggesting that all new land sales be temporarily halted. Many Northeastern interests feared that sales of cheap western land were syphoning off labor from industry in the North. This fear Van Buren as well as Clay had hoped to allay, and also to win Northern support for cheap land by offering high tariffs in return. The winter of 1829–30 saw a hard Senate battle which began on land policy but soon broadened to include other sectional issues, particularly the tough resistance that South Carolina was offering to the federal tariff of 1828. The climax was a historic confrontation between the brilliant orator Daniel Webster of Massachusetts and Robert Hayne of South Carolina.

The Webster-Hayne debate left the issue of land sales far behind, as the two men argued the nature of the Union, the function of government, the rights of states, and nullification. Daniel Webster, whose skill and dramatic presence had dominated several Supreme Court cases (*Dartmouth College, McCulloch* v. *Maryland*), was a nationalist and politically close to Henry Clay. Yet fate would bring him to the side of the agrarian Andrew Jackson, because both men placed the Union higher than the states. Hayne was drawn into making a full statement of a states' rights, separatist, strict-construction position, and Webster seized the opportunity to attack this philosophy head-on, ending with his famous peroration:

> Liberty and Union, now and forever, one and inseparable!

Somewhat as an anticlimax, Benton's Graduation Bill passed the Senate in May but was stopped in the House and a Pre-emption Act of 1830 became law the same month. Squatters could have first chance to buy 160 acres at $1.25.

The South and Calhoun

As the South and the North fought for the allegiance of the West in Congress, South Carolina became increasingly alienated from the Union and the administration. On a personal level, Calhoun and Jackson drifted further apart.

A Cabinet crisis occurred in 1831, over the strange issue known as "Eaton malaria." Jackson had been genuinely naive in encouraging his War Secretary, John Eaton, to marry the woman he had been courting for so long, once her husband had conveniently died while serving in the navy at sea. Jackson closed his mind to possible scandal that surrounded this vivacious, blue-eyed brunette, Peggy Eaton. His own beloved wife, Rachel, had died in December 1828, and she also had suffered from malicious gossip throughout her life. The ladies of Washington society, however, were not blinded by chivalry and they coldly ostracized Eaton's beautiful and no doubt, threatening, wife. Worse, the ladies were led in their campaign by Floride Calhoun, the wife of the vice president. Jackson, in a temper, at a cabinet meeting went so far as to declare Peggy Eaton "chaste as a virgin"—as if to purify the girl by fiat. In 1831 he entirely reshuffled the cabinet and his friend Eaton resigned. Calhoun came out badly. Van Buren made the most of it. Floride was not really to blame for the rift, because Calhoun himself could have stopped her. But he was jealous of Eaton and disliked Jackson's choice of cabinet officers.

More important than the Peggy Eaton scandal was the role Calhoun had played earlier, as War Secretary in 1818, when Jackson had exceeded his orders, invaded Spanish Florida after winning the Seminole War of 1816–18, and executed two British citizens, Arbuthnot and Ambrister. The cabinet had debated censuring Jackson, but the tough John Quincy Adams had defended him and accused Spain of incompetence in administering the Florida territory. Calhoun had voted to censure Jackson. The outcome had been that the United States bought Florida from Spain, and made Jackson its Governor.

A Jefferson birthday dinner, 1830

Calhoun chose to throw down the gauntlet of extreme states' rights at a Jefferson birthday dinner of April 13, 1830. Following on the explosive Webster-Hayne debate and Webster's attack on the "South Carolina doctrine," this was perhaps a foolhardy decision. Yet Calhoun still hoped for some support from Jackson and the Democratic party. The dinner in Washington was arranged by Hayne and Benton to symbolize the alliance of West and South in the party. This fond hope was shattered when Jackson made his toast:

Our Federal Union: it must be preserved!

This came with some exasperation, after having listened to dozens of states' rights toasts already; but Calhoun responded angrily:

The Union—next to our liberty, most dear. May we all remember that it can only be preserved by respecting the rights of the States, and distributing equally the benefit and burden of the Union.

"The benefit and burden of the Union"—here laid bare was the source of the inner political struggle of these years.

Meanwhile the full story on Calhoun's move to censure Jackson in the cabinet in 1818 was revealed to the president. Calhoun tried to defend himself in a 52-page letter, but Jackson was not persuaded. The February of the following year, 1831, Calhoun was foolish enough to give the correspondence to the press and embarrass Jackson still further. The rift between the two men was complete. The scene was set for the drama of nullification.

The theory of disunion: Calhoun's "concurrent majority"

Hatred of the Tariff of Abominations went to extremes in South Carolina, where economic problems brought on by the migration of cotton-planting to the Southwest helped to breed local tensions, in-group feelings, and separatism. Calhoun, after his *volte face* and conversion from nationalism to states' rights, developed an ingenious theory to rationalize the idea of nullification (the notion that individual states could ignore and nullify federal laws they did not like). This theory of the "concurrent majority" claimed that under the Constitution, decisions should be made only with the concurrence of the major conflicting interest groups. Instead of a mere "numerical" majority in which the South would be swamped, Calhoun desired a sort of functional representation, based on economic sections.

Majoritarian democracy has its problems, and mere numbers alone can be oppressive. But Calhoun's plan would certainly give no safeguard to minorities. On the contrary, by allowing a state or section to veto federal law, and opt out of the system, the "concurrent majority" theory would empower local elites to do precisely whatever they wished.

The intellectual honesty of Calhoun's new political philosophy was questionable, as he evolved other theories, clearly sectional, to defend the planter, slaveholding interests. He went so far as to declare chattel slavery to be a "positive good," much superior morally to Northern "wage slavery:" Equality could be enjoyed only by those who are truly equal. Calhoun, with his great prestige, guided the South down the road toward secession and bloody civil war. He did not live to see the outcome of his work, since he died in 1850. The tragic diversion of Cal-

John C. Calhoun

Mathew Brady, Library of Congress

houn's enormous talents into the defense of slavery and extreme states' rights was but one of the many costs of the Southern social system before the War.

Nullification and the threat of force

Jackson's Tariff of 1832 was a mild reform of the 1828 act, which still aided ironmasters. In South Carolina, Calhoun led the resisters to achieve the needed two thirds majority in the legislature to call a state convention. This body nullified the federal tariff law, in November 1832, and Calhoun resigned from the vice presidency in December to enter the Senate. Once again the American Union was threatened with disruption and possible break-up, as in 1798 and in 1814.

Andrew Jackson, just reelected for a second term on December 5th, had no intention of allowing this to happen. He assumed he had a popular mandate to fight the two major crises of the day: South Carolina's truculence, and his own war on the Second Bank of the United States. He adopted his famous "firm stand," with the Proclamation of December 11th, which declared nullification an "absurdity," and any threats of disunion to be "treason." He would use force to uphold federal laws, if necessary. This was Jackson, the Jeffersonian agrarian, using the tough Union rhetoric of Hamilton and Marshall. Both the federal government and the state of South Carolina began military preparation.

In Congress Webster debated Calhoun furiously, and in March 1833 a compromise tariff was hammered out, mainly between Henry Clay, the veteran compromiser, and Calhoun himself. All tariff rates were to be cut by 20 percent over a ten-year period. Calhoun had shied away from full secession and military conflict at the last minute and thus saved the day; but Jackson demanded from Congress a *Force Act*, which authorized the president to use troops to uphold federal law. He failed, however, to get the last word—South Carolina defiantly nullified the Force Act as a final gesture. By then Jackson was deeply embroiled in another crisis: the Bank war.

Jackson's war on the U.S. Bank

When the charter of the Second Bank of the United States was proposed for premature renewal in 1832, Jackson used his presidential veto to destroy the bank for ever. This bank had been created in 1816 with the support of President Madison, who had fought against Hamilton's first bank. Why had Madison's attitude to the idea of a U.S. bank altered by 1816? In the years between had come the War of 1812, which was financed by extravagant loans instead of by taxation. Federal over-borrowing and a flood of bank notes issued by state banks created the highest inflation of the century. In 1814 cash payments had to be suspended. The postwar currency was made up of a mass of bank notes and a smaller number of federal Treasury notes, all of which fluctuated in value. It was difficult to conduct normal business. From many sides came a demand for some sort of national bank, to impose order on the currency. This led to a bill by Calhoun, enacted in March 1816.

The charter of the Second Bank was like that of 1791, with a 20-

year lease of life, a capital stock of $35 million, one fifth subscribed by the federal government, and 25 directors, of whom 5 were chosen by the president. The bank's notes were to be accepted as payment of government accounts and were redeemable in specie (hard currency). State banks also had to resume specie payments and make their paper notes reliable. The entire banking system was churned into activity. Stability came to the currency system.

In view of these solid advantages to the nation and to all classes, why did Jackson hate the U.S. Bank so much? Why was he intent on destroying it? Jackson saw the Bank as an instrument of an elite, working against the "People." He thought it a dangerous money monopoly, a bastion of "privilege." He attacked what he called:

Lavish public disbursements and corporations with exclusive privileges . . . the means by whose silent and secret operations a control would be exercised by the few over the political conduct of the many by first acquiring that control over the labor and earnings of the great body of the people.

What "political" controls did he fear from the Bank? Jackson's Treasury Secretary, Roger B. Taney, convinced him that its branch banks had worked against him politically. But the struggle between Jackson and the Bank was essentially personal, and Jackson used the Bank War as an opportunity to expand the powers of the presidency.

Jackson's neo-Jeffersonian vendetta was opposed by a brilliant and powerful figure, Nicholas Biddle, who took over the Bank in 1823. Forceful and aggressive, Biddle revolutionized the Bank's activities, expanding its circulation, loans, deposits, stocks, and real-estate investments. Biddle wanted to turn the Bank into a genuine, powerful central bank with control over the nation's money market. By 1828 he had the Bank earning a surplus of $1.5 million. By 1831 its note circulation was up to $19 million, as opposed to $4.5 million when he

Nicholas Biddle's mansion, Adalusia

Historic American Buildings Survey, photo by Jack E. Boucher

took over. The Bank paid dividends to its investors at the high rate of 7 percent a year until 1836.

Besides making money for the Bank's stockholders, however, Biddle also helped the nation's money market to grow. He promoted stable economic growth through providing a reliable national currency, as the Bank's notes were solid and could always be turned in for hard cash. Easier interregional credits and transfers were facilitated. The government itself could borrow when necessary. Yet, whatever its monetary policies, the Bank always annoyed one group or another. The general distrust of all banks—that strange money-phobia of Americans, which lasted for so long—was fully shared by Jackson himself. Jackson's anti-bank prejudices may have been conditioned by experiences early in life, but the truth was that Jackson himself was a successful land speculator and merchant.

Who were the "People" that Jackson wished to protect from the moneyed elite? The People, thought Jackson, were those whose "success depends upon their own industry and economy": a moralistic definition, not tied to sections or classes, but he usually would include planters, farmers, mechanics, and laborers, "the bone and sinew of the country." Excluded from the decent folk were the promoters, financiers, men of commerce. The distinction was somewhat hypocritical and hard to maintain. In any case, the Bank was *not* simply a tool of the Northeast moneyed elite. In fact, only one seventeenth of its stock was held by New Englanders. Pennsylvania held one fifth, South Carolina one sixth, Maryland and New York one seventh each. Foreigners controlled one third.

The jealousy of state banks

Jackson's rhetoric did not exactly describe the realities of the Bank War. The greatest hostility to the Bank came from the jealous state-chartered banks. To some extent the war was not one of the People versus the Bank, but a civil war within the banking community. From the outset the state banks had tried to cripple the Second Bank by persuading their states to tax its branches. In the case of *McCulloch v. Maryland* (1819), Justice Marshall's Supreme Court saved the Bank. A new director, Langdon Cheves, then brought financial solidity and good credit to the Bank through a cautious and restrictive monetary policy. When Nicholas Biddle took over from Cheves in 1823 he brought this policy to an end and began a more expansionist phase. The power of the Second Bank, like that of all central banks, to regulate credit according to its own policies frightened the state commercial banks. One long-run outcome of the Bank War in fact was the rise of "Wall Street" in New York City, eventually surpassing Chestnut Street in Philadelphia, where the Second Bank had its headquarters.

Whatever policy the Bank pursued, some group hated it. When Cheves restricted credit between 1819 and 1823 and had to foreclose on unpaid mortgage loans, the Bank became the owner by default of real estate in western cities. The Second Bank was then attacked as the "Monster," eating up people's property. State banks, however, had been profiting out of the postwar inflation and from the confusion of the currency. These banks had no particular desire for stability or for a return to cash payments and sound, conservative financing. They were forced to do so only by the actions of the Second Bank and they resented this pressure. State bankers blamed the Panic of 1819 on the Second Bank's deflationary policies and the calling-in of loans. Yet, when Biddle took over and began the opposite policy, one of credit expansion, he met deep opposition from "hard money" men. In truth, some critics indiscriminately distrusted all banks, all paper money, and all money men. While we may sympathize with their fears and prejudices, they unrealistically blamed on banks alone such problems as inflation, speculation, and the boom-and-bust business cycle.

Besides the state banks, small businessmen and entrepreneurs distrusted the Second Bank because they feared its powers over the credit system. This fear cut across sectional lines. The "creditor" commercial and industrial Northeast did not consistently support the U.S. Bank; nor did the "debtor" South and West consistently oppose it or defend a decentralized monetary system with free local banking and credit expansion. Even debtors, presumably, could see the bad results of too many small banks making too many loans which they could not support. The Jacksonian philosophy preferred to stimulate free-enterprise state banks, with no federal controls or aid, in the hope that this system of laissez-faire banking would breed less "privilege." It seems doubtful that it would do that. Many of Jackson's supporters were would-be capitalists, "incipient entrepreneurs," rather than simple agrarians, who resented the Bank for its restraining influence on the wilder aspects of state banking. Jackson himself, once the fate of the Bank was assured, proceeded to strengthen the state banks.

Death of the Bank

Encouraged by Henry Clay, who had his own political reasons, "Tsar Nicholas" Biddle made a tactical error by demanding the rechartering of the Second Bank four years before it was necessary and in an election year. The legislation passed Congress but was vetoed by Jackson in July 1832 in an angry, rhetorical message, which Biddle denounced as "a manifesto of anarchy." The veto presumably meant the end of the Bank, but Jackson was determined to harass it during its remaining years under the charter.

Jackson's veto stood the risk of losing him some sectional votes in the 1832 election in the Middle states, but the outcome was reassuring. He won 219 electoral college votes and the combined opposition did not muster 70. Henry Clay was trounced (49 votes). The contest had been a three-way fight with *party conventions* now fully organized at the national level. The Democrats chose Jackson; the old National Republicans chose Clay. A third party was born, the *Anti-Masons*, the first of a series of third party movements in U.S. history, which drew some Whig support away from Clay and so helped Jackson, who, ironically, was a Mason, as was Clay. The Anti-Masons emerged in 1826 in New York, after the mysterious disappearance of a worker who allegedly revealed Mason secrets. They were a short-lived party,

Jackson fights the many-headed U.S. Bank

New York Historical Society

built partly on fear and popular prejudice against the Masons and against all "secret societies." This was one of the recurrent seasons of popular prejudice and fear of "conspiracies." Anti-Catholic feeling also ran high. The Anti-Masons included people of democratic mind, however, who opposed special privilege and monopoly. The Anti-Mason party succumbed and vanished after Jackson's victory in 1832, but one must note that Jackson himself used the fear of conspiracy as a powerful tool against the Second Bank. Fear of "secret societies" and fear of monopoly have much in common, however real or not the fear.

Armed with his mandate, Jackson attacked the Bank by allowing no further federal money to be deposited in it. Existing federal funds were allowed to drain out as the Bank made payments. Selected state banks, the so-called pet banks, were subsequently favored with federal deposits. As for the national bank itself, Biddle scorned the president who had "scalped Indians and imprisoned judges"; he was determined to fight. An internal power struggle within the Bank (his officers resented his dictatorship) proved disastrous to Biddle. He restricted credit in August 1833 and helped to create a financial crisis in 1834, at a time when he was seeking to convince the nation how badly it needed a central bank. The Jacksonians were sure they had been right all along about giving too much power to one bank. The charter of "Biddle's Bank" expired in 1836. State banks continued to be used as government depositories, and in 1841 Henry Clay's vain attempt to charter yet a third Bank was vetoed by President Tyler. For good or evil, the United States faced the age of industrialism with no formalized central banking structure until 1913.

Jackson's money policies had the opposite effect from his desired goal. As a hard-money zealot, he aimed to drive out all paper money from circulation and to get the nation to depend on specie. He would force the "pet banks" to stop using, first, all notes of under $5 denomination, then notes of higher denominations. In addition he would cajole state banks to reduce all loans and overall note issues and to keep enough cash in hand. If this had worked it would have been an economic disaster for the nation. At a time of rapid economic growth the nation badly needed credit facilities far beyond the capabilities of the mere gold and silver coinage. The checking system had still not appeared and paper bills were vital to economic life, as were loans. They were essential to farmers and planters, as well as to moneyed Easterners and industrialists. Jackson's agrarian, anti-money prejudices could have proved fatal.

However, the policy failed. Instead of restriction, the nation was hit by inflation and a great speculative boom. Without the federal bank to check on them, state banks multiplied, and states chartered them indiscriminately, thereby exhibiting much less responsibility than the federal government would have shown. The new banks could not be intimidated by Jackson because they did not need his federal deposits. They printed paper bills by the thousand and expanded credit. A wild speculative boom built up.

Jackson reacted strongly with a drastic "cure," the *Specie Circular* of 1836. The federal government would not accept payment for public land except in specie or redeemable, sound notes. This policy struck a blow to the already weakened credit structure of the nation. It may have accelerated the Panic of 1837 and the depression which followed. Henry Clay's Distribution Act of 1836, which transferred a federal surplus of about $40 million to state treasuries, made the situation worse, for it deprived the pet banks of these federal funds, leaving them still weaker.

Van Buren, who became president in 1837, was left with the problem. Obviously, the nation did need some sort of central banking policy after all. Laissez-faire in banking did not work. Jackson's maneuvers alone did not cause the Panic of 1837. The crisis was international and it began in Britain with the collapse of a railroad boom. Long-term factors were present, like a sudden influx of Mexican silver caused by changes in the way the distant opium trade was being financed in China. Jackson had no control over such elements. But a strong central bank might have operated to restrain the new state banks in their lax loan policies and their lowering of reserve ratios after about 1834. Jackson had removed the instrument that might have affected the situation.

Finally the destruction of the Bank did nothing for Jackson's worthy "farmers, mechanics and laborers." The moneyed men were as rich as

What was the outcome of the Bank War?

ever. Wall Street began to supplant Chestnut Street but this had no effect on the frontier. Intervening massively in the economy, contrary to his own philosophy, Jackson stimulated the rapid growth of state banks and then shook them badly by damaging confidence in all paper with his Specie Circular. With his anti-bank, anti-credit, anti-paper-money notions, Jackson stood for an obsolete *economics of scarcity*, ill-fitted to the age of expansion. He appealed to "a society drawn fatally to the main chance." Jackson was no mere symbol of the times or a figurehead, but an aggressive president who shaped his era. His personal war on the Bank crystallized a political party.

How "democratic" was Jacksonian Democracy?

In matters of foreign policy Jackson was not markedly "democratic." He was involved in a war scare with France, resolved in 1835. He signed the first U.S. treaty with an Asian power, Siam. He had little success with the new republican nations of Latin America, disagreeing over Texas and the idea of an Isthmian canal. Jackson, in fact, was best at dealing with the old enemy of the American Republic, Britain. He negotiated with the English over Canadian boundary disputes and West Indies trade. But the world itself was changing and after the Reform Bill of 1832, which extended the middle-class vote in England, that nation was becoming democratic by gracious degrees. In Canada in 1837 rebellions broke out that were the product of a democratic, popular unrest which was very Jacksonian in spirit.

Jackson carries Van Buren to the Capitol, making him vice president after the Senate refused to confirm him as ambassador to England in 1831

New York Historical Society

The new politics of the Jackson era is known for the *spoils system,* which has remained a feature of American democratic life. Andrew Jackson believed in the spoils, not because he supported corruption but out of feeling for *rotation in office.* While Jefferson had faith in the "People's" judgment in choosing officers, Jackson went a step further. Any honest citizen, he believed, was fit to *hold* office. The public had the right to participate in the actual governing of the nation as much as possible. Public offices should therefore be rotated. In practice, of course, one tends to rotate them in favor of a victorious party.

Contrary to popular belief, Jackson did not remove as many men from office as his political opponents claimed he did—perhaps no more than 10 percent of all federal officeholders lost their jobs. This was a small turnover, far short of any revolution. The pressure for rotation, in any case, came from the grass roots. At the state and local level, government jobs were often elective to begin with. Federal offices were the issue. Rotation could be a handy way of getting rid of aging or lazy federal officials of long standing, as well as being a party tool.

Jackson resisted the notion that public office was any one person's right or privilege, but the main era of removals from office and use of the spoils system came *after* Jackson in the 1840s and 50s. Both parties, Whig and Democrat, resorted to these party-building measures. The question of the spoils system came to a head in the administration of President James Buchanan on the eve of Civil War. Even so, while transient party hacks came and went, a more able and permanent corps of civil servants was being built up. True, Andrew Jackson did make some gross patronage blunders—such as appointing Samuel Swartwout the customs collector at the port of New York, where this thief amassed $1.25 million before running off to England.

Rotation in office and the spoils

Labor groups were not generally a part of the Democratic party coalition behind Jackson. He has actually been dubbed a "strikebreaker." Yet Jackson did share with labor leaders and theorists that general sense of humanitarianism and broad, egalitarian reform of the day. This feeling did not include, for Jackson any more than for most Americans, minorities like the Indians and the Negroes. So far as Negroes were concerned, Andrew Jackson owned slaves. He had them chastised when necessary and unlike Jefferson, did not seem to have been personally oppressed by any sense of guilt over owning slaves. Yet Jackson was no Calhoun on the slavery issue. If he had lived, he surely would have supported Lincoln against the Southern secessionists. Like Lincoln, he would not have believed that Negroes could ever be truly equal to white men.

Jackson's actions towards Indians betray little real understanding of their cultures or sympathy for their plight. In this he was an orthodox Westerner, who carried out faithfully the Jeffersonian era's policy of "Indian removal" west of the Mississippi. He did not share Jefferson's expressed opinion that the Indian was the potential equal of the white man. Thus Jackson helped to force thousands of Indian families

Jackson and the underprivileged

The U.S.A.

westward while whites grabbed their ancestral lands. The tribes were decimated by hunger, disease, and brutality. Resistance was put down by superior force.

The Indian "Trail of Tears"

The name "Trail of Tears" is given to the removal of the Five Civilized Nations (Cherokee, Creek, Choctaw, Chickasaw, and Seminole) from Georgia and the Gulf states westward to Indian Territory (Oklahoma) in the 1830s. The Seminoles, however, were almost wiped out as a tribe by 1843 after continuing resistance to the whites. The Indian Removal Act of 1830 provided for this policy and an act of 1834 created the special Indian Territory. When the Seminoles took to the warpath again in 1835 they were led by a brilliant chief, Osceola, who resisted for three years the army sent against him by Jackson. Jackson's two administrations produced 94 Indian treaties designed to eliminate Indian land titles. In Georgia the highly developed Cherokee Nation would not give up titles. They were settled in northwest Georgia in a well-organized community with frame houses, good roads, and well-kept farms. None of the standard white arguments could be used easily against the Cherokee—they were obviously not nomads and hunters but a settled, agrarian people. They had a newspaper, the

Map 5. The "Trail of Tears" —Removal of the Five Civilized Nations to Indian Territory under the Acts of 1830 and 1834

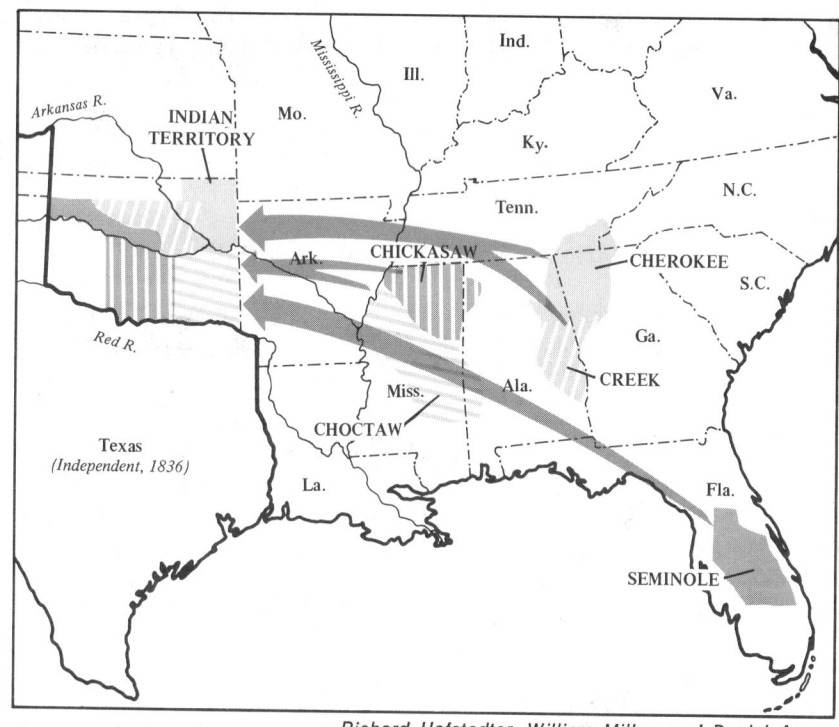

Richard Hofstadter, William Miller, and Daniel Aaron, *The American Republic, Volume One, to 1865,* © 1959, p. 401. By permission of Prentice-Hall, Inc., Englewood Cliffs, New Jersey.

Cherokee Phoenix, edited by Elias Boudinot, a full-blooded tribal member. Books they printed in Cherokee used the syllabary devised by Sequoya. The simple fact was that the whites of Georgia wanted their land, and the Cherokee were forced to give way in the end. Ignoring so-called treaties dating back to 1791, the state of Georgia legislated in 1828 to nullify all laws of the Cherokee Nation by 1830. When gold was discovered on Cherokee lands in 1829, pressure from the whites increased.

In 1832 (*Worcester* v. *Georgia*), Chief Justice Marshall ruled that the federal government had exclusive jurisdiction in the Cherokee Nation and that Georgia state laws were invalid there. Georgia ignored the ruling, and Jackson is said to have declared: "John Marshall has made his decision, now let him enforce it!" His concern for federal dignity was genuine but he had no intention of enforcing this decision against Georgia and in favor of the Cherokee. Far away in what would become Oklahoma the "Cherokee Strip" was set aside, and in 1838 President Van Buren completed the story by ordering the final removal of all the Cherokee. On the Cherokee Trail of Tears across the South through Arkansas to Indian Territory—a bedraggled forced-migration accompanied by army detachments—at least 4,000 died. (Perhaps one quarter of the 60,000 or so Indians of all tribes removed from the South died on the painful trek.)

The impact of the removal policy is seen in the bitter reply of an old Creek chieftain, Speckled Snake, to Jackson's demand that his tribe move across the Mississippi in 1829:

> When the first white man came over the wide waters, he was but a little man. . . . His legs were cramped by sitting long in his big boat, and he begged for a little land. . . .
>
> But when the white man had warmed himself at the Indian's fire, and filled himself with the Indian's hominy, he became very large. He stopped not at the mountain tops, and his foot covered the plains and the valleys. His hands grasped the eastern and western seas. Then he became our Great Father. He loved his red children, but he said: "You must move a little further, lest by accident I tread on you."
>
> Brothers! I have listened to a great many talks from our Great Father. But they always began and ended in this: "Get a little farther; you are too near to me."

In the Midwest a hasty movement to oust all remaining tribes was stimulated by the Black Hawk War, which was fought out in the upper Mississippi region in April–August 1832. The Sauk and Fox Indians were defeated in the Illinois-Wisconsin country, and in 1833 the Black Hawk Purchase lands of the Iowa region were opened up for white settlement. By 1837 Chicago was a small incorporated city. The future of the entire Midwest was clear.

A well-known journal of the day, *Niles' Weekly Register*, reported as early as 1815 that America was characterized by an "almost universal ambition to get forward." This was the driving force of the economic revolution and the dynamism behind Jacksonian society. The assault

"Making it": The world of Jackson

on the American wilderness was advanced. The Age of Competition was upon Americans. It was the beginning of the end of the Agrarian Dream, or at least of the chance that it might ever be realized. The simple, homogeneous, unified, agrarian society, insofar as it had ever existed, went out with the expiration of the Virginia dynasty. The search began for something else and would end up in machine technology and mass, urban society, though intermediary chapters of great importance to the American national experience were still to come. Jackson's anomalies were the anomalies of the age—of "making it" in a new world of opportunity with very few built-in restraints. A majoritarian democracy rode roughshod over unprotected, unorganized minority rights. Harbored within this self-conscious democracy, and at variance with many of its principles, was the institution of slavery-racism. This institution was certain to produce open social conflict in a democratic republic which worshiped at the public shrine of egalitarianism. Andrew Jackson realized the danger and the inherent contradiction in American values. During the nullification struggle he observed:

> the next pretext will be the Negro or slavery question.

To that question American thinkers more radical than Jackson had already been turning their attention.

Bibliography

G. Dangerfield. *The Awakening of American Nationalism, 1815–28.* New York: Harper, 1965).

R. V. Remini. *The Election of Andrew Jackson.* Philadelphia: Lippincott, 1963. *Andrew Jackson and the Bank War.* New York: Norton, 1968.

V. I. Armstrong. *I Have Spoken: American History Through the Voices of the Indians.* Chicago: Swallow, 1971.

R. Kent Newmeyer. *The Supreme Court Under Marshall and Taney.* New York: Crowell, 1969.

W. V. Freehling. *Prelude to Civil War: the Nullification Controversy in South Carolina.* New York: Harper, 1968.

10

Revivalism and radicalism: America as Utopia

The radical style: facing up to slavery . . . radical groundswell: origins . . . Romanticism: the cult of Nature . . . radical ideas in education . . . revolution for the American child: Horace Mann . . . heredity versus environment . . . the American worship of self-improvement . . . the High Culture: Transcendentalism . . . Brook Farm: elite commune . . . Emerson: mysticism, self-reliance, and cultural nationalism . . . the religious impetus: evangelicalism . . . the cult of "Love" . . . Beecher and Finney . . . religious undercurrents: anti-Catholic prejudice . . . communes: the search for Utopia . . . Shakers and Mormons . . . secular utopias: New Harmony and Nashoba . . . French phalanxes and communities . . . sexual radicalism: Oneida . . . women's leadership in a galaxy of reforms . . . Seneca Falls Convention, 1848 . . . labor and capitalism . . . humanitarian reforms: the Jacksonian underworld . . . the Cold-Water Army . . . reform as a way of life.

The radical style: Facing up to slavery

The 1830s and 40s were years of intense radical ferment in the United States, associated with years of religious experimentation and revivalism. Said one radical leader, John Humphrey Noyes, "Revivals breed social revolutions." Little of this revolution was seen at the level of national party politics. For example, the party system translated radical abolitionism into the more moderate and acceptable opposition to the *extension* of slavery into the western territories. Also women, who took a major role in many reform movements before the Civil War, achieved very little at the federal level for themselves.

The Jeffersonian-Jacksonian political tradition flourished for 60 long years, down through the administration of President James Buchanan to the election of Lincoln in 1860. Its agrarian, small-business, local rights, value system was morally flawed by the existence of human slavery in America, the central moral problem of the age. When the astonishing persistence of that institution so late in modern history could no longer be ignored, it was love of the Union and not moral antipathy to slavery which brought on the Civil War. The overwhelming value of Jacksonianism, preservation of the American Union, swamped everything else.

The new radicals of the 1830s and 40s, however, did face up to slavery. They also dragged out other issues for public exposure, ranging from temperance and women's rights to the treatment of the mentally ill and the horrors of war. Some of these reformers were zealots who have been accused of moral absolutism, intolerance, selfish status-anxieties about their own place in American society, and other sins. Some abolitionists were violent, some even unstable. But these radicals, black and white, men and women, whatever their faults as people, did attack slavery head-on. The more moderate or less sensitive majority managed to ignore the issue and were skilfully led through one political crisis after another by astute compromisers like Henry Clay.

Radical groundswell: Origins

Where did the new radicalism come from? The problem of its origins continues to puzzle historians, for the movement had multiple roots, particularly intellectual and religious. Its economic origins cannot be tied to any particular depression. Some writers have tried unsuccessfully to link radicalism with the post-Panic economic conditions after 1837, but in fact the general aura of the 30s and 40s was one of expansion, not failure. Economic growth may cause as much social dislocation and unrest as economic contraction.

The question of origins is complicated by international aspects. Parallel reform movements struggled in South America and Canada. Conservatives on both sides of the Atlantic fought back vainly against the tide of suffrage extension, trade union organization, and demand for women's rights. The influence of German philosophy, French socialism, and, above all, of British radical thought was profound. A constant interaction took place among the personnel of the Anglo-American reform cadre: visits, letters, conferences, and formal organizations. The British played the leading world role in the antislavery crusade. Reformers cooperated in the peace movement, feminism, postal reform agitation, temperance, and factory legislation campaigns, creating a transatlantic radical community that helped to seal the bond of Anglo-American understanding after the War of 1812. Naturally, radicalism cannot be merely injected into a nation from foreign sources: conditions at home must somehow encourage a positive native response.

Native American radicalism was at least 200 years old. The ferment of the 1830s and 40s was the fruition of earlier ideals like the Puritans' "City Upon a Hill" and the dream of Man's Redemption in a New World, or the contrasting rationalism of the American Enlightenment of Franklin and Jefferson. More immediate origins such as the Romantic movement, the evangelical revival, and Transcendentalism in philosophy also helped to create radical reformism in America, though in some other nations the same influences proved to be conservative. For instance, there is nothing inherently radical about religious revivalism: The search for men's souls has often ignored their bodies. Nor is Romanticism necessarily radical. One difference with Europe was that the United States had no fixed conservative ideology, despite the vestiges of the Federalist-Whig tradition. Here the barrier to change was not the opposition of entrenched landed elites, as represented by Metternich in Austria, or Palmerston in Britain, but *popular inertia* and the busy-ness of the Jacksonian generation—their commitment to material progress. To divert Americans from the engrossing occupation of "getting ahead" took dramatic means, such as revivalism.

In Germany, France, Britain, and America, the early 19th-century Romantic movement in literature, painting, and music was a reaction against the Classical tradition and an affirmation of Nature over Society, of human instinct and emotion over reason and intellect. One set of abstractions was exchanged for another. American radicalism is confusing because it combined inspiration from the rationalistic Enlightenment tradition together with this Romantic countermovement. With the "return to Nature" the painters and writers of Europe and America glorified things deemed "natural": children, allegedly simple peasants, and the "noble savage." North America, with its In-

Romanticism: The cult of Nature

The Hudson River School— Thomas Cole's "The Oxbow," 1836

The Metropolitan Museum of Art, gift of Mrs. Russell Sage, 1908

dians, its physical scenery, and its West, was ideally suited to fit the Romantic image. Human society was regarded as artificial and corrupt, while Man in a state of Nature was noble and perfectible. Jacksonian Americans responded to such attitudes with sympathy.

From Jean Jacques Rousseau down to Thoreau, the dogma of Nature and of the noble savage implied that Man was plastic and could be molded. He was innately good; only a bad environment and society corrupted him. Once the restraints of society were removed from him, the individual could be made perfect and could find complete self-realization. The Jacksonian negative concept of freedom, freedom from, thus received extra support from the individualism and anti-state, anti-society visions of the Romantics. The Romantic hero, if released from the trappings of a corrupt society and willing to trust his instincts and feelings, would triumph in the battle for selfhood.

Romantic mythology was embedded in the work of the American painter Thomas Cole and the Hudson River school. These native artists depicted a Romantic view of nature in dramatic landscapes of mountains, valleys, swirling clouds, and storms. The content was direct and emotional. Gone was the cool, classical portraiture of New England worthies. Cole's *Last of the Mohicans* (1827) or his famous *Oxbow of the Connecticut* (1836) marked a new school of nationalist American painting, one entirely suited to the age of western expansionism and frontier pride. Meanwhile George Catlin abandoned his Philadelphia law practice and in 1830 set out on an eight-year journey, painting some 500 canvases of Indians and scenes of tribal life. Catlin did for the Indian tribes, of which he came to know about 50, what the creole artist-scientist, John James Audubon, had done for American birds: He established a scientific record for all time. Catlin was not above showmanship. He traveled in Europe with a "Wild West Show" long before the creations of Buffalo Bill Cody.

The Romantic West was portrayed in literature by James Fenimore Cooper, whose 30-odd books, especially the "Leatherstocking" series, made him almost as popular as Sir Walter Scott. In truth, Cooper was a critic of American democracy, whose views did not fit the Jacksonian popular mold. Most readers did not discover this in his adventure stories. George Catlin's exhibitions and Cooper's tales linked the "high philosophy" of Transcendentalism and Romanticism with the masses, forming a model for popular culture. Lesser writers and artists soon turned sentiment into sentimentality. The popular music of Stephen Foster, for example, expressed the alleged feelings of the frontier and of Negroes, in ballads like *Old Folks At Home* (1851), *My Old Kentucky Home* (1853), and *Old Black Joe* (1860). Foster's knowledge of the frontier or Negroes was less than profound, being derived chiefly from "minstrel shows" and camp meetings. Yet his music traveled west with the pioneers throughout the 19th century and has survived remarkably well. Stephen Foster died of poverty and drink, not on the frontier or in the rural South of his songs, but in the Bowery of New York City in 1864 at the age of only 38.

Though the Romantic cult of Nature influenced popular culture as profoundly as high culture and has had much to do with American worship of the Great Outdoors, few Americans felt guilty about what they were actually doing to their rich natural environment or to the Indians during the antebellum years. The conscience of James Fenimore Cooper was troubled. But Progress rushed by amid popular acclaim. The work of one American stands out, that of Frederick Law Olmsted, the Connecticut-born landscape architect who designed many city parks, such as New York's Central Park, 840 acres acquired by the city in 1856. Olmsted gave American cities "lungs"—green spaces —so that they could still breathe in the years ahead. His personal contribution to popular culture and to Romantic ideals was very concrete and of immeasurable value for the quality of American life.

Radical ideas in education

The Romantic nexus of views on the nature of man, his potentiality and perfectibility, produced in Europe a revolution in ideas about the education of children. The French philosopher Jean Jacques Rousseau was again the fountainhead of many of these new notions. In his novel, *Émile* (1762), and in other writings, he had advanced the belief that the child should be allowed to develop with little interference, to find his own self-realization. Rousseau's disciples in Switzerland, particularly J. H. Pestalozzi, influenced several generations of American reformers, including Robert Dale Owen (son of the founder of British socialism, Robert Owen), the Jacksonian historian and Democratic politician George Bancroft, and Horace Mann. Bancroft used the Swiss concept of the free development of the child according to natural stages of growth at his Round Hill School in Northampton, Massachusetts. Robert Dale Owen visited Pestalozzi and agitated in the United States for a federal system of public schools on the Swiss model.

The new view of the child was also picked up by German reformers, notably F. W. A. Froebel, who introduced the first *kindergarten* in 1837 for infant care and training. The German philosopher J. F. Herbart tried to establish the field of education as a viable separate academic discipline. Herbart said that all learning must be "relevant" to the child's life-experience. Froebel's kindergartens gave the child pleasant surroundings, emphasizing physical activities and the working out of problems by the child himself. None of this may appear very radical today, but before this revolution of ideas the child was commonly regarded as a savage, whose "spirit" must be "broken" by school discipline. No thought was given to the training of teachers or to methods of how to teach. All learning was by rote, the simple parroting of information under harsh discipline. The Pestalozzi school introduced a friendlier child-teacher relationship and encouraged the child's own instinctive and creative feelings through the use of play devices. Rote learning was underplayed. The school became the means of the child's self-discovery. All of this, of course, was the hoped-for goal; the reality, whether in Switzerland, Prussia, or the United States, fell short, then as now. So much depended on the quality of the teachers.

Reality for the average American child meant frontier life or urban factory labor. The industrial revolution was partly built on child labor, in America as in other countries. New England was no exception. At least there had been a revolution in ideas and in the adult's view of the nature of children. A great educational reformer, Horace Mann, worked to provide the schools that would bring this educational revolution closer to reality for the American child.

Revolution for the American child: Horace Mann

The first Froebel kindergarten opened in Wisconsin in 1856. For older children of school age, Mann fought for the creation of free, tax-supported, nonsectarian public schools: the "Common School." Horace Mann was a Brown University graduate and a Massachusetts state senator who practiced law until 1837. He gave up this lucrative profession for a low-paid and untried public office, which he had helped to establish: Secretary of the Massachusetts State Board of Education.

Popular opinion, the Jacksonian rhetoric of equality, and the Romantic faith in the individual's capacity for growth were all on Mann's side in the struggle, but education in New England had sadly declined over the years. The original enthusiasm of the 17th-century Puritans with their first Massachusetts School Law of 1647 had long since evaporated. That law had provided for compulsory free elementary schools in the smaller townships and secondary schools in larger towns. Over the decades the decentralized character of the system, together with changing religious and ethnic patterns had left New England with destitute, tax-starved public schools, staffed by incompetent teachers, drilling by rote and corporal punishment. Teachers were low-paid and sometimes were forced to take their pay in kind, boarding out with pupils' families. The school year was a bare three months long. In contrast, private schools and colleges flourished in New England.

Outside the private institutions the great learning of the 17th-century Puritans was lost. Learning and Godliness were no longer related in the public mind. In fact rivalry among religious faiths had retarded education and brought the compromise of nonsectarian teaching. The religious revivals created new private sectarian colleges and schools, but in 1837 Mann faced a decaying public school system. Almost single-handedly he brought about a revolution. When he gave up the post in 1848 the anarchic district school system was more centralized, teachers' pay was twice as high, and the school year had been doubled to six months. Mann had seen 50 new high schools built. In 1839 he had begun the first state teacher-training "Normal School" in the United States at Lexington (1839). Stodgy curricula and teaching methods had also been radically altered in Massachusetts.

Horace Mann was bitterly attacked for his so-called Godless schools, though in truth he never favored a wholly secular system and fell back on Bible training as the chief source of moral education. In his famous *Seventh Annual Report* of 1843 Mann made clear that, given the religious conflicts of the day, only nonsectarian teaching would work. As more Irish Catholics flooded into Boston the religious and

Horace Mann, champion of public education

United Press International

cultural makeup of the eastern states altered. The possibilities of tension were enormously increased. The Massachusetts law of 1827 had already ruled for nonsectarian education in public schools, as Mann constantly reminded his opponents. Few today would question the vision of Mann's policies.

Mann's silent revolution was advanced by his editorship of the *Common School Journal* and by his friendships with many reformers. He entered Congress in 1848 as an abolitionist. Failing to win the Massachusetts governorship on a Free Soil, antislavery extension ticket in 1852, he became the first president of the liberal, coeducational Antioch College in Ohio. There he tried to extend his revolution from primary and secondary to higher education. Mann's ideas spread rapidly. In Connecticut and Rhode Island the reformer Henry Barnard achieved similar results propagandizing educational theories through his editorship of the *American Journal of Education*. Barnard also served as the first U.S. Commissioner of Education. In Pennsylvania the abolitionist Thaddeus Stevens had already won a common school law as early as 1835.

Like most reformers of the day Mann was a determined *environmentalist*. He believed that Man was shaped by his environment. Improved human ecology would therefore improve humans. In contrast, the "conservative" position has emphasized, down to the present day, that heredity is more important than environment. This view tends to blame individuals and groups for their own misfortune—the poor, the illiterate, the unemployed, and minorities. Horace Mann would not have gone as far as modern liberal environmentalists who

Heredity versus environment

demand a full welfare state or redistribution of income. He believed that all that was necessary was to provide a decent free public education for all children. After that the individual was best left alone to make his own way in a world of opportunity.

A similar argument still rages today as educationists and social psychologists debate nature versus nurture all over again in an age of controversy over the rights of ethnic and racial minorities. For Horace Mann, free public education—the Common School—was the gateway to a democracy of opportunity. Education was a social ladder, or as Mann explained in his final report to the people of Massachusetts in 1848:

a great equalizer of the condition of men—the balance-wheel of the social machinery.

Mann contrasted the European class system with American equality:

According to the European theory, men are divided into classes—some to toil and earn, others to seize and enjoy. According to the Massachusetts theory, all are to have an equal chance for earning, and equal security in the enjoyment of what they earn.

The American worship of self-improvement

Education became an American fetish, a nationally acknowledged value, and an integral part of the American Dream. Outside the classroom and formal education, self-improvement became the rage. It helped to create a mass, middle-class reading and voting public. It has been estimated that by 1860 over 90 percent of the U.S. population were literate—a very high proportion for the mid-19th century. Library associations, book clubs, debating groups, and "mechanics' institutes" abounded. The *lyceum movement* flourished before the Civil War. This was a form of adult education in manual arts and academic subjects begun in 1826 by Josiah Holbrook in Connecticut. By 1834 America had about 3,000 town lyceums, several state lyceums, and a national headquarters in Manhattan. Here the interested public could study public affairs issues like capital punishment, curriculum reforms, and popular science. Famous men gave public lectures, among them Ralph Waldo Emerson and Oliver Wendell Holmes. The public lecture circuit supplemented the royalty income of many a writer. The lyceum movement faded after the Civil War, having declined into a form of cheap public entertainment which merged into the music halls. From 1874, however, its place was taken by the *Chatauqua* movement for adult education.

Generations of Americans learned to read and write with the *McGuffey Readers*, six of which appeared between 1836 and 1857. They provided a mass market for the "penny press," the cheap, one-cent newspaper whose production was made possible by technical advances in the paper and printing industry, such as the rotary press of 1847. The penny press began in the United States with two New York papers, the *Sun* (1833) and the *Herald* (1835), both of which offered titillating human interest stories of crime and sex, with sensationalist banner headlines. The new presses cost about $20,000, so newspaper production became a highly capitalistic affair with conservative owners pressing their own economic views on editors. Radical ideas were left to the smaller papers or to ventures like Horace Greeley's *Tribune* (1841), which cast its sights a little higher than the mass market. Monthly and weekly magazines, like *Harper's* (1850), and the first women's journal, *Godey's Lady's Book* (1830), raised the horizons of countless families. In addition a host of denominational religious papers were available.

The High Culture: Transcendentalism

Advances in public education and mass literacy underlay much of the new radicalism of the 1830s and 40s. Far removed, a tiny intellectual elite in New England, the Transcendentalists, influenced the High Culture of the day. Their favorite journal, *The Dial*, enjoyed a miniscule circulation of about 300, compared with about 20,000 a day for the New York *Sun*. Transcendentalism was an intellectual branch of the Romantic movement, deriving its intellectual inspiration from the German idealist philosopher Immanuel Kant and from the British idealists like Samuel Taylor Coleridge. Several of the American Kantians were or had been Unitarian ministers, including Ralph Waldo Emerson, George Ripley, and Theodore Parker.

The members of the Transcendental Club who met at Concord, Massachusetts (1836), were emotionally unsatisfied with current Unitarian faith, "corpse-cold Christianity," as Emerson called it. In Massachusetts the old Protestant fire had long since died out. The Club was trying to revive it in new form. Borrowing heavily from Kant, they relied on intuition and subjectivism for some judgments, those "Great Moral Truths" which "transcend" mere orthodox proof and the obvious evidence of the senses. Great questions, they felt, such as man's immortality or the existence of God, depend not upon normal rules of evidence so much as upon will and faith and what they called "transcendent verification." Thus Theodore Parker (1810–60), master orator and strenuous advocate of social reform and abolition of slavery, rejected what he termed the "sterile rationalism" of those Unitarian clergy who opposed him. Parker was the indefatigable conscience of the reform movement. He wore himself out by the age of 50 in the cause of social uplift.

Transcendentalism was the counter-philosophy of the age of materialism and industrial revolution. The elite group of young intellectuals who met at Concord despised the commercial values of Boston and what they regarded as the decaying quality of American life. They would generally support Jacksonian political candidates, but normally eschewed all politics as sordid. How did they seek to change the world, given the fact that they were anti-capitalist, anti-political, and even anti-institutional altogether? The Transcendentalists worked through the pulpit, the press, and the school. Like most religious-minded or ethical reformers they pinned their hopes on the conversion of individual consciences, not on legislative programs or government policies. They also sought to teach by example—the collectivists among them tried to establish an ideal cooperative community, confident that the rest of the world would then copy.

The Transcendentalists were not revolutionary except in personal ways: Their outlook favored a *personal anarchism*. For example, Henry David Thoreau opted out of society for two years and chose to live in relative isolation and self-sufficiency at Walden Pond (1845–47). Society, however, was always close by. Thoreau was jailed for one night because he refused to pay his poll tax, on the grounds that such taxes supported the immoral war against Mexico (1846–48), which he viewed as a mere excuse for American territorial aggrandizement and the extension of slavery. Thoreau appealed to a "Higher Law"—the individual conscience—which rated above the demands of the state. His essay on *Civil Disobedience*, a major statement of the philosophy of passive resistance, influenced the Indian leader Gandhi in the 20th century and through him many young anti-war Americans of the 1960s, and the black leader, Dr. Martin Luther King.

Brook Farm: Elite commune

Emerson, too, was a strong individualist, but other Club members were prepared to experiment with collective living. Led by George Ripley, they established a small commune, Brook Farm, at West Roxbury, Massachusetts. Begun in 1841 and dedicated to the old New England principle of simple living and high thinking, the commune remained small for its first three or four years. Emerson visited it but would not stay. Brook Farm, he said, was a "perpetual picnic." The novelist Nathaniel Hawthorne was a member, along with Bronson Alcott, Margaret Fuller, W. H. Channing, and Orestes Brownson, all Brahmin intellectuals. Hawthorne was one of the few "nay-saying" writers of the period. He did not accept the idea of Man's innate nobility and perfectibility and was readier to face up to the problem of

Nathaniel Hawthorne

Mathew Brady, Library of Congress

Edgar Allan Poe

Mathew Brady, Library of Congress

evil. Hawthorne later wrote *The Blithedale Romance* (1852), based on his Brook Farm stay. After leaving the commune he developed into a major novelist and short-story writer, his work being shot through with a deep sense of guilt and sin. He did much to spread the gloomy, distorted view of the Puritans, in his *Scarlet Letter* (1850) and *House of the Seven Gables* (1851). Hawthorne was copied by legions of hack popular writers of "Gothic" novels of mystery and terror, leaving out his essential religious and philosophical core. The tale of terror was developed by that other nay-sayer, Edgar Allan Poe.

Brook Farm was enlarged and transformed into a socialist commune in 1844–45 by Albert Brisbane, a follower of the French socialist Fourier, but a fire destroyed the main building in 1846 and the community failed. It had never been a paying proposition. At its height Brook Farm housed about 140 people.

Emerson: Mysticism, self-reliance, and cultural nationalism

Ralph Waldo Emerson (1803–82) gave up his Boston church in 1832 because the higher voice of his own conscience would no longer allow him to administer Holy Communion. When traveling in Europe Emerson got to know the English idealists and Romantic poets, Coleridge, Wordsworth, and Carlyle. He also assimilated the mysticism of Emmanuel Swedenborg and acquired a taste for Orientalism in the ancient scriptures of India. Modern students find much that is familiar in Emerson once they overcome his style.

Emerson's lecture "The Over-Soul" entirely abandoned Unitarian orthodoxy in favor of a vaguely pantheistic doctrine in which all human souls commune together within a universal soul. Man is thus not regarded as depraved or sinful but as divine. "I am part and parcel of God!" exclaimed Emerson at a moment of revelation. The idea of a universal soul is directly derived from Hindu thought. In the ancient Indian books, the *Upanishads,* the souls of all men are finally reunited after the illusion of time and space are conquered. Modern readers may be reminded of the doctrine of the "collective unconscious" of the 20th-century psychoanalyst, C. G. Jung. More than Emerson before him, Jung was widely read in Oriental religions. His concept is less mystical than Emerson's, for the collective unconscious is the common, inherited tendencies of a people, represented by archetypes or model dream-figures and seen in folk-lore, beliefs, and dreams. Contemporaries of Emerson such as Walt Whitman were also impressed by Oriental ideas, but the doctrine of the Over-Soul received little general attention at that time.

More general excitement was aroused by two addresses Emerson gave in a traditional native vein. In "Self-Reliance" (1841) he pushed optimistic faith in the individual to its uttermost. Here was the inner-directed hero of 19th-century pioneer America. "Whoso would be man," Emerson declaimed, "must be a nonconformist." The individual must accept himself and maintain his total integrity. If this meant a public change of opinion occasionally, so what? The individual should abandon what Emerson called "foolish consistency." But which consistency is foolish? Emerson's argument could be used to sanctify

Ralph Waldo Emerson, American individualist

Harvard College Library

eccentricity for its own sake. Nevertheless, the individual must realize his potential, he insisted:

The power which resides in him is new in nature, and none but he knows what that is which he can do, nor does he know until he has tried.

It is well to remember that Emerson's extreme individualism was tempered because it was based on the belief, taken for granted, that man's personal intuition was always *divinely* guided.

In his Harvard University address of 1837 for the Phi Beta Kappa Society, "The American Scholar," Emerson put forward a strong claim for "self-reliance" for the United States itself—cultural nationalism. Throw off the apron strings of European thought, said this man who had learned so much from foreign philosophies. Do not bother to travel, one can learn more at home. "Travelling is a fool's paradise," Emerson now proclaimed. The United States should stand free of European dominance in architecture, literature, and general taste. Imitation should be rejected in all matters of style. "The American Scholar" was America's intellectual Declaration of Independence. It came a little early.

Though Emerson felt deeply about social matters he was too introspective to engage in overt reform activities and organizations. He was usually impatient with reformers, though in the late 1850s he did emerge for a while as an abolitionist propagandist, going so far as to praise John Brown's attack on the federal arsenal at Harper's Ferry (1859), in a Boston lecture, "Courage." This contained his famous and perhaps misguided eulogy of Brown as

The Saint, whose fate yet hangs in suspense, but whose martyrdom, if it shall be perfected, will make the gallows as glorious as the Cross.

John Brown was no Jesus Christ, but a fanatic for whom violence was an acceptable means to a just end. We must now turn from the complex ideas of this Brahmin intellectual, Emerson, to consider the radical activists.

The religious impetus: Evangelicalism

The Virginia pro-slavery conservative George Fitzhugh attacked the Transcendentalists for their "German learning and research" and for fomenting a "presumptuous revolutionary Utopian spirit, restless under restraint and ever anxious for change." Americans, however, were restless for many reasons; one cannot blame "German philosophy." Fitzhugh complained that the Transcendental Club had reduced religion to a mere "set of moral maxims and fine sentiments." In fact, a popular religious revival of vast proportions was under way in America, which was more significant for radical change than the thought of New England's intellectuals.

Emerson, Parker, and Ripley found orthodox Protestantism too cold and formalized, but they were equally repelled by the hyper-emotionalism of the crowds that surrounded the popular, revivalist hot-gospelers. The new evangelicalism with its passionate camp meetings filled a spiritual and emotional vacuum in the lives of many people. The 1820s and 30s saw a growth of this revivalism and evangelism. Its prime relation to the radical movements was that it thoroughly democratized theology and repeated, yet again, the now-familiar message of the importance of the individual and the need for an ethic above and beyond the "cash nexus" of commerce. Caught between the High Culture of Unitarianism and Transcendentalism and the Popular Culture of a rough frontier democracy and involvement in the material world, American Calvinism was forced to change its image and become more inviting and more meaningful and relevant for the masses.

Partly to fill churches and partly out of deep conviction, the clergy turned toward forceful leadership in social reform movements. They began with the temperance movement and moved on to abolitionism. The traditional preoccupation with individual sin and the saving of souls was not shoved aside, but supplemented. To some degree the churches were aiming at social *control* as much as social reform in their larger role in reform agitations. They managed to keep the reform trend largely inside the Protestant orbit. The churches organized rapidly. The American Bible Society, American Home Missionary Society, American Sunday School Union, American Tract Society, American Education Society, and other groups worked to keep alive the religious ideal. Meanwhile, as they became involved with worldly affairs, the orthodox theology of the denominations crumbled. Dogma was simplified and then resimplified to capture the masses of the unchurched, revival audiences at camp meetings. Liberal "Arminianism," the belief in the salvation of all believers and men of goodwill, replaced the doctrines of hell fire, and of eternal damnation for the majority and salvation for the favored few. The only requirement for salvation was repentance and admission of past guilt. Forgiveness of sins and redemption would follow for all: "Repent, for the Kingdom of God is at hand!"

The cult of "Love"

The ubiquitous phrase, "God is Love!" covered all contingencies. Love was the chief theme of many revivals, as of the backwoods utopias founded all over the nation. At one commune, Oneida, New York, the cult of love was taken literally and sexually. The most popular hymn of the day was "Jesus Loves Me." Thousands responded to this direct appeal and greater longevity and strength was thus given to American popular religion.

New faiths and new cults swept the land. The area from western Vermont, across the Mohawk Valley, past Albany, and up to Buffalo in western New York became known as the "Burnt-over District" because it had seen so many religious revivals come and go. Shakers, Millerites, Mormons, and others passed through the region in succession.

Beecher and Finney

Lyman Beecher and Charles G. Finney were two of the most popular revivalists of the day. Beecher (1775–1863) was the father of 11 children, including Henry Ward Beecher and the famous Harriet Beecher Stowe. A Yale graduate and a Congregationalist, Lyman Beecher made it his life's work to combat heresies such as Catholicism, Deism, and Unitarianism and to engage in selected social reforms: temperance, Sabbatarianism, and antislavery. The disestablishment of the Congregational Church in Connecticut in 1818 convinced Beecher of the need for the clergy to set a leadership example in social questions and thus to maintain its position. Beecher was most effective as a preacher and haranguer, concentrating his efforts on "moral awakening" rather than group actions or politics. Unlike the Transcendentalists, Beecher approved of most existing institutions and worked to preserve them. He hoped that a change of heart on the part of men would suffice to bring social change. Like many who are fluent with words, he exaggerated their power. As president of the new Lane Theological Seminary in Cincinnati from 1832, Beecher witnessed the dramatic walkout in 1836 of the fiery student, Theodore Weld, when the trustees suppressed an abolitionist society on campus. Weld helped to convert Lyman Beecher to a more radical antislavery position.

Charles Finney (1792–1875), another Connecticut Congregationalist, taught at Oberlin College, a defection from Lane Seminary created by Weld's walkout, and he later became Oberlin's president (1851–65). Oberlin was a hotbed of abolitionism and radical reform. It was coeducational when that was unusual if not unique and was the first college to admit Negroes. Finney had gained experienced as a revivalist preacher in the Burnt-over District of New York in the 1820s. His emotional brand of reform, New Calvinism, was called the "Oberlin theology." He was more genuinely reformist than Beecher. Weld was his greatest disciple. Their achievements went well beyond wringing tears from sinners or inducing the jerks in hysterical crowds.

Religious undercurrents: Anti-Catholic prejudice

Many evangelists fought for noble causes but shared undercurrents of deep prejudice. Denominations could be intensely jealous of each other. As theology grew more fuzzy and distinctions became harder to maintain, charges of "heresy" increased. Even Lyman Beecher was accused, though he was acquitted. Beecher was an outstanding anti-Catholic at a crucial time for Catholics in American history, when their numbers were being greatly increased by mass immigration from Germany and Ireland.

Irish Catholics were 40 percent of all foreign-born by 1860, numbering about 1,600,000. In the 1840s and 50s they labored as construction workers and took the roughest jobs at the lowest wages. No American immigrant group was ever poorer or more oppressed. The Irish were fearful and violently anti-Negro and anti-abolitionist. They fought among themselves and suffered harsh discrimination. Nevertheless, because of their numbers, the Irish soon swamped the American Catholic church, took it over, and imposed their own clergy, Saints' Days, and more orthodox faith upon it. The Irish thus bore the brunt of anti-Catholic violence and prejudice. Both Finney and Beecher used fears of "Popery" in their appeals to the unlettered.

In one inflammatory speech at "Brimstone Corner" in Boston in 1834 Lyman Beecher attacked Catholics for allegedly building a sinister global conspiracy against free institutions. A mob of 50 workers left his speech, marched on the Ursuline Convent in Charlestown, and burned it to the ground. They attacked Irish people on the way and stoned their homes. Ten years later mobs burned 2 churches in Philadelphia and killed 13 people. The myth of Catholic conspiracy, like the later myths of Jewish conspiracy and radical conspiracies, was kept alive by lurid propaganda: the pornography of prejudice. One tale, Maria Monk's *Awful Disclosure of the Hotel Dieu Nunnery of Montreal* went through countless editions after its first printing of 1836, sold an estimated 300,000 copies by the time of the Civil War and was still being read in the 20th century. The tract described the forced sexual submission of nuns to priests and the hiding of infant bodies. The real Maria Monk, a professional prostitute with some commercial imagination, died in jail in 1849. Her tale was one of many, some of which had been in circulation in various forms since the religious wars of 16th- and 17th-century Europe. The Protestant zealots who labored for so many reform causes seemed unable to see the gross discrepancy between such goals and their bitter sectarian prejudice. The cult of Love did not harmonize with anti-Catholic agitation.

Communes: The search for Utopia

Those Christian reformers who were more radical than the majority tried to create the Kingdom of God and the Brotherhood of Man here on earth by settling in communes of various sorts. The *Christian Socialists* looked back to the allegedly cooperative life of primitive Christianity.

The search for a Christian Utopia was no new thing in American history; it had lain at the heart of the separatist Pilgrim migrations.

In the 19th century numerous groups experimented with communal living—Shakers, Mormons, and brands of German separatists (such as the Amana Society, Rappites, Mennonites, Dunkers, Ephratists) and others. Many little colonies were secular. Several hundred small utopian settlements were begun in New England, the Midwest, Texas, and (after about 1850) in California. Fewer were established in the South but no state was without its commune before the Civil War. Paradoxically, despite the growth of prejudice, nativism, and anti-immigration fears, Americans seemed usually tolerant of eccentricity and experimentation within limits. It was possible in those days to begin a colony devoted to communism of property or to sex equality in a state like Ohio, Massachusetts, or Texas. In later years American orthodoxy hardened.

True, of the new groups, the Mormons suffered violent persecution. American society was generally open enough, however, and sheer love of novelty and change would enable fads and fancies to sweep the nation. It was an age of self-conscious experimentation. For example, the Yankee revivalist, William Miller, took the Bible literally and predicted that the world would end in 1843, according to his own calculations. Though 1843 came and the globe continued to spin, his followers did not lose faith in his predictions. "Millenialists," who expect the Second Coming of Christ, still exist today and still forecast the Coming (or the End), updating their calculations with the passage of time. In 1861 a group of Miller's people formed the *Seventh Day Adventist* church.

Meanwhile *Spiritualists* promised a happy, universal brotherhood between living and dead, claiming to communicate with the departed, usually through psychics or "mediums." Their leader was Andrew Jackson Davis. The first professional mediums of note seem to have been the Fox sisters of Rochester, New York, but they later recanted their beliefs (1848). Even rationalists took a deep interest in spiritualism and in psychic phenomena in those pre-Freudian days. The Brook Farm members read Swedenborg, the 18th-century Swedish mystic popular with Emerson. Some secular socialists like Robert Dale Owen were drawn to these notions. Phrenology, hypnotism, and mesmerism were commonly accepted, or toyed with. Spiritualism was not an American invention, as was the religion of Christian Science in later decades, but both denied death. The pursuit of happiness could go no further than this.

Shakers and Mormons

At the opposite end of the social scale from Brook Farm or from Bronson Alcott's ascetic colony of Fruitlands, Massachusetts, (1843) were the more numerous and successful Shakers and Mormons who appealed to the underdogs, to poor folk, and European factory hands. The Shakers are remembered today chiefly for their pleasantly plain furniture styles. They were originally an English sect, sometimes called "Shaking Quakers" from a shaking dance which was part of their group ritual. They owed much to Quakerism, but had roots deep in 17th-century France. The great Shaker leader was an illiterate factory hand, the daughter of a Manchester blacksmith, "Mother Ann" Lee. Mother Ann's early life was violent and tragic. She was abysmally poor, labored hard, was unhappily married, lost four children and was severely persecuted in England. She was jailed, maltreated, and forcibly starved. Mother Ann came to regard all sexual activity as a sin. She emigrated to New York in 1774 with a few disciples, sworn to a life of celibate communism. The Shakers had colonies in four New England states at the time of her death ten years later. By 1850 they numbered about 6,000 with about 20 little communes and had spread westward to Ohio, Indiana, and Kentucky. They were saved from the worst sorts of active prejudice by their own pacifism and quiet separatism.

The Shakers were also millenialists, expecting Christ to reappear, and receiving divine revelations through group rituals and trances. They talked freely with the spirit world. Communal life was strict. The elders, women and men, governed separate "families," and all worked a 12-hour day in fields or workshops. The Shakers were prosperous and adopted labor-saving devices; they became excellent craftsmen. Equality of men and women was the hallmark, in fact it was a fundamental *religious* principle for Shakers: Jesus they saw as the "male principle" in Christianity, Mother Ann as the "female principle." Prohibition of sex and marriage meant that the sect could increase only through direct conversion of new members. The Shakers in-

Shaker furniture

The Shaker Museum, Lees Studio photo

evitably declined. They became fully American after the first generation and almost vanished before the Civil War.

More long-lasting were the Mormons, whose sexual doctrines were very different. The founder of the Mormon church was Joseph Smith, a man of the poverty-striken Burnt-over District of western New York. His family had seen many revivals and cults sweep through the region. Smith claimed to have discovered golden tablets in a field in 1827, inscribed with religious revelations written in a strange language. He published these in 1830 as the *Book of Mormon,* claiming to have translated them with the aid of magic spectacles. Smith organized a group of "Latter Day Saints" who were soon hounded out of New York, Ohio, and Missouri. They settled for a while at Nauvoo, Illinois, in 1840. The people of Illinois hated the Mormons. Rioting broke out around Nauvoo in June 1844 when many of Joseph Smith's stalwarts were out of town, campaigning for his election to the U.S. presidency. Smith was jailed, but a lynch mob dragged him out of custody and killed him, together with his brother in Carthage, Illinois.

Nauvoo had become a prosperous river town. Mormon missionaries sent to Britain had attracted several thousand factory workers from Lancashire and other northern English counties and had established a Mormon recruiting headquarters in Liverpool. The population of Nauvoo was about 15,000 by 1844. The settlement was governed as a theocracy under the Prophet, Joseph Smith. Unlike the Shakers, the Mormons had made themselves too visible. They voted *en bloc* in state elections, directed by Smith. He was politically incautious and over-ambitious, frightening Mormons and non-Mormons alike. The policy of polygamy was announced in 1843, which did not help to allay popular fears of the Mormons. Smith's presidential platform of 1844 included abolition of slavery (with compensation) and the U.S. annexation of vast territories such as British Canada and Mexico.

After Smith's murder his family and close friends broke away from the main body of the church, repudiated polygamy, and settled in Iowa as a separatist sect. Mainstream Mormonism was now led by a brilliant organizer, Brigham Young. The rump of the church made the fantastic overland journey to the West and eventually settled near the Great Salt Lake of Utah (1846–47), an arid region. Here they prospered again, making the desert bloom. Additional waves of emigrants followed from Europe, mainly workers who crossed the American continent on foot, sometimes pushing handcarts before them. Within 30 years Mormon missionaries had boosted the settlement in Utah from 6,000 to 200,000. The Mormon state called "Deseret" entered the Union in 1896 as Utah, having officially (if not actually) given up polygamy in 1890 as a prerequisite.

Secular utopias: New Harmony and Nashoba

The longest-lasting communes were usually religious, like the Mormons with their state-socialist theocracy. For example Zoar, a German pietist community, flourished in Ohio from 1817 right down to 1898, while the Amana colonies of Iowa still prosper (their products today include microwave ovens and refrigerators). The most famous of the nonreligious colonies was Robert Owen's socialist settlement, New Harmony, established in Indiana in 1825. New Harmony lasted only three years. Its fame was derived partly from its founder, an internationally known reformer and the founder of socialism in Britain. Owen, however, was committed to many ideas, ranging from trade unionism to secularism and the cooperative movement. His children all settled here and, among his four sons, Robert Dale Owen (1807–1860) became an Indiana representative in Congress, a leading western expansionist, feminist, and abolitionist. Owen's only surviving daughter settled at New Harmony. His son Richard wrote its history, and another son, William, administered the commune.

Robert Owen went to the United States in April 1825 to buy New Harmony from the Rappites, a celibate German pietist group, which then moved to Pennsylvania. Owen's settlement received much national publicity. He addressed Congress in 1825, incredibly urging them to convert to socialism. Owen dined with American public figures, including Jefferson and Madison. He paid out $95,000 from his private cotton-mill fortune for the settlement and sank more money into it later. The failure of New Harmony was a severe financial blow to Owen.

The colony began well, the Rappites having done preliminary work. New Harmony attracted talented members apart from Owen's own progeny. Too many radical ideas were combined, however, and New Harmony suffered from lack of simple direction, a characteristic of Robert Owen himself. Owen stood for the total regeneration of Man through environmental manipulation. He attacked the churches, the marriage code, and existing family structure, and private property, thus frightening off much "respectable" support. The American love of novelty rarely extended to marital or certain religious ideas. One could become an unorthodox Christian, even a Jew; one could not profess atheism or agnosticism, as Owen seemed to. Nevertheless about 1,000 had settled in New Harmony on the banks of the Wabash by 1825. They held property in common and rewarded work according to the worker's needs, not as a measure of effort, on the lines of the classic socialist saying: *"From* each according to his ability; *to* each according to his need." This was an unlikely idea on the American frontier where labor could earn very visible rewards. New Harmony dissolved, despite its cultural attractions, concerts, lectures, dances, and visiting dignitaries. By 1828 eight or nine smaller Owenite colonies had also failed around the nation; Owen tried to get the Mexican government to give him a large land grant in Texas. This project did not work out, either.

Nashoba, Tennessee, was an entirely different sort of colony. There, another British-born reformer, Frances Wright, tried to create the ideal conditions under which freed black slaves could be educated and prepared for life in the outside world, mainly as farm workers and craftsmen. "Fanny" Wright was notorious for her radical views. In an age when women were not supposed to address public audiences (except of other women), she spoke out openly for socialism, feminism, agnosticism, abolitionism, and sex reforms. At Nashoba, near Memphis, the blacks and whites were to live together in a community, the Negroes doing most of the manual work, the white liberals training them. Wright appealed for government aid, publishing a booklet in 1825, *A Plan For The Gradual Abolition of Slavery in the United States Without Danger of Loss to the Citizens of the South.* She called for experimental farms like Nashoba on government land grants throughout the South. Here slaves could work for 10 to 15 years and farm profits would compensate former owners for their freedom. The slaves were to be prepared for a free life in some other nation. Her plan called for the compromise solution called "Colonization"—the shipping of freedmen abroad. The prospect did not please black abolitionist leaders.

Wright's colonization panacea did win her some white Southern support. Nashoba survived until 1829, though Frances Wright was rarely there and left the community altogether in April 1828. What destroyed Nashoba was her radical reputation, her open criticism of the institution of marriage, and her frank publication in the *Memphis Advocate* of implied approval of race mixing. Nashoba's few blacks and the poor location never paid off. The luckless Negroes were liberated but shipped out to Haiti. Wright turned her attention to other matters.

French phalanxes and communities

The impact of French socialism was felt in America through the spread of the ideas of Charles Fourier (1772–1837), who designed what he called "phalanxes" or combined industrial-farming communities of precisely 1,620 people living under socialism. The idea won various supporters, including the influential journalist Horace Greeley and Fourier's Yankee disciple, Albert Brisbane (1809–90), whose *Social Destiny of Man* (1840) was the most complete American exposition of Fourierism. On the phalanxes, each of an ideal size of 5,000 acres, men and women would exchange jobs, working at whatever they found most interesting. The machine society with its enforced specialization and narrowness was rejected. The individual would be free to develop his own talents and desires in "joyous labor."

Fourier's ideas went beyond Owen's, to a rejection of industrial society itself. Brisbane began several phalanxes and 30 or so were attempted in the Middle states and the Midwest. The North American Phalanx at Red Bank, New Jersey, consisted of about 100 or so people, far below Fourier's ideal, working on about 700 acres. Men and women received equal pay and all lived in a large three-story building. They worked a 30-hour week, in contrast with the long day of many Utopians, and had an active intellectual life in the evenings, with plays, debates, and concerts. A serious fire in 1854 brought the phalanx to an end after 11 years. It had not failed financially and in many ways it was one of the most interesting experiments, especially in its rewards system—higher pay for repulsive and unpleasant work and lower pay for agreeable labor. The members decided to disband in 1854, though the venture was successful and they could have continued with a loan from Horace Greeley.

Other French-inspired communities, the Icarians, were followers of Étienne Cabet (1788–1856). Their Utopias, which spread into the Midwest, Texas, and California, were strongly centralist. The Icarian communes were torn by dissension and declined soon after Cabet's death. Many had remained purely French and German emigrant colonies.

Sexual radicalism: Oneida

One long-lived Utopian colony more radical than most was Oneida, founded in upper New York in 1848 by John Humphrey Noyes (1811–86). Noyes came from a respectable, wealthy Vermont family who sent him to the best schools, Dartmouth, Andover, and Yale theological school. He was set for a clerical career when the ministry rejected him for his open avowal of the heresy called perfectionism—the belief that the act of conversion and direct contact with God made the individual totally free from all sin. Noyes was against sin, but in a novel way: He wished to *define* it out of existence. He refused to recognize sin in sexual relations. True conversion, he thought, was to liberate oneself from selfishness. He considered the exclusive love of one man for one woman to be selfish.

Forbidden a ministry, Noyes studied for 12 years, living off his wife's income. He read Owen, Fourier, the radical religions, and other philosophies, and in the early 1840s gathered a small group of relations and friends about him in a small, well-knit community at Putney, Vermont. Communism of property, the reduction of "kitchen slavery" for women to the preparation of only one formal meal a day, and shared tasks were one thing, but the local Putney folk were angered when this group began to share wives and husbands. The whole idea began in 1846 when Noyes, himself married, began to share a colleague's wife. This act was not impetuous: It had been preceded by months of verbal onslaught against the institution of marriage during intense discussions among the group.

Noyes invented a doctrine he called "complex marriage," which was not Free Love or promiscuity. Every woman was considered married to every man, but sexual union was not an individual choice. So far as possible, male continence was the general rule. Complex marriage was a form of multiple polygamy-polyandry, pairs being selected by group decision. "Special love" was outlawed and no permanent relationships were allowed; exclusive love between two people was antisocial. Complex marriage evolved gradually and became a full-grown institution only after the community had been driven from Vermont to New York State in 1848.

The second home of the perfectionists prospered. An original investment of $100,000 and 51 people, it had grown to over 200 members by 1851 with many additional buildings. Soon it was a miniature town. Women and men were equal and worked side by side at first, even at the roughest excavation work and building. In later years outside labor was hired for menial tasks. Iron-hoop skirts, petticoats, and corsets soon vanished in favor of the more convenient long Turkish-style knickers and short tunic, designed by the dress-reformer Amelia Bloomer. "Bloomers," with their greater freedom of movement for women, became the typical dress at Oneida. Women's equality was at the heart of the Oneida experiment, and in complex marriage there was no false double standard of relative sexual freedom for men, and male-imposed restraint for women.

Despite its outraged critics, Oneida was a great success. It survived until 1880, by which time the early economy of farming and logging had given way before various stages of industrialization. First the colony began to manufacture steel traps for the national market, then sewing thread, then cutlery. In the post–Civil War boom years Oneida thrived. A complex but efficient structure of committees governed this socialist economy; participatory democracy was the rule. Group encounter sessions were held for mutual criticism and the exposure of complaints and anxieties. Child education was relaxed and "progressive" before its day. The community remained founded on religion.

In 1879 Noyes gave way to outside pressure and abandoned complex marriage. The next year communism went, along with group marriage. The colony became "Oneida Community Inc.," a joint-stock business. The shares were divided. Noyes was a genuine iconoclast seeking to overthrow primary institutions, the family, and marriage. He opposed what he once called "the Sin system, the Marriage system, the Work system, and the Death system." Most Utopias are supposed to have failed miserably. Oneida did not "fail"; yet it was in some ways the most radical.

Women's leadership in a galaxy of reforms

The equal role of women in the utopian settlements was one of the many examples of the rising self-consciousness of American women. Their role on the frontier and in the growing factories, and the advance of feminist ideas in Britain and on the Continent brought to some women a realization that they were an oppressed minority. In this age of crinoline and corsets, women had few legal rights. They were treated as "wards" in a patriarchal, male society. Women could not sue alone in the courts; they could be forcibly claimed by their husbands, almost like fugitive slaves, and physically "corrected." On marriage, all their property went to the man. Husbands could commit wives to asylums and had advantages in the divorce courts. Women reform organizers found that their signatures on financial documents were worthless—they had to get their husbands to sign for them. Apart from legal disabilities, general attitudes prevented women from appearing in public or taking the lead in demonstrations. Those who did so in the 1830s and 40s put themselves immediately into a special class, open to all sorts of criticism and abuse.

Yet women in America were economically better off than in many nations and had already thrown off semi-feudal institutions like close chaperonage. The wealthier middle-class women, with the help of male sympathizers, usually took the lead—like the intellectual Margaret Fuller among the Transcendentalists, whose *Woman in the 19th Century* (1845) became a sort of rebel feminist handbook. Women were inspired by their success in the abolitionist movement to work for their own liberation. They often combined women's rights with antislavery, temperance, free public schools, prison reform, and other concerns for which they led the struggle.

American women leaders felt that better education was crucial to their movement. Oberlin, as we have seen, admitted women in 1833. Its first female graduate was Lucy Stone, tough suffragette and abolitionist. Three years later Mary Lyon created the first separate women's college, Mount Holyoke, Massachusetts. Others, like Smith College, followed in due course. In these liberal arts colleges of high standards women were not limited to allegedly "female" subjects such as home economics or embroidery. Meanwhile the state teacher-training Normal Schools, which accompanied the reforms of Horace Mann and others, increased educational and job opportunities for women, above the level of keeping house, bearing children, or bending over a cotton loom in a factory. In many professions like medicine, opposition from the entrenched male chauvinist establishment was rooted. One way out was separate medical colleges for women, tried in New York and in Pennsylvania. The first woman to gain a full medical degree was Dr. Elizabeth Blackwell (1821–1910) with an M.D. degree from Geneva, New York (1849). Typically, Dr. Blackwell was middle-class, of an educated reform and abolitionist family. Her brother was married to Lucy Stone and her sister-in-law, Antoinette, was a Unitarian minister and suffragette. Dr. Blackwell was British and returned home after her pioneer work in American medical education.

At a more popular but still middle-class level, the growth of journalism improved the quality of life of American women. Journals, such as the *Godey's Lady's Book*, edited for half a century by the formidable Sarah Josepha Hale, did much to spread rational ideas of diet, dress, exercise and professional opportunities for women, despite their editorial limits. But for thousands of servants, the many impoverished immigrant girls who served the middle-class, very little was done.

Seneca Falls Convention, 1848

A major plank of the women reformers was the right to vote—a goal not achieved by American women until the 19th Amendment of 1920. This was one concern of the women's rights convention, the first of its kind, called at Seneca Falls, New York, in 1848 by two pioneers, Elizabeth Cady Stanton and Lucretia Mott.

The two women had turned to women's rights when, as antislavery advocates, they had been denied accreditation at a large abolitionist meeting in London (1840) because of their sex. The spectacle of a group of "radical" men, meeting to debate the sins of slavery and simultaneously refusing admission to mere women, was something they did not forget. Mrs. Mott had already been a very active antislavery worker and her credentials should have been impeccable. From 1827 her home in Philadelphia was a stage on the Underground Railroad. She followed her Quaker conscience in breaking the law in obedience to the Higher Law of morality.

In 1851 the ranks of women's leaders were joined by another extraordinary Quaker reformer, Susan B. Anthony, daughter of a Massachusetts manufacturer and abolitionist. Mrs. Anthony had been forced to create a separate women's group in the temperance crusade, the Daughters of Temperance, because of the inadmissability of women. The experience helped to make her a militant suffragette, and in the election of 1872 she openly broke the law by going to the polls to vote. In the 1850s these women did manage to induce the New York legislature to grant legal rights to women, including the right to sue independently and the right to have guarantees of private property and earnings. With the aid of male reformers, like Robert Dale Owen in Indiana, these reforms spread to other states. The first to give the vote to women was Wyoming Territory in 1869, followed by other western states in the 1890s (Colorado, Utah, Idaho). On the whole, the women workers did far better on behalf of others than they did for themselves before the Civil War. Their "Declaration of Independence" at Seneca Falls, was a long time bearing fruit:

We hold these truths to be self-evident: that all men *and women* are created equal . . .

Labor and capitalism

One group the national politicians were eager to win over were the growing number of American skilled and factory workers. Both Andrew Jackson and John Quincy Adams made flattering appeals to them in the campaign of 1828. The chief demands of labor were the ten-hour day, free public schools, and land reform. An English immigrant and friend of Robert Owen, George Henry Evans (1805–56), led the movement for cheap public lands, culminating after his death in the Homestead Act of 1862. Evans urged workers to use the party system and "Vote Yourself A Farm!" He opposed the Fourierist and other Utopias as unrealistic. Evans' own National Reform Association was Jeffersonian in style.

George Henry Evans was a leading member of the short-lived third party, the *Workingmen's Party* of New York (1829–30), one of the few labor parties in U.S. history. Other founders included Robert Dale Owen, Frances Wright, and a number of unemployed New York workers. Evans edited the nation's first labor newspaper, the *Workingmen's Advocate,* down to 1837. The group stood also for the abolition of imprisonment for debt, equal tax laws, reform of monopolies (e.g., banking charters—here they were close to Andrew Jackson), repeal of the conspiracy laws which retarded trade unions, and elimination of the militia system. Notably, they were not socialists. Their hatred of monopoly and debtor laws expressed their desire to become small businessmen and independent farmers, an attitude on the part of American labor which has always impeded the growth of socialism here. The aims of the worker's party of the 1820s were part of the American Dream; mass education was their hoped-for social ladder.

In Jacksonian America urban poverty was already a fact in New York, Philadelphia, Boston, and other towns, where people lived in tenements without windows or indoor toilet facilities. Labor leaders gave little thought to this sort of poverty, which they did not see as permanent in the American setting of opportunity. More important to organized, skilled labor was the long legal struggle to establish trade unions, so that they could meet the employers on their own grounds. The chief obstacle was the doctrine of "conspiracy" in restraint of trade, introduced from the English Common Law. In Philadelphia in 1806, in *Commonwealth* v. *Pullis*, a group of shoemakers were found guilty of conspiring to strike to raise wages and prices and their would-be "closed shop" policy (employment of union members only) was shattered. The judge's decision significantly made as many references to Adam Smith's *Wealth of Nations* and the "immutable laws" of economic competition as to any laws of the land the cobblers had broken. In 1810 a New York court made a similar decision *People* v. *Melvin*. This doctrine had to be reversed if trade unions were to emerge.

No genuine labor movement extending beyond any one special trade can be traced before 1827. Strikes had occurred. Printers in Philadelphia demanded $6 a week in 1786 and cobblers struck in 1799. By the 1830s each trade had its union, all of them skilled, upwardly mobile workers—hatters, printers, bookbinders, glassmakers, joiners, and so on. But in 1827 for the first time a *central* trade union was created, combining trades: the Mechanics' Union of Philadelphia. Carpenters on strike for a ten-hour day were joined sympathetically by glaziers, bricklayers, and painters. Fifteen unions joined together. Similar "city centrals" emerged in New York, Boston, and elsewhere; even *national* organizations became possible. Many of these unions went under in the depression after 1837.

Unionism picked up again in the later 1850s with the increase of railroad construction, gold discoveries, and general economic expansion. National unions were formed, such as the Typographical Union (1850), Machinists and Blacksmiths (1859), and National Molders (1859). Again the new organizations were badly hit by the depression after the 1857 Panic. The courts however had softened their attitude to labor with the decision of 1842, *Commonwealth* v. *Hunt*, in Massachusetts. The state supreme court threw out the 1806 *Commonwealth* v. *Pullis* decision and virtually legalized trade unions. Consequently the upper strata of the labor force could organize themselves for self-protection in the market economy. For the masses of unskilled there was less hope. In January 1834 when the mainly Irish, immigrant workers building the Baltimore and Ohio Canal began to riot against tough company policies of blacklisting, use of spies, and hiring of private police, President Andrew Jackson gladly cooperated with the canal owners in providing federal troops. Jackson's old crony and ex-Secretary of War, John Eaton, was a company director.

Humanitarian reforms: The Jacksonian underworld

The skilled workers wanted abolition of imprisonment for debt, to stimulate small business venturers, but humanitarian radicals demanded more—better conditions in all American jails and reconsideration of the meaning of punishment. The petty debt problem was huge. An estimated five sixths of all prisoners in 1830 in New England and the Middle Atlantic states were in jail for debts, mostly under $20, and for business failures. This was crippling to economic incentive and hurt the "little man." Life in jail was harsh, as bad as that described by Charles Dickens in British jails. The Quakers in particular pressed for prison reform, arguing that jail should stand for more than the revenge of society. Imprisonment should reform the individual. Once more the environmentalist argument appeared—man, even criminal man, is plastic and can be remolded.

At first the reformed jails, now called "penitentiaries" (where the penitent could be forgiven and reeducated), were themselves grim. Hating the overcrowding of early jails in which all sorts of criminals were herded together, the reformers had urged separate cells, as in the Eastern State Penitentiary in Pennsylvania. However, isolation proved to be too cruel, so men were later allowed out in work gangs. Usually a very capitalistic solution was found: The gangs were contracted out to private firms. In Boston's reformatory and in New York's "House of Refuge" (1824) young boys were separated from hardened criminals. Mixing of ages and sexes continued for decades and remains a problem even today. The traditional Quaker criticism that "jails breed crime" is still true. No separate court treatment of young people came until the state of Illinois opened the first "Juvenile Court" in 1899.

The underworld of this progressive, majoritarian democracy also included most of its blind, deaf, and dumb and its mentally ill citizens, often lumped together with criminals and even jailed by state authorities. A courageous woman of unbelievable fortitude and spirit, Dorothea Lynde Dix (1802–87), made a three-year investigation of the terrifying conditions under which the mentally ill were forced to live in America: in cages, in cellars and attics, hidden away in closets and cupboards, kept in chains, sometimes naked, ill-fed, beaten and degraded. Miss Dix visited hundreds of jails, state prisons, and almshouses. She wrote a bitter exposé for the Massachusetts legislature in 1843. The politicians were startled into activity. Twenty states soon copied the Massachusetts example by founding state hospitals for the insane. Miss Dix then went abroad and inspired movements for reform in Japan, England, and elsewhere. Congress even voted a land-grant bill to aid the blind, deaf, and dumb, and insane, although the inept President Franklin Pierce vetoed it. Despite the noble work of pioneers like Dr. Samuel Gridley Howe of Boston's Perkins Institute for the Blind, the sightless in pre–Civil War America lived little better than the mentally ill.

The Cold-Water Army

Revivalist influence was nowhere felt more strongly than in the "Cold-Water Army"—the American temperance movement. Today, in a more relaxed and permissive age, we tend to think critically of the "teetotallers" as religious zealots who wished to legislate morals. But drunkenness was a social disease of staggering proportions in early 19th-century America, as serious as the drug addiction problem of the mid-20th century. For this reason many feminist and antislavery advocates were equally ardent temperance workers. Those few who paid

Dorothea Dix, a woman of outstanding courage and empathy

Library of Congress

attention to the poor, like the New York Society for the Prevention of Pauperism, blamed drink as the chief cause of poverty (1818). The movement was chiefly dominated by Quakers and Methodists. The Catholic Church also entered the field in the late 1840s led by Father Theobald Mathew.

There were undercurrents of middle-class arrogance, nativism, and bigotry toward beer and whisky-drinking Irish and German immigrants in the temperance crusade, no doubt. Protestant reformers did not like the uncouth immigrants with their unholy, lively Sabbath and their Catholic faith. Drinking was nonetheless a genuine social problem. Neal Dow of Maine became the national leader of the temperance cause. Dow fought successfully for prohibition laws in Maine (1851) and other states went dry. Later Dow evangelized abroad.

The attack on drinking took many forms. Every known revivalist technique was adopted: large camp meetings in which fiery orators harangued guilt-ridden crowds, music, drama, tracts, journals, sermons, and books. Supported by maudlin popular songs, the play by Timothy Shay Arthur, *Ten Nights in a Bar Room*, became a long-lasting hit show. One group, the Washingtonians, persuaded half a million Americans to "sign the pledge." In 1826 the National American Temperance Society was founded, to send into the field scores of missionaries. The movement did not emerge into national politics until after the Civil War, with the creation of the Prohibition Party of 1869. Neal Dow was the party's presidential candidate in 1880.

The financing and organization of the temperance crusade, like that so many other reform movements, was pushed by the religious denominations. New York City became the headquarters for many

Reform as a way of life

religious groups and their benevolent and reform activities in the 1830s. Until he moved to Oberlin College, Charles Finney could be heard there in a large Free Church. Also in New York lived the two rich merchant brothers, Arthur and Lewis Tappan, who personally financed many do-good schemes. The Tappans were leading capitalists, founders of the *Journal of Commerce,* and for good or evil, creators of the first U.S. credit agency. They spent their money on abolitionism, social reforms, and projects like Oberlin. The radical movements of the 1830s and 40s were sustained from such sources.

By the 1850s, however, the steam was being let out of the temperance cause and other issues as the antislavery question assumed center stage. Abolitionism was the confluence of all these streams—Romanticism, Transcendentalism, Utopianism, and the evangelical revival. Almost everyone who had pursued a reform career in various crusades concentrated their efforts on antislavery in the 1850s. Meanwhile, as a region, the South had experienced little in the way of radical reform. Pro-slavery apologists built up a comforting image of the Cotton Kingdom as a perfect civilization, founded on the wise and benevolent institution of slavery and modeled on Ancient Greek democracy. Southerners became impervious to new ideas. Freedom of thought vanished in the Old South.

So it came about that the Civil War, fought over slavery-extension and preservation of the American Union, finally brought an end to the Southern plantation-slavery subculture. The war also terminated the era of radical reform in the United States.

Bibliography

Alice F. Tyler. *Freedom's Ferment.* New York: Harper, 1962.

A. Bestor. *Backwoods Utopias.* University of Pennsylvania Press, 1950.
T. L. Smith. *Revivalism and Social Reform.* New York: Harper, 1957.
M. Katz. *Irony of Early School Reform.* Harvard University Press, 1968.
F. O. Matthiessen. *American Renaissance: Art and Experience in the Age of Emerson and Whitman.* New York: Oxford University Press, 1968.

11

Frontier nationalism

The party politics of expansionism . . . birth of Manifest Destiny . . . the growth experience reinforced . . . frontier nationalism: Canada . . . election of 1840: professional campaigning . . . frontier nationalism: the Pacific Northwest . . . the Polk Doctrine . . . Oregon and Asia . . . the Americanization of California . . . frontier nationalism: Middle Border and Southwest . . . slavery and Texas annexation . . . frontier nationalism: the war against Mexico . . . Mexico is halved . . . triumphant nationalism . . . the Mexican War and the Civil War . . . the Wilmot Proviso and the election of 1848 . . . Zachary Taylor favors statehood for California and New Mexico . . . Whigs, Democrats, and the Compromise of 1850 . . . the Fugitive Slave Law . . . the territorial issues: "popular sovereignty" . . . the Compromise in practice . . . the role of Texas . . . aftermath of the Compromise: election of 1852 . . . further fruits of expansionism: the Ostend Manifesto . . . the slavery question reopened: Kansas-Nebraska . . . Civil War in miniature . . . the Republicans and the ideology of sectional conflict.

The party politics of expansionism

The one-party dominance of the Jacksonian Democrats was threatened in the election of 1836 by the new Whig party. Moreover, a small Democratic splinter-group, the Equal Rights party, grasped control of the party machinery in New York City. Its members were called *Locofocos* after the name of the matches they used to light candles when their rivals turned off the gaslight at Tammany Hall. These reform Democrats represented the ideas and interests of the former Workingmen's party, but they had returned to the national fold of the Democrats by 1840.

In 1840 the Whigs captured the White House with William Henry Harrison. Two-party politics followed for a while—Democrats, 1844 (Polk), Whigs, 1848 (Taylor-Fillmore), and Democrats, 1852 (Pierce), and again in 1856 (Buchanan). Whatever their differences, both major parties shared the general enthusiasm of the American public for territorial expansion and economic growth. Expansion could not take place, however, without creating grave differences in the nation at large. Consequently, issues were sometimes faced more squarely by third parties, such as those which took a firm stand on the issue of slavery.

Even more than in the time of Monroe and John Quincy Adams the American people exemplified the nationalism of a new nation and of a frontier society. This later nationalism was heightened by greater acquisitions of territory. The hunger for land fed off itself. Territorial growth became sanctified by the doctrine of "Manifest Destiny." The nation experienced a wave of superpatriotism and spread-eagle oratory in the 1830s and 40s. Many of the radicals and reformers went along with this spirit of adventure and national pride and acclaimed territorial extension as the inevitable destiny of the Republic. The nationalist poet of democracy, Walt Whitman, was one example. The spirit of Manifest Destiny crossed party lines. It was born in the Democratic party's propaganda, it spread to the Whigs, and was extended after the Civil War by the new Republican party.

Birth of Manifest Destiny

The group of ideas represented by Manifest Destiny had been around for some time. The actual phrase was coined in July 1845 by a Democratic lawyer and editor, John L. O'Sullivan. His unsigned piece in the *U.S. Magazine and Democratic Review* warned of foreign powers plotting to prevent the U.S. annexation of Texas. They must be resisted, said this active "hawk" who had himself joined a filibustering adventure to Cuba. American expansion was not merely expedient and profitable, according to O'Sullivan, but was divinely ordained and historically inevitable. He proclaimed that it was

the fulfilment of our *manifest destiny* to overspread the continent allotted by Providence for the free development of our yearly multiplying millions.

In December 1845 the notion was applied to the Oregon boundary dispute with Canada by the New York *Morning News*. Almost instantly the phrase became common currency. Congressmen eagerly linked it to Canada, Cuba, and Mexico, wherever they felt Americans should rule. O'Sullivan combined the land-hunger, population-pressure excuse for expansionism with the arguments of divine benediction, historical inevitability, and the need to spread free institutions.

The argument adopted against the Indians that they did not use the soil properly was now used against Mexicans. This "superior-use" reasoning claimed that the U.S. should annex vast stretches of the California and New Mexico territories of Mexico, virtually halving that republic. Allegedly the Mexicans were inferior farmers who had not fully developed their lands. Superior-use was harder to employ against Canadians in Oregon. Here American settlers outnumbered others.

Superior-use implied the superiority of the *user*, for instance the cultural and racial superiority of white over Indian, or Anglo-Saxon over Mexican and mestizo. North Americans regarded the Latin American nations as childlike, incorrigibly underdeveloped and unstable. This attitude impeded intercontinental relationships through the 20th century and was bitterly resented south of the border. More important, perhaps, was the fact that North Americans came to identify their own freedom with their ability to acquire territory at will. By the 1840s territorial expansion and "free" land to the West, notwithstanding whoever occupied it—scattered Spanish pueblos and missions, Indian tribes, British Canadian pioneers or Russian traders —was accepted as the foundation of continued American liberty and growth.

The growth experience reinforced

The typical American frontier experience was growth. For over 200 years Americans had come to the wilderness, suffered privation, but witnessed in their own lifetimes the development of farms, towns, and trade. This happened with each new wave of settlement and each new frontier. Successive frontiers constantly reinforced the experience of building a new civilization from very little. Down through the 1890s Americans were still settling new frontiers. Even in the 20th century, Alaska, which became a state in 1959, was a fresh frontier to be conquered. An ebullient optimism and *expectation* of growth was stamped into the group experience of North Americans.

As early as the 1830s this condition produced what Tocqueville called the "irritating patriotism" of Americans. Superpatriotism and "puffery" was marked in the West. One stump orator of the 1840s declaimed:

Europe—what is Europe? She's nowhar—nothing. . . . We have faster steamboats, swifter locomotives, larger creeks, bigger plantations, . . . higher mountains, deeper cataracts, louder thunder, forkeder lightning. . . .

Forkeder lightning: Here speaks the raw nationalism of a new, expansive republic. Beyond the arrogance and insularity lay the special frontier spirit, its activism and optimism. The American's reach always exceeded his grasp. He built not according to his means but according to his expectations. Those were high.

Frontier nationalism: Canada

Americans built internal and external empires. The expansion of American foreign trade took them to all corners of the globe. They sought markets in China and opened up Japan. They won the rich tea trade by developing specialized clipper ships and fought for openings in Africa and Latin America. They sent whalers, missionaries, and traders to the Pacific and settled in Hawaii, where their chief rivals were English (evidenced by the present state flag of Hawaii with its Union Jack in one corner).

More significant than foreign trade adventures was the U.S. claim to a vast internal territorial empire. The U.S. pushed outward against Canada and Mexico. A crisis in foreign relations with Canada and Britain came in Martin Van Buren's administration, brought on by American defaults on debts to English creditors in the Panic of 1837, by boundary disputes, and by U.S. interference on the side of the

The U.S.A.

rebels in the Canadian insurrection of 1837. In 1838 Canadian troops crossed to the U.S. side of the Niagara to burn a steamboat, the *Caroline*, which had supplied the rebels. One American was killed. President Van Buren had the border patrolled to prevent retaliatory raids, but private American citizens pillaged the frontier throughout the winter of 1838–39 all the same, and further east, fighting broke out over the boundary dispute in Maine. This so-called Aroostook War between Canadian lumberjacks and Maine militia was stalemated by a truce in March 1839. The issue was settled by the Webster-Ashburton Treaty of 1842. During the Whig regime of President W. H. Harrison, Daniel Webster became Secretary of State and immediately began peaceful talks with his British counterpart. The trade-minded British Prime Minister, Sir Robert Peel, was also eager for peace.

Election of 1840: Professional campaigning

The election of 1840 carried political professionalism to a new stage of gimmickry, with placards, floats, and slogans. No real issues surfaced. The Whigs pretended that their man, Harrison, was a great democrat and frontiersman who had been raised in a log cabin. They used log-cabin floats and gave away plenty of hard cider. Van Buren was caricatured as a rich aristocrat, dining with gold spoons and silverware. Harrison, who was indeed a frontier hero, was elected on such claims and on his prowess as a killer of Indians (Tippecanoe, 1811). He died after one month in office. His vice president, John Tyler, a traditional Jeffersonian from Virginia, became the first to succeed to the White House through the death of the president in office. Tyler soon turned the tables on the Whigs by forcing his Southern states' rights views on the government and remaking the cabinet. Thus he appointed John C. Calhoun, of all people, Secretary of State in 1844. Tyler alienated Henry Clay by twice vetoing his proposed banking acts and frustrating his Whiggish "American System." Ideologically, President Tyler was a southern Democrat despite his party affiliation. The Whigs became a northern party at odds with their own president.

The election carnival of 1840 and the sudden succession of Tyler did not radically alter America's territorial nationalism. Tyler supported the second Pre-Emption Act of 1841 giving squatters prior land rights. He also supported the U.S. annexation of Texas.

Frontier nationalism: The Pacific Northwest

The beautiful Oregon country of the Northwest was highly regarded by visionaries like the first American millionaire, John Jacob Astor, as essential for U.S. domination of the continent and for Oriental trade. National ambitions brought a second Anglo-American crisis in the mid-1840s over the *Oregon Question*. The Spanish had relinquished their Oregon claims in 1819, the Russians in 1824. An Anglo-American treaty of 1818 had provided for joint occupation of the region by British and American settlers. As the riches of the Pacific Northwest became evident both sides claimed priority to the region. British discoverers, Captain Cook (1778) and Captain Vancouver (1792), were offset by American pioneers: Captain Robert Gray (1792) and Lewis and Clark (1804–6). Both nations had fur traders in Oregon. John Jacob Astor had founded Astoria in 1811 at the mouth of the Columbia River, hoping it would be a port for future China trade. The British captured Astoria during the War of 1812.

Missionaries, fur traders, and scientists moved into the Far West in the 1820s and 30s. In 1834 the Reverend Jason Lee founded a Methodist mission in the Willamette Valley. The missionary doctor Marcus Whitman took the first women across the Rockies and settled Walla Walla in 1836. Further south, California was being overrun by American pioneers. California entered the Mexican stage of its history after the fall of Spanish authority in 1822. The new Mexican government took over the old Spanish missions (1834–36) and doled out the land in huge "ranchos" with 8,000,000 acres going to only 800 landholders in the years 1830–46. But Americans were moving in, as they also moved into Texas, the Great Basin, and Oregon. Jedediah Strong Smith, a New England Puritan armed with Bible and rifle, pioneered the overland route to California from the Great Salt Lake southwest, via the Virgin and Colorado rivers to the San Gabriel mission on the Pacific coast in 1826. Smith also penetrated the fertile San Joaquin and Sacramento inland valleys of California. On a second trip he traveled northward from the San Gabriel mission all the way to Vancouver.

In 1827–28 Sylvester Pattie and his son James, working out of Santa Fe, explored the Colorado River and the Grand Canyon and blazed the southwestern route from Santa Fe via the Rio Grande and Gila River to San Diego. Regular traders followed Jedediah Strong Smith and the Patties. The "Old Spanish Trail" was established between Santa Fe and southern California. Along this trail Americans took U.S. blankets, woolens, and silver from St. Louis and other points and returned with Chinese silks, mules, and horses.

The 1840s saw the opening up of overland migration in the northern regions, particularly by the "Pathfinder," John C. Fremont. "Oregon fever" struck in 1842–43 as midwesterners moved to the Pacific Northwest, usually along the famous *Oregon Trail* from Independence, Missouri, to Astoria. Five thousand Americans had settled the Willamette region south of the Columbia River by 1845. As this population grew they became restive under joint Anglo-American occupation, just as further south, Americans were restive in California. In 1843 a group of Americans formed a provisional government for Oregon, making ready for eventual U.S. assimilation. The British were not ready to give up their hopes of keeping the fine harbor area of Puget Sound. They rejected the U.S. plan to extend the existing boundary in the east along the 49th parallel to the Pacific coast. Some expansionist Americans, like the socialist Robert Dale Owen, strongly opposed the British view and demanded huge territories beyond the 49th parallel. A Cincinnati convention of 1843 claimed land stretching as far north as 54° 40′, taking in much of present-day British Columbia. The Oregon Question came to a head in the U.S. election year, 1844.

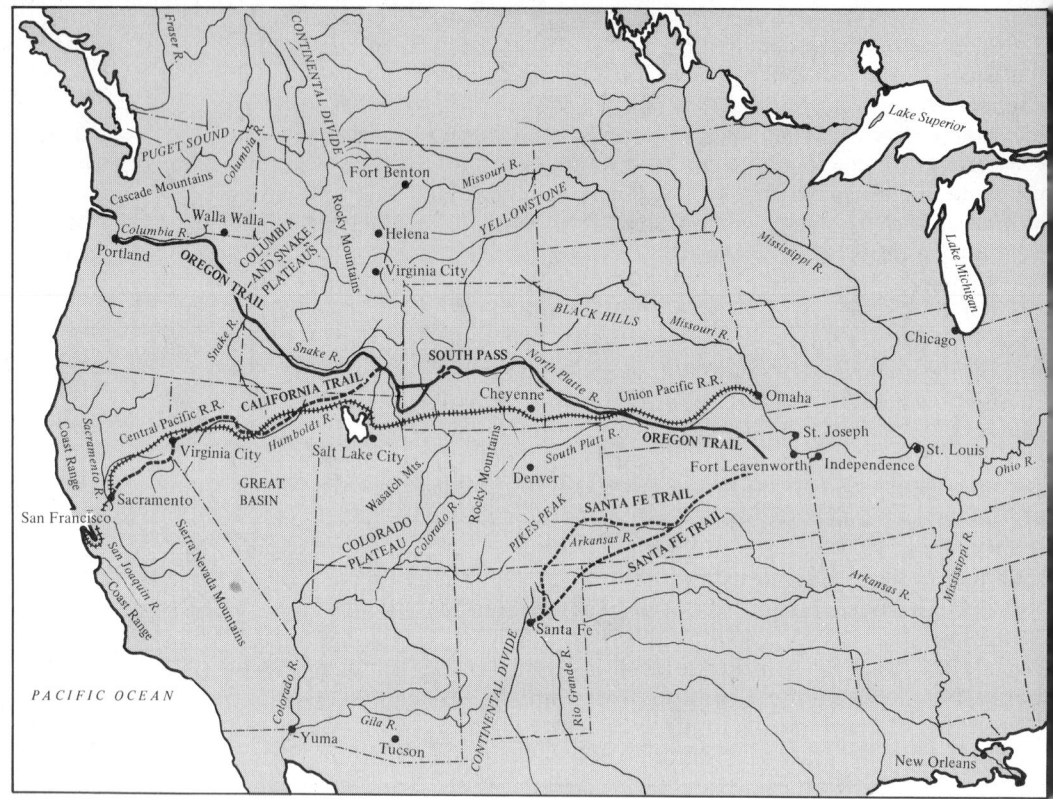

Map 6. Trans-Mississippi trails

Redrawn from R. W. Paul, Mining Frontier of the Old West (New York: Holt, Rinehart and Winston, Inc.).

The Polk Doctrine

The 1844 campaign brought another first in political techniques, use of the telegraph to report the Democrats' convention proceedings. The Whigs, not surprisingly, abandoned Tyler and selected the ever hopeful Henry Clay. The Democrats passed over the master-politician Martin Van Buren because he had publicly opposed the annexation of Texas. The aging Andrew Jackson did not share Northern fears about Texas annexation being a mere cover-up for slavery extension, and threw his support to James K. Polk who won the nomination and the election. Polk gained 170 electoral college votes and the luckless Clay, 105. The popular margin was narrower, 1,338,464 for Polk and 1,300,097 for Clay. A small third group, the Liberty party, led by James G. Birney, demanded abolition of slavery. Birney won only 62,300 popular votes, but his party helped Clay to lose New York, thus contributing to Polk's victory.

James K. Polk was a rigid disciple of Andrew Jackson, an ardent expansionist, and the mouthpiece of the interests and sentiments of the great Mississippi Valley. His administration saw the triumph of antebellum nationalism with the aggressive war against Mexico. President Polk added his own gloss to the Monroe Doctrine by warning the European powers still more emphatically that their interests had nothing to do with affairs in the Western Hemisphere and by decreeing that any independent nation in the hemisphere could unite with the United States if it wished. Polk had Texas in mind but was probably looking ahead also to new revolutions elsewhere. Texas had already been annexed on March 1, 1845; the "Polk Doctrine" was announced on December 2d. The second westerner to become president, Polk the Tennesseean, added more land to the nation than any chief executive since Jefferson.

Polk demanded the whole of Oregon. He was supported by cries of "54° 40' or Fight!" from Midwestern politicians like Stephen A. Douglas of Illinois, Lewis Cass of Michigan, and that old Jacksonian stalwart, Senator Thomas Hart Benton of Missouri. In a Manifest Destiny speech of 1846 Benton pulled out all the stops—race superiority, divine command, inevitability, superior-use, and the extension of liberty. Benton developed a surprising argument for U.S. expansion to the Pacific coast. He asserted that the appearance of Americans there would wake up the "torpid" civilizations of the Far East and bring about a mingling of the two superior cultures, yellow and white. The reds and blacks Benton thought to be inferior, the yellows *less* inferior to the whites.

Oregon and Asia

Whites and Chinese work together in a California gold mine, 1852

California State Library

The Mongolian or Yellow race is there (on the other side of the Pacific) . . . It is a race far above the Ethiopian, or Black—above the Malay, or Brown (if we must admit five races)—and above the American Indian, or Red: it is a race far above all these, but still, far below the White; and, like all the rest, must receive an impression from the superior race whenever they come in contact.

Not many years later Californians would writhe at such a semi-favorable view of the "Yellow" race. But Benton went on:

. . . the White race alone received the divine command, to subdue and replenish the earth! . . . The sun of civilization must shine across the sea (Pacific): socially and commercially, the van of the Caucasians, and the rear of the Mongolians, must intermix. They must talk together, and trade together, and marry together.

"Marry together"? Intermixing of yellow and white presented no "danger" said Benton, for

The White and Yellow races can marry together . . . Moral and intellectual superiority will do the rest: the White race will take the ascendant . . .

The White civilization then, would assimilate the Yellow. Thomas Hart Benton pointed out that the Red race had vanished from the eastern United States. The Capitol had replaced the wigwam. His argument was idiosyncratic and unusual, but Benton laid bare the links between "local" issues like Oregon, vast as that was, and the even wider ambitions of Americans in the entire Pacific area.

Oregon was taken bloodlessly. Americans did not annex lands as far north into Canada as the unreasonable demand of 54° 40′. England, in accordance with her usual 19th-century policy of sacrificing Canadian needs to her own, gave way to the United States. The Oregon Treaty of 1846 split the region in half along the 49th parallel though it allowed Canada to keep Vancouver Island, a beautiful and sizable foothold on Puget Sound waterway. In 1859 Oregon entered the Union, after intervening years of migration, and gold and silver booms in the Rockies of Colorado and Nevada.

The Americanization of California

The fate of California was settled after 1841 by the opening up of the California Trail to thousands of migrants. This trail ran from Independence, Missouri, westward along the Platte and North Platte rivers and through South Pass, Wyoming, a broad way through the Rockies in southwestern Wyoming at a height of about 7,500 feet, journeyed by Jedediah Strong Smith in 1824. The trail followed the Oregon Trail from Independence to South Pass and on to Fort Hall on the Snake River in what is now southern Idaho. At Fort Hall the two trails parted, the California Trail leading southwest to the Humboldt River valley and on to Sacramento and the coast.

Even the Mexican War failed to halt the tide of American migrants. A revolt of settlers led by William B. Ide in the Sacramento Valley resulted in the proclamation of the independent "Bear Flag Republic" in 1846 with the tacit approval of Colonel John C. Fremont. He arrived on the scene a few days after the proclamation and became head of the California Republic in July. During the winter of 1846 the *Donner Party* suffered terrible privations crossing the mountains in the snow and apparently resorted to cannibalism. Out of 87 pioneers, 47 survived. Today a multilane superhighway sweeps through the mountains at that point.

California was ceded to the Union in 1848 at the end of the war. Gold had just been discovered at Sutter's Creek and Polk publicized the strike one year later in his presidential farewell message. The "forty-niners" rushed to California and within one year the state was admitted to the Union (1850).

Frontier nationalism: Middle Border and Southwest

The greatest numerical population growth in the pre–Civil War decades took place not in the Far West but in the American heartland, the Mississippi Valley. Here the agricultural revolution was most thorough and successful. Midwestern cities grew to power as shipping and farm processing centers, such as Cincinnati and St. Louis. The section played a crucial role in the political alignments of the day and its extension to the west, the Iowa country, brought yet another land boom in the 1830s after the Black Hawk War. A timber frontier in Wisconsin and Minnesota was followed by a stage of commercial farming, large-scale production of dairy and grain foodstuffs. The transportation revolution, aided first by state and then by federal encouragement in the 1850s, brought canals and railroads to the Middle Border region. The Illinois Central Railroad, which was to link the Great Lakes to the Gulf, was chartered in 1851. By 1854 Chicago was struggling to be made the focal point for a projected transcontinental railroad.

In the Southwest, American intrusions in the Texas region were already giving the section its distinctive three-cultured character: Indian, Mexican, and Anglo-American. The Mexican Republic encouraged the process in 1821 by offering a land grant to Stephen Austin to bring American settlers into East Texas along the Colorado River. Southern slaveholders moved in and established cotton plantations, using black slave labor on this generous Mexican grant. By 1835 some 25,000 Americans had settled in Texas. Changes of government in Mexico City brought fluctuations in policy towards the Americans and their slaves. American immigration into Mexican Texas was restricted from 1829. In the 1830s violence became common as Americans resisted Mexican regulations. When the Mexican government banned further slave importations, open warfare broke out in 1835.

The war passed back and forth. General Santa Anna defeated the Americans at the Alamo, a mission in San Antonio, which he besieged for 12 days, leaving no Texan alive (1836). Among the dead was the legendary Davy Crockett. "Remember the Alamo!" became a useful political cry therefore on Mexican matters. One month after the Alamo defeat, Sam Houston captured General Santa Anna at the battle of

San Jacinto (April 1836) and the Texans created the independent Lone Star Republic of Texas.

Slavery and Texas annexation

Pressure to annex the Texas Republic built up rapidly after 1836 and was a major feature of Polk's election in 1844. Almost his first act was to confirm the annexation that outgoing President Tyler had signed a few days before. The assimilation of Texas was controversial not only because of its vast size but because slavery was legal and flourished there. Many Northerners, though not radical about slavery where it already existed in the South, were adamantly opposed to its spread. The outbreak of the Mexican War in 1846 thus brought this moral and political issue to a head.

Meanwhile French and British diplomats were conniving in the Texas Republic. Britain favored an independent, buffer state of Texas as a check to U.S. growth and as another source of raw cotton and a market for English manufactured goods. Britain's Texas policy was ambiguous in view of her leadership of the world antislavery crusade. An Anglo-Texas treaty was offered in 1840 after Sam Houston's plea for U.S. annexation was momentarily rejected by Washington. British and French agents acted as mediators in 1842 when Mexico re-invaded Texas. Fears that Texas might pass fully into the British orbit helped to push through the U.S. annexation in February 1845.

Frontier nationalism: The war against Mexico

The war of 1846–48 was a simple war of conquest by the United States, encouraged and engineered by President Polk with the aid of disciplined Democratic party majorities in Congress. As tension mounted between the United States and Mexico, Polk asked Congress for a declaration of war, which was slipped through two days later (May 13, 1846) by the addition of an amendment to a House appropriations bill. The amendment blamed Mexico and left a mere half hour for debate. "By the act of the Republic of Mexico, a state of war exists between that government and the United States," said the amendment. The Whigs opposed the war but the coalition of peace forces was too disorganized and slow to be effective.

Opposition to the Mexican War was nevertheless very strong inside the United States. The public anti-war debate brought in two former presidents, John Quincy Adams and Martin Van Buren, who opposed the war, as well as an obscure Whig Congressman from Illinois, Abraham Lincoln. Ralph Waldo Emerson commented that taking Mexico would be like taking arsenic. Thoreau was jailed for refusing to pay his poll tax; his essay on *Civil Disobedience* provided inspiration thereafter for generations of war-resisters. The American peace movement, one of the reform crusades of the period, was led by the wealthy, retired shipowner, William Ladd of Massachusetts. Ladd's *American Peace Society* (1828) condemned all use of war as an instrument of national policy. His *Essay on a Congress of Nations* (1840) suggested a sort of international tribunal for peaceful settlement of disputes. Ladd was years ahead of his time. It was an irony that the United States, whose reformers led the world peace movement, should embark on a purely aggressive, land-grabbing war.

Abraham Lincoln's strong hostility to the war was remarkable in the power of his rhetoric against President Polk and because he had previously taken little part in congressional debates. Polk gave Mexican hostilities on "American" soil as his excuse for the war. As Lincoln pointed out, the truth was that the disputed territory in southern Texas between the Rio Grande and the Nueces river had never been legally American. Indeed, it was Polk who had first sent United States troops there under General Zachary Taylor. Lincoln denounced Polk's war message as "the half-insane mumbling of a fever dream."

His mind, taxed beyond its power, is running hither and thither, like some tormented creature on a burning surface, finding no position on which it can settle down to be at ease. . . . He is a bewildered, confounded, and miserably perplexed man.

This attack on Polk and on the Mexican War hurt Lincoln badly among his expansionist Midwestern constituents; the Mississippi Valley was solidly pro-war. Some Americans would have gone right on to Mexico City and the assimilation of the entire Mexican Republic. The older states and the North resented the war as a power play by the South and slavery. For the end result was to strengthen temporarily the South's political position within the United States. In 1849 Lincoln abandoned politics and reverted to his law practice.

Mexico is halved

The young Mexican Republic was not strong economically or politically and was ineptly led by General Santa Anna. The military outcome of the war was not in doubt, though many young Mexicans died bravely. Three major U.S. campaigns thrust into Mexican territory: Stephen Kearny took New Mexico and California, joining up with Fremont's Bear Flag rebels and being supported by Commodore R. F. Stockton's sea invasion of California; Zachary Taylor invaded northern Mexico; General Winfield Scott captured the Gulf port of Vera Cruz and then entered Mexico City. The war was virtually over by the Battle of Chapultepec in September 1847. Santa Anna abdicated, peace being negotiated at the Treaty of Guadelupe Hidalgo in 1848.

The treaty was a crippling blow to Mexican pride. The United States took enormous stretches of territory: the whole of California, New Mexico, and Texas, north of the Rio Grande. This "Mexican Cession" eventually became the states of Texas, California, New Mexico, Arizona, Nevada, Utah, and parts of Wyoming and Colorado. The United States agreed to pay Mexico the sum of $15,000,000 compensation.

Triumphant nationalism

Frontier nationalism triumphed in 1848. A swift, relatively painless war for the United States, spurred by President Polk's hunger for New Mexico and California that was shared by other Americans, brought a rapid victory for the nation and more than incidentally for the Democratic party. The Mexican War reminds one of later American interventions and conflicts. The bitterness of anti-war feelings ran deep in the 1840s. The conflict was called "an outrageous war waged by the Executive, upon an offending people who merely oppose the robbery which we (are) attempting to perpetrate upon them." The war-making power was widely debated. Who had the right to make war, Executive or Congress?

John Quincy Adams, a vigorous anti-war leader, hoped that General Zachary Taylor's troops would actually desert, and that his own country would lose the war. In strong contrast, the poet Walt Whitman celebrated territorial expansion with a democratic argument in his Brooklyn *Daily Eagle:*

What has miserable Mexico—with her superstitions, her burlesque upon freedom, her actual tyranny by the few over the many—what has she to do with the great mission of peopling the New World with a noble race?

Whitman argued that the increase of U.S. territory was an "increase in human happiness and liberty." To some degree nationalism and moral fervor were buttressed by commercial interest. New England merchants, for instance, did not totally swallow the official Whig party anti-war line. Some eyed California's harbors and sought links for the legendary Japan and China trade. Of the various motives, frontier nationalism was the most encompassing.

Manifest Destiny, in truth, stopped short of annexing many actual "miserable Mexicans." Frontier imperialism assimilated "empty" lands. When American frontiersmen encountered Indians they decimated them; similar genocide against the numerous Indians and mestizos of Mexico was unthinkable and impossible. Manifest Destiny did not embrace large numbers of "natives" or aliens until the end of the 19th century. It is natural to reach for the catch-all argument of white racism to explain why Mexico proper was left alone, but throughout American history from the 17th century on, sparsely populated and undeveloped "free land" to the West had always been considered "empty." The American variety of land-hunger was slaked only by the taking of frontier lands, not the conquest of developed societies. The hotheads who had visions of grabbing British Ontario or of going beyond the Rio Grande into the ancient culture of Mexico, achieved nothing.

The Oregon Treaty lands became the states of Oregon (1859), Washington (1889), Idaho (1890) and parts of Montana (1889), and Wyoming (1890). Together with the Mexican Cession these additions doubled the size of the United States. Mexico had been halved, though the lands taken were her most undeveloped areas. In the 1853 *Gadsden Purchase,* a small part of Mexico, now in New Mexico and Arizona, which lay on the best possible route for a *southern* transcontinental railroad, rounded out the contiguous continental area of the United States. The vastness of Alaska was purchased from the Russians by

Seward in 1867. Frontier, democratic nationalism, and the exuberance of a new republic had accomplished this work.

The Mexican War and the Civil War

Two wars, the Mexican War and the Civil War, were inextricably connected. The inescapable fact is that the one war helped to cause the other, for the new acquisitions directly affected the sectional balance and created preconditions for civil conflict. The United States had truly swallowed Emerson's "arsenic" and the bitter question of human slavery in the Southern states and Western territories was now reopened.

The presidential election of 1848 brought in the hero of the Mexican War, General Zachary Taylor, "Old Rough and Ready," the victor over Santa Anna at Buena Vista (1847). With him came a Whig administration. The issue of the election was what to do with the captured lands. Should they be open to the spread of slavery or should they be kept free? Both major candidates, Democrat Lewis Cass of Michigan, himself a veteran of the War of 1812, and Zachary Taylor, a southern Whig, tried to confuse the slavery question. Both needed to straddle the issue to gain votes in the North and South.

Lewis Cass espoused "popular sovereignty": the idea that slavery as an issue should be taken out of the hands of Congress and left to the local discretion of voters in the Territories concerned. The disadvantage of popular sovereignty was that it was likely to produce violent conflict between pro-slavery and anti-slavery forces in the Territories. Meanwhile Zachary Taylor counted on his residence in Baton Rouge, Louisiana, and his ownership of a Mississippi cotton plantation with over 100 slaves to attract Southern voters to his fold. To placate North-

Zachary Taylor fights the Seminoles, 1837

Library of Congress

erners, Taylor promised a restrained use of the presidential veto—important because the House was more likely to pass measures blocking slavery than favoring it.

The Wilmot Proviso and the election of 1848

During the Mexican War a Pennsylvania Democrat, David Wilmot, had attached an amendment to an appropriations bill threatening President Polk with an inadequate supply of funds for negotiating with Mexico unless slavery were prohibited in any lands to be purchased or acquired from Mexico. The Wilmot Proviso passed the House twice though it was never successful in the Senate. The idea hung over the head of the administration throughout the war and in the peace that followed. The candidates of 1848 could not obscure the real electoral issue and a Free Soil party led by Martin Van Buren, which David Wilmot joined, openly opposed the spread of slavery in the Mexican Cession. This new third party attracted some antislavery "conscience Whigs" to its banner, as well as Van Buren's reform Democrats of New York, the "Barnburners," and the remnant of the Liberty party. The Free Soil party, like the Liberty party, was again crucial as a swing factor in the election in New York.

The 1848 election was very close. Both major parties gained 15 states. If Cass had won either Pennsylvania or New York he would have become president. The Free Soilers split the Democratic vote, causing Cass to lose New York and with it the White House. The results were: Taylor (Whig) 163 electoral college votes and 1,360,967 popular votes; Cass (Democrat) 127 and 1,222,342. Van Buren's Free Soilers gained no electoral college votes but polled 291,263 popular votes.

Zachary Taylor favors statehood for California and New Mexico

The Mexican Cession lands were administered by the U.S. Army at first, but the California Gold Rush of 1849 brought pressure for some form of civil government in the area. The problem was less acute in New Mexico, where population was sparse, no gold was found, and the land was developed mainly by Indians and Mexicans. In addition, Texas claimed a huge chunk of what later became eastern New Mexico. These complications delayed the push for New Mexico statehood, but in California a local constitutional convention was rapidly assembled and a state constitution drawn up which began to operate in December 1849. It excluded slavery in California. For his part, President Taylor favored statehood for both California and New Mexico; he also played with the notion of adding the Mormon state of Deseret to the Union as part of California. This would have created an impossibly huge state. Deseret had been proclaimed in March 1849 under the leadership of the Mormon pioneer Brigham Young. Theoretically it included most of modern Nevada, Utah, western Colorado, much of Arizona, and parts of southern and eastern California, including even the Pacific coast area which lies south of Los Angeles. At this stage of history the admission of the Mormon empire into the

Union was impossible because of its unorthodox religion and polygamy.

In Congress and the nation the atmosphere was tense: Members carried Bowie knives and pistols. In December 1849 it took 63 ballots to choose a Speaker of the House. A convention of all slaveholding states was called for June 1850 to meet the threat of a possibly hostile Congress. John C. Calhoun's "Southern Address" of January 1849 accused the North of conspiracy to destroy slavery in the South. His stance was radical even among Southerners but its appeal would grow.

Zachary Taylor, a professional soldier for 40 years with no previous political experience, was yet a confirmed patriot who did his best as president to follow what he thought to be the national interest. Southerners were dismayed by his encouragement of the rapid admission of California. However, Taylor died of acute gastroenteritis on July 9, 1850. He was replaced by his vice president, Millard Fillmore, a New York lawyer of no particular ability and a former member of the nativist Anti-Masons.

Whigs, Democrats, and the Compromise of 1850

Out of the sectional tensions over the Mexican Cession lands came Henry Clay's famous Compromise of 1850, which offered the admission of California as a free state; the organization of two new Territories, Utah and New Mexico, with no mention of the status of slavery there; the settlement of the Texas boundary dispute by the giving of land to New Mexico; payment of the Texas state debt; the restriction of the slave trade (not slavery itself) in the nation's capital city; and the passage of a more stringent law to enable masters to recapture runaway slaves. Each element was meant to balance the other in sectional appeal. No compromise could satisfy everyone. Some states—Georgia, Mississippi, Alabama, and South Carolina—seriously considered seceding from the Union. However, Southern extremists were attracted to the Compromise by the promise of the new Fugitive Slave Law.

Clay's compromise was eventually passed with heavy Democratic support, even though it was one measure for which the Whig administration of Millard Fillmore is remembered. Fillmore, the Whig president, did not command the full support of his party, and worse, was at odds with its leaders, including Thurlow Weed and W. H. Seward. By 1850 the Whigs were already breaking apart. Two years later antislavery men won control of the party. They dropped the inept Fillmore. With General Winfield Scott as their new presidential candidate the Whigs lost the 1852 election to the Democrats, who had wisely chosen a pro-compromise man, Franklin Pierce.

Clay's first compromise failed politically. The Senate Committee of Thirteen, which he chaired, announced an "Omnibus" compromise plan which lumped together too many controversial solutions for the Senate to swallow as a whole. The plan was saved by a Democrat, Senator Stephen A. Douglas of Illinois. Douglas broke the scheme down into five separate bills and steered them through by shrewd management. He was helped by President Fillmore who threw the weight of

300   The U.S.A.

Women shortage in California

MARRIED MUM ?   NO SIR!

Library of Congress

the White House behind the Compromise, and by those Whig opponents who decided to absent themselves. The names of Henry Clay and Daniel Webster will continue to be remembered for their brilliant oratory in defense of the Compromise.

The Fugitive Slave Law

The Fugitive Slave Law received the greatest publicity, partly due to the enormously successful abolitionist novel by Harriet Beecher Stowe, *Uncle Tom's Cabin*, which began to appear serially in 1851 and was published in book form in 1852. The novel sold 300,000 copies in its first year, was soon translated into the major world languages and was staged thousands of times in many towns as an immensely popular melodrama. *Uncle Tom's Cabin* painted a bleak picture of slavery and heightened public interest in the plight of runaways. Another reason for the attention paid to the Fugitive Slave Law was the dramatic nature of the work of the "Underground Railroad" in convoying slaves secretly out of the South into the free North and Canada, and the prominence of certain famous fugitive slave cases.

Despite the provisions of the federal constitution and the Fugitive Slave Law of 1793, which intended to make it compulsory for runaways to be returned, Northerners did not feel duty-bound to help masters recapture slaves. Actions against runaways depended on the willingness of local authorities to apprehend them, a willingness which was lacking. Moreover, apart from the moral issue of whites helping masters to re-enslave black men, a large number of *free* Negroes lived in the North. About 488,000 free Negroes lived in the United States in 1860, 46 percent in the North. These men were unprotected from the Fugitive Slave Laws and were sometimes seized as runaways. The situation helped to convince Northerners of their moral rectitude in refusing to obey the Fugitive Slave Law of 1793.

During the 1820s some Northern states began to demand full trial by jury for captured runaways. In 1842 the U.S. Supreme Court in *Prigg* v. *Pennsylvania* ruled that state-level officials were not *required* by law to assist in the return of fugitives. This loophole was used to enact "personal liberty laws" throughout the North. Strict documentary and other evidence was now needed in fugitive cases. Southern owners were infuriated. The new Fugitive Slave Law of 1850 was intended to placate them but it only created greater tension than before.

Under the new law, federal commissioners were to be appointed to aid local judges in seeing that fugitives were returned. All citizens were required to help and fines for rescuing slaves were doubled. These provisions rankled in the North, particularly the fact that federal commissioners were to be paid ten dollars for every arrest warrant issued but only five dollars for every Negro freed. Southern owners began a more vigorous search for slaves, and famous legal cases followed in the 1850s. For example, Jerry McHenry who had lived for some years in Syracuse, New York, as a free man was suddenly seized in 1851. Members of the Liberty party, meeting in convention at the time, freed McHenry and sent him to Canada via the Underground Railroad. In Boston an antislavery vigilance committee defied the new law by planning the escape of William Craft of Macon, Georgia. Craft traveled north with his light-colored wife, who pretended to be his owner, and the couple escaped to England. Again in Boston in 1854 a Virginia slave, Anthony Burns, was recaptured by his owner and defended in court by the author, Richard Henry Dana. Burns lost his case and a crowd failed to rescue him when they stormed the courthouse. He was shipped South, but a group of Bostonians bought him one year later and freed him. Such startling cases kindled the fire of sectionalism, though ironically the Fugitive Slave Law was not regarded as a major issue by the men who had debated the Compromise of 1850.

The territorial issues: "Popular sovereignty"

The central theme of the Compromise struggle was the future government of the new territories. Politicians divided along sectional lines, though prominent individuals could not be categorized in any simple fashion. Four types of opinion were discernible in the long debates. *Northern Whigs* usually demanded the complete exclusion of slavery throughout the new West, Daniel Webster being one notable exception. *Southern Whigs* came to favor the doctrine of "popular sovereignty," leaving the question of slavery to the vote of local settlers after Territorial forms of government had been created. *Northern Democrats* also went along with popular sovereignty, being led by Stephen Douglas and Lewis Cass. *Southern Democrats*, naturally, looked forward to the free expansion of slavery into at least parts of the West. The chief

Brigham Young, Mormon pioneer

Mathew Brady, Library of Congress

spokesman of the expansionists was John C. Calhoun, who died of tuberculosis in 1850 during the debates. He was aided by Senator Jefferson Davis of Mississippi. They argued that Congress lacked the constitutional power to interfere with slavery in the Territories.

The question of slavery in the Mexican Cession had not come out of the blue; there was of course the precedent of slavery in the Louisiana Purchase lands, as decided in the *Missouri Compromise of 1820*. That solution had seemed to give the North a reaffirmation of the principle debated in the federal constitutional debates of 1787, that Congress did have the power to legislate the status of slavery in the Territories. At the same time it had given the South the immediate goal of slavery in Missouri and the potential future admission of Arkansas and Florida as slave states. These were admitted in 1836 and 1845, respectively. The Missouri Compromise was effective for 30 years, and in 1849–50 some people argued that the new problem of slavery in the lands taken from Mexico should be solved by the simple extension of the 1820 principle—the extension of the 36°30′ line dividing slave and free all the way to the Pacific coast. This was President Polk's own view. The Wilmot Proviso challenged the whole idea directly and polarized public opinion by demanding the prohibition of slavery in *all* the lands of the Mexican Cession.

The Compromise in practice

There has been some confusion in texts over the meaning of the Compromise of 1850. What it meant in fact was that in New Mexico and Utah the Territorial legislatures would be free to legislate on slavery, subject to the possible veto by the Territorial governor or disallowance by Congress. When these Territories became sovereign states of the Union they would naturally have the right to decide on slavery in any way they wished, as the older states had done.

In practice, slavery persisted in legal form in California for some years after 1850 under that state's own supreme court rulings. There were few slaves in California but the state was pro-Southern and, in general, Democratic. Parties did not form around the slavery issue. By 1860 the commercial interests of northern California were dominant and voted to support Lincoln and the Union. As for Utah Territory, President Fillmore was sufficiently sensitive to make the Mormon leader, Brigham Young, its Territorial governor. Slavery was legally recognized there in 1852. The institution lasted down to 1863. However the Census of 1860 found only 29 slaves in Utah. As an issue, slavery was greatly overshadowed by polygamy and religion and by the federal intervention of 1857 in the "Mormon War." In New Mexico slavery was also protected, by an act of 1859, but there the dominant issue was the boundary struggle with Texas and Mexico.

The role of Texas

The congressional struggle over slavery and the Compromise of 1850 affected Texas, admitted into the Union since 1845, in two ways: First, how was Texas to be geographically defined? Second, what would happen to outstanding public debts of the former Texas Republic? It was suggested (shades of Alexander Hamilton) that Texas be given $10,000,000 to pay off its creditors. The debt was nominally over $11,000,000, though the Texas state auditor had pro-rated it as $5,600,000. The final Compromise measure of 1850 offered a federal payment of $10,000,000 to the state of Texas. In fact the full amount was never received by the state.

Some monied folk would benefit from this great windfall (as with the federal constitution of 1787) because they had bought depreciated Republic of Texas securities in anticipation of annexation. Speculators included prominent politicians and the influential Washington banking firm, Corcoran and Riggs. Thus William W. Corcoran was a central figure in the complex lobbying that surrounded passage of the Compromise of 1850. He entertained political figures lavishly, taking such steps as to pay off the debts of Daniel Webster after the latter's great 7th of March speech. Corcoran and Riggs received the largest federal payment, over $400,000, when the Texas debt was finally paid off. The bond lobby was a strong pro-Compromise force in Congress. The lobby also brought up the issue of the boundaries of Texas.

Debt and boundary questions were linked, since federal payment of the debt was partly a recompense to Texans for relinquishing land claims in eastern New Mexico. Northerners opposed and Southerners generally supported the Texan land claims. However the 1850 settlement was vague, and court cases continued for years. An anomaly was the so-called Cimarron Strip or "No-Man's-Land," for which no government was instituted. The Strip, now the panhandle of Oklahoma, was settled in the 1880s by squatters and cattlemen. An attempt to create a "Territory of Cimarron," named for the Cimarron ("Wild") River, failed in 1887. It was absorbed by Oklahoma Territory in 1890.

Aftermath of the Compromise: Election of 1852

Perhaps the compromisers gave the South more than was necessary. There is strong doubt that even if Calhoun had lived he could ever have united the South strongly enough to lead it in united secession over the issue of the admission of California as a free state. The Fugitive Slave Law was a major concession to Southern opinion and even the restriction of slave-trading in Washington, D.C., was only partial. Slaves were advertised and sold in the nation's capital after 1850.

Daniel Webster had pinned his oratorical arguments on *geographical determinism:* he believed that slavery could not survive economically in the climate and physical setting of the West. The idea was true of the arid zones though it did not apply to Texas. Henry Clay couched his rhetoric in noble, philosophical terms. "Life itself is but a compromise between death and life," he argued somewhat abstractly if not illogically, ". . . all society is formed upon the principle of mutual concession." Only four years later the struggle over Kansas vitiated most of the work of Webster, Clay, and Douglas. The future lay with more sectional-minded men like W. H. Seward and moralists who appealed to a Higher Law than the federal constitution—the moral law against human slavery.

The Democrats won the election of 1852 with Franklin Pierce, a New Hampshire lawyer and ex-Senator who had fought in Mexico with Scott and who supported the 1850 Compromise. Both parties, Democrat and Whig, included planks favoring the Compromise, but the Whig nominee, war-hero General Winfield Scott, was widely regarded as being too much under the influence of W. H. Seward. National sentiment in 1852 looked for conciliation, not sectional feeling. Though Scott's popular vote was respectable, 1,385,453 to Pierce's 1,601,117, his electoral college vote was poor, 42 to 254. Southern Whigs favored the Democratic candidate. Northern Whigs were divided, some taking W. H. Seward's moral stance over slavery, others—more conservative —rejecting both antislavery and the idea of fusion with the Democrats. In 1856 some of this group of Whigs ended up in the Know Nothing party.

The Democrats themselves were not united, despite their victory. It took them 49 convention ballots to select Pierce. His rivals for the nomination included men of the caliber of Stephen A. Douglas and Lewis Cass, as well as the weaker James Buchanan. A third party, the "Free Democrats," as they called themselves in their party platform, included Free Soil men from 1848, Liberty party men from 1844, and disaffected members of both major parties. Their candidate in 1852, the unknown John P. Hale, gained 155,825 popular votes.

President Franklin Pierce missed a historical opportunity after 1852 to bring the country together and heal its sectional wounds. He could have mounted a campaign on some popular issue such as free homesteads, education, or farm aid. He chose to do little. Pierce was genial but weak. He came under pro-slavery influence. In foreign affairs Pierce was an expansionist. He encouraged the Gadsden Purchase in 1853 and recognized the regime in Nicaragua of the American adventurer, William Walker in 1854. Pierce's support for the Kansas-

Nebraska Act of 1854 which opened up the possibility of a legal extension of slavery in that region, north of the 36°30′ line, gave ammunition to Northern radicals. Politics became very polarized. The White House exerted no leadership to reverse this trend.

Further fruits of expansionism: The Ostend Manifesto

Growing disunity over slavery did not diminish American expansionism abroad or in the West. Pierce sent Commodore Matthew Perry with an armed squadron to Tokyo to impress the Japanese in 1853. Perry's trip produced the Treaty of Kanagawa, opening Japanese ports to U.S. trade. Nearer home, Americans still lusted for Cuba. Jefferson and John Quincy Adams among others had realized the strategic importance of the island, located close to U.S. shores and commanding the entrance to the Gulf. Polk tried to buy Cuba from Spain in 1848. Constant raids were made by bands of American "filibusterers" and Cuban exiles. In 1851 the Spanish governor captured and executed about 50 American adventurers, among them a Kentucky colonel who had tried to start a Cuban revolution in favor of the émigré, General Narciso Lopez.

The mainly Democratic *Young America* movement of the 1840s was explicit in its intentions. Its followers identified with the European revolutionaries and nationalists of 1848, such as Louis Kossuth of Hungary who visited the United States in 1851–52 and was turned into an instant folk hero. Like Walt Whitman, the Young Americans linked sympathy for revolution abroad with U.S. expansionism. Stephen A. Douglas was a leading member. At its peak (about 1852) the Young America movement was demanding U.S. interventionism abroad and territorial expansion on the American continent, using its paper, the *Democratic Review* to spread the word. The Cuban issue, however, was clearly a slavery matter pushed by pro-Southerners.

In the North the pressure to "liberate" Cuba from Spain was seen darkly as yet another pro-slave plot. Slavery survived as an institution in Cuba until the late 19th century, unlike Mexico where slavery had been abolished from the beginning of its own independence. Cuba, too, had plantations. In 1854 some pro-slavery Democrats gained international publicity and a certain amount of ridicule for their cause. The American ministers to England, France, and Spain, James Buchanan, John Mason, and Pierre Soule, met at Ostend in Belgium to issue the *Ostend Manifesto*. If Spain did not agree to sell Cuba, they declared, the United States would be "justified in wresting it" from her. This arrogant manifesto was immediately repudiated by President Pierce, but damage had been done to U.S. diplomatic standing. Clearly, slave interests had their eyes on foreign policy. Northerners could no longer doubt the intentions of Southern expansionists and their "slave-power conspiracy."

The slavery question reopened: Kansas-Nebraska

The wound of slavery was reopened in 1854 by the debate over the Kansas-Nebraska Act. The problem of how to assimilate the remaining lands from the Louisiana Purchase still remained. Senator Stephen A. Douglas, master politician of the 1850 Compromise, now introduced a new bill to organize the territories of Kansas and Nebraska. His bill in its final form explicitly *repealed* the Missouri Compromise line of 1820 and opened up to slavery the Nebraska region north of 36°30′.

At first Douglas tried to attract southern support for the bill by using ambiguous language that neither excluded slavery from the region nor overturned the Missouri Compromise line. Later he gave way to Southern pressure and added an explicit provision for the principle of popular sovereignty: "all questions pertaining to slavery in the Territories and in the new States to be formed therefrom, are to be left to the people residing therein, through their appropriate representatives." Presumably, by this provision Kansas would become a slave state and Nebraska a free state. A later amendment angered antislavery elements by overtly declaring that the Missouri Compromise was to be "inoperative and void."

Why did Douglas, the compromiser of 1850, introduce this explosive bill in 1854? He has been accused of gross personal interest, even of seeking to promote slavery because his wife inherited a plantation of 150 slaves. The evidence shows he did not want the slaves and had already turned them down as a wedding present. More substantial issues were his large real-estate holdings in Chicago, where he had lived since 1847, and his eagerness to have the lands west of Iowa opened up for settlement. Douglas wanted Chicago to become the chief terminal of a transcontinental railroad. Beyond crude personal advantage, however, or a local interest in helping to reelect David R. Atchison of Missouri to the Senate, Douglas had a large vision for America of "a continuous line of settlements to the Pacific Ocean," made possible by the railroad and the removal of the "barbarian wall" of Indian tribes. Douglas wrote in December 1853:

The Indian barrier must be removed. The tide of emigration and civilization must be permitted to roll onwards until it . . . mingles with the waters of the Pacific. We must therefore have Railroads and Telegraphs from the Atlantic to the Pacific, through our own territory. Not one line only, but many lines . . .

Stephen Douglas at this point spoke with the authentic voice of frontier nationalism, not simple self-interest.

Douglas's desire to open up the West overcame any doubts about dividing the nation again on the slavery issue. His belief in popular sovereignty was probably genuine. He saw it as a device to ease political tensions and to keep the federal government out of the slavery question. His Kansas-Nebraska Act had the opposite result.

Civil War in miniature

For the next five years what soon became known as "Bleeding Kansas" suffered a tragic civil war, a tiny preview of the major conflict to come. Pro-slavery and abolitionist groups fought it out, grabbing land and making claims in Kansas Territory in order to forestall possible settlement by their rivals. Since the question of slavery depended on the votes of the local residents, many rushed in to vote illegally, to intimidate other voters, and gain political control. A pro-slavery government was set up. In retaliation, a Free Soil government was also created. Neither was strictly legal in form. In New England the *Emigrant Aid Society,* organized by the abolitionist Eli Thayer and stirred up by the revivalist oratory of Henry Ward Beecher, sent about 2,000 abolitionist settlers into Kansas Territory, with boxes of Sharp's rifles —"Beecher's Bibles," as they were known. Meanwhile, pro-slavers from Missouri flooded in, the so-called border ruffians. There was violence on both sides. News of the violence was also exaggerated in the press and in rumors. The "ruffians" attacked a Free Soil settlement at Lawrence, Kansas; in reply, the zealot John Brown raided an allegedly pro-slavery village and savagely executed five men at night. This "Pottawatomie Massacre" of May 1856 produced a brief reign of terror. These were the fruits of popular sovereignty.

In December 1857 the pro-slavery faction in Kansas proposed the LeCompton Constitution for the Territory. They cleverly avoided any genuine process of ratification, but the new U.S. President, James Buchanan, one of the writers of the Ostend Manifesto of 1854, was easily pushed by pro-Southern advisers to ask Congress to admit Kansas on the basis of the LeCompton Constitution. By his clearly partisan act Buchanan split open his Democratic party and lost the support of Douglas, who resented the flouting of the popular sovereignty principle by pro-slavery Kansans. Congress submitted the LeCompton Constitution to a searching vote in Kansas in a well-policed election. The local residents rejected it. Despite the furor and violence over slavery in Kansas, only *two* Negro slaves were actually living there in 1860.

Antislavery forces had during this time become convinced that *political* action was necessary. In July 1854 at Ripon, Wisconsin, a new third party was formed, the *Republicans*. They were made up of northern Whigs, Free Soilers, and dissident Democrats, all of whom were able to agree in their opposition to the Kansas-Nebraska Act and the overturning of the Missouri Compromise. They took their name from Jefferson's old party. The Republicans were strongly supported in the Midwest. Embracing moderate and radical antislavery opinion alike, they spread into the Northeast.

The Republicans and the ideology of sectional conflict

The chief plank of the new party was opposition to slavery extension, but their heart was ideological: the ethic of "free labor," Free Soil, social mobility, and economic growth—the very way of life of the northern middle and working classes. Republicans saw Southern civilization as the antithesis of everything that the American Republic should stand for. The Pursuit of Happiness, called later the American Dream, was threatened by the existence of human slavery and by the determined self-aggrandizement of the South as a section. In the presidential election of 1856 the new party carried 11 states and a strong popular vote, led by their candidate, the explorer-hero John C. Fremont of California. They won 114 electoral college votes and 1,339,932 popular votes to the Democrats' 174 and 1,832,955. James Buchanan was the new Democratic president.

Meanwhile a showing had been made by Millard Fillmore for the nativist Know Nothing, or American, party. They won 8 electoral college votes and 871,731 popular votes. The Know Nothings were anti-Catholic and anti-foreign. They dated back to the early 1840s and the "Order of the Star Spangled Banner." Ritualistic and secretive, their members always answered that they knew nothing when asked questions, hence the name. The party touched a popular nerve—fear of the mass immigration of German and Irish Catholics who entered the country in the two prewar decades. They were paranoid about "Popish plots" and wished to deny the vote to foreigners until after a residence of 21 years, a throwback to the ideas of the Naturalization Act of 1798. The party attracted a number of different sorts of Americans, including temperance reformers, who sometimes regarded the Irish as drunkards and the Germans as guilty for their breweries. Even some Northern abolitionists who resented the anti-Negro feelings associated with Irish immigrants saw some value in the Know Nothing party. Its political strength had already peaked by 1854, however. The party split over the decision of its national convention to support the Kansas-Nebraska Act.

James Buchanan of Pennsylvania was 65 when he attained the presidency. He had been a disciple of Andrew Jackson in his youth, was a strong nationalist, and had served as Polk's Secretary of State during the years of great territorial expansion. As Secretary, Buchanan had witnessed the Texas annexation, the Mexican Cession, and the settlement of the Oregon territory. Thus it was Buchanan's fate to take a part in the territorial building of the United States and, subsequently, as a rather weak, pro-Southern chief of state, to preside over its disintegration. In Buchanan's administration the fears of the decades were realized. The American Union finally fell apart.

Bibliography

Henry Nash Smith. *Virgin Land.* Harvard University Press, 1970 ed.

R. A. Billington. *The Far Western Frontier, 1830–60.* New York: Harper, 1956.

Ramón E. Ruiz. *The Mexican War: Was It Manifest Destiny?* New York: Holt, 1963.

Frederick Merk. *Manifest Destiny and Mission in American History: A Reinterpretation.* New York: Random House, 1963.

Holman Hamilton. *Prologue to Conflict: The Crisis and Compromise of 1850.* New York: Norton, 1966.

12

The survival of the Union

Love of Union versus secession . . . a conflict of sections? . . . former sectional issues: banking and tariffs . . . internal improvements: the allegiance of the West . . . from anti-slavery-extension to abolitionism . . . evolution of abolitionist thought . . . gradualism and immediatism . . . black and white abolitionists . . . abolitionism becomes political: the gag rule and the Liberty party . . . the drift to Civil War: Dred Scott . . . radical stereotypes: Cavalier and Yankee . . . the slave and the Negro . . . the emergence of Abraham Lincoln . . . the Lincoln-Douglas debates . . . escalation: John Brown's raid . . . the last straw: Lincoln's election . . . Lincoln and the secession crisis: Upper versus Lower South . . . the Upper South and last-ditch compromise . . . Jefferson Davis and the Confederacy . . . the final issue: federal bases in the South . . . the South shoots first: Fort Sumter, April 1861 . . . war strategy: the odds . . . First Bull Run and naval blockade . . . the campaigns of 1862: Second Bull Run and Antietam . . . diplomacy and slavery . . . origins of the Emancipation Proclamation . . . campaigns of 1863: Chancellorsville and Gettysburg . . . Vicksburg: cutting the Confederacy in two . . . troubles on the home front: the Radicals, draft riots, and the election of 1864 . . . the final campaigns: Chattanooga; Sherman's March . . . the ending: Appomattox and Lincoln's death . . . was it worth it?

Love of Union versus secession

When the Civil War came it was fought chiefly for the survival of the American Union. Love of the United States was a tentative growth in the Early National period: it had much to oppose it, including a rooted fear of executive power and the traditions of nearly 200 years of colonial separatism and jealousies. Was the Union a mere grouping of states? This was the issue between those who "thought continentally" and those who valued local rights and liberties above everything. Federalist v. Antifederalist, Hamiltonian v. Jeffersonian, Whig v. Jacksonian, all reflected in part a fundamental division between opposing visions of what the American Union was meant to be. Paradoxically, Jefferson and Jackson did much to strengthen the federal power, despite their states' rights and agrarian outlook. Jefferson and Polk were territorial nationalists, Jackson a tough executive and charismatic leader. Ambiguity about the nature of the Union was built-in to the American historical situation.

For some men like Andrew Jackson love of the Union came to override all else: it became mystical, part of a personal identity and value system. Feeling for the Union took time to grow, yet somehow the U.S. survived a series of shocks and crises and hints of possible secession. Jefferson himself raised the first hint of a threat with the Virginia and Kentucky Resolutions of 1798. Then in 1814 came another hint, the Hartford Convention. More serious was the South Carolina secession crisis of 1828–33. There was even a vague suggestion of Northern secession over slavery, though this was never much more than the rhetoric of the abolitionist propagandist, William Lloyd Garrison, who publicly burnt the federal constitution to symbolize his hatred of slavery.

The secession of the slave-owning Southern states in 1861 thus came at the end of an uncertain tradition of separatist reasoning. What did secession imply? South Carolina did not merely leave the Union in 1861, she opened fire on the federal garrison at Fort Sumter. In 1861 secession *without* war was improbable. The Union government's tough resistance to the idea of separation proved that no state could abandon the Union over a particular grievance, however sorely felt.

A conflict of sections?

The Civil War has often been presented as a "war between the sections." It was not truly a war between the sections but between one "section," or 11 Southern states, and the rest of the American nation. The "North," "South," and "West" were not monolithic or easily defined in 1861. The North was made up of the Northeast, the Middle Atlantic, and the Old Northwest (Midwest). The Northeast in turn was a subregion of conflicting economic interests. New England and New York contained farming, mercantile, shipping, and manufacturing interests. An "English'" type of industrial-urban civilization was beginning to emerge there, based on the Industrial Revolution. But in the Midwest, also part of the "North," an "American" type of civilization was emerging, shaped by the Agricultural Revolution and the productivity of the homestead farm. Even such generalizations characterizing subregions are too broad.

The South was also varied, with at least three subregions, the Upper South, older and suffering economic displacement; the Southeast; and the newer and wealthier Southwest, where cotton plantations now stretched into Texas. Southeast and Southwest together made up the "Deep South." Meanwhile a contrasting section of the nation, the Far West, was attracting settlers, though only one state, California, could have made much difference in the line-up in the Civil War. California supported the Union, as did Oregon, admitted in 1859.

The sectional makeup of the nation was, thus, far more complex than any North-South division. A greater difficulty in blaming the war on sectionalism is that the causes of sectionalism were not necessarily

12 / The survival of the Union

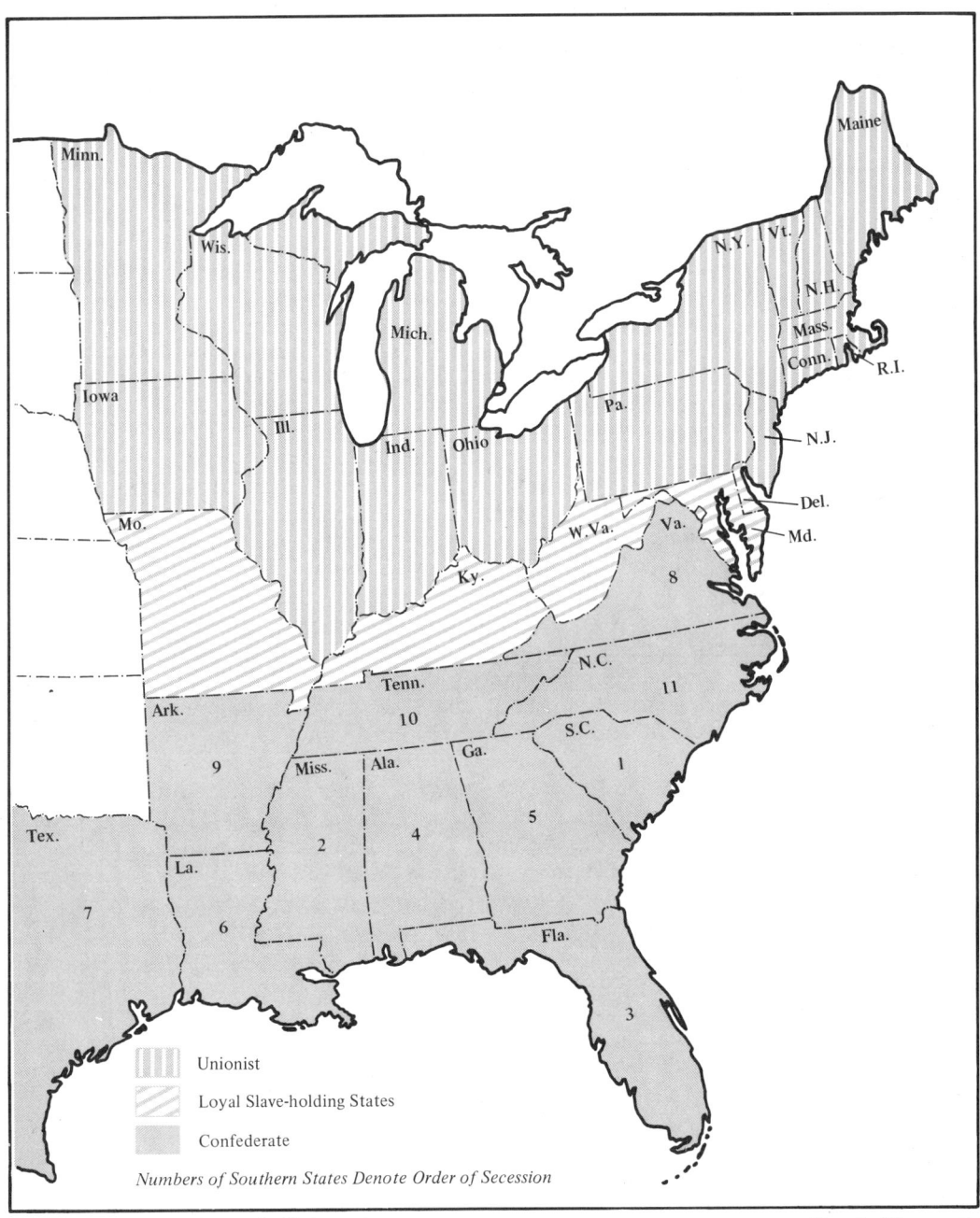

Peter d'A. Jones, An Economic History of the United States since 1783 *(London: Routledge, 1964)*.

Map 7. Alignment of states in the Civil War

the same as the causes of war. Sectional crises had occurred in 1820, 1850, and 1854. In 1832 the federal government and South Carolina had reached the point of military preparations, but no war came. Why did the war come when it did, in 1861, when many of the intersectional issues such as internal improvements, central banking, land policy, and tariffs had been resolved or shelved? The timing of the war was determined by the slavery question, that overarching issue which reached a crisis in the election of Abraham Lincoln. Slavery was the one issue which could bind together 11 states against the rest. The timing of the outbreak of war also arose out of particular historical circumstances.

Former sectional issues: Banking and tariffs

Let us review the issues of sectional conflict in the past. The furor over the Bank of the United States had never been clear-cut as a sectional dispute. Generally the Northeast, being a creditor area, had favored a unified monetary system with a central bank exercising control over the note-issue of local banks. But state-chartered banks in New England and New York, no less than in other sections, were jealous of the power of the central bank. In the North, too, workers hated the steadily devaluing paper money as much as did farmers in the South or West. Politicians nonetheless voted along sectional lines in the House. The vote to re-charter the Second Bank of the United States (July 3, 1832) was purely sectional. Northeast and Middle Atlantic states supported the renewal of the bank's charter, 68 to 35. The Southeast opposed renewal, 12 to 35. Three Southwestern states were indecisive, 8 to 8. So the Second Bank was re-chartered with a total vote of 107 for, 85 against. President Andrew Jackson's veto put a stop to the proceedings.

Like the bank issue, the tariff was not in hot dispute in the immediate antebellum decade, but was one of the most divisive questions which created the sections. The tariff crisis came in the 1820s and 30s. In the House the vote on the Tariff of 1828 was clearly sectional (April 22, 1828): Northeast, 73 to 34 in favor; South, 3 to 59 against; West (Illinois, Indiana, Kentucky, Missouri, and Ohio), 29 to 1 in favor. The South felt it was being made to pay higher prices for foreign imports in order to protect Northern industry. Tariffs did not loom large in 1861 but the memory of nullification was strong and used as a precedent. The *general* economic argument that the North was exploiting the South was more powerful. In fact, both the actual condition and the argument survived the Civil War itself.

Internal improvements: The allegiance of the West

The struggle over federal aid to rivers, canals, roads, and railroads was very divisive. In the long run this issue was dangerous to the economic and political status of the South because it split off the Northwest from its old natural trade alliance, via the Mississippi, with Southerners. The state and federally aided highways, canals, and railroads effectively removed the Allegheny barrier between east-west trade and travel, provoking the fear and hostility of planters and merchants alike in the South.

So in 1830 the vote on the proposed Maysville Turnpike bill, ultimately vetoed by Andrew Jackson, brought almost unanimous Western approval of the turnpike, 27 to 1; Southern opposition, 12 for, 51 against; and Northern favor, 63 to 35. By 1830 Northeastern businessmen and politicians had come around to support internal improvements and cheap land policies in return for Western backing for higher tariffs. The general usefulness of social overhead developments was now recognized in the East. Lincoln's Republican administration lost no time in approving a transcontinental railroad, higher tariffs, and a form of central banking. The absence of Southern members after 1860 allowed these measures to be swept through Congress.

Of all sectional problems, territorial expansion most dominated the immediate prewar years. After 1830 the South diverged sharply from the other two sections on this issue. The continuing expansion of cotton cultivation brought fearful Southern planters into collision course with Western frontiersmen and speculators who demanded a policy of cheap or free public lands. Cheap lands would mean individual farms rather than plantations worked by slaves. The slavery system had to expand to survive. Though Texas had been won for slavery in 1845, each new state added to the Union brought two new senators and a representative to Congress to represent sectional interests, slave or free. In the long run the South was fighting against the Census returns. As a region its fate was linked to the admission of new states, hence the crises of 1820, 1850, and 1854. Lincoln's party pushed through a radical Homestead Act in 1862 which gave 160 acres *free* to any bona fide settler after five years' residence, or allowed him to buy the land for $1.50 an acre after six months.

From anti-slavery-extension to abolitionism

Gradually opposition to slavery-extension evolved into opposition to slavery itself—abolitionism. Neither the North nor the West became fully abolitionized before the outbreak of war, however. White Americans did not think Negroes their equals intellectually or morally. Yet the feeling grew that slavery was an evil, whatever one thought of Africans or their American descendants. Respect for property rights remained strong; few went along with the radicals who began to demand abolition without proper compensation to owners for their heavy losses.

Were the slaves "ready" for freedom? Most whites, North or South, doubted it. Even abolitionists devised halfway schemes to delay the entry of freed Negroes into white society. Frances Wright and Robert Dale Owen at their Nashoba community sought to train Negroes in menial tasks, to groom them for later admission into society. James C. Birney, the Tappan brothers, and Theodore Weld entertained ideas of training freed slaves for the status of full citizenship, believing, with some evidence, that slavery debased men. Freedom would not imply the right to vote or to participate fully in the majority world.

These racial attitudes help to account in part for what happened to the freed Negroes after the Civil War. Americans before 1861 did not move beyond the intellectual position that slavery itself was a moral evil and that its further expansion could not be tolerated. By the 1850s opposition to slavery-extension was general outside the South. On the issue of slavery where it existed and the status of freed Negroes, ambiguity characterized most white opinion.

Evolution of abolitionist thought

Slavery was repugnant to some of the Founding Fathers, like Thomas Jefferson, and they did manage to restrict it to the South. They held high hopes for voluntary manumission, but what would happen to slaves voluntarily released by their owners? Few whites felt that such men could be accepted into the majority society. Many fell back on "colonization": freed slaves would be shipped "back" to Africa or elsewhere. The *American Colonization Society* found much support for this policy in the Upper South as well as in the North. In 1827 it solicited a Congressional grant to help in "colonizing" Africa. The appropriation was supported by Virginia, Maryland, and Kentucky. The Deep South—the Cotton Kingdom—blocked the aid. The Society did buy land in Africa which later became the republic of Liberia, and built a capital called Monrovia after the U.S. president. Because of inadequate funding only about 15,000 Negroes out of a total population of over 4,500,000 had been sent to Liberia by the outbreak of the Civil War. Removing the black population of the United States was much more difficult than the removal of the few thousand Indians.

Colonization was a white solution, designed more to rid the nation of free Negroes than to ameliorate slavery. *Black* abolitionists rejected the insulting idea. Not surprisingly, the Negro leaders from among the small number of Northern Freedmen were the most radical of abolitionists. As early as 1829, David Walker, a North Carolina runaway slave who lived in Boston as a secondhand clothes dealer, published one of the most bitter attacks on slavery, known as *Walker's Appeal*. He asked all "colored citizens of the world" to unite and throw off the shackles of slavery.

> Are we men!! I ask you . . . are we MEN? . . . America is more our country than it is the whites—We have enriched it with our *blood and tears*. The greatest riches in all America have arisen from our blood and tears . . .

Walker's Appeal, which openly advocated Negro action, was an early expression of black nationalism and pride. He rested his case on the Declaration of Independence itself. But Walker was no separatist. Most black leaders before the Civil War demanded freedom *at home*—not miles away in Africa, a place they did not know. "America is our country," said David Walker. Negroes joined with white abolitionists and also formed their own groups.

Gradualism and immediatism

Down to about 1830 the basis of the antislavery movement was clearly religious. A leader in this period was the Quaker preacher, Benjamin Lundy, who published an early antislavery weekly. Lundy's attack on the extension of slavery, *The War in Texas* (1836), did much to expose territorial nationalism as an excuse for slavery expansion.

Lundy believed in colonization as a solution for freed Negroes. Most early abolitionists were moralistic and Christian in reasoning, though they would also adapt arguments from the Rights of Man, the Romantic idea of human perfectibility and economics. They argued that slavery would die out because it was uneconomic, an argument not without force in the North and Northwest where slavery was generally outlawed by 1827.

After about 1830 a new radicalism infused the antislavery campaign. The call for *immediatism* was heard. Radicals demanded at least an immediate start on the process of eliminating slavery. The most ferocious in rhetoric, though he was an avowed pacifist, was Boston's William Lloyd Garrison (1805–79), who had worked with Lundy but then broke with him. Garrison's journal, *The Liberator*, totally transformed the style of the movement. Its first number of January 1, 1831 shouted forth:

On this subject I do not wish to think, or speak, or write with moderation. . . . I am in earnest—I will not equivocate—I will not excuse—I will not retreat a single inch—AND I WILL BE HEARD.

The reiteration of the "I" betrayed Garrison's total confidence that he was the chosen instrument of God's word and of the divine plan for the future of the United States. Many reformers believed that God had a plan for America of which their work was a part. Few made the identity as close as Garrison.

Soon after the founding of the *Liberator*, antislavery groups sprang up over the North and Midwest. Colleges and seminaries became

Uncle Tom's Cabin—Eliza escapes

New York Historical Society, lithograph, c. 1852

radical centers in the West—places like Western Reserve (established in 1828), Lane Theological Seminary in Cincinnati (1832), and Oberlin (1833). Oberlin was the fount of Western abolitionism, succored by revivalism and the spirit of moral regeneration. We have observed that Charles Finney taught there and that the original Lane faction included Theodore Weld, with whom Garrison worked briefly and then disagreed. Theodore Weld was the antithesis of Garrison in personality: he was a tireless, behind-the-scenes worker, who hated to hold office or subject himself to publicity. In some ways more influential than Garrison, Weld had brought the Tappans into the movement as well as James G. Birney, founder of the Liberty party, and Lyman Beecher. Weld's outlook was less aggressive than Garrison's; he was a self-doubter, a cautious, complex man who was never sure what God's plan was. Unlike Garrison he concentrated fully on one subject, abolition of slavery. Weld married Angelina Grimké, one of the two abolitionist Grimké sisters from South Carolina. He is best remembered for his tract, *Slavery As It Is: The Testimony of a Thousand Witnesses*, which was the factual basis for Harriet Beecher Stowe's popular novel, *Uncle Tom's Cabin* (1852). Weld also worked politically, helping to rally the antislavery wing of the Whig party in Congress. A group of missionary reformers whom he trained, known as "The Seventy," spread the abolitionist gospel. Weld's *Slavery As It Is* appeared in 1839; the following year this diffident man retired from the movement.

Another abolitionist leader who was free of neurosis or self-aggrandizement was Lydia Maria Child, known for her many children's books and for creating the first American children's magazine in 1826, the *Juvenile Miscellany*. Lydia Child was far in advance of her day in racial matters: she felt that Negroes were as educable as whites. Her plea for racial toleration, *An Appeal in Favor of That Class of Americans Called Africans* (1833), hit the nail on the head with its title. Were Negroes to be considered "Americans"? Lydia Child answered strongly, Yes, and extended it to Indians as well. She was an early, almost unique, racial egalitarian.

The abolitionists thus included men and women of considerable social vision and broad humanity, though not all shared these qualities. Not least among the abolitionists were the black leaders, David Walker, Henry Garnet, William Wells Brown, and Frederick Douglass. White *Southerners* also played some part, like the Grimké sisters and James G. Birney.

Black and white abolitionists

Relations between white and black leaders were not always smooth. The New England Antislavery Society was founded in the African Baptist Church in Boston's black quarter in 1832. The first nationwide antislavery group, the American Antislavery Society, owed much to black leadership in 1833. Prominent Philadelphia Negroes took part in it, like the abolitionist dentist, Dr. J. C. McCrummell, whose home was often the center for meetings with William Lloyd Garrison and others. However, black leaders were sometimes restive under white patronage.

Sojourner Truth

Schomburg Center for Research in Black Culture, The New York Public Library

The Negro-dominated Moral Reform Society of Philadelphia, created in 1835, refused to adopt the use of the word "African." They thought it was demeaning to Negro Americans and that it implied they were less than whites and not true Americans.

Garrison and the most famous of all Negro leaders, Frederick Douglass, soon broke. Douglass (1817–95), an escaped "mulatto" slave, came from Maryland, and became famous in the North and in Europe as an inspired orator on behalf of abolitionism. His life story was published in 1845. Two years later Douglass was made president of the New England Antislavery Society. He moved to Rochester, N.Y., and began his own journal, the *North Star*, which led to much jealousy and the split with Garrison. A few of the most pious black leaders disliked Garrison's anti-religious and anti-Bible rhetoric because it offended them. More important, his disunionism after 1842 scared them because it would leave slaves at the mercy of the South. His many reform commitments also seemed weakening to their cause. He was an advocate of nonviolence, an anti-Sabbatarian, and a nonvoter who refused to consider politics as a channel for reform. In contrast, Frederick Douglass actually held public office after the Civil War and served as U.S. consul to Haiti, 1889–91.

Besides David Walker, several Negro leaders were ready to inspire more violent action. In Cincinnati and St. Louis, Rev. Moses Dickson's *Knights of Liberty* were organized to overthrow slavery, and Rev. Henry H. Garnet, a black minister who served a white congregation in New York, urged a black convention in 1843 to rise and be numbered.

"Let your motto be resistance," Garnet urged, in contrast to Garrison's group, the New England Non-Resistance Society of 1838.

Abolitionism becomes political: The gag rule and the Liberty party

As the mounting criticism of slavery began to hurt, the South took measures against it. In Georgia an act of 1835 imposed the death sentence for abolitionist agitation or publication. Other states ejected reformers, banned writings, and mobbed offenders. Louisiana put a reward of $20,000—an enormous sum—on the head of the Northern reformer Arthur Tappan. Georgia enticed bounty hunters with a price of $4,000 for the arrest of Garrison. Anyone distributing Garrison's *Liberator* or *Walker's Appeal* could be subject to citizen's arrest in South Carolina: The citizen's reward would be $1,500. In Charleston in 1835 a mob grabbed antislavery journals from the post office and burned them in the public square. Suspected abolitionists were mobbed, like the unsuspecting Bible salesman from Ohio who was publicly whipped in Tennessee. Freedom of thought vanished from the South.

At the federal level Andrew Jackson suggested a law to ban antislavery literature from the U.S. mails in 1836, but it failed to pass the Senate. A Congressional climax came in 1837 when the continuing flood of petitions demanding abolition of slavery and of the slave trade in Washington, D.C., caused the House to adopt the "Gag Rule" by which petitions were simply tabled and received in silence. For eight years, thereafter, ex-President John Quincy Adams, in his 70s but still an active Representative for Massachusetts, eloquently opposed use of the gag rule to stifle debate. Adams was no abolitionist, because he thought Congress did not possess the constitutional authority to interfere with slavery in the individual states (unless war broke out). But he opposed slavery and felt strongly about the citizens' right to petition. The gag rule was used each year until 1844.

Fear and dislike of antislavery agitators affected the North and South alike. Congressional reactions like the gag rule simply reflected general public attitudes. Abolitionists were often attacked by mobs. The first antislavery martyr was Elijah P. Lovejoy, whose printing press was attacked four times by mobs in Alton, Illinois: he was killed in 1837. Northern whites, as yet unprepared to go to war to free blacks from slavery, committed violence in fear of violence, a common event in history. Garrison was himself mobbed in October 1835, being dragged through Boston's streets wearing a halter.

The antislavery movement split apart in 1839–40. Garrisonians wrested control of the New York meeting of the American Antislavery Society in 1839 and so their opponents created the separate American and Foreign Antislavery Society. The latter rejected Garrison's antipolitical stand and his diversion of funds and energies to the peace movement, feminism, and other reform activities. A man of many enthusiasms, Garrison had been corresponding with John Humphrey Noyes of the Oneida community and in 1837 he published these letters. They proclaimed his conversion to Noyes's view that all social institutions, including marriage and the family, were obsolete. This was too much for many of Garrison's colleagues. Garrison was a universal radical: in later years he denounced the U.S. Constitution as "a covenant with death and an agreement with Hell."

In 1839 the more moderate antislavery forces grouped behind James G. Birney, the Kentucky planter who had freed his slaves and gone into politics as a Whig abolitionist after 1833. Birney edited an antislavery journal and worked on the Underground Railroad in Ohio, the state which smuggled the most slaves out of the South. Reformers of the Weld variety were attracted to Birney's banner and he became the Liberty party's presidential candidate in 1844. The Liberty men linked up with the Free Soilers four years later to oppose extension of slavery into the Mexican Cession lands; both became part of the Republican party in 1854. Thus was abolitionism politicized. Respectable men were drawn into the movement, like the poets John G. Whittier and James Russell Lowell and the scholars Francis Wayland and William Ellery Channing. The party system absorbed the new tide of reform—aided by public hostility to the working of the repugnant Fugitive Slave Law.

The drift to Civil War: Dred Scott

The American Union fell apart in stages. The Mexican War set the scene, the Compromise of 1850 did not keep the peace for long, and the Kansas-Nebraska Act of 1854 produced the running sore which two years later became Bleeding Kansas. In the midst of this fear and confusion came the election of James Buchanan and the emergence of the Republican party, only two years old, as the nation's second major party. Though the Democrats attacked the "Black Republicans" for appealing to sectional prejudice, Buchanan's Democratic victory was made possible only by capturing the South as a sectional bloc.

In 1857 the Supreme Court led by Chief Justice Roger B. Taney, entered the fray. In a complex test case involving a Negro, Dred Scott, the court majority declared the Missouri Compromise of 1820 to be unconstitutional and void. They said Congress had no authority to legislate the status of slavery in the Territories. Dred Scott belonged to a St. Louis doctor who joined the army and served in Rock Island, Illinois, a free state, and later at Fort Snelling, in federal territory north of the line 36° 30′. When the army surgeon died in 1846, Scott, who had saved up some funds and got married, asked his master's widow to let him buy his freedom. She refused, so he sued for his liberty in a lower Missouri court in St. Louis on the grounds that, having lived (*a*) in a free state and (*b*) in federal territory from which slavery was banned by the Missouri Compromise, he was a free man. The state supreme court overruled the lower court's findings, which had been in Scott's favor. Scott, they said, was *not* made free under Missouri law by having lived in Illinois and in Indian Territory, because he had voluntarily returned to servitude in Missouri.

The situation altered in November 1853 when the doctor's widow remarried, ironically, to a Massachusetts antislavery politician. By law she lost control of her former husband's estate to another executor, her brother, who was a resident of New York state. Dred Scott's lawyers brought a new case, in federal court, on the grounds of diverse citizenship: *Scott* v. *Sanford*. Sanford, the brother, claimed that Scott, being a Negro, was not a citizen and therefore the federal circuit court had no jurisdiction. The case was lost by Scott, but he appealed to the U.S. Supreme Court in 1856. It was finally decided in 1857, but word of the probable decision, against Scott, was leaked to the incoming Democratic president, James Buchanan, who spoke about it in his inaugural address, hinting that the vexed question of slavery in the territories would soon be "speedily and finally settled" by the Supreme Court. Buchanan went beyond this indiscretion and brought White House pressure to bear on the Court to ensure the sort of decision he and Southerners wanted—nullifying Congressional authority over slavery in the Territories.

Thus Chief Justice Taney ruled, with majority support, that Dred Scott could not sue, because being a slave he was not, and could not become, a citizen. Moreover, Scott's temporary stay in a territory from which Congress had excluded slavery did not make him free. Congress had no power to exclude slavery from that territory. The Missouri Compromise, said Taney, was "not warranted by the Constitution" and was void. The Compromise was an unconstitutional deprivation of personal property without due process of law and contrary to the Fifth Amendment. The decision was prolix and turgid, but its impact was immediately felt. Rather than allaying political tensions, the Court polarized the nation more sharply because it struck directly at the Republican party's central plank, anti-slavery-extension. Coming on top of the bloody events in Kansas and the LeCompton Constitution, this partisan decision helped by White House interference hardened the North against the South. Moderates were left increasingly with no grounds on which to stand.

Radical stereotypes: Cavalier and Yankee

Propaganda by Southern "fire-eaters" and pro-slavery apologists on the one hand and by immediate abolitionists on the other helped create the popular stereotypes and myths that filled the public mind in the prewar years. To many Yankees, their Southern cousins were seen as planter-aristocrats, uneducated, and insular, yet overbearing. Conceited braggarts, men of violent passion, self-indulgent, impatient, jealous, avaricious, improvident, lazy, and despotic, they treated slaves like animals and were sadistically cruel. The abolitionist writer, Richard Hildreth (*Despotism in America*, 1840; and *The Slave: or Memoirs of Archy Moore*, 1836), depicted the southern whites as made degenerate by the institution of slavery. Hildreth described the personal impact of slavery, and sexual liberties taken with slaves. Harriet Beecher Stowe's *Uncle Tom's Cabin* was only slightly less critical in its portrait of the South.

To the Southerners on the other hand, the "Yankees" often were seen to be wild, Puritan extremists, hypocrites, and misanthropists, who lacked all feeling for the qualities of life and culture. Yankees were crude, dollar-chasing materialists who lived in "moral deformity and hideous gloom." Their "fierce, fantastic intolerance" made them unfit for the exercise of true civil and political liberty, according to the leading southern journal, *De Bow's Review* (1860). The *Review* in contrast found the southern planters, for all their human failings, to be gallant, high-spirited, chivalrous, and generous as a race. They were the direct descendants, it was claimed, of Anglo-Saxon blood; they lived by the Holy Bible, not the Almighty Dollar. The social system of the South *including slavery* was "founded on the revealed laws of God." If all that the North could produce was the wild ideas of Horace Greeley, whose New York *Tribune* was the sounding board of a great variety of reform ideas (abolitionism, feminism, communitarianism, socialism), then, argued George Fitzhugh of Virginia, "free society is a failure." Fitzhugh was anti-Negro, not simply pro-slavery. His defense was to attack and his various writings (*Sociology for the South*, 1854, and *Cannibals, ALL!*, 1857) developed the argument that Northern workers labored under far worse conditions than Southern slaves. Northern "wage slavery" was worse than the paternalistic system of the plantation. This was a clever argument at a time when the radical fervor of the day had brought a deep questioning of the working of the capitalist system. It contained enough truth to make men think, and it harked back to an older, agrarian and Jeffersonian tradition which would always appeal to Americans.

The slave and the Negro

The North, to be sure, was less than perfect. No one understood this better than the *free* Negroes who lived in Northern states and suffered from racial discrimination of all sorts. Everywhere the free Negro was a pariah. In Ohio, Indiana, and Illinois, centers of abolitionism, state laws prevented Negroes from voting, serving on juries, or testifying against whites. Their children could not attend public schools. Even in Massachusetts, Negroes were segregated on trains and in social life. The legal definition of "Negro" in the North, as in the South, was based on blood. Curiously, the addition of "white" blood did not make a Negro white, but the addition of "black" blood, even in small degrees, turned a white into a Negro. Churches, the very centers of evangelism, revivalism, and reform, kept blacks apart in special "Negro pews."

Free Negroes fought for their rights. In Massachusetts, for example, the black historian, William C. Nell, worked for almost 30 years to force local school districts to admit Negro children. Nell won passage of a state law in 1855, which some other states later copied. Sympathetic whites helped the cause of free Negroes. Charles Sumner (1811–74), the Massachusetts Senator, defended a great desegregation case in 1849, *Roberts* v. *City of Boston*. Sumner argued for "equality before the law," as against the brief of the Chief Justice of Massachusetts, Lemuel Shaw, who formulated an early version of the "separate but equal" dogma in the field of Negro education.

Sumner, Garrison, Wendell Phillips, and Salmon P. Chase were among the abolitionist leaders who were prepared to go further for the Negro than merely establish his legal freedom. They would try to secure his civil rights and give him a real chance through education and financial aid to compete in the white world. Few reformers would go along with them. Anti-extensionists hoped, like the Founding Fathers, that if slavery were kept cooped up in the South it would somehow die of its own accord. Violence would not be necessary. On the other hand, total abolitionists recognized the inhumanity of slavery wherever it existed, but rarely looked beyond its abolition to the condition of the free Negro. Like the Romantic reformers they were, most abolitionists conceived of freedom as the absence of restraint. But the ex-slave would need more than this negative concept of freedom if he were to survive after the war.

The emergence of Abraham Lincoln

For many fearful Southerners the last straw was the election of Abraham Lincoln in 1860. Rightly or wrongly, they felt that Lincoln was a direct threat to the entire Southern way of life. In truth, Lincoln was in many ways a moderate. Unpretentious and seemingly a crude, backwoods, homely sort of man, Lincoln would surprise his opponents and supporters alike in his superb command of language; his state papers and addresses would reach the heights of great literature. He emerged in June 1858 as the Republican nominee at Springfield, Illinois, for U.S. Senator. The son of an impecunious and improvident pioneer family of the Kentucky and Illinois frontier, Lincoln was already known locally as a self-made man and politician, a lawyer who had served four terms in the Illinois legislature and a term in the U.S. House. He had married upward socially, into a well-to-do Kentucky family, and emerged first as a Whig and then as a prominent Illinois Republican.

Lincoln was a tough match for Stephen A. Douglas in the electoral fight for the Illinois seat in the U.S. Senate in 1858. Douglas himself was under fire, not only for his act of 1854 but because the Democrats were split and he had courageously opposed the Buchanan leadership over their support for the LeCompton Constitution in Kansas. He had presidential hopes and could not afford to lose his Northern or Midwestern Democratic supporters by going along with the forcing of slavery upon the Kansans. Thus Douglas was fighting for his political life in 1858 when he engaged in the famous public debates around Illinois with Abraham Lincoln.

The Lincoln-Douglas debates

Lincoln, a moderate-to-conservative, had taken no strong stand on abolishing slavery where it already existed and had serious doubts about the potentialities of Negroes compared with whites. In the debate at Freeport, Illinois (August 27, 1858), Lincoln cleverly pinned his opponent: How did Douglas reconcile his theory of popular sovereignty with the Supreme Court's decision in the case of Dred Scott? Douglas's answer was very ingenious. True, the Court had *legally* deprived the Territory from banning or instituting slavery, said Douglas, but as a practical matter, slavery could exist in no locality unless the people who lived there chose to protect it with an adequate code of slave laws and regulations and a positive policy of policing and safeguarding slave property. This *Freeport Doctrine* ("slavery cannot exist a day or an hour anywhere, unless it is supported by local police regulations"), with its clever distinctions between *de jure* and *de facto* conditions, was Douglas's attempt to keep the support of the Northern voters without totally alienating the Southerners in his party. He did lose the Southerners, who thought he had sold out to abolitionism. Lincoln found the Freeport Doctrine slippery and easy to criticize. He is reported as having said after this debate:

You can fool all of the people some of the time, and some of the people all of the time, but you cannot fool all of the people all of the time.

If he did not say it, perhaps he should have, for the doctrine was too clever. It backfired for Douglas, who won his reelection to the Senate in 1858 but lost the bigger battle later.

Escalation: John Brown's raid

Meanwhile, moderate opinion in the North suffered a grave blow when one of the most unbuckled, violent antislavery zealots, John Brown (1800–59), planned the wildest military action of his career to publicize the antislavery position. Brown intended to encourage a slave uprising in Virginia, to collect escaped slaves in a mountain stronghold there, and gradually to subvert the South. He was supported in this plan by money from Northeastern abolitionists, including Rev. Theodore Parker (see Chapter 10), Gerrit Smith, and Rev. Thomas Wentworth Higginson, the Unitarian minister who was to lead a Negro regiment in the Civil War. If Brown was a "maniac," then these more respectable financiers of his scheme deserve psychoanalysis also. Clearly, the popular view sometimes expressed that John Brown was insane is too easy a judgment to make.

Brown was surely bloody minded. He had left his debt-ridden farm in New York to join his five sons in the Kansas Territory in 1855 with the explicit intention of raising trouble. The Pottawatomie Massacre carried out by his little band was a brutal execution and mutilation of five innocent men. The band with which Brown attacked the federal arsenal at Harper's Ferry, Virginia, in October 1859 was not much larger: 18 men, including 5 Negroes. After a two-day battle they were captured by federal marines led by Col. Robert E. Lee. What carried Brown through this poorly-conceived scheme was his burning conviction that God had chosen him to wage war on human slavery. During his treason trial Brown was perfectly lucid, noble, and courageous. He rejected his attorney's plea of insanity, lost all chance of a lighter sentence, and stood his ground, saying that at all times his sole aim was to free the slaves. John Brown was hanged and immediately became a martyr for some, like Emerson, who sanctified him, but an evil symbol for others.

Slaves did not flock to Brown's banner in 1859 though several black leaders felt by then that a Negro revolt was the only possible way of bringing drastic change. White Southerners were terrified of the possibility of slave uprisings, with some reason. The Gabriel Plot of 1801 in Virginia, the Denmark Vesey uprising in South Carolina in 1822, and the bloody Nat Turner revolt in Virginia in 1831 were but three

The U.S.A.

of a series of insurrections over the years. Southerners lived in constant fear of slave plots and conspiracies. They did all they could to keep Negroes apart from each other, to deny them any communion, and to prevent them from being educated or becoming organized. The John Brown raid therefore touched a raw and exposed nerve in Southern society in 1859.

The last straw: Lincoln's election

The outcome of Lincoln's victory in the presidential election of 1860 was that a national decision seemed to have been made, a decision which a large part of the nation—ultimately 11 states—refused to accept. The consensus was shattered. There was no longer any acceptance of the principle of peaceful transfer of power between rival administrations. The campaign itself was formally a four-way struggle among Democrats, Republicans, Constitutional Unionists, and Southern Rights Democrats.

The last bonds of union seemed to snap when the political parties, like the churches, split and re-formed along sectional lines. The Whigs had disintegrated after 1852. The Democrats suffered their final splintering at the Charleston, South Carolina, convention of 1860. Factionalism was rife in the only party that could have united the

The Chicago Wigwam, seat of the Republican convention for the 1860 election

Chicago Historical Society, photo by Alexander Hesler

nation and representatives of the Deep South gained the whip hand. The Alabama "fire-eater" and rabid states' righter, W. L. Yancey, featured prominently as the orator of the day. Years earlier his "Alabama Platform" of 1848, in answer to the Wilmot Proviso of that year, had won the endorsement of four Southern states. It demanded that Congress clearly protect slavery in the Territories. Yancey resubmitted this platform in 1860 and most southerners at the convention followed him. During the debate one Georgia slave-trader went so far as to demand reopening of the African slave trade. The convention split wide open. Disrupted, it met again in Baltimore, fought a bitter delegate-seating battle, and split once more. What was left of the meeting nominated Stephen A. Douglas as the Democratic candidate for the U.S. presidency, flanked by a Georgia moderate for vice president, Herschel V. Johnson. Two conventions of Southern bolters were held, at Baltimore and Richmond, and both chose John C. Breckinridge of Kentucky for president and Joseph Lane of Oregon for vice president. Douglas's hopes of winning the election were thereby dimmed.

The Constitutional Union party, whose candidates were John Bell of Tennessee and Edward Everett of Massachusetts, was a composite group made up of ex-Whigs and nativist Know Nothing party members. They tried to unite pro-Union southern opinion, of which there was still a great deal, with moderate opinion in the North and West. Unfortunately from the viewpoint of preventing open conflict, their stand was necessarily vague. The Constitutional Unionists lacked a real platform and were dubbed the "Do Nothing" rather than Know Nothing party. They carried Virginia, Kentucky, and Tennessee in the election, border states which supported compromise and which stood to suffer the most from heavy fighting.

In Chicago, by contrast, the robust Republican party chose Abraham Lincoln on the third ballot. It framed an anti-slavery-extension platform and a promise of no interference with slavery where it already existed in the South. The superficially more radical W. H. Seward of New York had been the leading presidential contender and had led the first two ballots. Seward had declared his doctrine of an inevitable conflict in 1858 when he said that sectionalism was

an irrepressible conflict between opposing and enduring forces, and it means that the United States must and will, sooner or later, become either entirely a slaveholding nation or entirely a free-labor nation.

This view appealed to many Republicans, who saw the whole Northern and Western way of life, based on free soil and free labor, as being threatened by the spread of the slavery system. But Seward's failure to win the party nomination in Chicago signified that a more moderate attitude had won the day.

The Republicans wished to spread their net to catch the small farmer and were aided in this shrewd tactic by the after effects of the Panic of 1857 which they could readily blame on the Democrats, along with other accumulated evils like Bleeding Kansas and the pro-Southern Supreme Court majority. In 1857 a different sort of voice was heard from the South: it dissented sharply with the pro-slavery consensus. A North Carolina poor-white, Hinton Rowan Helper (1829-1909), published his *Impending Crisis of the South*. Helper was anti-Negro, but anti-slavery. He denounced slavery abusively because he thought it was ruining the South's economy and crushing out the small, white farmer. Horace Greeley, the New York reformer and publisher, printed about 100,000 copies of a short version of Helper's book as Republican campaign material in 1858. In many parts of the South Helper's work was banned: to read it was a crime. The reprint was seen as yet another Northern trick. Lincoln was clearly a wild, backwoods radical!

In the final electoral outcome, Stephen Douglas was the sole candidate with any genuine nationwide support. His chances of winning were hurt by the unedifying and bitter debate in which he was embroiled in the Senate shortly before the election—a fight with a party colleague, Jefferson Davis of Mississippi. Davis had long opposed the popular sovereignty panacea of Douglas. The debate gave the electorate the spectacle of a badly divided Democratic party engaged in internal battles. Lincoln was elected to the White House though only by a minority of the popular votes. The Republicans gained support by toning down their radical image and broadening their appeal with internal improvements, free homesteads, protective tariffs, and federal aid to transcontinental railroads. The Republican slogan, "Vote Yourself A Farm!" was a promise partly fulfilled by the Homestead Act of 1862. In the popular vote, Douglas gained 1,382,713; Lincoln, 1,865,593; Breckinridge, 848,356; and Bell, 592,906. The electoral college result was: Douglas, 12; Lincoln, 180; Breckinridge, 72; and Bell, 39. Owing to Lincoln's large excess of electoral college votes the election did not have to be decided by the House of Representatives as some had feared. But Lincoln's support was decidedly sectional.

In the popular vote Lincoln failed to win a *single* supporter in ten states of the South. His vote in the other Southern states was smaller than Breckinridge's vote in the North. Lincoln won because he carried the most populous states with their big blocks of electoral college votes, such as New York's 35, Pennsylvania's 27, and Ohio's 23. The biggest Southern blocs, Virginia's 15, Kentucky's and Tennessee's 12 each, went to Bell. Lincoln carried the electoral college votes of all the Northern, free states except New Jersey, split between himself and Douglas. Douglas's 12 votes came from New Jersey and Missouri. Breckinridge, the Southern Rights candidate, took the entire Deep South, though he was no radical "fire-eater" of the Yancey type. Among the border states and Upper South he carried North Carolina, Maryland, and Delaware. Breckinridge, however, did not win even a majority of the popular vote in the slave states. They were not united behind him.

The die was cast. With the most sectional mandate of all four contestants, Abraham Lincoln inherited the White House and faced the immediate crisis of probable Southern secession from the Union.

Lincoln and the secession crisis: Upper versus Lower South

Between the November election of 1860 and early February of 1861 seven states of the Deep South left the American Union and formed a separate nation, the Confederate States of America (CSA). As in past crises, fiery South Carolina led the way. The Upper South was more reluctant to move. This situation was the clue to Lincoln's policy during the ensuing confrontation. Lincoln hoped to win over some of the northerly states of the South.

The essential moderation of Lincoln was lost on most of the South. Its basis was his own ambivalent attitude towards Negroes and his deep love of the Union. As far as blacks were concerned, Lincoln shared the ambiguities of his era, though he strived to rise above them. Black leaders felt no initial surge of enthusiasm for Lincoln. They could find little to cheer in any of the four parties. Frederick Douglass warmed up to Lincoln but then cooled off again as the campaign progressed and the Republican party disavowed any intention of abolishing slavery. It was painful for Negroes to hear their friends, like the white radical Horace Greeley, say: "Never on earth did the Republican party propose to abolish slavery." Politics involves the art of winning. Frederick Douglass threw his support away on the minor party led by Gerrit Smith, called the Radical Abolitionists. Douglass claimed:

Ten thousand votes for Gerrit Smith at this juncture would do more . . . for the ultimate abolition of slavery in this country, than two million for Abraham Lincoln, or any other man who stands pledged before the world against all interference with slavery in the slave states.

One Illinois black leader was even more critical of Lincoln:

Take Abraham Lincoln. I want to know if any man can tell me the difference between the antislavery of Abraham Lincoln, and the antislavery of the old Whig party, or the antislavery of Henry Clay? Why, there is no difference . . . In the State of Illinois . . . we have a code of black laws that would disgrace any Barbary State.

By this he meant that free Negroes could not vote in Lincoln's own state of Illinois. By 1860 a handful of New England states alone had given Negroes the franchise.

President-elect Lincoln spent the entire lame-duck period between election and inauguration working on his party organization and giving out patronage jobs. The nation was disintegrating around him. Lincoln seemed to underestimate the seriousness of the secession actions, or he placed too much hope on the wisdom of the putative "silent majority" of Southern moderates. He thought that the non-slaveowning, moderate Southerners were pro-Union, and he blamed a minority of "fire-eaters" for the crisis. As a result of this misjudgment of the situation, Lincoln blocked many compromise efforts by privately and quietly opposing any relaxation of the anti-slavery-extension principle. He felt that the South was bluffing and called that bluff. Yet one must remember that anti-extension was the Republican party's reason for being.

The Upper South and last-ditch compromise

Though Lincoln got no votes in one third of the nation he did win some degree of support in five *slaveholding* states: Missouri, Delaware, Virginia, Kentucky, and Maryland. These same border states stayed in the Union, though Virginia split apart. The small farmers of West Virginia separated in June 1861 and formed a new state which entered the Union in 1863. The rest of Virginia joined the Confederacy in April 1861. Richmond, Virginia, became the Confederate capital. Lincoln was never sure that the slaveholding border states would remain loyal to the Union. He struggled to win them over, especially Maryland and the state of his own birthplace, Kentucky.

Southern secessionists also worried about the border states. If these states joined the Confederacy, secessionist unity would present a more solid front to the North. South Carolina, the first state to leave the Union (December 20, 1860) gave as its chief reason the election of a president "whose opinions and purposes are hostile to slavery." The Deep South had good reason to fear that Lincoln could win over the Upper South by use of federal patronage and by private political deals. The less monolithic and united was the front of the slave states, the more they feared division among themselves and the more extreme became the demands of the firebrands like Senator Robert Toombs of Georgia and Robert Barnwell Rhett of South Carolina. In an atmosphere of excitement and revolution the process of secession passed through the states of the Deep South. The Georgia convention was a crucial breakthrough. Here the vote to secede was narrow: 164 to 133. Many who voted did not anticipate the full implications. Instead of tragic war they expected the Union to be reorganized in some fashion more favorable to Southern interests. They believed they had a better chance of negotiating from strength *outside* the Union than inside it. Votes in other states were more decisive, as in Texas—166 to 8 in favor of secession. Texas had been in the Union only 16 years.

Six cotton states had followed South Carolina by February 1, 1861: Mississippi, Florida, Alabama, Georgia, Louisiana, and Texas. Later, four states of the Upper South also seceded, but only after the outbreak of hostilities: Virginia, North Carolina, Tennessee, and Arkansas. These harbored pockets of pro-Union sentiment.

Last-ditch pleas for compromise came from the threatened border states. The leader of pro-Union sentiment in the South was Kentucky's venerable Senator J. J. Crittenden, whose compromise proposal in Congress was the chief of several schemes to prevent war. In the House a special "Committee of Thirty-three" was created, made up of one man from each state, to offer plans to avert war. At this juncture few Republicans were in the mood to throw away the political advantages they had won in the 1860 election. As for secessionists, they announced with a great air of finality on December 13, 1860:

> The argument is exhausted. All hope of relief in the Union, through the agency of committees, congressional legislation, or constitutional amendments, is extinguished.

This negative *Southern Address* came before South Carolina had left the Union and before any scheme of compromise had yet been offered.

It was signed by Robert Toombs of Georgia and Jefferson Davis of Mississippi, former mouthpiece of President Buchanan, and it set a bleak uncompromising tone for the weeks that followed. The idea of Southern independence appeared attractive:

We are satisfied the honor, safety and independence of the Southern People are to be found only in a Southern Confederacy.

Southern Democrats in Congress refused to sit on compromise committees. They gave long speeches on Southern rights and on the dangers of Lincoln. In the House 16 out of 22 Southerners refused to vote to create the Committee of Thirty-three (December 4). They scuttled one conciliation plan after another.

The *Crittenden Compromise* was the personal work of the aged Senator from Kentucky. The plan was to overturn the Dred Scott decision by reestablishing the 36° 30' line. Slavery would once more be banned in Territories north of the line, while Congress would guarantee it south of the line. Future states would enter the Union on the basis of popular sovereignty, with or without slavery according to popular vote. The Fugitive Slave Law would be fully enforced: if a locality refused to comply in arresting a runaway, the federal government would pay the slaveowner compensation and retrieve the damages from the local authorities. Congress was not to abolish slavery in Washington, D.C. These measures were to be embodied in full amendments to the federal constitution and no future amendment was ever to give Congress the power to interfere with slavery in any of the states.

Crittenden's proposals were well-meaning but too pro-Southern. The attempt to legislate for the future was foolish. Lincoln himself opposed the Crittenden Compromise, writing privately to an Illinois representative:

Entertain no proposition for a compromise in regard to the extension of slavery. The instant you do, they have us under again; all our labor is lost, and sooner or later must be done over.

In Lincoln's words of December 11, 1860:

The tug has to come, and better now than later.

He would agree to withdraw Republican opposition to the Fugitive Slave Law but would not budge on slavery-extension. Crittenden's plan would have allowed slavery expansion by way of U.S. penetration of Cuba or Mexico. It failed in the Senate. His unusual scheme of organizing a *national referendum* on the proposals came to nought.

The final plea for peace was made when Virginia led the *Washington Peace Conference* of the border states in February 1861. They met in camera, chaired by ex-President John Tyler of Virginia. Lincoln did not answer their plea for a public airing of his views; he kept silent until the inaugural of March 4, thus projecting to the South a sterner, less compromising image than he in fact possessed. But the peace conference met too late anyway; the Confederate Constitution had already been drawn up in Montgomery, Alabama, and Jefferson Davis was chosen as President of the Confederacy on February 9.

There were two American nations.

Jefferson Davis and the Confederacy

The Confederate Constitution was not in itself a radical departure. Modeled on the existing federal document, it gave stronger guarantees to slavery, was more explicit on states' rights, prohibited protective tariffs, and contained no "implied powers" clause under which Congress could accrue power. The constitution banned the importation of fresh slaves from abroad, chiefly as a sop to British opinion. From the outset the Confederacy hoped to win foreign sympathy and diplomatic recognition.

Suspicion of all central executive power dogged and weakened the Confederacy as a form of effective government. Eventually these fears made the system unworkable. Six executive departments were created but no department of the Interior. Jefferson Davis tried desperately to exert some authority from the center. Moreover he excluded from his cabinet the most radical fire-eaters such as W. L. Yancey and Robert Barnwell Rhett. Like Lincoln, Davis faced the problem of having to win over the border states and Upper South. To do this he had to act with moderation. Yet, given the strong states' rights feelings, Davis also needed to have every Confederate state represented in his cabinet.

The final issue: Federal bases in the South

Though President Buchanan has gone down in history as a weak and vacillating man, his policy was rational at this stage of the crisis: an attempt to avoid open military conflict but still somehow maintain the authority of the Union. In earlier years Buchanan had without question pursued pro-Southern policies. Faced now with open rebellion he had to choose between love of the Union and sympathy for the South. Unionism came out on top. His message to Congress of December 3, 1860 was a careful statement accusing Northern agitators of inflaming the South but denying the right of individual states to leave the Union. Lincoln's election was no justification for secession, said Buchanan. The Union was not a "rope of sand" but was "perpetual." He pleaded with both sides to save the Union from dissolution, to preserve it as an example to the world. At a cabinet meeting a month earlier Buchanan had suggested that a national convention be called to draw up a plan for conciliation between the sections.

Secession was one matter, war another. The military crisis came with the acute dilemma over the ownership of federal forts in the South. Some federal forts were simply taken over by the Confederates. Buchanan decided to hold the line by resisting the takeover of Fort Pickens, Florida, and Fort Sumter on an island in Charleston harbor, South Carolina. There were three forts in the Palmetto State but federal force there was only sufficient to defend one of them. So Buchanan ordered Major Robert Anderson to move his men from Fort Moultrie to Fort Sumter in order to consolidate them in one fort that was defensible. South Carolinians regarded this move as a provocation and subsequently occupied the other forts. When President Buchanan

*Mathew Brady,
Library of Congress*

Mr. and Mrs. Jefferson Davis

sent an unarmed supply ship, the *Star of the West,* to Sumter to provision Anderson's garrison, the ship was turned back by Confederate shore fire. Meanwhile, in Florida, the Fort Pickens relief ships stayed offshore to avoid any irreversible confrontation. Until Lincoln took over the White House in March 1861 the issue remained in limbo, with the luckless Anderson and his men besieged at Sumter and low on supplies.

President-elect Lincoln played a close hand. He kept to his party platform, made no official statements, and privately indicated that all federal property would have to be retrieved. Lincoln spent most of his time selecting a geographically balanced cabinet—three Easterners, two Westerners, two from border states; three ex-Whigs, two ex-Democrats, two who had been both. He failed to find a Southerner. To keep an image of moderation was as much his goal as to remain noncommital. As early as 1858 Lincoln had said on the slavery issue: "I, as much as any man, am in favor of having the superior position assigned to the white race." His opposition to the spread of slavery, he explained, was so that *"white* men may find a home."

The question must be asked: was it necessary to hold or to take back the federal forts? Perhaps Lincoln could have waited for a cooling-off period. Perhaps he could have evacuated Fort Sumter temporarily. But Lincoln, like Buchanan, had to balance the risks of war against the risks of federal compliance with the dissolution of the Union. His opponent, President Jefferson Davis, faced a similar dilemma. Davis's strong defiance of the Union could have two opposite results. It could force Lincoln into firing the first shot, thus producing a wave of sympathy for the beleaguered South and bringing the wavering border states over to the Confederate side. Or it could alienate those same border states, pushing them into the Union camp. How far could Davis afford to press his defiance of federal authority? It was a gamble. He

The U.S.A.

needed the support of Virginia, Tennessee, North Carolina, Arkansas, and if possible Maryland, with its enclave, the capital city of the Union, Washington, D.C. In the end, Jefferson Davis took a provocative course of action: he ordered General Pierre G. T. Beauregard to demand the surrender of Fort Sumter.

The South shoots first: Fort Sumter, April 1861

William H. Seward, the exponent of the "irrepressible conflict" theory and now Lincoln's Secretary of State, advised the president against precipitate action over the federal forts. Seward negotiated with Confederate commissioners and, in fact, suggested that Sumter be evacuated, while Fort Pickens be retained. On March 15th Seward swung the cabinet with him but Lincoln had to make up his own mind, whatever his friends and his cabinet appointees might advise. His attitude was hardening: he ordered reinforcements to be sent to both Pickens and Sumter. Lincoln's inaugural pledged that no invasion or force would be used anywhere, though he insisted that federal property must be protected. He told the South:

The government will not assail *you*. You can have no conflict without being yourselves the aggressors. *You* have no oath registered in Heaven to destroy the government, while I shall have the most solemn one to "preserve, protect and defend" it . . .

Lincoln's peroration called up the "mystic chords of memory, stretching from every . . . patriot grave to every living heart and hearthstone."

The new president made it clear that it was up to the South to fire the first shot. The drama in Charleston harbor worked itself out. The federal relief force was inadequate and could not enter the harbor with safety. After a series of exchanges between Anderson and Beauregard, South Carolina shore batteries bombarded Fort Sumter at 4:30 A.M. on April 12, 1861. These were the first official shots of the Civil War.

War strategy: The odds

In Washington, D.C., President Lincoln immediately called for 75,000 Union volunteers to augment his small federal army of about 16,000. The number was far too low. In time, vast armies totalling well over one and a half million men on the Union side and one million on the Confederate side would man the field of battle. In terms of numbers and geographical range, the Civil War was the greatest military conflict until World War I. It was also the first war of the Industrial Revolution, involving not only armies but civilian populations and the entire economy of both sides. The long-term odds weighed heavily against the South, which lacked the industrial, transportation, and manpower resources of the North and West. Twenty-three Union states faced 11 Confederate states, a population of 23,000,000 faced 9,000,000, over one third of whom were black slaves whose loyalty to the Confederacy was presumably less than enthusiastic. By July 1861 Congress gave Lincoln the power to enroll 500,000 men. The Confederate capital was moved to Richmond, Virginia, (as part of the strategy to placate the Upper South) and the war largely settled down to a struggle of each side to capture its opponent's capital.

Despite the numerical and material odds, the South hoped to win. Many foreign observers thought the Confederacy had a good chance. In the first place, the South was defending, the North attacking. Second, the region to be invaded was vast. Union armies would need to stretch their supply lines into unfamiliar terrain. The South was, on the whole, better led, at least at the beginning of the war. Its military traditions had kept alive the arts of war and many of the best generals joined the Confederacy. The South began well, with bold victories and high morale.

Southern strategy aimed at driving a wedge between the Northeast and the Northwest, by moving north after capturing Washington. Northern strategy aimed to blockade the Atlantic and Gulf coast, keep out foreign trade and supplies, and prevent cotton exports from leaving the South; to capture Richmond; to win control of the Mississippi river system and choke off its waterways, and then to divide the South. The strategy of both sides was based on prewar sectional realities.

First Bull Run and naval blockade

Neither side had much luck in working out its strategy. The struggle for Richmond and Washington extended over four years. (Richmond did not fall until April 2, 1865, seven days before the end of the war.) It was popular clamor in the North that obliged Winfield Scott, commander-in-chief in the field and "Old Fuss and Feathers" of Mexican War fame, to order a Union move against Richmond in July 1861. The result was an initial Union defeat in the first battle of Bull Run (July 21, 1861). Bull Run was brought about largely by the resistance of the Southern general, "Stonewall" Jackson. It was a bad blow to Lincoln, who still had no idea how long the war was to last. Southerners, triumphant and overjoyed, believed that early victory was in sight. Union successes in West Virginia in June, however, proved more important in the long-term struggle to win control over the border states. Bull Run stiffened the North's resolve. Lincoln replaced Winfield Scott with General George B. McClellan, whose minor victories helped to create the separate state of West Virginia in June 1861 (admitted in 1863). Further west a civil war broke out in Missouri and was finally decided by the pro-Union forces.

At sea, Lincoln's order to establish a blockade of Southern ports brought Union naval victories and considerable success in cutting off the lifeline of Southern trade. In 1861–62 the Union navy controlled most of the Atlantic coast, captured Southern outlets like Port Royal, South Carolina, (November 7, 1861) and made Southern blockade-running increasingly perilous. By 1864 it was said that one in three blockade-runners were captured, though several hundred ships were engaged in the business. Many used the British port of Nassau in the Bahamas as their base. In a spectacular move, Commodore David Farragut captured New Orleans in April 1862 and thus sealed off the mouth of the Mississippi.

A "first" in naval history took place in Hampton Roads, Virginia, with the battle of the two ironclad vessels, *Merrimac* and *Monitor* (March 9, 1862). The Union engineer, James B. Eads, famous after

The U.S.A.

the war for his bridge over the Mississippi at St. Louis, had been ordered to design a fleet of ironclads—which subsequently helped to clear the Mississippi River of Confederate shipping in its lower reaches. The *Monitor* was built by the Swedish immigrant, John Ericsson, and launched by the Union in 1862. The *Merrimac* had been captured by the Confederates from the Union navy. The *Monitor* was little more than a floating armored battery; it was low in the water—its deck, sheathed in iron-plate, a mere eight inches above the waterline. On top was a revolving turret, like that of a modern tank, with two 11-inch guns. The *Monitor* fought the *Merrimac* to a draw, but the battle is often incorrectly claimed as a Union victory. John Ericsson foresaw the nature of modern armored warfare. He cabled Lincoln in 1862:

> The time has come, Mr. President, when our cause will have to be sustained not by numbers, but by superior weapons. By a proper application of mechanical devices alone, will you be able with absolute certainty to destroy the enemies of the Union.

The campaigns of 1862: Second Bull Run and Antietam

The Union goal of cutting the Confederacy in half and taking its capital was good on paper. The price was very high and progress slow. General McClellan proved to be an unhappy choice; he was dilatory and for months took little action. Lincoln had great difficulty in finding a suitably aggressive general. He was unlucky until the

Civil War drill

U.S. Army Photograph

emergence of Ulysses S. Grant in 1863. There were, however, important Union advances in the West and in river warfare. Grant invaded Tennessee in the early days of 1862 and fought the battle of Shiloh (April 6–7), a tragedy for both sides, with heavy casualties: 13,000 Union soldiers and 11,000 Confederates fell in the battle, which involved over 100,000 men. General Grant's efforts were impaired by poor tactical decisions on the part of the Union commander in the West, General H. W. Halleck.

In the eastern sector McClellan stirred himself into the Peninsular Campaign against Richmond, which failed in July 1862. Lincoln pinned his hopes on Halleck's armies in the West, where Union ironclad vessels attacked Memphis and combined Union forces invaded the state of Mississippi. In the East the tide of war continued to go badly for the Union. Stonewall Jackson was victorious and General Robert E. Lee was given high command of Confederate forces in Virginia. After a Southern victory at the second battle of Bull Run (August 29–30), Lee began a general invasion of Maryland. Harper's Ferry fell readily to Stonewall Jackson (September 15) and with it went rich supplies, munitions, and 11,000 Union prisoners. The Union capital of Washington, D.C., was endangered.

McClellan gathered himself slowly and finally met Lee at the bloody battle of Antietam (September 17) which cost nearly 5,000 lives and over 18,000 wounded, equally divided between Confederate and Union troops. Lee retired to Virginia and McClellan hesitated as usual, failing to pursue him. Had he done so, the war might have been drastically shortened.

Diplomacy and slavery

The rival forces also competed for favor and aid in Europe. Britain was the chief target of their attention and both sides had much to recommend them to the English government. The North's antislavery and the South's position as a would-be independent small nation attracted different groups in Britain. The government did not extend full diplomatic recognition to the Confederacy but it did recognize a state of belligerency. This solution pleased neither North nor South. The Confederates hoped that British need for raw cotton would force the government in London to bring diplomatic pressure against the Union. At first, however, English manufacturers had adequate supplies of cotton on hand. Later a serious cotton famine struck badly at the textile county of Lancashire and brought intense suffering and unemployment to British workers.

The traditional myth that the British workers supported the North and Lincoln, despite their own suffering, while the British upper classes favored the South, we now know to be incorrect. Many Englishmen of all classes regarded Lincoln with suspicion and wondered why he took so long to free the slaves. They did not sympathize with his position that the war was a conflict over the Union, not over slavery. The Emancipation Proclamation brought some change of attitude toward the North but even that was thought by many to be a trick of Lincoln's to raise the freed slaves against the Confederacy. Some English public leaders were pro-Southern, as were the major journals, especially the London *Times*. A crisis in Anglo-American relations was caused by the *Trent* affair in December 1861 when a Union gunboat stopped and boarded the British steamer *Trent* and took off two Confederate diplomats, J. M. Mason and J. Slidell, who were on their way to negotiate in Europe. Seward wisely released the two men and the sudden war fever abated in Britain. More important was the *Alabama* incident two years later.

The French and British governments both allowed private shipyards to equip vessels for the Confederacy. Several raiders were built in England, including the *Alabama*, launched at Liverpool in July 1862. The raiders destroyed about 300 Union ships during the war. French loans from the house of Erlanger had helped to finance their construction. The Union government strongly complained and the practice stopped. Direct English aid to the Confederacy was thus cut off abruptly. French intervention in American affairs went one step further with the imposition of Archduke Maximilian of Austria on the throne of Mexico, while the United States was otherwise engaged in the Civil War. The Empire of Maximilian in Mexico did nothing to help the Confederate cause and gradually, after 1863, British opinion came around to support the Union.

Sheridan's attack at Five Forks

Library of Congress

Origins of the Emancipation Proclamation

Abraham Lincoln was anxious to woo the British and published a direct address to the British workers. European feelings about slavery affected his decision to issue the Emancipation Proclamation but the "victory" at Antietam decided the precise timing. Though the Republican Radicals, men like Charles Sumner, Thaddeus Stevens, and Benjamin Wade, continually pressed for abolition, Lincoln was advised by Seward not to issue the declaration in July 1862, during a period of military setbacks, in case his motive would be questioned. As the war continued with its growing death-toll of battles like Shiloh and Antietam, public opinion in the North became more open to the idea of completely abolishing slavery. Liberation would release freed Negroes as troops for the Northern armies and would also deprive the South of its labor force. No doubt some Northerners also hoped to see slave uprisings in the Confederacy.

Politically, Lincoln needed the Proclamation to help him to weather the storm at home, to win over or undercut the Radicals in his own party, and perhaps also to meet the rising criticism of the small number of black leaders. At the same time he could not afford to alienate the loyal slaveholding states which still supported the Union side.

Negro leaders were not silent. Some had even derived hope from Union military setbacks, which might cause antislavery opinion to harden in the North and force a reluctant Lincoln to abolish slavery. The escaped slave and leader of the Underground Railroad, Harriet Tubman (1821–1913), is reported as having said (in poorly imitated southern dialect) in 1861:

> God won't let Massa Linkum beat de South till he do the right ting!

When some of Lincoln's generals abolished slavery in captured territories, the cautious president revoked their military decrees. Black leaders were enraged. In an editorial of July 1862, a furious Frederick Douglass declared:

> Abraham Lincoln is no more fit for the place he holds than was James Buchanan, and the latter was no more the miserable tool of traitors and rebels than the former is allowing himself to be. . . . The country is destined to become sick of both McClellan and Lincoln, and the sooner the better.

But when Lincoln finally took the plunge and issued the declaration (September 22, 1862; published in final form on January 1, 1863), Douglass was overjoyed:

> We shout for joy . . .

President Lincoln explained to Congress: "In giving freedom to the slave we assure freedom to the free." He was less than candid. The Proclamation was a theoretical proscription. Total abolition still lay in the future.

Campaigns of 1863: Chancellorsville and Gettysburg

After Antietam, McClellan relapsed into inactivity. Lincoln took steps to find a new general and tried Ambrose Burnside, who failed disastrously at the battle of Fredericksburg in December 1862. Burnside was quickly replaced by Joseph Hooker, who had the political

A dead Confederate

Mathew Brady, Library of Congress

support of Salmon Chase and the Republican Radical wing. Robert E. Lee's victory over Burnside at Fredericksburg, about halfway between Washington, D.C., and Richmond, left him in a strong military position. About four months later the two armies met in a bloodbath at Chancellorsville (May 2–4, 1863). Lee divided his forces, as at Second Bull Run, and sent Stonewall Jackson against Hooker's right flank. The outcome was a Southern victory at a high price. The brilliant Jackson was shot in error by his own men while surveying the battlefield in the evening. Both sides lost about 1,600 men each, and over 9,000 were wounded on each side. Hooker retired in confusion and Lincoln replaced him with General G. G. Meade.

Robert E. Lee, emboldened by his victories, launched an offensive into Pennsylvania. Lee wished to penetrate as deep as he could and give Northerners a taste of the war for a change. Here Lee failed. Two great armies met at Gettysburg, Pennsylvania, and fought it out (July 1–3, 1863): 70,000 Confederates against 93,000 Union troops. Advance parties began this crucial battle and at first neither commander was present—they stumbled into the battle. Reinforcements arrived and the two armies locked. The Confederates were winning after the first day, but Meade regrouped along Cemetery Ridge. On July 3d came Pickett's charge, the turning point of the battle, when Lee ordered General George E. Pickett with 15,000 men to charge the center of the Union position on the Ridge. Well-placed guns on the hilltop mowed his men down, killing and wounding about half. The rest were captured. Lee withdrew and was attacked again as he crossed the Potomac. Total casualties in this three-day battle were about 28,000 Confederates and about 23,000 Union dead, missing, and wounded. Lee's daring onslaught into the North had failed, and Gettysburg, with the simultaneous Union victory at Vicksburg in the West, turned the tide of war.

Vicksburg: Cutting the Confederacy in two

Just as the South had hoped to cut the Northwest from the Northeast, the Union's Vicksburg campaign in Mississippi was fought to separate the South from the rich Southwest. It was a decisive campaign. Vicksburg itself was a prosperous steamboating and cotton city where the Yazoo River meets the Mississippi. It was situated in the heart of the fertile lands of cotton migration in the Southwest. General Grant moved south from his earlier victories in Tennessee and headquartered at Memphis, as several futile attempts were made to take Vicksburg by land and by river. The town stood on a seemingly impregnable bluff.

Though Farragut had taken New Orleans in April 1862, a stretch of the Mississippi river between that city and Memphis was still in Confederate hands. Grant therefore moved an army down the west bank to below Vicksburg. He crossed the river with boats and besieged the city for almost seven weeks. Vicksburg fell in July 1863 with a loss of about 9,000 Union soldiers and 10,000 Confederates. Over 30,000 rebels were taken prisoner. A few days later Port Hudson, Louisiana, also fell, and the entire Mississippi was under Union control. The South was severed from the Southwest. The way was open eastward for a march to the sea. With Robert E. Lee in defeat and Vicksburg in enemy hands, the end was in sight.

Troubles on the home front: The Radicals, draft riots, and the election of 1864

Political unrest at home dogged every move Lincoln made. He had to fight two simultaneous battles. The Radical Republicans were suspicious and frustrated by the war's slow progress. They wanted to exert greater *congressional* control over postwar planning for "Reconstruction" and for future treatment of the ex-rebel states. Some Radicals were more sensitive to the needs and civil rights of freed Negroes after manumission. In the House, Thaddeus Stevens, and in the Senate, Charles Sumner, were far more committed to racial equality than was Lincoln. Though the Emancipation Proclamation had strengthened the president's position with the Radicals and had undercut some of their appeal, many could point out that it freed few if any slaves. The Proclamation applied only to areas over which the Union had as yet no control. It excluded Union-occupied zones. Radicals opposed Lincoln's conciliatory plan for the readmission of rebel states to the Union. He would readmit a state when 10 percent of its voters of 1860 were willing to take an oath of allegiance to the Union. The Radicals proposed the Wade-Davis Bill of 1864 which was much harsher to the South.

In addition to this tension, Lincoln faced popular hostility to his Conscription Act of March 1863, the first in U.S. history. The Union needed troops and could not depend on the state militia. The act was unfair because those who could afford it were allowed to buy themselves out for $300 or to provide a substitute. Irish, and other workers, in the poorer sections of New York City rioted for four days in July 1863. They pillaged, and they lynched Negroes. Troops had to be spared from the battlefield after Gettysburg to put the rioters down and maintain order. The Confederacy had adopted conscription a year earlier and its law was equally divisive and unfair.

Nevertheless, Lincoln had at last found his generals in Meade and Grant. He had built a workable war machine by trial and error. His armies were winning, if at terrible human cost. Generally the Northern economy was prosperous, even booming in some sections. About 800,000 foreign immigrants came in during the war. Farming continued to expand to meet growing war demand. In contrast, Jefferson Davis faced enormous difficulties both in the battlefield and in the lack of political and economic support at home. Strong states' rights convictions and tough state governors in the Confederacy were hard for Davis to control.

In November 1863 Lincoln delivered the short, stunning *Gettysburg Address*, to dedicate the cemetery at that battlefield. He had reached the peak of his political greatness and maturity. His address was a moving poem to the hopes of mankind. It expressed what the Civil War had come to mean for him. The participants' views of what the war was all about evolved over time, as they fought its battles. First, the political resistance to the expansion of slavery into the Territories became a hot war against secession and to save the Union. Then the war to save the Union became a war against slavery as an institution.

Lincoln was reelected in 1864 with a sweeping victory. He ran, not as a Republican, but as a "Union National" candidate, flanked by a Unionist Democrat for vice president, Senator Andrew Johnson of Tennessee. The Radical Republicans gave Lincoln trouble by demanding another convention. They had opposed his pocket veto of the Wade-Davis Bill. But the choice of Lincoln was unanimous. The Radicals had been unable to agree on a candidate of their own. Lincoln's Democratic opponent, General McClellan, did not stand much chance. The Democratic platform had demanded a quick end to the war on terms of an armistice. McClellan was too Unionist to accept this plank. Undoubtedly the victories of the Union forces came at precisely the right moment for Lincoln's reelection. Opposition to his alleged dictatorship was growing. The good military news from Georgia swept it all aside. Lincoln won 212 electoral college votes and 2,206,938 popular votes in the truncated nation. McClellan gained 21 and 1,803,787 for the Democrats. Lincoln had jailed some "Copperheads" (Northern Democrats) who opposed him. He refused them a trial. Civil rights suffered under wartime conditions and under the fear of civil unrest like the draft riots. But the issue was still the course of the war itself.

Lincoln's second inaugural placed the blame for the Civil War squarely on the South:

Both parties deprecated war; but one of them would make war rather than let the nation survive, and the other would accept war rather than let it perish. And the war came.

The final campaigns: Chattanooga; Sherman's March

After the Vicksburg victory the Union launched its Chattanooga campaign to split the Confederate armies in Virginia from those in the West. Much fighting took place in Tennessee and began with a Union defeat at Chickamauga under the poor command of General W. S. Rosecrans (September 19-20, 1863). But at least one Union general, George H. Thomas, earned distinction in that battle. His troops put up stiff bayonet resistance to the Confederates until help arrived. For this feat, Thomas became known as the "Rock of Chickamauga." Rosecrans and the Union army were now pinned down in Chattanooga. Hurriedly, Lincoln placed the hero of Vicksburg, General Grant, in control in the West. Grant immediately gave G. H. Thomas the command of the army of Chattanooga and rushed to the zone himself. Two Northern victories then drove the Confederates under General Braxton Bragg off Lookout Mountain, overlooking the city, and off Missionary Ridge. Thomas had the final victory over Bragg on the crest of Missionary Ridge (November 23-25).

The southern rout at Chattanooga opened the way for the Union army to turn east and cut the Confederacy in half again the other way, by driving across Georgia to the Atlantic coast. General William Tecumseh Sherman, who had fought at Lookout Mountain, led the Union army out of Tennessee and marched on Atlanta, Georgia, in May 1864. This move was timed to coincide with an attack by General Grant in the east against Richmond. Atlanta fell in September 1864. Sherman ordered survivors out of the stricken city and then promptly burned it down.

With an army of 60,000 men and few supplies, Sherman ordered his "March to the Sea." The army was told to forage and to live off the land. All the way to Savannah, about 250 miles, they burned and looted a path about 60 miles wide, destroying and pillaging all the means of communication and supply, methodically wrecking plantations, factories, cotton gins, and bridges. Railroads were meticulously destroyed: even the ties were pulled up and the tracks twisted. The idea of this was to strike terror and destroy the morale of the population. Sherman's theory of total war, a precursor of 20th-century warfare, deliberately involved civilian populations. In December he took the port city of Savannah, then turned north to join up with Grant.

At Richmond, Grant slugged out the much slower Wilderness Campaign in May and June 1864. The fighting was bloody and indecisive in this region west of Fredericksburg, Virginia, as in the battles of Spotsylvania and Cold Harbor. The campaign cost Grant 60,000 men and cost Lee 30,000. Grant recouped, then did an "end run" around Lee to Petersburg, 20 miles below Richmond. He hoped to take the

The U.S.A.

Confederate capital from there. Petersburg refused to give way, however. The campaign bogged down into a nine months' siege of the city. Losses were heavy and morale often faltered through the long winter months. The campaigns of 1864–65 were bloody and heartbreaking, but Grant persisted. He hardly realized that the end was in sight. Lincoln gave him necessary moral support.

The ending: Appomattox and Lincoln's death

Things went badly for Jefferson Davis and Robert E. Lee. The Union naval blockade became almost total when the North closed the port of Wilmington, North Carolina, in February 1865. The Confederate armies were low in supplies and the Union controlled large sections of the countryside. Urban riots in the South protested shortages and the activities of speculators. Desertions from the once-proud army forced Davis to the extreme position of actually *arming* the slaves to fight against the North. Yet states' rights feelings had not abated in the Confederacy. Even at the height of tragedy and defeat, independent-minded South Carolinians nullified a law of the Confederate Congress

Free Negroes in Richmond, 1865

Mathew Brady, Library of Congress

(December 1864). The Congress had tried to save the situation by imposing central control of goods and services. The Palmetto State refused to relinquish any of its sacred sovereignty. The Southern Confederacy foundered on its own philosophy of localism.

Lee evacuated Petersburg and Richmond in April 1865 and fell back toward Lynchburg where he hoped a rail connection would take him to join up with Confederate forces under General Joseph E. Johnston. Sherman was advancing north against Johnston, however, and Lee was encircled before he could reach him. Lee surrendered in the McClean farmhouse in the village of Appomattox, west of Richmond, Virginia, on April 9, 1865. The elegant Southern hero, wearing a fresh, full-dress uniform, surrendered to the mud-stained, disheveled Grant, who wore battle fatigues. But General Grant maintained the amenities: he silenced the cheer of his own men as the Confederates piled up their rifles. The rebel army surrendered in an honorable, eerie silence.

Five days after Appomattox, on April 14, 1865, President Lincoln took the evening off to watch a performance of the play, *Our American Cousin*, at Ford's Theater in Washington, D.C., An unhinged actor, John Wilkes Booth, shot the president in the back of the head with a derringer. Lincoln was carried to a boardinghouse across the street, his life ebbing. Before 7:30 A.M. the next morning the president died. His last public speech, given on April 14th, had been a call for reconciliation and forgiveness in the spirit of the second inaugural of the 4th of March: "with malice toward none, with charity for all."

As an anticlimax to this bitter outcome, General Johnston finally surrendered to Sherman at Durham, North Carolina, on April 26. The remaining Confederate forces gave up the struggle at New Orleans a month later (May 26). The long and bloody anguish was over.

The most devastating question one can ask of a major war is: Was it worth it? The Civil War in America was a human tragedy on a vast scale. It cost many lives and casualties: 360,000 Union dead, 258,000 Confederate dead; 275,000 Union wounded and maimed and at least 100,000 Confederate wounded. A total of upwards of 1,000,000 men, dead and injured; incalculable property damage and economic retardation; civilian hardships and sorrows; atrocious prison camps like the Confederate prison at Andersonville; the crude shock treatment of Sherman's ecological warfare in the South—a horrifying total picture of waste and devastation. What was the outcome?

Was it worth it?

The Civil War produced two major results. First, and fully intended by the North, the war sealed the American Union in blood. It proved conclusively that secession was not permissible. Second, and less intended at the beginning of the war, the black slave was legally emancipated. Slavery was abolished in the American Republic. Few Americans today would doubt the ultimate wisdom and value of having preserved the Union and having eliminated the blot of human slavery. Some would still question the means used to achieve these ends. As for emancipation itself, 100 years later a generation of black Americans still found it necessary to ask: What did the Civil War truly achieve for Negroes? The transition from a condition of legal servitude to one of de facto peonage or serfdom in the South, together with the maintenance of racial segregation and discrimination in the North, begs the question: Who really won the Civil War?

Bibliography

J. G. Randall and David Donald. *Civil War and Reconstruction.* Boston: Heath, 1969.

Louis Filler. *The Crusade Against Slavery.* New York: Harper, 1960.

Eric Foner. *Free Soil, Free Labor, Free Men.* New York: Oxford University Press, 1971.

John Hope Franklin. *The Militant South.* Boston: Beacon, 1964; *The Emancipation Proclamation.* New York: Doubleday, 1963.

E. Genovese. *The World the Slaveholders Made.* New York: Random House, 1971.

B. Quarles. *Black Abolitionists.* New York: Oxford University Press, 1969.

PART III
A nation of strangers

13

From slavery to serfdom: The unreconstructed South

Who won the Civil War? . . . Reconstruction: an unusual idea . . . if Lincoln had lived . . . fears of the Republican Radicals . . . Andrew Johnson and Confederate Reconstruction . . . Negro and Radical dissatisfaction rises . . . the battle for Negro civil rights: white violence . . . civil rights amendments . . . election of 1866: the coming of Radical Reconstruction . . . impeachment of President Johnson . . . political arms of the Radicals . . . Negro education . . . the hooded Klan . . . black reaction to Reconstruction: what did Freedmen want? . . . why were ex-slaves not given land? . . . collapse of Negro land schemes . . . election of 1868: the 15th amendment and women's rights . . . strange death of Reconstruction . . . why did the North acquiesce? . . . myths of Reconstruction . . . was Radical Reconstruction "corrupt"? . . . why did Reconstruction fail? . . . Southern cultural nationalism. . . the Redeemers and the New South . . . control of blacks in the New South: the Supreme Court . . . black accommodation: Booker T. Washington.

Once the tragedy and horror of Civil War was over the United States underwent rapid social and economic change. A major shaping force was mass immigration, which underlined yet again that America was a complex nation, united more by common beliefs and common goals than by common origins and history. By the late 1890s some western farm states were as "foreign" in their population makeup as were the industrial northeastern states. The country was to a large degree a nation of strangers, yet was driven forward by a massive, common, popular impulse toward economic and territorial growth. By the end of the 19th century the United States was a world economic power. She soon also acquired colonial possessions.

During these dramatic changes the South was left behind. As a region the South was conservative and unyielding, despite attempts in the 90s to create a more economically diversified "New" South. White

Southerners retained their distinctive attitudes and subculture, and from the 90s onward, racial segregation and discrimination against the freed Negroes became even more severe. Radical reformers could well ask: Who really won the Civil War?

Who won the Civil War?

The Southern armies had resisted bravely against heavy odds during the war and were matched only by Northern doggedness in seeing the conflict through to the end. The price the South paid for its resistance was physical devastation. Three major blows stunned the region's economy. First, the abolition of slavery without any compensation wiped out about two billion dollars' worth of Southern capital at one stroke. Second, the collapse of the Confederate banking system reduced currency and bills to worthless scraps of paper and destroyed Southern savings. Third, the war utterly disrupted the plantation system and Southern farming. Many Southerners, nonetheless, still stubbornly refused to admit defeat, even as they struggled to pick up the pieces and to make slow, painful efforts to rebuild their way of life. Psychologically, the determined Southern nationalists turned defeat into victory, and later generations built up the guiding myth of Southern society—the myth of the heroic "Cavalier" nation, fighting for its survival in the gallant "War between the States."

It is thus fair to ask the question, who won the war? The South resisted the North in peace and military occupation as firmly as she had resisted in war. Southerners would not accept the idea of "Reconstruction" and by 1900 had turned the ex-slaves into virtual peons, tied to the land by indebtedness and bereft of basic civil rights. The war destroyed the hopes of secession, but the dogma of states' rights remained as strong as ever.

Reconstruction: An unusual idea

Reconstruction was historically unusual. The idea was that the South was to be remade and reintegrated into the American national community after it had been suitably purged of Confederates. Modern students may think of "de-Nazification" in post–World War II Germany as a sort of parallel, or the U.S. attempt to remold Japanese society under the leadership of General Douglas MacArthur. Of course, Reconstruction was much milder: only a handful of Republicans demanded a complete uprooting of Southern society and only a few Confederate statesmen were temporarily jailed. The brief "war crimes" trial of the Civil War was that of the luckless Swiss-American commander of the infamous Confederate prison stockade at Andersonville, Georgia, Henry Wirz. The hanging of Wirz on November 10, 1865, was probably unwarranted, but in no way measures up to the large-scale trials and purges by the victorious Allies in Germany and Japan after 1945.

Reconstruction meant different things to different observers. For Unionist Southerners and Northern Democrats, it meant the simple readmission of the ex-rebel states into the Union, imposing only the abolition of legal slavery and denial of the right to secede. As the war became more bitter and bloody the idea of postwar reconstruction evolved with it. Radical Republicans came to claim that the Confederate states had committed political suicide by leaving the Union. They were to be readmitted only after a period of internal rehabilitation and renewed status as Territories.

When is a state not a state? The federal constitution was no guide. It gave the president, as commander-in-chief, the power to pardon. Yet Congress alone had the power to admit new states or to pass laws regulating the Territories. Clearly, the rebel states were not "new," but Congress also had the right to judge the qualifications of its own members. The explicit doctrine of Separation of Powers prevented the executive from telling the legislative branch who could sit in Congress. If the president chose to pardon the rebels and readmit Southern states he would be dictating to Congress on that body's own membership. On the other hand, his right to pardon was meaningless if the Southerners could not have representation in Congress. Immediately a struggle broke out between Congress and the White House for control over the fate of the ex-rebel states.

The concept of Reconstruction evolved. First came "rehearsals" for Reconstruction, as the Union armies overran Confederate areas and imposed military rule in Tennessee, Arkansas, Louisiana, and the Sea Islands off the coast of South Carolina. Here experiments took place in freeing slaves and giving them land grants and civil rights. The experiments were short-lived. Second, came a phase of *Confederate* Reconstruction (April to December 1865) under which ex-rebel states were readmitted by Lincoln and by his successor, President Andrew Johnson, with most of their prewar institutions and prejudices left intact except for legal slavery. Third, came military occupation of the South, brought about when the frustrated Radical Republicans in Congress took over control from the White House in a series of measures during 1866–68. This *Radical* or *Black* Reconstruction, so-called, continued down through 1877 though its force waned heavily in later years. Finally, came conservative resurgence in the South, the creation of all-white, "Redeemer" state governments and the Northern abandonment of freed Negroes to their own fate.

If Lincoln had lived

Lincoln is correctly characterized as moderate, conciliatory, and magnanimous in victory. From one viewpoint, if he had not been assassinated, the "tragedy" of Reconstruction might have been avoided and the South would not have suffered military occupation in peacetime. From a contrasting view however, Lincoln's moderate plan of Reconstruction capitulated to white Southern demands and subverted some very aims of the Civil War. The ex-slave would be forced to pay for Lincoln's eagerness to forgive, forget, and bind up the terrible wounds of war.

Lincoln's *Ten Per Cent plan,* proclaimed in December 1863, allowed rebel states to reenter the Union if 10 percent of those who had voted in 1860 took an oath of allegiance to the Union and accepted the emancipation of Negroes. The plan said nothing of the condition of the freed slaves. It made no provision for Negroes to vote or hold office in these reconstructed states. Before the war's end three states, Louisiana, Arkansas, and Tennessee, administered by Union generals, had been reorganized and they sent representatives to the wartime Union Congress. Lincoln clung to the constitutional doctrine that since the Union was inviolable the rebel states *had never left it*. His position was self-contradictory because he did not wish to amnesty all Confederate personnel and he insisted that the readmitted states should accept the principle of slave emancipation without compensation to former owners.

The Ten Per Cent plan was a scheme of white man's reconstruction. It brought angry opposition from Radical Republicans in Congress led by the fiery pro-Negro from Pennsylvania, Thaddeus Stevens, and by the eloquent and courageous idealist, Charles Sumner of Massachusetts. Black leaders were bitterly disappointed in Lincoln's plan. A group of well-to-do New Orleans blacks complained directly to the White House. Lincoln softened to the point of suggesting that blacks be admitted into political life in Louisiana, ruled by his military governor, General N. P. Banks. The argument that ex-slaves were worthy of the right to vote was based on Negro military service, on the taxes they paid, and on the education and property some blacks had managed to acquire. Few whites suggested total suffrage for the Freedmen. The allegedly "reconstructed" white electors of Louisiana voted a solid *No* to Lincoln's mild suggestion. The president still wanted Louisiana to be readmitted all the same and used his influence to persuade Congress. In 1864 Congress refused to seat the members from Lincoln's three "reconstructed" states. A political impasse followed.

President Lincoln had been at loggerheads with the Radicals for some time. We have already seen their opposition over war policy and the selection of generals; but the bitterest disagreement concerned slaves and Freedmen. Lincoln's personal beliefs about blacks went little further than those of Thomas Jefferson, whom he often quoted. Like Jefferson, he aimed merely to limit slavery geographically where it existed at the outset of the war. He never felt that blacks were potentially the equal of whites or that the two races could live peacefully together, both equal. His plan, like Jefferson's, was the colonization of the Freedmen abroad, though he used the harsher word "deportation." In his famous Cooper Union speech in New York (February 27, 1860) Lincoln took Jefferson's words. The nation, he said, should

direct the process of emancipation and deportation, peaceably, and in such slow degrees as that the evil will wear off insensibly . . .

He thus hoped that "emancipation and deportation" would allow the places of Negroes to be filled by "free white laborers." Gradually, the Negroes would vanish and the nation would "whiten."

Lincoln appointed a Commissioner of *Em*igration in 1862 (an unusual post for the United States), to push for Negro colonization in Africa, Haiti, and Central America. In one sorry episode he allowed himself to be taken in by a fraudulent scheme of an American adventurer who suggested a black colony at Chiriqui (Panama). Under Lincoln's scheme it has been estimated that emancipation-deportation could have taken up to the year 1900 for completion.

Fears of the Republican Radicals

Many moderate Republicans questioned Lincoln's trust in the ex-Confederates, while some Radicals demanded direct proof that the Southerners were fully humiliated and submissive. Their fears of the effect of "presidential reconstruction" were understandable. As it stood, Lincoln's plan would simply restore the South of 1860, minus slavery. What had the war been all about? The president's overriding concern for border-state opinion and his dependence on the use of moral suasion and states' autonomy in matters of Negro policy, promised little hope of further racial justice beyond emancipation. He had adopted the Emancipation Proclamation only after the rejection by the pro-Union border states in Congress of his appeals to abolish slavery voluntarily.

So in 1864 the frustrated Radicals, fearing a Confederate comeback, introduced the Wade-Davis Bill which offered a far harsher plan for reconstruction. Before consideration for readmission, a *majority* of the electorate in each Southern state must pledge an oath of loyalty to the Union. Only those able to take an ironclad oath of *past* and present loyalty would be allowed to vote for delegates to the new state constitutional conventions. No ex-Confederate officials could act as delegates or hold office or vote under the new state constitutions. They were to be purged from the body politic of the South. Lincoln wished to avoid a direct confrontation. To bypass throwing out the Wade-Davis Bill altogether he gave it a "pocket veto"—failed to sign it into law. The Radicals were angered and issued the *Wade-Davis Manifesto*, published in Horace Greeley's liberal paper, the New York *Tribune*, in August 1864. The Manifesto attacked Lincoln for his expansion of executive powers during the war and tried to reassert Congressional authority over the South.

The President . . . must understand that the authority of Congress is paramount . . . If he wishes our support he must confine himself to his executive duties—to obey and execute, not make the laws—to suppress by arms, armed rebellion, and leave the political reorganization to Congress.

Lincoln was saved from a major constitutional crisis only by General Sherman's military victories in the fall of 1864. The conflict eventually would come to a head with the impeachment of his successor, President Johnson. At the federal level the Radicals had won a victory and had rejected Lincoln's representatives from the three states. At the local level the victory was his, since all-white civil governments had been established in these states, at least temporarily. The Radical Republicans still lacked widespread national support for their views. Lincoln won reelection in the fall of 1864, running on a Union Nationalist ticket flanked by the war Democrat, Andrew Johnson.

Andrew Johnson and Confederate Reconstruction

The murder of Lincoln left the Republican party to the control of the Radicals and gave the White House to his Democratic vice president. Andrew Johnson never escaped his past. He was a poor-white tailor from east Tennessee, illiterate until marriage, when his wife taught him to cipher and read and write. Johnson thereafter made good in state politics, subsequently serving in both houses of Congress. He rose by sheer hard work, determination, and uncompromising class ideals. Johnson was driven by his hatred of the Southern gentry and by a bitter class-consciousness in all things. He never liberated himself from the memories of his own past poverty and rarely forgave. He opposed slavery mainly because it was the device which kept the rich planters in power; he was never pro-Negro in his abolitionism. Johnson was a stalwart Jacksonian Democrat (he had been named after Jackson) and was strongly pro-Union and a strict devotee of the letter of the federal constitution.

At first some of the Radicals, like Ben Wade and George Julian, thought well of Johnson though he did not share their general anti-Southern prejudices. All he wanted was to destroy the power and prestige of the rich planters and leave the South in the hands of the white yeomen farmers. Johnson's hope was not realized. He began with fierce denunciations of Confederate "traitors" but under the influence of the office of the presidency, and of moderate and nationalist advisers like Secretary of State W. H. Seward, Johnson came to follow Lincoln's plan for reconstruction. He aimed, like Lincoln, at the rapid readmission of ex-rebel states with no prolonged Territorial or reeducational stage.

What Representative Julian of Indiana called "Mr. Lincoln's known policy of tenderness towards the rebels" now became Johnson's, though he could not resist the temptation of forcing wealthier Southerners (owners of taxable property of over $20,000 in value) to make humiliating personal applications to the president himself for pardon. Johnson adopted Lincoln's claim that legally the rebel states had never left the Union. With Congress out of session, he readmitted the remaining seven states by proclamation. President Johnson did not ask for an electoral majority to take the oath in these states, as did the Radicals, nor for 10 percent of the voters of 1860 (Lincoln's plan). Instead he was more liberal than Lincoln and allowed readmission when "that portion of the people . . . who are loyal" had created a de facto government. Meanwhile, he gave the states civil governors.

Thus by the end of 1865, state constitutional conventions having been held, all the rebel states had passed through reconstruction in the eyes of Andrew Johnson. This was the great missed opportunity of the ex-Confederates. If the Southern whites had now acted with moderation and had given Johnson their full political support, the story of Reconstruction might have ended there. Instead they remained recalcitrant and arrogant, they wrote strongly anti-Negro constitutions and passed rigid "Black Codes" in 1865–66 to impose a new sort of serfdom on the liberated blacks. They thus invited criticism and opposition from the Radical Congress.

Negro and Radical dissatisfaction rises

As the ex-Confederates returned to power in the South (Johnson even placed an ex-rebel colonel in charge of pardons), the Republicans came to fear for their political life. Former rebels would dominate the new federal Congress if they were allowed to take their seats. The abolition of slavery had taken with it the old rule whereby the state population count for representation in the House allowed only three fifths of a count for each Negro. Now each Freedman counted as one full citizen and the representation of the Southern states would therefore be 12 votes higher in the lower chamber. Moreover, under the Johnson plan, Congress as of December 1865 would contain almost 60 ex-Confederate Congressmen, 4 ex-generals, 5 ex-colonels, 6 ex-cabinet members, and the former vice president of the Confederacy, A. H. Stephens. Many of these men were openly hostile and personally unreconstructed. In Louisiana, ex-Confederates wore their army uniforms in the state legislature. The Confederate flag was common and Southern ladies sported Confederate badges and buttons whenever they could. Even Andrew Johnson was taken aback by some of the gestures of the Southern leaders. The Republican Congress refused to seat members from these "reconstructed" states.

Johnson's political failings were his obstinacy and narrowness. He never made clear to the South what he expected in return for his leniency and he gave way too easily to their blank refusal to reform. Thus the president let down the Southern moderates and seemed to encourage the extremists. Even the racist Wade Hampton of South Carolina might have supported partial voting rights for Negroes if pressed by the White House; but that pressure never came. A rigid Jacksonian, Johnson allowed his states' rights beliefs to cripple his initiative in handling such issues. He misread the political mood and underestimated the violence of Northern hostility to his pro-Confederate policies.

Whatever Johnson's personal failings were, two elements doomed his reconstruction plan: his own disregard for the fate of the Freedmen (he cared only for middle-class whites), and the stand of the Southern whites themselves. The Republicans were angered; Negroes organized political conventions across the South to demand full civil rights; Confederate Reconstruction was attacked by liberal papers such as Greeley's *Tribune* and E. L. Godkin's *Nation*, and by Radical leaders like Thaddeus Stevens, Wendell Phillips, and W. L. Garrison. Representative Stevens emerged as virtual leader of the nation for two years, using his position on the congressional Joint Committee on Reconstruction. President Johnson blocked a series of countermeasures passed by Congress. His opposition to any practical compromise with the Republicans forced them into taking tougher action, ending up in Johnson's own impeachment trial.

The battle for Negro civil rights: White violence

Confederate Reconstruction was not entirely reactionary or backward-looking. State social reforms were introduced which benefited middle-class and lower-class whites, such as abolition of imprisonment for debt, "stay" laws to delay mortgage foreclosure, and free public

354   The U.S.A.

Thomas Nast attacks Andrew Johnson, I

education. The Johnson states hoped to encourage immigration from Europe to the South. They were ingenious in raising revenues for internal improvements despite the terrible postwar poverty of the South. However, some of these white governments were corrupt, long before the alleged introduction of political corruption by "Black" Reconstruction state governments. More important, the central goal of their policies was to re-enserf and subdue the liberated Negroes. Their Black Codes imposed harsh vagrancy laws and labor regulations on black workers. They restricted black voting rights, jury service, and office-holding. Poll taxes, forced labor on highways, and banning of interracial marriage, dubbed "miscegenation," very clearly expressed the racial attitude of the new governments. Violence against black Freedmen was common in the South. As the civil rights struggle deepened in Congress, the North was shocked by so-called race riots, actually white *pogroms* against blacks, such as those in Memphis in April and May 1866 and New Orleans in July.

In Memphis, tension between black troops and whites led to mob attacks by poor whites and city police on Negro quarters, which were burned and pillaged. Negro churches and schools were set in flames, 46 blacks died including women and children, and over 80 were wounded. In contrast, one white man was injured. Federal troops imposed order on Memphis after three days of chaos. A few weeks later in New Orleans a political struggle over the Negro franchise produced a "riot" which killed 34 blacks and injured about another 200. Four white men, of whom three were Negro sympathizers, lost their lives. The Congressional investigation of the New Orleans election riot exposed police brutality. General Philip Sheridan reported the riot as:

an absolute massacre by the police . . . A murder which the mayor and police . . . perpetrated without the shadow of necessity.

Northern reaction was prompt. Violence did most to harden Northern opposition to Confederate Reconstruction and to Johnson's policies. Since Northerners were themselves ambiguous about the whole question of full Negro civil rights, they had needed some outside force to unite them in a demand that the South, at least, must give the vote to freed slaves. The riots and the more generalized anti-Negro violence and lynching in the South performed this role.

Civil rights amendments

The most notable outcome of Reconstruction was the new radical amending of the constitution. The *13th Amendment* which abolished slavery came into effect in December 1865 after ratification by 27 states. Beyond this move any further step toward progress for Negro Americans was temporarily blocked by the bitter contest between President Johnson and Congress. Johnson stood between the South and a more radical approach to reconstruction, but the Radical Republicans, though never a majority, gained an ever widening segment of Northern and moderate opinion. In February 1866 Congress tried to expand the work of the *Freedmen's Bureau,* a small government agency created in

Thaddeus Stevens

The Bettmann Archive

March 1865 to administer abandoned Confederate lands and to help succor the freed slaves. Johnson vetoed the bill but the enlarged Bureau did become an essential arm of Radical Reconstruction later, after Congress simply revoted the measure.

Andrew Johnson also vetoed the Stevens-Sumner *Civil Rights Act* of 1866, designed to reverse the Supreme Court's Dred Scott decision of 1857 and to give Negroes full U.S. citizenship. Notably, nothing was said at this time about citizenship for the American Indians. Johnson's rhetoric and pro-Southern arguments became legalistic: He opposed the Civil Rights Act on traditional grounds of infringements of states' rights. The Radicals decided it was necessary to settle the issue definitively through a constitutional amendment which would guarantee full citizenship to black Americans.

So was born the famous *14th Amendment,* hammered out in Thaddeus Steven's Joint Committee by the Radicals and first introduced in June 1866. The president immediately opposed the amendment. He took a broad swing through the northern and midwestern states, haranguing crowds in towns like Cleveland with bitter stump speeches. Johnson became somewhat unhinged in these attacks, yelling at the crowds, "Hang Thad Stevens!" It was a strange cry to come from the mouth of a president of the United States. He grossly caricatured the Radicals as bloodthirsty, angry men, bent on vengeance—a caricature which has stuck to them through the ages. Johnson was unable to hide his dislike of Negroes in these wild speeches. Naturally, Southern states were encouraged by Johnson's words to reject the 14th amendment out of hand: only Tennessee ratified it.

Several *northern* states had misgivings over the amendment and about granting full civil rights to Negroes. They delayed ratifying the amendment as long as possible. The measure was felt to be a revolutionary and futile attempt to make the black man the equal to the white by decree, or to be a deliberate trick to help perpetuate the Republican party in office with the aid of Negro votes. Certainly this idea had not escaped some Republican leaders, though the opposite danger was always a possibility—that Southern Negroes would be intimidated by the white elite and vote *Democratic*. The idealistic Thaddeus Stevens, an early abolitionist and one of the minority who wished to go beyond mere emancipation to full civil rights for Freedmen (he was a genuine egalitarian, quite apart from the fact that he loved his black mistress), pointed out with great practicality in January 1867 that the enfranchisement of the Negro could ensure "the ascendancy of the Union party." Give Negroes the vote, Stevens argued, because in the Southern states:

they form the great mass of the loyal men. Possibly with their aid loyal governments may be established. . . . Without it all are sure to be ruled by traitors; and loyal men, black and white, will be oppressed, exiled or murdered.

So the Negro vote would also protect the minority of loyal *white* men in the South against the ex-Confederates and their Northern "Copperhead" supporters. But above all, Stevens argued, Negroes should have the right to vote because "it is just."

At first, however, even the consistent reformer Stevens had hesitated on the voting issue. The value of the vote as a form of political protection was questioned. By 1867 Stevens had thrown off these earlier doubts and saw the right to vote as essential to the whole package of Negro civil rights for which he fought. In his own state of Pennsylvania, where his iron works and his law practice were to be found, Stevens fought against the toughest opposition to the 14th Amendment. He never compromised his moral principles for any self-interest. Gradually the Northern states did ratify the amendment in 1867 and the Radicals determined to force it upon the South as an extra condition for readmission to the Union.

The voting rights provisions of the amendment were not very strong. The *15th Amendment* was adopted in 1870, to make up for this weakness. It said:

The right of citizens of the United States to vote shall not be denied or abridged by the United States or by any State on account of race, color, or previous condition of servitude.

The added amendment was still weak: Negroes were not to be *denied* the right to vote on account of their skin color, but qualifications for voting were still left to the individual states. Negroes were subsequently denied the franchise by a series of devious poll tax laws, by "grandfather clauses" limiting the vote to descendants of the voters of 1867, by intimidation, and by force, sometimes organized by terrorist groups like the Ku Klux Klan, sometimes not.

Election of 1866: The coming of Radical Reconstruction

The Congressional election of 1866 tipped the scales against Andrew Johnson and his Democratic supporters. The Republicans won two thirds of both houses and control of key committees. The Joint Committee on Reconstruction became the true center of political gravity in the nation. For some years the presidential form of government was subverted. The United States was ruled mainly by Congress in a quasi-parliamentary, though largely one-party, system.

The Democratic party did not evaporate; it showed surprising strength in the later elections of 1868 and 1872. The nation was never unquestioningly behind the Republicans, still less behind the Radicals. Northern Democrats had opposed secession, but little more; they hoped to restore the Union "as it was." The Republicans themselves were divided and held together only by Southern violence and stubbornness. Perhaps President Johnson could have done better by exploiting economic issues: the Republicans had passed crucial banking, tariff, and railroad laws, and they feared that this legislation would be overturned if Johnson's Southern members entered Congress. It is unlikely, however, that clever exploitation of this issue could have won elections for Johnson at this time.

Empowered by the electoral mandate of 1866 the Radicals now pushed for what they regarded as true reconstruction. Existing reconstruction was wiped out. No state could be readmitted until it repealed its Black Code, guaranteed voting and office-holding rights to Negroes, and established a state government sufficiently "republican" in nature to satisfy the Joint Committee. All whites who had been in active rebellion during the war were disqualified from office-holding, despite any pardons granted by Lincoln or Johnson. The 14th and 15th Amendments had to be accepted. The political theory of state suicide was now the sole guide to reconstruction policy.

Congress passed the Freedmen's Bureau and Civil Rights bills over Johnson's veto. The first *Reconstruction Act* of March 1867 divided the South into five military districts, each subject to martial law under the command of a general. Existing state governments were abolished except in Tennessee. Conventions were called, based on adult male suffrage, including blacks but still excluding all women, black and white. The Supreme Court tried to oppose the Reconstruction Act so Congress simply withdrew some types of cases from the court's jurisdiction. The Radicals had attacked presidential power and were ready to take on the Supreme Court too.

Impeachment of President Johnson

Andrew Johnson brusquely rejected the Reconstruction Act as a measure "in palpable conflict with the plainest provisions of the Constitution." He accused the Radicals of forcing the franchise on blacks who did not want it and of trying to "Africanize" the South for their own political advantage. But it was far too late for Johnson to pretend to any degree of objectivity on the black civil rights issue.

The same day as the Reconstruction Act was passed over the veto, March 2, 1867, the Radicals took two severe steps to limit executive power. The *Tenure of Office Act* forbade the president from sacking

13 / From slavery to serfdom

Thomas Nast attacks Andrew Johnson, II

officials appointed with the Senate's consent. It strictly reduced his patronage power and his control over his own cabinet personnel. Johnson tested the act by trying to dismiss his War Secretary, E. M. Stanton, who refused to vacate his office. Stanton was a holdover from Lincoln's cabinet, so there was some question whether this contravened the act. Meanwhile the *Command of the Army Act* actually forbade the president from issuing military commands except through General U. S. Grant. His role in making Supreme Court appointments was also questioned. These were deliberate attempts to humiliate the proud and fierce chief executive, who had blankly opposed the Radicals' favorite proposals. Johnson's open encouragement of anti-Negro and anti-Freedmen's Bureau feelings in the South had stirred up the entire Republican party against him.

On February 24, 1868, a historic House resolution called for the impeachment of the president for "high crimes and misdemeanors." Johnson was tried by the Senate, according to Article I, Section 3, of the Constitution and was saved from conviction by only *one* vote short of the necessary two thirds majority. The vote of May 16, 1868, was 35 to 19. Seven Republican senators hesitated to convict Johnson, perhaps because they did not want his potential successor, the acting president of the Senate, Benjamin Wade. As an all-out radical, a feminist, and a labor reformer, Wade was feared by a majority of senators.

The man behind the original House impeachment resolution, Thaddeus Stevens, died in August 1868. Stevens was far ahead of his time as a genuine racial egalitarian. He defended the poor and downtrodden and stood for public education for black and white alike. Stevens pushed the boundaries of American majoritarian democracy outward to new limits. He insisted on being buried in a Negro cemetery. His epitaph read:

> I repose in this quiet and secluded spot
> Not from any natural preference for solitude
> But, finding other Cemeteries limited as to Race
>   by Charter Rules,
> I have chosen this that I might illustrate in my
>   death
> The Principles which I advocated through a long life:
> Equality of Man Before His Creator.

The political arms of the Radicals

Radical Reconstruction had two arms in the South itself: the Freedmen's Bureau and the Union League. The League was political, an extension of the party, working to get out the vote among blacks. It was an early version of the Southern voter-registration drives of the 1960s, though intimidation of black would-be voters was much greater in the 1860s than a century later. It took enormous courage for an ex-slave to stand up and vote. The Union League had branches in many states and was armed with ritual and secrecy; it delivered the Republican vote and managed to muster over 700,000 black voters in time for the 1868 election. It was hoped that this would lay the foundation for Republicanism in the South.

By contrast, the Freedmen's Bureau was a major though short-lived organ of radical social change. It began with measures of war rehabilitation for whites as well as blacks. For example, the Bureau handed out 25,000,000 food rations by 1869; it staffed nearly 50 hospitals by 1867; it reduced the death rate among blacks very sharply.

Negro education

The Bureau's greatest triumph was in public education at all levels for blacks, ranging from night school and Sunday School to college. Hundreds of Northern teachers, usually courageous New England women, descended upon the South to teach the Freedmen. The Negro leader, Booker T. Washington, said it was like witnessing a whole race going to school, young and old alike. The ideal of many older blacks was to be able to *read* the Bible before they died. The black enthusiasm for education was overwhelming, but in 1870 the educational work of the Bureau was terminated. By that date there were over 4,000 schools and nearly a quarter of a million pupils. Black colleges begun in this period included Howard University, Atlanta University, Hampton Institute, and Fisk University, all segregated and many aided by the Bureau directly. Various religious denominations created schools for blacks also. The rule in most of these institutions was a de facto segregation, though not until later, in the 90s, did states in the South openly legislate segregation. Occupied Louisiana and South Carolina had integrated school systems until 1877. Tennessee, admitted as a state because it accepted the 14th Amendment immediately, could afford to create separate schools for blacks and whites as early as 1867. In the North, of course, schools were normally segregated.

Separate or integrated, all schemes to educate the ex-slaves filled Southern whites with horror as a step toward inevitable sexual "amalgamation" and "Africanization" of the South. Public educational facilities for blacks and whites alike remained backward in the South well into the 20th century, owing to unsympathetic public attitudes towards education and a poor tax-base. Poor whites suffered from this backwardness as well as Negroes.

The Freedmen's Bureau also exerted limited judicial powers. It fought for fairness in labor contracts between blacks and white employers. Its chief failure was in the inability to redistribute "abandoned" and confiscated lands to the needy Freedmen. When it did so, the government usually quickly reversed the decision and gave the land back to white owners. Freed slaves were thus left with little means of independent support in the market economy.

The hooded Klan

Southern whites attacked the Bureau and the Union League by fair means and foul. The *Ku Klux Klan* was one of a number of white terrorist groups, usually made up of army veterans, created to maintain white supremacy by frightening the ex-slaves into submission and by intimidating white liberals and sympathizers. The Klan rode at night dressed in white sheets and pointed hoods. They burned down schools and beat up or mutilated Negroes and their friends. Other groups included the Knights of the White Camellia, who were probably larger in number, and many local groups such as the "Rifle Clubs" of South Carolina. It was difficult for federal troops to counter these guerrilla organizations; the soldiers were often sympathetic in any case. Murder and mayhem became the general rule in the South. An angry Congress passed two *Force Acts* in 1870 and 1871, which gave the president extraordinary powers to suspend habeas corpus in order to put down these "armed combinations."

The Klan itself was officially dissolved in 1869. Anti-Negro violence continued for several years despite many arrests and convictions under the Force Acts. The Klan and similar groups could wield political pressure. They helped to push Louisiana into the Democratic camp in 1868 and brought Democrats back into power in Virginia, North Carolina, and Georgia by 1870. Many times federal troops had to apply martial law; hundreds of Negroes were murdered; in 1871 troops intervened in the South 200 times to maintain order. In 1872 they had to take over three cities—Montgomery, Little Rock, and New Orleans—in order to settle violent election riots. A famous Confederate cavalry officer made the white attitude clear—General Nathan Bedford Forrest, a hero of Chickamauga, who was now Grand Wizard of the Klan. Forrest opposed the Radical governor of Tennessee, W. G. "Parson" Brownlow, whose state militia had enlisted black troops. The Klan's aim, said Forrest, was to "kill Radicals." He claimed a Klan membership of over 40,000 in Tennessee in 1868, and 550,000 throughout the South. "I am not an enemy to the negro (*sic*)," said Forrest. "We want him here among us; he is the only laboring class we have . . ."

This Negro, however, was not to be allowed to vote or to enjoy other civil rights in return for his labor. He was to remain a menial at all times.

Black reaction to Reconstruction: What did Freedmen want?

The ex-slaves were not passive or lacking in opinions and aims. What did they want? This is not easy to elucidate since the mass of slaves were kept illiterate and uneducated and were largely inarticulate. At least two indications of their desires are available: first, their remarkable reserve and moderation with the coming of freedom. Emancipation did not bring attacks on the master class or widespread bloodshed, despite the history of intermittent, often bloody, slave uprisings in the South. Abandoned white homes were briefly vandalized in South Carolina and elsewhere by freed slaves. Examples of Negro violence amount to little when compared with the destruction by Sherman's forces and the white attacks on blacks as Union armies approached. Thus the fears of Lincoln's critics that his Emancipation Proclamation would stir up race violence, came to nought. The conservative London *Times* had attacked Lincoln in sex-charged rhetoric (October 7, 1862):

He will appeal to the black blood of the African, he will whisper of the pleasures of spoil and of the gratification of yet fiercer instincts; and when the blood begins to flow and shrieks come piercing through the darkness, Mr. Lincoln will wait till the rising flames tell that all is consummated . . .

The blood did not flow and the Freedmen's calm acceptance of freedom made pure nonsense of the political pornography of the *Times*.

A second indication of the mood of the ex-slaves was their courage in registering to vote, in the face of white intimidation and the obvious return to power of ex-Confederates during presidential reconstruction, and their general enthusiasm to go to the new schools. The *vote* and *education*, many blacks realized, were the keys to future security and progress. After Reconstruction most Negroes were deprived of both. The ex-slaves did not desire to fulfill General Forrest's white Southern dream and become a permanent class of menials, though the failure of Reconstruction and the rise of Populism eventually made them so.

Some field hands immediately gave up working upon receiving news of emancipation. The "day of jubilo" did not bring an end to hard labor for blacks, however. Many had hoped it would bring them a free plot of land per family—a goal shared by very few whites, even among the radical abolitionists. "Forty acres and a mule" proved to be a politically impossible dream.

Why were ex-slaves not given land?

The dream of free land was not impossible economically. The federal government, under the Railroad Act of 1850, gave away many millions of acres to private corporations, including 40,000,000 acres to one company alone—a single grant which would have meant 40 acres each for a million black families. As for the "mule" (or a little working capital), the cotton tax could have been diverted for that use: it yielded about $68,000,000. If this had been done, the entire course of later history for black Americans might have been different.

Thaddeus Stevens fought for the idea, and one ex-slave from Virginia gave testimony to Stevens' Joint Committee on Reconstruction in 1866. Asked if Freedmen were willing to emigrate and leave America, this man, Richard R. Hill, said No.

Question: Are they not willing to be sent back to Africa?
Answer: No, sir. . . . They say that they have lived here all their days and there were stringent laws made to keep them here; and that if they could live here contented as slaves, they can live here when free. . . . if we can get lands here and work and support ourselves, I do not see why we should go to any place that we do not want to go to.

Freedmen, however, were not helped with public lands, though the Freedmen's Bureau was authorized to settle them on forfeited *Confederate* lands.

Under the Homestead Act of 1862 the newly-freed Negroes as well as whites could take up public land through normal channels. The federal government did try to encourage this by placing public lands on the homestead market in the Southern states—Alabama, Mississippi, Arkansas, Louisiana, Florida—regardless of race. Some Freedmen took up these lands, but for successful settlement by Freedmen some *exceptional* treatment of Negroes would be needed—more advice and help with modest capital needs. The white majority did not choose to go that far. A bill by Charles Sumner to give ten acres to every black soldier failed in the Senate in February 1863. Another Radical abolitionist, Wendell Phillips, gave an oft-repeated address, *Amen to the Proclamation*, reiterating the Negro's need for more than mere emancipation. Representative George Julian of Indiana, tough Homestead Act reformer, demanded in 1863 that plantations be confiscated and divided up among Freedmen, rather than sold to land speculators.

One notable experiment was tried in 1863 at Port Royal, South Carolina, on the Sea Islands. Here Negroes took over and redivided confiscated Confederate land with which they were already familiar. They did not have to move further west to homestead strange crops in new terrain. Like other black settlers on such lands, they were soon thrown off, as ex-Confederate owners reasserted their claims and received rapid presidential pardons. The Port Royal plan allowed the military governor to reserve certain tax-delinquent lands for ex-slave families. The bulk were to be sold at public auction, but a group of New England reformers known as *Gideon's Band*—who hoped to remake South Carolina in the image of Massachusetts, with free labor and a mixed economy—went South to organize resistance to auction sales.

Thomas Nast and the Negro, I

The reformers themselves were divided. Some were paternalistic toward the Freedmen and feared that a gift of land would ruin the Negroes; they preferred that a consortium of Northern capitalists should buy the land and employ Negroes to work it by free labor. A group of Boston capitalists led by E. S. Philbrick bought up about 8,000 acres at under $1 an acre and made a huge profit with free black labor in 1863. They touted this success in the Northern press. Other "Gideonites" did not favor this profit-making scheme and like the American Antislavery Society, which was still going strong, demanded outright confiscation and free donation of land to Freedmen. In December 1863 the government allowed Negroes to *preempt* up to 40 acres per family, i.e., settle land adjoining the land they had already bought at $1.25 an acre. The tax commissioners sent to Port Royal to administer the problem disagreed; their deliberate delaying tactics added to the legal confusions. Washington reversed its decision. The outcome was that most of the Confederate lands did go for public auction and the price was driven up by white speculators to as high as $11 an acre on occasion. A mere 2,000 acres went to the Freedmen (at $1.25), who bought it out of pooled savings. There were 15,000 Freedmen on the Islands.

Collapse of Negro land schemes

The Port Royal experiment was confused, divided, and given no real chance to succeed. In 1864 as he advanced to the Georgia-Carolina coast, General Sherman issued his Special Field Order No. 15, setting aside the coastal and river lands up to 30 miles inland, from Charleston to Jacksonville, for segregated black settlement. Forty acres were allowed per family and no whites were to enter the region except on military business. Abolitionists and true egalitarians like W. L. Garrison objected to this segregation, but about 40,000 Negroes had settled the area by June 1865. Their "possessory titles" were then swept aside by returning white owners, and they lost everything. Congress was simply not ready to wipe out private property rights, even of ex-rebels.

The land schemes were allowed to collapse (they cannot be said to have "failed") for a complex of reasons. Many whites thought the freed slaves were not competent to work independent farms by themselves. They confused illiteracy with farming skills. There was little evidence for the argument—after all, slave labor had built up the King Cotton economy; many slave cabins had their plots for household crops; slaves had good, all-round country knowledge, and many of them were local craftsmen and artisans, who kept the well-nigh self-sufficient plantations going. In this pre-factory stage of the South's economic development, the region might have become partly one of small farmers, living on a modest but ample subsistence level, a *black* Jeffersonian Dream come true.

Larger economic issues, such as what would have happened to the cotton export crop, are more difficult to estimate. The argument of slave incompetence was a weak one, however. More logical was the desire to protect private property (of whites); but this could only apply to confiscated or temporarily abandoned Confederate lands and does not explain why more was not done to encourage Negro homesteading. Many white reformers drew back from giving exceptional privileges to freed Negroes; like true Romantic reformers they only wished to make the slave free, then leave him to run the American individualistic race. This would have meant running the gauntlet, as more radical and far-sighted reformers, like Stevens and Sumner, realized. As late as 1880, the well-known ex-slave, Frederick Douglass, complained about land policy:

> Could the nation have been induced to listen to those stalwart Republicans, Thaddeus Stevens and Charles Sumner, some of the evils which we now suffer would have been averted. The Negro today would not be on his knees, as he is, supplicating the old master-class to give him leave to toil..

With an adequate land-grant policy for Freedmen the transition from legal slavery to de facto serfdom would not have happened in the postwar South.

As Wendell Phillips said in lectures in 1863–64:

> The Negro has *earned* land, education, rights. Before we leave him, we ought to leave him on his own soil, in his own house, with the right to the ballot and the schoolhouse within his reach.

Too few whites agreed with this outlook.

Election of 1868: The 15th Amendment and women's rights

The Republicans were wary of the issue of the Negro vote, at least until they had secured a party mandate by the election of Grant to the presidency in 1868. Northern states were slow to give the vote to blacks: in the state elections of 1867 Negro suffrage candidates lost in Minnesota, Ohio, Kansas, Connecticut, and New York. In the Southern states, ironically, the Reconstruction Act imposed Negro voting. The Republican party decided to endorse the 15th Amendment despite the risk of a political backlash from Northern white voters. The safe election to the White House of a Republican war hero, General U. S. Grant, assured general acceptance of the voting rights amendment. Grant was a moderate and a known conciliator. The high tide of Republican Radicalism had turned. Grant's electoral college margin was wide, 214 to 80, though his popular vote was less definitive, 3,013,421 to 2,706,829. His victory was certainly aided by the 700,000 Negro voters. The continuing strength of the Democrats however should have been a warning to the victors.

The 15th Amendment left a large loophole by which individual states could subvert its spirit and aim. They could limit the vote of both blacks and poor whites, maintaining power safely in the hands of the Southern upper classes and planter elite. For the women's movement the amendment was a major setback and bitter disappointment. After all their years of leadership in reform activities since the 1830s, women were now abandoned in their own struggle by the male radicals. No provision was made in the amendment to protect the rights of women to vote. This lost opportunity, unnoticed by the majority of

Americans, male and female, set back the women's cause for half a century. As for Negro Americans themselves, the voting rights amendment remained a paper agreement until the 1960s.

Strange death of Reconstruction

Conservative strength in the South grew steadily from 1870. The conservatives were determined never to give way on white supremacy and restriction of Negro civil rights. They combined political organization, economic pressure, and violence against Negroes. They opposed the government through organized tax-resistance. This *Counter-Reconstruction* paid off and helped to reduce Reconstruction to a shambles throughout the South. The Republicans fought a losing battle in this respect. Though no candidate could have defeated Grant in 1872, the party did split, a reformist Liberal Republican faction being led by the erratic but well-known liberal editor, Horace Greeley. Supported by a mixed bag of Eastern and Western reformers, free traders, and protectionists, such as David A. Wells, C. F. Adams, Ignatius Donnelly, and Carl Schurz, the once-intransigent abolitionist Greeley now campaigned for national unity and forgiveness, a handclasp across the "bloody chasm" of war. Greeley personally signed the bail bond for the release of Jefferson Davis. With Grant's reelection the Liberal Republican party fell apart.

The presidential election of 1876 was disputed. The Democrats thought they had captured the White House at last, with the victory of the reform mayor from New York City, Samuel J. Tilden. Despite his popular vote majority of 250,000 however, Tilden's electoral college total in the South came under scrutiny. The issue was fine: a question of *one* vote. An electoral commission gave the White House to his Republican opponent, Rutherford B. Hayes of Ohio. The Southerners were apparently won over to this decision by the promise of a speedy end to Reconstruction. The federal occupation of South Carolina and Louisiana came to an end in April 1877.

The termination of Reconstruction had long been in sight. After 1875 the "Shot Gun" or "Mississippi" Plan spread in the South: the Mississippi white conservatives rejected caution and abandoned any hopes of winning over the freed blacks by allowing them minimal rights under a paternalistic system. Poor economic conditions after the Panic of 1873 helped this conservative revolution along. A so-called riot in Vicksburg in December 1874 brought the death of two whites and 35 blacks. Physical intimidation of Republicans and their supporters produced a Democratic resurgence in the state. Federal protection was entirely lacking. Grant and his party took no steps and Mississippi's example was quickly copied.

So after 1876 the misnamed "Redeemer" governments of white supremacists took over the Southern states. The great social advances of the Reconstruction years were largely repudiated. Blacks and poorer whites were left to fend for themselves. The return of the planter oligarchy assured the survival of the modified plantation system with *peon*-type labor, tied to the soil by ignorance (the schools were now closed), by debt, and by intimidation. The *sharecropping system* was a form of neo-serfdom: the planter and farmer provided tools, seed and other necessities, and the poor-white and Negro croppers worked the soil but gave a large portion of the crop to the master. Sharecroppers had no choice of what crops to cultivate and they never got out of debt. Thus the slave had become a debt-serf. Other forms of indebtedness included the *crop-lien system,* in which poor farmers borrowed on the future crop. Such techniques for meeting the desperate shortage of liquid capital, and the inability of Freedmen to pay for the land, retarded the progress of the Southern regional economy for another 75 years. Of course, they were also means of labor control and social submission of Negroes.

Why did the North acquiesce?

Economic interest is often cited for the North's acceptance of this state of affairs and its abandonment of the Negro. Business interests in the North were very divergent and not at all monolithic, and there was no *united* effort to exploit the Southern economy during or after Radical Reconstruction; but many Northerners recognized the profit potential in Southern investments all the same. This recognition stretched even to reformers like Philbrick of Gideon's Band. Also, the reform editor Greeley did not limit his editorials to advising Americans to "Go West, young man!"; he pushed for northern "colonization" of the South and sold the advantages of states like North Carolina (cheap land, "docile" labor, good timber), South Carolina (textiles), and Tennessee (iron, coal, zinc, copper). Greeley was frank in his hot opposition to the Radicals whose vindictive anti-Southern policies, he claimed, were driving away valuable business. Economic investment by the North would not only bring development and profits but would "Republicanize" the South. Certainly in the years that followed Northern investments did increase in the South, though the nation was chiefly taken up by the industrialization of the Northeast and Midwest and the drive to the West. Even the Supreme Court, for one telling example, spent much of its time on economic cases.

Republican ideology contained distinct weaknesses. Their 19th-century distrust of central power and sympathy for local rights, and their skepticism regarding Negro equality with the white man, were *two* of them. After all, the conventional wisdom, 19th-century science, and experience did not seem to support the idea that the Negro was merely a white in black-colored skin. Lacking scientific proof, white men, North and South, remained fundamentally racist. Also, Republicans were not ready to sacrifice local self-government, a treasured liberal principle, and to exert the *continuous* federal pressure that it would have taken to safeguard Negro civil rights throughout the period. The growth of central prerogatives through civil war powers and war financing already scared many liberals. They could not go along with the Stevens-Sumner demands that the full force of the federal branch be used to guarantee Negro rights and nondiscrimination at the polls, in education, and in all public places. Why select Negroes alone for this special protection? Stevens and Sumner were now both dead. Laissez-faire, local rights, and the principle of private property were all at stake, and Negroes lost in this tug-of-war.

Myths of Reconstruction

The Reconstruction era is shrouded in myths. First, the extent of Radical Reconstruction has been exaggerated and the length of time and the degree of military occupation of the South overstated. Actual federal troop strengths were negligible, especially in contrast with the rising violence of these years in the South. Federal soldiers were kept out of the way in their barracks and inadequate federal protection led to greater dependence on state militias, which did enlist some black troops. They were hated and often murdered in their uniforms by whites. But the South was never dominated by black or white Union forces.

Among the three groups credited with Radical Reconstruction—the blacks, the *Carpetbaggers* from the North, and the Southern white *Scalawags* who cooperated with Radicals—the last were the largest in number. But the Scalawags were not white ruffians and traitors who sided with blacks and Northerners for private profit; they were often Southern Whigs, pro-Union Democrats who opposed secession but did not oppose slavery itself during the war. Usually they represented whites other than the rich planter class and they looked toward a more democratic, middle-class South. Andrew Johnson shared these ideas, which lingered on after Reconstruction in aspects of Southern Populism.

The Carpetbaggers, though not all made up of pure-minded, idealists of the more modern "Peace Corps" type, did include respectable Northern businessmen seeking legitimate investments, together with Union veterans and federal employees who decided to settle in the South, schoolteachers committed to Negro education, and a few Northern Negroes intent on reform. The Carpetbaggers, despite their bad reputation, did much to diversify and strengthen the economy of the area—like the two men from Ohio, Captain H. S. Chamberlain and General J. T. Wilder, who stayed on to develop coal and iron plants in Tennessee. The average Carpetbagger, though accused of trying to "Africanize" the South, was racially conservative, like most Scalawags, and would go no further than enfranchising the Negro. The black vote was conceded on pragmatic grounds alone, to buttress the Republican party in the South. Carpetbaggers, like investors and entrepreneurs throughout history, stood chiefly for law and order.

As for the blacks, there was no real Black Reconstruction, as the Negro leader W. E. B. Du Bois pointed out decades ago. Negroes did not win control of any single state government during Reconstruction, not even in South Carolina where they outnumbered whites in the lower house, or in Mississippi, where blacks outnumbered whites in the state population. The 16 blacks who served in Congress down through the early 1880s scarcely made a "Black" government out of Washington.

As a group, black politicians were not illiterate, uncouth, self-seeking ruffians. They were self-educated and usually they were ministers or teachers. They represented varied economic interests, normally quite conservative in tone. They were conciliators, choosing to work within the system, even on behalf of the re-enfranchisement of ex-Confederate whites. They did not demand racial integration, still less intermarriage, the two deep fears of white supremacists, though they occasionally opposed segregation in public schools. Du Bois quoted an English observer, Sir George Campbell, on the essential moderation of these Freedmen politicians:

> The white serfs of European countries took hundreds of years to rise to the level which these Negroes adopted in America.

The three groups were at loggerheads with each other in Reconstruction. No single, unified Radical policy existed. "Negro rule" was a myth. For some whites the sight of Negroes voting and holding office was a terrible shock, though in fact under one fifth of the nation's Negroes registered to vote. Also the new candor in black-white relationships and the rejection of the countless minor regulations of Negro social conduct in dress and deportment must have seemed like a great social upheaval to the supremacists.

Was Radical Reconstruction "corrupt"?

Some Reconstruction state governments were corrupted. Yet political corruption began long before, during the period of white Confederate Reconstruction, and it was rife *nationally* during this Gilded Age. Rapid economic growth, federal bond issues, and hasty railroad financing, encouraged a relaxation of morality in public and business affairs. Political machines in northern cities were more corrupt than Reconstruction governments in the South, and huge scandals like Crédit Mobilier (railroads) and the Whisky Ring belittled Reconstruction stories. Yet the traditional image of Radical Reconstruction long remained the drunken Negro politician, rolling a whiskey barrel out of a state Capitol. This sort of propaganda against the social revolution that the Radicals aimed for was very effective.

The partly bogus issue of corruption obscures the genuine problem faced by Reconstruction states: how to finance state government in an impoverished region. The wartime destruction of tax-producing property and a general low tax-base in an agrarian society, together with massive need for public spending on highways, buildings, and internal improvements produced a financial crisis. Necessary transportation improvements and repairs and public welfare and education took large sums of money. White conservatives were reluctant to pay taxes, especially since the tax rates were now uniformly assessed and no longer favored the planters as they had before the war. In view of these problems the achievements of Reconstruction government were considerable.

Why did Reconstruction fail?

Ultimately Reconstruction failed as a revolution in the South because it did not create the *permanent* institutions that would be needed to sustain its work, apart from the new state constitutions. The South

Thomas Nast and the Negro, II

needed a permanent Freedmen's Bureau, a national school system for blacks, and a host of supportive institutions. These would include savings banks, black building and loan associations, social settlements, and a special labor office for Negro placement. In the atmosphere of the day there was no chance for such a comprehensive reform plan.

The Supreme Court lent its prestige to the policy of Negro abandonment by refusing to protect black Americans from Jim Crow segregation laws in the 1870s, by wiping out Civil Rights Acts in the cases of 1883, and by inventing the convenient legal doctrine of "separate but equal" as an excuse for segregated schools and public facilities in 1896. White supremacy received the Court's sanction.

Above all, Reconstruction did not fully succeed because it did not last long enough. It takes a great time to "reconstruct" the way of life of an entire region and subculture. In this sense, at least, the Radicals were correct in demanding a long period of Territorial status for the ex-rebel states. In many ways Reconstruction did not fail, any more than did the land settlement schemes that were a brief part of it. It was deliberately *destroyed*. The white South never fully accepted defeat after the war and remained staunchly unreconstructed. Southerners successfully resisted: by use of political organization and pressure (with a divided Republican ideology and a strong Democratic party), with the support of local bastions of economic power and social prestige, by passive resistance, and by open violence.

Southern cultural nationalism

The whole edifice was supported by and suffused with a well-developed Southern ideology, expressed in verse, letters, novels, and popular thought. Before the war, poets like Henry Timrod of South Carolina had used nationalist themes, but it was after the conflict that the Southern myth was created. The "Cavalier" South, the Southern lady, the cultured elite, the Big House, the happy slave, the cohesive, meaningful society—these fictions became realities in the minds of most white Southerners. Cultural nationalism survived down through the 20th century, along with the Confederate flag and rebel yells.

The other tradition in Southern letters, that of failure, despair, frustration and rural poverty, was kept alive in the richer works of Ellen Glasgow, Thomas Wolfe, William Faulkner, and more recently, Robert Penn Warren. The first three were born, respectively, in 1874, 1897, and 1900; they did not live through the Civil War and Reconstruction, and though they were not exactly popular writers, their greater realism should have balanced the distorted image that the South had of its own past. The image survived because it served a clear political purpose.

Earlier writers like George Washington Cable (born in 1844) and Joel Chandler Harris (born in 1848) stand out among a host of lesser romanticizers and distorters. Cable depicted New Orleans and its rigid caste society and was driven into exile in Massachusetts. Harris created a whole semi-folk world of the Uncle Remus and Brer Rabbit stories of Negro and poor-white life. In Harris the underdog often comes out on top in various life situations.

From the viewpoint of social and economic progress, Southern cultural nationalism, like some sorts of nationalism elsewhere in world history, was a retarding factor. The return to power of the conservative white Redeemer governments in 1876–77 was no real victory for the South as a region. Traditionalism and class locked the section in the grip of rural poverty and economic backwardness for years to come. Cultural nationalism might have helped to give the Southerners an identity and a pride, but did little for the poor whites and Negroes. Meanwhile mass immigration, the westward movement, and industrialization were enriching the rest of the nation. Could the South share in this growth?

The Redeemers and the New South

The Redeemer governments allowed the plantation system to reassert its authority in the Southern states, but the Redeemers themselves tended to be businessmen and industrialists rather than planters. Georgia in the 70s and 80s, for example, was politically dominated by railroad, coal, and iron masters, while Mississippi was governed by corporate lawyers. The Redeemers were not wholly "Bourbons" in their aim and character and at first they sometimes invited Negro political support. They stood between the Radical years of Reconstruction in Negro history and the tragic years of Negro-baiting which were still to come. Complete disfranchisement of blacks did not occur immediately after Reconstruction but was delayed until the 1890s. Sometimes the black vote was used by Democratic state governors, like Wade Hampton of South Carolina, who gave public jobs to Freedmen in return for political support.

Essentially the new Redeemer governments stood for laissez-faire in most matters: tax-cutting, encouragement to industries such as railroads, public utilities, and textile mills, and reduced powers of government. These policies encouraged those Southern dreamers who had long demanded an economically diversified "New" South, no longer dependent on the export of staple crops to the Northeast and to Europe. They wanted a Southern urban civilization with mills, mines, factories, and railroads. City newspapers pushed the New South idea, especially the Atlantic *Constitution*, edited by Henry W. Grady. In 1886 Grady delivered a speech in New York City entitled "The New South":

> The Old South rested everything on slavery and agriculture, unconscious that these could neither give nor maintain healthy growth. The New South presents a perfect democracy, the oligarchs leading in the popular movement . . . a hundred farms for every plantation, fifty homes for every palace; and a diversified industry that meets the complex needs of this complex age.

Grady wanted Northerners to invest in the South; the race problem could safely be left in Southern white hands.

During the late-1800s some industry did move South: iron and steel to Birmingham, Alabama, for example, and textile mills to the southeast. Yet the region remained relatively backward well into the next century; it was underdeveloped and with a status of neocolonialism, still serving Northeastern masters and foreign nations as a supplier of raw materials and semifinished goods.

Control of blacks in the New South: The Supreme Court

The Supreme Court buttressed white supremacy in the South with a series of decisions. In *U.S.* v. *Reese* (1876) the Court crippled the Force Acts. In *Hall* v. *De Cuir* (1878) the justices struck down a Louisiana state law that forbade discrimination in transportation, calling it an illegal interference with Congressional authority over interstate commerce. Anti-Negro decisions came swiftly in the 1880s. The case of *U.S.* v. *Harris* (1883) argued that the lynching of four Negroes by a white mob was a matter beyond the Court's jurisdiction because it was committed by individuals, not by the state. The infamous *Civil Rights Cases* of 1883 virtually wiped out the Civil Rights Act of 1875, which had banned segregation in transportation and public accommodation. Justice Bradley argued:

The U.S.A.

It would be running the slavery argument into the ground to make it apply to every act of discrimination which a person may see fit to make as to the guests he will entertain, or as to the people he will take into his coach or cab or car, or admit to the concert or theater . . .

Finally, in *Plessy* v. *Ferguson* in 1896 the legal doctrine of "separate but equal" was invented to justify segregated facilities for Negroes. One strict constructionist, Justice J. M. Harlan, strongly dissented from this legalized racism, declaring:

The destinies of the two races in this country are indissolubly linked together. . . . What can more certainly arouse race hate . . . than state enactments which in fact proceed on the ground that colored citizens are so inferior and degraded that they cannot be allowed to sit in public coaches occupied by white citizens?

Segregation rules became general in the South in the 1890s. They were called derisively "Jim Crow" laws, after a minstrel character created by a black-faced white entertainer, Thomas D. Rice of New York. Along with segregation came disfranchisement. For a short time during the 1890s the advent of Populism and farm reform movements of blacks and whites alike, in response to depression conditions, brought the possibility of black-white cooperation among poorer farmers in the South. Populist agitators like Tom Watson of Georgia frightened the conservatives by appealing to Negroes for support. White Democrats revived the race-scare and Negroes were rapidly disfranchised in a series of state laws, poll taxes, literacy requirements, and other tricks. The Negro lost his vote in Mississippi (1890), South Carolina (1895), and in other states. The status of black Americans reached its lowest ebb by the time of World War I.

Dr. George Washington Carver, 1864–1943, American scientist

Library of Congress

Black accommodation: Booker T. Washington

The chief black spokesman of these increasingly harsh years was Booker T. Washington (1856–1915). His theme was sheer survival for Negroes. He counseled his brothers to accept a policy of accommodation: voluntary segregation, Negro self-help, and emphasis on acquiring manual and trade skills, while going along with white policies. Washington addressed a white audience at the Atlanta Cotton States Exposition of 1895, the first time a black was allowed to share a public platform with whites in the South. This ex-slave and principal of an industrial training school for Negroes, Tuskegee Institute, told the whites that accommodation was the only answer for blacks. Southern whites should not seek the immigration of white European labor but should depend on Negroes. Blacks in turn should abandon claims of political or social equality and become good skilled workers. He argued:

We shall prosper in proportion as we learn to dignify and glorify common labor. . . . No race can prosper till it learns that there is as much dignity in tilling a field as in writing a poem. It is at the bottom of life we must begin, and not at the top . . .

Booker T. Washington is often accused of selling his people short by demanding that they become good laborers. In his day, however, they *were* mainly laborers, and his argument taught them race-pride—laborers were as good as poets. Washington continued:

The wisest of my race understand that the agitation of questions of social equality is the extremest folly . . . The opportunity to earn a dollar in a factory just now is worth infinitely more than the opportunity to spend a dollar in an opera house.

His appeal to the dignity of labor was Jeffersonian and religious. His policy in this famous *Atlanta Compromise* speech was pragmatic and tied to the local situation. Yet it also seemed to accept white prejudices. For Washington, accommodation was a purely temporary policy; for the whites who enjoyed his address it was permanent. Other Negro leaders attacked Washington as an "Uncle Tom." Bishop Henry M. Turner, a black nationalist who wanted to start a colony in Africa, said that "a man who loves a country that hates him" was contemptible. W. E. Burghardt Du Bois (1869–1963), the gifted black historian and writer with a Ph.D. from Harvard, whose career spans black history down to the 1960s, bitterly opposed Washington's position.

In his *The Souls of Black Folk* (1903) Du Bois emphasized activism instead of accommodation, liberal arts higher education for blacks rather than mere trade schools, race-pride instead of servility to whites, political and social demands instead of purely economic advances for Negro Americans. Du Bois helped to create the nationalist *Niagara Movement* in 1905, which demanded the right to vote, the abolition of segregation and race distinctions, and complete freedom of expression for all blacks. In 1909 Du Bois also helped to found the *National Association for the Advancement of Colored People* (NAACP).

Booker T.
Washington

Library of Congress

In national politics and in the Republican party, however, it was Booker T. Washington who exercised influence on behalf of blacks. He controlled the small number of patronage posts open to Negroes and administered whatever funds were spent on black causes. Despite the strict limitations of his accommodation policy, Washington managed to keep alive a modest participation by blacks in American public life during this tragic period of Negro neo-serfdom.

Bibliography John Hope Franklin. *Reconstruction, After the Civil War.* University of Chicago Press, 1961.

Fawn Brodie. *Thaddeus Stevens, Scourge of the South.* New York: Norton, 1966.

W. R. Brock. *An American Crisis: Congress and Reconstruction.* New York: Harper, 1963.

R. P. Sharkey. *Money, Class and Party.* Baltimore: Johns Hopkins University Press, 1967.

J. M. McPherson. *The Struggle for Equality.* Princeton University Press, 1964.

Useful readings are: Charles Crowe (ed.). *Age of Civil War and Reconstruction, 1830–1900.* rev. ed. Homewood, Ill.: The Dorsey Press, 1975.

Appendixes

Appendix A: The Declaration of Independence

THE UNANIMOUS DECLARATION OF THE THIRTEEN UNITED STATES OF AMERICA

When, in the Course of human events, it becomes necessary for one people to dissolve the political bands which have connected them with another, and to assume, among the Powers of the earth, the separate and equal station to which the Laws of Nature and of Nature's God entitle them, a decent respect to the opinions of mankind requires that they should declare the causes which impel them to the separation.

We hold these truths to self-evident, that all men are created equal, that they are endowed by their Creator with certain unalienable Rights, that among these, are Life, Liberty, and the pursuit of Happiness. That, to secure these rights, Governments are instituted among Men, deriving their just Powers from the consent of the governed. That, whenever any form of Government becomes destrustive of these ends, it is the Right of the People to alter or to abolish it, and to institute new Government, laying its foundation on such Principles, and organizing its Powers in such form, as to them shall seem most likely to effect their Safety and Happiness. Prudence, indeed, will dictate that Governments long established should not be changed for light and transient causes; and, accordingly, all experience hath shewn, that mankind are more disposed to suffer, while evils are sufferable, than to right themselves by abolishing the forms to which they are accustomed. But, when a long train of abuses and usurpations, pursuing invariably the same Object, evinces a design to reduce them under absolute Despotism, it is their right, it is their duty, to throw off such Government, and to provide new Guards for their future Security. Such has been the patient sufferance of these Colonies; and such is now the necessity which constrains them to alter their former Systems of Government. The history of the present King of Great Britain is a history of repeated injuries and usurpations, all having in direct object the establishment of an absolute Tyranny over these States. To prove this, let Facts be submitted to a candid world.

He has refused his Assent to Laws the most wholesome and necessary for the public good.

He has forbidden his Governors to pass Laws of immediate and pressing importance, unless suspended in their operation till his Assent should be obtained; and when so suspended, he has utterly neglected to attend to them.

He has refused to pass other Laws for the accommodation of large districts of People, unless those People would relinquish the right of Representation in the legislature; a right inestimable to them and formidable to tyrants only.

He has called together legislative bodies at places unusual, uncomfortable, and distant from the depository of their Public Records, for the sole Purpose of fatiguing them into compliance with his measures.

He has dissolved Representative Houses repeatedly, for opposing, with manly firmness, his invasions on the rights of the People.

He has refused for a long time, after such dissolutions, to cause others to be elected; whereby the Legislative Powers, incapable of

Annihilation, have returned to the People at large for their exercise; the State remaining in the mean time exposed to all the dangers of invasion from without, and convulsions within.

He has endeavoured to prevent the Population of these States; for that purpose obstructing the Laws for Naturalization of Foreigners; refusing to pass others to encourage their migrations hither, and raising the conditions of new Appropriations of Lands.

He has obstructed the Administration of Justice, by refusing his Assent to Laws for establishing Judiciary Powers.

He has made Judges dependent on his Will alone, for the tenure of their offices, and the amount and payment of their salaries.

He has erected a multitude of New Offices, and sent hither swarms of Officers to harrass our People, and eat out their substance.

He has kept among us, in times of Peace, Standing Armies, without the Consent of our legislatures.

He has affected to render the Military independent of and superior to the Civil Power.

He has combined with others to subject us to a jurisdiction foreign to our constitution, and unacknowledged by our laws; giving his Assent to their Acts of pretended Legislation:

For quartering large bodies of armed troops among us:

For protecting them, by a mock Trial, from Punishment for any Murders which they should commit on the Inhabitants of these States:

For cutting off our Trade with all parts of the world:

For imposing Taxes on us without our Consent:

For depriving us, in many cases, of the benefits of Trial by Jury:

For transporting us beyond Seas to be tried for pretended offences:

For abolishing the free System of English Laws in a neighbouring province, establishing therein an Arbitrary government, and enlarging its Boundaries, so as to render it at once an example and fit instrument for introducing the same absolute rule into these Colonies:

For taking away our Charters, abolishing our most valuable Laws, and altering fundamentally the Forms of our Governments:

For suspending our own Legislatures, and declaring themselves invested with Power to legislate for us in all cases whatsoever.

He has abdicated Government here, by declaring us out of his protection, and waging War against us.

He has plundered our seas, ravaged our Coasts, burnt our towns, and destroyed the Lives of our People.

He is at this time transporting large Armie of foreign Mercenaries to compleat the works of death, desolation and tyranny, already begun with circumstances of Cruelty and perfidy scarcely paralleled in the most barbarous ages, and totally unworthy the Head of a civilized nation.

He has constrained our fellow Citizens, taken Captive on the high Seas, to bear Arms against their Country, to become the executioners of their friends and Brethren, or to fall themselves by their Hands.

He has excited domestic insurrections amongst us, and has endeavoured to bring on the inhabitants of our frontiers, the merciless Indian Savages, whose known rule of warfare, is an undistinguished destruction of all ages, sexes and conditions.

In every stage of these Oppressions, We have Petitioned for Redress, in the most humble terms: Our repeated Petitions, have been answered only by repeated injury. A Prince, whose character is thus marked by every act which may define a Tyrant, is unfit to be the ruler of a free People.

Nor have We been wanting in attentions to our British brethren. We have warned them from time to time of attempts by their legislature to extend an unwarrantable jurisdiction over us. We have reminded them of the circumstances of our emigration and settlement here. We have appealed to their native justice and magnanimity, and we have conjured them by the ties of our common kindred, to disavow these usurpations, which, would inevitably interrupt our connexions and correspondence. They too have been deaf to the voice of justice and consanguinity. We must, therefore, acquiesce in the necessity, which denounces our Separation, and hold them, as we hold the rest of mankind, Enemies in war, in Peace Friends.

WE, THEREFORE, the Representatives of the UNITED STATES OF AMERICA, in GENERAL CONGRESS assembled, appealing to the Supreme Judge of the World for the rectitude of our intentions, DO, in the Name, and by Authority of the good People of these Colonies, solemnly PUBLISH and DECLARE, That these United Colonies are, and of Right, ought to be FREE AND INDEPENDENT STATES; that they are Absolved from all Allegiance to the British Crown, and that all political connexion between them and the State of Great Britain, is and ought to be totally dissolved; and that, as FREE AND INDEPENDENT STATES, they have full Power to levy War, conclude Peace, contract Alliances, establish Commerce, and to do all other Acts and Things which INDEPENDENT STATES may of right do. AND for the support of this Declaration, with a firm reliance on the protection of divine Providence, we mutually pledge to each other our Lives, our Fortunes, and our sacred Honour.

Appendix B: The Constitution of the United States

PREAMBLE

We the People of the United States, in Order to form a more perfect Union, establish Justice, insure domestic Tranquility, provide for the common defence, promote the general Welfare, and secure the Blessings of Liberty to ourselves and our Posterity, do ordain and establish this Constitution for the United States of America.

ARTICLE I

Section 1 All legislative Powers herein granted shall be vested in a Congress of the United States, which shall consist of a Senate and House of Representatives.

Section 2 The House of Representatives shall be composed of Members chosen every second Year by the People of the several States, and the Electors in each State shall have the Qualifications requisite for Electors of the most numerous Branch of the State Legislature.

No Person shall be a Representative who shall not have attained to the Age of twenty five Years, and been seven Years a Citizen of the United States, and who shall not, when elected be an inhabitant of that State in which he shall be chosen.

Representatives and direct Taxes shall be apportioned among the several States which may be included within this Union, according to their respective Numbers, [which shall be determined by adding to the whole Number of free Persons including those bound to Service for a Term of Years, and excluding Indians not taxed, three fifths of all other Persons.][1] The actual Enumeration shall be made within three Years after the first Meeting of the Congress of the United States, and within every subsequent Term of ten Years, in such Manner as they shall by law direct. The Number of Representatives shall not exceed one for every thirty Thousand, but each State shall have at Least one Representative; and until such enumeration shall be made, the State of New Hampshire shall be entitled to chuse three, Massachusetts eight, Rhode-Island and Providence Plantations one, Connecticut five, New-York six, New Jersey four, Pennsylvania eight, Delaware one, Maryland six, Virginia ten, North Carolina five, South Carolina five, and Georgia three.

When vacancies happen in the Representation from any State, the Executive Authority thereof shall issue Writs of Election to fill such Vacancies.

The House of Representatives shall chuse their Speaker and other Officers; and shall have the sole Power of Impeachment.

Section 3 The Senate of the United States shall be composed of two Senators from each State, [chosen by the Legislature thereof,][2] for six Years; and each Senator shall have one Vote.

Immediately after they shall be assembled in Consequence of the first Election, they shall be divided as equally as may be into three Classes. The Seats of the Senators of the first Class shall be vacated at the Expiration of the second Year, of the second Class at the Expiration of the fourth Year, and of the third Class at the Expiration of the sixth Year, so that one third may be chosen every second Year; [and if Vacancies happen by

---

[1] Superseded by the Fourteenth Amendment.

[2] Superseded by the Seventeenth Amendment.

Resignation, or otherwise, during the Recess of the Legislature of any State, the Executive thereof may make temporary Appointments until the next Meeting of the Legislature, which shall then fill such Vacancies.][3]

No Person shall be a Senator who shall not have attained to the Age of thirty Years, and been nine Years a Citizen of the United States, and who shall not, when elected, be an Inhabitant of that State for which he shall be chosen.

The Vice President of the United States shall be President of the Senate, but shall have no Vote, unless they are equally divided.

The Senate shall chuse their other Officers, and also a President pro tempore, in the Absence of the Vice President, or when he shall exercise the Office of President of the United States.

The Senate shall have the sole Power to try all Impeachments. When sitting for that Purpose, they shall be on Oath or Affirmation. When the President of the United States is tried, the Chief Justice shall preside: and no Person shall be convicted without the Concurrence of two thirds of the Members present.

Judgment in Cases of Impeachment shall not extend further than to removal from Office, and disqualification to hold and enjoy any Office of honor, Trust or Profit under the United States: but the Party convicted shall nevertheless be liable and subject to Indictment, Trial, Judgment and Punishment, according to Law.

Section 4 The Times, Places and Manner of holding Elections for Senators and Represenatives, shall be prescribed in each State by the Legislature thereof; but the Congress may at any time by Law make or alter such Regulations, except as to the Places of chusing Senators.

[The Congress shall assemble at least once in every Year, and such Meeting shall be on the first Monday in December, unless they shall by Law appoint a different Day.][4]

Section 5 Each House shall be the Judge of the Elections, Returns and Qualifications of its own Members, and a Majority of each shall constitute a Quorum to do Business; but a smaller Number may adjourn from day to day, and may be authorized to compel the Attendance of absent Members, in such Manner, and under such Penalties as each House may provide.

Each House may determine the Rules of its Proceedings, punish its Members for disorderly Behaviour, and, with the Concurrence of two thirds, expel a Member.

Each House shall keep a Journal of its Proceedings, and from time to time publish the same, excepting such Parts as may in their Judgment require Secrecy; and the Yeas and Nays of the Members of either House on any question shall, at the Desire of one fifth of those Present, be entered on the Journal.

Neither House, during the Session of Congress, shall, without the Consent of the other, adjourn for more than three days, nor to any other Place than that in which the two Houses shall be sitting.

Section 6 The Senators and Representatives shall receive a Compensation for their Services, to be ascertained by Law, and paid out of the Treasury of the United States. They shall in all Cases, except Treason, Felony and Breach of the Peace, be privileged from Arrest during their Attendance at the Session of their respective Houses, and in going to and returning from the same; and for any Speech or Debate in either House, they shall not be questioned in any other Place.

No Senator or Representative shall, during the Time for which he was elected, be appointed to any civil Office under the Authority of the United States, which shall have been created, or the Emoluments whereof shall have been encreased during such time; and no Person holding any Office under the United States, shall be a Member of either House during his Continuance in Office.

Section 7 All bills for raising Revenue shall originate in the House of Representatives; but the Senate may propose or concur with Amendments as on other Bills.

Every Bill which shall have passed the House of Representatives and the Senate, shall, before it becomes a Law, be presented to the President of the United States; If he approve he shall sign it, but if not he shall return it, with his Objections to that House in which it shall have originated, who shall

---

[3] Modified by the Seventeenth Amendment.
[4] Superseded by the Twentieth Amendment.

enter the Objections at large on their Journal, and proceed to reconsider it. If after such Reconsideration two thirds of that House shall agree to pass the Bill, it shall be sent, together with the Objections, to the other House, by which it shall likewise be reconsidered, and if approved by two thirds of that House, it shall become a Law. But in all such Cases the Votes of both Houses shall be determined by yeas and Nays, and the Names of the Persons voting for and against the Bill shall be entered on the Journal of each House respectively. If any Bill shall not be returned by the President within ten Days (Sundays excepted) after it shall have been presented to him, the Same shall be a Law, in like Manner as if he had signed it, unless the Congress by their Adjournment prevent its Return, in which Case it shall not be a Law.

Every Order, Resolution, or Vote to which the Concurrence of the Senate and House of Representatives may be necessary (except on a question of Adjournment) shall be presented to the President of the United States; and before the Same shall take Effect, shall be approved by him, or being disapproved by him, shall be repassed by two thirds of the Senate and House of Representatives, according to the Rules and Limitations prescribed in the Case of a Bill.

Section 8   The Congress shall have Power To lay and collect Taxes, Duties, Imposts and Excises, to pay the Debts and provide for the common Defence and general Welfare of the United States; but all Duties, Imposts and Excises shall be uniform throughout the United States;

To borrow Money on the credit of the United States;

To regulate Commerce with foreign Nations, and among the several States, and with the Indian Tribes;

To establish a uniform Rule of Naturalization, and uniform Laws on the subject of Bankruptcies throughout the United States;

To coin Money, regulate the Value thereof, and of foreign Coin, and fix the Standard of Weights and Measures;

To provide for the Punishment of counterfeiting the Securities and current Coin of the United States;

To esablish Post Offices and post Roads;

To promote the Progress of Science and useful Arts, by securing for limited Times to Authors and Inventors the exclusive right to their respective Writings and Discoveries;

To constitute Tribunals inferior to the supreme Court;

To define and punish Piracies and Felonies committed on the high Seas; and Offences against the Law of Nations;

To declare War, grant Letters of Marque and Reprisal, and make Rules concerning Captures on Land and Water;

To raise and support Armies, but no Appropriation of Money to that Use shall be for a longer Term than two Years;

To provide and maintain a Navy;

To make Rules for the Government and Regulation of the land and naval Forces;

To provide for calling forth the Militia to execute the Laws of the Union, suppress Insurrections and repel Invasions;

To provide for organizing, arming, and disciplining, the Militia, and for governing such Part of them as may be employed in the Service of the United States, reserving to the States respectively, the Appointment of the Officers, and the Authority of training the Militia according to the discipline prescribed by Congress;

To exercise exclusive Legislation in all Cases whatsoever, over such District (not exceeding ten Miles square) as may, by Cession of particular States, and the Acceptance of Congress, become the Seat of the Government of the United States, and to exercise like Authority over all Places purchased by the Consent of the Legislature of the State in which the Same shall be, for the Erection of Forts, Magazines, Arsenals, dockYards, and other needful Buildings;—And

To make all Laws which shall be necessary and proper for carrying into Execution the foregoing Powers, and all other Powers vested by this Constitution in the Government of the United States, or in any Department or Officer thereof.

Section 9   The Migration or Importation of such Persons as any of the States now existing shall think proper to admit, shall not be prohibited by the Congress prior to the Year one thousand eight hundred and eight, but a Tax or duty may be imposed on such Importation, not exceeding ten dollars for each Person.

The Privilege of the Writ of Habeas Corpus shall not be suspended, unless when in Cases of Rebellion or Invasion the public safety may require it.

No Bill of Attainder or ex post facto Law shall be passed.

No Capitation, or other direct, Tax shall be laid, unless in Proportion to the Census or Enumeration herein before directed to be taken.[5]

No Tax or Duty shall be laid on Articles exported from any State.

No Preference shall be given by any Regulation of Commerce or Revenue to the Ports of one State over those of another; nor shall Vessels bound to, or from, one State, be obliged to enter, clear, or pay Duties in another.

No money shall be drawn from the Treasury, but in Consequence of Appropriations made by Law; and a regular Statement and Account of the Receipts and Expenditures of all public Money shall be published from time to time.

No Title of Nobility shall be granted by the United States: And no Person holding any Office of Profit or Trust under them, shall, without the Consent of the Congress, accept any present, Emolument, Office, or Title, of any kind whatever, from any King, Prince, or foreign State.

Section 10 No State shall enter into any Treaty, Alliance, or Confederation; grant Letters of Marque and Reprisal; coin Money; emit Bills of Credit; make any Thing but gold and silver Coin a Tender in Payment of Debts; pass any Bill of Attainder, ex post facto Law, or Law impairing the Obligation of Contracts, or grant any Title of Nobility.

No State shall, without the Consent of the Congress, lay any Imposts or Duties on Imports or Exports, except what may be absolutely necessary for executing its inspection laws; and the net Produce of all Duties and Imposts, laid by any State on Imports or Exports, shall be for the Use of the Treasury of the United States; and all such Laws shall be subject to the Revision, and Control of the Congress.

No State shall, without the Consent of Congress, lay any Duty of Tonnage, keep Troops, or Ships of War in time of Peace, enter into any Agreement or Compact with another State, or with a foreign Power, or engage in War, unless actually invaded, or in such imminent Danger as will not admit of delay.

ARTICLE II

Section 1 The executive Power shall be vested in a President of the United States of America. He shall hold his Office during the Term of four Years, and, together with the Vice President, chosen for the same Term, be elected, as follows.

Each State shall appoint, in such Manner as the Legislature thereof may direct, a Number of Electors, equal to the whole Number of Senators and Representatives to which the State may be entitled in the Congress: but no Senator or Representative, or Person holding an Office of Trust or Profit under the United States, shall be appointed an Elector.

[The Electors shall meet in their respective States, and vote by Ballot for two Persons, of whom one at least shall not be an Inhabitant of the same State with themselves. And they shall make a List of all the Persons voted for, and the Number of Votes for each; which list they shall sign and certify, and transmit sealed to the Seat of the Government of the United States, directed to the President of the Senate. The President of the Senate shall, in the Presence of the Senate and House of Representatives, open all the Certificates, and the Votes shall then be counted. The person having the greatest Number of Votes shall be the President, if such Number be a Majority of the whole Number of Electors appointed, and if there be more than one who have such Majority, and have an equal Number of Votes, then the House of Representatives shall immediately chuse by Ballot one of them for President; and if no Person have a Majority, then from the five highest on the List the said House shall in like manner chuse the President. But in chusing the President, the Votes shall be taken by States, the Representation from each State having one vote; A quorum for this purpose shall consist of a Member or Members from two thirds of the States, and a Majority of all the States shall be necessary to a Choice. In every Case, after the Choice of the President, the Person having the greatest Number of Votes of the Electors shall be the Vice President. But if there

---

[5] Modified by the Sixteenth Amendment.

should remain two or more who have equal Votes, the Senate chuse from them by Ballot the Vice President.][6]

The Congress may determine the Time of chusing the Electors, and the Day on which they shall give their Votes; which Day shall be the same throughout the United States.

No Person except a natural born Citizen, or a Citizen of the United States, at the time of the Adoption of this Constitution, shall be eligible to the Office of President; neither shall any Person be eligible to that Office who shall not have attained to the Age of thirty five Years, and been fourteen Years a Resident within the United States.

In Case of the Removal of the President from Office, or of his Death, Resignation, or Inability to discharge the Powers and Duties of the said Office, the Same shall devolve on the Vice President, and the Congress may by Law provide for the Case of Removal, Death, Resignation or Inability, both of the President and Vice President, declaring what Officer shall act accordingly, until the Disability be removed, or a President shall be elected.

The President shall, at stated Times receive for his Services, a Compensation, which shall neither be encreased nor diminished during the Period for which he shall have been elected, and he shall not receive within that Period any other Emolument from the United States, or any of them.

Before he enter on the Execution of his Office, he shall take the following Oath or Affirmation:—"I do solemnly swear (or affirm) that I will faithfully execute the Office of President of the United States, and will to the best of my Ability, preserve, protect and defend the Constitution of the United States."

Section 2 The President shall be Commander in Chief of the Army and Navy of the United States, and of the Militia of the several States, when called into the actual Service of the United States; he may require the Opinion, in writing, of the principal Officer in each of the executive Departments, upon any Subject relating to the Duties of their respective Offices, and he shall have Power to grant Reprieves and Pardons for Offenses against the United States, except in Cases of Impeachment.

He shall have Power, by and with the Advice and Consent of the Senate, to make Treaties, provided two thirds of the Senators present concur; and he shall nominate, and by and with the Advice and Consent of the Senate, shall appoint Ambassadors, other public Ministers and Consuls, Judges of the supreme Court, and all other Officers of the United States, whose Appointments are not herein otherwise provided for, and which shall be established by Law: but the Congress may by Law vest the Appointment of such inferior Officers, as they think proper, in the President alone, in the Courts of Law, or in the Heads of Departments.

The President shall have Power to fill up all Vacancies that may happen during the Recess of the Senate, by granting Commissions which shall expire at the End of their next Session.

Section 3 He shall from time to time give to the Congress Information of the State of the Union, and recommend to their Consideration such Measures as he shall judge necessary and expedient; he may, on extraordinary Occasions, convene both Houses, or either of them, and in Case of Disagreement between them, with Respect to the Time of Adjournment, he may adjourn them to such Time as he shall think proper; he shall receive Ambassadors and other public Ministers; he shall take Care that the Laws be faithfully executed, and shall Commission all Officers of the United States.

Section 4 The President, Vice President and all civil Officers of the United States, shall be removed from Office on Impeachment for, and Conviction of, Treason, Bribery, or other high Crimes and Misdemeanors.

ARTICLE III

Section 1 The judicial Power of the United States, shall be vested in one supreme Court, and in such inferior Courts as the Congress may from time to time ordain and establish. The Judges, both of the supreme and inferior Courts, shall hold their Offices during good Behaviour, and shall, at stated Times, receive for their Services, a Compensation, which shall not be diminished during their Continuance in Office.

Section 2 The judicial Power shall extend to all Cases, in Law and Equity, arising

---

[6] Superseded by the Twelfth Amendment.

under this Constitution, the Laws of the United States, and Treaties made, or which shall be made, under their Authority;—to all Cases affecting Ambassadors, other public Ministers and Consuls;—to all Cases of admiralty and maritime Jurisdiction;—to Controversies to which the United States shall be a Party;—to Controversies between two or more States;—between a State and Citizens of another State;[7]—between Citizens of different States,—between citizens of the same State claiming Lands under Grants of different States, and between a State, or the Citizens thereof, and foreign States, Citizens or Subjects.

In all cases affecting Ambassadors, other public Ministers and Consuls, and those in which a State shall be Party, the supreme Court shall have original Jurisdiction. In all the other Cases before mentioned, the supreme Court shall have appellate Jurisdiction, both as to Law and Fact, with such Exceptions, and under such Regulations as the Congress shall make.

The Trial of all Crimes, except in Cases of Impeachment, shall be by Jury; and such Trial shall be held in the State where the said Crimes shall have been committed; but when not committed within any State, the Trial shall be at such Place or Places as the Congress may by Law have directed.

Section 3 Treason against the United States, shall consist only in levying War against them, or in adhering to their Enemies, giving them Aid and Comfort. No Person shall be convicted of Treason unless on the Testimony of two Witnesses to the same overt Act, or on Confession in open Court.

The Congress shall have Power to declare the Punishment of Treason, but no Attainder of Treason shall work Corruption of Blood, or Forfeiture except during the life of the Person attainted.

ARTICLE IV

Section 1 Full Faith and Credit shall be given in each State to the public Acts, Records, and judicial Proceedings of every other State. And the Congress may by general Laws prescribe the Manner in which such Acts, Records and Proceedings shall be proved, and the Effect thereof.

Section 2 The Citizens of each State shall be entitled to all Privileges and Immunities of Citizens in the several States.

A Person charged in any State with Treason, Felony, or other Crime, who shall flee from Justice, and be found in another State, shall on Demand of the executive Authority of the State from which he fled, be delivered up, to be removed to the State having Jurisdiction of the Crime.

No Person held to Service or Labour in one State, under the Laws thereof, escaping into another, shall, in Consequence of any Law or Regulation therein, be discharged from such Service or Labour, but shall be delivered up on Claim of the Party to whom such Service or Labour may be due.

Section 3 New States may be admitted by the Congress into this Union; but no new State shall be formed or erected within the Jurisdiction of any other State; nor any State be formed by the Junction of two or more States, or Parts of States, without the Consent of the Legislatures of the States concerned as well as of the Congress.

The Congress shall have Power to dispose of and make all needful Rules and Regulations respecting the Territory or other Property belonging to the United States; and nothing in this Constitution shall be so construed as to Prejudice any Claims of the United States, or of any particular State.

Section 4 The United States shall guarantee to every State in this Union a Republican Form of Government, and shall protect each of them against Invasion; and on Application of the Legislature, or of the Executive (when the Legislature cannot be convened) against domestic Violence.

ARTICLE V

The Congress, whenever two thirds of both Houses shall deem it necessary, shall propose Amendments to this Constitution, or, on the Application of the Legislatures of two thirds of the several States, shall call a Convention for proposing Amendments, which, in either Case, shall be valid to all Intents and Purposes, as Part of this Constitution, when ratified by the Legislatures of three fourths

---

[7] Modified by the Eleventh Amendment.

of the several States, or by Conventions in three fourths thereof, as the one or the other Mode of Ratification may be proposed by the Congress; Provided that no Amendment which may be made prior to the Year One thousand eight hundred and eight shall in any Manner affect the first and fourth Clauses in the Ninth Section of the first Article; and that no State, without its Consent, shall be deprived of its equal Suffrage in the Senate.

ARTICLE VI

All Debts contracted and Engagements entered into, before the Adoption of this Constitution, shall be as valid against the United States under this Constitution, as under the Confederation.

This Constitution, and the Laws of the United States which shall be made in Pursuance thereof; and all Treaties made, or which shall be made, under the Authority of the United States, shall be the supreme Law of the Land; and the Judges in every State shall be bound thereby, any Thing in the Constitution or Laws of any State to the Contrary notwithstanding.

The Senators and Representatives before mentioned, and the Members of the several State Legislatures, and all executive and judicial officers, both of the United States and of the several States, shall be bound by Oath or Affirmation, to support this Constitution; but no religious Test shall ever be required as a Qualification to any Office or public Trust under the United States.

ARTICLE VII

The Ratification of the Conventions of nine States, shall be sufficient for the Establishment of this Constitution between the States so ratifying the Same.

(Signatures omitted.)

AMENDMENTS

Articles in addition to, and Amendments of the Constitution of the United States of America, proposed by Congress, and ratified by the Legislatures of the several States, pursuant to the fifth Article of the original Constitution.

(The first ten articles were declared in force in December 1791.)

ARTICLE I

Congress shall make no law respecting an establishment of religion, or prohibiting the free exercise thereof; or abridging the freedom of speech, or of the press; or the right of the people peaceably to assemble, and to petition the Government for a redress of grievances.

ARTICLE II

A well regulated Militia, being necessary to the security of a free State, the right of the people to keep and bear Arms, shall not be infringed.

ARTICLE III

No Soldier shall, in time of peace, be quartered in any house, without the consent of the Owner, nor in time of war, but in a manner to be prescribed by law.

ARTICLE IV

The right of the people to be secure in their persons, houses, papers, and effects, against unreasonable searches and seizures, shall not be violated, and no Warrants shall issue, but upon probable cause, supported by Oath or affirmation, and particularly describing the place to be searched, and the persons or things to be seized.

ARTICLE V

No person shall be held to answer for a capital, or otherwise infamous crime, unless on a presentment or indictment of a Grand Jury, except in cases arising in the land or naval forces, or in the Militia, when in actual service in time of War or public danger; nor shall any person be subject for the same offense to be twice put in jeopardy of life or limb; nor shall be compelled in any criminal case to be a witness against himself, nor be deprived of life, liberty, or property, without due process of law; nor shall private property be taken for public use, without just compensation.

ARTICLE VI

In all criminal prosecutions, the accused shall enjoy the right to a speedy and public trial, by an impartial jury of the State and district wherein the crime shall have been committed, which district shall have been previously ascertained by law, and to be informed of the nature and cause of the accusation; to be confronted with the witnesses against him; to have compulsory process for obtaining witnesses in his favor, and to have the Assistance of Counsel for his defense.

ARTICLE VII

In Suits at common law, where the value in controversy shall exceed twenty dollars, the right of trial by jury shall be preserved, and no fact tried by a jury, shall be otherwise reexamined in any Court of the United States, than according to the rules of the common law.

ARTICLE VIII

Excessive bail shall not be required, nor excessive fines imposed, nor cruel and unusual punishments inflicted.

ARTICLE IX

The enumeration in the Constitution, of certain rights, shall not be construed to deny or disparage others retained by the people.

ARTICLE X

The powers not delegated to the United States by the Constitution, nor prohibited by it to the States, are reserved to the States respectively, or to the people.

ARTICLE XI (declared ratified January 1798)

The Judicial power of the United States shall not be construed to extend to any suit in law or equity, commenced or prosecuted against one of the United States by Citizens of another State, or by Citizens or Subjects of any Foreign State.

ARTICLE XII (declared ratified September 1804)

The Electors shall meet in their respective states, and vote by ballot for President and Vice-President, one of whom, at least, shall not be an inhabitant of the same state with themselves; they shall name in their ballots the person voted for as President, and in distinct ballots the person voted for as Vice-President, and they shall make distinct lists of all persons voted for as President, and of all persons voted for as Vice-President, and of the number of votes for each, which lists they shall sign and certify, and transmit sealed to the seat of the government of the United States, directed to the President of the Senate;—The President of the Senate shall, in the presence of the Senate and House of Representatives, open all certificates and the votes shall then be counted;—The person having the greatest number of votes for President, shall be the President, if such number be a majority of the whole number of Electors appointed; and if no person have such majority, then from the persons having the highest numbers not exceeding three on the list of those voted for as President, the House of Representatives shall choose immediately, by ballot, the President. But in choosing the President, the votes shall be taken by states, the representation from each state having one vote; a quorum for this purpose shall consist of a member or members from two-thirds of the states, and a majority of all the states shall be necessary to a choice. And if the House of Representatives shall not choose a President whenever the right of choice shall devolve upon them, before the fourth day of March next following, then the Vice-President shall act as President, as in the case of the death or other constitutional disability of the President.—The person having the greatest number of votes as Vice-President, shall be the Vice-President, if such number be a majority of the whole number of Electors appointed, and if no person have a majority, then from the two highest numbers on the list, the Senate shall choose the Vice-President; a quorum for the purpose shall consist of two-thirds of the whole number of Senators, and a majority of the whole number shall be necessary to a choice. But no person constitutionally ineligible to the office of President shall be eligible to that of Vice-President of the United States.

ARTICLE XIII (declared ratified December 1865)

Section 1 Neither slavery nor involuntary servitude, except as a punishment for crime whereof the party shall have been duly convicted, shall exist within the United States, or any place subject to their jurisdiction.

Section 2 Congress shall have power to enforce this article by appropriate legislation.

ARTICLE XIV (declared ratified July 1868)

Section 1 All persons born or naturalized in the United States, and subject to the jurisdiction thereof, are citizens of the United States and of the State wherein they reside. No State shall make or enforce any law which shall abridge the privileges or immunities of citizens of the United States; nor shall any State deprive any person of life, liberty, or property, without due process of law; nor deny to any person within its jurisdiction the equal protection of the laws.

Section 2 Representatives shall be apportioned among the several States according to their respective numbers, counting the whole number of persons in each State, excluding Indians not taxed. But when the right to vote at any election for the choice of electors for President and Vice President of the United States, Representatives in Congress, the Executive and Judicial officers of a State, or the members of the Legislature thereof, is denied to any of the male inhabitants of such State, being twenty-one years of age, and citizens of the United States, or in any way abridged, except for participation in rebellion, or other crime, the basis of representation therein shall be reduced in the proportion which the number of such male citizens shall bear to the whole number of male citizens twenty-one years of age in such State.

Section 3 No person shall be a Senator or Representative in Congress, or elector of President and Vice President, or hold any office, civil or military, under the United States, or under any State, who, having previously taken an oath, as a member of Congress, or as an officer of the United States, or as a member of any State legislature, or as an executive or judicial officer of any State, to support the Constitution of the United States, shall have engaged in insurrection or rebellion against the same, or given aid and comfort to the enemies thereof. But Congress may by a vote of two-thirds of each House, remove such disability.

Section 4 The validity of the public debt of the United States, authorized by law, including debts incurred for payments of pensions and bounties for services in suppressing insurrection or rebellion, shall not be questioned. But neither the United States nor any state shall assume or pay any debt or obligation incurred in aid of insurrection or rebellion against the United States, or any claim for the loss or emancipation of any slave; but all such debts, obligations, and claims shall be held illegal and void.

Section 5 The Congress shall have power to enforce, by appropriate legislation, the provisions of this article.

ARTICLE XV (declared ratified March 1870)

Section 1 The right of citizens of the United States to vote shall not be denied or abridged by the United States or by any State on account of race, color, or previous condition of servitude.

Section 2 The Congress shall have power to enforce this article by appropriate legislation.

ARTICLE XVI (declared ratified February 1913)

The Congress shall have power to lay and collect taxes on incomes, from whatever source derived, without apportionment among the several States, and without regard to any census or enumeration.

ARTICLE XVII (declared ratified May 1913)

The Senate of the United States shall be composed of two Senators from each State, elected by the people thereof, for six years; and each Senator shall have one vote. The electors in each State shall have the qualifications requisite for electors of the most numerous branch of the State legislatures.

When vacancies happen in the representation of any State in the Senate, the executive authority of such State shall issue writs of election to fill such vacancies: *Provided,* That the legislature of any State may empower the executive thereof to make temporary appointments until the people fill the vacancies by election as the legislature may direct.

This amendment shall not be so construed as to affect the election or term of any Senator chosen before it becomes valid as part of the Constitution.

ARTICLE XVIII (declared ratified January 1919)

Section 1 After one year from the ratification of this article the manufacture, sale, or transportation of intoxicating liquors within, the importation thereof into, or the exportation thereof from the United States and all territory subject to the jurisdiction thereof for beverage purposes is hereby prohibited.

Section 2 The Congress and the several States shall have concurrent power to enforce this article by appropriate legislation.

Section 3 This article shall be inoperative unless it shall have been ratified as an amendment to the Constitution by the legislatures of the several States, as provided in the Constitution, within Seven years from the date of the submission hereof to the States by the Congress.[8]

ARTICLE XIX (declared ratified August 1920)

The right of citizens of the United States to vote shall not be denied or abridged by the United States or by any State on account of sex.

Congress shall have power to enforce this article by appropriate legislation.

ARTICLE XX (declared ratified February 1933)

Section 1 The terms of the President and Vice President shall end at noon on the 20th day of January, and the terms of Senators and Representatives at noon on the 3d day of January, of the years in which such terms would have ended if this article had not been ratified; and the terms of their successors shall then begin.

Section 2 The Congress shall assemble at least once in every year, and such meeting shall begin at noon on the 3d day of January, unless they shall by law appoint a different day.

Section 3 If, at the time fixed for the beginning of the term of the President, the President elect shall have died, the Vice President elect shall become President. If a President shall not have been chosen before the time fixed for the beginning of his term, or if the President elect shall have failed to qualify, then the Vice President elect shall act as President until a President shall have qualified; and the Congress may by law provide for the case wherein neither a President elect nor a Vice President elect shall have qualified, declaring who shall then act as President, or the manner in which one who is to act shall be selected, and such person shall act accordingly until a President or Vice President shall have qualified.

Section 4 The Congress may by law provide for the case of the death of any of the persons from whom the House of Representatives may choose a President whenever the right of choice shall have devolved upon them, and for the case of the death of any of the persons from whom the Senate may choose a Vice President whenever the right of choice shall have devolved upon them.

Section 5 Sections 1 and 2 shall take effect on the 15th day of October following the ratification of this article.

Section 6 This article shall be inoperative unless it shall have been ratified as an amendment to the Constitution by the legislatures of three-fourths of the several States within seven years from the date of its submission.

ARTICLE XXI (declared ratified December 1933)

Section 1 The Eighteenth article of amendment to the Constitution of the United States is hereby repealed.

Section 2 The transportation or importation into any State, Territory, or possession of the United States for delivery or use therein of intoxicating liquors, in violation of the laws thereof, is hereby prohibited.

Section 3 This article shall be inoperative unless it shall have been ratified as an amendment to the Constitution by conventions in the several States, as provided in the Constitution, within seven years from the date of the submission hereof to the States by the Congress.

ARTICLE XXII (declared ratified February 1951)

Section 1 No person shall be elected to the office of the President more than twice, and no person who has held the office of President, or acted as President, for more than two years of a term to which some other person was elected President shall be elected to the office of the President more than once. But this Article shall not apply to any person holding the office of President when this Article was proposed by the Congress, and shall

---

[8] Superseded by the Twenty-first Amendment.

not prevent any person who may be holding the office of President, or acting as President, during the term within which this Article becomes operative from holding the office of President or acting as President during the remainder of such term.

Section 2 This article shall be inoperative unless it shall have been ratified as an amendment to the Constitution by the legislatures of three-fourths of the several States within seven years from the date of its submission to the States by the Congress.

ARTICLE XXIII (declared ratified March 1961)

Section 1 The district constituting the seat of government of the United States shall appoint in such manner as the Congress may direct:

A number of electors of President and Vice President equal to the whole number of Senators and Representatives in Congress to which the District would be entitled if it were a State, but in no event more than the least populous state; they shall be in addition to those appointed by the States, but they shall be considered, for the purpose of the election of President and Vice President, to be electors appointed by a State; and they shall meet in the District and perform such duties as provided by the twelfth article of amendment.

Section 2 The Congress shall have power to enforce this article by appropriate legislation.

ARTICLE XXIV (declared ratified January 1964)

Section 1 The right of citizens of the United States to vote in any primary or other election for President or Vice President, for electors for President or Vice President, or for Senator or Representative in Congress, shall not be denied or abridged by the United States or any State by reason of failure to pay any poll tax or other tax.

Section 2 The Congress shall have power to enforce this article by appropriate legislation.

ARTICLE XXV (declared ratified February 1967)

Section 1 In case of the removal of the President from office or of his death or resignation, the Vice President shall become President.

Section 2 Whenever there is a vacancy in the office of the Vice President, the President shall nominate a Vice President who shall take office upon confirmation by a majority vote of both Houses of Congress.

Section 3 Whenever the President transmits to the President Pro Tempore of the Senate and the Speaker of the House of Representatives his written declaration that he is unable to discharge the powers and duties of his office, and until he transmits to them a written declaration to the contrary, such powers and duties shall be discharged by the Vice President as Acting President.

Section 4 Whenever the Vice President and a majority of either the principal officers of the executive departments or of such other body as Congress may by law provide, transmit to the President Pro Tempore of the Senate and the Speaker of the House of Representatives their written declaration that the President is unable to discharge the powers and duties of his office, the Vice President shall immediately assume the powers and duties of the office as Acting President.

Thereafter, when the President transmits to the President Pro Tempore of the Senate and the Speaker of the House of Representatives his written declaration that no inability exists, he shall resume the powers and duties of his office unless the Vice President and a majority of either the principal officers of the executive departments or of such other body as Congress may by law provide, transmit within four days to the President Pro Tempore of the Senate and the Speaker of the House of Representatives their written declaration that the President is unable to discharge the powers and duties of his office. Thereupon Congress shall decide the issue, assembling within forty-eight hours for that purpose if not in session. If the Congress, within twenty-one days after receipt of the latter written declaration, or, if Congress is not in session, within twenty-one days after Congress is required to assemble, determines by two-thirds vote of both Houses that the President is unable to discharge the powers and duties of his office, the Vice President shall continue to discharge the same as Acting President; otherwise, the President shall resume the powers and duties of his office.

ARTICLE XXVI (declared ratified July 1971)

Section 1 The right of citizens of the United States, who are eighteen years of age or older, to vote shall not be denied or abridged by the United States or by any State on account of age.

Section 2 The Congress shall have power to enforce this article by appropriate legislation.

Appendix C

Growth of U.S. population

Census	Population of contiguous U.S.	Percent increase over the preceding census	Population per square mile
1790	3,929,214		4.5
1800	5,308,483	35.1	6.1
1810	7,239,881	36.4	4.3
1820	9,638,453	33.1	5.5
1830	12,866,020	33.5	7.3
1840	17,069,453	32.7	9.7
1850	23,191,876	35.9	7.9
1860	31,443,321	35.6	10.6
1870	39,818,449	26.6	13.4
1880	50,155,783	26.0	16.9
1890	62,947,714	25.5	21.2
1900	75,994,575	20.7	25.6
1910	91,972,266	21.0	30.9
1920	105,710,620	14.9	35.5
1930	122,775,046	16.1	41.2
1940	131,669,275	7.2	44.2
1950	150,697,361	14.5	50.7
1960*	178,464,236	18.4	59.9
1970†	204,765,770		

* Without Alaska (population 226,167) and Hawaii (632,772).
† With Alaska and Hawaii (632,772).

Appendix D

Admission of states

State	Admission	State	Admission
Vermont	March 4, 1791	Oregon	Feb. 14, 1859
Kentucky	June 1, 1792	Kansas	Jan. 29, 1861
Tennessee	June 1, 1796	West Virginia	June 20, 1863
Ohio	March 1, 1803	Nevada	Oct. 31, 1864
Louisiana	April 30, 1812	Nebraska	March 1, 1867
Indiana	Dec. 11, 1816	Colorado	Aug. 1, 1876
Mississippi	Dec. 10, 1817	North Dakota	Nov. 2, 1889
Illinois	Dec. 3, 1818	South Dakota	Nov. 2, 1889
Alabama	Dec. 14, 1819	Montana	Nov. 8, 1889
Maine	March 15, 1820	Washington	Nov. 11, 1889
Missouri	Aug. 10, 1821	Idaho	July 3, 1890
Arkansas	June 15, 1836	Wyoming	July 10, 1890
Michigan	Jan. 26, 1837	Utah	Jan. 4, 1896
Florida	March 3, 1845	Oklahoma	Nov. 16, 1907
Texas	Dec. 29, 1845	New Mexico	Jan. 6, 1912
Iowa	Dec. 28, 1846	Arizona	Feb. 14, 1912
Wisconsin	May 29, 1848	Alaska	Jan. 3, 1959
California	Sept. 9, 1850	Hawaii	Aug. 21, 1959
Minnesota	May 11, 1858		

Appendix E

Presidents and vice presidents

Term	President	Vice president
1789–1793	George Washington	John Adams
1793–1797	George Washington	John Adams
1797–1801	John Adams	Thomas Jefferson
1801–1805	Thomas Jefferson	Aaron Burr
1805–1809	Thomas Jefferson	George Clinton
1809–1813	James Madison	George Clinton (d. 1812)
1813–1817	James Madison	Elbridge Gerry (d. 1814)
1817–1821	James Monroe	Daniel D. Tompkins
1821–1825	James Monroe	Daniel D. Tompkins
1825–1829	John Quincy Adams	John C. Calhoun
1829–1833	Andrew Jackson	John C. Calhoun (resigned 1832)
1833–1837	Andrew Jackson	Martin Van Buren
1837–1841	Martin Van Buren	Richard M. Johnson
1841–1845	William H. Harrison (d. 1841) John Tyler	John Tyler
1845–1849	James K. Polk	George M. Dallas
1849–1853	Zachary Taylor (d. 1850) Millard Fillmore	Millard Fillmore
1853–1857	Franklin Pierce	William R. D. King (d. 1853)
1857–1861	James Buchanan	John C. Breckinridge
1861–1865	Abraham Lincoln	Hannibal Hamlin
1865–1869	Abraham Lincoln (d. 1865) Andrew Johnson	Andrew Johnson
1869–1873	Ulysses S. Grant	Schuyler Colfax
1873–1877	Ulysses S. Grant	Henry Wilson (d. 1875)
1877–1881	Rutherford B. Hayes	William A. Wheeler
1881–1885	James A. Garfield (d. 1881) Chester A. Arthur	Chester A. Arthur
1885–1889	Grover Cleveland	Thomas A. Hendricks (d. 1885)
1889–1893	Benjamin Harrison	Levi P. Morton
1893–1897	Grover Cleveland	Adlai E. Stevenson
1897–1901	William McKinley	Garret A. Hobart (d. 1899)
1901–1905	William McKinley (d. 1901) Theodore Roosevelt	Theodore Roosevelt
1905–1909	Theodore Roosevelt	Charles W. Fairbanks
1909–1913	William H. Taft	James S. Sherman (d. 1912)
1913–1917	Woodrow Wilson	Thomas R. Marshall
1917–1921	Woodrow Wilson	Thomas R. Marshall

Presidents and vice presidents *(continued)*

Term	President	Vice president
1921–1925	Warren G. Harding (d. 1923) Calvin Coolidge	Calvin Coolidge
1925–1929	Calvin Coolidge	Charles G. Dawes
1929–1933	Herbert C. Hoover	Charles Curtis
1933–1937	Franklin D. Roosevelt	John N. Garner
1937–1941	Franklin D. Roosevelt	John N. Garner
1941–1945	Franklin D. Roosevelt	Henry A. Wallace
1945–1949	Franklin D. Roosevelt (d. 1945) Harry S Truman	Harry S Truman
1949–1953	Harry S Truman	Alben W. Barkley
1953–1957	Dwight D. Eisenhower	Richard M. Nixon
1957–1961	Dwight D. Eisenhower	Richard M. Nixon
1961–1965	John F. Kennedy (d. 1963) Lyndon B. Johnson	Lyndon B. Johnson
1965–1969	Lyndon B. Johnson	Hubert H. Humphrey, Jr.
1969–1973	Richard M. Nixon	Spiro T. Agnew
1973–1974	Richard M. Nixon	Spiro T. Agnew; Gerald R. Ford
1974–1977	Gerald R. Ford	Nelson A. Rockefeller

INDEX

Index

A

Abolitionism, 87, 219, 221, 233f, 240, 257f (nature of), 263, 265, 269f, 274f, 278f, 279 (women leaders), 284, 290, 299f, 304, 306f, 308, 310, 313f (evolution of), 321f, 323f, 327
British-led, 221, 258, 294
Adams, C. F., 367
Adams, John, 52, 83f, 86f, 90f, 96, 98, 116, 137f, 149, 151, 152f, 155f, 165, 167f, 171
Adams, John Quincy, 158, 168, 178, 228, 234f, 236f, 244, 280, 286, 294, 296, 305, 318
Adams, Sam, 80, 83f, 86f, 110
Adams-Onis Treaty (1819), 229, 234
"African," use of name by black Americans, 317
Agrarian Dream, 107, 145, 171f, 186, 256, Ch. 7 passim; see also Agrarianism and American Dream
Agrarianism, 157, 173, 243f (Jacksonians), 246, 257f, 310, 321
Agricultural Revolution, 211f, 221f, (in the South), 293 (Midwest), 310
Alabama, 159, 163, 183f, 198, 215f, 216 (population table), 220, 299, 325, 330, 363
Alamo, 293f
Alcott, Bronson, 266, 272
Algonquin Indians, 25, 65
Alien and Sedition Acts, 154f
Amana Society, 272, 274
Amendments, constitutional, 122, 124, 155, 175, 183, Appendix
Amendments 1–10 (Bill of Rights), 127f, 138
5th, 127f, 320
12th, 122, 153, 156, 169, 236

Amendments—*Cont.*
13th, 14th, and 15th, 122, 355f, 366f
17th, 119, 122
19th, 122, 279
24th, 122
American Antislavery Society, 314, 316, 318, 365
American Colonization Society, 234
American Dream, 264, 280, 307, 365 (blacks); see also Agrarian Dream
American and Foreign Antislavery Society, 318
American Insurance Co. v. *Carter* (1828), 166
American Peace Society, 294f
American Roman style, 135
"American" self-consciousness and identity, 51, 81f, 135f; see also Nationalism, American
American System (Henry Clay), 213, 223, 228, 237, 288
American System (of manufacture), 210f
"Americanization" (industrialization), 211
Andersonville, 343, 348
Anglicans, 29, 31, 32f, 39, 64, 75f
Anglo-America, heritage, 82
Anglo-American crisis, 288f (1840s), 330 (1861)
Anglo-American understanding, 177, 237, 258f
Anglo-French rivalry, 22f, 24f, 28, 61f
Anthony, Susan B., 279f
Anti-Catholic prejudice, 38f, 48, 84, 250, 270f, 308
Antietam, battle of, 335, 337
Antifederalists, 106, 113f, 125f, 126 (name discussed), 146f, 309
Anti-Mason party, 249f
Anti-Negro prejudices and arguments, 174, 271, 308, 321, 326, 352, 355,

Anti-Negro prejudices and arguments—*Cont.*
360, 373; see also Racism *and* Slavery
Antinomianism, 43
Anti-war feelings, 258, 266, 294f, 296; see also Peace movement
Apache Indians, 9
Arawak Indians, 14f
Architecture, American, 135, 163, 209, 222
Arizona, 295f, 298
Arkansas, 223f, 234, 302, 328, 332, 349f, 363
Arminianism, 73f, 161f, 269f
Army, U.S., 152, 155, 178f, 190, 298, 319
Arnold, Benedict, 96, 98
Aroostook War, 288
Art, American, 134f, 259f
Astor, J. J., 280f
Athabascan Indians, 9
Atlanta, Georgia, burnt, 341
Atlanta Compromise, 374f
Attucks, Crispus, 87, 110
Audubon, J. J., 260
Austin, S., 293

B

Back-country, 48, 61f, 70f, 87, 113, 160f, 212
Bacon's Rebellion, 18, 20, 48, 71
Ballads, frontier, 260
Baltimore, Lord, 39f
Baltimore, Maryland, 56, 70, 136, 163, 191, 196, 325
Baltimore and Ohio Railroad, 193, 196, 281
Bancroft, George, 241, 261
Bank of the United States, First, 143f, 145, 165, 173, 229f, 237
Bank of the United States, Second, 121, 136, 241, 246f, 312
Banking, 58 (colonial), 112f, 121, 143f, 165, 187, 205f, 227, 229f, 241, 246f, 303, 312, 348, 358
Banks, Gen. N. P., 350

XXV

Banneker, Benjamin, 137
Baptists, 47, 49, 75, 161f
Baranov, Alexander, 64, 234
Barnburners, 298
Baroque style, 15, 22, 135f
Beauregard, Gen. P. G. T., 332
Beecher, H. W., 270, 307
Beecher, L., 270f, 316
Bell, John, 325f
Benton, Sen. Thomas Hart, 243f, 291
Bering, Vitus, 63, 234
Bible, first in United States (1661), 65
Biddle, Nicholas, 247f
Big House (plantation), 163, 215, 219f, 372
Bill of Rights
 1689, 51, 127
 U.S., 104, 127, 138
Bills of exchange, 57f
Birney, J. G., 290, 313, 316, 319
Birthrate, colonial, 26, 60f
Bishops, Anglican, 31f, 78f, 75f
Black Americans, 13, 36f, 37 (contributions to colonial life), 39, 121, 137, 173f (Jefferson and blacks), 190 (contributions to economic growth), 231f (Indian-black relations), 240, 253, 270, Ch. 10 passim, 323 (fight in Civil War), 327 (criticize Lincoln) 340, Ch. 13 passim; *see also* Reconstruction; Slavery; *and* Voting rights
Black abolitionists, 258, 275, 314, 316f, 337; *see also* Abolitionism
Black Codes, 352f, 355, 358
Black Hawk War, 255, 293
Black nationalism, 375f; *see also* Nationalism, black
Black nationalists, 314, 317f
Black Reconstruction, 369, 375f
"Black Republicans," 319
Black troops, 350, 362
Blackwell, Dr. Elizabeth, 279
Blair, Frances P., 242
Blake, Lyman, 207
"Bleeding Kansas," 306f, 319f, 325
Blind, in America, 282
Blockade, 170f, 333f, 342
Bloomer, Amelia, 277f
Board of Trade, 25, 54, 56, 67, 80, 142, 188
Body of Liberties (1641), 46
Boone, Daniel, 61, 190

Booth, John Wilkes, 343
Border raids (Canada), 288
"Border ruffians," 307
Border states, 228, 325f, 328f, 330, 351
Boré, J. E., 223
Boston, Massachusetts, 32f, 42, 45, 47, 67, 70, 72, 79f, 85f, 87 (Negroes organize), 88, 91f, 93 (siege), 113, 158, 187, 193, 196, 199, 204f, 206, 262f, 265, 271, 274, 280, 282, 301, 314f, 316, 318
Boston Associates, 204f
Boston Manufacturing Co., 204
Boston Massacre, 86f, 93, 110
Boston Tea Party, 88f
Boston town meeting, 87
Boudinot, E., 255
Boundary disputes
 Canada, 184, 287f
 colonial, 39, 71f
Bourbons, Southern, 373
Bowie knife, 161, 299
Boycott, 85f
Braddock, General, 67
Bradford, Gov. William, 41, 65
Bragg, Gen. Braxton, 341
Brandywine, battle of, 93
Breckinridge, J. C., 325f
Breweries, 211, 308
Brewster, William, 39f
Bridge building, 191, 209
Brisbane, A., 267, 276
Britain, British, 58, 145, 148f, 175f, 192, 200 (in China trade), 206f, 209f, 213, 231f, 235, 237, 240, 252, 287 (in Hawaii), 292, 294 (in Mexico); *see* understanding; *and* Anglo-French rivalry
 British and American Civil War, 330, 333, 335f
 British America, character of, 32, 81f
 British colonization, 13, 15, 22, 26f, 108
 British immigrants, 49, 154, 212, 274 (Mormons)
 British influence on American radical reformers, 221, 258f, 278
 British investments in United States, 192, 197
 British-U.S. trade, 198f, 216f, 229
British Columbia, 289
Broad construction (Constitution), 121
Brock, Isaac, 182

"Broken voyage," legal principle, 171f
Brook Farm, 266f, 272
Brown, John, 268f, 307, 323f
Brown, Moses, 204
Brownlow, W. G. "Parson," 362
Brownson, Orestes, 266
Buchanan, Pres. James, 253, 257, 285, 304f, 307, 319f, 329f, 337
Buena Vista, battle of, 297
Buffalo herds, 66, 193, 214, 224f
Bull Run, battle of, 333 (first), 338 (second)
Bunker Hill, battle of, 91
Burgesses, House of (Virginia), 27, 37f, 68f, 84
Burgoyne, Gen. J., 93, 96
Burke, E., 89, 147f
Burns, Anthony, 301
Burnside, Gen. A., 337f
Burnt-over District (New York), 270f, 274
Burr, Aaron, 153, 155f, 168f, 240
Business cycle, 249
Business failures, 281f
business organization, 22, 39f, 58, 191, 194, 202, 204f, 369, 372f
Byrd, William I and II, 71

C

Cabet, Etienne, 277
Cabildos, 38
Cabinet system, 55, 80, 138, 360
Cabinets
 Jackson, 242f
 Lincoln, 331f
 Washington, 138, 146
Cable, G. W., 372
Cabot, J., 26
Cajuns, 163
Calhoun, John C., 175f, 228f, 236f, 239, 242f, 244f, 253, 288, 299, 302 (death), 304
 Mrs. Floride C. Calhoun, 244
California, 195, 199f, 201, 272, 277, 286, 289f, 292f, (Americanized), 298f, 303, 310
California Trail, 292f
"Calling," 30
Calvert family (Maryland), 38f, 55, 64
Calvinism, 73f, 82, 269f
Cambridge, Massachusetts, 45, 207

Index

Camp meetings, 160f, 268f, 283
Canada, 9, 20, 22, 25, 61f, 64, 81f, 89, 93, 98, 150, 163f, 176, 178f, 182f, 184, 188, 191f, 212, 229, 234, 252, 258, 274, 286f, 288f, 292, 300; see also French Canada
population, 182, 188
Canada Act (1791), 98
Canals, 112, 145, 164f, 175, 187, 191f, 194 (rail v.), 196, 206, 214, 224f, 229f, 281, 293, 312f
Cannibals, ALL! (1857), 321
Canning, George, 177, 235, 237
Cannonichet, Chief, 65f
Canoe trails, 62
Capital, as an economic factor, 188f
Capital, foreign (in America), 197f, 265
Capital goods, 189
Capital punishment, 128, 264
Capital scarcity, 143f, 166, 197, 189f, 204, 368
Capital-intensive conditions, 223
Capitalism
American, 42, 108, 128, 141f (Hamiltonian variant), 197, 204f, 230f, 265, 284
industrial, 202, 204f
meanings of, 141, 188f
merchant, 27, 202, 206
questioned, 265, 321
state capitalism, 145
Capitol, 135f, 239, 292
Caravel, 19
Caribbean, 13, 16, 27f, 36f, 56, 150
Carnegie, Andrew, 194
Carpetbaggers, 369
Carroll, Bishop John, 163
Cartier, J., 24, 26
Casa de contratación (1503), 54
Cass, Lewis, 291, 297f, 301, 304
Caste values, 70
Catalogues, retail, 187
Catholics
Spanish America, 13, 15, 22
North America, 18, 31, 32, 38f (Maryland), 48, 61f, 89 (Old Northwest), 136, 163, 262f (schools), 271 (immigrants), 283, 308
Catlin, George, 260

Cattle, 45, 164, 212, 214f, 224f
Caucus, party, 156, 167, 229, 235f (opposed)
Caudillos, 239
"Cavalier" South, myth of, 71, 163, 217, 320, 348, 372
Census, U.S., 119, 313
Centralism, political, 19, 105f, 108, 114f, 171f; see also Antifederalists; Federalists; *and* States' rights
Champlain, S. de, 25
Chancellorsville, battle of, 338
Channing, W. E., 266, 319
Charisma, 310
Charleston, South Carolina, 59, 64, 68, 70f, 88, 97, 114, 196, 220, 224, 318, 324, 330f, 365
Chase, Judge S., 154
Chase, Salmon P., 321, 338
Chatauqua movement, 264
Chattanooga campaign, 341
Chauvinism, male, 278f
Checks and balances (Constitution), 117, 124
Cherokee Indians, 12, 61, 66, 184, 215, 237f, 254f
Chesapeake Bay, 35, 58, 97
Cheves, L., 248
Chicago, 164, 196f, 198, 214, 255, 293, 306, 324f
Chickamauga, 341, 362
Chickasaw Indians, 12, 62, 254
Child, Lydia Maria, 316
Children, American view of, 261f
Children's literature, 316
China trade, 3, 14, 200f, 251, 287, 289, 296
Chippewa Indians, 66f
Chitterlings, 219
Choctaw Indians, 12, 254f
Christian Scientists, 272
Christian Socialists, 271f
Church and state, separation of, 103
Churches, 321 (segregated), 324 (divided, Civil War); see also Religion
Cincinnati, 158, 164, 194, 214, 270, 289, 293, 316f
Cities, 49, 56f, 59, 67f, 145, 158, 164, 187, 194f, 211, 221f, 261, 280f, 293, 373
city rivalries, 136f, 193, 196
Citizen-soldier concept, 93
Citizenship, 154, 165, 308, 313, 356

"City Upon A Hill," 39, 41, 258
Civil Disobedience, 206, 294
Civil liberties, 154f
Civil list, 52
Civil rights, 38, 42, 89, 321f, 340 (Civil War), 349f, 371
black, 313f, 320, 339, 353f, 355f, 368
Civil Rights Acts, 356, 371, 373
Civil service, 253
Clark, G. R., 97
Class, social, 47, 59f, 68f, 71f, 75f, 77, 108f, 110f, 128, 139, 162f (frontier), 205, 248, 251f, 264, 274, 280, 283, 335f
Classical revival, 135f, 259
Clay, Henry, 176f, 213, 223, 228f, 230, 234, 236f, 241, 243, 246, 249f, 251, 258, 288, 290, 299f, 303, 327
Clinton, Gov. De Witt, 156, 183, 193
Clinton, Gov. G., 147, 149, 169
"Clinton's Big Ditch," 193
Clipper ships, 199f, 287
Cod fishing, 24, 45, 56, 203
Cody, Buffalo Bill, 260
Coffee, American consumption, 172, 201, 203
Colbert, 22, 25, 27, 141f
Cold Harbor, battle of, 341
Collectivism, American, 265f, 272f
Colleges, American, 68, 75, 116, 162f, 163 (Catholic), 230, 262f, 270, 279, 315f (radical centers), 361
Colonialism, 25, 53f (theory of), 78, 141
Colonization, European, 19f, 64f, 107, 158, 199, 235, 288
"Colonization" (of blacks to Africa), 174, 276, 314, 350f, 375
"Colonization," internal, 187, 206, 224
Colorado, 280, 289, 295, 298
Columbus, Christopher, 3, 7, 13f, 34
Command of the Army Act (1867), 360
Commerce clause (Constitution, 120f, 173, 231
Common law, 52, 128, 281
Common Man, Age of, redefined, 238f
Common School, 262f
Common School Journal, 263
Common Sense, 91, 106

xxviii
The U.S.A.

Commonwealth v. Hunt (1842), 281
Commonwealth v. Pullis (1806), 281
Communism, 272f, 277f
Communitarianism, 41f, 266f, 270f, 321
Company of 100 Associates, 25
Comparative advantage, 224
Competition, economic, 196f, 256
Compromise
  1820, 233f
  1850, 233, 299f, 302f, 319
  1861, 327f
Concord, battle of, 91, 265
"Concurrent majority," 245f
Confederacy, Southern, 165, 327f, 329f (Constitution of), 332f (strategy of), 335f (foreign policy), 342f (difficulties of), 353
Confederacy, Northern, 168f
"Confederate Reconstruction," 349f, 352f, 363
Confederation (13 colonies), 96, 100, 104f, 106f, 114f, 125f, 128, 142 (debts)
Confederation Congress, 112f, 174
Congregation, idea of, 41f
Congregationalists, 31f, 46f, 74f, 161f, 270
Congress, U.S., 106f, 137f, 143f, 146, 154, 159, 166, 168, 173, 176f, 182, 197f, 233f, 236f, 249, 263, 275, 282, 294, 296, 298f, 302f, 312f, 316, 320, 328f, 330f, 339f (opposes president), 349, 352f, 355f, 358f, 369f, 373
Congreve, W., 71
Conquistadors, 15f, 21f, 213
Connecticut, 23, 45f, 55, 61, 70, 110, 126f, 135, 164, 168f, 183, 211, 216, 236, 243, 263f, 366
Connecticut Valley, 45, 47
"Conscience Whigs," 298
Conscription Act (1863), 340; *see also* Draft laws
Consensus, 43, 229, 324f
Conservation, 213
Conservative political tradition, lacking in America, 259f
Conspiracy, American popular fear of, 78f, 82, 154, 178, 206, 250, 271, 281, 299, 305, 308, 324
Conspiracy laws, 280

Constitution, Federal, 40, 71f, 133, 143f, 159, 166, 173, 175, 183f, 228, 230f, 245f, 302, 304, 310, 318f, 322, 350f
  analyzed, 117–25
  full text, Appendix B
Constitution, colonial, 55f, 81
Constitutional Unionists, 324f
Consumer goods, 189, 207, 237
Containment of revolution, 109f, 111f, 128, 157,
Continental Congress, 89f, 91, 100, 104f, 140
Continental System, 171f, 177
Contract clause (Constitution), 230
Contracts, law, 121f, 211
Cooper, James Fennimore, 260f
Cooper, Peter, 196
Cooperative movement, 275
Copperheads (Northern Democrats), 340, 357
Corporations, 209, 230
Cotton, John, 46
Cotton, 53, 59, 112, 160, 162, 171f, 184, 196, 198f (exports), 219 (prices), 237 (exports), 294, 297, 204f, 216f (yields), 218, 240, 310f, 313, 321, 328f, 333, 335f, 365
Cotton gin, 198
Cotton Kingdom, 184, 215f, 284, 314, 365
Cotton plantations, 212, 215f, 310f, 328f; *see also* Plantation system *and* Slavery
Counter-Reconstruction, 367f
County fairs, 213
Cowpens, battle of, 97
Coxe, T., 145
"Crackers," 162f, 215
Craft, William, 301
Craft unions, 281
Crash; *see* Panics
Crawford, W. H., 228, 236f
Credit mechanisms, 189, 284 (first U.S. credit agency)
Creek Indians, 12, 64f, 183f, 215, 231f, 237f, 240, 254f
Creek War, 183f
Creoles, 26, 109f
Crimean War, 201
Critical Period, re-examined, 112f
Crittenden, J. J., 328f
Crittenden Compromise, 329
Croatan Indians, 26
Crockett, Davy, 293
Cromwell, Oliver, 31, 46, 49, 53

Crown colonies, 35, 39, 55
Cultural baggage, Ch. 2 passim, esp. 26f
Cultural differentiation, New World, 21f
Cultural pluralism, 262f, 291
Culture-shock, 12f
Cumberland, Maryland, 191, 193
Cumberland Gap, 61, 190
Cumberland Revival, 160f
Cumberland Road, 191
Currency, 57f, 106, 112f, 143f, 189, 246f, 348; *see also* Banking *and* Paper money

D

Dakota Indians, 66
Dare, Virginia, 26
Dart, Joseph, 214
Dana, R. H., 199f, 301
Dartmouth College v. Woodward (1819), 230
Daughters of Temperance, 280
Davis, A. J., 272
Davis, Jefferson, 326, 329
  family, 165
  President of Confederate States of America, 330f, 340, 367
Davis, John, 26
Deaf and dumb in America, 282
Dearborn, Gen. H., 182
Death-rate, Negro, 361
De Bow's Review, 321
Debts and debtors, 48, 70f, 82, 112, 167, 172, 189, 249f, 280
  debt reform laws, 121f, 235, 281f, 353
  debtors' jails, 112, 172, 280
Decatur, Stephen, 166
Deciduous forests, 218
Declaratory Act (1766), 84
Deep South, 162, 194, 211f, 215f, 310f, 314, 325f, 327f; *see also* South, as a section
Deere, John, 212
De Grasse, Admiral, 97
Deism in America, 73f, 76, 270
Delaware, 126f, 156, 169, 326
Delaware Indians, 67
Delaware River, 23, 195
Demand (as economic factor), 121, 128
  British, 198
  elasticity of demand, 202

Demand (as economic factor) —*Cont.*
　home demand, 121, 141, 206, 210; *see also* Market economy
Democracy, American view of, 75, 92, 159 (and slavery), 160f (frontier), 172f, 236, 245f, 250, 252f, 278, 308
Democratic Societies, 149
Democratic Unionists, 340
Democrats (1860s), 322f, 324f, 326
Democrats, Jacksonian (Democratic-Republicans), 146f, 158, 237, 244, 253, 285f, 290, 294, 296, 299f, 352, 358, 366; *see also* Jeffersonians
Depopulation, 12f, 15f
Depression, economic, 42, 111f, 172, 188, 204f, 230, 235, 251, 281, 367
Deseret, 274, 298
Dickinson, John, 85
Dickson, Rev. Moses, 317
Diet, American, 162f, 219
Diffusion theory, 5, 203f (industrialization), 206f (technology)
Diocese, first American Catholic, 163
Discrimination, racial, 175, 321f, 344, 373; *see also* Racism *and* Segregation
Diseases, colonial, 62, 66
Dissent, political, 236
Distribution Act, 1836, 251
District Courts, U.S., 123, 138
Division of labor, 141f, 187, 210, 220, 276
Divorce, 278
Dix, Dorothea, 282
Dixie; *see* South
Dollar, U.S., 144
Domestic service, 218, 222, 279
Dominion of New England, 46f
Dongan, Gov. Thomas, 62
Donnelly, Ignatius, 367
Donner party, 293
Double-entry bookkeeping, 204
Double jeopardy, 127
Double standard, 278
Douglas, Stephen A., 291, 299f, 301, 304f, 322f (debates with Lincoln), 325f
Douglass, Frederick, 316f, 366 and Lincoln, 327, 337
Dow, Neal, 283
Draft laws, 332, 340 (riots)

Drake, Sir Francis, 26
Dress reform, 279
Drug addiction, 282
Drunkenness, 282f, 308
Du Bois, W. E. B., 369f, 375f
Due process of law, 85, 320
Dutch colonies, 23 (Dutch West India Company), 24, 27f, 37, 40, 48, 54, 56 (Dutch Americans), 64
Dyer, Mary, 46

E

Eads, J. B., 333f
Eaton, Peggy, 243f
Eaton, John, 243f, 281
Ecology, 15, 263, 343
Economic growth, 28f, 45f, 47, 67f, 100, 112f, 121, 141, 159, Ch. 8 *passim*, 227f, 240 (Jackson and growth), 248, 251, 258, 281, 285f, 287f, 340, 370, 373
Economic growth, expectation of, 29, 287f
　conditions for, 202, 206f
　political basis for, 285f
Economic nationalism, 141f; *see also* Nationalism
Economic revolution (industrialization), 19f, 26f, 82, 186f, 224f, 228 (political basis for), 347f, 365f
Economic theory, 140f, 193, 202, 281; *see also* Gallatin, A.; Hamilton, Alexander *and* Mercantilism
Education in America, 44f, 69f, 161, 163f, 163 (Catholic), 210, 213 (farm), 222 (slaves), 230, 261f, 279 (women's), 361 (blacks)
　as social ladder, 264, 280, 321
Edwards, Jonathan, 74f
El Dorado myth, 34
Elections
　1789, 137
　1792, 147
　1796, 152f
　1799 (Congressional), 155
　1800, 155f, 165, 169
　1804, 169
　1808, 175
　1812, 156, 183
　1816, 228
　1820, 229
　1824, 235f
　1828, 184, 229, 237f

Elections—*Cont.*
　1832, 246, 249f
　1836, 285f
　1840, 183, 285f, 288
　1844, 237, 274, 285, 289f, 294, 319
　1848, 285, 298
　1852, 288, 299, 304
　1856, 285, 307f
　1860, 228, 257, 322, 324f, 326 (statistics)
　1864, 340, 351
　1866, 358
　1868, 361, 366f
　1872, 367
　1880, 283
Electoral college, 122, 137, 147, 153, 169, 175, 236, 239, 249, 290, 298, 307, 326, 340, 366
Electorate, growth of, 238f
Elevator, grain, 211, 214
Elevator, passenger, 210f
Eliot, John, 65
Elite, social, 69f, 114, 121f, 128, 139, 206, 218, 220, 223, 228f, 235f, 238, 245, 248f, 259, 265f (intellectual), 352, 357, 366, 369
Emancipation (of slaves), 220, 335f
　by Union Army, 337, 349
　voluntary, 174f, 221, 314
Emancipation Proclamation, 335f, 337, 339, 348, 351, 362f
Embargo, 171f, 183, 188
　Embargo Act (1807), 171f, 223
Emerson, Ralph Waldo, 241, 264f, 266f, 294, 297, 323
Emigrant Aid Society, 307
"empire for liberty," 157, 159
"Empty" continent, myth, 8, 232f, 296
Enclosure movement, 28
Enlightenment, in America, 72f, 82, 92, 110, 161, 258f
"Entangling alliances," 152, 165, 170f
Enterprise, private, 230f
　small enterprises, 209f
Entrepreneurs, American, 196, 204f, 209f, 249, 255f, 281f, 369
"Enumerated commodities," 53
Enumerated powers (in Constitution), 120, 143f
Environmentalism, American faith in, 82, 173, 260f, 263f, 275, 282
Equal Rights Party, 285f

Equality, American doctrine of, 69f, 92, 103, 236, 240, 253, 256, 262f, 316
and blacks, 313, 321, 357, 360, 368, 374f
Equality of opportunity, 240, 264; see also American Dream
Ericsson, John, 334
Erie Canal, 104, 192f, 194, 199, 209, 212, 224f
Erie, Lake, 164, 182, 190, 193, 195
Essex case (1805), 171
Essex Junto, 168
Ethnicity, 238 (voting), 262 (education)
Evangelicalism, 269f
Evans, G. H., 280f
Evans, Oliver, 195, 211
Everett, Edward, 325
Exchange, foreign, 188
Executions, public, 65
Executive branch (departments of), 106, 138
Executive power, American suspicion of, 106f, 351, 368
Executive privilege, 170
Expansionism, American, Ch. 11 passim, 175f, 215, 260, 274f, 285f, 305f
Exploration, western, 166, 289f
Exports, 35, 37f, 45f, 100f, 158, 171f, 187f, 190, 198f, 223f
cotton, 216, 333, 335f
Extended family, 44f
Extensive agriculture, 211f

F

Faction, American spirit of, 32, 50, 71f, 80, 146, 152, 229, 234f
Factors of production, 188f, 199, 206, 211
Factory system, 202f, 258 (factory reform), 280f
factory hands, 219, 222, 272, 321
Fairs, county, 213
Family structure, 22f, 44f, 161, 186, 275, 318
Farmers, farming, 56f, 71, 112f, 126, 128, 143, 145, 148, 157f, 160f, 170, 179, 186f, 189, 204f, 207, 211f (prices), 213f, 222f
mechanization, 209, 213f
productivity, 179, 213f
Farragut, D., 333

"Father of the Constitution," 114
Federal aid to economic growth, 141f, 145, 165f, 173, 189, 191, 197f, 209, 211, 213, 223, 228f, 240, 312f, 326; see also Internal improvements
Federal bases in the South, 330f
Federal style, 133, 135f
Federalism, Ch. 9 passim
evolution of federal system)
origins, 104f, 111
Federalist Papers, 109, 126, 143, 146
Federalists, Ch. 6 passim, 112f, 114f, 125f, 146f, 148f, 156f, 167, 175, 178, 228f, 309
choose name, 106, 125f, 140
High Federalists, 154, 168, 183
Feminism, 241, 258, 275, 278f, 282, 318, 321, 360
Feudalism, in America, 20 (definition), 25f, 30, 38f, 41f, 48, 83
Filibuster raids, 286, 305
Fillmore, Millard, 285, 299f, 307f
Fink, Mike, 165
Finney, C. G., 270f, 284, 316
Finns, 23
"Fire-eaters," 320, 325f, 327
Fires, in cities, 163
First Families of Virginia, 71
Fishing industry, 24, 45, 54, 68, 198
fishing rights, 98, 184
Fitch, John, 195
Fitzhugh, George, 269, 321
Five Civilized Tribes, 12, 254f
Fletcher v. *Peek* (1810), 230
Florida, 25, 82, 97f, 113, 151, 154, 167, 172, 176, 183f, 190, 215, 220, 229, 231f, 241, 244, 302, 328, 330f, 363
Flour milling, 57, 149, 194, 198, 201, 207, 211 (machinery), 214f
Folklore, 267, 372
Foot, Sen. S. A., 243
Force Acts, 246, 362, 373
Foreclosures, mortgage, 112
Foreign capital in United States, 189, 202
Foreign policy, American, 113f, 133, 137, 140, 148f, 150f (control of), 156, 166f, 170f, 175f, 228, 234f, 237, 252, 305f, 335f

Forests, American, 59, 201, 208, 218
Forrest, Gen. N. B., 362f
Fort Caroline, 24
Fort Dearborn massacre, 164
Fort Duquesne, 63
Fort Hall, 292
Fort Jackson, treaty of, 184, 231
Fort Mims massacre, 231
Fort Moultrie, 330f
Fort Pickens, 330f
Fort Snelling, 319
Fort Sumter, 213, 310, 330f
"Forty acres and a mule," 363f
Forty-Niners, 293
Forty-Ninth Parallel, 229
Foster, Stephen, 260
Founding Fathers, 71f, 102f, 109f, 146, 168, 213
as a cohort group, 113, 115f
and slavery issue, 110, 314, 322
Fourier, Charles, 267, 276f, 280
Fox Indians, 62
Fox sisters, 272
Franchise, 122, 236, 238, 279f (women); see also Voting rights
Franklin, Benjamin, 69f, 72f, 74, 76, 80, 92, 96, 98, 106, 108, 113, 117, 122, 137, 258
Fredericksburg, battle of, 337f
Free Democrats, 304
Free labor, 205, 220f, 307, 325f, 364
"Free land," 296
Free Love, 277
Free Negroes, 219, 221, 234 (Liberia), 275f, 301, 313f, 321f (in North), 320, 327, 337
Free Soil Party, 263, 298, 304, 307, 319, 325f
Free trade, 120f, 128, 141 (imperialism), 142, 189, 199, 227, 239, 330, 367
Free Will, 161
Free Will Baptists, 162
Freedmen, 353, 361f (desires)
Freedmen's Bureau, 355f, 360f
Freedom
American negative concept of, 241f, 260, 287, 322, 366
of press, 83, 154f
of seas, 148f
of speech, 83, 154f

Index

Freedom—*Cont.*
  of thought, Old South, 318f, 326
Freemen, 40f, 42
Freeport Doctrine, 322f
Freethinkers, 76
Frelinghuysen, Rev. T., 73
Fremont, J. C., 289, 293, 295, 307
French, 66f (and Indians), 103f (influence on American Constitution), 108, 137, 142, 145, 148, 149 (French-American alliance), 151f, 153, 154 (spies), 163, 167, 170, 175f, 195, 198, 213, 231, 235, 252 (French-American crisis), 276f (socialism), 294, 336
  colonies, 22, 24f, 28, 60f, 93f
  French-Americans, 32, 159, 163
  immigration to America, 154, 163, 223, 277
  influence on American radicalism, 258, 267, 276f
  slavery, compared with American, 163, 219
French Canada, 22, 62, 64, 79, 82, 89, 188f
Frobisher, Martin, 26
Froebel, F. W. A., 261
Frontier, 60f, 62f (wars on), 71, 73f (religion), 75, 109, 150, 158f, 190, 197f, (and railroads), 224f, 231, 256, 260, 275, 287 (and American character), 288, 313, 322
  democracy, 240f, 269
  nationalism, 159, Ch. 11 passim, 293f, 306
  society, 150f, 159f, 163f, 183, 262, 286, 293
  towns, 164, 187, 195, 278
Fugitive Slave Law, 299f, 301 (cases), 304, 319, 329
Fugitive slaves, 121, 124, 174, 278
Full faith and credit clause, 124
Fuller, Margaret, 266, 278
Fulton, Robert, 194f, 230f
Fur trade, 23f, 42, 45, 61f, 64, 234, 289
Furniture styles, American, 272

G

Gabriel plot, 323
Gadsden Purchase, 296, 304

Gag rule, 318f
Gage, General, 91f
Gallatin, A., 165f, 197
Galloway, J., 90, 98
Garnet, Henry H., 316, 317f
Garrison, William Lloyd, 310, 315f, 317, 318 (mobbed), 321, 353, 365
Gaspé Peninsula, 24, 62
Gaspee incident (1772), 87f
Gates, Horatio, 96
General welfare clause (Constitution), 118, 127
Generation, first American, 133f
Genêt, Citizen E., 148f
Geneva, New York, 279
Geographic determinism, 304
George III, 78, 89, 91f, 99, 134
George, Lake, 190
Georgia, 48, 59, 64f, 68, 89, 97, 104, 112, 121, 126f, 158f (frontier), 195f, 205, 216, 223, 230f, 236f, 254f, 299, 318, 325, 328, 340f, 362, 372f
German immigrants, 49, 56, 60f, 92, 163, 190, 212, 271f, 274f, 277, 283, 308
German influence on U.S. culture, 258, 268f, 274f
Gettysburg, 328
Gettysburg Address, 340
Ghent, treaty of, 183f
Gibbon v. *Ogden* (1824), 121, 230f
Glagow, Ellen, 372
Glass industry, 35, 45, 85, 281
Godey's Lady's Book, 265, 279
Gold, 15, 22, 30, 42, 57, 112, 144, 195, 198f, 201, 251, 293, 298
  gold fever, 13f, 15f
  gold strikes, 281, 292, 298
Good Feelings, Era of, redefined, 229f
Gothic novels, 267
Government
  American view of, 186, 227f
  by assembly, 118f, 122
  by consent, 30f, 83f, 98
Governors, colonial, 52, 55f, 84f
Governors, of states, 104f, 116
Graduation Bill, 243
Grain trade, 56f, 149, 194, 198, 201, 212, 224f, 293
Grand jury system, 127
Grant, U. S., 335, 340f, 343, 360, 366f
Grass-roots politics, 149, 167, 235f, 238f, 253
Gravity-feed machinery, 211

Gray, Capt. R., 288
Great Awakening, 72f
Great Chain of Being, 174
Great Collaboration (Madison and Jefferson), 146
Great Compromise (Constitution), 117, 126
Great Lakes, 25, 62, 98, 164, 184, 192, 196, 229, 293
  militarization of, 184, 229
Great Migration, 42, 45, 56
Great Plains, 66
Great Salt Lake, 274, 289
Greek Revival style, 136f
Greeley, Horace, 265, 276, 321, 326f, 351, 353, 367f
Greenbacks, 144
Greenville, treaty of (1795), 150
Grenville, George, 82f
Grimké, Angelina, 316
Guadelupe Hidalgo, treaty of (1848), 295
Guerilla warfare, 61, 93f

H

Habeas corpus, 121, 362
habitants, 25
Hale, Sarah Josepha, 279, 304
Halfway Covenant, 47, 72
Hall v. *De Cuir* (1878), 373
Hamilton, Alexander, 102, 104, 108, 110, 114, 116, 119, 121, 123, 126, 133, 137f, 140f (his thought), 146f, 148 (foreign affairs), 152f, 154f, 157f, 165, 168f, 169 (death), 173, 175, 186, 202, 229f, 246, 303
Hamiltonian System, 140f, 165, 228
Hampton, Wade, 353, 373
Hancock, John, 9, 69, 86, 92
Harper's Ferry, Virginia, 268, 323f, 335
Harris, Joel Chandler, 372
Harrison, William Henry, 176f, 183, 285f, 288
Hartford Convention, 183, 310
Hawaii, 37, 201, 287
"Hawks" (foreign policy), 228, 286
Hawthorne, Nathaniel, 241, 266f
Hayes, Pres. R. B., 367
Hayne, Sen. R., 243
Headrights, 35, 38
Helper, Hinton Rowan, 326
Hemings, Sally, 173f
Henry, Patrick, 84, 87, 90, 110, 118, 138

The U.S.A.

Hereditary principle in government, 119
Heredity versus environment argument, 263f
Heresy trials, 271
Higginson, Thomas W., 323
High-wage economy, in America, 188f
"Higher Law" argument, 266, 279, 304
Hildreth, Richard, 320
Hillbillies, 162f, 215
Hillsborough, Lord, 85
Hindu thought, influence in America, 267
Holbrook, Josiah, 264
"Hollywood Indian," 8f
Holmes, Oliver Wendell, 264
Home market, 187f, 190, 206, 210; see also Demand and Market economy (as economic factor)
Homespun, 137, 202, 219, 223
Homestead Act (1862), 280, 313, 326, 363f
Homesteads (family farm), 56f, 68, 107, 157f, 162, 212, 218, 280, 310, 326, 363f, 366
homo sapiens, in America, 3, 5
Hooker, General Joseph, 337f
Hooker, Rev. T., 45, 46f
Horses, in America, 66, 196, 213f, 289
Horseshoe Bend, battle of, 184, 231
Hot gospellers, 161f, 269f
Hotels, American, 209
House slaves, 222
Housebuilding, 27
Houston, Sam, 293f
Howe, Elias, 206f
Howe, Dr. S. G., 282
Howe, Sir W., 93
Hudson Bay Company, 62f, 234
Hudson River School, 134, 259f
Hudson River valley, 23, 48, 56, 93, 169, 183, 190, 192, 194, 196, 205
Hull, Gen. William, 182
humanitarian reforms, 253f, 281f
Hussey, Obed, 212
Hutchinson, Anne, 43f, 46
Hutchinson, Gov. T., 79, 84
Hypnotism, 272

I

Icarians, 277
Ice-cream industry, 214f
Iceland, 6, 14
Idaho, 280, 292, 296

Ide, W. B., 292
Identity, national, 81f; see also American self-consciousness and identity
Ideology in America, 82 (Revolution), 227f
 relative absence of), 236
Illinois, 97, 159, 164f, 198, 212f, 216 (population), 255, 274, 282, 291, 299, 312, 318f, 321f, 327
Illinois River, 193, 198, 293
Impeachment process, 118f, 123, 154, 351, 358f
Imperialism, American, 141, 287f, 305f; see also Expansionism, American; Internal empire, America's; Manifest Destiny; and Territorial growth, United States
Implied powers (Constitution), 147, 230f, 330
Imports, 189, 197, 202, 237, 239, 312
Impressment, 150f, 171f, 175, 177, 184
Inaugurals
 Jackson, 239
 Jefferson, 157f, 165
 Lincoln, 327, 332, 341
 Washington, 138
Income distribution, 69f, 194, 264
Indentured labor, 7, 36, 49, 56f, 68, 70
Independence, Declaration of (U.S.), 69, 78, 91f, 102f, 104, 106, 112, 116, 129, 227, 268, 314
Independence, Declaration of (Women, 1848), 280
Independence, theory of, 90f
Independent judiciary, 78, 103f, 123f
Indiana, 159, 164, 273
Indian, American, 3f, 7f, 15f, 21f, 25 (French view), 26, 32f, 35, 42f, 62f, 64f, 66, 71, 87, 97 (in Revolution), 108, 118f (in Constitution), 151, 159, 173 (Jefferson), 176f, 213, 215, 231f (Indian concept of land-ownership), 233 (Supreme Court), 240, 244, 259f, 260 (portrayed), 275, 286, 288, 292f (white view), 296, 306 (seen as "barrier"), 312, 316
 British view, 60f, 66f, 177
 Indian policy, 13, 60f, 66f, 80, 82, 231f, 237f, 314

Indian—*Cont.*
 Jackson, Andrew, 231f, 253f
 named "Indians," 3, 37
 removal, 253f, 314
 wars, 46, 61f, 64f, 113, 150, 231f, 256
Indian Removal Act (1830), 254
Indian Springs, treaty of (1825), 237f
Indian Territory, 176, 254, 319
Indigo, 58f, 100, 145, 215
Indirect election of senators, 122
Individualism, American version of, 43, 53, 66, 103, 106, 108f, 127f, 142 (economic), 186, 228, 260f, 265f, 267f, 366
Industrial Revolution; see also Economic revolution and Industrialization process
 American, 82, 100, 112f, 172, 187f, 198, 202f, 207, 262, 310
 British, 27, 123, 145, 215f
"Industrial" slavery, 218, 222f; see also Slavery
Industrial society, 202f, 276f (rejected), 310
Industrialization process, 82, 112f, 145, 158, 193, 202f (social impact of), 205f (conditions), 207 (world), 212f, 321, 368f, 372f
Inertia, popular, 259
Inflation, 28f, 112, 246f, 249, 251
Infrastructure, 15, 193
Inner Light doctrine, 31, 46
Innovation, 199
Insane, in America, 282
Intellectuals, American, 240, 265f
Intermarriage, racial, 22, 26, 65; see also Race-mixing
Internal empire, America's, 159, 184, 287f
Internal improvements, 141f, 145, 165f, 175, 191, 227, 237, 240, 312f, 326
Interposition, doctrine of, 155, 171f
Interstate commerce, 231, 373
Interstate and intercolonial conflicts, 81, 87, 110f
Intertribal wars (Indian), 66
Intolerable Acts (1774), 88f
Investment, capital, 145, 165f, 188, 191, 196f (railroads), 202f, 369
"Invisible hand," 141

Iowa, 193, 219, 255, 274, 293, 306
Irish in America, 6, 49, 154, 163, 188, 190 (contributions), 199, 219, 262f, 271, 281, 283, 308, 340
Iron Act (1750), 60
Iron industry, 35, 60, 68, 100, 145, 206f, 239, 246, 357, 368f, 373
Ironclads, 333f
Iroquois Confederacy, 48f, 62f
Iroquois Indians, 25, 45, 64, 66f
Isolationism, 149, 184

J

Jackson, Andrew, 24, 78, 120f, 123, 158, 167, 183f, 228f, 229 (Jacksonians), 231f (and Indians), 236f, 238f (Jacksonian Revolution), 240f (life), 241–56 (presidency), 257f, 280f, 290, 308f, 310 (love of Union), 312f, 318
  Jacksonian Democracy, 229, 240f, 246–56
  Rachel Jackson, 240, 244
Jackson, Stonewall, 333, 335, 338 (death)
Jamestown, Virginia, 32, 34, 58, 64
Japan, 3, 14, 287 (opened to trade), 282, 296, 305, 348
Jay, John, 98, 126, 150f
Jay Treaty (1794), 150f
Jeans, 59
Jefferson, Thomas, 38, 64, 73f, 76, 92, 107, 110f, 113, 115, 121, 123, 128f, 134f, 135 (and architecture), 137f, 143f, 145f, 148f (foreign policy), 151, 153f (vice-presidency), 155f (1800 election), 157–75 (presidency), 173f (on race), 175, 188, 191, 195, 212 (as farmer), 213, 220, 223, 228, 234 (death), 236, 240, 253, 257f, 275, 291, 307, 309f, 314 (slave-owner)
  Jeffersonianism, evolving, 157f, 172f, 246
  Jeffersonians, 228f, 280, 288, 321, 350, 375
  realism, 165
  vision of America, 157f
Jefferson Birthday Dinner (1830), 244f
"Jerks," 161, 270
Jesuits in America, 64, 223

Jews in America, 13f, 28, 32, 275
Jingoism, 154
Johnson, Andrew, 123 (impeachment), 349, 351f, 353, 358f
Johnson, H. V., 325
Johnson, Lyndon B., 122
Johnson's and Graham's Lessee v. McIntosh (1823), 232f, 340
Johnston, General Joseph E., 343
Joint stock companies, 27, 39, 42, 48
Jones, John Paul, 93, 97
Judicial nationalism, 156, 167f
Judicial review, 124, 138, 168
Judiciary Act, 1789, 123f, 138, 168
Judiciary Act, 1801, 165, 167
Judiciary, independent, 78, 103f, 123f
Julian, G., 352, 364
Junto, 79f
Jury trial, 124, 128, 301, 355
Justices of the Peace, 30f, 167
Juvenile courts, 282

K

Kanagawa, treaty of, 305
Kansas, 190, 305f, 323, 366
Kansas-Nebraska Act, 304f, 308, 319
Karlsefni, Thorfinn, 6
Kearny, Stephen, 295
Keelboat era, 164f
Kelly, William, 209
Kennedy, John F., 122
Kentucky, 61, 151, 155, 158f, 160, 163, 165, 176, 190, 197, 209, 213, 216 (population), 220, 223, 236, 242, 273, 312, 314, 319, 322, 325f, 328f
Kettell, T. P., 195f
Kindergarten, 261f
"King Mob," 239
King Street, Boston, 86
King's Mountain, battle of (1780), 97
"Kitchen cabinet," 242
"Kitchen slavery" (of women), 277
Knights of Liberty, 317
Know Nothing Party, 308, 325
Kosciuszko, Thaddeus, 96, 116
Ku Klux Klan, 357, 361f
Kwakiutl Indians, 9

L

Labor, 166, 188f, 204f, 253, 280f

Labor-intensive economy, 189f
Labor mobility, 28, 194
Labor movement, 281, 360
Labor parties, 280
Labor reservoir, 206
Labor-saving devices, 190, 210, 212, 273
Labor scarcity in America, 35f, 37 (and slavery), 42, 70, 188f, 210f, 212, 217
Ladd, William, 294f
Lafayette, Marquis de, 97, 149
Laissez-faire, 140f, 242, 249, 251, 255f, 369, 373
Lame-duck period, 327, 331f
Lancaster Turnpike, 191, 195
Land abundance, 188f
Land Act (1820), 230
Land companies, 61, 107f, 159
Land grants, federal, 166, 189, 195, 197f, 363f
Land hunger, 6, 215, 286, 296
Land Ordinances
  1785, 107f, 159
  1787, 159, 174
  1790, 159
Land speculation, 70f, 107f
Landholding, 25, 186
  Indian concept of, 66, 231
Lane, Joseph, 325
Lane Theological Seminary, 170, 310
Las Casas, B. de, 13f, 15f
Latin America, 70, 109f (revolutions), 138, 219, 229, 234f, 252, 286f (North American view of)
Latrobe, B. H., 135f
LeCompton Constitution, 307, 320, 322
Lee, "Mother" Ann, 273f
Lee, Henry, 106
Lee, Rev. Jason, 289
Lee, Robert E., 323, 338f, 342f
LeHigh Crane Ironworks, Pennsylvania, 208
Leisler's Revolt (1689), 48, 89
L'Enfant, Major Pierre Charles, 136f
Letter from a Pennsylvania Farmer, 85
Lewis and Clark expedition, 159, 288f
Liberal freedoms, 84, 127f, 154f
Liberalism, American, 84, 92, 103, 127f, 154f, 367
Liberals, French, 103f
Liberator, 315, 318
Liberty, American view of, 91, 127f, 129
Liberty Party, 290, 298, 301, 304, 316, 319
Libraries, 264
Life-style, colonial, 56f

Lincoln, Abraham, 165 (family), 253, 294f (opposes Mexican War), 303, 322f (Lincoln-Douglas debates), 342f (elected president), 327 (views on Union), 331, 337, 340 (as orator), 343 (death), 350 (views on Negro) emancipation, 327f, 337
Literacy, 264f
Living standards, American, 218
Livingston, R. R., 167, 195, 213
Loans, government, 96, 106, 246, 336
Locke, John, 40, 51f, 66, 74, 92, 99f, 102f, 116, 129
Locofocos, 285f
Log cabins, 23, 162
London government and its views, 32f, 35, 49, 52, 55, 58, 60f, 67, 71, 78, 80f, 100
Long Island, battle of (1771), 93
Lost Colony, 26, 33
Louis XIV, 24, 25, 31, 52, 61
Louis XVI, 147
Louisberg, 63f
Louisiana, 61f, 64, 113, 159, 163 (lifestyle), 169, 184, 197, 215f, 216 (population table), 218, 220, 233f, 297, 318, 328, 349f, 353, 362f, 367, 373
Louisiana Purchase, 123, 151, 154, 157, 159, 163, 166f, 229, 234, 305f
Love cult, 270, 277f
Love-match marriages, 44f
Lovejoy, E. P., 318
Lowell, Massachusetts, 205f
Lowell, F. C., 204f
Lowell, J. R., 319
Loyalists, 77f, 110, 93, 97f, 182 ("Late Loyalists")
Lumber industry, 45, 56f, 198, 201, 206f, 293, 318; see also Timber
Lundy, Benjamin, 314f
Lyceum movement, 264
Lynching, 161, 340, 343, 355, 373

M

McClellan, Gen. G., 333, 337f, 340
McCormick reaper, 209f, 212, 222
McCrummell, Dr. J. C., 316

McCulloch v. Maryland (1819), 121, 230f, 243, 248
McGready, Rev. J., 161
McGuffy Readers, 264
McHenry, Jerry, 301
McKay, Donald, 199
Madison, James, 38, 108f, 114, 117f, 123f, 126, 133, 137f, 158, 142f, 146f, 149, 150f, 152, 155, 165, 167f, 171f, 175-184 (presidency), 228, 230, 233, 236, 246, 275
Mail, U.S., 198; see also Post office
Maine, 32, 45, 159, 187, 196, 234
 boundary dispute, 151, 283, 288
Majoritarian democracy, American, Part II passim, 236f, 245f, 256, 283, 313f, 360, 364
Malnutrition, 163, 219
Man-land ratio, 25, 35f, 47, 64, 166, 188f, 197, 211, 213
Mandamus, writ of, 167f
Manhattan, 23, 48, 193, 264; see also New York City
Manifest Destiny, 159, 286f (origins), 291, 296f
Mann, Horace, 261f, 279
Manufactures, Report on (1791), 145f
Manufacturing industries, 57f, 145f, 188, 202f, 204f, 310f
Marbury v. Madison (1803), 124, 167f, 230
Marbury, William, 167f
Marcy, William L., 239
Maritime rights, 176, 184; see also Impressment
Market economy, 109, 112f, 120f, 126, 128, 141, 187f, 189, 206f, 224, 281, 237, 361
Marriage, changing ideas of, 44f, 275f, 277, 310
Marshall, John, 118, 121, 124, 128, 156 (becomes Chief Justice), 166f, 170, 230f, 232f (on Indians), 242, 244, 248, 255
Maryland, 32, 35, 37, 38f, 41f, 46, 55, 58, 64, 68, 70, 126, 137, 193f, 220, 223, 230f, 242, 248, 314, 317, 326, 328, 335
Mason, J. M. and Slidell, J., 336
Mason, John, 305
Mass society, 256
Massachusetts, 29, 42f, 46f, 59f, 65f, 70, 79f, 84, 90f,

Massachusetts—Cont.
 111f, 126f, 143, 158, 165, 168f, 183, 193, 196f, 202f, 207f, 216, 234, 236 (Constitution of 1820), 241, 262f, 272, 279, 282 (legislature), 318f, 321, 325
 education in, 262f, 321
Massachusetts Circular Letter (1768), 85
Massachusetts School Law, 262 (1647), 263 (1827), 321 (1855, desegregation)
Massachusetts State Board of Education, 262
Materialism, American, 186, 259, 320f
Mather, Increase, 65
Mathew, Father Theobald, 283
Mayflower, 39
Mayflower Compact, 27, 40, 52, 102
Maysville Turnpike, 241, 313
Meade, Gen. G. G., 338, 340
Meatpacking industry, 164, 201 (exports), 211, 214f
Mechanical ingenuity of Americans, 188, 210f
"Mechanics," 70, 110
Mechanics' institutes, 264
Mechanization, 190, 210f, 212f, 216f, 222
Medical profession, women enter, 279
"Men on the make," 218, 230, 240, 249, 255f
Mennonites, 49, 272
Mental illness in America, 258, 282
Mercantilism, 19, 22, 25, 53f, 56, 81, 100f, 140f
Merchant capitalism, 27; see also Capitalism
Merchant navy, 166, 177, 218
Merchant seamen, 110, 199f
Merchants, 47, 56f, 65, 68f, 70f, 84, 88f, 100, 109, 149f, 170, 171f, 177f (1812 War), 183, 190, 201, 204f (enter manufacturing), 296, 312f
 in Revolution, 84, 88f
Merino sheep, 202, 213
Meritocracy, 69f
Merrimace Manufacturing Co., 205
Mestizos, 13, 286, 296
Methodists, 73, 161f, 283, 289
Metropolis, 164
Mexico, 5, 7, 12f, 20, 23, 63, 176, 196, 235 (independence), 251, 274f, 286, 289, 293f, 295 (halved by the United States), 296, 305, 329, 336

Michigan, 164, 212, 216 (population table), 291
Michigan, Lake, 193, 195
Microwave ovens, 274
Middle (Atlantic) states, 56f, 91f, 173, 183, 187, 198, 224f, 239, 281f, 310f
Middle class, 205, 228, 236, 252, 264, 283
"Middle Passage" (slaveships), 56
Middle West (Midwest), 7, 97, 164, 187, 192f, 194, 196, 202, 204, 212, 215f, 215 (population table), 222, 255, 276f, 272, 293f, 295, 307, 310f, 315 (antislavery); see also Old Northwest
"Midnight judges," 167
Migration
  emigration (to Canada), 182
  immigration, 5f, 23, 27f, 48f, 56, 59f, 64, 141, 154, 163, 189f, 190 (contributions), 194, 198f, 201, 205, 217, 219, 223, 237, 271, 274, 277, 279, 291f, 308, 340
  internal, 21, 25, 29, 37f, 42, 45, 47f, 59, 164f, 193, 212, 239, 289f, 292f
Militia, 155, 178f, 183f, 231, 280, 288, 340, 362
Miller, William, 272
Minimal government, idea of, 158, 166, 172f
"Ministerial" policies, 55f, 78f, 91
Minnesota, 7, 293
Minorities, 28, 245f, 253f, 263
Minstrel shows, 260
Mint, U.S., 144f
Mint Act (1792), 144
Minuit, Peter, 23
Minutemen, 91
Miracle of peaceful transfer of political power, 228, 324f
"Miscegenation," 174; see also Intermarriage, racial and Race-mixing
Missionaries, American, 287, 289
Missions, 234, 287, 289, 293
Mississippi, 9, 12, 22, 159, 163, 165, 184, 198, 215f, 216 (population table), 224, 297, 299, 328, 335, 339, 363, 374
Mississippi River and Valley, 60f, 64, 89, 108f, 151, 159, 164, 184, 188, 193, 196, 212, 215, 224f, 256, 290f, 295, 333f, 339

Missouri, 159, 190, 223, 233f, 243, 274, 302, 306, 312, 319f, 326, 328, 333
Missouri Compromise, 218, 229, 233f, 302, 306f, 319f
Mob, fear of, 104, 139, 239
Mobile and Ohio Railroad, 198
Mobility, social, 28, 69f, 100, 281, 307
Modernization, 17f
Mohawk Indians, 88
Mohawk valley, 62, 205, 270
Molasses, 56f, 82f
Molasses Act, 83
Monarchy for America, 102, 122, 138
Monetary issues, 189 (roots), 248f
Money, American phobia about, 248f
Money bills, 119f
Monk, Maria, 271
"Monocrats," 128, 148
Monoculture, 58f, 222
Monopoly, American fears of, 143, 197f, 230f, 247f, 280
Monroe, James, 158, 167, 228f (presidency), 234, 286, 314
Monroe Doctrine (1823), 184, 234f, 237, 291
Montana, 296
Montgomery Ward, 187
Morgan, Justin, 213
Morgan horse, 213
Mormons, 270, 272, 274, 303 (Mormon War)
Morris, Gouverneur, 114
Morris, Robert, 57, 112f, 114
Mortgages, 198, 205
Mosquitoes, 194
Mott, Lucretia, 279
Mount Vernon, 114, 117, 213
"Mulatto," 37 (use of word), 163, 173, 317
Music, American, 259f, 283
Music halls, 264

N

N.A.A.C.P., 375
Narragansett Indians, 43, 45, 65
Nashoba, Tennessee, 275f, 313
Nashville, Tennessee, 158, 190, 240
Natchez, 195
Natchez Indians, 9
Natick Indians, 87
National American Temperance Society, 213
National consciousness, 64 (Canadian nationality), 228; see also Nationalism, American

National debt, 109, 142f; see also Loans, government
National Republican party, 158, 237f, 239, 249f
National Road, 191, 237
Nationalism
  black, 314, 317, 375f
  British, 28f, 30f, 81
  Canadian, 64, 98, 182
  judicial, 156, 167f, 230f
Nationalism, American, 23, 81f, 91, 113f (Founding Fathers), 124, 128, 134f (nationalism and the arts), 140f, 154, 156f, 159, 166, 172f, 192f, 224, 228f ("new"), 243f, 260, 268 (cultural), 272, 290f, 293f, 305f, 308, 310; see also Expansionism, American
  economic, 229f, 236
  frontier, 293f, Ch. 11 passim
  territorial, 175–85, 214f, 231f, 234f
Nativism, 215, 260, 271, 283, 291f, 308
Natural Law, 64, 92, 98, 103f
Naturalization Act (1798), 154, 165, 308
Nature, American cult of, 134 (art), 259f
Navajo Indians, 9
Naval stores, 28, 35, 56, 58, 198
Navigation Acts, 45, 53f, 57f, 81, 100f, 201
Navy, American, 149, 166, 182f, 333f, 336
Nebraska, 214, 305f
"Negro," use of word, 37, 321
Negro Americans, see Black Americans
"Negro" pews, 321
Nell, W. C., 321
Neo-Federalism, 228f
Neo-Jeffersonianism, see Jacksonian Democracy
Neo-mercantilism, 140f, 145, 158, 173
Neutral rights, 148f, 175f
Neutral trading by United States, 100f, 146, 148f, 154, 179f, 184
Nevada, 3, 295, 298
New Amsterdam, 23, 64
New Bedford, 45
New Brunswick, 98
New Calvinism, 27
New Deal, 121
New England, 7, 22, 26, 28, 32 (named by John Smith), 39f, 41f, 46, 48, 56f, 62, 65f, 70f, 75, 82f, 91f, 112, 126f, 156, 164f, 168, 173,

New England—Cont.
183, 187, 202f (Industrial Revolution), 205, 211, 224f, 239, 248, 262, 265f, 273, 296, 307, 327, 337
New England Antislavery Society, 316f
New France, 22, 25f, 40, 62, 64
New Hampshire, 45f, 55, 126, 230, 304
New Harmony, Indiana, 275
New Haven, Connecticut, 45f
New Jersey, 14, 48, 50, 59f, 73, 93, 110, 117f, 143, 168, 174, 197, 209, 218, 276f, 326
New Jersey Plan, 117f, 223
New Mexico, 3, 62, 190, 286, 295f (statehood), 298, 302f, 303 (slavery)
New nation, America as the first, 102f, 286
New Orleans, Louisiana, 61, 113, 151, 158, 163f, 167, 172, 195f, 199, 220, 223, 333, 339, 343, 350, 355 (riot), 362, 372
New Orleans, battle of, 180, 236, 240
New Plymouth, 32f, 64
New South, 205, 372f
New Spain, 40
New Sweden, 23
New World, idea of, 5f, 17
New York Central Park, 261
New York Central Railroad, 196, 224
New York City, 23, 68, 109f, 126, 158, 172, 183f, 193f, 196f, 199, 206, 224f, 248, 253, 260, 283f (radical center), 285, 290, 340 (draft riots)
New York state, 48, 55f, 59f, 62, 70, 78f, 84, 93, 96, 113, 117f, 120, 136f, 139f, 143, 147, 149, 153, 155f, 168f, 178, 190f, 192f, 218, 231, 234, 236 (constitution, 1821), 238f, 242, 248f, 253, 270, 272f, 274, 279f, 283, 298, 310, 312, 317f, 319, 323, 325f
Newfoundland, 7, 24, 26, 62, 98
Newspapers, 68, 83, 150, 154, 167, 238f, 264f, 286, 305
Newport, Rhode Island, 67, 70, 97
Newport, Captain Christopher, 35
Newton, Isaac, 73f
Niagara, 66, 178, 182, 288
Niagara Movement, 375

Niña, 14
"No taxation without representation," 52, 55f, 83
"Noble Savage" concept, 259f
Non-Importation Act (1806), 171f
Non-Intercourse Act (1809), 177
Nonsectarian public education, 262f
Nonviolence, 317
Normal Schools, 262, 279
North, Lord, 87f, 97
North, as section, 173, 196, 211, 218, 224f, 243f, 295, 297f, 310f
North American Phalanx, 226
North Carolina, 55, 58f, 61, 71, 87, 126, 163, 220, 223, 314, 326, 328, 332, 343
North Sea, 53, 97
North, Simeon, 211
North-South political axis, 146f
North-South sectional division too simplistic, 310f
Northampton, Massachusetts, 74, 261
Northeast, as section, 171f, 190, 194, 243, 248f, 310f; *see also* New England *and* New York state
Northern Confederacy, 168f
Northwest, as section, 62f, 288f; *see also* Old Northwest
Northwest Ordinance (1787), 108
Northwest Passage, 24, 33, 192
Northwest Territory, 164
Notes on Virginia (1784), 135, 174
Nova Scotia, 45, 62
Novanglus Letters (1774), 90
Novelists, American, 267
Noyes, J. H., 257, 277f, 318
Nuclear family, 44f
Nullification, 155, 243f, 245 (definition), 246
"Number Seven," 148

O

Oath, presidential, 122
Oberlin College, 270, 279, 284, 316
Ogden, A., 230f
Oglethorpe, J., 48, 64f, 231
Ohio, 60f, 87, 97, 159, 163f (frontier lifestyle), 187, 191, 209, 212, 214, 216 (population table), 223, 225, 237, 263, 272f, 274, 312, 319 (Underground Railroad), 321

Ohio Canal, 164, 212
Ohio Company (1747), 61, 108
Ohio River, 60, 89, 108, 164, 191, 193, 212, 214
Oil, 188
Oklahoma, 255, 303 (Panhandle)
"Old Hickory" (Andrew Jackson), 240
Old Northwest, 97f, 98 (forts), 103 (Catholic settlers), 108, 150f, 158f, 171f, 174 (slavery excluded), 183, 211f, 214f, 221f
Old Southwest, 108, 113, 151f, 160f (frontier lifestyle), 171f, 175 (boom lands), 183f, 211, 215f, 218, 221, 224
Old Spanish Trail, 289
Olmsted, Frederick Law, 222, 261
One-party system, 158, 229, 235f, 285f
Oneida, 270, 277f, 318
Opecancanough, Chief, 35, 64
Opium trade, 251
Opportunity, in America, 240f, 256, 264, 275, 280f; *see also* American Dream *and* Economic growth
Optimism, American, 28
Orders-in-Council (British), 149f, 171f, 177f
Oregon, 195, 229, 288f, 292, 296, 308, 310, 325
Oregon Question, 184, 237, 286, 288, 289f
Oregon Trail, 289f, 292
Oregon Treaty (1846), 292, 296
Oriental influence in America, 267
Oriental trade, 200f, 288f
Osceola, Chief, 254
Ostend Manifesto, 305
O'Sullivan, J. L., 286
Otis, E. G., 210f
Otis, James, 84, 87
Ottawa Indians, 67
"Oversoul" doctrine (Emerson), 267
Owen, Robert, 261, 275, 280
Owen, Robert Dale, 261, 272, 280 (supports women's movement), 289 (on Oregon Question), 313

P

Pacifism, 273, 315; *see also* Anti-war feelings *and* Peace movement
Paine, Tom, 73f, 76, 91f, 98, 100, 103, 108f, 110f, 147f,

Index

Paine, Tom—*Cont.*
   152 (split with Washington)
Painting, American, 134f, 259f
Pamphleteers, 68, 76, 78f, 83, 85f, 114
Panics
   1819, 198f, 230, 244
   1837, 193f, 199, 251, 258, 281, 287f
   1857, 201, 281, 325
Paper money, 57, 83, 91, 112f, 143f, 146, 248f, 251f, 312
Paris, treaty of (1783), 98f, 150, 177
Parkman, Francis, 81
Participatory democracy, 278
Parties, political, 23, 80, 125f, 143, 146, 166, 167 (local), 173, 226, 229 (one-party dominance), 235f, 238f, 249f, 253, 285f, 319 (party system absorbs radicals), 324f, 327; *see also* Congress, U.S.; Grass-roots politics; *and* One-party system created, 125f, 146f
Partisanship, political, 147f, 173
Party conventions, 249f
Party discipline, 167, 173, 236
Party press, 167; *see also* Newspapers
Passive resistance, 266, 317f; *see also Civil Disobedience*
Pastoral agriculture, 164, 212
"patents" (land), 36
Paternalism, 219, 235, 321
Paterson, W., 117f
Patriotism, 287; *see also* Nationalism
Patronage, political, 55f, 79f, 99, 167, 169, 239, 253, 327f
Patroons, 23, 25, 48
Pattie, S. and J., 289
Pawtucket, R. I., 204
Paxton Boys (1763), 71
Peace movement, 258, 294f, 318
Peaceful transfer of political power, 152f, 155f
Peale, C. W., paintings by, 134, 147
"Peculiar institution," 175
Peddler, Yankee, 160
Penn, William, 48f
Pennsylvania, 39, 48f, 55f, 61, 70f, 72, 76, 93, 104, 114, 117f, 127, 149f, 183, 191, 193, 196, 206, 208f, 236, 239, 248f, 263, 275, 298, 308, 326, 338

Pennsylvania Dutch, 49
Penny press, 264
Peonage, black, 344
"People," 104, 241f, 247f, 251f, 253f
People v. *Melvin* (1810), 281
Pepper trade, 203
Pequot War (1637), 65
Percheron horse, 213
Perfectibility, belief in, 82, 260f, 266f (opposed), 275, 315
Perfectionism, doctrine of, 277
Perkins Institute for the Blind, Boston, 282
Perry, Commodore Mathew, 200, 305
Persecution, religious, 272, 274; *see also* anti-Catholic prejudice
Personal liberty laws (states), 301
Pestalozzi, J., 261
Philadelphia, 49, 68, 70f, 85, 89f, 92f, 96, 114f, 127, 136, 158, 191, 193, 196f, 211, 248, 252, 271, 280f, 316f (blacks)
Philip, King (Wampanoag chief), 65
Phillips, Wendell, 321
Philosophy, American, 265f
Physical setting of America, 134, 188f, 259f
Pickering, Sen. Timothy, 108
Pickett, Gen. G. E., 338f
Pierce, Franklin, 282, 285, 299, 304–308 (presidency)
Pietism, 274f, 317
Pilgrims, 32, 64f, 271, 398
Pinckney, C. C., 169, 175
Pinckney, Thomas (treaty), 151f
Pinta, 14
Pioneers, western, 158f, 164, 190
Pirates, 25, 28, 54, 82, 93, 149, 166
Pitts, H. and J., 212
Pittsburgh, 63, 193f
Placer gold, 16
Plains, Great, 190
Plains Indians, 9, 213
Plank roads, 192
"Plantation," use of word, 223
Plantation system, 36f, 41, 56f, 58f, 110f, 145f, 194, 198, 218f (dominates South), 237, 240
Planters, as elite interest, 68f, 70, 87, 160 (lifestyle), 171f, 184, 206, 211f, 215–22, 245f, 312f, 320, 328f
Plural executive, idea of, 117, 122

Pluralism, in colonies, 32, 49f, 68f, 100, 125
Plymouth, New, 35, 39f, 42
Pocahontas, 35, 64
Poles in America, 18, 96
Political thought, American, 51f, 116, 245f
Polk, James K., 241, 285, 290f (presidency), 294f, 298, 302, 305, 308, 310
Polygamy, 274, 277, 299, 303
Pontiac's Conspiracy (1763), 67, 82
Poor Richard's Almanac, 69
Poor whites, 162f, 215, 219, 222f, 326
Popular culture, 260f, 269, 283
Popular science, 264
Popular sovereignty, 297f (defined), 301f, 306f, 322f, 326, 329
Population growth, 8 (Indian), 12f, 15 (Indian), 21, 26, 28, 47, 51, 60f, 62, 67f, 100, 108, 117f, 139, 160, 182, 187f, 193, 199, 202, 206, 211f, 215–16, 260, 293, Appendix C
Population pressure, 6, 47, 286
Port Royal, S.C., 337
Portuguese colonization, 14, 16f, 28, 37, 110
"Positive good" theory (slavery), 245f
Post office, 120, 138, 187, 258, 318
Potlatch ceremony, 9
Pottawatomie massacre, 307, 323, 339
Poverty, 69f, 160f (frontier), 280f, 282f
Powhatan, Chief, 35
Powwow, 65
Pragmatism, American, 82, 116f, 228
Prairie, 163f, 212
Pre-emption Acts, 243 (1830), 288 (1841)
Presbyterians, 31, 40, 47, 60, 74f, 139, 161f
Prigg v. *Pennsylvania* (1842), 301
Prisons, 235f, 279, 282, 343
Private enterprise, 54, 193, 196f
Private property, 66 (and liberty), 127f (in Constitution), 186, 230f, 236, 313, 320 (and slavery)
Proclamation of 1763, 67, 82, 89, 97
Progress, dogma of, 73, 82, 159, 184, 228, 232, 259f, 261, 306
Prohibition party, 283

xxxviii
The U.S.A.

Proprietary colonies, 48f, 55
Proslavery arguments, 218, 220f, 234, 245f, 269f, 284, 306f, 318f
Prostitution, 271
Protestant Ethic, 42
Pueblo Indians, 9
Pulaski, C., 96
Puritans, 8, 25, 29f, 37, 39f, 43f, 47f, 65f, 72, 74, 258, 262, 267, 289
  family, 41, 44
"Pursuit of happiness," 103, 186 (defined), 211, 217, 224, 226f, 307, Ch. 8 passim

Q–R

Quakers, 31f, 46f, 48f, 75, 204, 272, 279, 283f, 314
Quebec Act (1774), 81f, 89, 97
Quetzacoatl, 13
Race-mixing, 22, 26, 36, 65, 163, 173f, 276, 291f, 316
Racial egalitarianism, 316
Racism, 65, 218, 219 (and sex), 220f, 286f, 291f, 296, 321f
Radical Abolitionist party, 327
Radical mercantilism, 141
Radical Republicans, 337f, 339f
Radicalism, American, Ch. 10 passim, 43, 70f, 84f, 87f, 89f, 100, 229, 235f, 240, 253f, 258f, 283f (financing), 315f, 320f
Radicalization of middle class, 110
Railroad Act (1850), 198
Railroads, 164, 187, 190f, 193f, 194 (were railroads premature), 197 (federal aid), 202, 206f, 212, 214, 219f, 224f, 281, 293, 306, 312f, 341 (South)
Rails, manufacture of, 197, 201, 208f
Raleigh's colony, 26, 31f
Ranchos, 289
Randolph, John, of Roanoke, 176, 221
Range cattle industry, 189
Rappites, 272, 275
Ratification struggle (Constitution), 115f, 124f
Rationalism, 53, 72f, 265f, 272
Real estate speculators, 107f, 159, 247, 306
Reapers, 212, 222
Reconstruction, 123, 339, Ch. 13 passim
Redcoats, 67, 86f

Redemption Act, 269f, 316
Referendum, national, 329
Regionalism, 187, 221f, 310f; *see also* Sectionalism
Regulators (North Carolina) 1771, 71, 87
"Relevance" in American education, 261f
Religion, 22, 31f, 38f, 46f, 72f, 75f, 80, 160 ("old-time"), 236, 258f, 269f, 283f, 315
Report on Manufactures, 202
Report on Roads and Canals, 165f
Representative government, idea of, 48 (origins), 52f, 75, 78f, 104f, 117f
Representatives, House of, 117f (origins), 138, 150f, 155f, 165, 233f, 235f, 239, 294f, 312f, 318f, 322, 326, 328f, 339f
Republican Party, Jeffersonian, 143, 146f, 149, 152f, 154f, 156f, 167, 171f, 177f, 228f, 236f, 286
Republican Party, of Lincoln, 197, 307f (origins), 313, 319f, 322, 324f, 327f (and slavery)
Republicanism in America, 49, 70, 90f (idea of), 99f, 102f, 110, 121, 124 (and slavery), 148, 152, 177f, 236, 245f, 253
Reservations, Indian, 215
Retail trade, 187
Revere, Paul, Jr., 89, 187
Revere, Paul, Sr., 70
Revivalism, religious, 72f, 160f, 177 (Indians), Ch. 10 passim, 316f, 321
Revolution, agricultural, 211f
"Revolution of expectations," 27
Revolution, American, 38, 56, 59f, 62, 69, 73, 75f, Ch. 4 passim, 99, 102f, 149, 152, 240
  interpretations, 77f, 99f
"Revolution of 1800," 155
Revolution, general nature of, 52, 77, 82, 109f, 152, 257
Revolutions elsewhere
  England (1688), 31, 47, 49, 51f, 103
  France (1789), 77, 82, 89, 92, 100, 104, 147f (impact on America), 163
  Latin America, 82, 92, 100, 235, 291
Rhett, R. B., 328, 330
Rhode Island, 32, 45 (charter), 47, 55, 75, 87, 91,

Rhode Island—*Cont.*
  121, 126, 168, 183, 203, 263
Rice plantations, 37, 58f, 68, 70f, 160, 198, 215, 222f
Richmond, Virginia, 135, 325, 328, 333, 335, 339, 341
Right of deposit, 151, 177
"Rights of Englishmen," 30f, 37, 56, 64, 80, 99, 127
Ripley, George, 265f, 269
Roberts v. *City of Boston* (1849), 321
Rochambeau, Gen., 97
Rockingham, Lord, 84, 97
Rolfe, John, 35f, 58
Rolling mills, 208f
Romantic movement in America, 259f, 267, 315, 322
Rosecrans, Gen. W. S., 341
Rotation in office, 70, 253
Round Hill School, 261
Rousseau, J-J., 40, 260f
Ruffin, E., 213
Rum trade, 25, 54, 56f, 83
Russians in North America, 23, 63f, 192, 234f, 287
Rutgers v. *Waddington* (1784), 140
Rutledge, John, 114

S

Sabbatarianism, 65, 160f, 270, 317
St. Louis, 163, 191, 195f, 214, 225, 293, 317, 319, 334
Salem witchcraft trials, 72
"Salutary neglect," 55, 87
San Jacinto, battle, 294
San Joaquin valley, 289
Santa Anna, Gen., 293f, 297
Santa Fe Trail, 190, 289
Santa Maria, 14
Saratoga, battle of, 93, 96
Saugus, Massachusetts ironworks, 60
Sauk and Fox Indians, 255
Savannah, Ga., 96, 196, 216, 220, 224, 341
Scalp-hunting, 64
Science, faith in, 18
Scientific agriculture, 173, 211, 213f
Scotch-Irish, 16, 49, 60f, 71, 240
Scott, Dred, 168, 319f, 322
Scott, Gen. W., 295, 299, 304, 333
Scott v. *Sanford* (1856), 320
Sea Islands, Ga. and S.C., 216
Seamen, merchant, 53
Seapower, 64, 97, 120

Secession, threats of, 105, 126f (New York City), 155, 168, 171, 175, 183, 197, 245f, 299, 304, 309f, 326f (process, 1860–61), Ch. 12 passim
Sectionalism, 56f, 71, 87, 108f, 110f, 117f (constitution), 144f, 158f, 173, 177f, 183, 187, 194, 196f, 221f, 224f, 228f, 237f, 245f, 249, 293, 310f, 319, 326f
  interdependence, 221f, 224f
  sectional crises, 242f, 312f
Secularization, 47f, 72, 275
Segregation, 321 (north), 344
Self-consciousness (women), 278f
Self-improvement, an American value, 264f
Seminoles, 184, 244
Seneca Falls Convention, 279f
"Separate but equal" dogma, 321
Separation of Powers, 55f, 103f, 123f, 128, 138, 197f
Sequoya, 255
Seventh Day Adventists, 272
Seward, W. H., 297, 299, 304, 325f, 332, 336
Sewing machine, 206f, 211
Sexual attitudes, 219
Sexual radicalism, 170, 272, 274f, 277f
Shakers, 279, 272f
Shaw, Justice L., 321
Shawnee, 183
Shays' Rebellion (1786), 111f, 118
Sheriffs, 30f
Sherman, Gen. W. T., 341
Shipbuilding, 27, 45, 56f, 68, 100, 199f, 201
Siam, 200, 252
Silver mining, 12f, 16, 22, 57, 144, 187, 251, 289, 292
Singer, Isaac, 207
Sitka, Alaska, 64, 234
Slater, Samuel, 203f
Slave breeding, 220f
Slave revolts, 163, 221, 223, 323f, 337
Slave trade, 25, 28, 56f, 121, 173, 175, 218, 220, 299, 304, 325, 329f
Slavery, 13, 35f (origins), 39, 41, 45, 49, 56f, 58f, 64f, 65 (of Indians), 68, 70, 92 (in Declaration of Independence), 108, 110f, 118 (Constitution), 124, 145 (opposed by Hamilton), 151, 158 (Jefferson), 159 (progress and), 162 (prices), 163 (French-

Slavery—Cont.
  speaking slaves), 168, 173f (Jefferson), 184, 205f, 209, 211 (prices), 215f, 217f (lifestyle), 219 (family, religion), 220 (did it pay), 221 (retarded South), 228f, 231, 233f, 240, 245f (defended), 253, 256f, 263, 275f, 284, 286, 290, 293f, 297f, 300f, 304f, 307 (and American Dream), 312f, 315 (was it dying), 319f, 321f (and racism), 325f (and Southern economy), 327, 329, 331, 340, 342f
Smith, Adam, 140f, 187, 210, 281
Smith, Gerrit, 32, 323
Smith, Capt. John, 32, 39, 45
Smith, J. S., 289, 292
Smith, S. H., 167
Smuggling, 82, 86
Social contract, theory of, 40f, 51f, 98
Social overhead capital, 165f, 193, 202, 205, 221f, 313
Socialism, 120, 271f (Christian), 275f, 280, 321
Soil erosion, 210f, 221, 223
Sons of Liberty, 83f, 86f, 91, 106, 110
Soul food, origins, 219
South, as a section, Ch. 10 passim, 37, 56f, 67f, 91f, 110f, 117f, 121, 124, 145f, 155, 159f, 187, 194, 205f, 215f, 221f, 224f, 228, 233, 243f, 284, 295, 297f, 299, 305, 307, 310f, 326
South Carolina, 55, 59f, 68, 70f, 97, 114, 143, 152, 194, 196f, 213, 216, 220, 236f, 240f, 244f, 299, 310, 312, 316, 323f, 327f, 330f, 342f
South Dakota, 62
Southern Rights party, 324f
Spanish America, 5, 12f, 21f, 27f, 32, 37, 48, 54, 62f, 82, 91, 97, 113, 234 (slaves), 288, 305
Spanish Florida, 184, 215, 229, 241, 244
Specie, 57, 112, 143f, 159, 189, 247, 251f
Specie Circular (1836), 251f
Speckled Snake, Chief, 255
Spiritualism, 272
Spoils system, 227, 253
Spotsylvania, battle, 341
Squanto, 64f
Stamp Act (1765), 79f, 83f
  Congress, 84

Stanton, Elizabeth Cady, 279f
Staple Act, 1663, 53f
"Starving Time," 34f
"State capitalism," 145
State Department origins, 137f
States' rights, Ch. 12 passim, 105f, 108, 110, 114f, 126, 156f, 173, 175, 178f, 228f, 236f, 243f, 257, 288, 309f, 325f
  in Confederacy, 330, 340, 342f
Status anxiety, 29, 258
Steamboat Act, 195
Steamboats, 158, 164, 194f, 199f, 224, 230f
Steel industry, 164, 201, 208f
Steuart, Sir J., 141
Steuben, Baron Von, 96
Stevens, Thaddeus, 263, 337, 339f
Stock exchange, 221
Stockton, Commodore R. F., 295
Stoddard, Rev. S., 47, 74
Stone, Lucy, 279
Story, Justice J., 230
Stourbridge Lion, 196
Stowe, Harriet Beecher, 270, 300, 316, 320
Strict construction (Constitution), 143f, 156, 175, 228, 243
Strikes, 235, 253, 281
Strutt, J., 203
Stuart, Gilbert, 134
Sturges v. Crowninshield (1819), 230
Stuyvesant, Peter, 23
Subsistence farming, 162f, 224f
Suffolk Resolves, 89
Suffragettes, 279f
Sugar Act, 83
Sugar plantations, 22f, 28, 36f, 53, 56f, 82f, 89, 160, 163, 218f, 222f
Sumner, Charles, 321, 337, 339f
Superior-use argument, 232, 254f, 286f, 291
Supremacy clause, 125, 127, 140
Supreme Court, 52, 91, 100, 119, 123 (Constitution), 166f, 170, 230f, 232f, 243, 248, 255, 301, 319f, 325f
Swedenborg, I., 267, 272
Swedish colonies, 23f
Swiss in America, 49, 165, 212, 261
Syllabary, Cherokee, 255
Synagogue, first, 32

T

Takeoff, industrial, 202, 211
Tallmadge, Rep. J., 234
Tammany Hall, 285
Taney, Justice R. B., 242, 247, 319f
Tappan, A. and L., 284, 313, 316, 318
Tariffs, 128, 138 (1789), 141f, 145, 165, 173, 197, 199, 208, 223, 227f, 230 (1816, 1824), 237f (1828), 239, 241 (1832), 243, 245f (1828), 246 (1832), 312, 326, 330 (Confederate States of America)
Taylor, John of Carolina, 155, 173
Taylor, Zachary, 285, 295f, 297f, 299
Taxes, 55f, 70f, 80f, 96, 106, 111f, 118, 155, 173, 197, 230, 262f, 266, 280
Tea Act (1773), 88f
Tea trade, 85, 87f, 199f, 287
Teacher training, 262f, 279
Technology, American, 66, 145, 188, 190, 206f, 210f, 212f, 216f, 222, 224, 231, 264f
Tecumseh, Chief, 177, 183f
Teedyuscung, Chief, 67
Tehuacan, 5
Temperance movement, 258, 269f, 280, 282f, 308
Ten Percent Plan, 339
Tennessee, 62, 113, 151, 158f, 160, 163, 183, 190, 213f, 216 (population), 231f, 240f, 224, 236f, 242f, 275f, 318, 325f, 328, 332, 340f
Territorial growth, United States, 60f, 107f, 158f, 165, 172, 211, 229, 231f, 285f, 293f, 306, 313
Territorial system, 108, 159, 233f, 257, 297f, 301f, 319f, 325
Texas, 176, 197, 215, 220, 223, 252, 272, 275, 277, 286, 289f, 293f, 299, 303f (state debts), 308, 310, 313, 328
Textile industry, 28, 112, 145, 188f, 202, 204f, 211, 216f, 219, 237, 239, 335
Thames, battle of, 183
Theocracy, 31, 41, 274
Theology, 75
 on frontier, 161f, 269f
Third parties, 249f, 286, 304, 324
Thomas, David, 208
Thomas, Gen. G. H., 341
Thoreau, 260, 266, 294
Tidewater elite, 48, 59f, 70f, 87, 215, 223
Timber, 28, 59f, 192, 208; see also Lumber industry
Tippecanoe, 177, 288
Tobacco, 33, 35f, 41, 46, 53, 56, 58f, 68, 70f, 100, 112, 162, 198, 215f, 222f
Tocqueville, A. de, 70, 101, 172, 188, 209, 287
Toilets, 280
Tom Thumb, 196
Toombs, R., 328f
Tories, American, 98
Toussaint L'Ouverture, 163
Towns, New England, 41f, 47, 107f, 159, 164, 262
Townshend, Charles, 81, 84f, 87
Trade unions, 235f, 275, 280f
Trails, 190, 290
Trail of Tears, 253f, 254
Transatlantic reform community, 258f
Transcendentalism, 258f, 260, 265f, 278, 293
Transcontinental railroads, 196f, 296, 306, 313, 320
Transferable fee title, 66
Treason, 170, 246
Treatise on Civil Government, 51f
Treaty power, 106, 118, 121f, 151, 166
Trial by jury, 89
Triangular trade, 56f, 82f
Tribune, New York, 265, 321
Trumbull, J., 135
Turner, Nat, 221, 323
Turnpike highways, 112, 135, 158, 165, 187, 191f, 224f, 312f
Two-party system, 237f, 285, 319
Tyler, John, 251, 288, 290, 329f
Tyler, Judge R., 178

U–V

Uncle Tom's Cabin, 300, 316, 320
Underground railroad, 300f, 319, 337
Unemployment, 48, 172, 280
Unitarians, 265f, 269, 323
Universalists, 162
Ursuline convent, Massachusetts (burnt), 271
Utah, 274, 280, 295, 298f, 302f
Values, American, 82, 91f, 263f
Van Buren, Martin, 237f, 242f, 244, 250f, 287f, 290, 294, 298
Vérendrye, P., 62
Verrazano, G. de, 24
Vermont, 159, 168, 178, 183, 213, 270, 277
Vesey, Denmark, 323
Veto, presidential, 120, 241, 246, 249, 298, 312f
Vicksburg, battle of, 339, 341
Vikings, 6f, 11f
Virginia, 7, 16, 22, 26, 32f, 40f, 45f, 53, 58f, 64, 68, 70f, 75, 87f, 97, 107, 112, 114, 117f, 126f, 135f, 137f, 143, 146, 151, 155, 158, 160, 163, 165, 171, 173, 190, 193f, 196, 220f, 223, 228, 236, 269, 288
Virginia Dynasty, 35, 158, 228f, 235f, 256
Virginia and Kentucky Resolutions, 171f, 310
Visible Saints, 46
Volunteer army, 332
Voting rights
 black: 122, 313, 321, 323
 women, 279f

W

Wade, Benjamin, 337, 352, 360
Wade-Davis Bill, 339f
Wage-slavery argument, 219, 245f, 321
Wages, U.S., 69f, 188f
Walker, David, 314, 316
Walker, William, 304
Waltham Plan, 204f
Wampanoag Indians, 65, 289
Warhawks, 175f, 228
War powers, 106, 120f, 166, 183, 294, 296
Wars
 Civil War, Ch. 12 passim; 165, 174, 184, 197, 201f, 207f, 213f, 223, 228, 245, 253, 257f, 264, 274, 284, 297f, 312f (timing), 319f (escalation), 322 (first shots), 333f (course), 340f, 343 (cost)
 1812–14, 97, 137, 156, 171f, 175f (origins), 178f (course), 191, 198, 202, 204, 215, 223, 226, 228, 240, 246, 258, 281, 297
 Independence, 67, 82, 86, 92f, 94, 101, 112, 126, 142, 218

Index

Wars—*Cont.*
 Mexican, 266, 292, 294f, 319, 333
 Napoleonic, 170
Washington, George, 38, 61, 89, 91f, 107f, 113f, 116, 133f, 137f (presidency), 152 (Farewell), 174, 213
Washington, D.C. Peace Conference (1861), 329f
Wayland, Francis, 319
Wayne, Gen. Anthony, 150
Webster, Daniel, 212, 230, 242f, 289, 300f, 303f
Webster-Ashburton treaty, 288
Weed, Thurlow, 299
Weld, Theodore, 270, 313, 316
Welfare state, 264
Welsh, 5f (discovery of America)
 immigrants, 49, 60f
West Indies, 7, 13, 25, 45, 57, 59, 81f, 65, 100, 139, 150, 171, 198, 223, 237f, 252
West Virginia, 328, 333
Western expansionists, 175f
Western Reserve, 164, 316
Westward movement, 60f, 67f, 82, 198, 296
Whaling, 87, 287
Whigs, American, 83f, 87, 110, 119, 134, 253, 259, 285f, 288, 290, 294f, 296f, 299f,

Whigs—*Cont.*
 301f, 304, 309, 316 (antislavery wing), 319, 322f (split), 327, 331
Whisky Rebellion (1794), 149
Whitefield, G., 73
Whitman, Dr. Marcus, 286, 289, 296
Whitman, Walt, 267, 305
Whitney, Eli, 198, 211, 215f, 218
Whittier, J. G., 319
Wilkinson, Gen. J., 170
Williams, Roger, 40, 43, 45, 65
Wilmot, David, 298f
Wilmot Proviso, 298f, 302, 325
Wilson, James, 114, 117
Winthrop, John, 29, 32, 42f, 46
Wisconsin, 25, 67, 164, 212f, 216 (population), 255, 262, 293, 307
Wise, Rev. J., 75
Wolfe, Gen. J., 63
Woman in the 19th Century (1845), 278
Women, 70, 204f (work), 241, 265, 278, 289 (cross Rockies)
Women, civil rights of, 122 (Constitution), 278, 280 (New York)

Women, radical leaders, 278f, 282, 316f
Women's Appeal, 318
Women's equality, 273f (Shakers), 276f (communes)
Women's magazines, 265, 279
Women's movement, 240, 247f, 275f
Wood, Jethro, 22
Woolens, 27f, 112, 202, 213, 239, 289
Worcester v. *Georgia* (1832), 232, 255
Working class, 70, 204f, 280f, 307, 340
Workingmen's Party, 280, 285
Wright, Frances, 275f, 280, 313
Wyoming, 280, 292, 295f

X–Z

XYZ affair, 154
Yancey, W. L., 325f, 330
Yazoo River lands, 212, 215, 339
Yeardley, Gov., 37
Yorktown, battle of, 97
Young, Brigham, 274, 298, 303
Young America movement, 305
Zoar (commune), 274f

This book has been set in 9 and 8 point Primer, leaded 2 points. Part numbers and titles are 30 point Deepdene. Chapter numbers are 60 point Caslon Old Style #540 and chapter titles are 30 point Deepdene italic. The size of the type area is 33½ x 46½ picas.